The Right Hon.ble Richard Lord Cobham
Lieutenant General of His Majesty's Forces &c.ª

GEORGE THE FIRST'S ARMY
1714–1727

CHARLES DALTON, F.R.G.S.

IN TWO VOLUMES
• VOLUME 2 •

The Naval & Military Press Ltd

Reproduced by kind permission of the Central Library,
Royal Military Academy, Sandhurst

Published by

The Naval & Military Press Ltd

Unit 10, Ridgewood Industrial Park,

Uckfield, East Sussex,

TN22 5QE England

Tel: +44 (0) 1825 749494

Fax: +44 (0) 1825 765701

www.naval–military-press.com

© The Naval & Military Press Ltd 2005

*In reprinting in facsimile from the original, any imperfections are inevitably reproduced
and the quality may fall short of modern type and cartographic standards.*

Printed and bound by Antony Rowe Ltd, Eastbourne

PREFACE

First and foremost I wish to express my hearty thanks to the Press in general for the very kind reception accorded to the first volume of this present work. Out of a total of sixteen reviews the first fifteen were eulogistic. Having said this, I have no wish to conceal the fact that the sixteenth notice, which made its belated appearance in a London Weekly, was of a different kind altogether. The *critique* in question seems to have been penned by a veritable Justice Shallow, whose knowledge of the class of book he attempted to criticise was manifestly not on a par with his ill-concealed anxiety to belittle my work.

One of the leading features of the present volume is the series of early Royal Artillery Muster Rolls (pp. 227–255), the value of which is set forth in a separate preface (pp. 225–226). The thirteen regiments raised in Ireland in 1716 and disbanded in 1717 are now printed for the first time, with my annotations (pp. 129–147); while all the Commission Registers on both the British and Irish Establishments, ranging from January 1719 to the death of George I., transcribed from the War Office Books at the Public Record Offices of London and Dublin, are given chronologically in the forthcoming pages. To the uninitiated the great mass of printed military commissions, representing the preferments and appointments in George I.'s Army for the last eight and a half years of that monarch's reign, is merely a collection of names and dates ; but to the literary searchers, either civil or military, who have toiled through heavy folio manuscript volumes, at the aforesaid Public Offices, looking for commission entries which the Civil Service clerks of the period had dumped down in chaotic and hopeless confusion, a carefully collated series of chronological registers must be considered a boon. It may be many years before the State Papers for the reign of George I. are calendared and

printed.   And when they are it is hardly likely that the two sets
of Commission Registers for above reign will be included, viz., the
War Office series, and that set known formerly as the Home Office
Entry Books, but now classed among the S.P. Domestic Entry
Books.   While adhering mainly to the War Office series, I have
had perforce now and then to give commission entries from the
second-named set of books.   Both sets are imperfect, and the
phonetic spelling of proper names by the clerks who entered the
commission registers in their respective ledgers from dictation has
given me an infinity of labour, not only in my text, but in the
index nominum.

Owing to lack of space in my first volume, I was obliged to
curtail my annotations.   I have now amply made up for this
enforced abstinence by giving many hundreds of notes, biographical and otherwise, in the following pages.   I have no intention of
descanting on this laborious portion of my work ; but now that
my series of *English Army Lists and Commission Registers*, 1661–
1714, is out of print, I feel at liberty to say that my annotations
in aforesaid *Army Lists* have proved useful to, and been in nearly
every case acknowledged by, compilers of Regimental Histories
during recent years.

I referred in the Preface to Volume I. of *George the First's
Army* to a wish that had been expressed relative to my carrying on
my *Army Lists and Commission Registers* from the death of George I.
to the close of the year 1739, so as to complete the bridge between
1661 and 1740—the date that the War Office prepared an official
Army List which was published the same year "by Order of the House
of Commons."   I bound myself to no further publication of Army
Lists subsequent to the death of George I., and now definitely,
though reluctantly, say I cannot attempt to bridge the first twelve
and a half years of George II.'s reign. In the first place the period
from June 1727 to December 1739 is one of the most stagnant in
British history. ´Secondly, the military MSS. for the years in
question at the Public Record Office, London, are few in number
and lamentably incomplete.   Take, for instance, the so-called
"Gradation List for 1730."   This valuable MS.—which I have
drawn upon largely for my annotations—lacks the names of

officers composing seven entire infantry regiments, six of which corps were then serving in the Colonies. Add to this that the date "1730" is somewhat misleading, because there are very few entries in this "Gradation List" for 1729, and none for 1730. Once more, the bulky MS. volume which bears in gold letters on the back "Army List, 1736," is a very deceptive volume, and full of surprises for the unwary searcher. Some of the cavalry regiments are conspicuous by their absence, and others wrongly placed by the binder. The date "1736" is an anachronism, as this Army List is undoubtedly for 1738, with additions and corrections up to 1748! This statement is borne out by the fact that lists are given therein of the "Twelve Independent Companies going on an Expedition under the command of the Hon. Admiral Boscawen, May 1747." MS. corrections to above companies give the names of subalterns who entered the service of the East India Company in 1748. The value of this "amalgamated" Army List does not consist in the regimental lists, as a large proportion of the officers' names have been erased, but in the contemporary official notes and additions.

It is a well-known fact to military historians that in the year 1751 regimental numbers were first "served out" to the British cavalry and infantry according to the precedence of each corps in the Army. It so happens that at the Public Record Office, London, there is a MS. "Army List, 1752," wherein the historic numbers first appear. This valuable MS. is in two volumes, having corrections and additions up to 1756. It is my ambition to evolve a 1752–1753 Army List out of the above MS., and edit the same with my own annotations. The *raison d'être* for such a volume is that the consecutive series of printed Army Lists, issued "by permission of the Secretary at War," begins in 1754, and the yawning retrospective gap between that year and 1740 would thus be shortened by two years. If granted a continuation of good health, I hope to attempt this labour of love. I know such a book will only appeal to an eclectic circle, so I do not propose to publish the projected volume, but to issue a few copies for private circulation.

It is my pleasant duty to acknowledge various items of information I received for my annotations from the late Mr. G. E.

Cokayne (the venerable Clarenceux-King-of-Arms), Major-General Sir Thomas Fraser, K.C.B., and Colonel W. O. Cavenagh; also to Major M. L. Ferrar (compiler of the recently published *History of the Services of the* 19*th Regiment*); Mr. George Holden (Librarian, All Souls College, Oxford); Mr. F. V. Rainsford; and Major E. M. Poynton, late Somerset Light Infantry. With regard to the illustrations, I wish particularly to draw public attention to the reduced copy of the engraving representing the great Duke of Marlborough's funeral procession on its way to Westminster Abbey, and the key to the same printed in the Appendices (pp. 110–114). I am indebted to Major J. W. Malet, late Editor of *The St. George's Gazette,* for his courtesy in permitting me to reproduce the portrait of Colonel Charles Whitefoord, Colonel 5th Regiment of Foot, which appeared in aforesaid *Gazette* in August, 1899. And I am likewise indebted to the Rev. F. J. Cannon for kindly sending me, through Colonel Cavenagh, the photograph of Major-General John Orfeur's portrait. Nor must I omit to thank Lt.-Colonel Sir Henry Smith, K.C.B., for information regarding a portrait in oils of a distinguished Scottish General who fell at Fontenoy.

Lastly, I wish to acknowledge the help I have received from Mr. G. T. Longley, of the MS. Department of the British Museum, whose intimate acquaintance with the various collections of MSS. connected with his sphere of work has been of great assistance to me; I also am indebted to him for the extracts he made for me from the parchment pay-list described on page 427.

The Index has been prepared by Mr. Longley, which is a guarantee of its excellence. I alone am responsible for the identification of names—mis-spelt or otherwise.

The Irish Commission Registers given in this particular volume were copied for me by Miss Gertrude Thrift, a well-known searcher of experience at the Dublin Record Office.

CHARLES DALTON.

1*st December*, 1912.

CONTENTS

APPENDICES TO VOLUMES I. AND II.

English Establishment.

ILLUSTRATIONS

KEY TO REFERENCE LETTERS

MSS. AT PUBLIC RECORD OFFICE, LONDON.

a = War Office Commission Entry Book, 1714–1716.

b =   „   „   „   1717–1718.

c =   „   „   „   1718–1724.

d =   .,   „   .,   1724–1727.

f = War Office MS. Gradation List, 1730.

p = S.P. Domestic Entry Book, 1717–1726.

MSS. AT PUBLIC RECORD OFFICE, DUBLIN.

h = Commission Entry Book, 1709–1716.

i =   „   „   1715–1717.

j =   „   „   1716–1720.

r =   „   „   1724–1730.

ABBREVIATIONS

See Volume I., p. xiii.

ERRATA

VOLUME I.

Page xlvi., 7th line, *for* "1870" *read* "1871."

„ 151, note 2, also p. 165, note 3, *for* "special memoir" *read* "biographical notice."

„ 194, last line, *for* "Chapean" *read* "Chapeau."

„ 223, note 77, *for* "8 May, 1739," *read* "8 May, 1732."

„ 294, note 5, *for* "1 Oct. 1715" *read* "1 Oct. 1714."

„ 308, note 4, to read as follows :—"Acclom Milbanke, third son of Sir Mark Milbanke, 2nd Bt. of Halnaby, co. York. Capt. 25th Foot, 28 March, 1712. Re-commissioned Capt. in do. 24 Aug. 1715. Left said Regt. 31 March, 1721. D. at Halnaby and was buried at Croft, 30 June, 1766. Said in *Gentleman's Mag.* to have been then aged 90 ; he was probably about 80."—(Communicated by Major E. M. Poynton, late Somerset Light Infantry.)

„ 361, *for* "Richard Chalmer Cobb" (in list of Captains) *read* "Richard Chaloner Cobb."

„ 379, 12th line, 1st column, *read* "Richard Chaloner Cobb."

VOLUME II.

Page 313.—The heading ought to read "The Prince of Wales's Own Royal Regiment of Welsh Fuziliers."

„ 422, notes 4 and 5.—The references are to Vol. I. and not the present volume.

ADDITIONAL NOTES.

Page 208, note 14.—Lt.-Col. Wm. Erskine was son of Col. Wm. Erskine of Torry, co. Fife, Deputy-Governor of Blackness Castle. Lt.-Col. Wm. Erskine of the 7th Dragoons is said to have tied the regimental standard to his son Cornet Wm. Erskine's leg on the morning of the battle of Fontenoy, and thus addressed him : "Go, and take good care of your charge ; let me not see you separate. If you return alive from the field, you must produce the standard." After the battle "the young cornet rode up to his father and showed him the standard as tight and fast as in the morning." Cornet Wm. Erskine attained the rank of Lt.-Gen. and Col. of the Cameronians. He was created a Bart. in 1791 and died at Torry in 1795.

Page 302, note 15.—Col. Robert Fraser got his majority in the 15th Foot, 10 Sept. 1733. Lt.-Col. of Lowther's Marines, 26 Nov. 1739. According to the *Gentleman's Mag.* for 1741 Lt.-Col. Fraser was transferred back to his old regiment (15th) as Lt.-Col. till he was appointed, 14 June, 1741, Col. of the 2nd Marines *vice* Robinson decd.—(Communicated by Maj.-Gen. Sir T. Fraser, K.C.B.)

Page 376, note 14.—"Capt. Claude Fraser was commissioned Capt. in 2nd Batt. 1st Foot, 7 Sept. 1741. He served with the 2nd Batt. forming the relief to West Indian Expedition of 1740 from Oct. 1741 when it sailed from Cork, to Dec. 1742 when it returned home. It was too late for the San Jago Expedition. He also, presumably, served in the Rising of 1745–46 in England and Scotland."—(Note by Sir T. Fraser, K.C.B.)

THE EARLY GEORGIAN ERA

PART II

THE declaration of war with Spain, coming as it did directly after the disbandment of many British regiments, necessitated, for the second time within four years, Dutch and Swiss auxiliaries being brought over to England in 1719. Some weeks earlier, news had reached the British Government of a sudden invasion intended to be made from Spain upon George I.'s dominions. The cost of transporting 6,000 men from a Dutch to a British seaport was at the rate of seven shillings a head; the return sea trip being sixpence a head dearer.* It is only fair to record that the former foreign levies, brought over in 1715, had behaved remarkably well in Scotland on the whole, and though practically in an " enemy's country " the Dutch regiments had generally kept their hands from picking and stealing. One corps, however, disgraced their cloth by some looting. A contemporary Scottish chronicler writing under date of March, 1716, reports that—

> " Count Vanso's regement of Dutch were much complend of and General Cadigen [Cadogan] repremanded him for not keeping disciplin which he refuisd with some warmth, but was told that he had incuriged such practices and that with his own hand had cut out from the fraime a picture of Mary Qween of Scots and had it in his baggage. The Count stormd at this but General Cardigen (*sic*) was plainer then plesant and said if he talked more so he would call a Councill of war and have him brock upon the spott and that his behaviowr showld be represented to the States." †

The same writer records that Colonel Newton, colonel of an English dragoon regiment, had in his baggage " a fine sowd bed lind with welwet valowd at one hundred and 50 pownd sterling taken out of Garentilly howse. It had belonged to the family of

---

* *Treasury Papers*, Vol. CCXIV., No. 17.
† *News Letters of* 1715-16 (published in 1910), p. 142.

Newwarke." * The gallant Colonel Newton managed to smuggle the above luxurious bed on board one of the artillery ships at Leith, with the rest of his baggage, but by General Cadogan's orders the stolen property was taken out of the ship and restored to the owners. †

In March, 1719, a Royal Warrant authorised the formation of a Regiment of Invalids which became the 41st Regiment of Foot (p. 324). This anomalous corps consisted of ten companies, of fifty men each, formed from the out-pensioners of Chelsea Hospital. Eight companies were sent to Portsmouth and two to Plymouth. In addition to this regiment, ten Independent Companies of Invalids, recruited from out-pensioners of Chelsea Hospital were likewise formed in March (p. 339), and in April following fifteen more Invalid companies were raised (p. 340). The object of these new levies was to free regiments doing duty at English seaports, and coast defences, for service in Scotland and in expeditions by sea. The substitution of war-worn veterans, many of whom had lost limbs in the service, for able-bodied young soldiers was a doubtful experiment at the very time that a Spanish invasion was expected. The history of the first corps of Invalids and Invalid companies is not devoid of humorous incidents. Take, for instance, an order issued in 1779 concerning Invalids in general which says : " If Invalids cannot march they are with due discretion *to ride on horseback or be placed in carts.*" ‡ Then again, take the respective ages of the officers nearly fifty years after the raising of the corps of Invalids. In 1767, a regimental return shows that Major Edward Strode (p. 334) was aged 82 ; Lieutenant Lawson 80 ; Ensign Chaman 71. Both subalterns being returned as "stone blind," while Ensign Stopforth's age is given as 79 ! § In 1787, the Regiment of Invalids (41st) was reorganised and served on the same footing as all other infantry corps.

One of the half-pay officers appointed Captain of one of the ten Independent Companies of Invalids, 3rd April, 1719, merits special

---

* *News Letters of* 1715–16 (published in 1910), p. 143.
† *Ibid.*
‡ *Hist. of the Services of the* 41*st Regt. of Foot,* by Lieut. David Lomax, p. 22.
§ *Ibid.,* p. 18.

mention here as he has left his mark behind him. Captain Mordaunt Cracherode (p. 340) had seen service in Spain, as a subaltern, during the War of Succession. In November, 1739, he was appointed commander of five newly-raised companies of Invalids and given the rank of Lieutenant-Colonel by commission dated 25th December, 1739. These five companies sailed with Commodore Anson's squadron of five ships in September, 1740, destined to attack Spanish vessels in dangerous and unfrequented seas. The British Government had promised Anson a whole regiment of marines; but this promise was not kept. "Of the 259 invalids embarked with Anson in 1740," writes the regimental historian of the 41st Foot, "not one ever saw his native land again." This sweeping statement does not apply to Colonel Cracherode, of whom a well-known writer of the far past has left this record :—

> "A curious anecdote not altogether unbibliographical belonged to Anson's Voyage round the World. Mordaunt Cracherode, the father of the Rev. C. M. Cracherode, of celebrated book fame, went out to make his fortune as a commander of the marines (*sic*) in Anson's ship. He returned in consequence of his share of prize money a wealthy man. It was said he returned from the Ansonian circumnavigation in the identical buckskins which he wore on leaving England, they having been the object of his exclusive attachment during the whole voyage ! It is said there is one particular volume in the Cracherode collection which is bound in a piece of the identical buckskins." *

Chroniclers of Commodore (afterwards Lord) Anson's adventurous voyage, 1740–44, state that it took the great circumnavigator forty days to round Cape Horn, two ships being lost in the terrible storms he then encountered. It must have been in remembrance of the buffeting he received during this fateful period that Colonel Cracherode afterwards utilised a portion of his sea-going buckskins for binding a book. As his son and heir left the Cracherode library to the British Museum (with the exception of two books which afterwards found their way thither) it goes without saying that the volume bound in the best portion of the old Colonel's cherished buckskins is now housed in the aforesaid national treasure-house.

* Dibdin's *Library Companion*, p. 394, note.

b

It has been truly said of the second Duke of Ormond that " he never accomplished anything of importance." Ormond's descent on the Devonshire coast, in 1715, with a mere handful of officers and men was a quixotade barely worthy of mention. No better success attended his appointment as Capt.-General of the Spanish fleet intended for the invasion of Great Britain. The well-appointed Armada had hardly lost sight of Cape Finisterre before it encountered a violent tempest and was scattered far and wide. Only two Spanish frigates succeeded in reaching the Scottish coast. On one of these ships was the valiant George Keith, Earl Marischal (Vol. I., pp. 87-90), who was in command of the Spanish troops on board. An interesting letter,* hitherto unpublished, from Captain George Gibbon, the Lieut.-Governor of Plymouth, who had the custody of an officer in the Spanish service, taken prisoner in June, 1719, throws fresh light on Earl Marischal's adventurous voyage to Scotland :—

> " Royal Citadel,
> " Plymouth,
> " July the 14, 1719.

" To Charles Delafaye, Esq., Secretary to the Lords Justices.

" SIR,

" Captain Peter Stapleton has a Company in the Regiment of Galicia, which Commission I have. Half of which Regiment embarked at Port Passage in two ships carrying about three and twenty guns each and sail'd Jan. 7th, N.S., but were oblig'd by contrary winds to put into Port Reō where they stay'd 14 or 15 days. Their orders were to sail some leagues West of Cape Finisterre before they open'd them. As soon as arrived they open'd them. They imediatly steer'd the North Course. Then the Spaniards knew where they were sailing to. They were seven weeks before they made Scotland and coasted three weeks there before they landed, which was at Donan † on April 24th, O.S. There were on board the two ships six or seven Scots gentlemen, but he says he saw none but Earle Marishall whom he did not know was aboard before he saw Scotland. When the Earle came upon deck [he] said they were all under his command. He believes the reason this was kept so secret was, that the Court of Spain thought the Spaniards would mutiny if they had known their design before they sail'd, for 'twas report'd they were to go to Scicily (*sic*). He told me about a fortnight before he sail'd he saw the late ‡ Duke of Ormond who goes by the name of Lord Cummelforth (*sic*), at a town call'd Villa Valid, that he has a Commission as

---

* *S.P. Dom. George I.*, Bundle 17, No. 102.

† The little island of Eilean Donan, Ross-shire.

‡ It was customary to apply this adjective to noblemen who had been attainted.—ED.

Generalissimo of the King of Spain's Forces and one of his Vice Admirals, and that he was sure he design'd to go aboard the Fleet that was lately dispers'd. He likewise says that tho Alberoni has been baulk'd in his late design he will certainly attempt it again. If I can hear anything more from him [Captain Stapleton] I shall report it to their Excellencys [the Lords Justices].

"I am, Sir, your most obedient humble servant,

"G. GIBBON."*

On 30th April, Earl Marischal sent the two Spanish frigates back to Spain, after the stores were landed, and on 10th June the Highlanders and Spaniards were defeated by General Wightman at Glenshiel as already narrated (Vol. I., p. 52).

The prospect of a Spanish invasion in the spring of 1719 was made use of, all over the Kingdom, by Jacobite agents, to set the people against the Hanoverian dynasty. In the country inn-keepers found it a profitable trade to propose the health of "Jemmy King of Scots" when their tap-rooms were fairly full and to encourage the singing of Jacobite songs. Now and again these little-worthy publicans got into trouble, being reported for their disloyalty by some chance loyalist. Among the Georgian State Papers are several cases of soldiers who gave evidence against inn-keepers who played the part of rebels. Here is an instance. Privates Chadock and Griffith Davies of Captain Hyde's Company, Royal Welsh Fusiliers, made a statement before a Justice of the Peace at Leominster on the 15th June, 1719, to the effect that a publican in the town had sung a Jacobite song about "King James being on the sea with thousands of men and that when he landed the English would all fight for him." The witnesses went on to say that when the song was finished the landlord invited them and the five countrymen in the bar-room to drink "King James's health," which the five civilians thereupon did. The case in question was referred to the Lords Justices, who ordered the inn-keeper to be prosecuted at the Government's expense and deprived of his licence.

King George's departure for Hanover early in the summer of 1719 set loose a flood of scurrilous pamphlets and ballads in the streets of London. This class of pestilential literature had been

* D. in Jan. 1746 as Lieut.-Governor of Plymouth.—*Gentleman's Mag.*

bad enough before the King's departure. The Lord Mayor of London (Sir John Fryer) writing to Mr. Delafaye, the Under-Secretary of State, in April, 1719, enclosed "a villainous ballad," and went on to say: "You see here what ballads are sung about the streets. I think if your messengers were diligent examining the Presses of these beggarly fellows, that print ballads, it might stop the practice which continues to alienate the minds of the common people by these things." *

One of the most objectionable pamphlets surreptitiously printed in London during the early years of George I.'s reign was: *Vox Populi, Vox Dei*; and one of the most scurrilous ballads: *The Old Turnip Man's hue and cry after more money.†* John Mathews, a well-known printer of treasonable literature, was apprehended, tried, sentenced, and executed at Tyburn 6th November, 1719. He was made a hero of by the class to which he belonged and a rough wood-cut portrait of this eighteen-year-old youth adorns the broadside headed: *The Last Dying Words, Character, Portraiture, Prison Prayers, Meditations, and Ejaculations of Mr. John Mathews, Printer, &c.* A low-class ballad-singer was arrested, at a later date, when plying his trade in London, and committed to Newgate. He managed to find a ready letter writer in prison who penned the following petition, which was forwarded to Mr. Delafaye: —

"Petition of William Turner sheweth that your Petitioner being a very illiterate person and likewise out of all employment was obliged in regard of himself and family to sing Ballads about the Streets, and buying a parcell of Ballads and not knowing they were prejudicial did sing them about the City and suburbs by which means your Petitioner was carried before Hon. Justice Dene and by his direction was committed to prison." ‡

The endorsement of "libels" on the back of above document by Secretary Delafaye tells its own tale. Another petition on the

---

* *S.P. Dom. George I.*, Bundle 16.

† George I. is reported to have said, when he first came to St. James's Palace, that he would turn St. James's Park into a turnip field—hence his nick-name of "The Turnip Man."—*Notes and Queries*, 30th March, 1912.

‡ *S.P. Dom. George I.*, Bundle 17.

subject of ballads, pasquinades, &c., was from "a Major of the Royal Horse Guards of Saxony" who, being in London during King George's absence in Germany, was so hurt by the disloyal literature hawked about the streets that he offered "to bring about the assassination of the Pretender whose *valet de chambre* the writer knew." *

During the late spring and early summer of 1719 preparations were made for a descent upon the north-west coast of Spain, while the French Government agreed to send a force at the same time to attack some Spanish towns in Catalonia. Owing to the absence of George I. in Germany, the Regents of the Kingdom directed affairs—civil and military. It is surprising to find an English bishop writing to Mr. Secretary Delafaye on a subject which manifestly only concerned the military authorities:—

"Duke Street,
"Westminster,
"Aug. 3, 1719.

"DEAR SIR,

    "I am desired by a friend to procure him an answer to the following queries :—

        "Hath anything been done by the Regents with regard to furnishing the Surgeons' Chests for this Expedition, and if anything, what ?

    "Your enabling me to answer this query will much oblige,

"S^r
"Your affec^{te} Friend,
"EDM. LINCOLN." †

Unfortunately the replies to the bishop's queries are not forthcoming among the State Papers.

The account of the expeditionary force to the Spanish coast under Viscount Cobham and the success thereof are fully detailed in his memoir (pp. 1–8); but it may interest military readers to hear of the vicissitudes which befell a young English

---

  * *S.P. Dom. George I.*, Bundle 17.

  † Dr. Edmund Gibson, Bishop of Lincoln 1716–23. Translated to the See of London in 1723. D. at Bath, 6 Sept. 1748. Above letter is among the *S.P. Dom. George I.*, Bundle 17, No. 6.

gentleman who accompanied the aforesaid expedition as a volunteer with the 34th Foot :—

"PETITION TO LORD CARTERET.
"THE MEMORIAL OF RICHARD WOOLLASTON,* ESQ.

"His son Richard Woollaston went over with Colonel Chudleigh's Regiment to the late Expedition to Vigo and was taken prisoner with several others. After seven months imprisonment, living upon bread and water, he was forced into the Spanish Service and was tryed twice for his life for endeavouring to escape ; and was after [that] chain'd to others almost naked and march'd from that part of the Country through all Spain to Barcelona where he is now a common soldier—La Capane de Carlon Cap. de Regimento de Real Artilaria in Barcelona. Memorialist not having heard of him for three years concluded him to be dead, till last week by a shipp receiv'd the account from him wherein he begs for a discharge. Memorialist humbly begs your Lordship to get him discharged that he may return to England." †

A scholar, whose name is not given, also accompanied Lord Cobham's expedition. He is vaguely referred to in a military journal quoted in *The Political State of Europe*, 1719, as "an ingenious gentleman." This would-be poet wrote some very flattering Latin verses in Lord Cobham's honour and then turned them into French for the benefit of those officers who were unacquainted with the former dead language. The French lines are as follows :—

"Perkin ce Heros en peinture
    Du Lion Espagnol ayant pris le Minois,
La Grippe, la Dent, la Posture
    Menacoit, mais de loin, le Leopard Anglois
De cette fausse et étrangere Armûre
    Tu dépouilles, Cobham, ce Lion contrefait ;
Alors malgre son imposture,
    Il nous paroit ce qu'il est en effet,
    Un ridicule es[t] vil Baudet."

By way of diverting Spanish attention the French sent a force overland to besiege the town of Rosas, in Catalonia, at the same time that Lord Cobham bombarded Vigo. Ill luck attended the French expedition. While crossing the Pyrenees a violent storm

---

* A certain Richard Woollaston in the 17th century was appointed Master Gunner of England by the Committee of National Safety in 1649.

† *S.P. Dom. George I.*, Bundle 25, No. 32.

hurled some of the gun-carriages down a steep precipice, and about twenty mules laden with provisions shared the same fate. A London paper, dated 19th November, 1719, quoting advice from Paris two days earlier, chronicles :—•

> " There appears yet some hopes of recovering the carriages of the Artillery which was intended for the siege of Rosas and were lost in the great storm which was so violent that 15 or 20 mules, loaded with provisions for the Army, were blown off the side of a precipice betwixt Collioure (*sic*) and Rosas ; upon this disaster we look upon that siege to be disappointed for the present." *

One of the most remarkable, as well as dangerous, men of the Early Georgian Era was John Law the financier. In 1719 he was at the height of his fame, and his " system " had turned the Parisians into half-crazy gamblers. The Earl of Stair, as British Ambassador in Paris, thought it his duty to warn his Government against the Scottish financier's growing power and ambition to be " first minister " at the French Court. On the 1st September, 1719, Mr. Crawford, Lord Stair's secretary, enclosed in one of his official letters to London the following clever epigram † on John Law :—

" TO MR. L—W.

" O Toy que la France revere
Comme son unique Soutien
Esprit qu'un feu divin éclaire
Createur qui fait tout de rien
Par un espoir imaginaire
Tu nous seduis tout pour nous plaire
Ton génie est notre Trèsor
Et tu scais nous montrer de l'or
Ou tu ne vois qu'un Chimère."

In May, 1720, Lord Stair was recalled. and a month later Law's boasted " Mississippi scheme " collapsed, and the shares fell to nothing; while the projector fled for dear life to Brussels. Among those Britons who had bought Mississippi shares at an inflated price was Captain Alexander Abercrombie (p. 347), of the Royal North British Fusiliers. Here is his letter to

* *The St. James Evening Post*, 19–21 Nov. 1719.
† *S.P. Foreign, France*, P.R.O., Vol. 165, fol. 113.

one of the Secretaries of State, asking for leave to go to Paris and giving the reasons why :—

> "SIR,   Sept. 15, 1720.
>
> "Having been so unluckie to send over any little money I had some tyme agoe to France, I am afrayde that next arret (*sic*) may take the remains and therefore I would gladly goe over and take what I can if you will doe me the honour to procure me two Months Leave to goe for Paris. I beg you will excuse this truble from
>
> "Your most faithfull and most obedient humble servant,
> "ALEX. ABERCROMBIE."

Secretary Craggs endorsed this letter "Allowed" ! *

John Law's evil influence communicated itself to the directors of the English South Sea Company, who, prior to 1720, had acted with honourable intent. In April, 1720, the South Sea Bill—the main public intention of which was the re-purchase of what had hitherto been unredeemable annuities granted by the Government during the last two reigns—passed both Houses of Parliament. The rage of speculation that had turned Paris into one big gambling hell now descended upon London. The result is a matter of history. Numbers of Army officers bought South Sea Stock at a very high figure, and were ruined, or nearly so, when the gigantic bubble burst. Some of the cases were very pitiable. Here is a sample :—

> "PETITION OF LT.-COLONEL JAMES CUNNINGHAM OF THE
> EARL OF ORKNEY'S REGIMENT OF FOOT.
>
> "Petitioner had served in above Regt. from 1686 and was a Major and Brevet Lt.-Colonel. He had made twenty-two campaigns in Flanders and received several dangerous wounds—one through the body at Hochstadt [Blenheim]. He sold his commission in 1718 and laid out his money in Government Securitys at a very high rate in 1720. He not only lost the product of his post but also the greatest part of all he had in the World, and having so numerous a family to subsist, and provide for, and nothing to do, appeals for half pay." †

This petition bears the callous Treasury endorsement, "No Order." On 25th December, 1726, Lt.-Colonel Cunningham was

---

* *S.P. Dom. George I.*, Bundle 25, No. 176.
† *Ibid.*, Bundle 24, No. 277.

transferred from his post as Lieutenant-Governor of Fort William to a similar command at Inverness (p. 347). Other military holders of South Sea Stock who suffered were General Owen Wynne, who lost £10,000, and General John Pepper, £2,000; while Major Testefolle (whose head was evidently not his guiding star) petitioned the King "for half-pay in Ireland as Captain of Horse, the little fortune he had got in the Service was lost in the fatal and general calamity of the South Sea project." *

The Duke of Portland and Lord Belhaven had to solicit the King for West India governments. The former was made Governor of Jamaica (p. 351) and the latter Governor of Barbados (p. 332). A sad fatality befell Lord Belhaven directly after leaving England. His ship (the *Royal Anne*) was wrecked on the Stag Rocks, near the Lizard Point, on 10th November, 1721, and he was drowned. Lady Belhaven, the widow, is described by a Scottish verse-writer as having gone mad :—

> "Thus she raves, in sad distraction,
>   In her bed with cords she's bound ;
> Crying night and day, my tender jewel,
>   He is in the ocean drown'd."

Some hard things have been said by an able military historian on the subject of Secretaries-at-War during the first half of the eighteenth century. They are made out to have been more officious than official. Without going into this matter, it may be well to show how that celebrated statesman, William Pulteney (created Earl of Bath), who was Secretary-at-War from 1714 to 1717, defined, in last-named year, the duties of his office: "A Secretary-at-War is a ministerial, not a constitutional, officer, bound to issue orders according to the King's directions." Comparisons are said to be odious; but, for all that, they are sometimes useful. The Secretaries-at-War during the first ten years of the reign of George I. showed far more zeal to ameliorate the condition of both officers and men than the Board of Ordnance did for the *personnel* of the Army during the same period. Owing to failing

* *S.P. Dom. George I.*, Bundle 35.

health during the last few years of his life, the Duke of Marl-borough, as Master-General, had left things much as he found them, and official slackness was the order of the day. Archbishop King, one of the Lords Justices of Ireland, in a letter to his brother-in-law, Colonel Irvine, of the Royal Regiment of Foot, thus wrote from " Dublin, 3 July, 1722 " :—

> " My Lord Cadogan being now Master of the Ordnance, I believe I shall give him the trouble of a letter about our powder. We have had several supplies from the Tower and are now to have a considerable quantity from thence ; but they have generally sent us the refuse of what was there and such as was not fit for use. I intend to intreat his care in that particular." *

In the *Military Entry Books* for the reign of Charles II., there are occasional Royal Warrants to the Board of Ordnance, authorising "the sale of wet and decayed powder to Our best advantage"; but it was not thereby intended that at any future time the powder in question should be palmed off on the sister Kingdom! And there is abundant evidence to show that the Honourable Board of Ordnance were quite content to serve out obsolete arms of different kinds to the Regiment of Invalids raised in 1719, as well as to the Independent Companies of Invalids who were garrisoning towns on the coast and manning important forts. When the exigencies of circumstances necessi-tated an Independent Company of Foot being raised and sent out to South Carolina, five men were drafted from each of the ten companies of Colonel Fielding's Regiment of Invalids and sent to Plymouth to await embarkation. Brigadier-General Francis Nicholson (pp. 53–62) found when he came to inspect his company, that the men's arms were both old and unserviceable. He wrote at once to the Secretary-at-War, and enclosed a certificate from Captains Twynihoe and Sedgeley, commanding two companies of Invalids at Plymouth, to the effect that the firelocks complained of "were old ship's arms of different sorts, and not at all fit for his Majesty's service."† Mr. Treby (Secretary-at-War) wrote

---

* *A Great Archbishop of Dublin, William King, D.D.*, 1650–1729, p. 238.
† *Ordnance Warrants*, W.O. 55/347.

as follows to the Board of Ordnance, with reference to Nicholson's letter :—

"Whitehall, Jan. 7th, 1720/1.

"MY LORDS AND GENTLEMEN,

"I hereby desire you give order to the Storekeeper at Plymouth to deliver out of His Majesty's Stores a sufficient number of good Firelocks to the soldiers that compose General Nicholson's Independent Company in the room of those they now have, to the end that when they arrive at South Carolina they may be useful for the defence of the Fort they are to construct there.

"GEORGE TREBY." *

And here comes a wail from the distant and lonely Bermuda Islands :—

"THE HUMBLE PETITION OF BENJAMIN BENNETT, ESQ., HIS MAJESTY'S LT.-GOVERNOR OF THE BERMUDA IS-LANDS, AND CAPTAIN OF THE INDEPENDENT COMPANY THERE.

"That it is about fifteen years since the said Company received any bedding which is long since worn out; having no quarters allow'd them by the Country, but barracks, and your Petitioner having even after His Majesty's happy accession to the Throne sent over an officer to lay their deplorable case before His Majesty, and to pray for a supply of bedding many of the soldiers being very ill and in the winter season ready to starve.

"That His Majesty was pleased to order the Council of the 31st August, 1715, to refer the matter to the Board of Ordnance, but by reason the said officer was soon oblig'd to return to Bermuda nothing further had been hitherto done therein, and for want of such supplys of bedding many of the soldiers have since perish'd. Petitioner begs their Excellencies to order the bedding to be sent." †

The callousness so often exhibited by the heads of the Board of Ordnance—the storekeepers of the Kingdom—for the mortality among British soldiers in the Colonies, was on a par with that shown by the Rector of Holy Island, when the plague raged there in the year 1639. This reverend gentleman got tired of enumerating in his parish register the deaths of soldiers garrisoning the island fort, and saved himself further trouble by recording that "About this time were sundrie sogers buryed." ‡

In 1725 the great Duke of Argyll was chosen Master-General of the Ordnance, and many changes for the better took place.

---

* *Ordnance Warrants*, W.O. 55/347.

† *Ibid.*

‡ Canon Raine's *History of North Durham.*

It was under his *régime* that, in 1727, two additional companies of Royal Artillery were raised, thus putting the Royal Regiment on a more respectable footing. Three and a half months after Argyll's appointment as Master-General appeared the following eulogistic notice in a popular London journal :—

> "They write from Sevenoaks, Kent, October 3rd, that Sunday last being his Grace the Duke of Argile's birthday, Sir Henry Fermor in respect to that noble Peer made a very sumptuous entertainment where was the greatest Assembly of Gentry that ever was seen in so small a town. The bells rung all day and the evening was usher'd in with a fine Consort (*sic*) of Musick perform'd by Gentlemen whilst that celebrated song *Genius of England* began and ended it." *

On the 10th July, 1720, that unfortunate Prince known in history as the Old Pretender issued, from Rome, the Declaration which appears on Plate opposite.†

On 31st December (N.S.) 1720, the expected child first saw the light and was, in due course, christened Charles Edward. It was only to be expected that the Jacobites received this news with great joy.

A fresh impetus was given to "Stuart literature" which was surreptitiously sold in London and the provinces. A new Jacobite drinking song ‡ was printed and circulated on 10th June, 1721, the exiled "monarch's" birthday. A copy was sent by a Hanoverian loyalist to Mr. Secretary Delafaye, who endorsed it "Treasonable News." The song ran as follows :—

(1)

> "To J——s our Lord let's drink a health
>   Now on this glorious day,
> And though we're forc'd to do't by stealth
>   To his success let's pray.

(2)

> "And that he to us may be given
>   Our grief for to redress,
> Incessantly we'll ask of Heaven
>   From whence comes happiness.

---

* Mist's *Weekly Journal*, 16th October, 1725.

† There are several printed copies of this Declaration among the *S.P.D. George I.*

‡ *S.P. Dom. George I.*, Bundle 24, No. 196.

JAMES REX.

JAMES by the grace of God King of England, Scotland, France, and Ireland, Defender of the Faith, &c.

To all our Loving Subjects of what degree or quality soever Greeting.

WHEREAS it is thought our Royal Confort is now in her sixth month with Child, and whereas wee are informed that persons of the first rank in our three Kingdoms have been formerly summon'd to be present at the birth of an Heir to the Crown. That wee may conform our selves, as much as is possible to the Customs of our Contry, and do every thing in our power for the satisfaction of our People, Wee have thought fit hereby to invite all and every one of the Peers of our said three Kingdoms to come and be present at the delivery of our said Royal Confort. Given at Rome the tenth day of July 1720. in the nineteenth year of our Reign.

J. R.

(3)

" Then fill a bumper to the Queen
And let the health go round,
Let Peace attend her virtuous steps
And nought but joy abound.

(4)

" Let angels guard the Prince of Wales
That his virtues may be known,
And that himself and Father may
Reign on his Grandsire's Throne."

On the aforesaid birthday anniversary a Jacobite riot took
place at Bridgwater, where a detachment of Brigadier Philip
Honywood's Dragoons (11th) was then stationed under the
command of Lt.-Colonel Archibald Hamilton. This officer sent
an account of the riot in question to the Ministry. After detailing
how some of the Bridgwater magistrates went out of town early
on the 10th of June, and the Mayor prevented the Proclamation
against rioting being published, Colonel Hamilton goes on to say :—

" The Magistrates hid themselves on the 10th, leaving no one to appear but
their Incendiarys to stir up the people to insult the Government, which they did
att nine in the morning by stoning of the Guard as they march'd by the Butchers
Row, assaulting myself soon after with cleavers and knives when no one was
with me, but my Drum[mer] whom they beat without any provocation ; 'twas
then I applied to the Magistrates but could meet with no one to doe justice to the
troops nor to examine who put Roses, Horns, and Turnips * over the door of my
quarter and in the Market Place ; the apparent unwillingness of the Magistrates to
check the insolence with which the people shew'd their disaffection encourag'd
them to continue the Ryott all day by flinging stones and setting dogs at the
Dragoons as they pass'd ; these Insults I say my Lord I believe they [the
magistrates] will not take any notice of. About eight at night a whole street rose
upon some of the Dragoons and flung stones at them as they pass'd, and one man
L°° Farly presented his pistol loaded and prim'd to the breast of one Dragoon
(who did not so much as see him he being then looking another way) they [the
soldiers] indeavoring to seize the man to bring him before a Justice, two persons
who were in the Crowd received some blows with a stick and [one] a slight cutt
in the arm . . . . . .

"ARCH. HAMILTON."†

* See explanatory note on p. xx.—ED.
† S.P. Dom. George I., Bundle 27, No. 23.

The Mayor of Bridgwater having been commanded by the Ministry to reply to the charges made against him and the Magistrates by Colonel Hamilton, wrote the following:—

" On ninth June it was unanimously agreed that the common bellman should cry it about the Towne on the Tenth of the same they should be bound over to the next Sessions to answer the same ; but the bellman going out of Town that morning very early that Order was not perform'd, but we took such care that none but some few ignorant women and children, and one man whose name we know not, wore any White Rose that day within this Burrough.

" JONATHAN THOMAS,
" Mayor." *

This remarkably lame story, particularly well told, did not go down with the authorities. Colonel Hamilton's version of the Bridgwater riot was entirely satisfactory to Lord Townshend as is exemplified in a letter from the Colonel to Mr. Delafaye :—

" June 28, 1721.

" SIR,

" My Lord Townshend ordered me to desire you'l prepare a letter for his Lordship to sign, to reprimand the Magistrates of Bridge Water for their misbehaviour on the 10th June the Pretender's birthday ; 'twill make the King's troops all wayes easy there, which I am sure will be agreeable to you.

" I am, &c.,
" ARCH. HAMILTON.

" To Charles Delafaye, Esq., Deputy Secretary of State." †

Time has preserved an unbiassed account of the Bridgwater riot in a letter by the historian John Oldmixon, who happened to be collector of the port at aforesaid town. This letter ‡ was also to Mr. Delafaye and was dated 1st July, 1721.

In the spring of 1722 a far-reaching Jacobite conspiracy was brought to light. The project included a foreign invasion of 5,000 troops under Ormond and a simultaneous rising in Great Britain. Among the conspirators were two former British general officers, Lord North and the Earl of Orrery. The Duke of Norfolk and the Bishop of Rochester were both deeply implicated. All four were sent to the Tower; also Christopher Layer, a barrister of the

---

* *S.P. Dom. George I.,* Bundle 27, No. 26.

† *Ibid.,* Bundle 29, No. 324.

‡ See facsimile facing p. xxxii. The original letter is among the *S.P. Dom. George I.,* Bundle 27.

Middle Temple, who was sent to trial 21st October, at King's Bench, most incriminating papers being found in his writing. One of these documents was Layer's "Scheme" which bore for a motto "Au defaut de la Force il faut employer la Ruse." Other papers contained lists of soldiers and non-commissioned officers whom he professed to have won over to the Jacobite conspiracy; also lists of officers belonging to regiments in the London district. After some of the names in last-named lists occur the significant words "To be secured." While yet another list of officers was addressed to "Colonel Duncan Mackenzie at Mr. Hilliards a saddler and corner house as you goe in to Craig's Court over against the Devil's Tavern at Chairing (sic) Cross, or at Old Man's Coffee House."*

It goes without saying that when Colonel Duncan Mackenzie was "wanted" he was not found at the above addresses!

Layer was executed at Tyburn, 17th May, 1723, and his head affixed to Temple Bar. According to a modern writer, Layer's head happened to be blown off its lofty perch one windy night and the finder sold it to Dr. Richard Rawlinson, the Jacobite antiquary. He kept the skull in his study and was buried with it in his right hand.†

The heads of the Jacobite conspiracy had planned the rising to take place while the King was at Hanover and Parliament not sitting. George I. gave up his intended visit to Germany and a large force of troops, including artillery, were encamped in Hyde Park. Six infantry regiments were ordered from Ireland to England; but were shortly afterwards countermanded. A paragraph in a London paper for July, 1722, records that "Orders were sent to stop the transportation of the Irish Regiments into England, but the express being detained at Park Gate [Cheshire] by contrary winds, several transports arrived before he could put to sea."

Important evidence regarding the great conspiracy was given by Captain Andrew Pancier, late Captain-Lieutenant of Lord

---

* *S.P. Dom. George I.,* Bundle 40.
† Nichols' *Literary Anecdotes,* Vol. V., p. 497.

Sir

It is at the Desire & the Earnest Entreaty of the King's Friends in this Town, that I presume to continue the Advice I gave in my Last of the Riot here on the 10th of June

As I then hinted Coll Hamilton of Brigadier Honeywoods Regimt of Dragoons, wrote to the Ministry, & by Mondays Post a Letter came to him from My Lord Townshend intimating that his Majesty approvd of the Colls Zeal and Conduct and directing a farther hint of the Affair, to see if the Rioters should be prosecuted at the Kings Charge. Another Letter came from his Lordp to the Mayor and tho they keep the Contents of it very secret, yet I understand the Substance is to direct them to explain themselves why an Order of the Mayor & Common Council (drawn up by Mr Sloane himself) was not published as they promisd Instead of which the Mayor & his Officers employd on those Occasions, withdrew Themselves, This Order was to prevent wearing White Roses, What else there is in the Mayors Letter I cannot Learn, But they have ever since been practising their Old way of Affidavits with which I suppose they rather intend to perplex than clear the Matter.

Coll Hamilton had with good precaution orderd the Dragoons to be drawn up in the Morning & sent a Guard to a Post assignd by the Magistrates, which Guard were pelted with Stones in their March hither and this Sir, was the Beginning of the Riot. The Soldiers finding that Post not convenient were returning to the Cross, & a Drum going thro' the Shambles the Butchers fell upon him. The Coll Himself passing that Way afterwards the same Butchers took up their Cleavers & ripping Knives as the Mayoress had threatend if they were disturbd in their White Roses, & said they would cut the Dragoons to pieces if they came there, or Words to that Effect of which Coll Hamilton has made an Affidavit. They had early in the Morning hung out a Garland of White Roses on the Cornhill, & Another Such Garland decorated with Horns at the Colls Quarters Which with other Signs of Insolence & Sedition continued all the Day, did indeed put some of the Soldiers so out of temper towards the Evening That they bang'd two or three of the Offenders & broke 2 or 3 Panes of Glass, for which Coll Hamilton gave them immediately more Satisfaction than they desird Laid aside All thoughts of prosecuting One of the Fellows, who was taken with a Pistol laden & primd in his Pocket.

& But notwithstanding this Satisfaction All the Magistrates do to

justifie their Conduct & to stirr up those very persons to make New
Affidavits of Injuries, for which they have been much over paid
in procuring these Oaths, which have not the least Relation to their
refusing to publish the Order of Council, nor to the Morning Joyfully
nor to the Riot in & near the Shambles, Nor to the Mayors
Wife & Children marching about Town Seven Jrulling with
their White Roses, They aggravate as far as they are capable
The Soldiers beating off Some of the Accomplices of the Rioters
& I'm informd money has not been wanting to encourage the
Swearers, which they are certainly the best provided with of any
Body of Men in England, as appeard Justiciously in the Corporation
Cause

By this You will perceive Sir, that the Charge of Disaffection
Stands good against Them & that they are incorrigible in it
This will also confirm the just Character given of them in former
Representations to the King & Council & His Majesty has lately
heard how they are affected to him. The Ministers have it fresh
in Consideration, Their Charter is declard Void by the most
able Lawyers, for Want of a regular Surrender of the Old
One Thus the Authority they abuse reverts to the Crown
The Matter is gone through already & their Demerits Notorious

It is not for me to draw any Conclusions from these Premises
but in the Name of the Honest Men for Whom I write most
humbly to assure You of the Utmost Devotion On All Occasions
to Your Service & Interest

I am With Respect & Gratitude

Sir

Your most Obedient
most faithful
& most oblig'd Humble Servant

Customhouse Bridgwater
1 July 1725

J. Oldmixon.

Cobham's Dragoons. This officer was sworn before Secretary Delafaye, 24th August, 1722, and testified that "he had become acquainted with one James Skeen, who was at Preston and Glenshiel in the Rebel Army and had commanded 100 men at Preston under [Brigadier] Mackintosh." Skeen (? Skene), who was cousin to the Earl of Mar, got on very friendly terms with Pancier and offered to procure him a good post in the military service of King James. Pancier also testified to having been told

"THE KING OVER THE WATER"

by Skeen that "the design for placing the Pretender on the throne of three Kingdoms would be put in execution before the end of November." * Pancier owned that "he had been undone by the South Sea Scheme and had to sell his commission." This accounts for his indecent haste to denounce the brave Scottish soldier with whom he had been on very friendly terms. Skeen was sent to the Tower where he underwent a long and rigorous imprisonment; while Pancier was rewarded some years later by being appointed Captain of an additional troop in the Royal Dragoons (p. 205).

* *S.P. Dom. George I.*, Bundle 35.

c

George I. showed great leniency to the Duke of Norfolk, Lord North, and the Earl of Orrery, all three being discharged from the Tower in May, 1723. The Bishop of Rochester was tried by the House of Lords for high treason. All his papers were seized and among them was a small engraving of the "King over the Water" which portrait is now preserved at the Public Record Office, London. (See previous page.)

The great popularity of Bishop Atterbury in London was shown by the following anonymous letter warning Secretary Delafaye that an attempt might be made to rescue the Bishop when being escorted by a detachment of Guards to the House of Lords :—

"HON^BLE SIR,   "April 21, 1723.

"I love King George ; I live in Newgatt Markett and keep an Ale House and I hear a great many things. The Bishop of Rochester is to go on Thursday to his Tryol ; there is several in my hearing have aggread to go with him and shout [for] him. I hope you will tak care he is garded well or else by what I find, and by what I can hear they intend to take him away from the Gards. Do not dispicse this from your well meaning Servant unkno'n.

"T. S.

"The Hon.
        "Mr. La fea
    "The Secetary's Office
        "in Whit Hall
            "London." *

Bishop Atterbury was banished the Kingdom and died an exile in France.

A good idea of the state of Ireland in 1718 may be gathered from a general order issued by the Lords Justices to the commanding officers of certain regiments in that Kingdom :—

"Whereas His Grace the Lord Archbishop of Dublin, one of the Lords Justices of the Kingdom, is going on his Visitation to Kilkenny, and that it will be for His Grace's safety to have a guard to attend him on some parts of his Road thither and back again, where the country is infested with Tories, Robbers, and Rapparees, these are to direct and require you to send with his Grace the Lord Archbishop such a number of men through such parts of the Road, leading to and from Kilkenny as His Grace shall think fit to attend him for his safety. Each party when relieved are to return to their former Garrison ; the Civil magistrates being to provide them with convenient quarters on their march according to Law. Given, &c., 28 May, 1718.†

* *S.P. Dom. George I.*, Bundle 31.
† *Military Entry Book*, P.R.O. Dublin.

By the Lord Lieutenant General
and General Governour of IRELAND,

A

DECLARATION.

CARTERET.

WHEREAS upon Viewing the last Muster taken of his Majesty's Army in this Kingdom, it appeared to Us, That divers Officers have taken liberty, at their own pleasure, to leave the Places wherein they are Garrison'd or Posted, without Licence from the Government; and many others who did obtain Licence do stay from their Duty, beyond the time allowed them, to the detriment of His Majesty's Service, and contrary to all good Order and Discipline. For prevention therefore of so great neglect of Duty, and the Inconveniences that may happen thereupon, We have thought fit hereby to Require and Command all Officers and Soldiers, now absent without Licence, immediately to repair to their respective Garrisons or Quarters, and there remain at their Duty; and all such as are absent by Licence to return at the expiration of such Licences, to their several Garrisons or Posts where they are to continue. And for the future, no Officer is upon any pretence, whatsoever, to absent himself from his Garrison or Quarter, without special Licence in Writing first obtained from Us, otherwise they must expect to be answerable for their Disobedience.

Given at His Majesty's Castle of *Dublin* the Twenty Eighth Day of *June* 1725.

By His Excellencie's Command,

Tho. Clutterbuck.

God Save the King.

DUBLIN: Printed by *Andrew Crooke,* Printer to the King's most Excellent Majesty, at the *King's-Arms* in *Copper-Alley,* 1725.

All regiments on the Irish Establishment were recruited in Great Britain. In 1724, Viscount Shannon, Commander-in-Chief in Ireland, issued a general order to Colonels of regiments on the subject of recruiting for filling up vacancies by death and desertion in regiments in Ireland :—

".... you are to give orders to the officers appointed to raise Recruits for your Regiment that they do not only avoid Inlisting any natives of this Kingdom, but likewise Inlisting any men in Ireland on any pretence whatsoever." *

Here is an early instance of "no Irish need apply."
In the summer of 1724, Lord Shannon reviewed

     4 regiments of Horse,
     6   do.   of Dragoons,
     21 battalions of Foot.

Out of a total of thirty Colonels Commandant twenty-four were absent! And in 1725 when the above regiments were again reviewed fifteen Colonels were conspicuous by their absence. In consequence of this growing evil among all ranks of officers serving in Ireland, Lord Carteret, Lord-Lieutenant and General-Governor of Ireland, issued a printed Declaration from Dublin Castle, 28th June, 1725, "commanding all Officers and Soldiers, now absent without Licence immediately to repair to their respective Garrisons or Quarters." †

Notwithstanding the aforesaid Proclamation the curse of absenteeism continued, and at a review in 1726 the field-officers of Colonel Bowles's Dragoons (12th) were "all absent." Eleven regiments were found to have "bad arms"; while the arms for two other corps were "not yet delivered." ‡

Officers were not permitted to go abroad without obtaining a pass from the King. It seems somewhat strange that in the time of peace a crack corps like Colonel Churchill's Dragoons (10th) should have to procure horses from Denmark and North Germany. Yet so it was, and on 24th August, 1724, Captain

* Miscellaneous Military Papers relating to Ireland, *Add. MS.* 23636.
† From Copy in the Brit. Mus. MS. Department. See facsimile.
‡ *Add. MS.* 23636.

Wm. Elliot (p. 196) of above regiment wrote as follows to Mr. Delafaye * :—

> " SIR,
>
> "Colonel Churchill desires the favour of you to procure a Pass from his Majesty for Captain Elliot, Cornet Edward Cator, a Quarter-Master, and five Private Dragoons of the Regiment to Hamburgh, Copenhagen, and the Places adjacent, our business is to buy horses to mount our Officers.
>
> " I am, &c.,
> " W. ELLIOT."

Throughout George I.'s reign Jacobite agents in London and other towns lost no opportunity of surreptitiously enlisting British subjects and shipping them off to Calais where they were to be drafted into a Jacobite legion. Writing to Secretary Delafaye under date of 23rd January, 1720, Sir John Fryer says :—

> "I send my friend Mr. Nicholas herewith to inform you of a very treasonable design of many persons being listed, and just going off to the ships for France. They are taken up by my Warrant and are now in the Compter. I guess there may be more on board the ship that was to carry them ; if you can get an order sent away to stop all ships that are going for Calais I hope I shall shortly know the ship's name which in this haste I cannot learne. Pray direct me what I shall do in this matter. I am lame or would wait on you." †

On the same day that above letter was written a London Justice of the Peace issued the following warrant :—

> "TO THE KEEPER OF NEWGATE.
>
> " Receive into your custody the body of John Grant he being charged on oath for Inlisting Peter Collins for the Service of the Pretender to go with others on board a ship for France to be imployed in the Service of the said Pretender called King James. Keep him in safe custody untill discharged by due course of Law and this shall be your Warrant for so doing. Given under my hand and seal this 23rd day of January, 1719/20.
>
> J. SAUNDERS." ‡

Three months later came a wail from Newgate in the shape of a " Petition from John Grant, prisoner in Newgate, concerning his great sickness and pitiable condition."

The Channel Islands were favourite hunting-grounds for recruiting officers from France. One of these emissaries, sent by

---

* *S.P. Dom. George I.*, Bundle 51.
† *Ibid.*, Bundle 20, No. 17.
‡ *Ibid.*, No. 20.

General Dillon to Guernsey, calling himself the Chevalier de Bomblade, got on intimate terms with Lieutenant Dupray (*sic*),* an officer of the garrison, and unfolded a wondrous Jacobite scheme, in which he said: " one-third of the Kingdom of England was engaged and that several Lords had procured Arms and Magazines to further their design." The British officer felt it to be his duty to inform Colonel Spicer, Lieut.-Governor of Guernsey, of all the so-called Chevalier had told him, and the Colonel immediately despatched his son-in-law, Ensign Donovan, to London with a despatch for the Duke of Newcastle. It is interesting to know from the following letter that Colonel Giles Spicer had held commissions in the British Army since 1677. His quaintly spelt letter † is a fine sample of loyalty to his King, his country, and the profession which he so well adorned (Vol. I., p. 243, note 3) :—

" Guernzey,
" the 25 May 1724.

" SIR,

" It hath been a very sencable pleasure to mee to hear by your letter that my sonn [in-law] Mr. Donovan hath discharged his late commission soe well to the sattisfaction of his Grace of Newcastle. Ever since the year 1677 that our Sovrons have honored mee with Commissions in the Army it hath been my greatest pleasure and Glory to serve the Government faithfully, and I think it my greatest Happiness now to pass the residue of my dayes in protecting these Islands in their unanimous zeale to the Elustreous house of Hanover, and to nexclect noe opertunity in serving my King and Country. Pray make my very humble respects and duty exceptable to his Grace and believe me,

" Sir,

" Yo' most obedient,
" faithfull humble servant,

" To Charles Delafaye, Esq." "GILES SPICER.

Among the Governors of Scottish Forts and Castles during the latter half of George I.'s reign the name of Colonel Jasper Clayton (Vol. I., p. 340, note 1) stands out in bold relief. When Clayton was appointed Governor of Inverness the citizens were smarting under an " Act for levying duty of 2d. Scots, or one-

---

* In the *S.P. Dom. George I.*, Bundle 50, is the lengthy statement dated 3rd April, 1724, made on oath by Lieut. Dupray. This officer cannot be traced, but there was a Lieut. *Duprat* on the English Half-pay List in 1722.

† *Ibid.*, Bundle 49, No. 188.

sixth part of a penny sterling, upon every pint of ale or beer that shall be vended or sold within the town of Inverness, and privileges thereof, for paying the debts of the said town and for building a Church and making a harbour there." Clayton had not been long at his new post before he commenced fortifying Inverness and making the Castle proof against everything except cannon. He set many hands to work and erected a battery. Lord Carpenter, then Commander-in-Chief in Scotland, brought Colonel Clayton's diligence to the notice of the Duke of Roxburghe (Secretary of State for Scotland), and went on to say that the Governor "could erect another battery for ten or twelve pounds expense. Two or three pieces of cannon may be planted on it that would command the bridge, the hill, and all the woods both to the Town and Castle. This would be a very great security—the Town being entirely open." *

After reading the above it is very amusing to come across an Inverness magistrate's letter to the Lord Advocate dated 1726, in which the writer plainly sets forth his contempt for the military in general and the English law in particular.

"As we have at all times," he writes, "out of our affection to his Magesti's person and Government endeavoured to cultivate a friendship with the troops quartered amongst us, it is with the greatest reluctance that we declare it impossible for us to bear with the haughty, keen, and unsupportable government of these military and stranger judges set over us. We mean Coll. Clayton and Mr. Burt,† Justices of the Peace, and Major Ormisby of General Whitney's (sic) ‡ Regiment. It is not possible for us to give your Loyt [Lordship] due account of the many insults and indignities offered us, we have no better terms from Coll. Clayton than 'trucklers!'

"It is common for the last two to say in the coffee-house that we are corrupt and partiall Judges—that we have neither law nor Justice in our country—Dam our Laws.

"They, the Justices of the Peace above-named, will lay all matters before them and show up the English law, and they will support and execute their sentences by their military force.

* *S.P. Dom. George I.* for 1720.

† Edmund Burt was agent to General George Wade in connection with the forfeited estates in the Highlands. He was author of *Letters from a Gentleman in the North of Scotland.* The first edition of the *Letters* was published in 1754. Burt d. in London 4th Feb. 1755.—ED.

‡ There was no General Whitney at this date. The name ought to be *Whetham's* Regiment (12th Foot) then in Scotland.—ED.

"If at any time we complain to the Governor of the injustice done the inhabitants by the soldiers, we meet with haughtiness and flashes of passion instead of redress ; we are publickly certified every day almost by Major Ormisby. That if he see but three town's people in a tuilzee (or a mob as he calls it), that, by God, he will Disperse them that minute by Bullot, That he'l let us know that he is not oblidged to read a proclamation, or wait dispersing of a mob one minute, and to convince us that he is in earnest, the oyr day, when we were going by the Guard-room with a buriell, the Guard was turned out and ordered to charge their pieces with Ball, and put fresh powder in their pans, which was at our sight execute ; and as we know not how farr a man of Mr. Ormisby's complexion might mistake a buriell or some such occasion for a mob, we represented to the Governor that we did not understand such management, who told us in derision that what the Major did was to do us honour, and all the excuse for this threat to shoot us is that we (are ?) only fined in £90 Scots.

" My Lord, if such treatment as we meet with dayly be the effect of lodging a judicative power in the hands of strangers and military, we cannot longer boast of being free-born subject, but must acknowledge ourselves slaves to the pride and passion of such as profess not only ane ignorance of our law, but ane abhorrence of all our countrymen without distinguishing betwixt such as wish well to the present constitution or not." *

Two notable events occurred in Scotland in 1725, viz., the formation in the spring of the year of six Independent Companies of Foot (p. 344) in the Highlands—the nucleus of the famous corps known as "The Black Watch"—and the pardon by George I. of divers Scots lords and gentry against whom an attainder had been passed. "Robert Campbell, *alias* Macgregor, commonly called Rob Roy," was among those to whom the King extended his clemency.† It has already been stated (Vol. I., p. xlvi.) that the system of purchasing and selling commissions was highly disapproved of by George I., but that the Board of General Officers who had to be consulted in this weighty matter was too strong for him. The King, however, by a Royal Warrant of 27th February, 1719 (p. 109), regulated the prices to be paid for commissions in the Life Guards, Cavalry, Foot Guards and Infantry—which sums nominally held good for many a long day. But from the date of the aforesaid Royal Warrant to 1871, when purchase was abolished, the regulation prices for commissions were very seldom the respective amounts paid by the purchasers

* This letter was given in an article entitled " A Beautiful Capital," by John Macleay and appeared in *The English Illustrated Magazine.*

† *S.P. Dom. George I.*, Bundle 60.

to the vendors. The outgoing officer expected, and received, an over-regulation sum for the regimental post he was vacating. The military authorities had to wink at transactions of this kind for they could not stop them. Four years after George I. fixed the scale of prices for the purchase of commissions in the British Army, Ensign Smith, of the Independent Company of Foot, doing duty at Edinburgh Castle, made a written declaration, which ran as follows * :—

"I James Smith of the Garrison of Edinburgh Castle commanded by the Rt. Hon. the Earl of Orkney desire leave to resign my Commission of Ensign in the said Garrison to any such person as His Majesty shall please to appoint and am content to receive the sum of Two hundred and forty pounds Sterling in consideration thereof. As witness my hand at Edinburgh Castle the 28th day of February, 1722/3, before theis witnesses Major James Le Blanc of the aforesaid Garrison and Mr. Andrew Melvill Doctor of Medicine in Edinburgh.

"JAMES SMITH.

"JAS. LE BLANC
" witness.
"A. MELVILL
" witness."

The regulation price for an Ensigncy was £200 (p. 109) but Ensign Smith demanded £240 !

It will be seen from many annotations to Commission Registers, given in the latter half of this volume, that widows of officers of all ranks were granted pensions when their respective husbands died ; but it would seem there was no fund for full-pay retirement during the first half of the eighteenth century for superannuated officers—they must go on half-pay if they could not get appointed to Invalid Companies. There were one or two rare exceptions made in the case of subalterns of many years' standing. Here is a curious instance. Lieutenant Patrick Agnew of the Inniskilling Dragoons (p. 214), after twenty-four years' service in said corps, was, by a Royal Warrant signed 20th April, 1744, granted a pension of "nine shillings per diem for his natural life, the said sum being made up by one shilling per diem being deducted from the youngest Lieutenant's pay and full pay of the youngest Cornet, viz., eight shillings per diem which makes up the amount of nine shillings per diem, and Peter (*sic*) Agnew's wife to be entitled to the pension of a Lieutenant's widow in case she should survive. Same pension to commence 31st August, 1743."*

Two important colonies in the New World came under the rule of British Governors in the reign of George I., viz., the Bahama Islands and South Carolina. Captain Woodes Rogers the circumnavigator was sent out to the Bahamas early in 1718 with an Independent Company. He had the King's orders for fortifying the settlement and suppressing piracy. How well Rogers carried out his orders is told in his own letters given in this volume (pp. 96–97); but the rough reception he met with at the hands of the pirate chiefs on his arrival off the island of Providence is best described in the words of a nineteenth-century writer:—

"Governor Rogers arrived off Nassau on the 11th April, 1718, in the evening; when it being unsafe to venture over the bar in the dark it was resolved to lie off-and-on till daybreak, but the *Rose*, a 20-gun frigate, was sent in advance. The daring [pirate] Vane (p. 96), bidding defiance to mercy, caused a French ship of 22 guns to be set on fire after double-shotting the ordnance, in hopes of burning or destroying the King's vessel, and indeed she would have been in much danger had she not got off in time by cutting her cables. His own escape was next to be attempted, and as he had also to wait till it was light enough to steer through the passage it allowed of the *Rose*, *Milford*, and another man-of-war to make towards him. He, however, having a fast sailing brigantine, cleared the toils, and, hoisting the black flag, fired a shot at his opponents and saw the *Milford* and her second run aground. After the fleet was safely moored in the harbour Woodes Rogers took formal possession of the fortress, being met at his landing by the president of the council, the chief justice, and the principal people of the place, as well as by the [six] pirate captains [who had acknowledged Rogers], and others, with their crews drawn up in two lines, reaching from the water-side to the port. After reading his Majesty's commission in presence of all the inhabitants of the island, he proceeded to settle the government upon plans as moderate, though vigorous, as wise." †

Captain Edward Teach (p. 96), the most notorious of the pirates who defied the authority of Governor Rogers, has been thus described:—

"Teach was a most ferocious and depraved monster in whose iron breast mercy had never nestled and his person corresponded to his ferocity. . . . . In times of action he had a particularly brutal and furious aspect—with three

* *War Office Miscellany Book*, No. 20 at P.R.O.
† From a paper entitled "The Marooners, or successors of the Buccaneers," printed in the *United Service Journal*, 1835, Part I., p. 490.

brace of pistols suspended to him, and lighted matches under his hat, sticking out over his ears, flourishing his sabre, he shouted the most blasphemous execrations that vulgarity and wickedness could prompt. Even his jokes were in admirable unison with the audacious extravagance of his character. As his men it seems thought that he dealt with the devil, he resolved to show them a hell of his own creation. For this purpose he collected a quantity of sulphur and other combustible materials between decks, and shutting down the hatches he literally involved himself and companions in fire and brimstone. With oaths and frantic gestures he then acted the part of a demon, as little affected by the smoke and stench as if he had served his time in the infernal regions, till his comrades nearly suffocated and fainting, implored relief, when he opened the hatches, not a little pleased that he had held out the longest. . . . He was often married, indeed he had no fewer than fourteen women whom he called his wives." *

On 21st November, 1718, Teach met a better death than he deserved in a desperate action off the coast of Virginia with a royal sloop commanded by Lieutenant Maynard, R.N., which Teach had boarded. The victor cut the dead pirate's head off and attached it to his bowsprit end.†

Piping times of peace were productive of many duels and internecine quarrels in Great Britain and Ireland amongst military men and civilians. A nineteenth-century writer records that :—

"During the summer of 1717, on the evening of a levee, a large party of persons who moved in the sphere of gentlemen, had assembled at the Royal Chocolate House in St. James's Street. Disputes at hazard produced a quarrel, which became general throughout the room and a general *mêlée* ensued. As they fought with swords three gentlemen were mortally wounded. The affray was only ended by the interposition of the Royal Guards, who, as entreaties and commands were of no avail, were compelled to knock the combatants down indiscriminately with the butt-end of their muskets. A footman of one of the parties, a Colonel Cunningham, who was greatly attached to his master, seeing his danger, rushed through the swords, seized him round the body, and literally carried him by force out of the room."‡

A London paper,§ under date of 21st May, 1720, contains the following paragraph :—

"On Wednesday night last, about twelve, there was such a great riot in Windmill Street that near 100 gentlemen and others were all engaged at one time, some with swords and others with sticks and canes, wherein abundance were

* From a paper entitled "The Marooners, or successors of the Buccaneers," printed in the *United Service Journal*, 1835, Part I., pp. 492-94.

† *Ibid.*, p. 494.

‡ Article entitled "Progress of Duelling in England," in the *United Service Journal*, 1838, Part III., p. 301.

§ *The Original Weekly Journal.*

dangerously wounded ; the watchmen that came up to put an end to the affray were knocked down and barbarously used. At last the patrole of Horse Guards came, and, finding them obstinate, rode through them, cutting all the way with their swords ; yet we hear of none that were killed upon the spot, though many, it is thought, cannot recover of their wounds."

On 3rd May, 1726, Major John Oneby, a half-pay officer who had served during Queen Anne's wars, was convicted of murder under circumstances of peculiar aggravation. The Major* escaped execution by committing suicide the night preceding it.

The *Historical Register* for 1720 records, under date of 29th May, the death of Major Browne of Bowles's Dragoons, " killed in a duel in Dublin by Mr. Whologan (*sic*), a gentleman of County Cork." The details of this encounter are not forthcoming, but it is within the bounds of possibility that the above-mentioned Mr. Whologan may have given his name to that undesirable class now termed "hooligans."†

In 1720 Gibraltar was threatened by the Spaniards. The garrison consisted of three weak infantry regiments (5th, 13th and 20th), and only two field officers were in the fortress.‡ Colonel Richard Kane (p. 144), Lieut.-Governor of Minorca, was ordered to embark some troops from his garrison and proceed to Gibraltar under convoy of the Mediterranean fleet. Kane's timely reinforcement of men and supplies saved the situation, and the Spanish fleet sailed for Ceuta. Towards the close of the year 1726 a Spanish army began to assemble near Algeciras. As there had been no declaration of war between Great Britain and Spain the British fleet under Admiral Hopson, then at anchor in the bay, was powerless to act. In the meantime strained relations with Germany caused the British Government to prepare for war. The Army was increased by three additional troops to the Horse and Dragoon regiments in England,

---

* See biographical notice of this officer in Vol. V. of *English Army Lists and Commission Registers*, 1661–1714, p. 198, note 8.

† This word does not appear in *The New English Dictionary*, edited by Sir John Murray.

‡ *History of the XXth Regiment*, by Lieut. B. Smyth, p. 17.

while two companies were added to each infantry corps. The war-cloud with Germany passed away; but was followed by a rupture with Spain. Three complete infantry regiments embarked on board the fleet from Portsmouth in January, 1727, and arrived in Gibraltar Bay on the 2nd February. Two regiments were sent from Cork.* Ten companies of the 1st Foot Guards, "selected by lot," embarked for Gibraltar at the end of March. Colonel Jasper Clayton, who had succeeded Brigadier Kane as Lieut.-Governor, took over the command of the fortress until the arrival of the Governor—the veteran Earl of Portmore —who arrived in April, "accompanied by several persons of quality and distinction," whose names unfortunately are not given.

It is disappointing to find that the Colonial State Papers† at the Public Record Office, London, contain no records of the siege of Gibraltar which practically commenced on the 11th February, 1727, and continued until the middle of June following. The loss of the garrison, given in detail, appears in a contemporary periodical.‡ In Dodds's *History of Gibraltar*, it is stated that

---

* The Duke of Newcastle writing to Colonel Clayton on 21st March, 1726/7, says : "I hope the two Irish Regiments are with you by this time ; the further reinforcement mentioned in my last of 7th inst. of your own regiment, and a detachment of the Guards will put to sea in a very few days for Gibraltar."—*Gibraltar Papers*, Colonial Office, 91/1.

† *Gibraltar Papers*, Colonial Office, 91/1.

‡ *Political State of Great Britain*, Vol. XXXIV., p. 413.

—	Officers killed.	Men killed.	Men wounded.	Died of wounds.	Total.
Foot Guards -	—	2	19	2	23
Royal Artillery	1	11	16	2	30
Pearce's 5th Regiment -	—	4	9	—	13
Lord Mark Kerr's 13th Regiment	—	7	26	3	36
Clayton's 14th Regiment -	—	7	13	5	25
Egerton's 20th Regiment	1	8	12	8	29
Middleton's 25th Regiment	1	3	14	—	11
Anstruther's 26th Regiment -	—	6	29	3	38
Disney's 29th Regiment	—	2	12	—	14
Bissett's 30th Regiment	—	8	15	4	27
Hayes's 34th Regiment -	—	2	16	2	20
Newton's 39th Regiment -	—	6	4	4	14
Detachments from the Regiments at Minorca, under Col. Cosby, 18th Foot	—	6	17	1	24
TOTAL -	3	72	202	34	311

there was a heavy loss by sickness during this siege, and for some time after : —

> "The Guards lost upward of a hundred and six men, and the other regiments in proportion, but 'twas chiefly by sickness, and, as it appears, after the 12th June, so that by the lists [of casualties], which are most exact and true, above eight times as many died from distemper, occasioned, as it was thought, by want of fresh provisions, as well by all the accidents attending the siege."

The reference to the lack of fresh provisions by the historian in question may excite the curiosity of the reader as to what the soldiers' diet consisted of during the four months' blockade. The following copy of a document penned by the chief store keeper at Gibraltar, gives full particulars of the provisions served out to the garrison a few months before hostilities commenced :—

> "A REPORT of the manner of serveing out of the provisions for the Publick Serviss of the Garrisson.
> "Every Monday morning the Regiments receives all their provissions except bread, except in winter time when one regiment is serv'd in the after noon by reason of the days being short, & they take it by turns in being first serv'd. The biskett takeing up more time, it is served out every Tuesday morning, & when soft bread is issued out it is every fourth day, except to Officers every second day.
> "The Gunners, Ordnance & the severall odd Mess's receive their provissions on Mondays affter the regiments are severd (*sic*) in y⁰ afternoon.
> "The Spaniards receive their provissions twice a month, which is serv'd out every other Tuesday after the biskett is serv'd to the regiments, & when soft bread is issu'd, they receive it every fourth day as the regiments dos, I presume the reason of serveing the Spaniards only twice a month, was in regard to their haveing better conveniencys for preserveing, or secureing the provissions than the soldiers has in their barracks.
> "Wᵐ. SHERER.
> "Victualling Office yᵉ 3ʳᵈ August 1726, O.S."

> "The species that are issu'd in lieu of some others specified in the contract, on any emergency, or when some species may fall short, are Vizt.——
> "By the last contract oyle was issuable in lieu of butter or cheese, as it is now, except you disaprove, yᵉ proportion beeing one pint in lieu of a pound of butter or two pounds of cheese——
> "When in want of pease or oatmeal, rice is issu'd in lieu, one pint in lieu of four pints of pease, & halfe a pint in lieu of three pints of oatmeal/flower has allso been issu'd in lieu of those two species, & in lieu of one gallᵒ of pease, three pounds of flower & one pound Dᵒ in lieu of three pints of oatmeal——

" It has sometimes hapin'd that a larger quantity of beefe has been in the Stores then of pork, in such case sometimes there has been an issue of all beefe, giveing three for two of pork, in order to bring y⁰ speces more equall, the proportion being about equall in value, & is frequintly practis'd in the Navy——

           " Wᵐ. SHERER.

" The Allowance pʳ week for one man as pʳ contract, is seven pound of biskitt, two & half pound of beef, one pound of pork, four pints of pease, three pints of oat-meale, six ounces of butter & eight ounces of cheese, except oyl is issued as above, & if requir'd, flower may be issued in lieu of bread——

" There is no deduction in weight or measure of eights for waste &c." *

It is interesting to find that in 1796 the food of the British soldiers at Gibraltar was of the same kind as just stated. " They were given one meal a day of the King's own mess beef, or pork, and pease pudding. Such a diet was provocative to drink with the thermometer at 80°."†

A humorous incident during the siege of Gibraltar is recorded by an officer in the Spanish camp in a French letter which some-how fell into British hands and is still preserved with the following translation :—

" The day before yesterday the Duke of Wharton insisted on going to a [British] Battery to show his Garter Riband‡ crying out a thousand times ' Long live the Pretender,' and using a quantity of bad language. They represented to him repeatedly that he ought to withdraw, but he refused to do so. At last he was struck by a piece of a shell on the toe. He had been drinking brandy, otherwise perhaps he would have been wiser. . . . If the English do not have pity on us we shall all have our beards grey before Gibraltar is taken. Plenty of persons have engaged to write otherwise but I would rather hold my tongue than write falsehoods." §

On 3rd June, 1727, George I. left England for Hanover. As he never lived to return the under-mentioned official

---

* *Add. MS.* 23637, fol. 111.

† *United Service Journal*, 1843, Part III., p. 599.

‡ " Deposition of Samuel Crewe one of His Majesty's Messengers, who says that being sent with Dispatches to his Excellency Colonel Stanhope, His Majesty's Ambassador at Madrid heard there the 31st March last [1726] . . . having to employ one Thomas Don, a taylor there, he told the Deponent in discourse that he the said Thomas Don had some days before sewed upon the coat of the Duke of Wharton, who was then at Madrid, a star in the same manner as worn by Knights of the Garter." —*S.P. Dom. George I.*, Bundle 62.

§ *Townshend Papers*, printed by the Hist. MSS. Commission, p. 199.

arrangements for His Majesty's journey have an interest of their own :—

"MEMORANDUM.*

" À Son Excellence Mylord TownShend touchant les Escortes pour Sa Majesté de Vaert jusqu'à Nordhorn. Selon la Route cy jointe que Le Roy prendra :

" Et Sa Majesté s'Embarquera icy le 2ᵈ ou le 3ᵐᵉ de Juin.

" Mais Sa Majesté ne veut avoir plus que dix Cavalliers commandés par un lieutenant ou Cornet sur chaque Station.

" E. LOCHMAN.

" Londre le 25 du May, 1727."

" ROUTE

" De Postes que Sa Majesté prendra par l'Hollande, de Vaert jusqu'à Nordhorn. De Vaert jusqu'

à Utrecht - - - - -	2. heures.
Amersfort - - - -	4. heures.
Voerthuysen - - -	3. heures.
Appeldoren - - -	5. heures.
Deventer - - - -	3. heures.
Holten - - - -	4. heures.
Delden - - - -	4. heures.
Ottmarsen - - -	4. heures.
Jusqu'a Nordhorn - - - - -	4. heures."

Late on 9th June (O.S.) the King arrived at Delden, and resumed his journey at 7 next morning with the intention of visiting his brother the Prince-Bishop at Osnabrück. That forenoon His Majesty had an apoplectic fit in his coach and was heard to mutter : " C'est fait de moi."† These are the last words he is said to have spoken. After being blooded by his physician (Dr. Alders) "the King indicated by a nod, and a movement of his left hand, that it was his desire to proceed to Osnabrück."‡ On arrival at his destination at 10 that night, the unconscious monarch was placed on a bed and passed away in his sleep at forty minutes after midnight on 11th June. Thus ended King George's checkered career. His remains were interred at Hanover.

* Add. MS. 15867, fol. 240.
† The First George by Lewis Melville, Vol. II., p. 145.
‡ Ibid.

THE MILITARY CAREER OF
FIELD-MARSHAL VISCOUNT COBHAM

GEORGE THE FIRST'S ARMY

1714—1727

CHAPTER I

THE MILITARY CAREER OF FIELD-MARSHAL VISCOUNT COBHAM.

> "And you ! brave Cobham, to the latest breath,
> Shall feel your ruling passion strong in death."
>
> POPE.

RICHARD TEMPLE was eldest son of Sir Richard Temple of Stowe, Bart. He is said to have been born about 1669.[1] But this approximate date is given, by one of his biographers, on the assumption that the Richard Temple who was appointed Ensign in the Prince of Denmark's Maritime Regiment, 30th June, 1685, was the son of Sir Richard Temple, 3rd Bart. of Stowe. At first sight it seemed a certainty that the aforesaid Ensign Temple was identical with the Sir Richard Temple who won military fame in Queen Anne's reign under Marlborough, and was created Viscount Cobham in 1715. But, after weighing evidence on both sides, there is conclusive proof that Ensign Richard Temple, of the Maritime Regiment, was a kinsman of the Stowe Temples, and that when the Maritime Regiment was disbanded in 1689, Ensign Temple was appointed Captain in Babington's Corps—the present Royal Warwickshire Regiment. Under date of 1702 two Richard Temples appear in the Army List—one a Captain in Columbine's (late Babington's) Foot, and the other a Baronet, who was Colonel of a newly-raised infantry corps. The latter was the future Viscount Cobham. It is on record that on 31st October, 1694, Richard, son of Sir Richard Temple of Stowe, was admitted a fellow-commoner of Christ's College, Cambridge. The undergraduate's age is given in the College books as 18. It may therefore be taken that Richard Temple was born about 1676. As he took no degree at Cambridge he did not give much promise of any particular talent. That was to come afterwards. On leaving the University it is more than probable that he made a campaign in Flanders under William III. as a volunteer, which was a common practice, at the period in question, with "sprigs of quality." In

---

[1] *Dict. of National Biography.*

A 2

May, 1697, Richard Temple succeeded his father in the baronetcy and family estate, and on 17th December, 1697, he was elected M.P. for Buckingham. When England was confronted with the War of the Spanish Succession, many regiments were hurriedly raised. Sir Richard Temple was appointed Colonel of a new infantry corps by commission dated 12th February, 1702. This appointment goes far to prove that Temple had served a campaign under William III., as this soldier-monarch was not likely to have given a regiment to a young man who had no previous knowledge of war.

In July, 1702, Temple's Regiment was ordered to proceed to Ireland. The embarkation took place at Bristol. It is recorded in *The Post Boy* for 27th August, 1702, that one of the transports which had on board two companies of Sir R. Temple's Regiment "overset, whereby forty of the men were unfortunately drowned." Sir Richard Temple did not accompany his corps to Ireland, but got permission to join the Earl of Marlborough at The Hague, and serve as a volunteer in the coming campaign. The Hon. Harry Erskine, in a letter to his brother the Earl of Mar, from "Breda, 5th August, 1702," gives a list of the gentlemen volunteers who marched with the Anglo-Dutch troops to lay siege to Venlo :—

"My Lord Kuts (*sic*) commands the English foot as Major-Generall, and Brigadeer Hamilton under him as beeing his Brigadeer. Colonell Webs, the Lord Belhemoar's [1] (*sic*), Sir Mathew Bridges, and Brigadeer Hamiltou's regiment; the Earl of Huntington (*sic*), the Marquess of Lorn, Sir Richard Temple & the Master of Stears [Stair] are gone with them as wolntiers (*sic*)." [2]

Sir R. Temple and the above-named volunteers were with the storming party at the taking of Fort St. Michael, Venlo, in September, 1702. Lord Cutts's orders to the stormers, after the covered way had been gallantly carried by them sword in hand, was that the fort must be taken, "let the consequence be what it might." Captain Robert Parker, of the Royal Irish Regiment of Foot, who was one of the stormers, graphically described in his autobiography how Fort St. Michael was taken, after the capture of a ravelin and the bridge connecting this outwork with the interior of the fort :—

"Here like madmen, without fear or wit, we pursued the enemy over the tottering bridge, exposed to the great and small shot of the body of the fort. However, we got over the fausse braye and then our situation was such that we might take the fort or die. They that fled before us climbed up by the long grass that grew out of the fort, so we climbed after them. Here we were hard put to it to pull out the palisades which pointed down upon us from the parapet, and was it not for the surprise and consternation of those within we could never have surmounted this difficulty; but as soon as they saw us at this work they quitted the rampart and retired down to the parade in the body of the fort, where they laid down their arms. Part of the garrison, in attempting to swim across the Meuse, was drowned in the river. Thus were the unaccountable orders of Lord Cutts as unaccountably executed, to the great surprise of the whole army, and even of ourselves, when we came to reflect on what we had done; however, had not several unforeseen accidents occurred not a man of us could have escaped." [3]

[1] The Earl of Barrymore's Regiment—the present Somerset Light Infantry.
[2] *The Earl of Mar's MSS.* at Alloa House, p. 224.
[3] *Memoirs of the Most Remarkable Military Transactions from the year* 1683 *to* 1718, by Captain Robert Parker.

In the above business, from first to last, 136 British officers and soldiers were killed and 161 wounded. The town of Venlo surrendered soon afterwards. It is on record that Sir Richard Temple greatly distinguished himself before Venlo. He also served at the capture of Ruremond, and at the storming of Liège citadel.

In the spring of 1704 Temple's Regiment was ordered from Dublin to Holland, but did not arrive in the Low Countries in time to accompany Marlborough's Army to Germany. The regiment was sent to garrison Gorcum. The following year Sir R. Temple served with his corps under the Earl of Orkney, who was sent in June with 12,000 men to prevent a conjunction of two large bodies of French troops near Liège. Orkney used such expedition that he seasonably reinforced the Dutch, and prevented Marshal Villeroy retaking Liège citadel, about which the French troops were then formed. On 17th July the French lines were surprised, and forced between Neer Hespern and Felixheim. Many prisoners of distinction were captured by Orkney's troops.[1]

Temple's corps did not take part in the battle of Ramillies on 23rd June, 1706. Sir R. Temple was promoted Brigadier-General 1st June, 1706, and acted as such this month at the siege of Ostend, which surrendered to Marshal Auverquerque. Temple served during the greater part of the siege of Lille in 1708, and "having borne the brunt of the siege" was sent express by the Duke of Marlborough to Queen Anne, with the Duke's account of the surrender of that fortress.[2] On 1st January, 1709, Temple was promoted Major-General. He returned to Flanders in May, 1709, and in the following September took part in the sanguinary battle of Malplaquet. Temple's and Argyll's Regiments suffered severely; the former had three officers killed and twelve wounded. For his distinguished service Sir R. Temple was promoted Lieut.-General in January, 1710, and appointed 24th April same year Colonel of the Regiment of Dragoons,[3] lately commanded by the Earl of Essex. Sir R. Temple took an active part in the siege of Douai, June, 1710. A letter "from the camp before Douay, 25th June" (N.S.), printed in *The Post Boy*, 20th June (O.S.), 1710, narrates how Douai was surrendered on Marlborough's terms :—

> "Just now the enemy beat a parley and hostages were exchanged. General Withers, Sir Richard Temple, &c., went into the town, and the French sent out three hostages on their part, who came to my Lord Duke's quarters with an air of gaiety and good humour ; but his Grace insisting on the surrender both of the town and Fort L'Escarpe to save any further loss of men and time, they returned not so pleasant as they came out. They were told that if they insisted upon the delivering up of the town only, they should be all prisoners of war ; but in case they would capitulate for both they might have honourable terms. They have till ten to-morrow to confer on't or expect a good storm, all things being ready for the purpose."

Douai surrendered on 26th June, and the garrison marched out with the honours of war.

In the following year Temple served under Marlborough at the siege and surrender of Bouchain. Being a strong Whig he was, like his great

---

[1] "In this action Webb's Brigade was composed of Tatton's, Temple's, Farrington's, and Ingoldsby's Regiments, and formed the right of the 2nd line of Infantry."—*Hist. of the 29th (Worcestershire) Regiment.*

[2] *Marlborough Dispatches*, Vol. IV., p. 274.

[3] The present 4th Hussars.

chief, laid aside by the Home Government on his return to England, and the name of Sir Richard Temple is conspicuous by its absence in the list of General Officers nominated to serve under the Duke of Ormonde in Flanders, and on 12th October, 1713, Temple's Regiment of Dragoons was given to Major-General William Evans.

On the accession of George I. this monarch rewarded Sir Richard Temple for his eminent military services by creating him Baron Cobham on 19th October, 1714, and five days later he was appointed Ambassador to the Emperor Charles VI. at Vienna. These honours were followed by Lord Cobham being given the colonelcy of the Royal Dragoons, 13th June, 1715, and in the following year he was appointed Constable of Windsor Castle.

England and France declared war with Spain in December, 1718. Six months later preparations were made for an English descent on the Spanish coast. Lord Cobham (who had been given a viscounty in 1718) was appointed to the command of the above expedition,[1] although junior to many experienced Generals. Four Infantry regiments[2] were brought over from Ireland to the Isle of Wight. Thither was also sent a detachment of Cavalry and a battalion from each of the three regiments of Foot Guards—with the 3rd, 34th, and 37th Regiments. The total force numbered 4,000. Major-General Wade was appointed second in command. The two Brigadiers were Philip Honywood and Lord Mark Kerr. Colonel Albert Borgard commanded the Artillery. Colonel John Ligonier was Adjutant-General, and Colonel John Armstrong Quartermaster-General; Captains Richard Roberts and Andrew Hamilton were Majors of Brigade; and Major Devischer A.D.C. to Lord Cobham. The expedition sailed from Portsmouth 21st September. The objective was said to be Corunna; but this may have been purposely given out to deceive the Spaniards. Be this as it may the British fleet anchored off Vigo on 29th September, and on the same evening Cobham landed with the Grenadiers of the army, three miles from the town. The armed peasants in the neighbourhood fled to the mountains, from whence they carried on an ineffectual musketry fire against the British. The Vigo garrison left the town to its fate, after having spiked the cannon, and retired into the citadel. Lord Cobham sent 800 men under Brigadier Honywood into the deserted town to garrison the place, and on 1st October Colonel Borgard landed with the heavy artillery. From forty to fifty great and small cannon were placed in position and bombarded the citadel under cover of Fort St. Sebastian which had surrendered.[3] After the citadel had been battered for some days, Lord Cobham summoned the garrison to surrender. "He sent Colonel Ligonier," wrote an officer in his journal of the expedition, "with a message to the Governor to say that if the castle was not given up immediately there would be no quarter granted. Colonel Ligonier found that the Governor had been wounded and carried out of the citadel. The Lieut.-Colonel in command desired time to send to the Marquis de Risbourg

---

[1] Secretary Treby to Secretary Delafaye from Whitehall, 28th July, 1719, desiring him "to draw a commission for Lord Viscount Cobham to be Commander-in-Chief of the Forces to be employed in the present expedition, and to have it drawn in as full and ample a manner as hath been formerly granted to other Generals upon the like occasion."—S.P.D. George I., Vol. 17.

[2] George Grove's (19th), Howard's (24th), Barrell's (28th), and Hawley's (33rd).

[3] "Journal of the Expedition to Vigo," quoted in The Political State of Great Britain, 1719.

at Tuy for directions."[1] Lord Cobham declined to wait, and the Acting-Governor capitulated on 10th October.

During the bombardment 80 of the Vigo garrison were killed and 225 wounded ; 135 soldiers had deserted ; 319 officers and soldiers, with 148 peasants, marched out of the citadel with all the honours of war.[2]

On the British side only two officers and a few soldiers were killed.[3]

Sixty large cannon had been taken in the town, 43 pieces in the citadel, about 2,000 barrels of powder, and 8,000 muskets, "All these," wrote an English historian[4] of the 19th century, "relics of Ormond's armament, and seven sloops were seized in the harbour."

On 12th October General George Wade was sent to Pontevedra on a transport with 1,000 men and a bomb vessel. He burnt the arsenal there and spiked 86 big iron cannon. The brass guns and stores were shipped for Vigo. Wade also burnt Redondella. Fort Marine was blown up, and on 25th October the great cistern of Vigo citadel met a similar fate.

On 26th October Lord Cobham wrote to Secretary Craggs from aboard the *Ipswich*, and announced his immediate return to England.[5] This letter was sent with Major Roberts on board the *Speedwell* bomb vessel, which sailed on the 26th for Portsmouth.[6] The transports followed the next day. The Spanish Government were so alarmed by the success of Lord Cobham's expedition that they made peace with England and France before the close of the year. The captured brass guns, with the stores of arms and ammunition taken in the citadel of Vigo, and at Pontevedra, were sent to the Tower of London. Their aggregate value is said to have been £87,000.[7]

In 1721, Lord Cobham was transferred to the colonelcy of the 2nd Horse—now the 1st Dragoon Guards. The following year he was appointed Controller of Army Accounts, and a few months later the King bestowed on Cobham the governorship (non-resident) of Jersey.

In the spring of 1727, when Gibraltar was being besieged by the Spaniards, the Austrians threatened to attack the Dutch frontier towns "by way of diverting the attention of the British Government from Gibraltar." George I. ordered an army corps of 10,000 men to be equipped for service in Holland, and appointed Viscount Cobham to the chief command. At this juncture Las Torres, who was conducting the siege of Gibraltar, thought it well to propose a cessation of hostilities. On 12th June a truce was agreed upon, and shortly afterwards peace was restored between Great Britain and Spain. The expeditionary force under Cobham had not left England, and the troops returned to their former garrisons.

Cobham's active career as a soldier now ceased, but he played a leading part as a politician in State affairs during the early part of George II.'s reign. For his opposition to Walpole's Excise Bill, in June, 1733, Lord Cobham was deprived of his colonelcy of the King's Regiment of Horse. He retired to Stowe, his beautiful place in Bucks, and spent much of his time in the "pleasing toils" of landscape gardening. Some years

[1] "Journal of the Expedition to Vigo," quoted in *The Political State of Great Britain*, 1719.
[2] *Ibid.*   [3] *Ibid.*   [4] Lord Stanhope.
[5] *S.P. Spain.*   [6] *Ibid.*
[7] "Journal of the Expedition to Vigo," quoted in *The Political State of Great Britain*, 1719.

previously the poet Congreve (who died in 1729) had addressed some verses to Lord Cobham containing the following couplet :—

> " Say, Cobham, what amuses thy Retreat ?
> Or Stratagems of War, or Schemes of State ? "

Pope also immortalised Lord Cobham as a " patriot" in his *Moral Essays*. His Lordship's letter to Pope, dated " Stowe, Nov. 1st, 1733," is a model of good taste and perspicuity :—

> " Though I have not modesty enough not to be pleased with your extraordinary compliment, I have wit enough to know how little I deserve it. You know all mankind are putting themselves upon the world for more than they are worth, and their friends are helping the deceit, but I am afraid I shall not pass for an absolute patriot ; however I have the honour of having received a publick testimony of your esteem and friendship, and am as proud of it as I could be of any advantage which could happen to me."

In April, 1742, Viscount Cobham was appointed Colonel of the 1st Troop of Horse Grenadier Guards,[1] and in the December following received a Field-Marshal's baton from the King. In May, 1745, his Lordship was nominated one of the Regents during King George's absence on the Continent. Cobham died 13th September, 1749, and leaving no issue by his marriage with Anne, daughter of Edmund Halsey, Esq., the barony and viscounty passed, according to the limitation, to the deceased lord's sister, Hester Grenville. This lady was created Countess Temple.

---

[1] At the time of his death he was Colonel of the 10th Dragoons—the present 10th Hussars.

FIELD-MARSHAL WADE

Lieutenant General Wade, Commander in Chief &c of his May.ᵗⁱᵉˢ Forces in Scotland

CHAPTER II

FIELD-MARSHAL WADE

1673-1748

GEORGE WADE was born in 1673. He is said to have been son of Jerome Wade of Kilavally, Westmeath, whose father, William Wade, Major of Dragoons in Cromwell's Army, had settled in Ireland. On 26th December, 1690, young Wade was appointed Ensign to Captain Richard Trevanion's Company in the Earl of Bath's Regiment (10th Foot). With this corps George Wade took part in the sanguinary battle of Steinkirk in August, 1692. Whilst serving in Flanders be was promoted Lieutenant, 10th February, 1692/3; Captain-Lieutenant, 19th April, 1694; and Captain of the Grenadier Company, 13th June, 1695. On the outbreak of the war with France, in March, 1702, Wade again served in Flanders with his corps (then commanded by Sir Bevil Granville) and was present at the sieges of Kaiserworth, Venlo, and Ruremond; also in action with the French near Nimeguen. His Grenadier Company was one of the attacking party at the storming of Liège citadel, one of the strongest in Flanders, in the autumn of 1702. Wade's gallantry on this occasion had doubtless much to do with his subsequent rapid promotion. He was appointed Major of his corps 20th March, 1703; and Brevet Lieut.-Colonel in Brigadier Blood's Regiment (17th Foot) 25th October following, after serving at the siege and capture of Huy. A few months later Wade volunteered to go with the expedition to Portugal; and through the influence of the Earl of Galway, who had been appointed Commander-in-Chief of the British contingent to serve in the Peninsula, he was appointed Adjutant-General, with the brevet rank of Colonel, 27th August, 1704.

Lord Galway took the field in Portugal in the spring of 1705, and laid siege to Valencia Alcantara, which was taken by storm. On 9th June Wade was given command of the corps subsequently known as the 33rd Foot. Colonel Hans Hamilton, writing to Lord Cutts from Lisbon on 26th June (O.S.), 1705, records: "Colonel Duncanson is dead of the wounds he received at [the siege of] Valencia and Wade has got his regiment, who was Brevet Lieut.-Colonel to Blood." [1] Wade took part in the subsequent operations [2] which culminated in the occupation of Madrid; and when the British and their allies had to evacuate the Spanish capital Wade accompanied Lord Galway's Army in the retreat to the province of Valencia. "The retreat was made in so good order," wrote Galway, "that the enemy, superior as they were in numbers, never durst venture to attack us after the warm reception twenty-two of their squadrons met with from two battalions under the command of Colonel Wade in the town of Villa Nova." At the fatal battle of Almanza, April,

---

[1] *Frankland-Russell Papers*, at Chequers Court.
[2] Wade was wounded at the siege of Alcantara, 10th April, 1706.

1707, Colonel Wade commanded, as a Brigadier-General in the Spanish Army, the third brigade of British infantry, which bore the brunt of the fighting during this deadly contest. Wade miraculously escaped capture and rejoined Galway at Alcira. Shortly afterwards the former was sent to England with despatches and was promoted Brigadier-General 1st January, 1707/8.

Wade returned to Spain a few months later and was chosen by General (afterwards Earl) Stanhope to be his second in command in the expedition to Minorca (September, 1708). Brigadier Wade led the stormers at the assault on Fort St. Philip (which defended Port Mahon) and captured a redoubt. This led to a surrender of the Castle. The capital and the rest of the Island submitted shortly afterwards and Minorca became a British dependency. Charles III., titular King of Spain, wrote a complimentary letter to Wade and bestowed on him a Major-General's commission in the Spanish Army. General James Stanhope sent Wade home with despatches in November, 1708.

On his return to the Peninsula, Wade remained in Portugal until 1710, when he rejoined Stanhope in Spain. He was given command of a British brigade of infantry, which he led to victory at Saragossa on 20th August. "All the colours, twenty-two pieces of cannon, and nearly 4,000 prisoners were captured. Also King Philip's plate and equipage. Wade was recommended by Stanhope for promotion to Major-General."[1] Wade was sent to England to ask for additional troops and supplies. He did not return to Spain. On 3rd October, 1714, Wade was promoted Major-General by George I., and a month later was appointed Major-General of the Forces in Ireland, but did not take up this command, having been elected M.P. for Hindon in Wilts, January, 1714/15.

On the breaking out of the Rebellion, in 1715, Wade was sent to Bath, a Jacobite centre, in command of two regiments of Dragoons. With his accustomed energy he soon discovered a *caché* of "eleven chests of firearms and swords, three pieces of cannon, one mortar, and moulds to cast cannon, which had been buried underground." This "find" gained for Wade great credit with the Government and made him a *persona grata* with the Bath loyalists.

In January, 1717, General Wade was sent to arrest Count Gyllenberg, the Swedish Ambassador, at his house in London, and seize his correspondence. The Count's papers disclosed a far-reaching Jacobite conspiracy, which is a matter of history. George I. showed his appreciation of Wade's past services and loyalty by giving him the colonelcy of the regiment now known as the 3rd Dragoon Guards, which became vacant by the retirement of Viscount Windsor, 19th March, 1716/17.

In the summer of 1719, when it was decided to send an expeditionary force to the coast of Spain, General Wade was chosen second in command under Viscount Cobham. Wade's share in the expedition to Vigo has already been recorded on page 7 and need not be recapitulated.

The Borough of Taunton selected General Wade for the Recordership of their town in April, 1720, and prayed the King to give his approbation to their request, which His Majesty did on 17th May following.[2] In

---

[1] Colonel Thomas Harrison's letter to Lord Dartmouth, 23rd September, 1710; see also General Stanhope's letter to Lord Dartmouth, dated 10th November, 1710.—*Dartmouth Papers.*

[2] Vellum document among the *S.P.D. George 1.*, dated 25th April, 1720.

1722 George Wade was elected M.P. for Bath, which he represented in Parliament to the time of his death.

The Disarming Act, which followed the Rebellion of 1715, had not worked well in the Highlands of Scotland; the loyal were said to be at the mercy of the disloyal, many of whom were reported to have concealed their arms. With a view to getting reliable information as to the state of affairs in the Highlands, George I. sent Wade to Scotland in July, 1724, with definite instructions as to the course he was to pursue, and to report on such remedies as in his (Wade's) observation "may conduce to the quiet of His Majesty's faithful subjects, and the good settlement of that part of the kingdom." Wade returned to London from the Highlands in the autumn of 1724, and issued a lengthy report.[1] Referring to this important document, the late Sir Kenneth S. Mackenzie, Bart., in his valuable paper on "General George Wade and his Roads,"[2] says :—

> "Confining attention mainly to the origin of the military roads, it may suffice to say that the report concluded by suggesting, under eleven different heads, what, from his own observation, Wade considered necessary to be done; and although he had in the body of his report observed on 'the great disadvantages regular troops are under when they engage with those who inhabit mountainous situations,' and the still greater impracticability of the Highlands, 'from the want of roads and bridges,' yet under none of those eleven heads does he make any recommendation that roads should be constructed. In April of the following year, however, he delivered to the King a supplement to his report, containing his scheme for reducing the Highlands to obedience, and among the purposes for which he says money would be required, he includes 'mending the roads between the garrisons and barracks for the better communication of His Majesty's troops.'"

It will be seen from the above extract that the military roads in the Highlands were not suggested by Wade until about six months after his return from his mission to Scotland in 1724. In the interim he had been appointed Commander-in-Chief of the Forces in North Britain by commission dated 25th December, 1724.

In the opening page of General Wade's "Letter and Order Book," preserved at the Junior United Service Club, London, appears this entry : "Major-General Wade arrived at Edinburgh 16th June, 1725." Previous to proceeding to Scotland Wade had received, under date of 1st June, a warrant for disarming the Highlanders, according to a recent Act of Parliament; also a set of instructions[3] for his guidance on taking up his post in Scotland. The Paymaster-General of the Forces was also authorised to pay Wade the sum of £1,000 "in consideration of his services and the charge and expense he was at in going through and visiting the Highlands of Scotland last year; as also the further sum of £500 upon account for expenses in regulating the said Highlands."[4]

Wade lost no time in carrying out his instructions relative to disarming the Highlanders. He set about this delicate task with remarkable tact and conciliatory spirit, "insomuch that he became personally popular, even though whilst faithfully obeying most distasteful orders."[5] Wade

---

[1] Printed in the Appendix to Jamieson's edition of Burt's *Letters from the Highlands.*
[2] Paper read at the Inverness Field Club, 13th April, 1897.
[3] Printed in the Appendices to this volume.
[4] Treasury Minute, dated 26th May, 1725.
[5] Lord Mahon's *History of England*, 1713–83, Vol. II., p. 86 (5th edition, 1858).

not only disarmed the tenants and vassals of the Earl of Seaforth, within a few weeks of his arrival in Scotland, but on his journey north quelled riots and disorders, both at Glasgow and Edinburgh, in consequence of the imposition of the malt tax. These facts are mentioned in the following draft of official letter [1] from Lord Townshend to General Wade, which has never before been printed :—

> "Hanover,
> "21st September/2nd October, 1725.
>
> "SIR,
>
> "The Duke of Newcastle transmitted to me your letter to him from Brahan Castle of the 21st August last, and I laid it before the King, who was so well pleased with the contents of it that His Majesty ordered me particularly to write to you to assure you how much he was satisfied with your conduct, as well as with your success, in disarming those Clans in the Highlands which were tenants and vassals to the late Earl of Seaforth. His Majesty makes no question but that you will with the same prudent and dexterous management go on to disarm the rest of the Highlands, and thereby render this part of His Majesty's dominions as obedient to the laws, and as submissive to his Government, as any other country within his realms. The King took particular notice of the handsome manner in which you performed this great service ; and ordered me to assure you that he will make good all the promises you have made in his name for the quieting the minds of the people in those parts.
>
> "You will give me leave, Sir, to congratulate you on this important success in the Highlands ; and I must tell you at the same time that the King gave no less commendation to what you did in the south, at Glasgow and Edinburgh, towards quelling the spirit of mutiny and rebellion that was growing to a dangerous heightth (sic), but is now in a fair way of being happily and totally subdued.
>
> "I am, &c.,
> "TOWNSHEND."
>
> "To Major-General Wade."

The formation, in the spring of 1725, of six Independent Companies in the Highlands (the nucleus of the famous Highland corps known as "The Black Watch") materially assisted Wade in disarming the Clans, and in furnishing detachments, in common with at least two other British regiments, for the construction of military roads. Before 1725 "everybody took the road he liked best in the Highlands," but in the autumn of aforesaid year the pickaxe and shovel altered the face of the country. "On his arrival in Scotland," writes the late Sir Kenneth Mackenzie, "Wade must have set to work with energy, for in a letter of 27th October —preserved among the Scottish Domestic State Papers at the Record Office—he already writes : 'I have made some progress in the roads of communication, and left the vessel for navigating on Lake Ness in such forwardness that I hope it will be finished in a fortnight's time.' When the year closed he was able to write of the roads still more confidently. On the 31st January, 1726, in reporting to the King how he had carried out the instructions he had received, he says : 'I presume also to acquaint your Majesty that parties of regular troops have been constantly employed in making the roads of communication between Killyhuimen and Fort William, who have already made so good a progress in that work that I hope before the end of next summer they will be rendered both practicable and convenient for the march of your Majesty's forces between those

[1] *S.P. Dom. Entry Book*, Vol. 272.

garrisons, and facilitate their assembling in one body if occasion should require." [1]

Wade was promoted Lieut.-General on 7th March, 1726/27, and on 20th June, 1727, George II. renewed this commission, as also that of Commander-in-Chief in Scotland.

During the first year of the new reign Wade reported progress to the King :—

> " I presume further to report to your Majesty that the great road of communication extending from the East to the West Sea, through the middle of the Highlands, has been successfully carried on upon the south side of the lakes from Inverness to Fort William, being near 60 miles in length, and is now practicable for the march of Artillery or other wheel-carriages, as may appear by my having travelled to that garrison the last summer in a coach and six horses to the great wonder of the inhabitants, who, before this road was made, could not pass on horseback without danger and difficulty. This work was very troublesome from the interposition of rocks, bogs, and mountains, yet was performed by your Majesty's troops quartered in those parts, without any assistance from the people of the country. The non-commissioned officers and soldiers are allowed double pay during the time they are employed on this service, and if it is your Majesty's pleasure to continue the same allowance out of the contingencies for the Army, as was granted by his late Majesty for the two preceding years, with provision for erecting stone bridges where they are wanting, a military way may be made through the mountains from Inverness southwards as far as Perth, which will open up a short and speedy communication with the troops quartered in the Low Country ; contribute to civilise the Highlanders ; and, in my humble opinion, will prove the most effectual means to continue them in a due obedience to your Majesty's Government." [2]

In the early summer of 1728 Wade commenced the road from Inverness southwards. On 20th July he wrote to the Right Hon. Henry Pelham :—

> " I am now with all possible diligence carrying on the new road for wheel carriages between Dunkeld and Inverness, of about 80 English measured miles in length, and that no time may be lost in a work so essential for His Majesty's service, I have employed 300 men on different parts of this road that the work may be done during the favourable season of the year."

Wade carried his military road as far south as Crieff.[3] From first to last he had opened out close on 259 miles of roadway,[4] and had built in

---

[1] Given in " General George Wade and his Roads," by Sir Kenneth Mackenzie, Bart.
[2] *Ibid.*
[3] Wildey's " Map of the King's Roads made by his Excellency General Wade . . . from Sterling to Inverness, with the adjacent Countries, &c.," published in 1746, ought not to have included the continuation of the road from Crieff to Stirling, as this was made by Major-General Jasper Clayton, Wade's successor in the Scottish command, about 1741.—*Ibid.*
[4] Taylor and Skinner's road distances, as quoted in " General George Wade and his Roads," are as follows :—

	Miles.	Furlongs.
Fort William to Inverness - - -	61	5
Inverness to Dunkeld (Inver Inn) -	100	4
Fort Augustus to Dalwhinnie -	31	4
Dalnacardoch to Crieff - - -	44	1
	237	6
Add Ruthven to Catcleugh - -	8	0
	245	6

twelve years forty bridges of sorts, the most notable of which was that over the Tay, at Weem, of "five arches, nearly 400 feet in length, the middle arch 60 feet wide, the starlings of oak, and the piers and land-breasts founded on piles shod with iron."[1] According to the tablets, containing both Latin and English inscriptions, this bridge was built in 1733, Wade himself having laid the first stone on 23rd April same year. This monumental work was a splendid triumph to Wade's engineering skill. William Caulfield[2] who had been appointed "Surveyor of the new roads throughout the Highlands," in 1734, is said to have written the well-known lines :—

> "Had you seen these roads before they were made,
> You would lift up your hands and bless General Wade."

In 1732 George II. conferred upon Wade the sinecure government of Berwick and Holy Island; and in 1733 he was appointed Governor of the newly-constructed Fort William, Fort George, and Fort Augustus. Wade was in England during the Porteous riots in Edinburgh; but it was owing to his application to Queen Caroline, then acting as Regent, that Captain Porteous was reprieved.[3]

On 2nd July, 1739, Wade was promoted full General. In 1740 he left Scotland for good, being succeeded by Major-General Clayton as Commander-in-Chief. In the summer of 1740 Wade was in command at Newbury, where some of the newly-raised forces were encamped. On 31st January, 1742, he was appointed Lieut.-General of the Ordnance, and on 24th June following was made a Privy Councillor.

After the British victory at Dettingen (1743) Field-Marshal the Earl of Stair resigned his command. On 14th December following Wade was promoted Field-Marshal, and appointed Commander-in-Chief of the British Forces in Flanders. He was allowed £3,000 for his "equipage."[4] The veteran Marshal, who was turned seventy, took over his important command in the spring of 1744. The British troops were allied with those of the Austrians under the Duke d'Aremberg and the Dutch under Count Nassau. From the very commencement of the so-called campaign of 1744, the three aforesaid commanders disagreed among themselves as to a united plan of action. Horace Walpole, writing in May, 1744, says : "We hear of great quarrels between Marshal Wade and Duke d'Aremberg"; and in June he tells his correspondent that while the Allies only numbered 36,000 men, the French, under the leadership of Marshal Saxe, had 90,000 in the field and were expecting 40,000 additional troops. Mr. Fortescue records in his *magnum opus* that the "Austrians and Dutch were apprehensive of leaving their towns on the frontier without garrisons," and goes on to say : "Wade, to do him justice, was for keeping all the troops together, crossing the Scheldt, and taking up a strong position to cover Ghent; but the Austrians would not consent lest they should expose Brussels."[5]

---

[1] *House of Commons Journal*, 7th Feb. 1734.

[2] Wm. Caulfield was the son of the Hon. Toby Caulfield (brother to the 2nd Viscount Charlemont). Appointed Barrack-Master-General and Inspector of Roads in North Britain in 1743. Served as Quartermaster-General at Prestonpans. In 1758 he was Deputy-Governor of Fort George and Major in the Army. His eldest son, called "Wade," after Field-Marshal Wade, was an officer in the 3rd Dragoon Guards.

[3] Duncan Forbes of Culloden, Lord Advocate, in a letter to Mr. Peter Lindsay, dated 11th Sept. 1736, writes : "Porteous's reprieve is owing, I perceive, to the application of General Wade. I wish it may have a good effect."

[4] Treasury Grant dated 24th Feb. 1743/4.

[5] *Hist. of the British Army*, Vol. II., p. 105.

A British officer who served under Wade, and who wrote " An Authentic Narrative of the Campaign in Flanders the year 1744," records what steps the Marshal took for the safety of Ghent :—

> " Asche, May $\frac{17\ N.S.}{6\ O.S.}$.—Marshal Wade, in order to prevent, if possible, their [the French] seizing on Ghent, which had no garrison for its defence, and lay the most exposed, proposed imediately (*sic*) the sending a detachment of 12 squadrons of Dragoons and 6 companies of Grenadiers, with 9 field pieces, to march all night so as to be at the gates of Ghent by break of day, which Lieut.-General Campbell, who commanded them, executed with such diligence that he for the present secured that place." [1]

Whilst the Allied commanders were trying to settle on some definite plan of operations, the French, within six weeks, had reduced Courtrai, Menin, Ypres, Fort Knoque, and Furnes. George II. alarmed at these conquests, made Lord Carteret write to Wade and inform him that "it was His Majesty's pleasure the Army should march upon the enemy and attack him with a spirit suitable to the glory of the British Nation." [2] The Allies crossed the Scheldt on 20th July, with a view to forcing an engagement with the French. The time was well chosen. Prince Charles of Lorraine, at the head of an Austrian force, had recently achieved marked success against the French in Alsace. Louis XV. had been driven to withdraw part of his troops from Flanders. Marshal Saxe, however, took up a strong position behind the Lys. At this juncture the Allies, impeded by the divided counsels of their respective leaders, were further hampered by two plans of campaign prepared in England by the Earl of Stair, and sent to Lord Carteret to forward to Marshal Wade. In this 20th century it is difficult to comprehend the lack of good taste and *savoir faire* shown by Lord Stair in thrusting his unasked advice on the Marshal who had virtually succeeded him (Stair) in the command on the Continent. Yet so it was! Stair, who had led his army into a "mousetrap" (as Marshal Noailles jubilantly exclaimed on the eve of Dettingen) was hardly the man to show Wade, d'Aremberg, and Nassau, how to outmanœuvre Maurice of Saxe—the first soldier of his time. The Allies effected nothing of importance. Wade and his colleagues were made the butts for pasquinades in the French papers and appeared as comic figures in Gallic plays. A translation of one of the lampoons in question appeared in the *Gentleman's Magazine* for 1744 and is as follows :—

> " On the 30th July they [the allied forces] encamped within four or five miles of Lisle [Lille]. On the 31st they lost a Scotch volunteer before it, and had a Captain wounded and taken prisoner. They looked also for a field of battle, but by good providence no enemy was near. On the 1st inst. they were put in fear, but, as it happened, danger was at a distance ; on the 2nd they slept sound ; on the 3rd the right wing foraged ; on the 4th the whole army was reviewed ; on the 5th they rested ; on the 6th the left wing foraged ; on the 7th did nothing ; on the 8th relieved the free companies of Austrians at Lanoy, and received a trumpet from Count Saxe about the exchange of prisoners ; on the 9th sent him back again ; on the 10th the Hanoverians foraged and had a gun fired at them from Lisle ; on the 11th the Britons foraged and had no gun fired at them, and the Captain that was taken at Lisle being exchanged, returned."

---

[1] *Add. MS.* 36251, Brit. Mus.
[2] *Carteret Papers* under dates of 13th July and 17th July (O.S.).

An English writer in *Temple Bar Magazine* thus refers to Wade in an article on " Fontenoy " and the abortive campaign of 1744 :—

> " He gave proof of considerable sagacity, however, in keeping out of reach of Saxe ; and at the end of the campaign he might have echoed the complacent boast with which Walpole once met Queen Caroline's demands for war : ' There are fifty thousand men killed this year in Europe and not one Englishman.' "

It is an act of simple justice to Marshal Wade to give, in his own words, some of the difficulties he had to contend with, not only from bodily ill-health, but from obstruction to his plan of campaign on the part of the Duke d'Aremberg and the Count of Nassau. In a letter to Lord Hardwicke, dated from " Château d'Anstein, near Lille, 2nd Sept., O.S., 1744," Wade writes :—

> " Having had a return of the astma (*sic*), together with a spitting of blood, it has for these three weeks rendered me so weak as to be hardly able to perform the necessary business that must daily occur to one in my situation. I fear we shall never be able to lay siege to any of the enemy's fortified towns, nor to bring them to a general engagement the last of which I have been extremely solicitous with my colleagues that we should attempt and, persuant to His Majesty's repeated commands, proposed it in a council of warr, but was so unfortunate to be single in my opinion ; in short, my Lord, partial and private consideration seem to influence our action here, and if we don't alter our measures our treasure will be exhausted for little purpose." [1]

Duke d'Aremberg had evolved a plan for having the Royal Artillery battering train, and stores, sent from Ostend to Antwerp, or Brussels, from whence it was to be conveyed to the place where it was to be employed. Wade had given his consent on the expressed stipulation that horses and wagons should be in readiness at the port where the train was to be disembarked.

> " He [Duke d'Aremberg] had always assured the Marshal," writes a British officer in Wade's Army, " everything should be ready ; but never dropped a word to any that it was to be at His Majesty's expense . . . . six weeks maintenance, by the Duke's confession, for 10,000 horses and 2,000 wagons [would amount] to £50,000 sterling." [2]

The Royal Artillery battering train was sent to Antwerp by Wade's orders ; but when it reached that port neither horses nor wagons were to be seen or heard of ! The sequel is best told in Marshal Wade's own words :—

> " Château de Huysson,
> " 12 Octr. 1744, N.S.
>
> " . . . . In relation to what yor Lord[p] mentions of our Artillery being continued on board the Vessels at Antwerp, I fear you have been misinform'd. For they continued on Board 3 weeks before any of the Dutch arriv'd, at an Expence of near 20[ll] a day Demurrage, & when they had laid there a month, Mr. Jones the Comptroller wrote word that the Skippers began to Mutiny at their being detain'd from home so long, & threatn'd to throw the Stores overboard if they were not dismiss'd, which obliged me to send an order for their being placed on the Key near the River Side in Sheds built for that purpose at a considerable Expence, where they may be ready to be reship'd when occasion should require.

---

[1] *Add. MS.* 35587, fol. 292.
[2] " An Authentic Narrative of the Campaign in Flanders the year 1744."—*Add. MS.* 36251.

"And when the Duc d'Aremberg in consequence of the Project before mentioned desir'd me to bring our Artillery & Stores to Ghent, which must cost a considerable Sum, I often told him, that if He would order the 18 peices that are at Brussells, which might be brought by Land Carriage in two days, I would send for as many of the Cannon & Stores from Antwerp as was necessary to be employed in any Siege that a Council of War should determine to undertake, which he never thought fit to comply with." [1]

Marshal Saxe's Army got their quota of fun out of the fact that the British Artillery remained at Antwerp, instead of being brought to batter down the walls of Lille when the allied forces encamped near that town.

"When in winter quarters," records Mr. J. A. Browne (formerly of the Royal Artillery), "a company of comedians from Paris played in the French camp, and among their performances was a pantomime in which the following dialogue was introduced :—

"An English officer is represented who is asked by the Clown : 'Where are you going ? '

"OFFICER : 'To the siege of Lisle, which we shall take in five days.'

"CLOWN : 'You have not a sufficient force.'

"OFFICER : 'Don't mind that. One Englishman will beat five French. Huzza, boys ! '

"CLOWN : 'But where is your artillery ? '

"OFFICER : 'Odd so (*scratching his head*) ; we have forgot it. Let me think. It is at Ostend or Antwerp, if it has escaped the last storm.'" [2]

On the 17th October (N.S.) the right wing of the British Army broke up their camp at Drogen and marched off to their winter quarters. Wade, with his headquarters staff, proceeded to Ghent. He had not been there long before he heard that a string of accusations had been drawn up against him by the Dutch generals and forwarded to the British Government. The first article of accusation was as follows :—

"That the Right Wing of the Army broke up the 17th October, at Drogen, in an unexpected, abrupt, and unconcerted manner, and marched, much to the surprise of the Duke of Aremberg, the Court of Brussels, the Dutch generals, and the Republic." [3]

Answer :—

"On the 16th October in the evening the General of the British Horse came to Marshal Wade in the camp at Drogen representing the distrest condition of the Cavalry, both men and horses, were in from the heavy rains and storms ; the men's tents being so much torn that it was not possible to pitch them, that their horses stood up to their knees in water, and their forage quite spoilt by the heavy rain that had fallen for 3 days together, and still continued with great violence ; desiring therefore that they might be ordered into Winter Quarters, to prevent the total destruction of that body. Representations were likewise made by the

---

[1] *Add. MS.* 35354, fol. 93. Copy of letter of Field-Marshal George Wade to Lord [Stair ?].

[2] *An Historical Narrative of the Services of the Royal Artillery*, p. 12.

[3] "Articles against Marshal Wade sent over to England at the end of the Campaign of 1744 with the Answers to them drawn up by Captain York, Aide-de-Camp to Marshal Wade." (*Add. MS.* 36251, fol. 51.) The Hon. Joseph *Yorke* was third son of the 1st Earl of Hardwicke, the Lord Chancellor. He was appointed Ensign in the Coldstream Guards 25th April, 1741. Served at Fontenoy as A.D.C. to the Duke of Cumberland. Capt. and Lt.-Col. 2nd Foot Guards, 27th May, 1745. A.D.C. to George II., 1749. Col. 8th Dragoons, 23rd Oct. 1758. Created Lord Dover in 1788. Col. 1st Life Guards, 1789. D. in 1792.

General of the Foot in regard to their tents being in the same condition. Numbers of the men being sent daily to the hospital, occasioned by the excessive bad weather. But the Marshal would not consent to their going into Winter Quarters till he had the approbation of the Duke d'Aremberg, for which purpose he sent the Quartermaster-General and Adjutant-General to the Duke to acquaint him with the situation the troops were in. . . . A quarter of an hour after these gentlemen set out with the said message, Major-General Gemmigem, Quartermaster-General of the Austrians, arrived at the Marshal's quarters, from the Duke's, with a message to the same purpose that the excessive bad weather made it necessary that the troops should march into Winter Quarters." [1]

The Duke and his Generals made no objection to Wade's proposal. On the contrary the Duke desired Brigadier Bland would draw out a disposition for the march of the right wing and sign it.[2] Wade's indignant letter to the Duke of Newcastle, when the former became aware of the charges made against him by his colleagues, has been preserved and is as follows :—

"Private.   "Gand, Nov. 7th, N.S., 1744.
"MY LORD,
"I had no sooner received the honour of your Grace's commands but I acquainted Coll. Russell of your favour in his behalf and gave him my consent to his setting out for England as soon as he pleased. Your Grace has, I daresay, been informed of the many heavy accusations laid to my charge by letters from Holland, which I was the more surprised at since neither I, nor any officers of the Army (neither English or foreign) had ever heard of before the Army was separated to their Winter Quarters, and it is somewhat strange that neither the Duke d'Aremberg nor the Barrons Ginkle and Cromstron (the last of which is said to be the author of those letters) should never say a single word to me on the subject when they severally made me a visit as they past through this Town on their way to Brussells. As to Cromstron having lived with him the whole Campagne in an amicable and friendly manner, I can't help thinking he has been made the instrument of the Duke to propagate these false and scandalous misrepresentations, who has probably taken advantage of his failure of hearing and memory, to impose this task on him ; for from the beginning his [d'Aremberg's] behaviour has been haughty and reserved as if he thought it an indignity to one of his Quality to act in his Military Capacity on an equall foot with a Commoner of Brittain, and I assure your Grace my patience has been sufficiently tryed on various occasions in hopes my aquiessance would be a means the better to execute the Trust his Majesty was pleased to repose in me, and to enable me to bring the operations of the latter part of the Campagne to a better issue. I have by this Messenger sent my Answers to the Accusations to the Earl of Granville which I hope will prove satisfactory to his Majesty and his Ministers, and convince all the world that the imputations laid to my charge are False, Scandalous, and without the least Foundation.
"I am very much oblidged to your Grace for your goodness in enquireing after my health. I wish it was better, but have reason to apprehend the frequent colds I have got in the field have brought it to a confirmed Astma and will render me unable to serve any more Campagns (sic), but whatever my condition is I shall be ever proud of being,
"My Lord,
"Your Grace's most humble and most obedient servant,
"GEORGE WADE." [3]

[1] "Articles against Marshal Wade sent over to England at the end of the Campaign of 1744 with the Answers to them drawn up by Captain York, Aide-de-Camp to Marshal Wade."—*Add M.S.* 36251, fol. 51.   [2] *Ibid.*   [3] *Add. MS.* 32703, fol. 389.

Shortly after this letter was written, Marshal Wade returned to London. It is on record that the King thanked him for his late services, which affords tangible proof that George II. fully recognised the difficulties Wade had to contend with from the beginning to the end of the abortive campaign in Flanders.

Wade resigned his command on the Continent early in 1745.

Stephen Poyntz, in a letter to Trevor, the British Minister at The Hague, writes: "Mr. Wade being entirely disabled from making another campaign, the command of our army is once more vacant."[1] On the 6th March, 1744/45, the Duke of Cumberland was appointed "Captain-General of all His Majesty's land forces within the Kingdom of Great Britain, and of all His Majesty's land forces which are or shall be employed abroad in conjunction with the troops of His Majesty's allies."

George II. showed his goodwill to Marshal Wade by appointing him Commander-in-Chief[2] of the Army sent to the North of England, in September, 1745, on the outbreak of the Jacobite insurrection in Scotland.

The landing of Prince Charles Edward Stuart in the West of Scotland, and the raising of the Royal Standard at Glenfinnan, were notable events which caused great consternation at St. James's Palace, whither George II. returned on 31st August from Hanover. Marshal Wade was sent to Newcastle with half-a-dozen regiments, and had orders to collect as many troops there as he could. Dutch auxiliaries, to the number of 6,000, were requisitioned from Holland to swell Wade's Army. The militia of several counties was also called out; but no enthusiasm was evinced for King George's cause. Henry Fox, in a confidential letter to Sir C. H. Williams, dated 5th September, 1745, writes: "England, Wade says, and I believe, is for the first comer, and if you can tell whether the 6,000 Dutch and the ten battalions[3] of English, or 5,000 French or Spaniards, will be here first, you know our fate."[4] A fortnight later the same writer again opens his mind to his former correspondent: "The French are not come, God be thanked! But had 5,000 landed in any part of this island a week ago, I verily believe the entire conquest would not have cost them a battle."[5] The end of September found Wade and his troops at Doncaster. The Marshal had for his second in command Lieut.-General Lord Tyrawly. The 6,000 Dutch, with some Hessians, joined Wade's forces at Newcastle early in October. The Highlanders, elated by their complete victory at Prestonpans on 21st September (O.S.), were reluctantly persuaded by their leaders to invade England. But they waited more than a calendar month before the forward movement began, which delay, however necessary it may have been, gave time to the Duke of Cumberland to collect an army in the south. Charles Stuart began his march on 1st November. His army marched in two divisions; the Prince led his troops to Kelso and made a feint of proceeding to Wooler which deceived Wade and kept the Northern Army at Newcastle. Lord George Murray

---

[1] From letter quoted in article on "The Battle of Fontenoy" given in *The Edinburgh Review* for July, 1911, p. 28.

[2] In *The War Office List and Administrative Directory for the British Army*, under "Commanders-in-Chief to 1870," Wade appears as "Commander-in-Chief, March to Dec. 1745"; while the Earl of Stair appears in same list as "Commander-in-Chief, Feb. 1744 to June, 1746." Lord Stair was Commander-in-Chief in South Britain at the time above mentioned while Wade was Field-Marshal Commanding-in-Chief the Northern Army.

[3] Certain English regiments serving in Flanders were ordered home in the autumn of 1745.

[4] Quoted by Lord Mahon in the *Hist. of England*, 1713–83.   [5] *Ibid.*

led the other division of the Highland Army to Moffat and thence into Cumberland, where he was joined near Carlisle by the Prince who had marched westward through Liddesdale. Carlisle was besieged and captured. Wade had marched to Hexham hoping to intercept the Highland Army there. Arriving there on 16th November in a very severe snowstorm, the roads were found to be impassable. The next day news was received by Wade that Carlisle had been taken after a slight show of resistance. The Highland Army now marched southwards. At Manchester the Stuart Prince was received with enthusiasm. Meanwhile Wade was following the Highlanders with his less mobile army. On 30th November Charles Edward issued a "Proclamation" from Manchester, concerning the repair of certain bridges which had been pulled down in the county, "particularly that at Crossford, which is to be done this night by his own troops, though his Royal Highness does not propose to make use of it for his own army but believes it will be of service to the country ; and if any forces that were with General Wade be coming this road they may have the benefit of it ! " [1]

The Duke of Cumberland, with 8,000 men, was marching across Staffordshire hoping to intercept the Highlanders while Wade was in the rear of the invaders. Lord George Murray out-marched and out-manœuvred both Cumberland and Wade, arriving at Derby 4th December. Two days later the Highland Army turned its face homewards. Once more Lord George Murray guided his troops between Scylla and Charybdis and reached the borders of Westmorland in safety. Cumberland was appointed Commander-in-Chief of the whole British Army in December, 1745, and Wade retired into private life.

General Hawley was appointed Commander-in-Chief in Scotland, 20th December, 1745, and marched there with the main portion of Wade's Army at Newcastle. "It is to be said for Wade," wrote the late Sir Kenneth Mackenzie, "that his army suffered much from sickness. 'The Volunteer'—supposed to have been a medical man—who has left an account of his journey with the Duke of Cumberland's Army, tells how, on arriving at Newcastle he 'heard of the great sickness amongst the men in Marshal Wade's Army occasioned by the inclemency of the weather, the hospitals being filled; these fevers raged also among the townspeople, and even amongst the surgeons and apothecaries that attended them, many of whom died.'" [2]

In 1746, Wade presided over the court-martial which tried Sir John Cope for his defeat at Prestonpans.

Field-Marshal Wade died on 14th March, 1747/48, and was buried in Westminster Abbey. A monument by Roubiliac was erected to Wade's memory over a door leading from the south aisle into the cloisters. The inscription thereon records Wade's rank and military appointments held by him at the time of his decease, but makes no mention of his having been Commander-in-Chief in Flanders or in England. It is said that Roubiliac used to cry when looking at Wade's monument on account of it being placed so high !

Wade died unmarried. He left about £100,000, the bulk of which went to his natural children—two of whom were officers in the Army. He also provided handsomely for the family of his brother, the Rev. William Wade, Canon of Windsor.

[1] Lord Mahon's *Hist. of England*, Vol. III., Appendix 1, p. xxx.
[2] "General George Wade and his Roads."

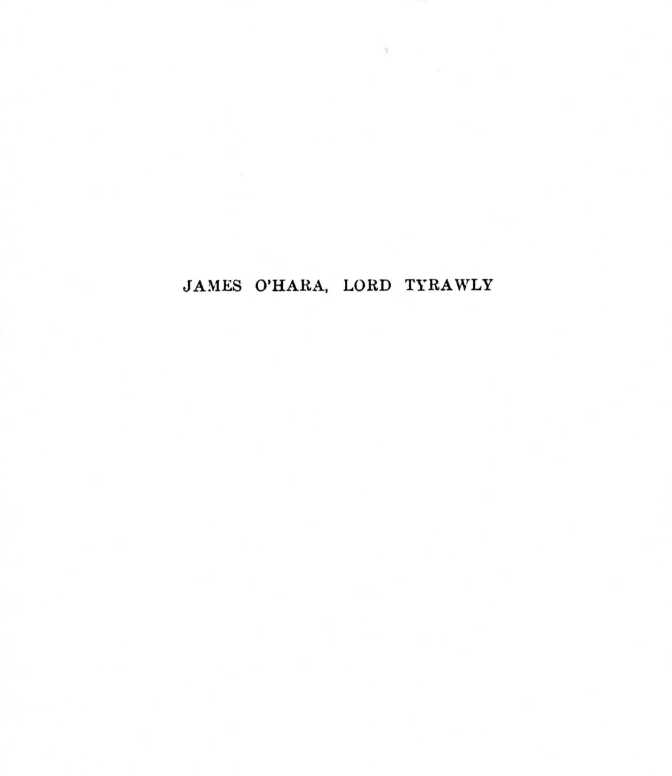

JAMES O'HARA, LORD TYRAWLY

CHAPTER III

JAMES O'HARA, LORD TYRAWLY,
SOLDIER AND DIPLOMATIST [1]

" A man of commanding talents both as a soldier and a diplomatist. —
Chatham Correspondence, I., 200.

THIS nobleman, who attained the rank of Field-Marshal, was son of
General Sir Charles O'Hara, first Baron Tyrawly, and was born in 1690.
His first commission ran as follows :—

> " James Hara, gent., to be [2nd] Lieut. in the Royal
> Regiment of Fuzileers whereof Sir Charles O'Hara
> is Colonel.   Dated 15 March 170$\frac{3}{4}$."

O'Hara was promoted Captain two years later, and embarked with his
corps for the Peninsula in February, 1706. He served at the relief of
Barcelona in May same year. In the following year he was appointed to
the staff of his father who commanded the left wing of the allied army at
the sanguinary battle of Almanza. It is recorded that Captain O'Hara
saved Lord Galway's life by interposing between his Lordship and a
dragoon whom he shot with his pistol, but was himself slightly wounded
by the French soldier. Shortly after this incident the one-armed Lord
Galway received two sabre-cuts over his right eye which bled so profusely
that he had to retire from the field to have his wounds dressed. It was
Captain O'Hara who piloted his gallant chief across the artillery-swept
field to the rear. For his gallantry at Almanza O'Hara was given a troop
in General Harvey's Horse and appointed to Marlborough's staff. He
served as A.D.C. to the Duke at Malplaquet, where he was wounded.[2]

James O'Hara succeeded his father in the colonelcy of the Royal
Fusiliers, 29th January, 1713, and took over the command of the corps in
the Island of Minorca, which had been ceded to Great Britain by the
Treaty of Utrecht. O'Hara was appointed A.D.C. to the King in 1717, and
in July, 1718, the Royal Fusiliers, under O'Hara's command, embarked on
Admiral Byng's fleet and proceeded to Naples, where they arrived on
31st July. The next day the troops were sent off to garrison the citadel
and fort of Messina, where they landed on 9th August. A day later,
Admiral Byng attacked the Spanish fleet and defeated it off Cape Pasaro.
"The exact action of the Fusiliers," writes the latest compiler of the
records of this distinguished corps, "cannot be determined, as the *London
Gazette* does not give details. For the remainder of the year the regiment

---

[1] A great part of this memoir is compiled from *Add. MSS.* 23627–23642, at the British
Museum, wherein are to be found the Tyrawly Papers—notably Lord Tyrawly's " Memorial"
referred to on p. 29.
[2] *Marlborough Dispatches*, Vol. IV., pp. 594 and 606.

was occupied in operations in Sicily." [1]   In April, 1719, the Royal Fusiliers were ordered home in consequence of a Spanish invasion being expected. Colonel O'Hara proceeded overland from Naples to Paris and thence to England.   His corps embarked on board Byng's fleet at Naples in company with Sankey's Regiment (39th).   The Spanish armada came to grief and the invasion scare was at an end.

In February, 1721, James O'Hara was created Baron Kilmaine of Kilmaine, co. Mayo, as a recompense for his military services during Queen Anne's reign.   Three years later he succeeded his father as second Baron Tyrawly, and was made a Privy Councillor same year.   From 1719–27 the Royal Fusiliers were stationed in Ireland.   Seven months after the accession of George II., Tyrawly, who received the appointment of A.D.C. to the King, was offered the post of Ambassador to Portugal.   On accepting, Tyrawly asked George II. "to allow him to put himself at the head of his regiment if employed on active service in the field." [2]   This request was granted.

Tyrawly soon became a *persona grata* at the King of Portugal's Court. He made a study of the Portuguese language and quickly mastered it.   In May, 1735, when disputes arose between Portugal and Spain, George II.'s Ministry deemed it expedient that Admiral Sir John Norris, who commanded the British Fleet in the Mediterranean, should act temporarily with Tyrawly as joint British Minister.   Norris accordingly was sent to Lisbon.   Whatever the advantages may have been to the Portuguese Government, certain it is that Tyrawly and Norris held divergent views concerning the course to be pursued.   "The misunderstandings grew to such a height that the two British Ministers found it necessary to execute separately the joint orders they had received."   Norris was an experienced naval commander who had rendered very valuable service to his country in the reign of George I.   This being so, George II. felt it his duty to uphold Norris's views in the matters that were at issue, and the Duke of Newcastle wrote to Tyrawly in March, 1736, to the effect that "His Majesty approved of Admiral Norris's conduct on the several late occasions."   In July, 1737, Admiral Clinton came to Lisbon to command the Mediterranean Fleet, his headquarters being at Gibraltar.

The strained relations between George II. and Frederick Prince of Wales came to a head in the autumn of 1737, and the Duke of Newcastle wrote the following letter to Lord Tyrawly :—

"MY LORD,

"Hampton Court,
12th Sept. 1737.

"I am commanded by the King to acquaint your Lordship that His Majesty, having had some reasons to be dissatisfied with the conduct of H.R.H. the Prince of Wales immediately before the delivery of the Princess, has thought proper to order H.R.H. to leave St. James's with all his family, and the Master of the Ceremonies was yesterday directed to wait upon all the Foreign Ministers to acquaint them with the resolution that His Majesty had taken, and to desire that, in consequence of it, they would avoid going to pay their court to H.R.H.

"I am very sorry for the occasion of giving you the trouble, and am, with great truth and regard,

"My Lord, &c., &c.,

"Lord Tyrawly."

"HOLLES NEWCASTLE."

---

[1] *Historical Record of the Royal Fusiliers*, by W. Wheater.
[2] Tyrawly to the Duke of Newcastle, January, 1728.

On 23rd November, 1735, Tyrawly was promoted Brigadier-General, and on 2nd July, 1739, a Major-General. George II. also transferred him to the colonelcy of the regiment of horse now known as the 4th Dragoon Guards, in August, 1739. Great Britain being at war with Spain in 1740, Lord Tyrawly pined for a military command, and petitioned George II. for leave to resign his post at Lisbon and return home. The Duke of Newcastle wrote to Tyrawly on 6th May, 1741, informing him that the King granted his Lordship's request to return "not only on account of your private affairs, but that you might at this time have an opportunity of serving His Majesty in your military capacity." Lord Tyrawly embarked at Lisbon for England on 17th July, 1741. The King of Portugal gave him a parting present of fourteen bars of gold. Horace Walpole, in a letter to Sir Horace Mann, gives a humorous account, which must be read with a grain of salt, of Tyrawly's arrival in London with his "harem" :—

> "My Lord Tyrawly has come from Portugal, and has brought three wives and fourteen children. One of the former is a Portuguese with long black hair, plaited down to the bottom of her back." [1]

On his return home Tyrawly pressed his claim for military employment. In March, 1743, he was promoted Lieut.-General, and a month later obtained the colonelcy of the 2nd Troop of Horse Grenadier Guards. The King appointed Tyrawly to the command of a brigade on the Home establishment, consisting of five regiments, which he was to review and to report on as to their fitness for foreign service. Tyrawly now thought the wish of his heart about to be realised, viz., to command British troops on active service. But this was not to be. In October, 1743, the King selected Tyrawly for the vacant post of Ambassador to the Russian Court, and the Duke of Newcastle pressed his Lordship to accept this important appointment. Newcastle informed Tyrawly that the Marquis de la Chetardie, Ambassador from France to Russia, was striving to bring about a triple alliance between Russia, France, and Sweden, to the exclusion of England from all affairs in the north. Putting his own cherished hopes in the background, Tyrawly patriotically accepted the diplomatic post offered him, and started for Russia about 1st April, 1744. His journey from London to Moscow *via* Germany cost him, inclusive of the expenses of his suite and an escort from the Russian frontier consisting of a subaltern, two sergeants, two corporals, and thirty soldiers, £2,500. On sending in his bill of costs to the British Government, Tyrawly wrote : "These are expenses in travelling unknown in any journeys but this." His Lordship was informed that he was not permitted "to charge his living expenses on the road to His Majesty of Great Britain—only the bare travelling."

In a letter to Lord Carteret from "Petersburg" in April, 1744, Tyrawly writes :—

> "I pray God to continue to bless His Majesty's arms with victory, and beg leave to congratulate your Lordship on Admiral Mathews's success and on the event of the ridiculous Don Quixotade from Dunkirk. I cannot conceal the mortification it is to me that His Majesty should choose to employ me in an Embassy at a time that he is engaged in a war, and I shall hope from your Lordship's long and experienced friendship for me that you will let His Majesty know my earnest desire of attending him in the Field."

[1] Horace Walpole to Sir Horace Mann.

On Tyrawly's arrival at Moscow the Vice-Chancellor waited on him and in course of conversation mentioned that the Empress Elizabeth much desired the Order of the Garter, being a crowned Queen in her own right. "I heartily wish we had a Garter for this lady," wrote Tyrawly to Carteret on 6th June, 1744, "it would be no equivalent to give it to the Grand Duke [of Holstein], it would not be taken well by Her Majesty." Tyrawly played his diplomatic cards so well that the before-mentioned French Ambassador's schemes for a triple alliance fell to the ground, and he himself had to leave Russia. "Chetardie had to give up all pictures and presents, given him by the Empress, on his arrival at the frontier in August, 1744, or else undergo ten years' imprisonment."

Tyrawly returned to England early in 1745. In April that year he was transferred to the command of the 3rd Troop of Life Guards, which gave him the privilege of taking the Court duty of Gold Stick. On 6th October same year Tyrawly was appointed Lieut.-General of the Army under Field-Marshal Wade, then at Doncaster. Wade's forces got as far as Newcastle, where sickness and heavy snowdrifts prevented their march into Scotland. The Jacobite Army gave Wade the slip, and so far as the Field-Marshal and Lord Tyrawly were concerned they never came within touch of the rebel forces.

So long as Great Britain was at war with France, Tyrawly was averse to accept any diplomatic post which would lose him an opportunity of active military employment. It may be that George II., knowing how well fitted Tyrawly was for ambassadorial work, had offered his Lordship some post abroad which had been declined. Be this so, or not, the King was temporarily offended with this particular nobleman. General (then Colonel) Wolfe in a letter to his own father, 18th September, 1749, writes: "Lord Tyrawly said humorously. being asked if the King spoke to him, and how he received his Lordship, that 'few words are best among friends.'"

The 3rd and 4th Troops of Life Guards having been disbanded in 1746, Lord Tyrawly was appointed Colonel of the 10th Foot in December, 1746, and transferred to the King's Dragoons (3rd) in 1752. In April, 1752, the King sent Tyrawly to Lisbon on a special mission. He returned in August same year. In May, 1753, Tyrawly was given the Governorship of Minorca, and two years later appointed Colonel of the Coldstream Guards. For reasons to be presently stated, Lord Tyrawly, who knew every inch of Minorca and its defences, was not permitted to take up his new post. Lieut.-General Wm. Blakeney acted as Lieut.-Governor, and made a most splendid, though unsuccessful, defence of Fort St. Philip when besieged by the French from the end of April to the end of June, 1756. Through an unfortunate error of judgment, Lieut.-General Thos. Fowke, Governor of Gibraltar, refused to send troops to the relief of Port Mahon when applied to for succours, for which he was recalled, tried by a court-martial, and cashiered. Lord Tyrawly was sent for from Blackheath, by express from the Duke of Cumberland, 1st June, 1756, to come immediately to London, where he was informed the King had appointed him Governor of Gibraltar, and Commander-in-Chief of all H.M.'s forces in the Mediterranean, for which he was to set out with all expedition. On 7th June Tyrawly left Blackheath with three A.D.C.s, viz., Sir Wm. Wiseman, Captain Rainsford, and Captain Charles O'Hara,[1]

---

[1] Illegitimate son of Lord Tyrawly. He accompanied his father to Portugal in 1762. Served at the siege of Toulon in 1793 as Lt.-General, and was taken prisoner. Appointed

who embarked at Spithead on H.M.S. *Antelope* for Gibraltar. Shortly after arrival there news came of the surrender of Fort St. Philip to the Marshal Duke of Richelieu after a record defence, and thus the whole of Minorca fell into the hands of the French. The garrison had military honours granted them and were transported to Gibraltar, viz., 2,400 regular troops, 80 gunners, 25 Greeks and Jews. Lord Tyrawly drew up " a plan for recapturing the Island of Minorca by first possessing ourselves of the Island of Corsica," but, like similar projects, it was pigeonholed and never taken into consideration. In his " Memorial" (of which hereafter) Tyrawly expressed his vexation at not having been in Minorca when the French descent took place.

> " It was not my fault," he wrote. " I had repeatedly offered my services to go there, and had, at two different times, made my preparations for it and embarked my servants and baggage, but had been contre-ordered (*sic*) on the rumours of an invasion at home. The care of the Royal Family, of the City of London [1] and the quiet thereof, in case of an attempt from the French to land, being committed to me, for which I had made a plan and disposition in writing which was approved of by H.R.H. the Duke and, as I was then informed, by H.M.'s Ministers."

Tyrawly found the defences of Gibraltar in a very neglected state. " I found all the old works," he wrote in his 'Memorial,' " in a ruinous condition and out of all repair to the land side, the batteries injudiciously crowded with guns in some places and at others no defence at all." The writer severely criticised Mr. Skinner,[2] the British engineer who was responsible for the fortifications in question. " One battery near the new mole, made by the chief engineer," wrote Tyrawly, " was so ill-constructed that the foundation sunk soon after it was erected and since is quite tumbled down." His Lordship also found the ordnance stores very unsatisfactory. " I did not find one musket-ball in the stores," he goes on to say, " that fitted our arms, being all too big for the calibre. I was obliged to have them all new cast in moulds made for that purpose since I found no moulds in the stores." Tyrawly's demands for putting Gibraltar in a fit state of defence " to stand a siege for six months by sea or land," were declared by the Board of Ordnance to be enormous. The Governor's plans for new fortifications were disapproved of by Mr. Skinner, who felt his own reputation as an engineer had been impugned by Tyrawly's report on the state of the military works at aforesaid garrison. In a letter to the Right Hon. Henry Fox, 20th August, 1756, Tyrawly wrote : " If anything can tempt anybody to besiege Gibraltar it will be the fatherless and motherless defenceless state it has been suffered to run into ; all which I have fully reported at home where I thought it was most proper." [3]

Commandant of Gibraltar in 1787 and held this post for four years. Governor of Gibraltar in 1795—and died there in 1801. " O'Hara's Tower " at Gibraltar still exists. This General died unmarried, but left two families by Spanish ladies at Gibraltar, who inherited his fortune.

[1] It was doubtless when he was in command of the London District that the present inn at the junction of High Street and Nottingham Street, Marylebone, was given the sign of " The Lord Tyrawly."

[2] See his commission as a Practitioner Engineer and note thereto on p. 259.

[3] *Chatham Correspondence*, Vol. I., pp. 200–1.

After hammering away at the home authorities, Tyrawly got permission to put Gibraltar into a fit state of defence. Before the new works were finished, Tyrawly was relieved at Gibraltar in April, 1757, by the Earl of Home, and returned to England. Horace Walpole has left the following pungent account of Tyrawly's appearance at the bar of the House of Commons to defend himself against the charge of undue extravagance, at the national expense, when refortifying Gibraltar :—

"While at Gibraltar Lord Tyrawly ordered great additions to the works with no more economy than Governors are apt to do, who think themselves above being responsible. Lord George Sackville caught at this dissipation and privately instigated Sir John Philips to censure the expense. To their great surprise Lord Tyrawly demanded to be heard at the bar of the House in his own defence. A day was named. He drew up a Memorial which he proposed to read to the House. It attacked Lord George roundly for having avoided all foreign command. Thus alarmed, Lord George got the day of hearing adjourned for near a fortnight, and having underhand procured the report of Skinner, who surveyed the works at Gibraltar, to be brought before the House, without mentioning what it was, Mr. Fox laid open the unhandsome darkness of this conduct, and Lord Tyrawly himself appeared at the bar, and made good by his behaviour all that had been taken for vapour before he appeared there; for, leaning on the bar he browbeat Skinner, his censor, who stood on his left hand, with such arrogant humour that the very lawyers thought themselves outdone in their own style of worrying a culprit. He read his Memorial, which was well drawn, with great art and frankness, and assumed more merit to himself than he had been charged with blame. Such tough game tempted few hunters; Lord George was glad to waive the sport, and the House dismissed the affair." [1]

In December, 1758, Tyrawly presided at the court-martial appointed to enquire into General Sir John Mordaunt's miscarriage at Rochfort. The following year Lord Tyrawly was appointed Governor of Portsmouth.

In 1760, Lord George Sackville was tried by a court-martial for wilfully disobeying the orders of Prince Ferdinand of Brunswick at the battle of Minden where the aforesaid Prince was in supreme command. It has been said that cowards have their moments of bravery and brave men their moments of fear. Be this as it may, there was a general consensus of opinion among British and German officers who served at Minden that Lord George Sackville had lamentably failed in courage on that historic battle-field. Lord Tyrawly was president of the court-martial which tried Lord George and found the charges against him proved. Sackville was dismissed the Army, and George II. ordered that the finding of the court-martial should be entered in every British Regimental Order Book at home and abroad.

In 1761, the King was pleased to promote Tyrawly a General on 10th March. On 10th February, 1762, Tyrawly wrote to the Secretary at War :—

"I had a letter yesterday from my Lord Egremont to tell me that the King had appointed me Commander-in-Chief of his troops to be sent to Portugal, and as such have had the honour of kissing His Majesty's hand this morning."

[1] *Chatham Correspondence*, Vol. II., p. 293.

Tyrawly was at the same time appointed Ambassador to the Portuguese Court. The British troops which embarked for Lisbon under their veteran commander consisted of 7,164 officers and men of all arms. This force had been despatched in consequence of the threatening attitude of France and Spain towards Portugal, whose monarch had declined to enter into an alliance with the above two Powers in order "to curb the pride of the British nation which aspired to become despotic over the sea." On arrival at Lisbon, Tyrawly wrote to Pitt that the Portuguese force was a mere rabble. This report was afterwards confirmed by a German writer, who says :—

> "The officers of the Portuguese Army at this time frequently followed mechanical trades in order to maintain themselves. Captains were tailors, and their wives washerwomen ; general officers gave their servants commissions in the army in lieu of wages ; and the guards on duty at the King's palace in Lisbon would, with outstretched hand and on bended knees, beg alms from passers by." [1]

Tyrawly, who was now in his 73rd year, had not been long in Portugal before he found that he was unequal to the fatigues incidental to a campaign. "The spirit was willing but the flesh was weak." He felt reluctantly compelled to send in his resignation and apply for leave to return to England. Carlyle says in his *History of Frederick the Great* that on the appointment of Count La Lippe to the command of the Portuguese Army, "Tyrawly resigned in a huff" ; but another able writer remarks, "There is reason to believe that Tyrawly himself suggested the choice of one with whom he had served and whose merits he appreciated, to supersede him in the fulfilment of an uncongenial duty." [2] On 22nd June, 1762, Lord Egremont wrote to Tyrawly relative to the latter's request to return home : "your infirmities," said the former, "making it impossible for an officer of your ability and experience to continue in command of the British forces in Portugal, where your Lordship's knowledge of the country, people, and language could not fail of being particularly useful to the King's service."

Tyrawly left Lisbon on board an English warship 26th August, 1762. He was succeeded by the Earl of Loudoun as Commander-in-Chief of the British forces in Portugal. George II. appointed Lord Tyrawly a Field-Marshal on 23rd July, 1763.

The veteran soldier and diplomatist spent the evening of his life at Twickenham where he had purchased a residence. The Earl of Chatham in a letter to his Countess dated 11th April, 1772, refers to "his fine old friend Lord Tyrawly," and goes on to say, "A how do you call from you to him would please and be proper." Lady Chatham made the suggested call, and though she did not see the aged nobleman she received the following characteristic note from him :—

> "Lord Tyrawly presents his respectful compliments to Lady Chatham. Lord Tyrawly is in good health, but so blind as to be forced to employ another hand to write, so deaf as not to hear half the nonsense said near him, and so simple of understanding as not to be able to conceal his own."

---

[1] Varnhagen von Ense in his *Denkmaale*, Berlin, 1824.
[2] *Life of General the Rt. Hon. John Burgoyne*, by E. de Fonblanque, p. 29, note 1.

Lord Tyrawly died 13th July, 1773, aged 83, and was buried at Chelsea Hospital. He had married in November, 1724, the Hon. Mary Stewart, daughter of Viscount Mountjoy. This lady predeceased her husband, leaving two daughters.

Horace Walpole has left the following word portrait of Lord Tyrawly :—

"He had a great deal of humour and occasional good breeding, but not to the prejudice of his natural temper, which was imperiously blunt, haughty, and contemptuous, with an undaunted portion of spirit."

LIEUT.-COLONEL WILLIAM CECIL

CHAPTER IV

LIEUT.-COLONEL WILLIAM CECIL, EQUERRY TO GEORGE I.; CHIEF JACOBITE AGENT IN LONDON, 1731-1744

THIS officer was born about 1679.[1] His father was John Cecil of Salton, Wilts., "one of the Exeter family."[2] There was some mystery about this John Cecil which has never been cleared up. In the register of his marriage to Ann Oglethorpe (daughter of Wm. Oglethorpe of Oglethorpe, Tadcaster, by the widow of the last Savile of Northgate Head, Wakefield) at East Ardsley, Yorkshire, in 1673, this same John Cecil is called "John Plantagenet," a surname to which he is said to have had no claim.[3] The only child of this marriage was William Cecil.

Interest in high quarters obtained for young Cecil a commission, as Cornet in Lord Cavendish's Regiment of Horse (the present 7th Dragoon Guards), 1st March, 1689, when he was only ten years of age. It may be taken for granted that he never joined this regiment, though his parents may have drawn his pay. On 16th February, 1694, Wm. Cecil was appointed Cornet in the Earl of Denbigh's newly raised regiment of Dragoons. His uncle, Wm. Oglethorpe, was Major of this corps, which was disbanded in 1697 and the officers placed on half-pay. On the outbreak of war with France in 1702, Cecil received a commission as Cornet in the Royal Dragoons, dated 13th February, 1702, from Lord Raby the Colonel. He quitted this corps before 3rd March, 1704, and joined Lord Mohun's Regiment of Foot, of which his uncle Wm. Oglethorpe was Major. After serving with this corps in Ireland young Cecil was given a company in the Earl of Orrery's Regiment, and proceeded to Flanders with the same in 1708. Cecil saw active service under Marlborough, and was seriously wounded in the sanguinary battle of Malplaquet. On 28th December, 1709, John Bromley, Lord Raby's Yorkshire agent, writes to his Lordship from Wakefield: "Poor Captain Cecil was sadly mawled (sic) at the [late] Battle; I am told his arme was all shattered to peices, the splent bones are still coming oute; he was also shoot through the side. He is at Brussells now."[4]

On 31st January, 1709/10 (O.S.), Cecil's mother writes to Lord Raby: "My Lord, give me leave to renew my request for my pore son. He has been in the hottest of sarvis this year,[5] to which the Duck of Orgile (sic) has been a witnes and haes given him his promise to do him all the kindness he can . . . He is in the Lord Orerie's Regiment in Brussels."[6] The outcome of this letter was a brevet majority dated 8th December, 1710. On 1st July, 1712, Cecil was made Brevet Lieut.-Colonel by Queen Anne. He served under the Duke of Ormonde in Flanders, and was with his corps

[1] In the *Half-Pay List for* 1739 Wm. Cecil's age is given as 60.
[2] *The Wentworth Papers* with notes by Cartwright.
[3] *Oliver Heywood's Diary.*
[4] *Wentworth Papers.*
[5] Meaning the battle of Malplaquet.
[6] *Wentworth Papers.*

at Ghent, in March, 1713. A dispute arose between Cecil and Lieut.-Colonel Goodwyn as to the command of the regiment in aforesaid garrison, which had to be referred by General Sabine to the Duke of Ormonde :—

> "Gand, March 11, 1713. . . . . Lt.-Colonel Cecill of Gen. Sybourg's Regiment having come here, there is a dispute between him and Lieut.-Coll'. Goodwyn of the Command of the Regiment, the first having a Brevett as Major of an elder date to it, than the Commission of the latter as actual Major, so that I desire you'll be pleased to lay this before My Lord Duke in order to have his Directions, till then to avoid all disputes the eldest Captain is to command. Pray do me the honour to present my most humble duty to his Grace.
>
> I am, with real truth and esteem, &c., &c.,
>
> "JOS. SABINE.
>
> "Both the Brevett and Commission is granted by Her Majesty." [1]

On 24th December, 1713, Cecil was promoted Major of Corbet's, late Sybourg's, Foot, and was placed on half-pay a few weeks later on the disbandment of the regiment in Ireland.

In the summer of 1715, when a number of new cavalry and infantry regiments were added to the British Army, Colonel Cecil was appointed Major of Brigadier Alexander Grant's Regiment of Foot, and served with said corps in the West of Scotland, 1716. In June, 1717, this regiment was sent to Ireland, and was disbanded in November, 1718. Cecil was again placed on half-pay. In recognition of his war services and loss of an arm, George I. appointed Colonel Cecil an Equerry,[2] which post in the Royal Household carried with it an annuity of £300 per annum and £5 "for linnen."

Soon after the death of George I. it became known that Colonel Cecil was on terms of intimate friendship with the Earls of Barrymore and Orrery, both of whom were Generals in the Army on the unemployed list and in correspondence with the Chevalier St. George. Cecil had served under Lord Orrery in Flanders for some years, and that nobleman's wife (*née* Lady Elizabeth Cecil) was the Colonel's kinswoman. When the Earl of Orrery died in 1731, Cecil took the former's place as chief Jacobite agent in London. What followed is best told in the words of the learned Dr. Wm. King who was one of Cecil's contemporaries :—

> "Colonel Cecil who was agent for the Chevalier St. George, and succeeded my Lord Orrery, the father of the present Earl of Cork, in that office, had a weak judgment, and was very illiterate, and in many other respects was wholly unqualified for such a delicate commission. I believe he was a man of honour, and yet he betrayed his master. For he suffered himself to be cajoled and duped by Sir Robert Walpole to such a degree as to be fully persuaded that Sir Robert had formed a design to restore the House of Stuart. For this reason he communicated to Sir Robert all his despatches, and there was not a scheme which the Chevalier's Court, or the Jacobites in England, had projected during Sir Robert's long administration, of which the Minister was not early informed, and was therefore able to defeat it without any noise or expense. The Duchess of Buckingham, who was closely connected with Cecil, . . . was induced by him to entertain the same favourable opinion with himself of Sir Robert Walpole, and consequently

---

[1] Letter addressed to Mr. Henry Watkins, Secretary to the Duke of Ormonde, in possession of Mr. George Mackey of Birmingham, who kindly contributed a copy of this epistle.
[2] His name occurs as Junior Equerry in Chamberlayne's *Angliæ Notitia* for 1723 and 1726.

all the letters and instructions which she received from Rome were, without reserve, communicated to him. After Sir Robert Walpole's resignation the new Ministry ordered Cecil, whose agency was well known, to be taken into custody, which gave Sir Robert the occasion of saying to some of his friends that the Government had taken up the man from whom he had received all his information of the Jacobite measures." [1]

It was on 24th February, 1744, that Colonel Cecil was arrested at his house in Masham Street. His papers were all seized, and he was examined before the Council at the Cockpit with several other prisoners. On the 27th of the same month Cecil was sent to the Tower. On 11th May following he was bailed in £4,000 and four sureties of £2,000 each. [2] A month later the Grand Jury for co. Middlesex found a Bill against Colonel Cecil for Misprision of Treason. He was ordered to continue on his recognisance till the first day of the following term. [3] Colonel Cecil and the Earl of Barrymore formed the subjects of a debate in Parliament when attention was drawn to the treasonable papers [4] found in the former's pockets. The Hon. Philip Yorke thus refers to Cecil and the Jacobite correspondence in his *Parliamentary Journal* :—

"Such of the Papers as were thought proper to be inserted in the Indictment which was afterwards found against him for misprision of treason I had a cursory perusal of. They were letters to the Colonel from one of the correspondents in France relating to an insurrection here and an invasion from abroad ; the writer seems very confident of success. That the Hanover Family was much despised and hated by the people. That he thought Lord Barrymore's scheme the most feasible of any, which was to land near London with a body of 16,000 men and march directly thither. Hopes friends in England would be ready to take up arms at the same time. The Cardinal [Fleury] approved the project, and gave strong hopes of supporting it ; has expectations from Sweden and Spain likewise." [5]

Cecil's case was not brought to trial. His having made a confidant of Sir Robert Walpole in the past stood him in favour. He was in poor health, and being a *persona ingrata* to the Jacobites, as well as to the Royalist party, the Government felt he could do no more harm. His punishment was great enough ; his name was struck off the half-pay list, and for the short remainder of his life he did not frequent fashionable circles. Death came to him on 9th December, 1745. In his will, [6] wherein he describes himself as "Wm. Cecil of the parish of St. John the Evangelist in the liberty of Westminster, being infirm in body but of sound mind," &c., he refers to a paper in his own handwriting and signed by himself, enclosed in a sealed cover, containing a list of legacies and bequests which he begs may be admitted to probate. All the residue of his property he bequeathed to "his faithful servant, Richard Clarkson," who was named executor. Cecil's will bore date 28th November, 1745,

[1] Dr. Wm. King's *Political and Literary Anecdotes*, 2nd Edition, pp. 36–39:
[2] *Gentleman's Magazine*, 1744.
[3] *Ibid.*
[4] A list of the papers found in Colonel Cecil's house, and in his pockets, is given in the "Report on Mr. Underwood's Papers," printed by the *Hist. MSS. Commission.*
[5] Quoted in *Parliamentary History of England*, Vol. XIII., 1743–47, pp. 668–69.
[6] Original at Somerset House.

and was proved on 16th December following by Clarkson, who produced the sealed packet referred to in the will, and swore to the contents being in the handwriting of Wm. Cecil, who died a bachelor. The will and the private paper were admitted to probate, and the executor was duly sworn to administer to the same.

Thus ended a career which began with great promise but terminated most miserably.

LIEUT.-GENERAL HENRY HAWLEY

CHAPTER V

LIEUT.-GENERAL HENRY HAWLEY, COMMANDER-IN-CHIEF IN SCOTLAND,
20TH DECEMBER 1745—30TH JANUARY 1746

" Very brave and able ; with no small bias to the brutal."—HORACE WALPOLE.

SIR WALTER SCOTT threw down the gauntlet for English genealogists to take up when he put into print the idle rumour that General Hawley was an illegitimate son of George II.[1] Several subsequent writers have proved the absurdity of this statement by pointing out that George II. was some years junior to Hawley.[2] So far back as 1805 the following query was inserted in the *Gentleman's Magazine*: " Can any of your correspondents give an account of General Hawley, who lost his life at one of the sieges where General Erle had a command, by taking up a hand-grenade which burst in his right hand ?"[3]

It was stated in reply that the aforesaid General Hawley was father of General Henry Hawley of Falkirk notoriety.[4] It was not until 1896 that the mystery of Henry Hawley's parentage was completely cleared up by the present writer.[5]

Henry Hawley was the eldest child of Lieut.-Colonel, and Brevet-Colonel, Francis Hawley of the Princess Anne of Denmark's Regiment of Dragoons (the present 4th Hussars), by his wife Judith Hughes.[6] Colonel Francis Hawley commanded his corps at the battle of Steinkirk in 1692, and was killed by the bursting of a grenade, as stated in the *Gentleman's Magazine*.[7] Colonel Hawley died intestate, and left his widow and children nearly destitute. They were befriended by Brigadier-General Thomas Erle, who was half-brother to the deceased Colonel Hawley. Erle was in high favour with William III., and this monarch was pleased on 1st August, 1692, to bestow a cornetcy in the 4th Dragoons on Edward Hawley, second son of the aforesaid Francis Hawley, then aged six years.[8] In January, 1694, Edward Hawley's elder brother Henry was given an

[1] *Tales of a Grandfather.*
[2] See article on " The Barony of Hawley " in *The Genealogist*, Vol. I., pp. 161–63.
[3] *Gentleman's Magazine*, Vol. 75, p. 135.
[4] *Ibid.* p. 251.
[5] See article on " The Parentage of General Hawley," by Charles Dalton, in *Notes and Queries*, 8th Series, Vol. IX., 15th Feb. 1896; also 10th Series, Vol. VI., 7th July, 1906.
[6] Marriage licence granted 21st Jan. 1683/84.—*London Marriage Licences.*
[7] There is, or was, a posthumous portrait of Colonel Francis Hawley at Charborough House, Dorsetshire, the seat of the late Mrs. Drax Erle. The picture represents Colonel Hawley being killed in the manner stated in the text. It has been wrongly calendared in Hutchins's *Hist. of Dorset* as " Portrait of General Hawley."
[8] See article on " Child Commissions in the Army," by Charles Dalton, in *Notes and Queries*, 8th Series, Vol. VIII.

ensigncy in Brigadier Erle's own regiment, subsequently known as the 19th Foot. Young Henry Hawley was barely nine years old when he received the above commission. It is needless to say that neither he nor his brother Edward joined their respective regiments for some years. On the 11th October, 1696, their mother, Mrs. Judith Hawley, petitioned William III. She stated that "her husband, Colonel Francis Hawley, was killed at Steinkirk, leaving her in charge of four children, with no other fortune but the hopes of His Majesty's royal favour which he had been graciously pleased to promise to the petitioner's brother[-in-law], Major-General Erle . . . petitioner, by her endeavours to fit her children for His Majesty's service has engaged herself in great difficulties."[1] The immediate outcome of the above petition was a grant of £40 to Mrs. Judith Hawley.[2] This sum was only a temporary annuity; and some time afterwards William III. bestowed a pension of £300 per annum on this widow.[3] On 10th March, 1702, Ensign Henry Hawley was appointed Ensign in Sir Richard Temple's newly raised Regiment of Foot, and presumably proceeded with said corps to Ireland same year. In March, 1704, Temple's corps embarked for Flanders; Hawley did not accompany it. A friend at Court got him the promise of preferment in the Cavalry. On 11th September, 1704, Henry Hawley was commissioned Cornet in the Royal Horse Guards; and on 27th May, 1706, was appointed Captain in his late father's old corps—the 4th Dragoons, then commanded by the Earl of Essex. A month later, the before-named Edward Hawley was appointed Lieutenant to his elder brother, Captain Henry Hawley.

In October, 1706, part of Lord Essex's Dragoons embarked with the Earl of Rivers's expedition for Spain. The following April Hawley's troop took part in the sanguinary battle of Almanza, where Colonel Charles Dormer of the above corps was killed. Hawley returned to England in April, 1707.[4] In 1708 the regiment took part in an expedition against Cherbourg. Hawley was promoted Major of above corps 27th January, 1711, and succeeded to the Lieut.-Colonelcy 4th April same year. On 16th October, 1712, he was given a brevet of Colonel. This rapid promotion seems to indicate that Hawley was considered a good soldier.

On the accession of George I. the 4th Dragoons, then under command of Major-General Wm. Evans, was in Ireland. In the autumn of 1715 Evans's corps embarked for Scotland and was actively engaged at the battle of Sheriffmuir. Colonel Hawley was severely wounded[5] when charging with the Royalist cavalry. As a reward for his services he was given the command of the regiment, subsequently known as the 33rd Foot, 19th March, 1717. This corps was then in Ireland. In 1719, Hawley served with his regiment in the expedition to Vigo. What he yearned for was a dragoon regiment. He got his wish on 7th July, 1730, when he was appointed Colonel of the 13th Dragoons, then stationed in Ireland. Five years later he was promoted Brigadier-General; and in 1739 advanced to the rank of Major-General.

---

[1] *Treasury Papers*, under date of 11th Oct. 1696.
[2] *Warrants for Pay and Contingencies*, 20th Nov. 1697, to 24th June, 1700.
[3] See p. 44.
[4] It appears from a "Muster Book" at the British Museum (*Add. MS.* 19023, fol. 16), that Captains Umfreville and Hawley returned to England in the spring of 1707, after handing over their horses to a regiment of French Huguenot Dragoons.
[5] " Colonel Hawley was shot through the body, but there is hope of his recovery."—*Colonel Harrison's Account of the Battle of Sheriffmuir.*

On 12th May, 1740, Henry Hawley was given the command of the Royal Dragoons, which he retained for the rest of his life.

In the summer of 1742, George II. having entered into an alliance with the Queen of Hungary against France, 16,000 British troops under the Earl of Stair were despatched to Flanders to co-operate with the Austrian Generals on the Continent. These troops were joined subsequently by 6,000 Hessians and 16,000 Hanoverians in British pay. The following letter from Major-General Hawley to the Duke of Richmond gives a lamentable report of the ill-preparedness of the British troops to enter upon a campaign :—

"Ghent, Sep. 16, 1742.

"I had the honour of your Grace's the day before yesterday, and yesterday by the poste wee had a full account of all your counter-orders at Gravesend, which I assure you nobody here is sorry for, for whatever the Plan of this Winter Campagne is nobody here (exclusive of us Englishe, who are quite in the darke) can conceave any prospects of success. Our Cantonement is fix'd, the right at Dixmude the left at Courtray, the regts. of Ligonier and Cope marche tomorrow. The regt. of Honywood march'd yesterday from Lierre, the rest are all to follow by regts. ; this by Count Neuperg's orders, for Lord Staire's came to Brussells but last night. As 'tis morning now he may be here tonight, but that's not yeat certain ; if all this goes on it points for the french lines at Dunkirke. Wee find the Austrians hold the party of Monsieur Neuperg very low, and our Gen'll's best Friende cant help saying, *qu'il joue gros jeu!* Our next G., tho' no more in the secrett, than I am, actes such a part as hurts all those that knew him before ; *cela fait pitié*. If I could describe the way wee are in you would not believe itt. The truthe will be knowne some day ; hitherto, 'tis plaine, 'tis not yeat knowne on youre side ; but marche wee muste into a Countrey which the inhabitants have deserted with all their Effects and Cattle, and as for the Troopes that joine us, if they are like six battallions that came thro' here Monday last wee are not like to do muche, they are very indifferent, one Regt. lost 190 deserted on the marche, they, the Hanovers and Hessians lye behind us ; as to numbers, I still say the English for a Day of Action will not be 9,000 men, rank and file, tho' they were call'd 16,000 upon paper, the sicke still continue aboute the same number, aboute 2,000 at Bruges, and some dying every day, the rest going into a worse countrey out of warme beds, no victuells to be got but Rye bread ; for the Boors having even dug up theyr potatoes and carryed them off ; you may guess if our numbers wont increase—I wish I could say, in the *hospitall*, for to this day there's no orders for any to goe with us, and what's more amazing is, wee are told by our Genll. here that this little one for 150 men is to goe two days back to Antwerpe, and wee goe three days forward from here, in short we cant believe what wee are tolde, 'tis so contradictory to comon sense ; 'tis no matter how many men the French have here next Spring, for this body of men who came with us muste be destroyed, exclusive of our Enemy. I put that out of the question, nor I dont speake as a Collonel, having been no more here this five weekes paste, but I speake as an Englishman, and so I am resolv'd to acte and speake too if I am ever to be looked on here above a Collonel, and so others besides me. Wee depend upon a great deale tomorrow when our Genll. is here, 'tis certain the Hanover Troopes and Hessians are stop't in theyr marche on this side the Maine and two Regts. of Austrian Dragoons are stop't at Brussells. What this meanes wee dont yeat know, may be wee shall before night ; in the meantime I am withe all sincerity

"Your Grace's most obedt. humble servant

"H. HAWLEY."

[P.S.] ". . . My Lord Staire has sent for our three Lt.-Genlls. to Brussells, to consult whats to be done, and as I guess, how wee are to subsist this Winter, for hithertoe it lookes more like starving for the Horse and Dragooues than other-ways ; the Dutche have forbid any more Forrage coming out of Holland and wee have been fed here only from hand to mouthe this three weekes ; there never has been at any time a fortnight's Forrage in the place." [1]

Somehow or other the British troops and their officers survived through a long and particularly trying winter in Flanders.   Towards the latter end of April, 1743, the Earl of Stair, at the head of a strong British contingent, crossed the German frontier.   A Council of War was held at Aix-la-Chapelle on 23rd April, and Hawley, who had been promoted Lieut.-General 30th March, 1743, was one of the British generals who voted that " the advance into Germany is absolutely necessary." [2]   Two months later the battle of Dettingen was fought and won by the British and their Allies.   Fate decreed that the second line of cavalry at this battle should be commanded by Lieut.-Generals John Cope and Henry Hawley, the two commanders who were in turn to be signally beaten by the Highland Army at Prestonpans and Falkirk.   On the return of the British troops to Flanders, after Dettingen, Hawley was appointed British Commandant at Ghent.   Horace Walpole, writing under date of December, 1745, tells the following characteristic anecdote about General Hawley :—

"Two years ago when he arrived at Ghent, the magistrates according to custom sent a gentleman with the offer of a sum of money to engage his favour. He told the gentleman in great wrath that the King, his master, paid him, and that he should go tell the magistrates so, at the same time dragging him to the head of the stairs and kicking him down." [3]

Hawley had a cavalry command under Marshal Wade in the latter's inglorious campaign of 1744.   There is still extant a letter to Field-Marshal Wade from General Hawley, in which the latter gives some interesting particulars regarding his immediate relatives and himself :—

"King William gave my two brothers and myself commissions.   They were both killed since in the service.   He also gave a pension of £300 to my mother and sister to maintain them, which a few years ago his Majesty ordered to be struck off as I was then one of his aides-de-camp.   I gave my sister the pay of that post (being called £200 a year) ; when his Majesty was pleased to employ me abroad he took that away.   I then was forced to make my sister the same allowance out of my pay." [4]

At Fontenoy, Hawley was second in command of the Horse to Lord Crawford, after Sir James Campbell received his mortal wound.   Shortly after this battle, Hawley was given the command of a detachment of troops to cover the march of an Austrian garrison to Mons, also to enable a body of British troops at Aeth to rejoin the army.   Having performed this service, Hawley returned to Brussels.   In the autumn he returned to England, and joined the Duke of Cumberland's Army at Lichfield.   Horace Walpole, in a letter to Horace Mann, under date of 9th December, 1745, writes : " The Duke has sent General Hawley with the Dragoons to harass the rebels."   On the night of 18th December, the Royalist advanced cavalry caught up the rear-guard of the Scottish Army on Clifton Moor,

[1] Extracted from *A Duke and his Friends*, by the Earl of March, Vol. II., pp. 397–400.
[2] *Add. MS.* 22537, fol. 240.   See copy of this document in the Appendices.
[3] *Walpole's Letters*, Toynbee Edition, Vol. II., p. 160.
[4] Undated letter, endorsed " 27 July, 1744."   Quoted in Mr. Skrine's *Fontenoy*, 1906.

near Penrith, and a skirmish took place. Two days later Hawley was appointed Commander-in-Chief in Scotland.

On arrival at Edinburgh, Hawley found twelve battalions of infantry —mostly raw levies—and three regiments of dragoons in garrison there. It was not till the middle of January that he was ready to take the field and attempt the relief of Stirling Castle. His letters from Edinburgh to the Earl of Harrington, Secretary of State, explain the causes of delay :—

> " I hope we shan't be blamed but it is not the name of twelve battalions that will do the business. No diligence in me shall be wanting, but a man cannot work without tools. The heavy artillery is still at Newcastle[1] for want of horses, which were sent to Carlisle for no use. The major of artillery is absent through sickness. . . . I have been obliged to hire a conductor of artillery and seventy odd men to act as his assistants for field artillery. I was three days getting them from the Castle to the Palace yard and now they are not ready to march."[2]

On the 13th January, 1746, Hawley's first division, under Major-General Huske, advanced to Linlithgow and drove a party of rebels from the town. On the following day three regiments quitted Edinburgh to support General Huske ; and on the 16th, Hawley, with his whole force, amounting to 9,000 men, marched to Falkirk and encamped near the town. On the same day Prince Charles Edward, who had lately undertaken the siege of Stirling, drew up his troops on Bannockburn, a field of happy augury to the Scots, and awaited an attack. Hawley stayed where he was. His contempt for the Jacobite levies led him to neglect even the most common precautions ; and on the morning of the 17th Hawley rode over to Callender House to breakfast with Lady Kilmarnock, leaving no orders behind him. While the English general was thus agreeably engaged the Highland Army was marching to attack the Royalist forces on their own ground. The English soldiers were preparing for their dinner about one o'clock in the afternoon, when some country people hurried into the camp with news that the Highlanders were in sight. The drums beat to arms and messengers were despatched to Hawley at Callender House, while General Huske formed the troops in line in front of their camp. Hawley soon galloped up—hatless. He instantly ordered the dragoon regiments of Ligonier, Hamilton, and Cobham, to advance with him, full speed, to the top of Falkirk Muir, and the foot to follow with fixed bayonets. Ever since Sheriffmuir, Hawley had been strongly imbued with the notion that " Highlanders could not stand a charge of dragoons who attacked them well."[3] This fixed idea was put to the test, and caused Hawley's defeat at Falkirk. The charge of the dragoon regiments was met by a steady

---

[1] "Newcastle, Jan. 16, 1745/6.—Yesterday 48 Gunners and Mattrosses marched hence to join General Hawley in Scotland, and were this morning followed by 16 pieces of Artillery."—*London Gazette.*

[2] Letters of 10th, 11th, 13th Jan., quoted in the Hon. John Fortescue's *British Army*, Vol. II., p. 138. The artillery to which Hawley refers got hard and fast in a bog during the engagement at Falkirk, and never came into action. "As soon as the peasant drivers, who had been engaged with the horses, saw the Royal Army waver they promptly fled, and of the eight guns which accompanied the King's troops, seven fell into the hands of the enemy."—*Hist. of the Royal Artillery*, by Col. Duncan, R.A., Vol. I., p. 128.

[3] " Hawley had once said to a group of officers in Flanders who were talking about the battle of Prestonpans that ' *he* knew the Highlanders ; they were good militia, but he was certain they could not stand a charge of dragoons who attacked them well.' "—Browne's *Hist. of the Highlands.*

and withering fire from the enemy's ranks, followed by an impetuous rush of the Highlanders, who dropped their muskets and charged sword in hand. Two of the dragoon regiments turned tail and fled. The elements were entirely in favour of the Jacobites, as a storm of wind and rain beat full in the faces of the English troops. When the dragoons bolted the Highlanders fell upon the flank of Hawley's two columns of foot, who were likewise furiously assailed in front. The infantry, partly composed of militia levies, could not stand the double onslaught. "In vain did their General," writes an historian, "attempt to animate them by his personal courage, his white head uncovered and conspicuous in the front ranks of the combatants; the whole centre gave way in confusion and betook themselves to flight."[1] The extreme right of the Royal Army, under Major-General Huske,[2] being protected by a bank, was able to keep the Highlanders at bay; and being joined by Cobham's Dragoons, inflicted heavy loss on the left wing of the Prince's Army, and compelled the Highlanders in that part of the field to retreat. Both armies had had enough. The Prince passed the night at Falkirk, while Hawley marched back with his dejected troops to Linlithgow and the day following to Edinburgh. Hawley had 16 officers and 300 to 400 private soldiers killed. From Edinburgh Hawley wrote to the Duke of Cumberland: "My heart is broke. I can't say we are quite beat, but our left is beat and their left is beat." The defeated General lost no time in utilising two gibbets to hang some of his soldiers who had shown cowardice in the late engagement. His severity on this and subsequent occasions earned for him the sobriquet of "The Hangman."

Hawley's plain speaking is well exemplified in his address to the Edinburgh civic authorities :—

" General Hawley's address to the civic authorities at Edinburgh, delivered at Holyrood House a few days after the battle of Falkirk :—

"Gentlemen, you pretend to have an extraordinary zeal for his Majesty's service, and seem to be very assiduous in promoting it; but let me tell you, you have either been mistaken in your own measures, or have been betraying his cause. How often have you represented the Highland army, and the multitude of noblemen and gentlemen, who have joined them from the low country with their followers, as a despicable pack of herds, and a contemptible mob of men of desperate fortunes? How have you, in your repeated advices, disguised and lessened the numbers and strength of his Majesty's enemies in your rebellious country? And how often have you falsely magnified and increased the power and number of his friends? These things you had the hardiness to misrepresent to some of the ministers of state, and generals of the army. If the government had not relied on the truth of your advices, it had been an easy matter to have crushed this insurrection in the bud. If your information had not been unluckily believed, that most part of the Highlanders had run home with their booty after the battle of Gladsmuir, and that they who remained had absolutely refused to march into England, what would have hindered the King to have sent down a few troops from England to assist his forces in Scotland, to have at once dispersed and destroyed them? But you, out of your views or vanity, made him and his ministry believe that you were able to do it yourselves. And what are the consequences of your fine politics and intelligence? The rebels have got time to

---

[1] Earl Stanhope's *Hist. of England* (5th Edition, Vol. III., p. 288).
[2] Served many years in the 1st Foot Guards and Coldstream Guards. Fought at Dettingen, Fontenoy, and Culloden. Severely wounded at first-named battle. Gov. of Sheerness, 1745. General, 1756. Gov. of Jersey, 1760. D. 1761.

draw to such a head, that the King has been obliged to withdraw more than ten thousand of his own troops from the assistance of his allies abroad, and as many auxiliaries from Holland and Hesse, to defend his own person and dominions at home. As to your diminishing their numbers, and ridiculing their discipline, you see, and I feel the effects of it. I never saw any troops fire in platoons more regularly, make their motions and evolutions quicker, or attack with more bravery and better order than those Highlanders did at the battle of Falkirk last week. And these are the very men whom you represented as a parcel of raw undisciplined vagabonds. No Jacobite could have contrived more hurt to the King's faithful friends, or done more service to his inveterate enemies. Gentlemen, I tell you plainly, these things I am now blaming you for I shall represent at Court, so that it may be put out of your favour to abuse it for the future. I desire no answer, nor will I receive any. If you have anything to offer in your defence or justification, do it *above*, and publish it here. It will not offend me. In the meantime I will deal with you with that openness and honour which becomes one of my station and character. I will send to you in writing what I have now delivered to you by word of mouth, that you may make any use of it that you think proper for your own advantage and exculpation. Farewell." [1]

When news reached the King of Hawley's defeat, His Majesty appointed the Duke of Cumberland Commander-in-Chief in Scotland. The Duke left London immediately and travelled so expeditiously that he reached Edinburgh on 30th January.

The siege of Stirling Castle, which was defended by General William Blakeney proved a fiasco. The French engineer who conducted the attack did not know his business and his batteries were silenced. Many of the Jacobite officers in the Prince's camp returned to their homes. The heavy guns were spiked and on 1st February the besieging army retreated to Inverness. The Duke of Cumberland, who had been reinforced by 6,000 Hessians, lost no time pursuing the Scots. Hawley was given the command of the cavalry in the Duke's Army. It was not till 16th April, 1746, that the two rival armies met in battle on Culloden Moor. Hawley's A.D.C. was the immortal James Wolfe, then an Infantry Captain.[2] This distinguished soldier was then only nineteen but had already taken part in several campaigns and had been appointed a Brigade-Major, in Flanders, 12th June, 1745. Wolfe wrote an account of the battle of Culloden to a military friend at York. In this letter[3] he thus refers to General Hawley's part in the engagement :—

"Gen[l]. Hawley who commanded the five Squadrons of Dragoons on the Left, had by assistance of 150 Argileshire [militia] thrown down two stone Walls and was (when the fire of the Foot began) posted with his Dragoons opposite to the Extremity of the Enemy's Right Wing, and as soon as the Rebels began to give way, and the fire of our Foot slacken'd, he order'd General Bland to charge the Rest of them with three Squadrons, and Cobham to support him with two. It was done with wonderful [spirit?] and compleated the Victory with great slaughter. We have taken 22 pieces of Brass Cannon or near it, a number of Colours and near 700 Prisoners, amongst which are all the Irish Picquets, most

---

[1] In a pamphlet published at London in 1746, entitled : *A few Passages showing the Sentiments of the Prince of Hesse and General Hawley, &c*.

[2] In Barrell's Regt. (4th Foot). In *The Spottiswoode Miscellany*, Wolfe is referred to as Major in 1746. He had been a Brigade-Major but was not a Major in the Army until 1748–49.

[3] Given in *The Genealogist*, Vol. VII., pp. 225–29 and reprinted in Beckles Willson's *Life of Wolfe*. The letter was to Capt. Henry Delabene and dated 17th April, 1746.

of the remainder of Fitz James's Horse and part of Drummond's Regim^t., great quantity of Powder, Muskets, Bayonets, Broad Swords and Plads innumerable. All the Troops acquitted themselves as Troops worthy the Comand of a great and gallant General."

A month later, Captain James Wolfe wrote to Captain Charles Hamilton of Cobham's Dragoons at Forfar :—

"Inverness, May 19, 1746.

"SIR,

"I am ordered by General Hawley to acquent you that he has shown your letter to His Royal Highness, who approves of everything you have done and desires you will continue that assiduity in apprehending such as have been in open rebellion or are known abettors, and that you will be carefull to collect all prooffs and accusations against them, and deliver them to Major Chaban, and let the Major know from General Hawley that he is to receive and keep together all such accusations as shall be sent him from you, or any other officer under his command, that they may be more conveniently had when called for : you know the manner of treating the houses and possessions of rebells in this part of the country.   The same freedom is to be used where you are as has been hitherto practised, that is in seeking for them and their arms, cattle, and other things that are usually found.   These that have submitted to his Royal Highness' Proclamation are to be treated as you have mentioned.   The list is to be keept, and their arms are to be taken from them.

"I am, Sir, your most obedient Servant,
' J. WOLFE,
"Aid de Camp to General Hawley." [1]

The Duke of Cumberland made his headquarters at Fort Augustus soon after Culloden.   Then followed the systematic cruelties and outrages on the Scottish population, far and near, which earned for Cumberland the nickname of "The Butcher."   The Duke was ably seconded in his barbarities by General Hawley whose vindictive nature never forgot, or forgave, his defeat by the Highlanders at Falkirk.   The following letter is painful reading :—

LIEUT.-GENERAL HAWLEY to the DUKE OF RICHMOND.[2]

"Augustus Camp, June 16, 1746.

"MY LORD,

"By laste poste I had the honour of youre Grace's of the first, I do most truly acknowledge your goodness to me in this affair, as to the good opinion you have of me indeed you over rate my merritt, I hope the world wonte thinke that I putt myself upon a foot to choose where I will serve, as some of late have done, for once more I assure you I am no longer fitt for this employ, for the very reason you are pleas'd to mention, if his Majesty would leave me the Foot here, and the Parliament give the men *a guinea and a pair of shoes for every rebell's head they brought in,* I would still undertake to clear this country, but as to Law and Polliticks I beg to be excused, I have no Tallent that way, but as Ld. Albemarle[3] is now declar'd, who I pitty, I assure youre Grace he was not one of those I hinted, my two were first Tyrawley who would, if I don't mistake, have worked them well for six months, by that time they would have trip'd up his heels, the other was Huske who if they had made a Lt.-Genll. 'twas but making two.

---

[1] *The Spottiswoode Miscellany,* Vol. II., pp. 511–12.   This letter has also been printed in Mr. Beckles Willson's *Life of General Wolfe.*
[2] Extracted from *A Duke and his Friends,* by the Earl of March, Vol. II., pp. 511–12.
[3] Second Earl.   D. 22nd Dec. 1754.

" . . . As to affairs here I can give you no actt. when the Duke goes, nay even from hence, for here's so many prisoners dayly coming in, old Lovett and above 50 more were brought in yesterday, theres still some hopes of theyr P. Charly too, there's still so many more houses to burn and I hope still some more to be put to deathe, tho' by computation there's about seven thousand houses burn'd allready, yeat all is not done.

" I won't, nor cant stire, untill the Duke does, and now he dont go to Flanders I believe he'll stay to try to breake theyr hearts, but I defye him to make any one of the Countrey honest or sincere, God did not make them so, and that you will all be convinced off at laste as well as youre Grace's most obed. humble servant,

" H. HAWLEY."

A letter from Captain James Wolfe to the aforesaid Captain Charles Hamilton written from Fort Augustus, in July, 1746, contains General Hawley's instructions about cattle seizures :—

" The General bid me tell you that when any seizures were made of cattle or otherwise in this part of the world, the commanding officer and every person concerned have shares in proportion to your pay. . . . It is not known when the troops will move from hence, or what road General Hawley will go." [1]

Hawley left Scotland for good with the Duke of Cumberland the end of July, 1746, and the Earl of Albemarle succeeded the latter as Commander-in-Chief.

On 11th April, 1747, Hawley was appointed second in command of the British cavalry in Flanders. He served under the Duke of Cumberland in the campaign of 1747 and took part in the sanguinary battle of Laufeldt.

The following letter [2] to the Duke of Newcastle refers to Hawley's appointment as Governor of Inverness, which post became vacant by the death of Field-Marshal Wade in March, 1748 :—

" MY LORD DUKE,

" By a letter from Mr. Fox, I find his Majesty is pleased to have the Goverments in Scottlande divided, ordering the pay of Fort William to be three hundred poundes a year, and Lᵗ Genll: Bland to have that ; as also to order Inverness, &c., for me, withe the pay of five hundred a year.

" Now as Mr. Bland gives his reasons, why he earnestly desyres to be excused, taking any Goverment, in that Countrey, I moste humbly beg of his Majesty, that he will be gratiously pleased either, to continue them goverments as they were, to me till somethinge else offers, or that he will voutsafe to put me on the staff in Ireland added to Inverness, this Sʳ John Ligonier quitts, as well as Kingsale, as I heard him say, I then should be upon a parr, withe severall of my Juniors, who have long had good goverments, while I have never had any marke of Royall favour, And if yʳ Grace will be so good, to be my Friend in this, to his Majesty you will lay ane eternall obligation on your Graces moste Obedient and moste faithefull humble servant,

" HE: HAWLEY."

[*Endorsed*]
    " March 174⁷/₈
      Lt.-Genˡ Hawley."

---

[1] *The Spottiswoode Miscellany*, Vol. II., p. 513.
[2] *Add. MS.* 32714, fol. 413, Brit. Mus.

Hawley was in command of the British troops at Breda in the spring of 1748. His letter[1] to the Duke of Newcastle explains his position there and his ambition to have the rank of full General :—

> "Camp at Breda,
> "May ye 4th 1748.

"MY LORD DUKE,

"The very disagreable, and cruell situation I am in here, comanded by so many Dutche Genlls: who are muche younger than me forces me to give youre Grace this impertinent trouble, and being a little encouraged by the many favours allready receaved from your Grace ;

"When I came to Williamstad, intending to have joined his R: H: imedeatly from thence ; my Equipage being all there, I founde his orders to take upon me the Comande of the Englishe troopes left here, and those that came withe me, whiche in all consist of seven battallions, three hundred recruits belonging to those Regts: withe his R: H: and three hundred Dragoones, by whiche I am comanded by no less than sixteen dutche Genlls: who are all muche younger than me in every degree,

"As I am the nexte to Sr John Ligonier except Mr Handaside, who I beleive will scarse ever be employed, I humbly beg of youre Grace, to mention this to his Majesty, if he would be gratiously pleased, to give me my Ranke withe them whiche is the sixteenthe of May laste, it appears to me only a peice of Justice and I cant see what injustice, it can be to Mr Handaside, if he has his ranke when ever he serves, there being two Presidents of the same nature. As I doubte this muste be the laste Campagne, I shall never gett my Ranke, if his Majesty wont please to have some compassion for me now, I desyre no adition of pay,

"I muste beg leave to acquaint youre Grace, that I had suche Offers made me last year, that I beleive, if his Majesty would have Permitted me to have gone into that service, I could have been Genll: of Horse, and have had the Regt of Dragoones and the Goverment of Mastrick, whiche Prince William of Hesse quitted, his R: H: knowes this, but he knowes also that I will never forsake him,

"I beleive the Prince of Orange would now give me a Brevett, to preserve my Ranke, as there has been severall Presidents in my time but I should be ashamed to aske his Majestys leave for suche a thinge,

"I humbly beg youre Graces pardon, and am withe the greatest respecte
> "youre Graces moste Obliged
> "and moste devoted humble Servant
> "HE: HAWLEY."

[*Endorsed*]
"Camp of Breda.
May 4, 1748 N.S.
Lt General Hawley
R[ec.] 29th Apl
(by Butson)."

On his return to England, in 1748, Hawley was appointed to the Staff in Ireland as he had desired. He held this post for four years. He was then given the governorship of Portsmouth, 8th July, 1752. He held this command till the time of his death which occurred 24th March, 1759, at his residence, West Green, near Portsmouth.

General Hawley died unmarried. He left some property in Scotland to which his sister Anne Hawley was served heir general.[2] His will dated "29 March, 1749," caused a sensation at the time from the truculent and objectionable style in which he had worded it. He left his "adopted son

[1] *Add. MS.* 32714, fol. 518, Brit. Mus.
[2] *The Genealogist,* Vol. I., p. 162.

Captain Wm. Toovey" his sole executor who, with his brother Captain John Toovey, was amply provided for. Captain Wm. Toovey was directed in said will to take the names of " Henry Hawley."

There is no portrait extant of General Hawley. It is known, however, that he weighed 17 stone in 1739. This fact is stated by the present Earl of March, in his book entitled *A Duke and his Friends*, who records that Hawley was an ardent lover of fox-hunting and goes on to say :—

> " His [Hawley's] name appears constantly among the pages of the Duke's Hunting Diary as having been well to the front in many a good hunt. In fact he was one of the favoured few that were up at the finish of the ' Great Chase,' in January 1739, ' when the Glorious Twenty Three Hounds putt an end to the Campaign and killed the Old Bitch Fox ten minutes before six ' [in *January*, mark you !] which they had found in East Dean Wood at a quarter before eight in the morning. ' Billy Ives, whipper in, His Grace of Richmond, and Brigadier Hawley were the only Persons at the Death, to the Immortal Honour of 17 stone and at least as many Campaigns.' "

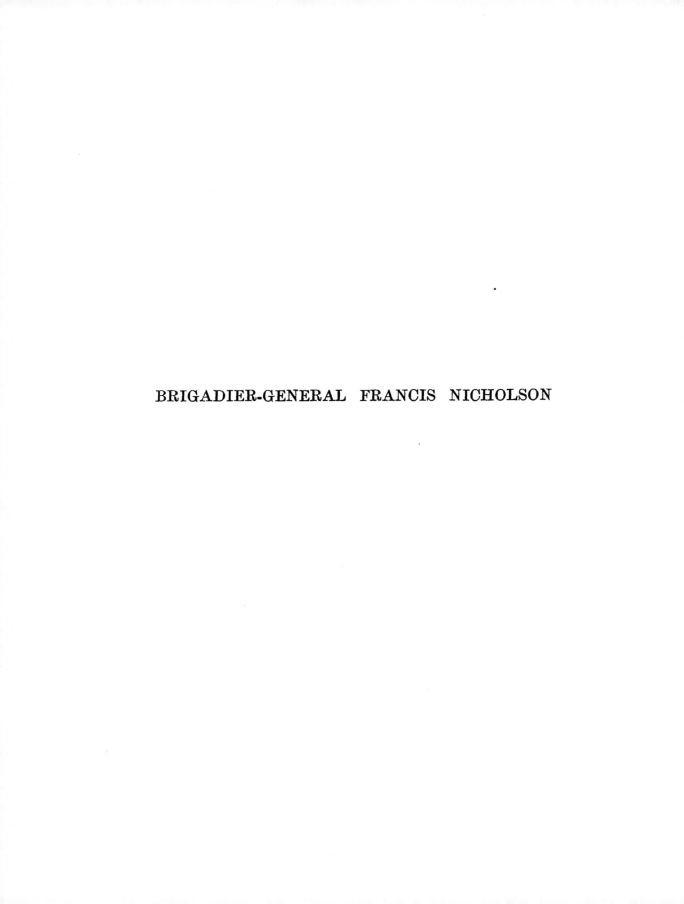

BRIGADIER-GENERAL FRANCIS NICHOLSON

CHAPTER VI

BRIGADIER-GENERAL FRANCIS NICHOLSON, GOVERNOR OF NOVA SCOTIA, 1712–1715; GOVERNOR OF SOUTH CAROLINA, 1720–1728

THE memoir of this distinguished soldier, and able administrator, in the *Dictionary of National Biography* is misleading in three essential points. The same remark applies equally to the article on this General in Appleton's *Cyclopædia of American Biography*. In the first place, Francis Nicholson was born in 1655 and not in 1660 as heretofore stated; secondly he was never knighted; and thirdly he was not made a Lieut.-General in 1720; the rank in question was local and temporary—in America. In his will, which was dated the day before his death, he describes himself as "Esquire," and, with a view to monumental inscription, says, "I was born at Downham [Downholme] Park, near Richmond, in Yorkshire, 12th November, 1655." Here is a clue to Nicholson's parentage which has always remained a mystery. Even that astute genealogist Dr. Whitaker, the Richmondshire historian, confessed he could never find out anything about the aforesaid Francis Nicholson, the native of Downholme, beyond the fact that Gale, in his *Registrum Honoris de Richmond*, dedicated a view of Richmond, in 1722, to General Nicholson. The dedication in question is somewhat pompous and fulsome, but that was the style of the period.

Downholme Park was the old seat of the Scropes, and on the death, in 1630, of Emanuel Scrope, eleventh Baron Bolton and first Earl of Sunderland, without legitimate issue, the extensive Scrope estates were divided between the late Earl's three natural daughters. Downholme Park fell to the lot of Mary the eldest of the three children. She married for her second husband, 12th February, 1655, Lord St. John, son and heir of the fifth Marquis of Winchester, who became possessed of the Bolton estate in North Yorkshire, and was created, in 1689, Duke of Bolton. This nobleman has been represented by two well-known contemporary writers, Sir John Reresby and Bishop Burnet, as one of the most extravagant livers of his time, and "a man who took all sorts of liberties to himself." Putting two and two together, and comparing several leading points of resemblance in the character of the Duke of Bolton, surnamed "the Proud," and General Nicholson, the present writer fully believes that the child born at Downholme Park on 12th November, 1655, was the natural son of Lord St. John, as he was then known. Nicholson may, or may not, have been the mother's surname; Francis was a name in the Paulet family. Unfortunately the Downholme parish registers only commence in 1736; and Nicholson's will, a lengthy document, makes no mention of relatives or kinsfolk. But sidelights are not wanting to bear out the writer's ideas as to Nicholson's father. In a letter from Lady Fauconberg (Cromwell's daughter) to Sir William Frankland, a Yorkshire neighbour, written on 5th May, 1683, her Ladyship says, "Captain Nichol-son, who was Lady Winchester's page, has been twice through Moratania (*sic*) as far as Mount Atlas, and is now returning again thither." Now this ex-page was undoubtedly Francis Nicholson, who was commissioned Ensign in the old Buffs (the present East Kent Regiment) 9th January, 1678, and appointed, in 1680, to an ensigncy in the newly raised corps commanded by the Earl of Plymouth, subsequently known as the 4th King's Own. This regiment embarked for Tangier three months after being raised for service against the Moors. Colonel Kirke, the Governor of Tangier, took special notice of young Nicholson, and appears to have employed him as an A.D.C., which may have obtained for him the local rank of Captain. This explains Nicholson's missions to the interior of Morocco [1] as well as his being sent with despatches to Lord Preston, British Ambassador in Paris, in 1682 and 1683.[2] In 1684, he was appointed Lieutenant in the Duchess of York's Regiment. Home interest and a well-filled purse accompanied Nicholson through life. The often repeated story of Nicholson winning James II.'s favour by kneeling when Mass was celebrated in the Royal tent at Hounslow is doubtless true; but it is unfair to attribute an unworthy motive for this action to a man who was a consistent Church of England devotee, and who, with all his faults, and possible vices, was a deeply religious man at heart.

On 30th July, 1686, Nicholson was appointed "Captain of a Company of Foot for the Colony of New England." Shortly afterwards he was made Lieut.-Governor of New York under Sir Edmund Andros, who, in 1685, had been appointed Governor of all the English Colonies in North America, between Maryland and Canada, excepting Pennsylvania. At the Revolution the colonists threw off Andros's yoke, which had long been burdensome to them, and imprisoned him with some of his subordinates. Shortly after, Andros was sent to England with some of his accusers and put on his trial. Nicholson had been head of the Administration at New York, in Andros's absence, from 1687–89; but he had quarrelled with the leader of the New York Militia and was unpopular with the colonists. Jacobite office-holders were in the minority in New York. The citizens made choice of Jacob Leisler, a German brewer, to be their leader. This man was Captain of one of the Militia companies and wealthy. A report was set on foot that the Jacobites in the city contemplated murdering the Dutch residents. On 2nd June, 1689, an armed mob seized the fort and Leisler was persuaded to accept the keys and assume the reins of government. Nicholson, expecting to be made prisoner like Andros, got on board a homeward-bound ship and returned to England. While at sea, a despatch arrived at New York from King William and Queen Mary directed "to Francis Nicholson, Esq., or in his absence to such as for the time being takes care for preserving the peace and administering the laws in his Majesty's Province of New York." Leisler took this as an appointment of himself as the King's Lieut.-Governor of New York, and assumed the aforesaid rank coupled with that of Commander-in-Chief.[3]

---

[1] In a letter to the Earl of Dartmouth from Tangier, 23rd Jan. 1682/83, F. Povey mentions that "Mr. Nicolson the Courier from England arrived here about ten days since . . . . and went on his journey to the King of Morocco." It is recorded in Mr. Routh's *Tangier* (London, 1911) that *Lieut.* Francis Nicholson was sent by Charles II. with an important letter, written in Arabic, which he was to deliver into the Sultan's own hands.

[2] *Graham and Verney Papers*, published by the *Hist. MSS. Commission.*

[3] This brave but misguided demagogue was tried by New York judges for high treason in 1691, on the arrival of Governor Sloughter from England, and hanged.

Francis Nicholson was back in England by the end of August, 1689. The Duke of Bolton[1] used his powerful interest to obtain for Nicholson the governorship of the Province of New York. "As to Captain Nicholson," wrote the Earl of Shrewsbury (Secretary of State) to the Duke of Bolton, 10th September, 1689, "his Majesty is undecided how he shall dispose of the government of New York; but however he succeeds in this I doubt not he will find the benefit of your recommendation." The Duke of Bolton replied: "You will do me a great kindness to assist Capt. Nicholson." These proofs of fatherly interest speak for themselves. Wherever Nicholson had been educated[2] he profited by the instruction he received. The late Mr. J. A. Doyle, of Oxford University, in *The English in America*, remarks on Francis Nicholson's letters and despatches, which were indicative of superior education and talents. When Bishop Burnet wrote that the Duke of Bolton "had the spleen to an high degree, . . . yet carried matters before him with such authority and success that he was in all respects the great riddle of the age," the description might have been fitly applied to Nicholson who was high-handed, arrogant, and given to uncontrollable fits of rage. It is recorded that when a North American Indian once saw Nicholson in one of his tempests of passion, he remarked to one of the officers in attendance: "The General is drunk." "No," answered the officer, "he never drinks any strong liquor." "I do not mean," said the Indian, "that he is drunk with rum. He was born drunk."

The governorship of New York was not given to Nicholson; but he was appointed Lieut.-Governor of Virginia early in 1690. It so happened that Sir Edmund Andros was sent out to Virginia in the spring of 1692, as Governor of Virginia—a post which Nicholson hoped to have received. The two men were antagonistic and did not pull well together. Nicholson was a strong Churchman and went hand in hand with Dr. Blair, the Bishop of London's commissary in Virginia, in forwarding the erection of churches in this colony and advancing religious education. Andros is credited with being the founder of the well-known " William and Mary College," but Nicholson is believed to have been the prime mover in this educational venture.[3] Nicholson resigned the lieut.-governorship of Virginia in 1693 and returned to England.

While residing in London, during the winter of 1693–94, Nicholson took out a Grant of Arms which affords another proof that he did not belong to any heraldic family. These are the arms he received: " Az., on a cross arg. between four suns or, a cathedral church gu. Crest, a demi man habited in a close coat az., the bottoms and the cuffs of the sleeves turned up or, his face and hands proper, armed with a head piece and gorget arg., the beaver open; holding in the dexter hand a sword erect proper, hilt and pommel of the second, and in the sinister hand a Bible open clasps arg."[4]

In March, 1694, Nicholson was sent out to America as Governor of Maryland and held this post for five years. In 1698, Andros was recalled from Virginia, great complaints having been made against him by Dr. Blair, the Bishop of London's commissary in that colony. Nicholson succeeded Andros as Governor of Virginia in 1699 and took over this post same year. He made a successful coup, early in 1700, by his capture of

[1] So created 9th April, 1689.

[2] A certain Francis Nicholson graduated from Magdalene College, Cambridge, in 1677.

[3] The late Mr. Doyle in his article on Francis Nicholson in the *D.N.B.* says that Nicholson contributed £300 to the " William and Mary College."

[4] Robson's *Heraldry*, art. " Nicholson of Virginia."

some pirates who had long been a terror to the Virginian traders. "A detachment of the Guards is sent down the river," wrote Narcissus Luttrell under date of 23rd July, 1700, "to bring to the Marshalsea the pyrates taken by Colonel Nicholson on the coast of Virginia, and sent over in the fleet newly arrived from thence." The same diarist records, under date of 29th April, 1703, that "Colonel Nicholson, Governor of Virginia, has founded two universities and 28 churches in that country." As a soldier, Nicholson was strongly of opinion that "all the Colonies should be placed under a Viceroy, and that a strong army should be maintained at their own expense." These recommendations were neither acceptable to the British Government nor to the American Colonies; and the Virginians having lodged complaints against their Governor's high-handed proceedings, particularly with regard to transferring the capital of the colony from Jamestown to Williamsburg, Nicholson was recalled in 1704 and the Earl of Orkney appointed Governor early in 1705.

In 1709, Nicholson and Colonel Samuel Vetch[1] were placed in joint command of a colonial expedition to invade Canada from the New York side, while a British fleet, with several regiments on board, was to sail up the St. Lawrence and besiege Quebec. The colonials under Nicholson and Vetch advanced to Wood Creek, near Lake Champlain, and there awaited news of the expected fleet having reached Boston. But it never came! The troops intended for the attempt on Quebec had been sent to Portugal instead. Nothing remained for Nicholson and Vetch but to disband their force, which had suffered much from sickness and privations. Nicholson returned to England in the winter of 1709–10 to promulgate his plan for the re-conquest of Nova Scotia, and ask for the sinews of war. He brought with him four Iroquois Indian chiefs, whom he presented to Queen Anne. On 4th May, 1710, Nicholson (who had been given the rank of Brigadier-General in the British Army on 1st January, 1710[2]) sailed from Portsmouth for Boston in New England. The Indian chiefs accompanied him, and, in addition to over 30 special service officers,[3] 400 Marines under Colonel Churchill sailed in the same transport. Nicholson's capture of Port Royal on 1st October, 1710, with 1,500 Colonial troops and 400 Marines, was a most important event as it established a permanent British foothold in Nova Scotia. Under date of 14th December, 1710, Luttrell records: "A ship arrived at Barnstaple from New England advises that Colonel Nicholson had taken Port Royal in Acadia, belonging to the French, with the loss of 10 men and a transport vessel, wherein the captain and 25 men were drowned; that he had left Colonel Vich (sic), with Sir Charles Hobby and 500 men in the fort, in which were 60 guns, the French Governor with 200 men made prisoners of war; and that he had sent to the Governor of Quebeck that if he still encouraged the Indians, as usually he had done, to barbarously scalp the English prisoners, he would retaliate the same on the French inhabitants at Port Royal who are about 500."[4] Nicholson's own account of the expedition to, and reduction of, Port Royal (which he named

---

[1] See biog. notice in *English Army Lists and Commission Registers*, Vol. VI., p. 192, note 20.

[2] Commission not given in the "Military Entry Books" but noted in List of Brigadiers given in Dr. Beatson's *Political Index*.

[3] A list of these officers is given in *English Army Lists*, Vol. VI., p. 287.

[4] Luttrell's *Short Relation of State Affairs*, 1678–1714, Vol. VI., pp. 664–65.

Annapolis in honour of Queen Anne) was printed in London, 1711.[1]   When Brigadier-General John Hill was sent to Boston, New England, in 1711, with a strong force of British troops destined for the reduction of Quebec and conquest of Canada, Queen Anne appointed Nicholson to be "Lieut.-General of all the Forces which shall be raised for Our Service in any of Our Colonies of North America and employed in the present intended Expedition against Our Enemies in those parts."[2]   Hill's forces arrived at Boston on board the fleet under command of Rear-Admiral Sir Hovenden Walker, 24th June, 1711.   Nicholson, at the head of a body of colonials again advanced as far as Wood Creek, near Lake Champlain, where he awaited news of the British fleet's arrival off Quebec.   When at last the expected intelligence reached his camp it was to the effect that nine transports, when entering the St. Lawrence, had been driven on the rocks and over 1,000 men perished.   So ended this unfortunate expedition.   Brigadier Hill returned to England after leaving detachments to reinforce the garrison at Annapolis Royal.

On 20th October, 1712, Queen Anne appointed Francis Nicholson "General and Commander-in-Chief of Our Forces in Nova Scotia and Newfoundland."   Nicholson succeeded Colonel Vetch as Governor of Nova Scotia same date, and took up the reins of government in 1713. He was likewise given "a sort of roving commission, to examine the accounts of the other Colonial Governors, from which fact he was termed the 'Governor of Governors.' "[3]

"As Governor of Nova Scotia," says the late Mr. J. A. Doyle, "Nicholson appears to have displayed that arrogant and over-bearing temper which constituted the worst side of his character."   During the two years that Nicholson held the governorship, his place, for the greater part of that time, was supplied by a deputy.

Great dissatisfaction was caused among the colonial loyalists in America by the British Government's change of policy with regard to the French settlers in Nova Scotia and Newfoundland after the signing of the Treaty of Utrecht.   Queen Anne had, by letter dated 18th March, 1709/10, made promises to Francis Nicholson that those colonials who contributed to the capture of Port Royal should

> "have the preference both with regard to the soile and trade of the country when reduc'd to any other of her Majesty's subjects.   This was signify'd to the several Governments by proclamations sign'd by Col° Nicholson, Col° Vetch, and by Col° Dudley, Govern' of the Massachusetts Bay.   Upon this the people readily and cheerfully came in, undertook the expedition and conquer'd the place. But when Col° Nicholson went over Govern' of Nova Scotia in 1713 he had a letter from her late Majesty in the words following :—
>
> " ' Whereas our good brother the most Christian King hath at our desire releas'd from imprisonment on board his galleys such of his subjects as were

---

[1] *Journal of an Expedition for the Reduction of Port Royal*, London, 1711, is in the Brit. Mus. Library.   [2] Commission dated 1st March, 1711.

[3] Extracted from a paper on "The Life of Major-General Jean Paul Mascarene" by James Mascarene Hubbard, Esq., of Boston, Mass.   In connection with Nicholson's appointment as Auditor of Colonial Governors' accounts, he had the invidious task of looking into Colonel Vetch's payments and receipts.   Under date of 17th Feb. 1713/14, Nicholson writes to the Earl of Dartmouth, Secretary of State, from Boston, New England : "I am now examining Colonel Vetch late Governor of Annapolis Royal, charged with arbitrary and illegal proceedings."   And in another letter to Lord Dartmouth, dated from Boston, 23rd April, 1714, Nicholson writes : "Colonel Samuel Vetch has scandalously run away from Boston when he should have stayed to make up his accounts."—*Dartmouth Papers.*

detain'd there on account of their professing the Protestant Religion ; we being willing to show by some mark of our favour towards his subjects how kindly we take his compliance therein, have therefore thought fit hereby to signify our will and pleasure to you that you permit, and allow, such of them as have any lands or tenements in the places under your Government in Acadie and Newfoundland, that have been or are to be yielded to us by virtue of the late Treaty of Peace, and are willing to continue our subjects to retain, and enjoy, their said lands and tenements without any let or molestation, as fully and freely as other our subjects do or may possess their lands, and estates, or to sell the same if they shall rather chuse to remove elsewhere. And for so doing this shall be your warrant. And so we bid you farewell. Given at Our Court at Kensington the 23rd day of June, 1713. In the 12th year of Our Reign.' " [1]

On 20th January, 1715, Nicholson was recalled from Nova Scotia and Colonel Vetch was reinstated as Governor.

Grievous complaints having been received by the Home Government, in 1719, from the settlers in South Carolina, against the Lords Proprietors of that colony, the Lords Justices and Privy Council, acting for the King who was in Hanover, declared that the said Lords Proprietors had forfeited their Charter to the Crown. George I., by the advice of the Lords Justices, appointed Brigadier Francis Nicholson to be Captain-General and Governor of South Carolina, also Captain of an Independent Company of Foot to be sent with him. The Letters Patent for first appointment were dated 26th September, 1720, and referred to "the great miscarriages and neglect in the government of the Territory of South Carolina and the incursions of the barbarous Indians, &c., &c." [2]

---

[1] "A Report prepared by the Board of Trade for the House of Commons, relating to Newfoundland, Nova Scotia, Cape Breton, &c." Printed in *Hist. MSS. Commission*, 11th Report, Appx. Pt. IV., pp. 295–96.

[2] Quoted in *War Office Commission Book*, 1718–23. The very rare pamphlet named below refers fully to the causes which led the British Crown to cancel the Charter of the Lords Proprietors of South Carolina, and the appointment of Governor Nicholson. The description of the tract is apparently from the pen of Mr. James Tregaskis the owner.

SOUTH CAROLINA. Yonge (Francis, Surveyor-General of S.C.). A Narrative of the Proceedings of the People of South Carolina, in the year 1719 ; and of the true Causes and Motives that induced them to Renounce their Obedience to the Lords Proprietors, as their Governors, and to put themselves under the immediate Government of the Crown. 4to, sewn, fine large copy, from the Townshend library. £27 10 0.

London (no name of publisher). Printed in the year 1726.

*** A rare tract of 40 pages, dedicated to John Lord Carteret, one of the principal Lords Proprietors of the colony. It does not appear to be known that the Lords Proprietors made an application to the king for a restitution of their government, the above narrative being set forth at the request of the people of the colony, in order to gain the sympathy of the king and his ministers for their cause. It relates the struggles of the colonists against the murderous depredations of the Cherokee Indians, the crushing debts caused by these continuous wars, the tyranny of the officials appointed by their noble "Proprietors," the futile appeals for help, and, finally, a state of open rebellion, when the people proclaimed their own Governor, chose a Council of Twelve, formed a Convention, and voted themselves an assembly. Sir Hovenden Walker, the admiral, was President of the Council. It all ended by the British Government cancelling the charter of the Proprietors, and sending Governor Nicholson to take charge of the colony on behalf of the crown. When he returned to England in 1725 he doubtless brought this Narrative with him for publication, or he may have caused a number of copies to be printed for private circulation amongst persons of influence. Its extreme rarity, and the absence of a publisher's name, would point to this latter as the most likely. I am unable to trace the sale of a copy prior to the one here offered.

An Acct of Severall things proper for Govr Nicholson to carry with him in Order to make presents to his Ma'ty more of the Indians in Carolina —

Six pieces of Broad Cloth of about 10s or 12s ye yard value of Black Blue Red and other Collours

Sufficient Linings and other Trimmings for to make them up into Cotts

2 Dozn Laced Hatts of about 12s value each

2 Dozn Course Stockins of about 3 or 4/ ye pair

2 Dozn pair of Shoes with Brass buckles

2 Dozn Course Neckcloths of Kenting or such like

2 Dozn Shirts of Garlicks

2 pieces of Strouds 1 blue the other red to be cutt into Flapps — Watch Coats and Stockens

a Dozn Fuzees of 20s value each with a few Ordinary Cutlaces and Belts — wth fine powder 1 barrl 2 cwt of lead in Barrs —

2 or 3 pieces of Course Callico or painted Stuffroll or Callaminco

2 Dozn Strings of Beads for Necklaces

Severall Toys at Discretion Joyo Trinklets & Looking glasses

2 Dozn Prints of his Majty & ye Royll ffamily in Small guilt Frames

Prints of his Maty Arms — a few Gere Guineas half Guineas Crowns half Crowns and Shillings to be Strung on Red Ribbons and wore by the Cheiffs

ffr: Nicholson

[signature]

Many years' acquaintance with the habits, customs, and idiosyncracies of North American Indian chiefs, had taught Nicholson how to best conciliate them. He made out a list of articles which he suggested taking out with him, as presents for the Cherokee chiefs, to be paid for by the British Treasury. The list[1] had to be sent to the Lords Justices, whose secretary, Mr. Delafaye, wrote as follows to the Lords of the Treasury[2] to whom he forwarded Nicholson's list:—

"MY LORDS,
          "Whitehall,
          21 Sept. 1720.

"Having laid before the Lords Justices the inclosed List of Presents to be given by Governor Nicholson to the Indians bordering on Carolina, in order to gain some and preserve others, in the interest of the British Nation, which is absolutely necessary for the peace and safety of that Colony now under His Majesty's more immediate care, and in the consequence of His Majesty's neighbouring Dominions in America, their Excellencys approving thereof have commanded me to signify by their Directions to your Lordships, that you order the several particulars mentioned in the said List to be provided and delivered to Governor Nicholson, or such Person as he shall appoint to receive them.

"I am, &c.,
"The Lords of the Treasury."   "CH. DELAFAYE."

[*Enclosing*]

"An Acco^t of Severall things proper for Govr Nicholson to carry with him in Order to make psents to the Head men of the Indians in Carolina.

"Six pieces of Broad Cloth of about 10^d or 12^d p Yard Value of Black Blue Red and other Collours.

Sufficient Linings and other Trimings for to make them up into Cloths.

2 Doz^n Laced Hatts of about 12^s value each.

2 Doz^n Course Stockins of about 3 or 4^s p pair.

2 Doz^n pair of Shoes with Brass buckles.

2 Doz^n Course Necloths of Kenting or Such like.

2 Doz^n Shirts of Garlicks[3]

2 pieces of Strouds[4] 1 blue the other red to be cutt into Flaps—Match Coats and Stockens.

A Doz^n Fuzees of 20^s value each with a few Ordinary Cutlaces and Belts—wth ffine powder 1 bar^ll 2^Ct w^t of lead in Barrs.

2 or 3 pieces of Course Callico or pointed fflanell or Callaminco.

2 Doz^n Strings of Beads for Necklaces, Severall Toys at Discretion some vermilion, & looking glasses.

2 Doz^n Prints of his Ma^ty & ye Roy^ll ffamily in Small Guilt Frames.

Prints of his Ma^tys Arms—a few New Guineas half Guineas Crowns half Crowns and Shillings to be Strung on Red Ribbons and wore by the Chiefs.

"FFR: NICHOLSON.
JOSEPH BOONE.
JN^o BARNWELL."

---

[1] See facsimile illustration.

[2] *Treasury Papers*, CCXXXII., No. 42.

[3] *Garlicks.*—(German) Görlitzer und Zittauer Leinwand, or (in French) Toile de Görlitz et de Zittau. This is taken from a technical dictionary. In English it is a linen cloth, or canvas, and as it came from Görlitz, evidently got corrupted into Garlicks.

[4] *Stroud.*—"A kind of coarse cloth made of strouding, worn by Indians of North America. Its etymology is doubtful, but perhaps originated from Stroud in Gloucestershire where flannel and cloth are manufactured."

Nicholson proceeded to South Carolina in the winter of 1720–21, and his Independent Company reached that colony on 7th March, 1721. It was a foregone conclusion that the new Governor would find many irregularities to redress on reaching Charlestown, the capital of South Carolina. Pirates infested the coast of this neglected colony ; and even captains of authorised trading vessels between Charlestown and the Bahama Islands did illicit smuggling on their own account. A few months after his arrival, Nicholson caused a search to be made on board the sloop *Recovery* belonging to the Bahama Company, and a certain cargo was found concealed which had not been entered on the bills of lading. The vessel was seized and condemned. This, with other similar instances, caused complaints against Nicholson to be sent to the Home Government, but it was subsequently shown in print [1] that Nicholson had not confiscated any cargo, or seized any ship, until the offending captains had been legally tried in Court and found guilty, and even then Governor Nicholson only received one-third of the confiscated ship and cargo, according to the law. This is duly set forth in the Judge's sentence *re* the sloop *Recovery* already mentioned :—

"Nov. 2, 1721.—I find (said Judge Smith) that the taking on board the Sloop *Recovery* 4 barrels of pitch, 2 barrels of tar, and 2 barrels of rice, without giving bond as the Court directs is a direct breach of the Act of Trade and that the Permit which has been produced in Court, sign'd by Colonel Wm. Rhett, Surveyor and Comptroller of the Customs in this Port [Charlestown] is unwarrantable and contrary to his Instructions, and therefore decree the said Sloop, with her tackle, furniture, and also all the goods and merchandize on board to be forfeited ; one third part to his Majesty ; one third part to his Excellency Francis Nicholson, Esq., Governor of this Province ; and the other part to Mr. Wm. Hammerton, Naval Officer of this Port who has informed and sued for the same ; and likewise ordain Landgrave Thomas Smith to pay such costs of Court as have become due since he enacted himself defendant in this case ; and the rest to be deducted out of the proceeds of the said Sloop and Goods." [2]

The late Mr. J. A. Doyle, a learned authority on British Governors of North American Colonies, has recorded in the *Dictionary of National Biography* that Francis Nicholson "ingratiated himself with the Colonists and conciliated the Cherokees."

In 1725, when Nicholson had attained the age of seventy, he returned to England and stayed there. He was allowed to retain his post as a reward for his many years of strenuous service in the interests of his country. He died in London, 5th March, 1727/28, and was buried in the parish of St. George's, Hanover Square, the following day. In the burial register of St. George's Church he is described as "The Honble. Governor Francis Nicholson, Esq." In his will, to which reference has already been made, he left the bulk of his property to the Society for the Propagation of the Gospel. His executors were Abel Kettleby, barrister-at-law, and Kingsmill Eyre, agent to Nicholson's Independent Company in South Carolina.

---

[1] *An Apology or Vindication of Francis Nicholson, Esq., His Majesty s Governor of South Carolina from the unjust aspersions cast on him by some of the Members of the Bahama Company,* London, 1724.

[2] *Ibid.*

COLONEL CHARLES WHITEFOORD

COLONEL CHARLES WHITEFOORD (COLONEL OF THE 5th FOOT, 1752-1753).

(From an Original Portrait in the possession of S. C. Whitefoord, Esq.,
of Whitton Paddocks, Ludlow.)

CHAPTER VII

COLONEL CHARLES WHITEFOORD, A.D.C. TO GENERAL LORD CATHCART, 1740;

COLONEL OF THE FIFTH REGIMENT OF FOOT, 1752–1754

THIS gallant and scientific Scottish soldier, whose conspicuous bravery at the battle of Prestonpans has been immortalised by Sir Walter Scott in *Waverley*, as " Colonel Talbot," was third son of Sir Adam Whitefoord,[1] first Baronet of Blaquhan, Ayrshire, by his wife the Hon. Margaret Cathcart, only daughter of Alan, seventh Baron Cathcart, and the Hon. Elizabeth Dalrymple, his wife, daughter of the first Viscount Stair.

Charles Whitefoord is believed to have been born about 1700. Being one of a large family his father could not purchase a commission for him or any of his brothers. This is clearly proved by a letter from the Countess of Cathcart to the Earl of Stair, dated 25th October, 1716, in which, after referring to the death of her son, Major James Cathcart, she goes on to say : " I beg my grandson John Whiteford (*sic*) may succeed him in your lordship's favor. John is mighty fond to be in the military ; but Sir Adam, having many children, cannot be brought to purchase for him, commissions now running so high." [2]

It is stated in the *Whitefoord Papers*[3] that " Charles Whitefoord entered the sea service in 1718 and served till he was qualified to be Lieutenant of a man-of-war, for which he passed an examination ; but the Lords of the Admiralty then taking a resolution to provide for half-pay officers only, he entered into the land service, carried arms two years in the Dragoons, and learned his exercises of riding, &c., in the Academy of Angers." [4]

It has been universally supposed, from the above statement, that Charles Whitefoord entered the Army as a private dragoon after quitting the Navy. But in the *MS. Army List* for 1745 Charles Whitefoord's first commission is dated " 3 May, 1720." From Lady Cathcart's letter, quoted above, it is quite certain Sir Adam Whitefoord was unable, or unwilling, to buy commissions for his sons. Lord Stair, the Colonel of the Inniskilling Dragoons, had been asked, and had promised,[5] to show favour to his young kinsman, John Whitefoord, " who was mighty fond

---

[1] Created a Baronet 30th Dec. 1701. Sir Adam registered arms 29th Feb. 1704, being described as " eldest son of James Whitefoord, of Dunduff, and heir served and retoured to John Whiteford, late of Blaquhan, his uncle, descended of the family of Whitefoord of that Ilk."—*The Genealogist*, Vol. V., p. 19.

[2] *Annals of the Viscount and First and Second Earls of Stair*, by J. Murray Graham, Vol. I., p. 326.

[3] Edited by W. A. S. Hewins for the Clarendon Society in 1898.

[4] The Earl of Stair being appointed Ambassador to the French Court, in 1715, doubtless led to Charles Whitefoord being sent to Angers for his education.

[5] Col. Charles Cathcart, in a letter to Lord Stair dated 22nd Jan. 1722, writes : " Lord and Lady Cathcart are most thankful for the kind assurances you are pleased to give them of taking care of their grandson [Whitefoord] when it is in your power."

to be in the military." His Lordship could not give him a Subaltern's commission, but he had the power of appointing the Quartermaster to each of the six troops in his own corps and commissioning them to that rank "under his hand and seal." [1] Both John Whitefoord and his brother Charles are stated in the *MS. Army List* for 1745 to have entered the Army in 1720; but as no entries for Whitefoord commissions are to be found in the Commission books under the latter date, the writer is strongly of opinion that the two Whitefoord brothers were made Troop Quartermasters in the Inniskilling Dragoons by the Earl of Stair. Many cavalry officers in the seventeenth and eighteenth centuries began their careers as Quartermasters—notably General Lord Carpenter.[2] It is noteworthy that cavalry Quartermasters got four shillings a day while Cornets only got five.

Sir Adam Whitefoord died in November, 1727. He was succeeded by his eldest son John,[3] who had raised one of the three new troops added to the Inniskilling Dragoons in December, 1726. Charles Whitefoord was now able to purchase, in 1728, an Ensign's commission in an infantry corps (the 31st), of which his uncle, the Hon. Charles Cathcart, had been appointed Colonel that year. In 1729, Ensign Whitefoord was appointed Adjutant to Colonel William Blakeney (afterwards Lord Blakeney), the officer commanding the aforesaid regiment on the Irish Establishment in Colonel Cathcart's absence. In 1733 Charles Whitefoord obtained his lieutenancy, and four years later his company. On 13th July, 1738, he exchanged to the Royal Irish Regiment of Foot, then serving in Minorca. There are several letters among the *Whitefoord Papers* from Captain Charles Whitefoord to his brother Hugh,[4] then a Cornet in the Inniskilling Dragoons, written from Minorca. The Royal Irish were recruited by drafts from Ireland, and the men sent over appear to have been "dear bargains." Writing to his brother Hugh from Ciudadella, on 15th December, 1738, Charles Whitefoord says: "By an agreement of our Captains that all men brought to the regiment shall be at the same rate my Irish draughts will cost me 7 lib. a man. . . . Pray send me an answer as soon as you can. How far is a Captain coming into a regiment bound to stand to the private agreements of the Captains?" Judging from his letters while in Minorca, Charles Whitefoord found his life there very monotonous and irksome. The general expectation, early in 1739, of a war between Great Britain and Spain is thus referred to in a letter from Whitefoord to his brother-in-law, Captain John Dalrymple, of the Inniskilling Dragoons: "12 April, 1739. . . . Would these damn'd Spaniards let us but alone, I shou'd soon be in a condition to leave what they call the pleasures of this world, but we are at present under no small apprehensions from the measures we (at least I) wish and dread will be taken. . . . A war I look on as inevitable."

[1] A few of these appointments are to be met with in the Commission Entry Books.

[2] See his commission on p. 46, in Vol. II., *English Army Lists and Commission Registers*, 1661–1714.

[3] Appointed Major of the Inniskilling Dragoons in 1743 and served in the Netherlands; Lt.-Col. 1744; Col. 12th Dragoons in Jan. 1750; Maj.-Gen. 1758; Lt.-Gen. 1760. D. at Edinburgh 1st March, 1763.

[4] Fourth son of Sir Adam Whitefoord; Cornet in the Inniskilling Dragoons 4th Oct. 1732; appointed Secretary to Lord Cathcart in July, 1740; Capt. in Col. Henry Harrison's Regiment of Foot same year. Served in the Carthagena Expedition. D. at Carthagena "from inclemency of the climate" in April, 1741.—*Gentleman's Magazine*, 1741, p. 332.

War having been declared with Spain in October, 1739, six regiments of Marines were ordered to be raised in November. Charles Whitefoord applied for and obtained an exchange with Lord Maitland of Colonel Wynyard's Regiment of Marines. Whitefoord's commission as Captain in said corps bore date 14th January, 1740. Through powerful interest, Charles Whitefoord was appointed Major[1] of the American Regiment, 4th April following. This corps was then raising in the North American Colonies. It was to consist of four battalions—each of 1,000 men. The Colonel-in-Chief was Major-General Alexander Spottiswood, Deputy-Governor of Virginia. Major Whitefoord did not join his new corps on promotion; he shortly expected to be appointed to the staff of his uncle, General Lord Cathcart, who was to command all the British forces in America. In July, 1740, Charles Whitefoord was gazetted an A D.C. to Lord Cathcart, and sailed with the Commander-in-Chief a few weeks later. It is on record in the *Whitefoord Papers* that the ship which conveyed Charles Whitefoord's baggage foundered, and that "he lost effects to a very considerable value without receiving any consideration." Lord Cathcart unfortunately died of dysentery at Dominica in December, 1740, and the command of the expedition devolved on Brigadier Wentworth.

The British Fleet, under Rear-Admiral Sir Chaloner Ogle, arrived at Jamaica in January, 1741, and joined Admiral Vernon's force. The conjoint squadrons numbered twenty-nine ships of the line, with many frigates, fireships, and bomb-ketches. The land forces, including the American Corps of four battalions, nearly totalled 12,000 men. The whole expedition arrived off Carthagena on 4th March. According to Admiral Vernon's despatch to the Duke of Newcastle, 1st April, 1741, the first step of the officers on board was to hold a Council of War in order to settle their respective shares of booty !

For the first fortnight Fortune smiled on the British expedition. A landing was effected on an island to the westward of the strong fort of Bocca Chica, which guarded the entrance to the straits of that name leading into the outer harbour of Carthagena. All the troops on board the fleet, with the exception of the 34th, 36th, and the major portion of the American Regiment, which was composed of raw and ill-disciplined men, took part in the operations on shore. A practical breach having been made, after fifteen days' siege, a panic seized the garrison of Bocca Chica, and when the stormers advanced against the walls the fort was found to be deserted. As only a detachment of the American Corps took part in the above short siege, it is quite uncertain whether Major Charles Whitefoord was with the troops on shore or not. The presumption is that he was, and that he then picked up some of his gunnery and engineering knowledge which stood him in good stead at the battle of Prestonpans in 1745, where he worked the Royalist guns with great skill. Among the *Whitefoord Papers* is a well-executed sketch of Castillo Grande by Whitefoord's pen, which important fort guarding the inner harbour entrance was relinquished by the Spaniards without firing a shot.[2] On

---

[1] In a letter to Capt. Alex. Wilson (regimental agent) from Chatham, 8th Sept. 1748, Col. Charles Whitefoord says : "I was one of the first nominated Field Officers to the Americans."

[2] "Castillo Grande mounted 59 guns, and might have cost much trouble and many lives to have reduced it. The enemy had the guns spiked in so great a hurry that many of them were soon rendered serviceable."—Beatson's *Naval and Military Memoirs,* Vol. I., p. 100.

5th April, a second landing of the British troops took place. While the guns from the fleet began to bombard Carthagena from the inner harbour, the soldiers and artillery invested the town from the land side. From lack of co-operation between Admiral Vernon and Brigadier Wentworth, who were antagonistic the one to the other, the troops on shore passed three nights in the open air for want of tents and tools. This exposure in an unhealthy season caused much sickness. General Wentworth thought it advisable to attack the strong fort of St. Lazaro by escalade. This fort was the chief outwork to Carthagena and built on an eminence overlooking the town. On 9th April, before daybreak, 1,500 picked men, who were under the immediate command of Brigadier Guise, made the fateful attempt. Colonel Grant, at the head of 500 grenadiers, was sent to storm the northern side of the fort, while Colonel Wynyard led a stronger force against the southern side. Spanish deserters, who acted as guides, ignorantly or purposely led the stormers to the strongest parts of the fortification. The result is well known. Although the soldiers never flinched, as they were mown down by hundreds from the murderous fire of the garrison, the leaders were at last obliged to give the order to retire.[1] Colonel Grant, of the 5th Marines, was mortally wounded. As he lay dying he is recorded to have said : "The General [Wentworth] ought to hang the guides, and the King ought to hang the General." Lieut.-Colonel Samuel Daniel, of Harrison's Foot (15th), succeeded Colonel Grant in the command of the 5th Marines; but Daniel died from fever on 24th April, and the colonelcy was bestowed on Lieut.-Colonel James Cochran. On 27th of same month Brigadier Wentworth selected Charles Whitefoord for the vacant lieut.-colonelcy of the 5th Marines—his commission being dated 27th April, 1741.

The historian Smollett, who was a surgeon on board a man-of-war during the expedition to Carthagena, gives the following harrowing account of the sickness and mortality among the troops on board the transports, when the rainy season had set in, after the failure of the attack on Fort St. Lazaro :—

> "The men were pent up between decks in small vessels where they had not room to sit upright ; they wallowed in filth ; myriads of maggots were hatched in the putrefaction of their sores, which had no other dressing than that of being washed by themselves in their own allowance of brandy ; and nothing was heard but groans and lamentations, and the language of despair, invoking death to deliver them from their miseries."

On 26th April, 1741, the British Fleet sailed for Jamaica. On arrival there only 1,700 soldiers were found fit for service! Among the many officers who died off Carthagena, in April, was Captain Hugh Whitefoord.

In July, 1741, a conjoint naval and military expedition was despatched from Kingston, Jamaica, to Cuba. The land forces consisted of 4,000 men, including 1,000 able-bodied Jamaica negroes for fatigue work. General Wentworth commanded the troops, which consisted of the "remnants" of the 15th and 24th Regiments, the Americans, and the six Marine Regiments.

---

[1] "One hundred and seventy-nine officers and soldiers were killed and four hundred and fifty-nine wounded, many of them mortally; sixteen were made prisoners, ten of whom had fallen wounded on the top of the hill ; of these three were officers, who, although they were treated with the greatest humanity by the Spaniards, died in two or three days."— Beatson's *Naval and Military Memoirs*, Vol. I., p. 106.

On 18th July the fleet anchored in a commodious Cuban bay.[1] It is recorded in the *Services of the Marine Corps* that, " after establishing a position on the side of the river, nearly three leagues from the mouth of the harbour, the General pushed some detachments into the country, which beat back the outposts of the enemy, and in a few days returned to the camp with plentiful supplies of provisions." Among the *Whitefoord Papers* is the following letter to Colonel Charles Whitefoord, who was in command of some troops sent some distance inland, and encamped on the shore of a river :—

" To Colonel Whitefoord, Commanding Officer at Guantanamo.

" Aug. 11th [1741].

" We the officers under your command . . . . to whom you have done the honour to desire that they might let you know whatever should occur to them for the good of the Service, beg leave to offer the following particulars to your consideration.

" That we have borne with great patience hitherto the great hardships we have suffered and still suffer, but that our stay in this place has already brought us into great difficultys, and are of opinion that unless a speedy resolution be taken to extricate us it will be out of our power to retreat from hence and rejoin our Army ; the river which separates us from Major Dunston's [Dunster's] party[2] grows sensibly deeper every day and Capt. North, Col. Lewis and Mr. Innes who came from the camp yesterday assure us the rivulet which hardly covered the shoes when we first passed it is now mid thigh deep ; so that in all probability our communication either with one ano' or w' the camp may be cut off in a few days.

" That if we by our delay suffer our retreat and communication w' the camp to be cut off we will expose ourselves to unavoidable ruin ; we have sufficiently experienc'd that we can have no provisions but from the camp, and at this present time we have only bread and rum for two days, and ano' supply is uncertain considering the accidents that may happen to it in passing the rivers, and the damage it may receive by rains, not to mention the possibility of it being cut off by the enemy.

" That in case of being attack'd it is morally impossible but we must have some men wounded, who, for want of proper care and assistance must be lost. The man who was wounded the other day when Cap. Web[3] was attack'd and who is now dead is a melancholy example of this.   The straits the soldiers are in makes them murmur already.

" The officers find it no easy matter to keep them within bounds, and if they find themselves much longer pinch'd the consequences may be terrible ; the Negroes are upon hard duty, and having nothing to subsist upon but what is spar'd from the soldiers' allowance it is very much to be fear'd that some of them will run into the woods and desert.   Should that be the case, the Enemy thereby coming to the knowledge of our situation will not fail to take advantage of it.

" That having no place where our ammunition or bread can be secur'd from the rains we might possibly be attack'd when it would not be in our power to make any defense.   Besides, the rains from which the houses that are here cannot

---

[1] Called " Walthenham Bay " in Beatson's *Naval and Military Memoirs.*

[2] " The General sent a detachment under Major Dunster, who penetrated as far as the village of Elleguava, the inhabitants of which abandoned it on his approach. Here he continued some days ; but not being supported, he seized some horses and cattle and returned with a very trifling loss to the camp."—*Ibid.*

[3] Richmond *Webb* of Cottrell's Marines, son of Major John Richmond Webb, Govr. of Upnor Castle. Richmond Webb, who served at Culloden, was Major of Battereau's Foot, and placed on half-pay in 1748. D. in 1785. Bd. in Westminster Abbey. His daughter Amelia md. Wm. Makepeace Thackeray, and was grandmother of the eminent author.

defend the men, join'd to their other hardships, must throw many into sickness who, for want of proper conveniences, cannot be recover'd, nor even carried away with us, and so must be entirely abandoned and lost.

"Sir, considering our present bad circumstances and our prospect of yet worse, we cannot help thinking it our duty to make this application to you our commanding officer, and to declare it as our opinion that no time should be lost in securing our retreat and joining our Army whilst the men's health and the little provisions that remain will permit us."[1]

"It was originally intended," writes the compiler of the *Services of the Marine Corps*, "to have made a joint attack upon St. Jago, but the want of unanimity ruined every purpose . . . . while the interests of the country and the lives of the troops were sacrificed to the prejudices and bad judgment of the officers entrusted with so important a command. After an interval of several months, during which nothing was attempted towards effecting the conquest of the island, and when sickness . . . . began its ravages it was determined to evacuate the island, which took place on the 20th November, 1741."[2]

On arrival at Kingston, Jamaica, Colonel Cochran's Marines, of which Charles Whitefoord was Lieut.-Colonel, numbered only 191 non-commissioned officers and men.[3] The original strength of this corps when raised in November, 1739, was 1,000!

No troops suffered more in the West Indies, during the years 1741–42, than the Marine regiments, as is plainly set forth in the *London Evening Post*: "April 13, 1743. Yesterday Brigadier-General Blakeney's Regiment of Marines—which consists only of 18 men out of 800, who either died or were killed in the West Indies—landed from Jamaica."

The same paper records in another issue: "Some marines arrived from Jamaica say that the unhealthiness of the climate is so great that of Cochran's and Robinson's Marine Regiments *hardly anything is left but the names*."

On arrival in England Colonel Whitefoord was stationed with the "remnants" of his corps at Chatham. Recruiting had to begin in earnest, while fresh officers were commissioned to the skeleton marine battalions. From Charles Whitefoord's letter to his brother Alan,[4] dated from "Chatham, Sept. 30, 1743, in my own house," the writer draws a very vivid picture of the dirt, discomfort, and insanitary condition of his quarters. After descanting on the number of drunken sailors in the town, he goes on to say :—

" . . . . You must know that I bore the marks of the favours I receiv'd from some sailors 24 years ago, for three years afterwards, and remember their compliments even unto this day. I could not eat where I lay and was reduced to the necessity of boarding. A large street door introduced you to a little dirty parlour on the ground floore ; a thin wooden partition divided you from the kitchen on the left, and another from the wash house and house of Office on the right, the side wall of which was the oven, all under the same roofe with our parlour. We were oblig'd to keep the great gate always open to let out the savoury smell [which] attacked us from right and left, which as I observ'd to you being very near as large as the roome, discover'd to us many delightful prospects.

---

[1] *Whitefoord Papers*, pp. 18–19.
[2] Cannon's *Records of 31st Foot and Services of the Marine Corps*, Pt. II., p. 30.
[3] *Ibid.*
[4] Appointed Receiver-General of the Land Tax in Scotland 1733, and d. in 1766.

Our diagonal on the left was the slaughter house of the most considerable butcher in the town, eternally employ'd, not even Sunday excepted ; that on the right the stable where the poor creatures bellowing dismal notes waited impatient their approaching fate at about 20 foot from us each.   Directly before us, at about 12 foot distance, was the Dunghill where all the filth was thrown and a wall built up to keep in the clotted blood."

In another letter Colonel Whitefoord dwells on the false position that a Marine officer finds himself in when sent to sea on board a man-of-war :—

"A Captain of Marines, tho' of the highest quality, may be confin'd by the cook of the Ship, the lowest of their officers haveing the command on board over the highest of ours.   He's allowed no other provision than the meanest sailor, and often lodg'd less comfortably than a dog in a kennel ; was I to say a hog in a sty it would be a nearer resemblance.   This year he's sent to be scorch'd under the Line ; the next he's starv'd under the Pole ; nothing certain but a variety of woes.   The only sweetner to ballance all this misery is the chance of a prise of which but a small part falls to his share and that purchas'd with the loss of health and a broken constitution." [1]

In the spring of 1745 Colonel Whitefoord proceeded to Scotland to visit his relatives and friends.   Writing from Edinburgh, early in August, to Lieut.-Colonel Wm. Congreve, he says :—

"We are alarmed here with an invasion, which I believe will end in smoke ; certain it is that a few people have landed in the West Highlands from a French man-of-war, but their number is so inconsiderable that they only seem to put us on our guard." [2]

The writer was wrong in his conjecture.   Affairs soon became serious. Whitefoord offered his services to Sir John Cope who wished to appoint him Adjutant-General, or A.D.C., but the Colonel preferred to go as a volunteer, "thinking it his duty to serve the King, to the utmost of his power, without any private view." [3]   Whitefoord accompanied Cope in the fruitless march to Inverness ; and from there was despatched to Aberdeen to make transport arrangements at that port.

Sir John Cope and his troops entered Aberdeen on 11th September, and the transports arrived in the harbour on the 12th.   Whitefoord acted as Commissary for providing stores for the troops.   He did his work so expeditiously that the little army was embarked on 15th September.   An adverse wind blew the transports to Dunbar, instead of Leith—the intended destination.   The first news that met Cope on landing was that the capital had surrendered to Prince Charles.

At the battle of Prestonpans Whitefoord acted as Engineer (though unqualified).   Owing to the early flight from the field of the gunners (sailors from the men-of-war), and the artillery drivers (hired countrymen), there was no one left to load and work the six mortars excepting the veteran Master-Gunner Griffith from Edinburgh Castle ; while Whitefoord was left quite alone to manage the six little galloper guns.   At the subsequent court-martial on Sir John Cope, in London, Whitefoord gave the following evidence in favour of the General :—

"You regretted the want of gunners and got six men from the men-of-war to supply their place, and sent to General Guest for the Ingeneer and Gunner from Edinburgh Castle who, unluckily missing their way, never reached you . . . .

[1] Lt.-Col. Charles Whitefoord to——? [1743].—*Whitefoord Papers.*
[2] *Ibid.*   [3] *Ibid.*

Then I went to the Cannon and had not the honor of speaking to you from that time . . . I continued all night with the Cannon, the post you was pleased to assign me where, alas, the sudden flight of the whole people I had to assist me, who carried with them the powder-horns, left me only the power of firing the guns that were loaded and primed . . . . Mr. Griffith met the same fate with the coehorns and both of us were made prisoners." [1]

It is recorded by a recent military writer that :—

"Whitefoord aimed and discharged his cannon as quickly as possible, but he could only accomplish five rounds in all. Some of them took effect and caused confusion (Lord Loudoun calls it a 'great shake') among the Highlanders. On noticing this the royal troops huzzaed; but the clansmen gave cheer for cheer and charged directly in face of the cannon." [2]

The sequel is graphically told by Sir Walter Scott :—

"Alexander Stewart of Invernahyle . . . . charged at the battle of Preston with his clan, the Stewarts of Appine; he saw an officer of the opposite army standing alone by a battery of four cannon, of which he discharged three on the advancing Highlanders, and then drew his sword. Invernahyle rushed on him and required him to surrender. 'Never to rebels,' was the undaunted reply, accompanied with a lunge which the Highlander received on his target; but instead of using his sword in cutting down his now defenceless antagonist, he employed it in parrying the blow of a Lochaber axe aimed at the officer. Thus overpowered Lieut.-Colonel Whitefoord gave up his sword, and with it his purse and watch, which Invernahyle accepted to save them from his followers."

Whitefoord was sent, with many other prisoners, to Perth. He was one of the British officers whom Viscount Strathallan, commanding the Jacobite forces at Perth, released on parole.[3] The Colonel duly surrendered himself by the appointed day and was sent with some other prisoners to Leslie. On 19th January following, Whitefoord and his fellow prisoners were rescued by the Angus Militia.[4] They were carried to Burnt-island and sent from thence to Leith on board a man-of-war. On arrival they were ordered by General Hawley to remain there till His Majesty's pleasure be known.[5] Among the *Whitefoord Papers* is a letter from Colonel Whitefoord giving a graphic account of the battle of Culloden in which he took part; but as he modestly omits all mention of himself there is no need to give any details of the Duke of Cumberland's victory.

One of the important prisoners taken by the Royalist troops in aforesaid battle was Alexander Stewart of Invernahyle—the chivalrous Highland gentleman who had saved Colonel Whitefoord's life at Preston-pans. It was now Whitefoord's turn to befriend Stewart. With this object in view the former went to the Lord Justice Clerk, to the Lord

---

[1] *Whitefoord Papers.*

[2] *Sir John Cope and the Rebellion of* 1745, by the late General Sir Robert Cadell, K.C.B., Royal Madras Artillery, p. 232.

[3] "Passport.—These are giving permission to Lt.-Colonel Whitefoord in Colonel Cochran's Regt. of Marines to pass to Edinburgh, with a servant, about his necessary business, he having given his Parole of honour to return to this place on 12th Dec. next. Given at Perth 26 Nov. 1745.—STRATHALLAN."—*Whitefoord Papers.*

[4] *London Gazette.* Lieut. Thos. White, of Cochran's Marines, in a letter to Col. Whitefoord "at his lodging in Edenbrowgh," dated "Chatham, Feb. 6, 1646," writes : "I wish you joy of your great delivery from the hands of those canibals."—*Whitefoord Papers.*

[5] It is recorded in the *Scots Magazine*, for 1745, that the rescued prisoners "did not dress like military men till the beginning of February. About that time they put on their swords and cockades by an order, as was said, from the King."—pp. 43–44.

Advocate, and to other State officials to plead for Stewart's life. All to no purpose. Whitefoord then went in person to the Duke of Cumberland and made the same request. The Duke refused point blank either to pardon Stewart or to grant a protection for this prisoner's house, wife, children, and property. As a last resort, Colonel Whitefoord produced his commission from his breast-pocket, laid it on the table before the Duke's eyes, and asked, with ill-concealed emotion, permission "to retire from the service of a Sovereign who did not know how to spare a vanquished enemy." The Duke was affected in his turn. He bade the Colonel take up his commission and granted the required protection for the family of Invernahyle. The Chieftain himself lay concealed in a cave near his own house and was fed by stealth. An Act of Indemnity released this brave man. He lived to narrate his adventures to Sir Walter Scott in the latter's childhood.

When Sir John Cope was summoned to appear before a court-martial, held in London, in the autumn of 1746, he wrote to Colonel Whitefoord and asked him to give evidence before the Board of General Officers ordered to sit in judgment upon him for his defeat at Prestonpans.

> "It is a very great happiness to me," wrote Cope, "that I had my Lord Loudoun and you to advise with, and assist me .... and that I have two officers of so much Honor and Reputation to appeal to, to give Evidence to the Board, in all these matters. You two were privy to, and consulted with, in every one step I took, from the first to the last of these affairs, and you were so good as to favour me with your advice and assistance there." [1]

It is not too much to say that Colonel Whitefoord's admirably drawn-up written account of Sir John Cope's whole conduct at Prestonpans, from first to last, had much to do with the finding of the Board which was to this effect: "Sir John Cope did his duty as an officer, both before, at, and after the action, and that his personal conduct was without reproach."

In November, 1748, all the Marine regiments were disbanded and the officers placed on half-pay. Colonel Whitefoord was too good an officer to be left on the shelf for good. He was appointed Lieut.-Colonel of General Irwin's Regiment of Foot (5th Fusiliers) in September, 1751, and joined his corps in Ireland. Whitefoord commanded the regiment during the first half of 1752, in General Irwin's absence, and devoted himself heart and soul to drill and recruiting.[2] For some time past, Colonel Whitefoord had been in failing health. Sir John Whitefoord, Colonel of the 12th Dragoons, in a letter to his brother Charles from Dublin (20th April, 1752), writes: "I am heartily sorry you have reason to complain of not being able to do anything you have done formerly."[3] Irwin's Regiment increased its high state of discipline and efficiency under Colonel Whitefoord's command. In a letter dated 6th June, 1752, his brother John writes:—

> "MY DEAR CHARLES,
>
> " .... I give you joy of the fine appearance as well as of the performance of your Regiment at last Review, of which the Earl of Rothes informed Lord George [Sackville] from Waterford, who was pleased to communicate his Lo⁸ sentiments to me. This I hope will do you great service, as the Earl of Rothes will do you

---

[1] Letter dated 2nd August, 1746.—*Whitefoord Papers.*
[2] See letter from Col. Whitefoord in Appendices.
[3] *Whitefoord Papers.*

justice in his report to H.R.H., which will be made some time next month. Honest Masterson said you did their Regiment great service, which occasioned their making a better appearance at the Review, than otherwise they wou'd have done." [1]

Within three weeks, General Irwin was dead and the Earl of Rothes, then in command of the troops in Ireland, had recommended Lieut.-Colonel Whitefoord for the command of the vacant corps.[2] The Duke of Dorset wrote to the Duke of Newcastle in favour of the same officer;[3] and on 25th November, 1752, the coveted command was given to Charles Whitefoord.

Colonel Whitefoord made his will on 23rd November, 1752, and set his house in order. On 2nd January, 1753, Charles Whitefoord died at Galway where his regiment was stationed. And so after his many travails, and travels, this brave and single-minded soldier died in harness as he must have wished to do, in the midst of his brother-officers and men who loved and respected him. It may be claimed for Charles Whitefoord as has been said of Sir Charles Napier that "he fulfilled all the conditions of the poet Wordsworth's exquisite portrait of ' THE HAPPY WARRIOR.' "

Colonel Whitefoord left a son, Caleb Whitefoord, who was born at Edinburgh in 1734. This well-known patron of art and literature was a wit and diplomatist who adorned the epoch in which he lived. His lineal descendant is the present S. C. Whitefoord, Esq., of Whitton Paddocks, Ludlow.

---

[1] *Whitefoord Papers.*
[2] Sir J. Whitefoord to his brother Charles, 27th June, 1752.
[3] MSS. of Mrs. Stopford Sackville at Drayton House, Northamptonshire, published by the *Hist. MSS. Commission.*

LIEUT.-GENERAL
THE HON. SIR JAMES CAMPBELL, K.B.

CHAPTER VIII

LIEUT.-GENERAL THE HON. SIR JAMES CAMPBELL, K.B.,

COLONEL OF THE SCOTS GREYS, 1717-1745 ;

COMMANDER OF THE BRITISH CAVALRY AT FONTENOY

THE HON. JAMES CAMPBELL, of Lawers, was third and youngest son of James, 2nd Earl of Loudoun. The year of his birth has never been ascertained.[1] He obtained a commission as Captain in the Royal Scots Fusiliers 25th February, 1702, and embarked with his corps for Flanders, from Scotland, on the outbreak of hostilities with France the same year. On arrival in Holland the Scots Fusiliers were sent to Breda, and in September marched towards Flanders. In 1703 the regiment served at the reduction of Huy and at the siege of Limburg, which was captured on 10th September. In 1704 Campbell fought at Schellenberg and Blenheim. His name appears in the "Bounty Roll,"[2] and his share of money was £30. James Campbell left the Scots Fusiliers in the autumn of 1704. Through family interest he obtained the lieut.-colonelcy of the Royal Scots Greys, 24th August, 1706, and took part in the splendid victory of Oudenarde. This battle was followed by the great military operation of the siege and capture of Lille, at which the Scots Greys, under Lord Stair, assisted. In September, 1709, was fought the most sanguinary of all Marlborough's battles—Malplaquet. "The Scots Greys," writes the historian of this corps, "were formed in brigade with the Royal Irish Dragoons, and were commanded by Brigadier Sybourg. They were posted near the centre of the allied army, to sustain the attacks of the infantry and protect the artillery. For some time they were only spectators of the fierce storm of battle which raged on every side; at length, however, they were ordered to file through a wood in their front and charge."[3]

Sir Robert Douglas, Bt., in his well-known *Peerage of Scotland*, gives the following account of Lieut.-Colonel the Hon. James Campbell's services at above battle, which account has been quoted in the memoir of this officer in the *Dictionary of National Biography* :—

"At the bloody battle of Malplaquet, 11th September, 1709, while the victory was as yet doubtful, Lieut.-Colonel Campbell, with a party of his men, marched with great fury against the French, and, cutting all before them, opened a way through the midst of the enemy, and returned the same way back. This successful sally, encouraging the confederates, and disheartening the French, contributed not a little to turn the fortune of the day. This conduct was made the subject of censure ; but Prince Eugene of Savoy, the commander-in-chief, who greatly

---

[1] According to his obituary notice in the *Gentleman's Magazine*, "he was nearly 78 when he died." This is a manifest error.

[2] Printed in *English Army Lists and Commission Registers*, 1661-1714, Vol. V., Part II.

[3] Cannon's *Historical Records of the Royal North British Dragoons*.

admired so gallant an action, and knew that junctures might exist, in which a transgression of rules might be justified by emergencies, thought it not sufficient that Colonel Campbell should pass uncensured; and therefore returned him thanks for exceeding his orders, in the face of the army, the day after the battle." [1]

Without going into the rights or wrongs of Colonel Campbell's disobedience of orders at Malplaquet, it may be well to recall a similar incident which happened at the battle of Vittoria in 1811. Major Norman Ramsay, in command of a battery of Horse Artillery, was posted with his six guns by the Duke of Wellington at a certain point, and told to remain there until he had orders from him. Ramsay was left waiting for orders while the battle went on in the far distance. Presently an A.D.C. galloped up and told Ramsay that General "Somebody" ordered him to bring up his guns. The Artillery Major asked if the order came from Lord Wellington. The reply was "No," but from another General. Ramsay repeated the orders he had had from the Commander-in-Chief. The A.D.C. explained that the General's entire brigade was being driven in and must be annihilated without the guns, and asked: "Would he let a whole brigade be slaughtered?" Ramsay was piqued at this remark. He ordered his guns to move and joined battle with the General. While he was away, an A.D.C. arrived on the spot where the guns had been posted, with an order from Lord Wellington. Nothing was to be seen of Ramsay and his battery. The French were repulsed and Ramsay's guns helped to turn the scale; but Wellington's preconcerted movement was seriously marred for want of the guns in question. Ramsay was put under arrest for his disobedience, and his name omitted from the Vittoria despatches. His punishment was severe, but it exemplified the necessity for implicit obedience.

In the campaign of 1710 Colonel Campbell was present at the siege of Douay, which he assisted in covering with the Scots Greys. He was given a brevet-colonelcy 15th November, 1711, having commanded the Greys during the sieges of Bethune, Aire, St. Venant, and Bouchain. In 1713 the regiment returned to England.

On 17th July, 1715, Colonel Campbell was given the command of the corps now known as the East Norfolk Regiment of Foot (the old 9th). This advancement was only a stepping-stone to the colonelcy of the Greys which was bestowed on James Campbell 15th February, 1717. For the next twenty-five years the Greys and their gallant commander saw no active service. But in June, 1742, Campbell's corps was sent to Flanders. Twelve months later was fought the battle of Dettingen. The Hon. James Campbell—now a Lieut.-General—commanded a cavalry division, and was conspicuous for his gallantry. He led the Greys in a brilliant charge against the French cuirassiers, which has been well described by a former writer on military records :—·

"Their grey horses and grenadier caps rendered them conspicuous,—their noble bearing excited admiration. Before them appeared the enemy's squadrons, formidable in numbers, and bright in polished armour; but, undismayed by the opposing ranks of war, the Greys raised a loud huzza, and rushed at speed upon their steel-clad opponents, who were overthrown and pursued to the rear of their own lines. Exulting in their success, and confident in their own prowess, the Greys dashed, sword in hand, upon the French household cavalry ;—the conflict was short, the result decisive; a British shout arose above the din of battle, and

---

[1] 2nd Edition (1813), Vol. II., p. 153.

the French horsemen galloped from the field in confusion. The Greys pursued their adversaries to the banks of the river and captured a white standard, with which they returned in triumph to their own lines."[1]

After the battle George II. created Lieut.-General Campbell a Knight of the Bath on the field of battle.

In March, 1744, Sir James Campbell proceeded to Flanders and joined his corps at Ghent. Lieut.-Colonel Charles Russell, of the 1st Foot Guards, writing to his wife on 14th April, 1744, mentions having dined with General Campbell, and, on 20th of same month, sends his wife the following interesting account of a great ceremony in which Prince Charles of Lorraine was the leading figure, and the Scots Greys a very picturesque addition to the procession :—

"On Monday [18th April] was the grand day when Prince Charles was inaugurated as a proxy, representing the Queen of Hungary as Countess of Flanders. In the morning he went to Mass . . . . about one he went in a grand procession with all the ensigns, standards, and trophies of the different provinces of Flanders, preceded by very fine equipages, the coaches and horses being finely ornamented belonging both to Church and State. Then came the Prince in but a moderate fine coach attended with one of our regiments of dragoons, the Scotch Greys, whose fine appearance was no small addition to the cavalcade.

"In this manner they proceeded to the further end of the Friday market, where there was prepared a very magnificent structure open to the square with grand arcades, above which were painted many emblems relating to the States of this country, and in the middle a very large picture of the Queen of Hungary with a representation of Flanders paying homage to her. Within this building was erected a stage all covered with red cloth, and in the middle a very noble throne and canopy made with crimson velvet embroidered richly with gold, where the Prince ascended, and when he was seated, there were all the states, bishops, abbots, and priors stood on each side of the throne, and the laity made a fine appearance with the richness of their clothes. At this time all their laws and statutes were read to him, which he in the name of the Queen ratified and confirmed to 'em, and by oath obliged himself to support 'em in all their ancient just rights and privileges ; they also took oath of allegiance to him. All this was performed in the grand square before all the populace, and the buildings all round thronged with people from the top to the bottom of the houses."[2]

Shortly after this ceremony at Ghent, Sir James Campbell joined Marshal Wade's Army at Asche Camp. While the English and their allies were debating and quarrelling as to how the campaign was to be opened, the French took Courtrai and other unprotected towns. Marshal Wade, in order to prevent the enemy seizing Ghent, which was very slenderly garrisoned, sent on 17th May (N.S.) a detachment of 12 squadrons of dragoons and 6 companies of grenadiers, with 9 field pieces, to march all night and be at the gates of Ghent by daybreak. Sir James Campbell was given the command of the above troops, and carried out his orders with such diligence that Ghent was secured for the rest of the campaign. Lord George Sackville, in a letter to the Duke of Dorset, dated "Bruges, 22 May (O.S.), 1744," narrates how a detachment of British troops under Major-General Wentworth, on the march from Bruges to Ghent, took the wrong side of the canal and fell in with a very strong party of French cavalry

---

[1] Cannon's *Historical Records of the Royal North British Dragoons.*
[2] Mrs. Frankland-Russell's MSS. at Chequers Court, printed by the *Hist. MSS. Commission,* p. 306.

and had to retreat to Bruges to avoid "being cut to pieces or made prisoners." An express was sent to Sir James Campbell to let him know what had happened. Two days later Sackville writes :—

> "I have only time to tell you that we are all safe arriv'd at Ghent. The garrison here was in great pain for us, and General Campbell march'd out to our relief the day we had like to have been demolish'd, with six companies of grenadiers and 300 dismounted dragoons, but he was not strong enough to venture on the same side of the river with the enemy." [1]

Sir James Campbell accompanied Marshal Wade's Army in its fruitless marches and counter-marches, from July to October, when the inglorious "campaign" came to an end.

The red-letter year 1745 witnessed one of the hardest fought engagements that ever took place in Flanders during the eighteenth century. This was Fontenoy, where the British infantry covered themselves with glory though eventually beaten. On 8th May (N.S.), in order to cover his operations at and around Fontenoy, Marshal Saxe had occupied the villages of Vezon and Bourgeon. On the 10th, British troops operating under Sir James Campbell occupied Vezon after driving back the Grassins,[2] while the Dutch possessed themselves of Bourgeon, which the French fired as they retired. The order for battle on the morrow was issued at midday on the 10th by the Commanders-in-Chief of the allied forces, viz., the Duke of Cumberland, Prince Waldeck, and Count Königsegs; it was as follows :—

> "Tomorrow at 2 a.m. the whole army will move to the position which the detachments will occupy today, and will form in order of battle in the manner which the generals shall find most suitable, having regard to the ground over which they may have to manœuvre. After which the army will march on the enemy." [3]

Sir J. Campbell's share in the great battle of 11th May, 1745, has been lately described :—

> "General Campbell was ordered to move forward with 12 squadrons of cavalry through Vezon on to the plain beyond, and there screen the infantry as they manœuvred into place. . . . During the night of the 10th, information was brought to Cumberland that a fort mounted with guns was situated slightly in advance of the French position and close to the wood of Barri. At about 5 a.m., and on the south side of Vezon, the Duke summoned to him Ingoldsby, a Brigadier-General, and explained to him that, cost what it might, he was to seize 'the fort or battery' [4] and either spike the guns or turn them on the enemy. . . . General Campbell, having learnt that Ingoldsby was to capture the cannon on the French left, determined to abide the success of that movement and delay the advance of his squadrons, thus saving them from the fire to which they would otherwise be exposed on emerging from Vezon into the plain. But he delayed in vain. The minutes passed, the infantry were pressing forward in rear, the cannon-fire of the enemy was becoming general, and at 5.30 he was compelled to resume his advance. Hardly had he got clear of the village and the ravine which crosses its front when he was struck by a shot which carried off his leg. He was

[1] Lord George Sackville to the Duke of Dorset. Ghent, 2nd June (N.S.), 1744.—Mrs. Stopford Sackville's MSS. printed by the *Hist. MSS. Commission.*

[2] "Irregular infantry called after Colonel Grassin by whom they had been raised in 1744."—"The Battle of Fontenoy" in *The Edinburgh Review* for July, 1911.

[3] *Ibid.,* p. 40.

[4] Redoubt d'Eu.

removed from the field in his carriage in a dying condition. Then no one knew what to do; Campbell had kept his orders faithfully to himself, the cavalry feebly drew aside, and the infantry, as they took ground in the plain, had to bear the brunt of a heavy cannonade from the French batteries."[1]

The gallant Earl of Crawford, a soldier of great experience and much distinction in war, succeeded Campbell as commander of the British cavalry. The former thus refers to Sir James Campbell's death in his *Memoirs* :—

"Lieut.-General Campbell formed the twelve squadrons which were, for a considerable time, all the cavalry we had up. But unhappily, and which [is] ever to be regretted, General Campbell had his leg shot off, at the head of his squadrons, which obliged him to be carried off the field and occasioned his death in 2 days. I am of opinion, by hints I heard him give, that if he could have remained in the field he would have distinguished himself this day; and heaven knows what turn he might have given to affairs! But the same decree which determined we should lose the battle likewise determined that he should be no more to prevent its being so. After his death the command of the twelve squadrons devolved upon me."[2]

In "A Dialogue between Thomas Jones, a Lifeguardman, and John Smith, late a Serjeant in the First Regiment of Foot Guards, just returned from Flanders," printed in London, 1749, Smith refers to the Duke of Cumberland obstinately going against the advice of the English generals at Fontenoy, by attacking the French, "as they were intrenched up to the chin"; and he goes on to say :—

"Poor G———l——— [Campbell] foresaw all this. Says he, when he was carried away after his leg was shot off, *Gentlemen, I have received my death in defence of my country, therefore die satisfied. But this day will never bring honour to E———d.*"

Another account of Fontenoy records that when General Campbell lost his leg he was "full of lamentation that he could take no further part in the action."[3] At the time of his death he was Governor of Edinburgh Castle.

The Hon. Philip Yorke, in a letter to Horace Walpole (the elder) dated 16th May, 1745, records Sir James Campbell's death the day after Fontenoy, under sad circumstances :—

"Doctor Wintringham was sent to visit him by the Duke, and found him lying in a cottage within the enemy's quarters, who had not been humane enough to give him any assistance. This has occasioned a pretty warm expostulation between the Duke and Marshal Saxe."

Sir James Campbell was buried at Brussels. By his wife, Lady Jane Boyle, eldest daughter of David, first Earl of Glasgow, General Campbell had a son, James Mure Campbell, of Lawers, who was born in 1736, appointed Captain in the Royal Scots Greys 29th May, 1745, and eventually succeeded as fifth Earl of Loudoun.

There is a portrait of Lieut.-General the Hon. Sir James Campbell, of Lawers and Rowallane, by Allan Ramsay, painted in 1744, at Loudoun Castle.

[1] Article on "Fontenoy" in *The Edinburgh Review*, pp. 41–42.
[2] *Memoirs of John Earl of Crawford* (Rolt's Edition), p. 362.
[3] *The British Army*, by the Hon. John Fortescue, Vol. II., p. 112.

F

CAPTAIN JAMES JEFFERYES

EXTRACT FROM CAPTAIN JAMES JEFFERYES'S LETTER TO EARL STANHOPE,
DATED "PETERSBURG, JAN. 9 (O.S.) 1718/9"

(From the Original Letter in the Public Record Office.)

or body, as their necessity requires, that I could not but admire both the zele and the robuste constitutions of those who in spight of the terrible frost we have acted in this farce; the devout parents to bring their little infants, just born, to be here baptized; and they do not fail at their leaving the place to fill their vessells with this holy-water, and to carry the same to their houses, which they keep by way of preservative against any evil that may befall them for the year to come. This is one of the ancientest customs among the Muscovites, to which His Czarish Majesty likewise submitts, to shew that in matters of religion he will not separate himself from one of the meanest of his people. I am with all dutifull respect

Thy Lord

I shall dispatch the Messenger
as soon as I receive from Boson
Shafirow the Czars resolution.

Your Lordships

most obedient and most humble servant

James Jefferyes.

CHAPTER IX

CAPTAIN JAMES JEFFERYES, OF BLARNEY CASTLE, GOVERNOR OF CORK, 1719–1739; BRITISH RESIDENT AT THE COURTS OF CHARLES XII. AND PETER THE GREAT.

SPECIAL interest attaches to this soldier and diplomatist, as he was the only British officer who attended Charles XII. in his campaign of 1708–09, including the battle of Pultawa, where he was taken prisoner.

James Jefferyes was the eldest son of Sir James Jefferyes, Knt., of Blarney Castle, a Brigadier-General in Queen Anne's Army, and Governor of Cork at the time of his death in 1719. The younger James Jefferyes was appointed Secretary to Dr. John Robinson, the British Envoy at Stockholm, in 1701. New levies were raised in England in 1705, and Sir J. Jefferyes applied for a Captain's commission for his son James. The applicant had a strong claim on his country, "having spent most of his substance in the service of the Crown, and abroad many years, and thereby almost ruined his numerous family. One of his sons was Lieutenant of the *Yarmouth*, and very instrumental in taking Gibraltar, where he lost his life."[1]

On 12th April, 1706, James Jefferyes was appointed Captain in Sir Roger Bradshaigh's Regiment of Foot, which corps was sent to Ireland. It is very doubtful if Captain James Jefferyes ever served with his regiment.[2] In May, 1707, he was still at Stockholm. Marlborough, in a letter to Harley, from The Hague, 10th May, 1707, writes :—

> "You know the King of Sweden will admit of no foreign Minister to attend him into the field, but as a particular mark of respect for the Queen the Ministers are willing to connive at Mr. Jefferies, Mr. Robinson's secretary, making the campaign as a volunteer, whereby H.M. may be truly informed of what passes."[3]

It was accordingly arranged that young Jefferyes was to accompany Charles XII.'s Army into the field, in reality as a combatant military attaché, but nominally as a volunteer. The British Treasury granted him an allowance for his equipage and subsistence.[4] From an editorial note in *The Marlborough Dispatches*, it appears that Jefferyes kept Marlborough informed of all that passed during the campaigns in which the former took part ; but that Count Piper (Charles's chief Minister) had to be heavily subsidised before he permitted Jefferyes to transmit the intelligence desired by the Duke.[5] In short, Marlborough had to *pay the piper !*

At the battle of Pultawa (8th July, 1709), which established the ascen-

---

[1] Sir J. Jefferyes's Petition to the Duke of Marlborough.—*War Office MS.*
[2] His name appears as Captain in this corps in 1712.
[3] *The Marlborough Dispatches*, Vol. III., p. 359.
[4] *Ibid.*, p. 379.
[5] *Ibid.*, Vol. V., p. 619.

dency of Peter the Great over his Swedish rival, Jefferyes was taken prisoner and lost all his equipage. He was given his liberty some months later; but it was not till the spring of 1710 that he reached London, and presented his bill of expenses to the Lords of the Treasury. Here it is :—

Taken from him on his being made prisoner by the Cossacks, eight horses, one baggage waggon, and all his goods and equipage to the value of - - - - - - -	£140	0	0
Extraordinary expenses from the Ukraine to Mosco - -	15	0	0
Extraordinary expenses from Mosco to Smolensko with a guard - - - - - - - - -	18	0	0
From thence for the rest of the journey home - - -	75	0	0
	£248	0	0

Endorsed : " Captain Jefferyes's Bill of Extraordinary Expenses and Losses." [1]

On 19th January, 1711, Jefferyes left London for Bender,[2] whither Charles XII. had retreated after his decisive defeat at Pultawa. Through Sir Robert Sutton, British Ambassador at Constantinople, promises had been obtained from the Grand Vizier that Captain Jefferyes, the accredited British Envoy to the King of Sweden, should have every facility given him in Turkey on his journey to Bender. For over five years Charles XII. was an exile of his own free will, and for most of that weary time Jefferyes remained in the neighbourhood of Bender, and assisted the iron-willed monarch with advice and money.[3] When Charles did elect to return to his own dominions he travelled with that marvellous rapidity which even Napoleon could not have outdone in his youngest days. Jefferyes describes the King's journey in a letter to Lord Townshend, written from Stralsund, 4th December (O.S.), 1714 :—

" His Majesty having dispos'd the small body of troops he had brought with him from Dimotico, and those that had joynd him from Bender, into 15 bands, and regulated their march, he departed from Pitest Oct. the 28th O.S., and by the 3rd of Nov. came to Vienna, where he only stay'd to take post, and passing by Lintz, Ratisbon, Nuremburg, Bamberg, Meiningen, Cassell, Brunswick, Leutzen on the Elbe, arriv'd at the gates of Stralsund the 11th at night, insomuch that his Majesty made in a fourtnight's time upwards of 200 German miles, and was in his own Dominions before any certain notice could be had of his going from Pitest ; at his arrivall here his legs were swelled to that degree that the Chirurgions were oblig'd to cutt open his boots, besides the wound on his left foot had open'd of it self, and he had receiv'd so many contutions by the falling of his post-horses, that he was in some danger of being attack'd with a fever. Nevertheless his Maj[ty] has conquer'd all this, and his wound is now allmost clos'd up again." [4]

The next landmark in Jefferyes's career is his marriage in London (marriage licence dated 14th October, 1717), to Elizabeth, widow of Edward Herbert, Esq., and eldest daughter of Colonel Philip Herbert. This lady died in November, 1718, and was buried in Westminster Abbey. Her husband was presumably in Russia when his wife died, as the *Historical*

[1] *Treasury Papers*, under date of 4th April. 1710.
[2] Mr. Rowe to Mr. Jackson, the British Envoy at Stockholm.—*S.P. Sweden*, 1704-14.
[3] Voltaire's *History of Charles XII.* (*translated from the French*). London, 1732. Page 96.
[4] *Stowe MS.* 227, fol. 528.

Register, under date of 9th October, 1718, says : "His Majesty appointed James Jeffreys, Esq., to be his Majesty's Resident at the Court of the Czar of Muscovy."

One of the first letters written by Jefferyes from Petersburg, to Lord Stanhope, gives an interesting account[1] of "the blessing of the River Neva by the chief ecclesiastics of the city," at which solemnity the Czar Peter was present.

A later letter from Jefferyes to Secretary Craggs refers to George I.'s recent "Proclamation," recalling his British subjects from foreign service :—

"St. Petersburg, May 29, O.S., 1719.

"RIGHT HONORABLE,

"On Tuesday in the afternoon I had a conference with Baron Shafirow upon the proclamation issued for recalling the King's subjects from foreign service, at which time I delivered to him a Memorial whereof I transmit to your Honour a copy. He immediately began to reproach me for having dispers'd and sent copies of the proclamation to some of His Majesty's Subjects here without giving him a previous notice of it ; to which I answer'd that he having on such a day and hour appointed me a meeting, I came to his house to wait on him, but not finding him at home I could not forbear putting His Majesty's orders in execution. He then began to spit his venom in a most vehement manner against the British Government telling me that the King and his Ministers doe all that lieth in their power to vex and torment the Czar, that the late Act of Parliament passed forbidding the subjects of Great Britain to employ foreign apprentices, and even this Proclamation, are evident proofs of their animosity and are levelled, the first solely against His Czarish Majesty's Subjects, and t'other to obstruct him in his Fleet ; that there are as able artificers and as experienced seamen in other Countrys as in Great Britain ; that the foreigners, especially the ship-builders, are more at their ease and have greater priviledges here than they can pretend to in Great Britain, and consequently that they rather choose to remain here than return home ; that the step is now too late, the Czar's own subjects being able to build Ships and will in time accustom themselves to the Sea likewise. . . ."[2]

In 1719 there were twenty-five British officers in the Czar's fleet,[3] including Admiral Gordon[4] and Rear-Admiral Sanders.

It is probable that Jefferyes's firmness in the matter of the proclamation, referred to in his letter to Secretary Craggs, made the British Resident's presence at the Czar's Court unwelcome. Be this as it may, it was thought desirable that Jefferyes should be transferred to Dantzic, an important Baltic port then under Russian rule. Accordingly Jefferyes bade the Czar farewell the first week in November, 1719, and proceeded to Dantzic, from whence his first letters to the British Secretary of State are dated.[5]

In 1719, Jefferyes succeeded to the Blarney Castle estate on his father's death ; and George I. appointed him "Governor of the City of Cork and

---

[1] See facsimile of Jefferyes's letter, dated from Petersburg, 9 Jan. (O.S.) 1718/19.

[2] *S.P. Russia*, Vol. IX.

[3] *Ibid.* The list of British officers in the Russian Navy is enclosed in one of Jefferyes's letters.

[4] Admiral Thomas Gordon. Had been Captain of a British merchant ship before 1717, in which year he entered the Russian Navy. Is said to have been nephew of Admiral Patrick Gordon (of Auchleuchries), who distinguished himself in Peter the Great's service. The above Thos. Gordon was Governor of Cronstadt at his death in 1741.

[5] Jefferyes to Lord Stanhope, 4th and 7th Nov. (O.S.) 1719.—*S.P. Russia*, Vol. IX.

the Forts adjacent in room of Sir James Jefferyes deceased," by commission dated 29th April, 1719.

On the accession of George II. Jefferyes was confirmed in his post as British Resident at Dantzic. There is no certainty as to the date of James Jefferyes's second marriage, but it must have taken place about 1730. It appears from his will in the Prerogative Court, Dublin, that he had, in 1734, two daughters (presumably twins), by his first wife; and a son by his second marriage to Miss Ann St. John (?). The will is as follows :—

"In the name of God, Amen. I James Jefferyes of Blarney in the County of Cork do make this my last Will and testament in manner and form following. Imprimis to my two daughters now in Dantzig Anne Louise and Elizabeth Jefferyes I give and bequeath two thousand seven hundred and two pounds three shillings capital stock in the Bank of England and two thousand pounds capital stock in the English East India Company to be equally divided between them. Item I devise unto my most dearly beloved wife to my son James St. John Jefferyes and to whatever my said wife Ann Jefferyes is now big with if born alive all the rest of my substance to be disposed of and divided in such manner as has been settled by my marriage settlement. . . . I do constitute and appoint my said wife Ann my sole executrix and have no doubt of her taking all care of my children even of her half daughters whom I most earnestly recommend to her. In witness whereof I have hereunto set my hand and seal this 11th day of June 1734."

From a memorandum attached to the above will, it appears that James Jefferyes died abroad in June or July, 1739. Ann Jefferyes, the relict, proved her husband's will 16th August, 1740. James St. John Jefferyes succeeded to the Blarney estate. This gentleman attained the rank of Major in the Army, and was Lieut.-Governor of Cork. He died in 1780, leaving a widow (*née* Isabella Fitzgibbon) whose ready wit and presence of mind saved the house, and probably the life, of her brother, the Earl of Clare, from the fury of a large Dublin mob who had assembled during the Fitzwilliam riots of 1795. The incident is graphically related in a letter from Mrs. Jefferyes, dated from 9, Molesworth Street, Dublin, July, 1807 :—

"My late brother, the Earl of Clare, always was an active, faithful servant to his King and country, and ever supported the Protestant interest both in Ireland, and in the House of Lords, in England, whenever that question was discussed. On the day Lord Fitzwilliam was re-called when my brother (as Chancellor) was returning from the Castle, after having assisted at the swearing in the newly arrived Lord Lieutenant, a ferocious mob of no less than 5,000 men, and several hundred women, assembled together in College Green, and all along the avenue leading to my brother's house. The male part of the insurgents were armed with pistols, cutlasses, sledges, saws, crowbars, and every other weapon necessary to break open my brother's house ; and the women were all of them armed with their aprons full of paving stones. This ferocious and furious mob began to throw showers of stones into my brother's coach, at his coachman's head, and his horses ; they wounded my brother in the temple in College Green ; and if he had not sheltered himself by holding his great square official purse before him, he would have been stoned to death before he arrived (through the back-yard) at his own house ; where with several smithy sledges, they were working hard to break into his hall door, *while some others of them had ropes ready to fix up to his lamp iron to hang him the moment they could find him*—when I arrived disguised in my kitchen-maid's dress, my blue apron full of stones. I mingled with this numerous mob and addressed a pale sickly man, saying, my dear jew'l, what will become of hus ! I am after running from the Castle to tell yeas all that a regiment of Hos is galloping down here to thrample hus, &c. Oh ! yea, yea, where will we go ? ' Then they cried, ' Hurry, hurry—the Hos is coming to charge and thrample hus ! Hurry for the Custom House.' And in less than a moment the crowd dispersed.

" I then procured a surgeon for my brother and a guard to prevent another attack, and thus I saved Lord Clare's life, at the risk of being torn limb from limb, if I had been recognised by any of the mob." [1]

[1] From the *Kilkenny Archæological Society Journal* (New Series, Vol. V., 416–17).

CAPTAIN WOODES ROGERS

Hogarth pinxt *Skelton sculp[t].*

Gov[r]. Rogers & family

CHAPTER X

CAPTAIN WOODES ROGERS,
GOVERNOR OF THE BAHAMA ISLANDS, 1717–1721, 1728–1732

GOVERNOR ROGERS, who was the son of Woodes Rogers and Frances his wife, is supposed to have been born at Bristol.[1] His father, who was master of a ship, removed to Poole where his younger son, John, was baptised.[2] The exact date of the younger Woodes Rogers's birth is unknown, but in January, 1705, a marriage licence was issued in London for " Woodes Rogers of the city of Bristol, merchant, bachelor, about 25, and Mrs. Sarah Whetstone, spinster, 18, with consent of her father the Hon. Rear Admiral William Whetstone of St. Paul, Covent Garden, Middlesex, Esq., at St. Mary Magdalen, Old Fish Street, London, 24 Jan. 1704/5."

In the summer of 1708, Woodes Rogers was appointed Captain of the *Duke*, and Commander-in-Chief of the *Duke* and *Duchess* privateers, fitted out by some Bristol merchants to cruise against the Spaniards in Southern Seas. The aforesaid vessels sailed from King Road, 2nd August, and after putting in at Cork steered for the Canary Islands. Rogers narrates in his log how he suppressed a serious mutiny on board the *Duke* by seizing the ringleader, assisted by some of the ship's officers, and " making one of the mutineer's comrades whip him, which method I thought best for breaking any unlawful friendship amongst 'em." Off Teneriffe, the *Duke* and *Duchess* captured some Spanish barks with cargoes of wine and brandy. The two privateers then sailed for Cape Horn which was rounded in January, 1709, after the officers and crews had endured hardships of all kinds. Rogers now determined to sail to the Island of Juan Fernandez on the west side of South America. The arrival of the *Duke* and *Duchess* off this desert isle, and what was found there, is clearly set forth in Captain Woodes Rogers's journal :—

" Jan. 31, 1708/9. At seven this morning we made the Island of Juan Fernandez ; it bore W.S.W. about 7 L[eague]s at noon W. by S. 6 Ls. We had a good Observ. Lat. 34-10-S."

" Feb. 1. About two yesterday in the afternoon we hoisted our pinnace out. Capt. Dover with the boat's crew went in her to get ashore, tho' we could not be less than 4 Ls. off. As soon as the pinnace was gone, I went on board the Dutchess who admir'd our boat attempted going ashore at that distance from land— 'twas against my inclination, but to oblige Capt. Dover I consented to let her go. As soon as it was dark we saw a light ashore ; our boat was then about a League from the Island, and bore away for the ships as soon as she saw the lights. We put out lights aboard for the boat, tho' some were of opinion the lights we saw were our boat's lights ; but as night came on it appear'd too large for that. We

---

[1] MS. note on dedication page of the copy of *A Cruising Voyage Round the World*, by Capt. Woodes Rogers, in the Granville Library, Brit. Mus.
[2] *Ibid.*

fir'd one quarter-deck gun and several muskets, showing lights in our mizen and fore-shrouds, that our boats might find us, whilst we ply'd in the lee of the Island. About two in the morning our boat came on board, having been two hours on board the Dutchess that took 'em up astern of us ; we were glad they got well off because it began to blow. We are all convinc'd the light is on the shore, and design to make our ships ready to engage, believing them to be French ships at anchor and we must either fight 'em or want water, &c.

"Feb. 2 . . . We sent our yall (*sic*) ashore about noon with Capt. Dover, Mr. Frye, and six men, all arm'd ; meanwhile we and the Dutchess kept turning to get in, and such heavy flaws came off the land, that we were forc'd to let fly our top sail sheet, keeping all hands to stand by our sails for fear of the wind's carrying 'em away—but when the flaws were gone we had little or no wind. These flaws proceeded from the land, which is very high in the middle of the Island. Our boat did not return so we put our pinnace with the men arm'd, to see what was the occasion of the yall's stay ; for we were afraid that the Spaniards had a garrison there and might have seiz'd 'em. We put out a signal for our boat and the Dutchess show'd a French ensign. Immediately our pinnace return'd from the shore, and brought abundance of craw fish, with a man cloth'd in goat skins who look'd wilder than the first owners of them. He had been on the Island four years and four months being left there by Capt. Stradling in the Cinque Ports ; his name was Alexander Selkirk a Scotchman who had been Master of the Cinque Ports a ship that came here last with Capt. Dampier who told me that this was the best man in her, so I immediately agreed with him to be a mate on board our ships. 'Twas he that made the fire last night when he saw our ships, which he judg'd to be English. During his stay here he saw several ships pass by, but only two came in to anchor. As he went to view them, he found 'em to be Spaniards and retir'd from 'em, upon which they shot at him. Had they been French he would have submitted ; but chose to risque his dying alone on the Island, rather than fall into the hands of the Spaniards in these parts, because he apprehended they would murder him, or make a slave of him in the mines, for he fear'd they would spare no stranger that might be capable of discovering the South Sea. The Spaniards had landed before he knew what they were, and they came so near him that he had much ado to escape ; for they not only shot at him, but pursu'd him into the woods, where he climb'd to the top of a tree at the foot of which they . . . kill'd several goats but went off again without discovering him. He told us that he was born at Largo in the County of Fife in Scotland, and was bred a sailor from his youth. The reason of his being left here was a difference betwixt him and his Captain which, together with the ships being leaky, made him willing rather to stay here, than go along with him at first ; and when he was at last willing, the Captain would not receive him. He had been in the Island before to wood and water, when two of the ship's company were left upon it for six months till the ship return'd, being chas'd thence by two French South Sea ships . . . After he had conquer'd his melancholy, he diverted himself sometime by cutting his name on the trees, and the time of his being left and his continuance there. He was at first much pester'd with cats and rats, that had bred in great numbers from some of each species which had got ashore from ships that had put in there to wood and water. The rats gnawed his feet and clothes while asleep, which oblig'd him to cherish the cats with his goats flesh ; by which many of them became so tame that they would lie about him in hundreds and soon deliver'd him from the rats. He likewise tam'd some kids, and to divert himself would now and then sing and dance with them and his cats, so that by the care of Providence, and vigour of his youth, being now but about 30 years old, he came at last to conquer all the inconvenience of his solitude and to be very easy. When his clothes wore out he made himself a coat and cap of goat skins, which he stitched together with little thongs of the same that he cut with his knife. He had no other needle but a nail ; and when his knife was wore to the back, he made others as well as he could of some iron hoops that were left ashore, which he beat thin and ground upon stones. Having some linen cloth by him, he sew'd himself shirts with a nail, and stitch'd 'em with the worsted of his old stockings which he pull'd out on purpose. He had his last shirt on when we found him in the Island." [1]

Alexander Selkirk was the prototype of Robinson Crusoe. Daniel Defoe never owned this to be the case; but Woodes Rogers's relatives the Harfords of Bristol, and other residents in same city, believed and averred that Selkirk had given Defoe particulars of his stay on Juan Fernandez. In the *Annals of the Harford Family* (edited by Alice Harford) occurs this testimony :—

> "Mrs. Damaris Daniel, daughter of Major Wade who was wounded at Sedgemoor, assured Joseph Harford that Selkirk had told her that he had 'placed his papers in the hands of Defoe.' Mr. Harford immediately wrote to the Editor of the *Gentleman's Magazine* who published the fact, adding 'Mr. Harford has thus proved what was always believed to be the case, namely, that Daniel Defoe wrote Robinson Crusoe from Selkirk's papers.'"

After leaving Juan Fernandez, the *Duke* and *Duchess* fell in with several small Spanish vessels which were captured, also one large ship. In April, 1709, the British privateers with their prizes arrived off Guayaquil, in Peru. This town was captured and sacked by the British. Rogers's brother, Thomas, was shot through the head on 15th April. After storing their plunder the English sailors passed the night in the churches, "where they were much annoyed by the smell of the recently buried corpses of the victims of an epidemic of plague." In less than two days after returning to the ships, these men fell ill. Captain Thomas Dover, second in command of Rogers's expedition, who was a Bristol surgeon,[2] ordered the ship's surgeon on board the *Duchess* to bleed the sailors in both arms "and thus about 100 oz. of blood were taken from each man. He then gave them a dilution of sulphuric acid to drink and only eight of the plague-stricken sailors died!"

Off the Californian coast, the privateers fell in with a large and rich Manilla ship, on 21st December, 1709, and engaged her. In this hard-fought action, Rogers was severely wounded. "I was shot through the left cheek," he records in his journal. "The bullet struck away a great part of my upper jaw and several of my teeth, part of which dropped down upon the deck where I fell." The rich prize was then taken. Five days later, a second large Spanish ship was sighted by the *Marquis* (an armed prize), which, in company with the *Duchess*, engaged her but was beaten off. On the next day the *Duke* came up with the same vessel and an action ensued. Rogers records in his journal: "I was again unfortunately wounded in the left foot with a splinter just before we blew up on the quarter-deck, so that I could not stand but lay on my back in a great deal of misery; part of my heel bone being struck out and all under my ankle cut above half thro' which bled very much and weakn'd me before it could be dress'd and stopt." The second Manilla ship got away. The expedition then crossed the Pacific and arrived off Batavia in June, 1710. The Cape of Good Hope was reached in December; and on 1st October,

---

[1] *A Cruising Voyage Round the World*, by Capt. Woodes Rogers, in the Granville Library, Brit. Mus., p. 123 *et seq.*

[2] Appointed F.R.C.S.L. in 1721. D. in London, 1742. There is a memoir of this learned physician, whose "powder" is still called by his name, in the *D.N.B.*

1711, the *Duke* and *Duchess*, with several rich prizes in tow, arrived in the Downs.

Woodes Rogers published, in 1712, *A Cruising Voyage Round the World*. He had reaped a fair share of prize money, and, in October, 1717, he rented, on a 21 years' lease, the Bahama Islands, from the Lords Proprietors.[1]

George I. appointed Woodes Rogers to be Governor of the Bahamas and Captain of the Independent Company of Foot to be raised for garrison duty there, by commission dated 6th November, 1717.[2]

On arrival at Nassau, in the Island of Providence, Governor Rogers found the place a nest of pirates. The enormous difficulties he had to contend with are plainly narrated in the following letters :—

> " South Carolina,
>   " Nov. 4th, 1718.
>
> " My last, if I forget not, gave you an account of the mortality that had been amongst the Soldiers and others that came over with Governor Rogers and the ill state of that place [Providence] both in regard to Pirates and Spaniards, unless speedily supported by a greater force than are yet upon the Place ; and especially the necessity that there is of Cruising Ships and Snows or Sloops of War to be station'd there, without which I do assure you it will at any time be in the power of either Pirates or Spaniards at their pleasure to make themselves masters of the Island.
>
> " The Pirates yet accounted to be out are near 2,000 men and of those Vain (*sic*), Shaitch,[3] and others promise themselves to be repossessed of Providence in a short time. How the loss of that place may affect the Ministry I cannot tell, but the consequence of it seems to be not only a general destruction of the Trade to the West Indies, and the Main of America, but the settling and establishing a nest of Pirates who already esteem themselves a Community and to have one common interest ; and indeed they may in time become so and make that Island another Sally [Salee] but much more formidable unless speedy care be taken to subdue them." [4]

Secretary Craggs forwarded this letter to the Commissioners of Trade and added a postscript from his own pen :—

> " Besides the Advices contain'd in the inclos'd letter, I am to tell you by way of confirmation that before Colonel Stanhope left Madrid he was made acquainted with a design of the Spaniards to possess themselves of the Island of Providence."

> " Nassau in Providence,
>   " May 29th, 1719.
>
> " I hope your Lordship will pardon my troubling you with but a few instances of the People I have to govern who, though they expect the Enemy that has surprized them within these fifteen years thirty-four times yet the wreches (*sic*) can't be kept to watch at night, and when they do they come very seldom sober and rarely awake all night, though our Officers or Soldiers very often surprize their Guard and carry off their arms, and I punish, fine, or confine them almost every day.

---

[1] On 1st Nov. 1670 Charles II. granted a Charter to the Lords Proprietors.— *S.P. Bahamas*, Vol. III.

[2] *George the First's Army*, Vol. I., p. 250.

[3] See notice of this famous, or infamous, buccaneer in the Introduction to this volume.

[4] Letter to Col. Thos. Pitt, Junr., Governor of Jamaica, from —— Gale of South Carolina, and enclosed by Secretary Craggs in his despatch to the Commissioners of the Board of Trade, 29 Jan. 1718'19.— *S.P. Bahamas*, Vol. I.

"Then for work they mortally hate it, for when they have clear'd a patch that will supply them with potatoes and yams and very little else, fish being so plentiful and either Turtle or Goanas (*sic*) on the neighbouring Islands, they eat them instead of meat and covet no stock of cattle but thus live poorly and indolently, with a seeming content, and pray for Wrecks or the Pirates ; and few of them have an opinion of a regular orderly life under any sort of Government and would rather spend all they have at a Punch house than pay me one tenth to save their familys and all dear to them.

"The Tax that I advised your Lordships they had agreed to pay to the Fortifications (though but a trifle had they been industrious) was the greatest grievance (*sic*) they ever met withall and did not hold three weeks, for I was glad to keep them in humour without money ; and had not I took another method of eating, drinking, and working with them my self, Officers, Soldiers, Sailors, and Passengers, and watch at the same time, whilst they were drunk and drowsy, I could never have got the Fort in any posture of defence, neither would they willingly [have] kept themselves or me from the Pirates if the expectation of a War with Spain had not been perpetually kept up and improved before I was certain of it, to make them do some work, after the Ships of War left us, and whilst they was here were too sickly to do any work. . . .

"WOODES ROGERS."[1]

Five months before this letter was written, Governor Rogers had hanged ten of the captured pirates.[2] And before he had been two years at Nassau he had built a strong fort, necessary cannon for which had been sent out from England at his request. In 1720 the Board of Trade made the following report to the Lords Justices who were acting as Regents in George I.'s absence :—

"To the Lords Justices.

". . . . A hundred men were sent, in 1717, to the Bahamas, with a great number of artificers to make a settlement. At their arrival they found about 700 Pirates whom they forced off the Island, tho' they continued afterwards for about eight months to infest that Coast, taking all vessells they met in those seas, insomuch that the Governor was necessitated to detain all the Lessees' Ships as Guard Ships until, at the expense of the Lessees, he had built a Fort with above 60 pieces of Cannon (100 small ones for the defence of the Harbour) 12 of which, with the necessary Stores and Ammunition, were forwarded by the Crown from home.

"Before the Governor could reduce the Pirates he was obliged, at the expense of the Lessees, to fit out 3 Ships which took some of the said Pirates and obliged others to surrender. . . . The Spaniards then threatened the Island of Providence with 5 Men of War, 3 Brigantines, 11 Sloops, and 1,400 regular troops. But the Governor having had timely notice thereof, he gave out Arms and Ammunition to about 700 men of the inhabitants who, by the assistance of the Fort and Guard Ship, drove off the Spaniards but they threaten a new attempt."[3]

In consequence of the above report the Lords Justices advised that " a hundred men be sent to Providence in one Independent Company if his Majesty thinks fit; also more cannon, arms, ammunition and stores."[4] So far as the proposed addition to the Nassau garrison was concerned, nothing was done.

[1] Letter to the Lords Commissioners of Trade.—*S.P. Bahamas*, Vol. I.
[2] Article on Woodes Rogers in the *D.N.B.*
[3] *S.P. Dom. George I.*, 1720, Bundle 23, No. 162
Ibid.

Early in the year 1721 Captain Woodes Rogers threw up his appointment as Governor of the Bahamas and embarked for England. His arrival at Bristol is notified in the *London Journal* of 12th August, 1721, as follows :—

"Capt. Woods Rogers late Governor of Providence is returned from thence by the way of Bristol, in a Carolina ship, and will be in town this week."

On the accession of George II. Woodes Rogers petitioned the King that he might be restored to the governorship of the Bahamas, and given command of the Independent Company there :—

"To the King's most Excellent Majesty.

"The humble Petition of Captain Woodes Rogers late Governor of the Bahama Islands in America, and Captain of the Independent Company there,

"Sheweth :

"The Petitioner had the honour to be employ'd by Your Royal Father to drive the Pyrates from the Bahama Islands, and he succeeded therein, he afterwards established a Settlement and defended it against an attack of the Spaniards. On Your Majesty's happy Accession he humbly represented the State of his great losses and sufferings in this Service, praying, that you would be graciously pleas'd to grant him such compensation for the same as might enable him to exert himself more effectually in your Majesty's Services having nothing more than the Subsistence of half Pay as Captain of Foot, given him, on a Report of the Board of General Officers appointed to inquire into his Conduct ; who farther recommended him to his late Majesty's Bounty and Favour.

"The Petitioner not having the happiness to know Your Royal pleasure, humbly begs leave to represent that the Bahama Islands are of very great importance to the Commerce of these Kingdoms, as is well known to all concern'd in the American Trade ; and the weak condition they now are in renders them an easy prey to the Spaniards, if a rupture should happen ; but if effectually secured, they will soon contribute very much to distress any power which may attempt to molest the British Dominions or Trade in the West Indies.

"The Petitioner therefore humbly prays, that your most Sacred Majesty would be graciously pleased to restore him to his former Station of Governor, and Captain of an independent Company of these Islands, in which he hopes to give farther proofs of Zeal for Your Majesty's Service. Or if it is Your Royal pleasure his Successor be continued there, he most humbly relyes, that thro' Your Great Compassion and Bounty he shall receive such a consideration for his past sufferings and present half Pay, as will enable him to be usefully employ'd for Your Majesty's and his Country's Advantage ; and in some measure retrieve his losses : that he may Support himself and Family, who for above Seven years past have suffer'd very much by means of this Employment wholly for the Publick Service.

"And Your Majesty's Petitioner, as in Duty bound, shall ever pray." [1]

At the same time that the foregoing Petition was sent to the King, twenty-eight influential gentlemen connected with the North American Colonies, amongst whom were Samuel Shute, ex-Governor of Massachusetts, Alexander Spottiswood, Deputy-Governor of Virginia, and Benjamin Bennet, ex-Governor of Bermuda, subscribed a petition to Sir Robert Walpole in favour of Captain Woodes Rogers :—

"London, February 29th, 1727/8.

"We whose names are hereunto Subscribed, being inform'd that Cap[tn.] Woodes Rogers, late Governor of the Bahama Islands, has deliverd the annex'd Petition to

Add. MS., Brit. Mus., 4459, fol. 101.

his Majesty, mentioning his sufferings and great loss of time in the Publick Service, which we can for the most part certify from our own knowledge, and the rest from credible Informations have been very severe. Therefore We take the liberty humbly to recommend him to Your protection, that he may either have the same employ or such [a] consideration according to the prayer of his Petition, as may enable him to retrieve his losses and be further Serviceable to the Publick of which he is very capable.

"We beg leave to instance his dislodging the Pyrates, who considerably spoil'd and Obstructed the American Trade, and were setled in great numbers at the Bahama Islands; and defending that Government afterwards against a formidable Attack of the Spaniards, proved of great consequence to the preservation of the West-India Trade. And We never heard any complaint against his Conduct in his Duty there, nor that he behaved otherwise in that Employ, than with the utmost resolution and fidelity becoming a good Subject, tho' to the ruin of his own Fortune."

[Here follow 28 signatures.]
"To the Rt. Honble. and Noble Sir Robert Walpole." [1]

In recognition of his past services to the Crown, George II. appointed Woodes Rogers Captain-General and Governor-in-Chief over the Bahama Islands, 18th October, 1728, and gave him the command of the Independent Company then garrisoning Nassau. Before leaving England, in 1729, Woodes Rogers and his family were sketched by Hogarth. They are represented disporting themselves outside the fort at Nassau. Governor Rogers arrived at the capital of the Bahamas, 25th August, 1729. When he did reach the Island of Providence he lost no time getting to work on the new fortifications at Nassau. On 2nd August, 1731, Rogers wrote to the Commissioners of the Board of Trade :—

"I can yet procure no assistance from the Inhabitants towards the Fortifications, though I have without any help from them built a good Barrack for the Garrison in the Fort, and have made upwards of 20 new carriages for guns of this Country timber, and shall continue to do all I can towards the Fortifications as soon as the heat of the summer is over, that I can put the Garrison to work again without endangering their healths. And as soon as possible will try in a new Assembly what I can do, though I fear little publick good is to be expected from them if Mr. Colebrooke and his Accomplices here can have any influence to prevent the Peoples working, they being too poor to contribute anything worth contributing in money." [2]

Two months before this letter was written, Governor Rogers had thus referred to Mr. Colebrooke :—

" . . . How great an enemy he has been to this Government, and what vile means he used to make the Garrison mutiny, and stirr up a spirit of sedition and discontent in the Islands, by the great influence which he had artfully gained over the most ignorant of them while he was Speaker of the Assembly, from all which I humbly hope that the method taken to prevent his proceeding in his wicked and pernicious design will meet with His Majesty's and your Lordships' approval." [3]

The "method" to which the Governor refers in above letter was nothing less than the arrest and indictment of the aforesaid Colebrooke. A true bill was brought in by the Providence Grand Jury on 28th May,

[1] *Add. MS.*, Brit. Mus., 4459, fol. 102.
[2] Letter written from " New Providence."—*S.P. Bahamas*, Vol. III.
[3] *Ibid.* Letter to the Board of Trade dated " New Providence, 10 June, 1731."

1731 ; three days later he was tried before Chief Justice Rowland of the Bahamas and found guilty of sedition by a petty jury.   The Judge pronounced this sentence :—

> " The judgment of this Court is that you Mr. John Colebroke be fined seven hundred and fifty pounds current money of these Islands, and that you be committed to the custody of the Provost-Marshal of these Islands until the same fine is paid and further remain confined during His Majesty's pleasure.   And that before you be discharged from this commitment you give sufficient security for your good behaviour during and for such time as His Majesty shall signify by his Pleasure for that purpose." [1]

Governor Rogers's last few months in the Bahamas were cheered by the just punishment meted out to his powerful enemy.   On 11th October, 1731, he wrote from New Providence to Alured Popple, Esq., Secretary to the Board of Trade, and sent the letter by his son who returned to England that month :—

> " My son who will wait on you with this having for near three years past resided here may be able to give your Lordships a farther information than is contained in this letter." [2]

Woodes Rogers died at his post in the summer of 1732.   Under date of September, 1732, the following notice appeared in the *Gentleman's Magazine* :—

> " Came Advice of the death of Woodes Rogers, Esq., Governor of the Bahama Islands, July 16.   He and Captain Cook, lately drowned, made a cruizing voyage to the South Seas and round the Globe, in the *Duke* and *Duchess*, in the Wars of Queen Anne."

He left one son, Whetstone Rogers, who was chosen one of the new Councillors for the Bahamas by the Lords Commissioners for Trade, 10th May, 1733, at a Council held at St. James's Palace, His Majesty being present. [8]

[1] *S.P. Bahamas,* Vol. III.
[2] *Ibid.*   Above letter is endorsed, " Recd. 3 Jan. 1731/2."
[8] *Ibid.*

APPENDICES TO VOLS. I AND II

APPENDICES TO VOLS. I AND II

MAJOR-GENERAL WIGHTMAN'S ACCOUNT OF THE BATTLE OF SHERIFFMUIR.

(See Vol. I., p. 50.)

Sterling, Nov. 14. 1715. *at Eleven at Night.*

Last *Friday* I arriv'd from *Edinburgh*, where I had finished all the Works and Barricadoes that I had Orders to do for the Security of that Town ; and as soon as I came to his Grace the Duke of *Argyle*, he told me he was glad to see me, and that as he intended to make a March towards the Enemy the next Morning, he had sent an Express to *Edinburgh* for me. Accordingly on *Saturday* the 12th Instant our whole Army marched over the Bridge of *Sterling* towards the Enemy, who lay at a Place call'd *Ardoch*, about seven Miles from this Place ; and in the Evening our Army came within three Miles of the Enemy's Camp. We lay all that Night on our Arms, and the next Morning, being *Sunday*, I went with his Grace where our advanc'd Guard was posted, and had a plain View of the Rebels Army all drawn up in Line of Battle, which consisted of nine thousand one hundred Men. They seem'd to make a Motion towards us, upon which the Duke order'd me immediately back to put our Men in Order, and soon after his Grace order'd them to march to the Top of a Hill against the Enemy ; but before all, or not half our Army was form'd in Line of Battle, the Enemy attack'd us. The Right of their Line, which lay in a hollow Way, vastly outwing'd us, which was not perceived by us, nor possible for us to know it, the Enemy having Possession of the Brow of the Hill ; but the Left of their Army was very plain to our View, the Moment we got to the Top of the Hill. Not half our Men were come up, or could form. The Enemy, that were within little more than Pistol-shot, began to attack with all their Left upon our Right ; I had the Command of the Foot, the Enemy were Highlanders, and as it is their Custom, gave us Fire, and a great many came up to our Noses Sword in Hand ; but the Horse on our Right with the constant Platoons of Foot, soon put the Left of their Army to the Rout ; the Duke of *Argyle* pursuing as he thought the Main of their Army, which he drove before him about a Mile and a half over a River. As I march'd after him as fast as I could with a little above three Regiments of Foot, I heard great firing on our Left, and sent my Aid-de-Camp to see the Occasion of it, and found that the Right of the Enemies Army that lay in the hollow Way, and were superior to that Part of their Army which we had beaten, was fallen upon our Left with all the Fury imaginable ; and as our Men were not form'd, they cut off just the half of our Foot and the Squadrons on our left. The Duke who pursued the Enemy very fast, was not apprised of this, and as he had ordered me to march after him as fast as I could. I was obliged to slacken my March, and send to his Grace to inform him of what had happened ; I kept what Foot I had in perfect Order, not knowing but my Rear might soon be attack'd by the Enemy that had beat our Left, which proved to be the Flower of their Army. At last when the Duke had put to flight that Part of the rebel Army he was engaged with, he came back to me, and could not have imagined to see such an Army as was behind us, being three times our Number ; but as I had kept that Part of our Foot which first engag'd in very good Order. His Grace join'd me with five Squadrons of Dragoons, and we put the best Face on the Matter ; to the right about, and so march'd to the Enemy who had defeated all the Left of our Army. If they had either Courage or Conduct, they might have entirely destroyed my Body of

Foot ; but it pleased God to the contrary.   I am apt to conjecture their Spirits were not a little damp'd by having been Witnesses some Hours before of the firm Behaviour of my Foot, and thought it hardly possible to break us ; we march'd in a Line of Battle till we came within half a Mile of the Enemy, and found them rang'd on the Top of a Hill, on very advantageous Ground, and above 4000 in Number ; we posted ourselves at the Bottom of the Hill, having the Advantage of Ground where their Horse could not well attack us, for we had the Convenience of some Earth Walls or Ditches about Breast high, and as Evening grew on, we inclined with our Right towards the Town of *Dumblain,* in all the Order that was possible.   The Enemy behaved like Civil Gentlemen, and let us do what we pleased ; so that we pass'd the Bridge of *Dumblain,* posted ourselves very securely, and lay on our Arms all Night. This Morning we went with a Body of Dragoons to the Field of Battle, brought off the wounded there, and came to this Town in the Evening.   General *Webb's* late Regiment, now *Morison's,* is one of the unfortunate Regiments that was not formed, and suffered most.   Major *Hammere* is kill'd, with young *Hillary,* and many other Officers.   General *Evans* and I had the good Fortune to be on the right Wing with the Duke.   General *Evans* had his Horse shot dead under him, and escaped very narrowly as well as myself.

  P.S.   Our whole Army did not consist of above a 1000 Dragoons, and 2500 Foot ; and but a little more than half of them engaged.   However, I must do the Enemy that Justice, to say I never saw regular Troops more exactly drawn up in Line of Battle, and that in a Moment ; and their Officers behaved with all the Gallantry imaginable ; all I can say, is, it will be of the last Danger to the Government if we have not Force to destroy them soon ; the Loss on both Sides I leave for another Time, when we have a more exact Account.

THE KING'S INSTRUCTIONS TO MAJOR-GENERAL WADE,

1st June, 1725.

(See Vol. II., p. 13.)

Instructions to our trusty and well-beloved George Wade, Esquire, Major-General of our Forces, whom we have appointed to take upon him the Command of our Forces, Castles, Forts, and Barracks in North Britain, given at our Court of St. James, the 1st day of June 1725, in the eleventh year of our reign.

Whereas it has been humbly represented to us that notwithstanding the many good laws that have from time to time been made to reduce our Highlands of Scotland to a more civilised and legal behaviour, and to a due obedience of our laws and Government; yet that many of the inhabitants of that part of our dominions do still continue possessed of great quantities of arms and warlike weapons, with which they commit robberies and depredations, and raise illegal exactions from our faithful subjects, now we, reposing especial trust and confidence in you, have by our Warrant under our Royal Sign Manual, bearing date with these presents, authorised and empowered you to summon, or cause to be summoned, such of the persons and clans as are therein described, to bring in and deliver up their arms and warlike weapons, pursuant to the Act of Parliament on that behalf.

But whereas it may be necessary for some of our subjects in that part of the kingdom (who may have occasion to travel to markets, fairs, or other places upon their lawful business, and for others who may be called on to assist the Civil Magistrate in the execution of the laws) to bear and use arms for their security and defence, you are therefore authorised and empowered in such cases to grant Licences under your hand and seal, taking care to specify in such Licences the particular arms and warlike weapons which such persons shall be authorised to keep, bear, or wear.

We have thought fit that six companies should be raised, consisting of Highlanders well affected to our Government, and you are to take care and direct that the regular troops under your command, together with the said companies, or any of them, do assist the Civil Magistrate as occasion may require.

As the tenants of the estate late of the late Earl of Seaforth have continued hitherto in a state of disobedience and defiance of our laws and Government, and notwithstanding that by the attainder of the said late Earl for high treason, the said estate became vested in the Crown (which through our love to our people we have given to the public), yet the said tenants have not only refused to pay in their rents in pursuance of our gracious intentions; but have paid them for the use of the said late Earl, and have supported themselves and one another in this disobedience by force of arms; and therefore, we have thought fit that when the troops are assembled and encamped, they shall be marched to the Castle of Brahan, which was the principal seat of the said late Earl, or any other part of the said estate as you shall judge most for our service, and to cause the summons above mentioned to be sent to the clans and tenants thereof, in order effectually to disarm them.

When you have used your utmost endeavour to perform this service, you are to proceed to send summons to such other clans or countries one after another, who are reported to be the most disaffected to our Government, or most addicted to robberies and depredations upon our faithful subjects; and in case you find it necessary to separate the troops under your command, you are to take care to send a careful officer with them, with orders to support the Civil Magistrate in the execution of the laws above mentioned.

In order to prevent, or subdue insurrection, and to hinder the Highlanders from passing into the low countries in times of rebellion, as well as for the better quartering of our Troops, you are, on your arrival at Inverness, to cause a barrack and fort to be erected upon the ground where our ancient Castle now stands (unless you shall find some other situation more proper and convenient), but if you shall think that the most proper situation, you are to cause the said Castle to be repaired, so that, together with the barracks to be there built, it may be sufficient to contain at least 400 men, as also the Governor and Officers appointed for the command of the said Fort, with such conveniency as the extent of the ground will admit of.

And whereas the situation of the Barrack Killiwemen has been represented to us to be insecure and inconvenient from its being built at too great a distance from the Lake Ness, We also think fit to empower you to contract with the Proprietors of such lands as shall be found to be necessary, if there shall be occasion for the same, and to cause a Fort or Barrack to be erected thereupon at the end of the said lake, which, together with the barrack already built, may be sufficient to contain a Battalion of Foot, with a communication between the said Barrack and Fort, as may be convenient for their mutual support.

You are likewise to give orders that Inspection be made into the present condition of the Castles and Forts in North Britain, and to cause necessary repairs to be made to secure them from the dangers of a hidden surprise.

And whereas Our service may sometimes require your presence in places far distant from the said Castles and Forts and Barracks when they are in building or repairing, you are hereby authorised to appoint such proper persons as you shall judge most capable to perform the said service and inspect the said works, in the execution whereof you are not to exceed the sums following, viz.—

For the Barracks to be Erected at Inverness	£7000
For the Fort and Barrack at Killiwemen	5000
And for the Repairs of the other Castles and Forts above mentioned ...	2000

Unless you shall receive our special order to exceed these sums.

And whereas it has likewise been represented unto us that the building of [a] vessel with oars and sails on the Lake Ness will be necessary for a better communication between the Garrisons of Inverness and Killiwemen, and for sending parties to the countries bordering on the said lake, you are to cause a vessel proper for that purpose to be built for the uses above mentioned, in which expense you are not to exceed £400.

And in order that all due encouragement may be given to such of the Highlanders who shall peaceably and quietly deliver up their arms in obedience to any summons that shall be sent them, or to such of them as shall contribute to facilitate the execution of the Disarming Act, or shall discover arms concealed, or persons outlawed, or attainted of High Treason, you are hereby authorised out of such money as shall come to your hands from time to time, to give reasonable gratuities to such persons, and in such proportions as you shall think fit and convenient, for the better carrying on this service.

And whereas some of the persons or Clans that are disaffected to our Government may presume to hide or conceal their Arms, or to carry or send them to distant Islands or other places, you are to use your best endeavours for the discovery of such concealments, by sending any ship or vessel that may be appointed to attend the service, to seize all such Arms as may be found to be so concealed, and to bring the concealers of such Arms to Justice.

And to the end that our Troops may be the better accommodated in their Incampment on the Mountains, and that proper provision may not be wanting during their continuance there, you are also authorised and empowered out of such money as shall come to your hands as aforesaid, to defray the extraordinary charges of such Incampment, and the carriage of soldiers' tents, ammunition, and provisions for the use of our said Forces, as also for the maintenance of Prisoners who shall be found in arms contrary to law ; and likewise for repairing the roads between the Garrisons and Barracks (where the same is practicable), for the better communication of our Troops , and also for such other contingent charges as shall be found necessary for our service.

And whereas Edmund Burt is appointed agent for the Estates late of the late Earl of Seaforth, and of Glenmorrison, not sold by the late Commissioners, you are to give him all legal assistance in the execution of the Trust reposed in him.

You are from time to time to correspond with one of our principal Secretaries of State, and to give account of the progress you make in the execution of these services, and of any difficulties that may arise in relation to the same.

When the season of the year shall require the troops to be sent into winter quarters, you are to report to us how far you have succeeded in the execution of these, our commands ; and to lay before us your opinion of what may be further necessary to be done towards settling the peace and quiet of that part of our kingdom.

G. R.

LIEUT.-GENERAL HAWLEY.

(*See* Vol. II., p. 44.)

My Lord Stair having been pleased to communicate to us the Measures taken between his Lordship and the Duke of Arenberg for the immediate march of the Head of the Army into Germany, we are of opinion unanimously, that those Measures were absolutely necessary at this very critical Time, and that they are entirely aggreeable to the Honour and Interest of the King and Kingdome, and to the Engagements so generously entered into by the King our Master for the Support of the Queen of Hungary and the Libertys of Europe.

At Aix la Chapelle the 23ᵈ. of March N.S. 1743.

Sign'd by all the Genˡ. Officers present.

JAMES CAMPBELL.
JNO. COPE.
J. L. LIGONIER.
HE. HAWLEY.
JOHN HUSKE.
CHA. FRAMPTON.

HUM. BLAND.

[*Endorsed*]   In Lord Stair's private
letter of the 23ᵈ. March
N.S. 1742/3.[1]

[1] Add. MS. 22537, fol. 240.

ACCOUNT OF THE BATTLE OF FALKIRK.

(See Vol. II., p. 46.)

LETTER FROM J. DE PESTER TO THE COUNTESS OF DENBIGH.

23 [Jan.] 1745.—Il est venu madame, un expres d'Ecosse qui a porté la nouvelle d'une action entre les troupes du Roy commandus (*sic*) par le General Hawley et l'armée des rebelles, ou ces derniers ont eû l'avantage, encore que nous eussions sept mille hommes contre cinq. Nous avons perdu sept canons et beaucoup de bagage, nos officiers se sont très bien comportez et les soldats très mal. Il y a plusieurs des premiers tuez ou blessez parmi lesquels je ne crois pas qu'il y ait personne que vous connoissiez. Enfin il y a resolu que le Duc partiroit incessament pour tacher de reparer le dommage. Cette mauvaise nouvelle a, comme vous le jugez bien, causé une sorte de consternation d'autant plus qu'on ne sait si c'est poltronièrie ou trahison qui a fait fuir ces soldats. Cependant on ne crois pas que le mal soit ireparable. On a appris d'un autre côte, que les officiers qui avoient été prisonniers à Preston Pans se sont échappez de l'endroit ou ils etoient aupres de Perth. J'oubliois de vous dire que dans l'action la première ligne a fait feu et s'est comportée médiocrement bien, et que la seconde qui etoit composée des mêmes troupes que le [General] Cope avoît à Preston Pans a pris la fuite sans tirez un seul coup. Enfin que Mr. Hawley s'etoit retiré à Edinbourg.[1]

EXTRACT FROM LETTER WRITTEN BY LIEUT.-COLONEL CHARLES WHITEFOORD, OF 5TH FOOT, IN 1752, TO MAJOR IRWIN OF SAME CORPS.

(See Vol. II., p. 73.)

I have the pleasure of yours, with one from Lieutenant McLaughlin, which gives me a good deal of concern. He says men are very hard to get, and has sent over but six, whereof two have been in the service. I have fatally experienced the bad consequence of giving the recruiting officers a latitude, and must have a very good opinion of the man to whom I give a discretionary power. To change low men for others no taller is folly, and not to be compleat in Aprile is dangerous; therefor lads under 18 of 5ft. 7in. I consent to take, but would alter the instructions no furthur. Now I must reveal my secret in order to make you easie, and procure the general's approbation, whose will shall always be to me a law. Our drummers are sightly fellows. I propose turning as many of them into the ranks as will compleat us, and listing boys in their roome. That saves us with the commissary, and does not exhaust the exchequer. After the review, I discharge the boys, and then shall have a fine sum in the stock purse. At the same time the general saves the cloathing. When winter comes, we will send a greater number of officers, by which method we shall save to the general, put money in the captain's pocket, and effectuat our scheme of not haveing (at least) the worst regiment in Ireland. I have a plot of making our serjeants fine at a small expence. You see their cloaths are new lapell'd. That I shall propose to alter, and have them looped like the men's with a half silver lace, which you must buy in England. By this means we shall make a show with economy, for the cloath saved will near purchase the lace, and as I have communicated this to nobody, I hope you will keep it to yourself.[2]

---

[1] "Earl of Denbigh's MSS.," printed by the *Hist. MSS. Commission*, 4th Report, Appendix.
[2] *Whitefoord Papers.*

ROYAL WARRANT, 27th February, 1718/19.[1]

(*See* Introductory chapter on "The Early Georgian Era," Part II.)

Previous to this Warrant it would appear that the seller of a commission had the power of recommending his successor. The 1719 Warrant provided :—

1. That whatever officer shall desire leave to sell shall be obliged to resign his command at the rate, and on the conditions hereafter mentioned ; to which end the seller is not to be admitted to interfere in any manner whatever in the recommendation of his successor.
2. That no officer above the rank of lieutenant be admitted as a purchaser whereby he may obtain any higher rank, unless he hath served as a commissioned officer upwards of ten years.
3. That no colonel shall sell but to such as have rank as colonel or lieutenant-colonel ; and no lieutenant-colonel but to such as have rank as major ; no major but to such as have rank of captain ; no captain but to such as have rank of lieutenant ; and no lieutenant but to a cornet or ensign.
4. That every officer having leave to purchase any higher commission shall be at liberty to dispose of his then present commission for the prices hereafter mentioned and according to the preceding rules.
5. Every officer desiring leave to dispose of his commission, shall sign such his request, and that he is content to resign at the price fixed, and lodge the same in the War Office, that a successor may be appointed to him.

The prices of commissions as established by this Warrant, were as follows :—

	Royal Regt. of Horse Guards.	Horse and Drag. Guards.	Dragoons at home.	Dragoons abroad.	Foot Guards.	Infantry Corps at home.	Infantry Corps abroad.
	£	£	£	£	£	£	£
Colonel and Captain ...	—	9,000	7,000	6,000	—	6,000	5,000
Lieut.-Col. and Captain...	4,000	4,000	3,200	2,700	6,000	2,400	2,000
Major and Captain ...	3,300	3,300	2,600	2,200	3,600	1,800	1,500
Captain	2,500	2,500	1,800	1,500	2,400	1,000	840
Captain-Lieutenant ...	1,500	1,500	1,000	850	1,500	450	380
Lieutenant	1,200	1,200	800	680	900	300	250
Cornet or Ensign ...	1,000	1,000	600	520	450	200	170
Quartermaster	300	—	—	—	150	150	125
Adjutant	200	200	200	172	200	150	125

At this period, it will be observed, there was a difference in the prices of commissions, both in cavalry and infantry, according as the corps happened to be serving in or out of Great Britain.

[1] *United Service Journal*, 1835, Part III., p. 2.

CONTEMPORARY ACCOUNT OF THE DUKE OF MARLBOROUGH'S FUNERAL AND KEY TO THE ACCOMPANYING PLATE.[1]

The Manner of His Grace's Lying in State at his late House in St. James's-Park.

The Hall was hung with Bayes, and adorn'd with Escutcheons, Ducal Coronets, and Electoral Caps, intermix'd with Stars, Crests, and *Mendleheims* within Garters. In the said Hall was four gilt Branches. At the Entrance Assistants in Mourning, to conduct the Lords in. The first Room was hung with black Cloth, where was a black Velvet Chair of State and Footstool on an Ascent of three Steps, in Mourning. It was enrich'd with Arms, Stars, &c. Over it was a Majesty Escutcheon on yellow Silk, one Yard and a half square, with his Grace's Arms, and the Eagle as Prince of *Mendleheim:* Round it were Badges, Stars, *Mendleheims*, and Sconces, &c. Over the Chair of State was a Velvet Canopy and Vallances, with Plumades of Feathers and Streamers ; and the Inside with Armes, &c. On the Right-Hand was the Standard, on the Left the Guidon, each Side having large Silver Candlesticks with Wax Tapers burning, and four Mutes in Mourning. Opposite the Chair was a Lozenge of Escutcheons, *Mendleheims*, Crests, Stars, Silver Sconces, and round the Room were double Rows, with Wax Candles burning in 'em ; the whole adorn'd with Escutcheons, Coronets, &c., and at the Entrance were Assistants in Mourning, to conduct the Lords in. The second Room was hung with four hundred Yards of new Velvet, and at the upper End was an Ascent of three Steps in Mourning, on which rested the Body. The Coffin was cover'd with Crimson Velvet, adorn'd with Watergilt Nails and Handles, Ducal Coronets, Stars, and a large Copper Plate, on which his Grace's Titles were engrav'd ; the whole being cover'd with a Velvet Pall trimm'd with Sarsenet, and drawn up in Festoons. On it was four large Escutcheons, half black Silk, with Ducal Coronets and Supporters, and half on yellow, with the Eagle as Prince of *Mendleheim*, and Mottos. On the Pall lay a compleat Piece of Armour, richly gilt, on a crimson Velvet Cushion : On the right side his Head stood a Ducal Coronet and crimson Cap, and on the other the Electoral Cap. In his right Hand was a General's Truncheon gilt ; on his left Side a rich Sword in a crimson Velvet Scabbard, girt round with a Velvet Belt ; the Collar of the Order about his Neck, with the *George ;* the Garter on his left Leg ; and at his Feet a silver Lion couchant, holding a Banner, being his Grace's Crest. Round the Body was a black Velvet Rail, adorn'd with Escutcheons, Stars, Plumades of Feathers, Silk Streamers, and Ducal Coronets. The ten Banner-Rolls of his Ancestors was plac'd on each side. On the right Side, at the Feet, stood the great Banner with all the Quarterings, and the Banner of the Order ; and on the other the Banner of *Mendleheim* and that of *Woodstock.* In the middle on a large Velvet Stool was the Regale, *viz.*, the Helmet, Crest, Mantle, Sword, Shield, Gauntlets, Spurs, and Surcoat of Arms. Round the Body was twelve large Silver Candlesticks with Wax Tapers burning, and eight Mutes on each side. At the Feet were two Pages of Honour. Over the Body was a Majesty Escutcheon, a Yard and half square, with his Grace's Arms as Prince of *Mendleheim*, adorn'd with Arms, Crests, Stars, Ducal Coronets, and Caps. On each side, at the Head, were two Gold Pillars of the *Corinthian* Order, embellish'd with Silk Badges, Stars, and *Mendleheims.* Over the Body was a large Velvet Canopy and Vallances bound with Gold, adorn'd with Plumades of Feathers and Streamers, and the Inside with Arms, &c. All was within a large Alcove, with two Pillars at the Foot cover'd with black Velvet, and adorn'd with Badges, Stars, Plumades, &c. From the Alcove hung a silver Branch. The whole Room was adorn'd with Arms, Silver Sconces, &c. Assistants waiting to conduct the Lords into their Rooms. The third Room was hung with deep Mourning, with Silver Sconces and Branches, and

---

[1] From the engraving in the British Museum.

adorn'd with two Rows of Escutcheons with his Grace's Arms, Crest, Stars, &c. Assistants waiting to sit (*sic*) the Company. The fourth was hung with black Cloth, and had Squabs cover'd therewith for the Lords to sit on. Here were four large Silver Branches and Sconces, double Rows of Escutcheons, Ducal Coronets, and Caps, intermix'd with Crests, Stars, &c. In the great Room was the Chief Mourners, Pall-Bearers, and Lords Assistants, fitted with their Cloaks, &c. About half an Hour after Twelve the Procession began, and march'd along the Road thro' *St. James's-Park*, and the *Upper Park*, to *Hyde-Park-Corner*, thence thro' *Picadilly*, down *St. James's-Street*, thro' *Pall-Mall*, and by *Charing-Cross* thro' *King-Street* to *Westminster-Abbey*, in the following Manner :

The Explanation of the Procession.

1. A Detachment of the First and Second Troops of Horse-Grenadiers, led by six Serjeants, three a-breast ; then a Lieutenant; then the private Men, four a-breast : After them two Lieutenants, two Captains, two Field-Officers a-breast ; then Col. *Fane*. Lastly, four Hautboys a-breast.
2. The Detachment of the First and Third Troops of Horse-Guards, commanded by the Lord *Newburgh :* The Artillery, with the two Companies of Cannoniers and Bombardiers, commanded by Colonel *Bourgard*, and march'd in the following Order :
3. Two Ranks of Pioneers, six in a Rank, with one on the Front, one in the Centre, and one in the Rear.
4. Six Tumbrils, or Cover'd Carts, the last Waggon having a Standard on it.
5. Twenty-four Matrosses, *Thomas James* Lieutenant, *James Richards* Captain.
6. Four Gunners, attending seven One and a half Pounders.
7. Two Bombardiers, attending two Howitzers.
8. Two Gunners, attending four Three Pounders.
9. *George Michaelson* Adjutant, and one Gunner, attending two Six Pounders, the last having a Standard on it.
10. A Kettle-Drum.
11. Master-Artificer ; six Artificers ; *James Deale* Captain-Lieutenant, *Richard Sommerfield* Lieutenant, and *John Winch* Fire-worker, a-breast ; 31 Matrosses in four Ranks, six a-breast, two in the Centre, and one at each Corner; then *Peter Stephins* Lieutenant, and as many Gunners, in the same Form, *Jonathan Lewis* and *George Minnens*, Lieutenants, following a-breast. Then *Thomas Pattison* Captain, and *Albert Bourgard* Colonel, closing the Rear.
12. The Detachment of the Third Regiment of Foot-Guards, commanded by the Earl of *Dunmore*.
13. The Detachment of the Second Regiment of Foot-Guards, commanded by the Earl of *Scarborough*.
14. The First Battalion of His Majesty's Regiment of Foot-Guards, of which his Grace was Colonel. The 1st Company led by Capt. *Courtney ;* the 2d by Col. *Lee* and Capt. *Webb* a-breast, Lieut.-Col. *Read* in the Centre, and four Lieutenant-Colonels in Rear ; the 3d and 4th by two Captains, a-breast each; the 5th by Ensign *Worley ;* the 6th by Ensign *Durand ;* the 7th by five Ensigns ; the 8th by Ensign *Hamilton ;* the 9th by a Captain and an Ensign ; the 10th and 11th by two Captains each, and Capt. *Reynolds* marching as Adjutant. Four Lieutenant-Colonels close the Rear.
15. Major-General *Tatton* alone ; then six Hautboys ; and then the General Officers as follows : Brig. *Honeywood*, Brig. *Crofts*, Brig. *Munden*, Brig. *Stanwix*, Brig. *Bisset*, Brig. *Bowles*, Maj.-Gen. *Wightman*, Maj.-Gen. *Wade*, Lieut.-Gen. *Macartney*, Lieut.-General *Wills*.
16. The Earl of *Cadogan*, General, and Commander in Chief of His Majesty's Forces, Master-General of the Ordnance, and Colonel of the first Regiment of Foot-Guards, attended by Col. *Otway* as Quarter-Master General, (in

the Place of Col. *Armstrong,* who being Surveyor General of the Ordnance, was oblig'd to attend at the *Tower,*) by Col. *Williamson,* Adjutant General, and by his Lordship's six Aids-de-Camp, *viz.*

Col. *Manning,*	Col. *Husk.*
Col. *Morton,*	Col. *Morgan.*
Capt. *Macartney,*	Lord *Carmichael.*

17. The eldest Company of Grenadiers of the first Regiment of Guards ; Capt. *Bagnel* led up the last Company.   Drums in the Centre ; Capt. *Herbert ;* and then Col. *Pitt* brought up the Rear.

All the Officers were in such Close Mourning as the Military Profession admits, the Colours furled and wrapp'd in Cypress, the Drums and Kettle-Drums cover'd with black Bays and Escutcheons, the Trumpets cover'd with Cypress, and having Banners of the Arms of the Deceas'd ; the Officers and Soldiers bearing their several Arms revers'd in a Funeral Posture.   All the Foot-Guards march'd eight a-breast, six deep.

18. Two chief Managers on Horseback, with Silk Scarves, and Velvet Furniture ; the Porter of the Herald's Office in a Gown of Cloth, with a black Staff in his Hand.
19. Eight Conductors in like Gowns, with black Staves in their Hands, to lead the Way, two and two.
20. Out-Pensioners of *Chelsea* Hospital, in Number 73, (answerable to the Years of his Grace's Age,) in Mourning Gowns, with the Badge of his Grace's Crest on one Arm, two and two, last single.
21. Three Trumpets on Horseback, with Banners of the Arms on the Standard, with Supporters.   Kettle-Drum in Mourning.   Three Trumpets more with like Banners.   Kettle-Drum in Mourning.
22. The Standard on a Lance, carried by Major *Gardiner,* supported by two Officers in their Military Mourning.
23. First Mourning Horse, cover'd with black Cloth, caparison'd with the same Arms as on the Standard, with Plumades before and behind, led by a Groom on Foot, with a Cap.   Then two Managers.
24. Forty Persons in Mourning Cloaks, Hatbands, and Gloves, on Horseback, two and two.   Then two Managers.
25. Three Trumpets, having Banners with the same Arms as the following Guidon.
26. *Rouge Croix,* Pursevant of Arms, in his Coat of Arms.
27. The Guidon on a Lance, carried by Major *Keightley,* supported by two Officers in their Military Mourning.
28. The second Mourning Horse, cover'd with black Cloth, caparison'd with the same Arms as on the Guidon, with Plumades, led by a Groom on Foot. Then two Managers.
29. Forty Persons in Mourning Cloaks, on Horseback.   Then two Managers.
30. Three Trumpets, having Banners with the same Arms as the Banner of *Woodstock.*
31. *Rouge Dragon,* Pursevant of Arms.
32. The Banner of *Woodstock* on a Lance, carried by Lieut.-Col. *Purcel,* supported by two Officers in their Military Mourning.
33. The third Mourning Horse, cover'd with black Cloth, caparison'd with the same Arms as on that Banner, with Plumades, led by a Groom on Foot. Then two Managers.
34. Forty Persons in Mourning Cloaks on Horseback.   Then two Managers.
35. Three Trumpets, having Banners of the Deceas'd as a Prince of the Empire.
36. Blue-Mantle Pursevant of Arms.
37. His Grace's Banner, as Prince of the *Empire,* on a Lance, carried by Lieut. Col. *Petit,* supported by two Officers in their Military Mourning.
38. The fourth Mourning Horse, cover'd with Cloth, caparison'd with the Arms of the Prince of the Empire, with Plumades, led by a Groom on Foot. Then two Managers.

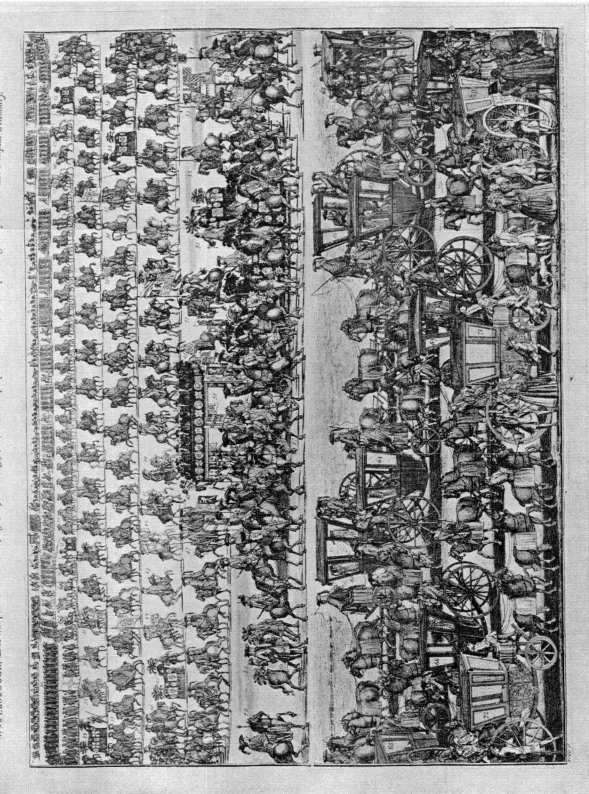

An Exact REPRESENTATION of the Solemn and Magnificent *Funeral PROCESSION* of His Grace *JOHN* late Duke of MARLBOROUGH, as it was perform'd on *Thursday* the 9th of *August*, 1722, with proper References, &c. explaining every Part of that *Pompous Solemnity*.

(From an Original Print in the British Museum.)

(See Key on p. 110.)

39. Forty Persons in Mourning Cloaks, on Horseback.   Then two Managers.
40. Mr. *Smith*, Secretary to the Deceas'd.
41. The Rev. Mr. *James* and Mr. *Cole*, Chaplains to the Deceas'd.
42. Three Trumpets in His Majesty's Livery, with Banners of the Order of the Garter.
43. Portcullis, Pursevant of Arms.
44. The Banner of the Order of the Garter on a Lance, carried by Col. *Pendlebury*, supported by two Officers in their Military Mourning.
45. The fifth Mourning Horse, cover'd with black Cloth, caparison'd with the same Arms as on the Banner of the Garter, with Plumades, led by a Groom on Foot.
46. Forty Persons in Mourning Cloaks on Horseback.
47. Mr. *Hodges* Chamberlain, Mr. *Lambert* Steward, Mr. *Humphreys* Treasurer, and Mr. *Pitts* Comptroler to the Deceas'd, with the white Staves of their Offices, a-breast.
48. Three Trumpets in His Majesty's Livery, having Banners with the same Arms as on the great Banner.
49. *Chester* Herald of Arms in his Coat.
50. The great Banner of his Grace's full Arms on a Lance, carried by Col. *Hopkey*, supported by two Officers in their Military Mourning.
51. The chief Mourning Horse, cover'd with Velvet, caparison'd with the said Arms, led by an Equerry, assisted by a Groom.
52. The Spurs and Gauntlets, carried by *Sommerset* Herald of Arms.
53. The Helmet and Crest, carried by *Lancaster* Herald of Arms.
54. The Target and Sword, carried by *Windsor* Herald of Arms.
55. His Grace's Surcoat of Arms, carried by *Norroy* King at Arms.
56. The Body, with the Suit of Armour, &c., as on the Bed of State, in an open Chariot, with Mr. *Ridley* and Mr. *Mitchel*, two Officers of his Grace's Bed-Chamber, sitting at the Head and Feet in close Mourning, bare-headed. The Chariot had four Columns, which bore up a black Velvet Canopy, lin'd with black Taffeta, with deep Gold Fringe, and Tassels at each Corner: On the Top with several black Plumes, with Trophies of War intermix'd with his Grace's Arms on the Eagle with Stars and Badges. The lower Part of the Chariot was adorn'd on both Sides with several Shields, representing his Grace's Victories and Conquests, under which was a Scroll with this Motto, *Bello hæc & plura.* The Chariot was drawn by eight Horses, cover'd with Velvet; the two first Horses caparison'd with the Arms of his Grace as Prince of the Empire; the next two with his Grace's full Arms, surrounded with the Garter, with the Supporters, surrounded with the Ducal Coronet; the next two with the same Arms as the first; and the two next his Body with his full Arms, surrounded with the Garter, as before.
57. On each Side of the said Chariot were five Captains in their Military Mourning, each carrying a Bannerol of the Arms of the Lineage of the Deceas'd. Each of the eight Horses were led by a Groom: The Coachman in deep Mourning. The Chariot was attended by a Party of Horse-Guards.
58. A Horse of State, caparison'd with Cloth of Gold, led with a silken Rein by Captain *Read*, his Grace's Master of the Horse, in his Military Mourning, walking on Foot, assisted by two Grooms on Foot.
59. *Garter* King at Arms, with the Rod of Office in his Right-Hand, and as Director of the Funeral.
60. His Grace the Duke of *Montague* chief Mourner, in deep Mourning, with the Collar of the Order of the Garter, with the Star of the Order on his Cloak, in the Dutchess Dowager's Coach and Six, Sir *Robert Rich*, his Train-Bearer, sitting over against him.
61. The Earls of *Godolphin* and *Sunderland* in the present Dutchess of *Marlborough's* Coach, as being Supporters to the chief Mourner, the former on the Right, and the latter on the Left.

	Right,	Left,
62.	The Duke of *Newcastle*, Ld. Chamb.	The Duke of *Sommerset*,
63.	The Duke of *Cleveland*.	The Duke of *Grafton*,
64.	The Duke of *St. Albans*.	The Duke of *Montrose*,
65.	The Duke of *Kent*.	The Duke of *Dorset*,
66.	The Earl of *Peterborough*.	The Earl of *Strafford*,

All (except the Duke of *Montrose*) having their Collars and Stars as Knights of the Garter; these Ten being Assistants to the chief Mourner.

67.	The Earl of *Cadogan*,	The Earl of *Leicester*.
68.	The Earl of *Bristol*,	The Earl of *Burlington*.

Who were to support the Pall in the Church.

69. A Horse of Honour richly caparison'd, led with a silken Rein by Capt. *Fish* in his Military Mourning, walking on Foot, assisted by two Grooms on Foot.
70. His Majesty's Coach.
71. His Royal Highness the Prince of *Wales's* Coach.
72. Then follow'd the Coaches of the Nobility, &c., according to their several Precedencies and Degrees.

Being arriv'd at the West-Door of the Abbey of *Westminster*, only those Persons who bore the Standard, Guidon, and Banners, above mention'd, and their Supporters, as also the Heralds, with his Grace's Secretary, two Chaplains, and his four White-Staff Officers, and those who carried the Banner-Rolls, enter'd the Church. The Chariot coming to the Door, the Armour was taken off, the Body carried into the Church, and rested near the Entrance, while the chief Mourner, his Supporters and Assistants, the Pall-Bearers, the Nobility, and others attending, alight out of their Coaches, the Organ playing during that Time. Having all enter'd into the Church, a Velvet Canopy being held over the Body, and the Pall-Bearers having taken up the Corners of the Pall, the Prebends in their rich Copes, and the Choir in their Surplices, placed themselves after the great Banner, and before the Heralds who carried the Trophies, and sung the Sentence in the Office for Burial, *I am the Resurrection and the Life*, and the two following Sentences, and continued singing till the Body was placed in King *Henry* the Seventh's Chapel. Then *Garter* King at Arms; the chief Mourner, with his two Supporters, Sir *Robert Rich* bearing his Train; the ten Assistants; and the Nobility according to their several Precedencies. In this Manner they proceeded through the south Isle of the Church, till they came near to the Choir; and then crossing into the north Isle, went up to King *Henry* the Seventh's Chapel, where the Body was rested on a Stand prepared for it in the middle of the Area. The Pall-Bearers were seated on Stools at each Corner of the Body: At the Head the chief Mourner with his two Supporters, one on each Hand; and his ten Assistants were seated five on each Side of the Body, the Nobility placing themselves in the Stalls. During the whole Solemnity in the Church, and also in this Chapel, the Banner-Rolls were held over the Body. An Altar, by the Dean's Order was erected at the Head of King *Henry* the Seventh's Tomb. After the Body was set down in the Chapel, an Anthem was perform'd with Vocal and Instrumental Musick, the Performers being placed on a Scaffold, hung from top to bottom with Mourning, erected for that purpose cross the Chapel, at the Entrance. The Anthem being ended, the Body was carried to a Vault at the Foot of King *Henry* the Seventh's Tomb, the Choir singing, *Man that is born of a Woman, &c.*, and the three following Sentences, and continued singing them till the Body was deposited in the Vault. Then the Lord Bishop of *Rochester*, Dean of *Westminster*, in his Cope, read, *For as much as it hath pleased Almighty God, &c.* Then the Choir sung, *I heard a voice from Heaven, &c.* The Service being ended, *Garter* King at Arms proclaim'd the Stile of the Deceas'd; and then his Grace's Officers breaking their Staves, deliver'd the Pieces to *Garter*, who threw them in upon the Coffin. During the Procession, and till the Body was deposited, the Guns of the *Tower* fir'd one every Minute. All the Troops and Artillery, being drawn up on the Parade, at a Signal given that the Body was deposited, fir'd three Volleys. Then they return'd to the Camp in *Hyde-Park*, the Horse first, the Foot next, and after them the Artillery.

LIST OF REGIMENTS WITH SUCCESSION OF COLONELS, 1714–1727

LIST OF REGIMENTS WITH SUCCESSION
OF COLONELS, 1714–1727

1st Troop of Life Guards.

John, Lord Ashburnham	7 July, 1713.
John, Duke of Montagu	10 May, 1715.
Henry, Lord Herbert	20 Sept. 1721.

2nd Troop of Life Guards.

George, Duke of Northumberland	4 Jan. 1712.
Algernon, Earl of Hertford	8 Feb. 1715.

3rd Troop of Life Guards.

Charles, Earl of Arran	2 Mar. 1703.
George, Lord Newburgh	8 Feb. 1715.

4th Troop of Life Guards.

John, Duke of Argyll	29 Sept. 1703.
John, Earl of Dundonald	11 Jan. 1715.
George, Lord Forrester	21 April, 1719.
Richard, Viscount Shannon	9 Mar. 1727.

1st Troop of Horse Grenadier Guards.

Hon. George Cholmondeley	4 Oct. 1693.
Richard, Viscount Lumley	8 Feb. 1715.
John, Earl of Westmorland	11 Dec. 1717.

2nd Troop of Horse Grenadier Guards.

George, Earl Marischal	5 Jan. 1714.
Henry, Earl of Deloraine	1 June, 1715.
George, Lord Forrester	17 July, 1717.
Hon. Henry Berkeley	21 April, 1719.

Royal Regiment of Horse Guards.

Charles, Earl of Peterborough	19 Aug. 1712.
John, Duke of Argyll	13 June, 1715.
Charles, Marquis of Winchester (Duke of Bolton)	8 Mar. 1717.

1st Dragoon Guards.

Hon. Henry Lumley	10 Aug. 1692.
Richard, Viscount Irwin	13 Dec. 1717.
Richard, Viscount Cobham	10 April, 1721.

2nd Dragoon Guards.

John Bland - - - - - - - -	1 Jan. 1712.
Thomas Pitt (Earl of Londonderry) - - -	9 Feb. 1715.
John, Duke of Argyll - - - - - -	26 Aug. 1726.

3rd Dragoon Guards.

Thomas, Viscount Windsor - - - -	18 May, 1712.
George Wade - - - - - - - -	19 Mar. 1717.

4th Dragoon Guards.

George Joceline - - - - - - -	20 Oct. 1713.
Sherington Davenport - - - - -	9 Feb. 1715.
Owen Wynne - - - - - - -	6 July, 1719.

5th Dragoon Guards.

George Kellum - - - - - - -	22 Dec. 1712.
Robert Napier - - - - - - -	27 May, 1717.

6th Dragoon Guards.

Leigh Backwell - - - - - - -	2 April, 1712.
Richard Waring - - - - - - -	15 Feb. 1715.
Richard, Viscount Shannon - - - -	17 June, 1721.
George Maccartney - - - - - -	9 Mar. 1727.

7th Dragoon Guards.

Charles Sybourg - - - - - -	12 Oct. 1713.
John Ligonier (Earl Ligonier) - - - -	18 July, 1720.

1st Royal Dragoons.

Thomas, Earl of Strafford - - - -	30 May, 1697.
Richard, Viscount Cobham - - - -	13 June, 1715.
Sir Charles Hotham, Bt. - - - -	10 April, 1721.
Humphry Gore - - - - - - -	12 Jan. 1723.

2nd Royal North British Dragoons (Scots Greys).

David, Earl of Portmore - - - - -	21 April, 1714.
Hon. James Campbell - - - - -	15 Feb. 1717.

3rd Dragoons (Hussars).

George, Lord Carpenter - - - - -	31 Dec. 1703.

4th Dragoons (Hussars).

William Evans - - - - - - -	12 Oct. 1713.

5th Royal Irish Dragoons.

Charles Ross - - - - - - -	16 July, 1695.
Thomas Sydney - - - - - -	8 Oct. 1715.

6th Inniskilling Dragoons.

Robert Echlyn	30 Dec. 1691.
John, Earl of Stair	4 Mar. 1715.

7th Dragoons (Hussars).

Hon. William Ker	10 Oct. 1709.

8th Dragoons (Hussars).

John Pepper	15 April, 1707.
Phineas Bowles	23 Mar. 1719.
Richard Munden	19 Nov. 1722.
Sir Robert Rich, Bt.	20 Sept. 1725.

9th Dragoons (Lancers).

Owen Wynne	22 July, 1715.
James Crofts	6 July, 1719.

10th Dragoons (Hussars).

Humphry Gore	22 July, 1715.
Charles Churchill	12 Jan. 1723.

11th Dragoons (Hussars).

Philip Honywood	22 July, 1715.

12th Dragoons (Lancers).

Phineas Bowles	22 July, 1715.
Phineas Bowles	23 Mar. 1719.

13th Dragoons (Hussars).

Richard Munden	22 July, 1715.
Sir Robert Rich, Bt.	19 Nov. 1722.
William Stanhope (Lord Harrington)	20 Sept. 1725.

14th Dragoons (Hussars).

James Dormer	22 July, 1715.
Clement Neville	9 April, 1720.

15th Dragoons (disbanded, 1718).

William Newton	22 July, 1715.

16th Dragoons (disbanded, 1718).

Charles Churchill	22 July, 1715.
Sir Charles Hotham, Bt.	17 July, 1717.

17th Dragoons (disbanded, 1718).

James Tyrrell - - - - - - - - 22 July, 1715.

18th Dragoons (disbanded, 1718).

Sir Robert Rich, Bt. - - - - - - 22 July, 1715.
James Crofts - - - - - - - - 17 July, 1717.

19th Dragoons (disbanded, 1718).

Richard Molesworth (Viscount Molesworth) - - - 22 July, 1715.

20th Dragoons (disbanded, 1718).

William Stanhope - - - - - - - 22 July, 1715.

21st Dragoons (disbanded, 1717).

Francis Palmes - - - - - - - 16 Feb. 1716.

22nd Dragoons (disbanded, 1717).

William, Viscount Mountjoy - - - - - 16 Feb. 1716.

23rd Dragoons (disbanded, 1717).

Thomas Ferrers - - - - - - 16 Feb. 1716.

24th Dragoons (disbanded, 1717).

Richard Morris - - - - - - - 16 Feb. 1716.

25th Dragoons (disbanded, 1717).

Lewis La Bouchetière - - - - - - 16 Feb. 1716.

Royal Regiment of Artillery.

Albert Borgard - - - - - - - 1 April, 1722.

1st Foot Guards (Grenadier Guards).

John, Duke of Marlborough - - - - - 26 Sept. 1714.
William Cadogan (Earl Cadogan) - - - - 18 June, 1722.
Sir Charles Wills, K.B. - - - - - - 26 Aug. 1726.

Coldstream Guards.

Charles Churchill - - - - - - 25 Feb. 1707.
William Cadogan (Earl Cadogan) - - - - 11 Oct. 1714.
Richard, Earl of Scarborough - - - - 18 June, 1722.

3rd Foot Guards (Scots Guards).

John, Earl of Dunmore - - - - - - 10 Oct. 1713.

1st Regiment of Foot (Royal Scots).

George, Earl of Orkney - - - - - - 1 Aug. 1692.

2nd Regiment of Foot (the Queen's).

Piercy Kirke - - - - - - - - 19 Sept. 1710.

3rd Regiment of Foot (the Buffs).

Archibald, Earl of Forfar - - - - - 14 April, 1713.
Charles Wills (Sir Charles Wills) - - - - 5 Jan. 1716.
Thomas, Earl of Londonderry - - - - 26 Aug. 1726.

4th Regiment of Foot (King's Own).

William Seymour - - - - - - - 12 Feb. 1702.
Henry Berkeley - - - - - - - 25 Dec. 1717.
Charles Cadogan (Lord Cadogan) - - - - 21 April, 1719.

5th Regiment of Foot (Fusiliers).

Thomas Pearce - - - - - - - 5 Feb. 1704.

6th Regiment of Foot.

Thomas Harrison - - - - - - - 14 June, 1708.
Robert Dormer - - - - - - - 7 Mar. 1716.
James Dormer - - - - - - - 9 April, 1720.

7th Regiment of Foot (Royal Fusiliers).

James O'Hara (Lord Tyrawly) - - - - 29 Jan. 1713.

8th Regiment of Foot (the King's).

John Richmond Webb - - - - - - 26 Dec. 1695.
Henry Moryson - - - - - - - 5 Aug. 1715.
Sir Charles Hotham, Bt. - - - - - 3 Dec. 1720.
John Pocock - - - - - - - 21 April, 1721.

9th Regiment of Foot.

William Steuart - - - - - - - 1 May, 1689.
Hon. James Campbell - - - - - - 27 July, 1715.
Hon. Charles Cathcart - - - - - - 15 Feb. 1717.
James Otway - - - - - - - 7 Jan. 1718.
Richard Kane - - - - - - - 25 Dec. 1725.

10th Regiment of Foot.

William, Lord North and Grey - - - - 15 Jan. 1703.
Henry Grove - - - - - - - 23 June, 1715.

11th Regiment of Foot.

John Hill - - - - - - - - -	8 May, 1705.
Edward Montague - - - - - - - -	13 July, 1715.

12th Regiment of Foot.

Richard Philipps - - - - - - - -	16 Mar. 1712.
Thomas Stanwix - - - - - - - -	25 Aug. 1717.
Thomas Whetham - - - - - - - -	22 Mar. 1725.

13th Regiment of Foot.

James, Earl of Barrymore - - - - -	15 Mar. 1702.
Stanhope Cotton - - - - - - - -	28 July, 1715.
Lord Mark Kerr - - - - - - - -	25 Dec. 1725.

14th Regiment of Foot.

Jasper Clayton - - - - - - - -	15 June, 1713.

15th Regiment of Foot.

Algernon, Earl of Hertford - - - - -	23 Oct. 1709.
Henry Harrison - - - - - - - -	8 Feb. 1715.

16th Regiment of Foot.

Hans Hamilton - - - - - - - -	23 June, 1713.
Richard, Viscount Irwin - - - - -	11 July, 1715.
John Cholmley - - - - - - - -	13 Dec. 1717.
Henry, Earl of Deloraine - - - - -	7 April, 1724.

17th Regiment of Foot.

Joseph Wightman - - - - - - - -	20 Aug. 1707.
Thomas Ferrers - - - - - - - -	28 Sept. 1722.
James Tyrrell - - - - - - - -	7 Nov. 1722.

18th Regiment of Foot (Royal Irish).

Richard Sterne - - - - - - - -	18 Feb. 1712.
William Cosby - - - - - - - -	24 Dec. 1717.

19th Regiment of Foot.

Richard Sutton - - - - - - - -	3 April, 1712.
George Grove - - - - - - - -	5 Aug. 1715.

20th Regiment of Foot.

John Newton - - - - - - - -	1 May, 1706.
Thomas Meredyth - - - - - - -	4 Oct. 1714.
William Egerton - - - - - - - -	7 July, 1719.

21st Regiment of Foot (Royal Scots Fusiliers).

Charles, Earl of Orrery	8 Dec. 1710.
George Maccartney	12 July, 1716.
Sir James Wood, Bt.	9 Mar. 1727.

22nd Regiment of Foot.

Roger Handasyde	3 April, 1712.

23rd Regiment of Foot (Royal Welsh Fusiliers).

Joseph Sabine	1 April, 1705.

24th Regiment of Foot.

Gilbert Primrose	9 Mar. 1708.
Thomas Howard	10 Sept. 1717.

25th Regiment of Foot.

William Breton	15 April, 1711.
Richard, Viscount Shannon	27 Jan. 1715.
John Middleton	17 June, 1721.

26th Regiment of Foot (Cameronians).

George Preston	24 Aug. 1706.
Philip Anstruther	3 May, 1720.

27th Regiment of Foot (Royal Inniskilling Fusiliers).

Thomas Whetham	29 Aug. 1702.
Richard Molesworth (Viscount Molesworth)	22 Mar. 1725.

28th Regiment of Foot.

Andrews Windsor	1 Oct. 1709.
William Barrell	27 Sept. 1715.

29th Regiment of Foot.

Lord Mark Kerr	7 Oct. 1712.
Henry Desney	25 Dec. 1725.

30th Regiment of Foot.

Charles Wills	13 Oct. 1705.
George, Lord Forrester	5 Jan. 1716.
Thomas Stanwix	17 July, 1717.
Andrew Bissett	25 Aug. 1717

31st Regiment of Foot.

Sir Harry Goring, Bt.	1 Mar. 1711.
Lord John Kerr	8 Sept. 1715.

32nd Regiment of Foot.

Jacob Borr - - - - - - - - - 5 Dec. 1704.
Charles Dubourgay - - - - - - - - - 28 June, 1723.

33rd Regiment of Foot.

George Wade - - - - - - - - - 9 June, 1705.
Henry Hawley - - - - - - - - - 19 Mar. 1717.

34th Regiment of Foot.

Thomas Chudleigh - - - - - - - - 30 Nov. 1712.
Robert Hayes - - - - - - - - 18 Feb. 1723

35th Regiment of Foot.

Richard Gorges - - - - - - - - 15 April, 1706.
Charles Otway - - - - - - - - 26 July, 1717.

36th Regiment of Foot.

Henry Desney - - - - - - - - 23 Oct. 1710.
William Egerton - - - - - - - - 11 July, 1715.
Sir Charles Hotham, Bt. - - - - - - - 17 July, 1719.
John Pocock - - - - - - - - - 2 Dec. 1720.
Charles Lanoe - - - - - - - - 21 April, 1721.

37th Regiment of Foot.

William Windress - - - - - - - - 1 May, 1710.
John, Earl of Westmorland - - - - - - 23 Aug. 1715.
Edward, Viscount Hinchinbroke - - - - - 11 Dec. 1717.
Hon. Robert Murray - - - - - - - 4 Aug. 1722.

38th Regiment of Foot.

Francis Alexander - - - - - - - - 27 Nov. 1711.
Richard Lucas - - - - - - - - - 23 Sept. 1717.

39th Regiment of Foot.

Nicholas Sankey - - - - - - - - 17 Mar. 1703.
Thomas Ferrers - - - - - - - - 11 Mar. 1719.
William Newton - - - - - - - - 28 Sept. 1722.

40th Regiment of Foot.

Richard Philipps - - - - - - - - 25 Aug. 1717.

41st Regiment of Foot (Invalids).

Edmund Fielding - - - - - - - - 11 Mar. 1719.

Six Regiments of Foot raised in England, in July, 1715, and disbanded in November, 1718.

Thomas Stanwix	22 July, 1715.
John Armstrong	17 July, 1717.
Sir Charles Hotham, Bt.	22 July, 1715.
Thomas Ferrers	17 July, 1717.
Alexander Grant of Grant, Junr.	22 July, 1715.
Maurice Nassau	17 July, 1717.
Charles Dubourgay	22 July, 1715.
John Pocock	22 July, 1715.
Richard Lucas	22 July, 1715.
Edward, Viscount Hinchinbroke	23 Sept. 1717.
Thomas Hales	11 Dec. 1717.

Eight Regiments of Foot raised in Ireland in February, 1716, and disbanded in the Summer of 1717.

Charles, Lord Tyrawly	16 Feb. 1716.
Francis, Marquis de Montandre	16 Feb. 1716.
David Creighton	16 Feb. 1716.
Sir John Wittewrong	16 Feb. 1716.
Edmund Fielding	16 Feb. 1716.
Theodore Vezey	16 Feb. 1716.
Richard Kane	16 Feb. 1716.
Maurice Nassau	16 Feb. 1716.

IRISH ESTABLISHMENT

LISTS OF OFFICERS IN THE REGIMENTS RAISED IN
FEBRUARY, 1716, AND DISBANDED IN JUNE, 1717;

ALSO

SUPPLEMENTARY COMMISSIONS IN ALL THE
REGIMENTS IN IRELAND, 1716–1718;
AND NON-REGIMENTAL COMMISSIONS, 1714–1718

LISTS OF OFFICERS IN THE REGIMENTS RAISED IN FEBRUARY, 1716, AND DISBANDED IN JUNE, 1717;

ALSO

SUPPLEMENTARY COMMISSIONS IN ALL THE REGIMENTS IN IRELAND, 1716–1718

LIEUT.-GENERAL FRANCIS PALMES'S REGIMENT OF DRAGOONS.

COMMISSIONS Sign'd by his Matie, and countersign'd by M^r. Sec^{ry}. Stanhope, dated at St. James's the 16th Feb^{ry}. 171⁵/₆ for a Reg^t. of Dragoons to be raised and commanded by Liev^t.-Gen^{ll}. Fran^s. Palmes. *h.*

CAPTAINS	LIEVTENANTS	CORNETS
Liev^t.-Gen^{ll}. Fran. Palmes,[1] Coll.	Willm. Entwisle,[7] Capt.-L^t.	Andrew Jack [9]
Elizeus Burgess,[2] L^t.-Coll^o.	William Hamilton	John Graham
William Blashford,[8] Maj^r.	Lodowick Peterson [8]	Charles Dering
Daniel Vere [4]	Henry D'Hourse	Edmond McNaghton [10]
Thomas Waldgrave [5]	Henry Harrison	Josiah Reed
Eliakim Studholme [6]	Richard Hanmaker	Thomas Knox

STAFF OFFICERS

Hugh Bolton—Chaplain
John Sutherland—Surgeon

[1] Appointed Capt. in Lord Cavendish's newly-raised Regt. of Horse (the present 7th D.G.), 31 Dec. 1688. Lt.-Col. of Col. Hugh Wyndham's Regt. of Horse, 2 Jan. 1694. Served several campaigns in Flanders and had command of a brigade. Col. of Horse, 1 July 1702. Brig.-Gen. at Blenheim. Maj.-Gen. 1 Jan. 1707. Lt.-Gen. 1 Jan. 1709. Envoy to the Duke of Savoy same year. Held the Colonelcy of the Carabiniers from 1 Oct. 1707 —2 April, 1712. D. 4 Jan. 1719.

[2] Appointed Brigdr. and eldest Lieut. in the 2nd Tp. of Life Guards, 13 March, 1693. Served under Gen. Stanhope in Spain. Lt.-Col. of Col. Lepell's Regt. of Dragoons, 8 Sept. 1711. In 1715 Secretary Stanhope offered Burgess the Governorship of Massachusetts, which the latter accepted. Countess Cowper, Lady of the Bedchamber to Caroline, Princess of Wales, thus refers to Col. Burgess in her *Diary* under date of 17 Feb. 1715 : "I told Baron Bernsdorff that my Lord had ordered me to speak to him to hinder Mr. Burgess from going Governor to New England. He is the most immoral man in the world ; was tried for the murder of two men, and was so common a swearer that the people,

I

who are rigid Puritans, and left the Kingdom before the Civil Wars, to enjoy their own way of worship in peace, would look at his being sent as a judgment upon them." The Agent for Massachusetts, being in London, advanced £1,000 to Col. Burgess to induce him to relinquish his appointment, and Col. Samuel Shute was given the Governorship.

[3] Served as Capt. in Col. Wm. Wolseley's Regiment of Inniskilling Horse at the battle of the Boyne and had a horse shot under him (*Records of the Inniskilling Dragoons*). His troop was reduced in 1691 (Petition for arrears dated 27 April, 1692, in *Treasury Papers*). Capt. in the Duke of Ormonde's Regt. of Horse in 1706 (*Add. MS.* 9762). Half-pay as Major of Lord Ashburnham's Regt. of Horse, 1713. Not in any List after 1717.

[4] Called *Weir* in former Comns. Served previously as Cornet, Lieut., and Capt. in the Earl of Hyndford's Dragoons, which Corps was disbanded in Ireland, 1712 or 1713, and the officers placed on half-pay.

[5] From half-pay. Had served in former reign as Capt. in Lord Mohun's Regt. of Foot (Comn. dated 25 May, 1707). Untraced after 1717.

[6] From half-pay. Served in former reign as Capt. in Lord Windsor's Regt. of Horse. Untraced after 1717.

[7] From half-pay. Served in former reign as Lieut. in Col. Samuel Masham's Regt. of Horse. Untraced after 1717.

[8] Served at Malplaquet as Ens. in the Earl of Orrery's Regt. Appointed Lieut. in Col. Ric. Lucas's Regt. of Foot in July, 1715. Capt.-Lieut. of the Earl of Harrington's Dragoons, 24 June, 1724. Capt. 1 July, 1734. Lieut.-Col. 13th Dragoons, 26 Feb. 1746. Retd. in 1747.

[9] and [10] Drawing half-pay in 1769.—*Army List*, 1769.

VISCOUNT MOUNTJOY'S REGIMENT OF DRAGOONS.

COMMISSIONS Sign'd by his Maṫiē, & countersign'd by M^r. Secret^{ry}. Stanhope, dated at S^t. James the 16th of February 171$\frac{5}{6}$ in the second yeare of his Reigne, for a Regim^t. of Dragoons to be forthwith raised and commanded by Willm. Lord Visco^t. Mountjoy. *h.*

CAPTAINS	LIEVTENANTS	CORNETS
W^m. L^d.Visc^t.Mountjoy,[1] Coll°.	Jam^s. Fleming, Capt.-L^t.	Adam Usher
Thom^s. Wilson,[2] Lt.-Coll°.	William Colhoon	William Charleton
Samuel Whitshed,[3] Maj^r.	William Witherington	Archibald Hamilton
Peter La Billiere	Richard Pearde [6] jun^r.	Charles Goullaine
Jacob Boyce	Stephen Ducasse [7]	Martin du Cloussy
William Titchborne (*sic*)[4]	Richard Pearde sen^r.	William Steuart

STAFF OFFICERS

Archibald Steuart (*sic*)[8]—Chaplain
John Darquier [9]—Chyrurgeon

SUPPLEMENTARY COMMISSION

Richard Tracey,[5] Esq. to be Capt. in room of Wm. Tichborne.
St. James's, 20 April, 1717.*j*

---

[1] Master-General of the Ordnance in Ireland.—See Vol. I., p. 372, note 1.
[2] Served previously as Lt.-Col. of Col. Richard Lucas's Regt. of Foot on the Irish Establishment, and had been on half-pay since 1713.
[3] See Vol. I., p. 155, note 4.
[4] Appears to have been second son of Baron Ferrard of Beaulieu. He md. a dau. of the 2nd Visct. Molesworth. Not in any subsequent List.
[5] Signed in England and issued in Ireland.—See Vol. I., p. 223, note 67.
[6] Of Carigeen, co. Cork. Will proved at Dublin 1772.
[7] D. in 1747. His will, proved at Dublin, describes him as "Lieut. of Dragoons on half-pay."
[8] The Rev. Archibald Stewart of Ballintoy, co. Antrim, d. in 1760. Will proved at Dublin.
[9] D. in 1732. Will proved at Dublin.

BRIGADIER-GENERAL THOMAS FERRERS'S REGIMENT OF DRAGOONS.

COMMISSIONS Sign'd by his Matie, and countersign'd by M^r. Secretary Stanhope, dated at S^t. James's the 16th Feb^ry. 171⁵/₆ for a Regiment of Dragoons to be raised and commanded by Brig^r.-Gen^ll. Thos. Ferrers. *h.*

CAPTAINS	LIEVTENANTS	CORNETS
Brig^r. Thos. Ferrers,[1] Coll°.	Robert King, Capt.-L^t.	William Wolsely [5]
George Whitehead,[2] L^t.-Coll°.	Richard Stedman	Edward Wilson
Gawin Hamilton,[3] Maj^r.	William Graham	William Berkeley [6]
George Barker	Joseph Dally	Reuben Roberts
Francis Browne	Thomas Fowke	Stephen Delfieu
S^r. Marcus Berresford [4]	James Carmichael	Mongo Campbell

STAFF OFFICERS

Peter Julian—Chaplain
Charles Melvill—Surgeon

SUPPLEMENTARY COMMISSIONS

James Miller to be Lieut. to Major Gawin (*sic*) Hamilton - - - - - - - - 5 July, 1716.*i*
Robert Smith,[7] Esq. to be Capt. in room of Francis Brown - - - - - - - - 13 March, 171⅞.*j*

---

[1] Appointed Ens. in the 1st Foot Guards, 24 Jan. 1692. Lieut. and Capt. 29 April, 1695. Capt.-Lieut. and Lt.-Col. 15 Feb. 1702. Wounded at Schellenberg. Capt. and Lt.-Col. 25 Aug. 1704. Bt.-Col. 25 Feb. 1705. Served at Ramillies and Malplaquet. Brig.-Gen. 1 Jan. 1710. Col. of a Regt. of Foot (late Hotham's), July, 1717 Half-pay in Nov. 1718. Col. 39th Foot, 11 March, 1719. Transferred to 17th Foot, 28 Sept. 1722. D. 20 Oct. 1722. He was of Bangaston, co. Pembroke. M.P. for Pembroke.—*Hist. Register,* 1722.

[2] Appointed Capt. in Sir Robt. Peyton's Regt. of Foot, 28 Feb. 1689. Served in Ireland 1690–91. Major, 17 March, 1694. Bt.-Lt.-Col. 29 Feb. 1704. Lt.-Col. of Col. Nich. Price's Regt. of Foot, 1 Sept. 1706. Half-pay, 1713. Not in any List after 1716.

[3] Appointed Capt. in the Earl of Hyndford's Regt. of Dragoons in 1702. Major of said Corps, 24 Aug. 1710. Serving as Major of Col. Phineas Bowles's Regt. of Dragoons in 1730. Out of the Army before 1740.

[4] Son of Sir Tristram Beresford, Bart. Succeeded his father in 1701. Created Baron Beresford and Visct. Tyrone, 4 Nov. 1720, in the Peerage of Ireland, and on 18 July, 1746, was made Earl of Tyrone.

[5] Appointed Cornet in Brigdr. John Pepper's Dragoons, 13 Feb. 1710. Out of said Regt. before 1715. Cornet in the King's Regt. of Horse (1st D.G.), 12 May, 1725. Out of the Army before 1740. Probably the eldest son of Capt. Richard Wolseley, M.P. for Carlow.

[6] Appointed Cornet in 8th Dragoons, 3 June, 1722. Lieut. 5 Dec. 1725. Serving in 1740.

[7] D. in 1720. Will proved at Dublin.

COLONEL RICHARD MORRIS'S REGIMENT OF DRAGOONS.

COMMISSIONS Sign'd by his Matie at S^t. James's the 16th of Feb^ry. 171$\frac{4}{5}$. Countersign'd by M^r. Secret^ry. Stanhope, in the second yeare of his Reign, for a Reg^t. of Dragoons to be raised forthwith, and commanded by Richard Morris Esqr. *h.*

CAPTAINS	LIEVTENANTS	CORNETS
Richard Morris,[1] Coll°.	Fred^k. Edmonds,[5] Capt.-L^t.	William Little
Robt. Johnson,[2] L^t. Coll°.	Robert Lambert	Chidley Blashford
George Weston,[3] Maj^r.	John Alexander	Edwd. Lovat Pearce [6]
Robert Moore	Thomas Toler	Francis Jemmat
William Whitaker	Henry Lawrence	Audley Mervin [7]
Lewis Delafaye [4]	William Flood	George Barnes [8]

STAFF OFFICERS

Nicholas Proude [9]—Chaplain
William Partinton [10]—Chyrurgeon

[1] A certain Richard Morris was appointed Capt. in Col. Edward Villiers's Regt. of Horse, 1 April, 1691. Col. Richard Morris was Capt. in Visct. Ikerrin's Regt. of Dragoons in 1706. Promoted Col. of last-named Corps, 24 Dec. 1710. Half-pay, 1712. D. in 1720 as Qr.-Mr.-Gen. and Barrack-Master-Gen. in Ireland. Will proved at Dublin.

[2] Capt. in Visct. Ikerrin's Regt. of Dragoons in 1706. Lt.-Col. 24 Dec. 1710. Half-pay in 1712. Untraced after 1716.

[3] Appointed 2nd Lieut. to the Grendr. Cy. in the Earl of Barrymore's Regt. of Foot, 1 Oct. 1694. Placed on half-pay as Major of Col. Edward Pearce's Regt. of Dragoons in 1712. He had served with last-named Corps in Spain under Lord Peterborough, but his Comns. therein are not forthcoming.

[4] From half-pay. Served in former reign as Capt. in Maj.-Gen. Nicholas Price's Regt. of Foot.

[5] See account of his services at the siege of Londonderry in Part II. of Vol. V. *English Army Lists and Commission Registers*, 1661–1714, p. 70, note 15. Wounded at Blenheim as Lieut. in 37th Foot.

[6] Appears to have been son of Capt. Sir Edward Lovet Pearce, Knt., whose will was proved at Dublin in 1734.

[7] Of Naul, co. Meath. Not in any subsequent List.

[8] Of Donore, co. Meath. D. in 1732. Will proved at Dublin.

[9] A descendant of Dr. Nicholas Proude, D.D., co. Meath.

[10] D. in 1725. Will proved at Dublin.

COLONEL LA BOUCHETIERE'S REGIMENT OF DRAGOONS.

COMMISSIONS Sign'd by his Matie, and countersign'd by M^r. Secretary Stanhope, dated at S^t. James's the 16th Feb^{ry}. 171$^5/_6$ for a Regiment of Dragoons to be raised and commanded by Charles La Bouchetiere Esqr. *h.*

CAPTAINS	LIEVTENANTS	CORNETS
Charles La Bouchetiere,[1] Coll°.	Francis Howard,[4] Capt.-Lt.	Gaspard du Petit Bosse
Robert Dalway,[2] Lt.-Coll°.	Thomas Williams	Henry Griffith
William Smith,[3] Maj^r.	Robert McMullan	John Carmichael
Sydenham Fowke [5]	John Knox	Daniel Cuningham
Daniel Harford [6]	John Maudsley	Melchior Guy Dickens [9]
James Norris [7]	Denny Cuffe [8]	Francis Godfrey

STAFF OFFICERS

Philip Fleury [10]—Chaplain
John Rapho —Surgeon

[1] This officer was given a Bt.-Colonelcy of Horse by William III. 22 Feb. 1694. Appointed Lt.-Col. of a Regt. of French Huguenot Dragoons in Portugal by Lord Galway 24 Feb. 1709. Taken prisoner at sea by the French *en route* for Portugal (see *S.P.D. Anne,* Bundle 22, No. 9). Aforesaid Corps was "broke" after the Peace of Utrecht, and the officers placed on half-pay. The will of " Col. Charles Janvre Bouchitière (*sic*) Lord of, in the Province of Poictu," was proved at Dublin in 1720.

[2] Appointed Cornet in Col. Fras. Langston's Regt. of Horse, 8 March, 1704. Capt. in Col. Sam. Masham's Regt. of Horse, 23 March, 1708. Lt.-Col. 1 Feb. 1713. Half-pay same year. Col. of the 13th Dragoons, 12 May, 1740. D. same year. Of Bellahill, co. Antrim.

[3] Capt. in Lord Ikerrin's Dragoons, 18 June, 1708. Major, 24 Dec. 1710. Half-pay, 1713. Untraced after 1716.

[4] A certain Francis Howard was appointed Capt. in the Rl. Regt. of Horse Guards, 21 July, 1719.

[5] See p. 156, note 17.

[6] Serving as Lieut. in the Duke of Ormonde's Regt. of Horse in 1706. Half-pay in 1712. Again placed on half-pay in 1717.

[7] A certain James Norris had served as Capt. in Pepper's Irish Dragoons previous to 1715.

[8] Half-pay, 1717. The will of " Denny Cuffe, Esq., of Sandhills, co. Carlow," was proved at Dublin in 1763.

[9] See his Comn. as Capt. in Brigdr. Jacob Borr's Regt. of Foot, 9 Aug. 1717, and note thereto.

[10] Will proved at Dublin in 1734.

LORD TYRAWLY'S REGIMENT OF FOOT.

COMMISSIONS Sign'd by his Majesty, and countersign'd by M[r]. Secretary Stanhope, dated at S[t]. James's the 16th Feb[ry]. 171$\frac{5}{6}$, for a Regiment of Foote to be forthwith raised, and commanded by Charles Lord Tyrawley. *h.*

CAPTAINS	LIEVTENANTS	ENSIGNES
Charles, Lord Tyrawley,[1] Coll[o].	Fred[k]. Gore, Capt.-Lievt.	Mathew Palen
William Sampson,[2] L[t].-Coll[o].	Thomas Drury	Charles Ohara
Peter Kerr,[3] Major	Thomas Doidge	Thomas Baxter
John Bolton [4]	John Lovell	Zachary Tiffen
Peter Combecrose [5]	Peter Delamander	Ralph Hadderton
John Concarret [6]	Jonathan Powell	James Knight
John Crow [7]	Edward Ford	Boyle Low
Christopher Dalston [8]	Thomas Steuart	Martin Skip
James Barry [9]	Robert Innes	Michael Norris
Abraham Swift [10] Gren[rs]. {	Robert Boyle	
	Thomas Bates	

STAFF OFFICERS

James Walsh—Chaplain
Lawrence Steele—Adjutant
James Macartney—Surgeon

[1] Charles O'Hara, of the county Mayo, is said to have come of an old Milesian family which had settled in the West of Ireland. He was appointed Lieut. in the Duke of York's Maritime Regt. of Foot, 14 Jan. 1678. Capt. of the Grendr. Cy. in said Corps before 1 March same year. Capt. in the Earl of Ossory's Regt. of Foot in the Dutch service, 15 Dec. 1679. Capt. in the 1st Foot Guards, 9 April, 1686. Lt.-Col. of do. with Bt. of Col. 16 March, 1689. Served in Flanders and was wounded at Landen. Brig.-Gen. 1 July, 1695. Col. of the Rl. Fusiliers, 12 Nov. 1696. Maj.-Gen. 9 March, 1702. Served at Cadiz and Vigo in 1702. Lt.-Gen. 1 Jan. 1704. Created Baron Tyrawly 10 Jan. 1706. Commanded the left wing of the allied forces at the battle of Almanza and was wounded. An Irish Privy Councillor in 1710. Gen. of the Foot in Ireland, 13 Oct. 1714. C.-in-C. in Ireland, 15 Oct. same year. D. 8 June, 1724. Bd. in St. Mary's Church, Dublin. See memoir of his son James, Lord Tyrawly, in this volume, pp. 25–32.

[2] Served in the late reign as Lt.-Col. of Col. David Creighton's Regt. of Foot Appears to have been of Inch, co. Donegal, and to have d. in 1732.

[3] Served previously as Major of Sir John Wittewrong's Regt. Half-pay, 1713. Lt.-Col. of the 13th Dragoons, 24 March, 1722. Comn. renewed in 1727. D. in 1744. Will proved at Dublin.

[4] From half-pay. Served in the former reign as Capt. in the Earl of Deloraine's Regt. of Foot. Untraced after 1717.

[5] Not in any subsequent List.

[6] D. in 1722. Described in his will, proved at Dublin, as "Capt. in Dormer's Regt. of Foot." His Comn. in latter Corps is not forthcoming owing to the registers between 1720–24 being lost.

[7] Not in any subsequent List.

[8] Served in the former reign as Lieut. in Col. Wm. Delaune's Regt. of Foot. Appears to have belonged to a Westmeath family. Untraced after 1717.

[9] A certain James Barry had served as Capt. in Stanwix's Regt. of Foot in former reign, and had been placed on half-pay in 1712.

[10] Served in the former reign as Capt. in Col. Edward Jones's Regt. of Foot. Half-pay, 1712. A.D.C. to Lord Tyrawly in 1718.

THE MARQUIS DE MONTANDRE'S REGIMENT OF FOOT.

COMMISSIONS Sign'd by his Majesty, and Countersign'd Mr. Secretary Stanhope, dated at St. James's the 16th Febry. 171⅚, for a Regimt. of foote to be raised and commanded by Francis Marquis de Montandre. *h.*

CAPTAINS	LIEVTENANTS	ENSIGNES
Marqs. de Montandre,[1] Collo.	Charles Brice, Capt.-Lieut.	Henry Lambert
William Berry,[2] Lt.-Collo.	William Hall	John Cassel
Josias Campbell,[3] Majr.	John Martin	Allen Julian
David Sutton [4]	John Hamilton	Samuel Davis
Robert Hawkins [5]	Henry Bolton	Theophilus Beaumont
John Baxter [6]	Gifford Craven [11]	John Bryand
James Hamilton [7]	Nicholas Ryland	John Barton
William Akie [8]	Philip Beranger	William Good
Edward Addison [9]	John Cunningham	Richard Bourne
James Abercrombie,[10] Grenrs.	{ William Watson { George Graham	

STAFF OFFICERS

William Somerfield—Chaplain
John Cassell—Adjutant
Intr. 12 March, 17¹⁶⁄₁₇. Stephen Cassan—Surgeon

SUPPLEMENTARY COMMISSION

Wm. Dalmas [12] to be Adjt. - - - - - - - 14 May, 1717.*j*

[1] See special memoir in Vol. I., pp. 39–47.

[2] Served as Lt.-Col. of Col. Wm. Wolseley's Regt. of Inniskilling Horse, 1689–97. Half-pay, 1697–1704. Major of Lord Henry Scott's Regt. of Foot in March, 1704. Out of said Regt. when it was disbanded in 1712. D. in 1717. Will proved at Dublin.

[3] Appointed Lieut. in Col. Skeffington's Londonderry Regt. of Foot in Jan. 1689. Served during the defence of Derry. Capt. of the Grendr. Cy. in Michelburne's (late Skeffington's) Regt. 12 March, 1692. Capt. in Visct. Charlemont's Regt. 1 March, 1702. Served with said Corps (36th Foot) in the Expedition to Cadiz and in the West Indies. Served subsequently in Spain with Visct. Dungannon's Regt., and was promoted Major of Montandre's Regt. (late Dungannon's) in 1706. Half-pay in 1713 as a Bt.-Lt.-Col. D. in 1722. Will proved at Dublin. His widow Lettice Campbell, in her petition to the Lords of the Treasury, stated that "her husband Lt.-Colonel Josias Campbell served the Crown above 30 years, and in the late war in Spain he expended £310 in the public service, which was not repaid, and £100 was due to him for loss of his baggage."—*Treasury Papers,* Vol. CCLXV., No. 39.

[4] Had served as Capt.-Lieut. in Lord Dungannon's Regt. of Foot in former reign. Untraced after 1717.

[5] Not in any subsequent List.

[6] Had served as Capt. in the Marquis de Montandre's former Regt. in 1711. Half-pay, 1713. Untraced after 1717.

[7] Untraced among many officers of this name.

[8] Served in Col. Hans Hamilton's Regt. in 1706. Of Fea, co. Tyrone. D. in 1734. Will proved at Dublin.

[9] Drawing half-pay in 1722.

[10] Half-pay in 1717. See his Comn. as Capt. in Col. Edward Montague's Regt. of Foot under date of 3 July, 1719, and note on this officer's war services.

[11] The will of "Jefford (*sic*) Craven of Cork, gent.," was proved at Dublin in 1723.

[12] Not in any subsequent List.

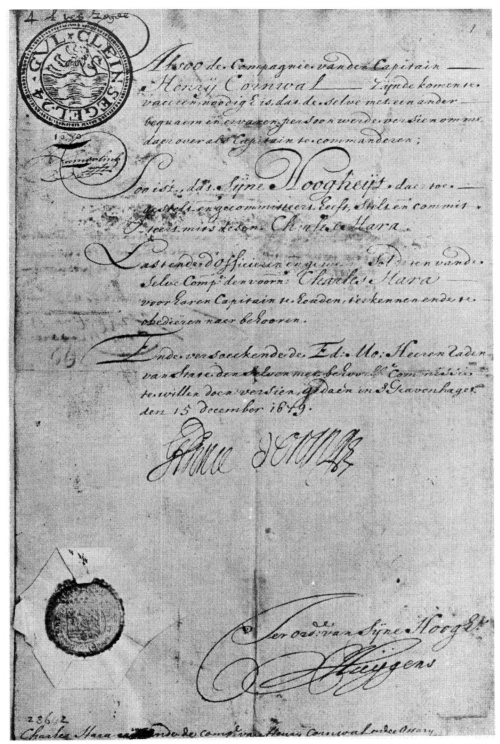

COMMISSION SIGNED BY THE PRINCE OF ORANGE APPOINTING CHARLES O'HARA CAPTAIN IN THE EARL OF OSSORY'S REGT. IN HOLLAND, 15th DECEMBER, 1679.

(See p. 135, note 1.)

(*From the Original in the British Museum.*)

BRIGADIER-GENERAL DAVID CREIGHTON'S REGIMENT OF FOOT.

COMMISSIONS Sign'd by his Majesty, and Countersign'd by M[r]. Secretary Stanhope, dated at S[t]. James's the 16th Feb[ry]. 171$\frac{4}{5}$, for a Regiment of foote to be raised and commanded by Brig[r]. David Creighton. h.

CAPTAINS	LIEVTENANTS	ENSIGNES
Brig[r]. David Creighton,[1] Coll[o].	Jam[s]. Hamilton, Cap[t].-L[t].	Lucius Henry Hibbins
John West, Liev[t].-Coll[o].	——	Michael Sampson
Patrick Fox,[2] Major	Lewis Meares	Richard Auchmooty
Robert Sampson [3]	George Graham	Algernoon Warren
Docwra Brooks [4]	Nicholas Budiani [10]	Samuel Morris
Benjamin Malide [5]	William Montgomery	John Nicholas
Abel Castlefrank [6]	Mathew Suberville	Wittle Frewin
Robert Saunders [7]	Charles Cotton	Edward Williams
Samuel Boyde [8]	Simon Sandys	Charles Turner
John Warburton,[9] Gren[rs]. {	{ John Crofton { Edward Wynne	

STAFF OFFICERS

Richard Weight—Chaplain
Mathew Bowen—Adjutant
Int[r]. 14 March, 171$\frac{4}{5}$.   Alexander Shurelock [11]—Surgeon

SUPPLEMENTARY COMMISSIONS

Ambrose Burrowes to be Lieut. to Lt.-Col. John West - 16 Feb. 171⁵/₆.*j
Do. to be Adjt. - - - - - - - ,, ,, ,, j
Mathew Bowen to be Lieut. to Capt. John Warburton - 4 May, 1717.j
Abraham Hamilton to be Adjt. - - - - - ,, ,, ,, j

[1] Son of Col. Abraham Creighton and father of Abraham Creighton, created Baron Erne, 15 July, 1768. David Creighton greatly distinguished himself in 1689 by his gallant defence of Crum Castle, co. Fermanagh, against James II.'s forces. Capt. in Col. Thos. Brudenell's Regt. of Foot in March, 1702. Served in Spain. Lt.-Col. before 1 Dec. 1706, on which date he was made Bt.-Col. by Lord Peterborough at Valencia. Succeeded Col. Toby Caulfield as Col. of a Regt. of Foot, 2 Aug. 1708. Brig.-Gen. 12 Feb. 1711. Half-pay as Col. in 1712. Promoted Maj.-Gen. by George I. 15 March, 1727. D. 9 June, 1728.

[2] Of Durrow, King's County. Appointed 1st Lieut. of the Grendr. Cy. in Lord Charlemont's Regt. 23 April, 1694. Bt.-Major, 10 Jan. 1706. Major of Col. D. Creighton's Regt. 16 Dec. 1709. Half-pay in 1712. D. in 1734. Will proved at Dublin same year.

[3] In April, 1708, this officer was appointed Ens. in Col. Toby Caulfield's Regt. Capt. 24 April, 1709. Half-pay, 1712. Serving as Capt. in Col. Johnson's Regt. of Foot in Jan. 1740. Major, 23 April same year. Lt.-Col. 7 June, 1741. Of Hillbrook, co. Dublin. D. 1764. Will proved at Dublin.

[4] Of Newbridge, co. Dublin. D. 1731. Will proved at Dublin. Called "Brooke" in said document.

[5] Appointed Capt. in Lord Ikerrin's Regt. of Foot in 1706.   Half-pay, 1712.   Untraced after 1717.

[6] Appointed Lieut. in Lord Ikerrin's Regt. of Foot in 1706.   Half-pay, 1712.   Untraced after 1717.

[7] Not in any subsequent List.

[8] Appointed Capt. in Col. Phineas Bowles's Regt. of Foot, 23 Jan. 1712.   Half-pay same year.   Untraced after 1717.

[9] Appointed Lieut. in Lord Ikerrin's Regt. of Foot in 1706.   Half-pay, 1712.   Untraced after 1717.

[10] This officer's Comn. as Lieut. in the Army is given as 1 Jan. 1706 in the Gradation List for 1730, in which latter year he was in Disney's Regt. (29th Foot).   Capt. in 29th Foot, 21 Jan. 1738.   Serving in 1740.

[11] Drawing half-pay in 1769.—*Army List*, 1769.

SIR JOHN WITTEWRONG'S REGIMENT OF FOOT.

COMMISSIONS Sign'd by his Majesty, and Countersign'd by M^r. Sec^{ry}. Stanhope, dated at S^t. James's the 16th February 171$\frac{5}{6}$, for a Regim^t. of foote to be raised and commanded by S^r. John Wittewrong Barr^t. *h*

CAPTAINS	LIEVTENANTS	ENSIGNES
S^r. John Wittewrong,[1] Bar^t., Coll°.	Robt. Parry, Capt.-Lieut.	Nathaniel Kerr
Rich^d. Cole,[2] Liev^t.-Coll°.	Benjam^n. McDowell	Christopher Simpson
Samuel Francis,[3] Major.	Samuel Hacket	Charles Fox [10]
George Gregory [4]	Barnet Connolly	Philip Haynes
David Cugley	Richard Hunter	John Gugleman [12]
James Painter [5]	Robert Brereton	Christopher Hewet-
Alexander Cumming [6]	George Webb	John Brahon [son [11]
John Burgeaud [7]	Alexander McWatty	Cuthbert Wade
John Silliock [8]	John Nelson	Thom^s. Bustaquet
James Menzies,[9] Gren^{rs}. {	{ Andrew Kerr { David Fairfield	

STAFF OFFICERS

John Shadwell—Chaplain
John Spicer—Adjutant
Thomas Collins—Surgeon

SUPPLEMENTARY COMMISSIONS

Charles Reding (*sic*) [13] to be Lieut. to Capt. James Menzies' Grenadier Cy. - - -	—	14 May, 1716.*i*
John Gore to be Ens. to Capt. Alex. Cumins	—	14 June, ,, *i*
George Wittewronge to be Lieut. to Major Samuel Francis - - - -	Hampton Court, 28 Aug. ,, *i*
Samuel Harrison, to be Ens. to Sir John Wittewrong's own Cy. - - -	St. James's, 15 Nov. ,, *i*

[1] 3rd Bart. of Stantonbury, Bucks. He had been Col. of a Regt. of Foot (disbanded in 1712) in late reign. Half-pay in Nov. 1718. D. 30 Jan. 1722.

[2] This officer had served as a Subaltern in Col. Edward Dutton Colt's Regt. in the West Indies in 1695. Subsequently served on board the Fleet as Lieut. in Dutton Colt's Regt. of Marines. Capt. in Lucas's Regt. (34th Foot) in 1704. Bt.-Lt.-Col. in 1712. Lt.-Col. of Chudleigh's Regt. (34th Foot) 1 Aug. 1713. Half-pay on reduction of Wittewrong's Regt. in Nov. 1718. D. in 1729. Will proved at Dublin.

[3] Appointed 1st Lieut. to an Indep. Cy. in Newfoundland, 6 March, 1701. Bt.-Capt. 10 Feb. 1703. Capt. in Lord Henry Scott's Regt. of Foot in 1704. Major of Col. Nich. Price's Regt. 1 Sept. 1706. Half-pay from said Corps in 1713. Again placed on half-pay in Nov. 1718. D. in 1745. Will proved at Dublin.

[4] Had served as Capt. in Lord Slane's Regt. of Foot from 1708 to 1712. Untraced after 1717.

[5] Had served in the former reign as Capt. in Col. Hans Hamilton's Regt. (34th Foot). Untraced after 1717.

[6] Believed to be identical with Capt. Alex. Cumming on half-pay from Grant's Regt., whose remarkable career is detailed at length in Vol. VI. of *English Army Lists*, p. 215, note 5.

[7] Served in former reign as Capt. in Brigdr. Grant's Regt. of Foot. Believed to be identical with " John Burjaud, of Kilmollog, King's County, Esq.," whose will was proved at Dublin in 1753.

[8] Appointed a Sub-Engineer, 3 May, 1705. Capt. in Col. Chas. Churchill's Regt. of Marines, 12 July, 1711. Served in Portugal, 1707 ; in Flanders, 1710 ; at Vigo, 1719. Capt. in 34th Foot, 25 Dec. 1726. D. on active service at Jamaica in June, 1741.

[9] Served previously as Capt. in Brigdr. Grant's Regt. of Foot. Probably a son of Sir Alex. Menzies of Castle Menzies, Bart.

[10] and [11] Drawing half-pay in 1769.—*Army List*, 1769.

[12] See his Comn. on p. 272, and note thereto.

[13] *Reading.* His will, as of " Ballycommon, King's County, gent.," was proved at Dublin in 1721.

COLONEL EDMUND FIELDING'S REGIMENT OF FOOT.

COMMISSIONS Sign'd by his Majesty, and Countersign'd by Mr. Secretary Stanhope, dated at St. James's the 16th February 171⅚ for a Regimt. of foote to be raised for his Mats. Service, & commanded by Edmund Fielding Esqr. *h.*

CAPTAINS	LIEVTENANTS	ENSIGNES
Edmund Fielding,[1] Collo.	Thoms. Theaker, Capt.-Lt.	Toby Caulfield
Thoms. Bellasyse,[2] Lievt.-Collo.	Walter Bagnold	William Budgell
George Purdon,[8] Major	Harry Meggs	Emanuel Harris
Anthony Jephson [4]	William Markham	John Bullock
Stanhope Yarborough [5]	Theophilus Creamer	Leonard Stamford
Jonathan Munsell (*sic*)[6]	Thomas Bulkely	Thomas Ballard
Francis Denty [7]	Paul Labastide	William Hull
Christopher Harrison [8]	Benson Cushen	Haestreet James [11]
George Wingfield [9]	Henry Gill	David Douglass
Julius Stirke,[10] Grenrs.	{ William Coleman	
	{ John Lunden	

STAFF OFFICERS

William Piers—Chaplain
William Coleman—Adjutant
Peter La Plant—Chyrurgeon

SUPPLEMENTARY COMMISSION

Henry Brook to be Ens. to Capt. Ant. Jephson - - 29 March, 1716.*i*

---

[1] Appointed Ens. in the 1st Foot Guards, 15 Dec. 1696. Capt. in Brig.-Gen. Webb's Regt. (8th Foot) before 1704. Fought at Blenheim. Major of Lord Tunbridge's Regt. of Foot, 12 April, 1706. Succeeded Col. Brasier in command of a Regt. of Foot in Ireland, 1 Aug. 1709. Half-pay, 1713. Col. of a newly-raised Regt. of Foot (41st), 11 March, 1719. Brig.-Gen. 16 March, 1727. Maj.-Gen. 8 Nov. 1735. Lieut.-Gen. 2 July, 1739. D. 20 June, 1741. He was third son of the Rev. John Fielding, Canon of Salisbury, and father of Henry Fielding, the novelist.

[2] Appointed Ens. in Sir Henry Bellasyse's Regt. 1 July, 1696. Lieut. 8 April, 1698. Capt. of the Grendr. Cy. in Lord Henry Scott's Regt. in Ireland, March, 1704. Lt.-Col. of do. before 1713, when he was placed on half-pay. On the reduction of Fielding's Regt. in Nov. 1718, was again placed on half-pay.

[8] Lieut. in Lord Lucas's newly-raised Regt. of Foot, 10 March, 1702. Capt. 6 March, 1703. Bt.-Major, 1 Jan. 1712. Major of aforesaid Corps, 1 Aug. 1713. Half-pay same year. D. in 1755. Described in his will as of Dysert, co. Cork.

[4] Of Mallow, co. Cork. Will proved in Dublin in 1756.

[5] Appointed Capt. in Maj.-Gen. Brudenell's Regt. of Foot, 20 Oct. 1707.

[6] Not in any subsequent List.

[7] Do.

[8] D. in 1727 as Capt. in Brigdr. W. Newton's Regt. of Foot. Will proved at Dublin.

[9] Served as Capt. in the Earl of Orrery's Regt. of Foot at Malplaquet. This officer came over with the Prince of Orange in 1688, and was placed on the Irish Half-pay List in 1697. Was an applicant that year for the vacant Governorship of Montserrat. Half-pay, 1713.

[10] Served in the former reign as Capt. in Col. Chas. Churchill's Regt. of Marines. Half-pay, 1713. Untraced after 1717.

[11] Appointed 2nd Lieut. in Col. Chas. Churchill's Marines, 6 Sept. 1711. Attained the rank of Major in Gen. Stanwix's Regt. of Foot, and was drawing half-pay in 1749.

BRIGADIER-GENERAL THEODORE VESEY'S REGIMENT OF FOOT.

COMMISSIONS Sign'd by his Majesty, and countersign'd by M^r. Secretary Stanhope, dated at S^t. James's, the 16th Feb^{ry}. 1714/5, for a Regiment of Foote to be raised, and commanded by Brigad^r. Theodore Vesey. *h.*

CAPTAINS	LIEVTENANTS	ENSIGNES
Brig^r. Theodore Vesey,[1] Coll^o.	Math^w. Norgate,[11] Capt.-Liev^t.	Edward Griffith
Rich^d. Ea. of Cavan,[2] Liev^t.-Coll^o.	Mathew Floyer	John Vernon
Dudley Cosby,[3] Major.	John St. Clair	John Norris
James Lloyd [4]	Allen Johnson	George Maxwell
John Montague [5]	Benjamin Theaker	Randal Berry
Maurice Wynne [6]	Marcus Smith [13]	Thomas Ashton
John Darby [7]	William Wright	John McCausland
Barnaby Purcell [8]	Thomas Griffeth	Charles Collins
Robert Lundy [9]	Joseph Lambert	Durand du Therond
Francis Cope,[10] Gren^{rs}.	{ Walter Walsh { Henry Francfort	

STAFF OFFICERS

Andrew Nixon—Chaplain
Edward Griffeth—Adjutant
William Dobbs—Surgeon

SUPPLEMENTARY COMMISSION

George Hungerford,[12] Esq. to be Capt. in room of
John Darby -   -   -   -   -   -   -   - 28 Jan. 171⁶/₇. *i*

---

[1] Appointed Ens. in Col. John Foulkes's Regt. of Foot, 8 Oct. 1691. Lieut. of Grendrs. 30 Oct. 1693. Served in the Martinique Expedition of 1693. Lieut. of Grendrs. in Prince George of Denmark's Regt. of Foot (3rd Buffs), 3 March, 1695. Capt. in Maj.-Gen. Gustavus Hamilton's Regt. before 1705. Col. of a Regt. of Foot in Spain (aftds. disbanded), 1710. Brig.-Gen. 30 Oct. 1735. Gov. of the Rl. Hospital, Kilmainham, at the time of his death in 1736. Believed to have been son of the Rev. Theodorus Vesey of Kinsale who d. in 1682.

[2] As Richard, Lord Lambert, this officer was appointed Lieut. in Visct. Charlemont's Regt. of Foot, 23 April, 1694. Capt. in Maj.-Gen. Gustavus Hamilton's Regt. of Foot, 10 March, 1702. Succeeded his father as 4th Earl of Cavan same year. Lieut.-Col. Fielding's Regt. of Foot, 1 Aug. 1708. Half-pay from Vesey's Regt. in Nov. 1718. Lt.-Col. of Dormer's Regt. (6th Foot) before 1726. Sold the Lt.-Colonelcy to John Murray in May, 1726.—*Dublin Journal*, 7 May, 1726.

[3] See p. 342, note 5. in Vol. I.

[4] Not in any subsequent List.

[5] Appointed Capt. and Lt.-Col. in 1st Foot Guards, 13 March, 1718. Lt.-Col. of the Rl. Irish Regt. of Foot. 20 Nov. 1719.

[6] D. in 1738. A copy of his will in the Dublin Record Office describes him as "Maurice Wynne of Carnarvon, Esq."

[7] Served at Malplaquet as Capt. in the Earl of Orrery's Regt. of Foot.   Appointed 2nd Major and Bt.-Col. in 3rd Foot Guards in Nov. 1723. Serving in 1728. D. in 1736.

[8] Had been Fort Major of Duncannon in former reign. Untraced after 1717.

[9] Believed to have been son of Col. Robert Lundy, or Lundie, of Londonderry notoriety. Had served in Gen. Tidcomb's Regt. of Foot in former reign. Untraced after 1717.

[10] A certain Francis Cope was appointed Lieut. and Capt. 3rd Foot Guards, 3 March, 1727. Out before 1740.

[11] Served subsequently as Capt.-Lieut. in Hargrave's Regt. of Foot. D. before 1735, in which year his widow was in receipt of a pension of £20 per annum. Latter's will proved at Dublin, in 1754, as "widow of Capt.-Lieut. Mathew Norgate of Hargrave's Regt."

[12] Appointed Major of the 13th Dragoons, 20 June, 1739. Out of said Corps before 1748. A certain George Hungerford of Studley, co. Wilts., d. in 1764.

[13] Appointed Capt. in the Royal Fusiliers, 4 Nov. 1724. Major, 13 Feb. 1741. Lt.-Col. 3 June, 1752. Col. 60th Foot, 11 Nov. 1761. Maj.-Gen. 10 July, 1762. D. in Nov. 1768.

COLONEL RICHARD KANE'S REGIMENT OF FOOT.

COMMISSIONS Sign'd by his Majesty, and countersign'd by M^r. Secretary Stanhope, dated at S^t. James's, the 16th Feb^{ry}. 171$\frac{5}{6}$ for a Regiment of foote to be raised, and commanded by Richard Kane Esqr. h.

CAPTAINS	LIEVTENANTS	ENSIGNES
Richard Kane,[1] Coll^o.	Brook Plukenet,[11] Capt.-L^t.	William Hamilton
James Allen,[2] L^t.-Coll^o.	Theophilus Taylor	Thomas Pennefather[14]
John Echingham Chichester,[3] Maj^r.	Archibald Wilson	Robert Ponsonby
John Walsh[4]	William Ford	Thomas Mounsey
William Wansborough[5]	William Supple	[Peter] Laprimaudaye[15]
Thomas Sinnot[6]	Andrew S^t. Leger	Robert Fowke
George Gledstanes[7]	John Mowberry	Robert Cooke
William Norcliffe[8]	Maurice Crosby	George Palfrey
Amateur Borough[9]	George Burston	John Preston
Solomon White,[10] Gren^{rs}. {	Samuel Lane / John Dyos	

STAFF OFFICERS

Samuel Webber—Chaplain
Willm. Wansborough—Adjutant
John McNeale—Surgeon

SUPPLEMENTARY COMMISSIONS

David Fairfield,[12] Esq. to be Capt. in room of John Walsh   14 May, 1716.i
Wm. Fullerton,[13] Esq. to be Capt. in room of Wm. Norcliffe   26 Mar. 1717.j

---

[1] Appointed Lieut. in Col. Skeffington's Londonderry Regt. of Foot in 1689 and served during the defence of Derry.   Lieut. in the Earl of Meath's Regt. of Foot (18th) 12 Nov. 1692.   Capt. 25 Sept. 1693.   Wounded at the siege of Namur.   Major, 24 Aug. 1704. Wounded at Blenheim.   Bt.-Lt.-Col. 1 Jan. 1706.   Commanded the Rl. Irish Regt. at Malplaquet.   Col. of a Regt. of Foot (late Maccartney's), 8 Dec. 1710.   Said Corps was disbanded in 1712.   Lt.-Gov. of Minorca, 16 Aug. 1712.   Comndt. of Gibraltar in 1720. Lt.-Gov. of do. 10 July, 1725 (Comn. signed by George I. at Pyrmont).   Col. of the 9th Foot, 25 Dec. 1725.   Lt.-Gov. of Minorca in 1730.   Brig.-Gen. 1 Nov. 1735.   D. 20 Dec. 1736 (M.I. in Westminster Abbey).   Bd. in St. Philip's Church, Minorca.   He was author of Narrative of Campaigns in the Reigns of William III. and Queen Anne, and New System of Exercise for a Battalion of Foot, published 1745.
[2] Had served as Lt.-Col. to Col. Kane's former Regt.   Probably kinsman to Sir John Allen of Dublin, who was created Lord Allen in 1717.
[3] His will, proved at Dublin in 1720, describes him as " of the parish of St. James, Westminster."
[4] D. or left the Regt. in May, 1716.
[5] Served in former reign as Capt. in Visct. Mountjoy's Regt. of Foot.   Half-pay in 1717. Major Rl. Welsh Fusiliers, 25 Dec. 1722.   Master of Kilmainham Hospital, 1737-39.
[6] Served in the former reign as Capt. in Col. Wm. Delaune's Regt. of Foot.   D. in 1726. Will proved at Dublin.
[7] Of Lisboy, co. Tyrone.   D. 1739.   Will proved at Dublin.

[8] See his Comn. as Cornet in the Princess Anne of Denmark's Regt. of Dragoons in Vol. IV., *English Army List*, p. 14, and note thereto. Capt. in Hawley's Regt. (33rd), 23 March, 1717. Left in Aug. 1717.

[9] Served at Malplaquet as Lieut. in the Earl of Orrery's Regt. of Foot. Capt. in Sir Richard Temple's Regt. of Foot, 1 April, 1710. Serving as Capt. in Col. Thos. Howard's Regt. of Foot in 1728. Called "Bouchereau" in the 1702–06 Army List.

[10] Appointed Capt. in Col. Wm. Southwell's Regt. (6th Foot), 20 May, 1714. Drawing half-pay in 1722.

[11] Deputy Commissary of Musters in Ireland, 18 Jan. 1718. D. in 1723. Will proved at Dublin.

[12] D. in 1733. Will proved at Dublin.

[18] Served in former reign as Capt. in Grant's Regt.

[14] Probably son of Col. Kingsmill Pennefather, on whom the Compsey and other estates were settled in 1730. (See Burke's *Landed Gentry*, under Pennefather of Lakefield, co. Tipperary.) This Thos. Pennefather was appointed Capt. in the Earl of Orkney's Regt., 22 Oct. 1723. Serving in 1737. Out before 1740.

[15] See under Warrant Commissions on p. 259, note 3.

COLONEL MAURICE NASSAU'S REGIMENT OF FOOT.

COMMISSIONS Sign'd by his Maᵗⁱᵉ at Sᵗ. James's the 16ᵗʰ of Febʳʸ. 171⅚, Countersign'd by Mʳ. Secʳʸ. Stanhope, for a Regᵗ. of foote to be forthwith raised for his Matiᵉˢ Service, & comanded by Morris (sic) Nassau, Esqʳ. h.

CAPTAINS	LIEVTENANTS	ENSIGNES
Morris (sic) Nassau,[1] Collᵒ.	Willᵐ. Cox, Capt.-Lievt.	——— Sᵗ. Leger
Lewis de la Boiragon,[2] Lᵗ.-Collᵒ.	John Ardes	John Johnson
Richᵈ. Brooks,[3] Major	Richard Abbot	Martin Needham
Stephen Tempie [4]	William Gurney	Thomas Turnbull
Walter Wolfe [5]	Benjamin Billingsly	Richard Burren
John Eyres [6]	Joseph Hill	Benjamⁿ. Willington [14]
Marsh Harrison [7]	James Rietfield	William Whitshed
Richard Rogerson [8]	Thomas Fitzgerrald	Charles O'Brien
Thomas Steuart [9]	William French	Thomas Browne
Michael Cole,[10] Grenʳˢ.	{ James Ducasse	
	Robert Jordan	

STAFF OFFICERS

Gamaliel Capell—Chaplain
—Adjutᵗ.
Daniel Gates—Surgeon

SUPPLEMENTARY COMMISSIONS.

Edmond Lesley,[11] Esq. to be Capt. in room of Thomas Stewart - - - - - - - - 5 June, 1716.i
Wm. Rynes to be Ens. to Capt. Stephen Tempie - - 14 ,, ,, i
Joseph Still to be Adjt. - - - - - - 11 July, ,, i
Banastre Maynard,[12] Esq. to be Capt. in room of Richard Rogerson - - - - - - - - 29 Aug. ,, i
Peter Brisac,[13] Esq. to be Capt. in room of Stephen Tempie - - - - - Hampton Court, 25 Sept. ,, i

[1] See Vol. I., p. 316, note 1.
[2] Served in the Marquis de Miremont's Dragoons in 1695. Appointed Major of the Earl of Galway's Regt. of Dragoons in Portugal, Feb. 1709. Lt.-Col. of said Corps, 24 June, 1710. Half-pay, 1712. Untraced after 1716.
[3] Appointed Capt. in Visct. Mountjoy's Regt. of Foot in Ireland, 28 June, 1701. Served with said Corps as Major at Almanza and was taken prisoner. Half-pay, 1712. Untraced after 1716.
[4] Appointed 2nd Lieut. of Grendrs. in Lord Mohun's Regt. in 1706. Served under the Earl of Peterborough in Spain and was made Bt.-Capt. by him, 19 Feb. 1707. Drawing half-pay in 1722.
[5] Uncle to Maj.-Gen. James Wolfe. Ens. in the Earl of Orrery's Regt. of Foot, March, 1706. Lieut. 1 Jan. 1708. Served at Malplaquet. Half-pay, 1713. Serving as

Capt. in Col. Chas. Lanoe's Regt. (36th Foot) on the accession of George II. Major of a newly-raised Regt. 1 April, 1742. Retd. before 1746. D. in Ireland, 1771. Will proved at Dublin.

[6] A certain John Eyres had served in the former reign as Cornet in the Duke of Ormonde's Regt. of Horse.

[7] Of Castle Martin, co. Kildare. D. in 1731. Will proved at Dublin.

[8] Left above Regt. in Aug. 1716.

[9] Left do. in June, 1716.

[10] A certain Nicholas Cole had served in former reign as a Subaltern in Col. Edmund Soame's Regt. of Foot.

[11] Serving as Capt. in Maj.-Gen. Chas. Otway's Regt. of Foot (35th) in 1740.

[12] Appointed Capt. in Col. Wm. Delaune's Regt. of Foot in Ireland, 25 Feb. 1709. One of the younger sons of Banastre, 3rd Baron Maynard. Untraced after 1717.

[13] Comn. signed in England and issued in Ireland. Appointed Capt.-Lieut. in Col. Rooke's Regt. of Foot, 24 Feb. 1705. Half-pay as Capt. in 1712. Untraced after 1717.

[14] *Wellington.* See p. 188, note 15.

IRISH ESTABLISHMENT

NON-REGIMENTAL COMMISSIONS AND APPOINT-
MENTS, 1714–1718

REGIMENTAL COMMISSIONS, 1716–1718

IRISH ESTABLISHMENT

NON-REGIMENTAL COMMISSIONS AND APPOINTMENTS, 1714–1718.

Charles, Lord Tyrawly,[1] to be General of Our Foot Forces [in Ireland] - - - -	St. James's, 13 Oct. 1714.*a*	
Do. to be Commander-in-Chief of Our Land Forces in Ireland in the absence of the Earl of Sunderland - - - - -	,, 15 ,, ,, *a*	
Morgan Ryan,[2] Gent. to be Town Major of Limerick - - - - -	Dublin Castle, 13 Jan. 1714/5.*h*	
James Wybault,[3] Esq. to be Major of the Trayne of Artillery in Ireland - -	St. James's, 1 June, 1715.*h*	
Rodolphe Corneille,[4] Esq. to be His Majesty's 2nd Engineer in Ireland - - - -	,, ,, ,, *j*	
John O'Hara, Gent. to be Town Major of Galway whereof George, Lord St. George is Governor - - - - -	,, 15 Aug. ,, *i*	
James Daubusargues,[5] Esq. to be Major-General of Our Forces as well Horse as Foot - - - - - -	,, 22 Sept. ,, *i*	
Capt. John Sterling[6] to be Governor of Ross Castle, co. Kerry - - - -	,, 10 Oct. ,, *i*	
Richard Whitworth,[7] Esq. to be Major of Brigade of the several Regts. of Horse and Dragoons in Ireland - - - -	,, 25 Nov. ,, *j*	

TRAIN OF ARTILLERY IN IRELAND.

SUPPLEMENTARY COMMISSIONS, 1716–17.

John Corneille,[8] Esq. to be 2nd Engineer of Ireland [in room of Rodolphe Corneille]	Hampton Ct., 15 Sept. 1716.*i*	
James Stuart (*sic*),[9] Esq. to be 3rd Engineer of Ireland in room of Arthur Gore, Gent.	,, 20 Dec. 1717.*j*	

IRISH ESTABLISHMENT, 1716–1717.*

COMMANDER-IN-CHIEF.

Charles, Lord Tyrawly -   -   -   - 15 Oct. 1714.

LIEUT.-GENERALS.

Richard, Visct. Shannon.
George Maccartney.

MAJOR-GENERALS.

Sherington Davenport.
[James d'Aubusargues]

BRIGADIER-GENERALS.

Lord Mark Kerr.
David Creichton.
Thomas Ferrers.
Robert Napier.
Jacob Borr.
Richard Munden.

QUARTER-MASTER-GENERAL.

Col. Richard Morris.

ADJUTANT-GENERAL.

Col. Huntington Manning   -   -   - 28 Jan. 1717.

PHYSICIAN-GENERAL.

Dr. John Campbell.

CHIRURGEON-GENERAL.

Thos. Proby,[10] Esq.

JUDGE-ADVOCATE-GENERAL.

Michael Tisdall,[11] Esq.

PROVOST-MARSHAL-GENERAL.

John Lumley, Gent.

* From the MS. Lists of Payments on the Military Establishment of Ireland, 1717–18, at the Public Record Office, Dublin.

MUSTER-MASTER-GENERAL.

Mat. Penefather (*sic*),[12] Esq.

AIDES-DE-CAMP TO THE LORD-LIEUT.

Major Charles Pawlet.[13]
Major Samuel Whitshed.[14]
Capt. George Maccartney.[15]
Major Peter Bettsworth.[16]

AIDE-DE-CAMP TO THE COMMANDER-IN-CHIEF.

Capt. Sydenham Fowke.[17]

SIX DEPUTY-COMMISSARIES OF THE MUSTERS.

John Brady -   -   -   -   ————
Edward Butler   -   -   - 16 Oct. 1717
Wm. Moore -   -   -   - 6 Dec. „
Brook Plukenet [18] -   -   - 18 Jan. 1717/8.

———————
———————

GOVR. OF CORK.

Sir James Jefferyes,[19] Kt.

GOVR. OF KINSALE AND CHARLES FORT.

Earl of Inchiquin.[20]

LIEUT.-GOVR. OF DO.

Lt.-Col. Henry Hawley.[21]

GOVR. OF DROGHEDA.

Henry, Lord Ferrard[22] -   -   -   - 3 Feb. 1715/6.

GOVR. OF GALWAY.

George, Lord St. George.[23]

GOVR. OF LIMERICK.

Major-General Thos. Pearce.[24]

GOVR. OF DUNCANNON.

Brigadier-Gen. Richard Sterne.[25]

GOVR. OF LONDONDERRY.

Lieut.-Gen. Meredyth.[26]

GOVR. OF CARRICKFERGUS.

Brig.-Gen. Lord Mark Kerr.[27]

GOVR. OF ROSS CASTLE.

Capt. John Sterling [28] -　　-　10 Oct. 1715.

GOVR. OF WICKLOW CASTLE.

[Henry Piercy,[29] Esq.]

GOVR. OF CHARLEMONT FORT.

[Henry, Lord Barry of Santry.[30]]

TOWN MAJORS.

John O'Hara = Galway　-　-　-　15 Aug. 1715.
Major John Reading [31] = Limerick　-　14 Feb. 1715/6.
succeeded by
John Miller -　-　-　-　-　-　15 April, 1717.
Thos. Sinnott [32] = Dublin.

FORT MAJOR AT DUNCANNON.

Charles Nicholson.[33]

FORT MAJOR AT CHARLES FORT, KINSALE.

Major Andrew Knox.[34]

LIEUT. FORT MAJOR AT KINSALE.

Alex. Heron [35]　　-　-　-　24 Sept. 1717.

CHAPLAIN OF CHARLES FORT, KINSALE

Jonathan Smedley [36] -　　-　26 Jan. 1716/7.

COMMISSIONS TO BARRACK-MASTERS.

Thos. Hewetson to be Barrack-Master of the Barracks
  built at Kilkenny, Callen, Thurles, Longford
  Pass, and Kilmaine, in the room of Griffith Lloyd [— March, 1716].*i*

John Shaw to be do. of the do. built at Clonmell,
  Carrickneshure, Nine Mile House, Four Mile
  Water, Dungarvan, and Cashell - - - - [— „ „] *i*

John Hodder to be do. of the do. built at Corke and
  Mallow, in the room of Richard Dawson - - 19 July, 1716. *i*

Samuel Bindon to be do. of the do. built at Limerick,
  Clare Castle, Bryan's Bridge, and Abbington, in
  the room of Abraham Sherigley - - - - „ „ *i*

George Baker to be do. of the do. built at Charlemont,
  Ardmagh (*sic*), Dungannon, Altmore, Bleck Bank,
  and Drumbote, in the room of Wm. Baker - - „ „ *i*

Hugh Galbraith to be do. of the do. built at Athlone,
  Portunna, and Banagher, in the room of Edmond
  Morris - - - - - - - - - „ „ *i*

James Dennis to be do. of the do. built at Bantry,
  Macroome, Rosscarbery, Kilmeedy, and Inshigaela,
  in the room of Francis Cornwall - - - 18 Oct. 1717. *j*

Francis Cornwall to be do. of the do. built at Nenagh,
  Roscrea, and Silvermines, in the room of James
  Dennis - - - - - - - - „ „ *j*

Luke Gardiner, Esq. to be Registrar of the Barracks - 18 Jan. 1717/8. *j*

Robert FitzSimons to be Barrack-Master of the do.
  built at Kilkenny, &c., in room of Thos. Hewetson,
  superseded - - - - - - - 23 Feb. „ *j*

Wm. Mortimer to be do. of the do. at Londonderry,
  Culmore, &c., in room of Richard Babbington - 10 July, 1718. *j*

Carncross Nisbit to be do. of the do. at Sligo, Colloony,
  &c., in room of Sidney Ormsby - - - - „ „ *j*

Sidney Ormsby, Esq. to be one of the General
  Inspectors of the Barracks in room of James Read „ „ *j*

VARIOUS COMMISSIONS.

Stephen Deane, Esq. to be one of the six Commis-
  saries of the Musters in Ireland - - - - 16 Aug. 1718. *j*

Henry Barry, Baron of Santry,[87] to be Governor of
  Charlemont - - - - - - - - 18 Sept. „ *j*

Richard Borough,[88] Esq. to be Town Major of Dublin 15 Nov. „ *j*

Capt. Abraham Swift [89] to be A.D.C. to Lord Tyrawly — „ *j*

---

[1] See biog. notice on p. 135, note 1.
[2] D. 10 Feb. 1717. Succeeded by Major John Reading, 14 Feb. 1717.
[3] See Vol. I., p. 369, note 3.
[4] Succeeded by John Corneille, 15 Sept. 1716.
[5] Served under William III. in Flanders, and was given a Bt.-Colonelcy of Dragoons 8 April, 1692. Appointed 2nd Col. of Lord Galway's Regt. of French Horse, 14 May, 1695. Commanded said Corps, 1695–98. Not in any List after 1716.
[6] Probably the Capt. John Sterling of Col. Disney's Regt. of Foot.
[7] See Vol. I., p. 326, note 3.

[8] Comn. renewed by George II. in 1727.

[9] Promoted Major of the Irish Train of Artillery in room of James Wybault, 13 Feb. 1728.

[10] Appointed Surgeon to the Duke of Ormonde's Regt. of Horse, 30 Dec. 1707.

[11] Of Mount Tisdall, co. Meath. D. 7 Dec. 1726.

[12] Second son of Mat. Pennefather of the Tipperary family of this name. Appointed Ens. in Col. Ric. Ingoldsby's Regt. of Foot, 1 June, 1695. Lieut. 31 May, 1701. Capt. 25 Aug. 1704. Served as an A.D.C. at Blenheim. Bt.-Lt.-Col. 1 Jan. 1707. Slightly wounded at Oudenarde. Commissary-Gen. of Musters in Ireland in May, 1709. Auditor of the Irish Revenue *temp.* George I. M.P. for Cashel from 1716 until his decease in 1733.

[13] See Vol. I., p. 135, note 10.

[14] See Vol. I., p. 155, note 4.

[15] See Vol. I., p. 212, note 65.

[16] In 1706, Peter Bettesworth applied to the Duke of Marlborough for a Comn. in the New Levies, and thus described himself : " A gentleman of a good estate and family in the County of Southampton, and who has served his country as a M.P. and J.P. with good reputation." He was appointed Capt. in Col. Wm. Evans's Regt. of Foot, 24 May, 1706. Half-pay, 1713. Lt.-Col. of Bisset's Regt. (30th Foot), 7 May, 1718. Comn. renewed by George II. Out of said Regt. in May, 1732.

[17] Appointed 2nd Lieut. of the Grendr. Cy. in Lord Henry Scott's Regt. of Foot in March, 1704. Capt. in Col. Vezey's Regt. of Foot, 24 June, 1710. Capt. in La Bouchetière's Dragoons in Ireland, 16 Feb. 1716. Major of the Tower Garrison, 1 Feb. 1721.

[18] D. in 1723. Will proved at Dublin.

[19] See special memoir of his son Capt. James Jefferyes of Blarney Castle, pp. 85–89.

[20] Wm. O'Brien, 3rd Earl. D. 24 Dec. 1719.

[21] Bro. to Col. Fras. Hawley of the Princess Anne of Denmark's Dragoons, who was killed at Steinkirk, and uncle to Col. (aftds. Lt.-Gen.) Henry Hawley, Gov. of Portsmouth. Henry Hawley was appointed Major of Col. Luttrell's Regt. (19th Foot) at its first raising in Feb. 1689. Lt.-Col. of Erle's (late Luttrell's) Regt. 15 April, 1691. Left the Regt. 23 March, 1709. He was a legatee under Gen. Thos. Erle's will proved 7 Dec. 1720. Lt.-Col. H. Hawley d. in 1724, and his will was proved 8 Sept. same year.

[22] Sir Henry Tichborne of Beaulieu, co. Louth, Knt. and Bart., created Baron Ferrard 26 Sept. 1715. D. 1731.

[23] Son of Sir Oliver St. George, Bart. Sir George St. George was created a Peer of Ireland in 1715. He was a Privy Councillor and Vice-Admiral of the Province of Connaught. D. in 1735.

[24] See Vol. I., p. 142, note 1.

[25] See Vol. I., p. 158, note 1.

[26] See Vol. I., p. 160, note 1.

[27] See Vol. I., p. 356, note 1.

[28] See note 6.

[29] Referred to in the Comn. of Samuel Warter Whitshed, Esq., who was appointed Gov. of Wicklow Castle, 25 March, 1726.

[30] Appointed Gov. of Londonderry, 19 June, 1719.

[31] See Vol. I., p. 340, note 4.

[32] Sold his post to Capt. Ric. Borough in 1718. D. in 1726. Will proved at Dublin.

[33] A certain Chas. Nicholson, Lieut. in the Royal Regt. of Foot of Ireland, d. in 1730. Will proved at Dublin.

[34] This appointment dated from Queen Anne's reign. Possibly the Andrew Knox who had served, previous to 1714, in Pepper's Regt. of Dragoons.

[35] His Comn., signed by the Duke of Bolton, directed him " to be Lieut. Fort Major under Major Andrew Knox, and to command in his absence." Had served in the late reign as Lieut. in Col. Ric. Lucas's Regt. of Foot. D. 1721. Will proved at Dublin.

[36] His Comn. describes him as " Rector of Ringcurran."

[37] 3rd Baron. Born 1680. Lt.-Col. of the Earl of Wharton's Regt. of Dragoons, 28 April, 1710. D. 1734.

[38] It appears from this officer's petition to the Lords of the Treasury that his real name was *Desherbiers*, and that he had a pension of 5s. p. diem under this name from King William for wounds and services. He also stated in aforesaid petition that " he had lost an arm in the late war on the Rhine," and had "purchased the post of Town Major of Dublin." (*Treasury Papers*, Vol. CCXX., No. 15.) Comn. renewed by George II.

[39] See his Comn. on p. 135. This officer's name appears as A.D.C. to Lord Tyrawly in the " List of Payments on the Establishment of Ireland, 1718." Further services untraced.

REGIMENTAL COMMISSIONS, 1716–1718

THE PRINCE OF WALES'S OWN REGIMENT OF HORSE.
[4TH DRAGOON GUARDS.]

Robert Wolseley [1] to be Cornet to Major David Renovard - - - - -	—	1 Jan. 1715/6.*i*
George Gilland [2] to be Qr.-Mr. to Capt. James Carr. Given under General Davenport's hand and seal the - - - -	—	20 Mar. „ *i*
Charles Lyons [3] to be Cornet to Lt.-Col. Thos. Hatton - - - - -	—	23 „ „ *i*
Peter Davenport [4] to be Cornet to Capt. James Carr in room of Price Hartstongue - -	—	25 June, 1716.*i*
Do. to be Lieut. to above Troop - -	Hampton Ct., 25 Aug. „ *i*	
John Walsh [5] to be Cornet to Capt. Carr in room of Peter Davenport - - -	„ „ 28 „ „ *i*	
Robt. Burton, [6] Esq. to be Capt. in room of John Fielding - - - - - -	St. James's, 17 May, 1717.*j*	
John Warburton, [7] Esq. to be Lieut. to Capt. Richard Stewart in room of Wm. Baldwin	—	28 Sept. „ *j*
Peter Renovard, [8] Esq. to be Major and Capt. of a Tp. in room of Major David Renovard - - - - - - -	—	18 Nov. „ *j*
Peter Davenport, [4] Esq. to be Capt.-Lieut. to that Tp. whereof Lt.-Col. Thos. Hatton is Capt. in room of John Lister, preferred to be Capt. in the Army in Ireland - - - - - - -	—	25 Mar. 1717/8.*j*
John Lister, [9] Esq. to be Capt. in room of James Carr - - - - - -	—	„ „ „ *j*
Robert Wolseley [1] to be Lieut. to Capt. John Lister in the room of Peter Davenport -	—	„ „ „ *j*
Richard Corbet [10] to be Cornet to Major Peter Renovard in room of Robert Wolseley -	—	„ „ „ *j*
Samuel Ogle [11] to be Lieut. to Capt. Ric. Allen in room of Francis Hurry - - -	—	„ „ „ *j*
Luke Ogle [12] to be Cornet to Capt. Robt. Burton in room of Samuel Ogle - -	—	„ „ „ *j*
John Lawson [13] to be Lieut. to Capt. John Lister in room of John Walsh preferred -	—	24 July, 1718.*j*

[1] Appears to have been younger bro. to Sir Wm. Wolseley, 5th Bart. of Wolseley, co. Stafford. Lieut. 25 March, 1718. Capt. 23 Sept. 1719. Serving in 1730. Out of the Regt. before 1736.

[2] Serving as Qr.-Mr. in same Regt. 1736.

[3] Left the Regt. in Oct. 1719.

[4] Comn. signed by George I. Issued in Ireland. From Cornet in Dormer's Dragoons. Lieut. 25 Aug. 1716. Capt.-Lieut. 25 March, 1718. Out of the Regt. 1 June, 1720.

[5] Comn. signed by George I. Issued in Ireland. Capt. in the Carabiniers, 24 July, 1718. Serving in 1730. Not in any subsequent List.

[6] Comn. signed by George I. Issued in Ireland. Left the Regt. in Sept. 1719. Major of the Rl. Irish Dragoons, 23 Sept. 1719. Left last-named Regt. in Nov. 1725.

[7] From Cornet in Brigdr. Jas. Crofts's Dragoons. Capt. in the Rl. Irish Dragoons, 23 Feb. 1724. Lt.-Col. of said Corps at the time of his death which occurred at Bath in Feb. 1750. —*Gentleman's Mag.*

[8] Served previously in the Rl. Dragoons and Ker's (7th) Dragoons. Brother-in-law to Lt.-Col. St. Pierre of the Rl. Dragoons. He is said to have served 12 campaigns abroad. Fought at Sheriffmuir. Lt.-Col. of the 5th Horse (4th D.G.), 10 May, 1738. D. in 1763. Will proved at Dublin.

[9] Serving in same Regt. in 1730. Out before 1737.

[10] Capt.-Lieut. 27 June, 1723. Capt. 10 May, 1738. Serving in 1740.

[11] Comn. renewed by George II. Probably son of "Samuel Ogle, Esq., of Dublin," whose will was proved in 1719 at Dublin.

[12] Lieut. 23 Sept. 1719. Comn. renewed by George II. Out before 1740. The will of a certain Luke Ogle, Gent., of Newcastle, Northumberland, was proved at Dublin in 1735.

[13] Not in any subsequent List.

MAJOR-GENERAL GEORGE KELLUM'S REGIMENT OF HORSE.
[5TH DRAGOON GUARDS.]

Maurice Bocland[1] to be Lieut. to Brigadier Robert Naper (sic)	—	24 April, 1716.*i*
John Sherigley[2] to be Cornet of above Troop	—	,, ,, ,, *i*
Alex. Leith to be Surgeon	Hampton Ct., 8 Sept. ,,	*i*
John Hall[3] to be Lieut. to Capt. Daniel Paul	—	13 Mar. 1716/7.*j*
Daniel Crespin,[4] Esq. to be Capt. in room of Washington, Lord Tamworth	—	26 ,, 1717.*j*
Thos. Rauden (sic),[5] Esq. to be Capt.-Lieut.	—	30 ,, ,, *j*
Robert Napper (sic),[6] Esq. to be Colonel and Capt. of a Troop in room of Major-General G. Kellum	—	27 May, ,, *j*
Wm. Hall,[7] Esq. to be Lt.-Col. and Capt. of a Troop	—	20 July, ,, *j*
John Waller,[8] Esq. to be Major and Capt. of a Troop	—	,, ,, ,, *j*
Peter Ormsby[9] to be Cornet to Capt. Thos. Bligh in room of Adam Cardonnel	—	6 Sept. 1718.*j*
John Daniel Degenes,[10] Esq. to be Capt. of Major Waller's late Troop	—	21 Oct. ,, *j*
Thos. Bligh,[11] Esq. to be Major in room of Waller and Capt. of a Tp.	—	11 Jan. 1718/9.*j*

[1] Son of *Maurice Bockland*, M.P. for Downton. Promoted Capt.-Lieut. of the 2nd Horse (1st D.G.), 2 Oct. 1719. M.P. for Lymington, 1734. Capt. and Lt.-Col. Coldstream Guards, 15 Dec. 1738. 2nd Major with rank of Col. 27 May, 1745. 1st Major, 21 Nov. same year. Col. of the 11th Foot, 1 Dec. 1747. Maj.-Gen. 18 Feb. 1755. Lt.-Gen. 23 Jan. 1758. D. in 1765.

[2] Not in any subsequent List. Possibly the " John Sherigley, Esq., of Bettyville, co. Carlow," whose will was proved at Dublin in 1746.

[3] Untraced.

[4] Appointed Cornet in the Earl of Arran's Regt. of Horse, 25 March, 1700. Lieut. 25 Aug. 1704. Served at Blenheim, Oudenarde, and Malplaquet. Capt.-Lieut. 22 Dec. 1712. Out of the Regt. before 1727. A scion of the ancient Norman family of " Bec Crispin " or " Crespin."

[5] *Rawdon.* Out before 1727.

[6] *Napier.* See Vol. I., p. 328, note 2. A pedigree of this officer's family is given in Burke's *Commoners*, Vol. II., pp. 639–42.

[7] Lieut. and Capt. 1st Foot Guards, 8 July, 1705. Capt. in Gen. Cadogan's Regt. of Horse, 8 April, 1708. Served at Oudenarde and Malplaquet. Major, 10 Feb. 1715. Left Napier's Regt. in Oct. 1719. Gov. of Kilmainham Hospital, Dublin, 1744. D. 1755.

[8] Left the Regt. 21 Oct. 1718. Probably identical with John Waller of Castletown, M.P. for Doneraile, grandson of Sir Hardress Waller.

[9] Capt.-Lieut. 14 Jan. 1738. Serving in 1740.

[10] Jean Daniel de Gennes of Portarlington. Was of the de Gennes Sieurs de la Pico-thière, established in Brittany *circa* 1100 A.D. Son of Nathaniel H. de Gennes. Jean md. at Sunbury-on-Thames, 1 Sept. 1720, Françoise, dau. of Antoine Hullin Sieur d'Orval and of his wife Suzanne Gonyquet de St. Elloy. His eldest dau. and co-heiress, Judith Suzanne de Gennes, md. George Fraser, aftds. Col. Fraser, of Parke and Cuba House, Banagher. Jean Daniel was gazetted Capt. in Robt. Napier's 6th Horse (now 5th Dragoon Guards), on 21 Oct. 1718; and on 2 Oct. 1719 was gazetted as Major in the same Regt.; and again on 18 Aug. 1739 Lt.-Col. in Maj.-Gen. J. Cope's Regt., the 9th Dra-goons (now 9th Lancers). D. at Portarlington on 5 Dec. 1766. Will proved same year —(Communicated by Maj.-Gen. Sir Thomas Fraser, K.C.B.)

[11] Younger son of the Rt. Hon. Thos. Bligh of Rathmore, co. Meath. Promoted Lt.-Col.
of above Regt. 2 Oct. 1739, the Colonel being Lt.-Gen. Robt. Napier, who was maternal
uncle to Lt.-Col. Thos. Bligh. Col. 20th Foot, 26 Dec. 1740. Transferred to the 12th
Dragoons in April, 1746, and to his old Corps, the 6th Horse (5th D.G.), 22 Dec. 1747.
Maj.-Gen. 15 Sept. 1747. He commanded the British troops in action at Melle, when
marching to Ghent to reinforce the garrison (*Records 4th Dragoons*). Lt.-Gen. 23 March,
1754. Appointed C.-in-C. of the expedition to the French coast in Aug. 1758. The British
troops landed at Cherbourg and met with little or no opposition—the town being deserted.
The forts, magazines, and batteries were destroyed ; 27 ships in the harbour were burnt.
Many brass guns and some French Colours were captured and sent on board the fleet. The
troops re-embarked and were landed at St. Lunar, in the bay of that name, on the coast of
Brittany. The plan was to march to St. Malo and attempt that place ; but the French
troops appeared on the scene, at St. Cas, in very superior numbers, and Bligh thought it
best to re-embark the force under his command. This was only effected with the loss of
nearly 1,000 men belonging to the rear-guard. The fleet, under Admiral Howe, then
returned home. The feeling in England was so strong at this disaster that Gen. Bligh
resigned his Regt. and retired into private life. He d. at Brittas, near Dublin, in 1775,
aged 91.

THE FIRST REGIMENT OF CARABINEERS, COMMANDED BY BRIGADIER-GENERAL RICHARD WARING.

[6TH DRAGOON GUARDS,—CARABINIERS.]

Samuel Close to be Chaplain - - - - - - -	13 Jan. 1715/6.*i*
Philip Chenevix,[1] Esq. to be Lieut. to Capt. Chas. Echlin	3 May, 1716.*i*
John Petry [2] to be Cornet to Capt. John Allen - -	„ „ „ *i*
Wm. Ball Waring [3] to be Cornet to Major George Robinson in room of Harry Gordon preferred - -	14 Aug. 1717.*j*
Henry Gordon to be Lieut. to Capt. Richard Edmonds in room of Lieut. Peck decd. - - - - -	„ „ „ *j*
John Arabin [4] to be Cornet to Lt.-Col. John Petry in room of Richard Backwell - - - - -	2 Sept. „ *j*
Urmston Pepys [5] to be Cornet to Capt. Chas. Echlin in room of Euseby Stratford - - - - -	22 May, 1718.*j*
Beaumont Astle (*sic*) [6] to be Lieut. to Lt.-Col. George Robinson in room of James Harrison - - -	10 July, „ *j*
John Aldcroun (*sic*) [7] to be Cornet to Capt. Richard Edmonds in room of Beaumont Astle (*sic*) preferred	„ „ „ *j*
Lord Nassau Paulet [8] to be Capt. in room of John Allen	15 „ „ *j*
John Walsh,[9] Esq. to be Capt. in room of Chas. Echlin	24 „ „ *j*

[1] Appointed Cornet in above Regt. 25 June, 1711. Capt. 19 June, 1722. Lt.-Col. of the Regt. 1 June, 1745. Serving in 1749. Retd. in Jan. 1750. D. in 1758. Will proved at Dublin. He was son of Major Philip Chenevix, of the Carabiniers, who fell at Blenheim ; and grandson of the Rev. Philip Chenevix, Protestant pastor of Limay, near Nantes.

[2] Son of Col. John Petry of same Regt. who served under Marlborough in Flanders and Germany, and d. in 1723. Cornet Petry left the Carabiniers before 1727. He subsequently served in the Infantry and was appointed Major of the 36th Foot, Feb. 1746. Killed at the battle of Laufeldt in 1747.

[3] Belonged to Brigdr. Waring's family. Out of the Regt. before 1727. D. in 1756. Described in his will, a copy of which is in the Dublin Record Office, as " of Thatcham, Berkshire."

[4] Capt.-Lieut. 11 June, 1733. Major 8th Dragoons, 7 Sept. 1742. Lt.-Col. 22 June, 1745. Col. 57th Foot, 26 Dec. 1755. D. in 1757. Will proved at Dublin. He was father of Lt.-Gen. John Arabin of the Royal Irish Artillery.

[5] Attained the rank of Major of above Regt. 1 June, 1745. Retd. in Aug. 1757. His death is recorded in the *Gentleman's Mag.* as having taken place at Bath, 15 Nov. 1774.

[6] Called " Astley Beaumont " in the 1715 List and " Beaumont Astle " in the Gradation List for 1730, where he appears as Capt.-Lieut. under date of 19 June, 1722. Not in any subsequent List. The *Gentleman's Mag.* for 1773 records the death of " Major Astle, ætat. 100, of Carlow, Ireland."

[7] *Aldercron* or *Adlercron*. This officer was appointed Col. of the 39th Regt. of Foot 14 March, 1752, and proceeded with this Corps to Madras in 1754 to uphold British interests in India. When it was decided, in 1756, to send an expeditionary force to Bengal from Southern India, the Madras Government made choice of Lt.-Col. Robert Clive, to command the Madras Army. But Col. Aldercron of the 39th aspired, as senior King's officer in India, to the command of the force to be sent to Bengal. He had had no experience of Indian warfare, and the Madras Government had wisely selected Clive, who had the rank of Lt.-Col. in the King's Army, to command the military part of the expedition. In consequence of this decision, Col. Aldercron stayed at Fort St. George with two-thirds of his Regt. while the remaining portion of the 39th sailed for Bengal, and in the following year participated in Clive's glorious victory at Plassey (see *Memoir of Col. Sir Robt. Barker, Kt. and Bt.*, by Charles Dalton, F.R.G.S., in Vol. XXVIII. of *Proceedings of the R.A. Institution*). Col. Aldercron attained the rank of Lt.-Gen., and d. in 1766.

[8] Born in 1698. Son of the 2nd Duke of Bolton by his third wife Henrietta Crofts, illegitimate dau. of James, Duke of Buccleuch and Monmouth. Appointed Cornet in Brigdr. Bowles's Regt. of Dragoons about Oct. 1715. Serving as Capt. in the Rl. Regt. of Horse Guards in 1730. D. 24 Aug. 1741. His only child md. the 3rd Earl of Egmont.

[9] Comn. renewed in 1727. Out before 1737.

L

MAJOR-GENERAL SYBOURG'S REGIMENT OF HORSE
[7TH DRAGOON GUARDS.]

Richard Prescot (*sic*)[1] to be Lieut. to Capt. Molineux Robinson - - - -	—	21 Jan. 1715/6.*i*
Michael Swift[2] to be Cornet to Major Robert Norton - - - - - - -	—	„ „ „ *i*
Sir Robert Denham,[3] Bt. to be Lieut. to Capt. Claude Testefolle - - - - -	St. James's, 14 July, 1716.*i*	
Edward Combe[4] [Senr.] to be Chaplain - -	—	10 Nov. „ *i*
Solomon Desbrisay[5] to be Cornet to the Colonel's Troop in room of Edward Hanbury - - - - - - -	—	22 Aug. 1717.*j*
Theodore Leeds[6] to be Cornet to Capt. Molineux Robinson - - - - -	—	2 Sept. „ *j*
Solomon Debrisay (*sic*)[5] to be Lieut. to Major Palms in room of Chas. Powlett - -	—	9 Dec. „ *j*
George Gore[7] to be Cornet to the Colonel's Tp. in room of Solomon Desbrisay preferred - - - - - -	—	„ „ „ *j*
Wm. Kenrick[8] to be Cornet to Major Norton in room of John Briggs - - -	—	2 Oct. 1718. *j*
George Bennet,[9] Esq. to be Capt. of Major Robt. Norton's late Troop - -	—	14 „ „ *j*
Michael Swift[2] to be Lieut. to Lt.-Col. Wm. Bray in room of George Bennet preferred	—	„ „ „ *j*
David de Charmes[10] to be Cornet to Capt. George Bennet - - - - -	—	„ „ „ *j*
Stephen Palmes,[11] Esq. to be Major - -	—	„ „ „ *j*
Henry Culpeper Fairfax,[12] Esq. to be Capt.-Lieut. in room of Francis Lawe - -	—	24 Feb. 1718/9.*j*

[1] See Vol. I., p. 330, note 2. He was father of Gen. Robert Prescott, Gov. of Canada and Nova Scotia 1793–99, and Col. 28th Foot.

[2] Appointed Ens. in Brigdr. Primrose's Regt. 25 March, 1705. Served at Malplaquet. 2nd Lieut. of Grendrs. 20 March, 1710. Lieut. in Sybourg's Horse, 14 Oct. 1718. Serving in same Regt. 1730. Out before 1736. The will of a certain Michael Swift, Esq., was proved at Dublin in 1737.

[3] Of Westshields, Scotland. Not in any subsequent List. D. in 1756.—*Gentleman's Mag.*

[4] Succeeded as Chaplain by his son Edward, 24 Dec. 1724.

[5] Lieut. 9 Dec. 1717. Capt.-Lieut. 15 Dec. 1738. Serving in 1740.

[6] Lieut. 9 May, 1722. Serving in 1730. Out before 1736.

[7] Out before 1727.

[8] Serving with same rank in 1727. Out before 1736.

[9] Cornet in above Regt. 24 Feb. 1708. Served at Oudenarde and Malplaquet. Lieut. 2 April, 1711. Major, 25 May, 1721. Serving in 1730. D. 1738.

[10] Lieut. 21 Jan. 1720. Serving with same rank in 1736. Out before 1740.

[11] Cornet in the Duke of Schomberg's Regt. of Horse, 23 April, 1691. Lieut. in 1702. Wounded at Blenheim. Capt. 25 March, 1705. Bt.-Major, 1 Jan. 1712. Served throughout Marlborough's campaigns. Left the Regt. in 1721 (?). D. in 1740. Will proved at Dublin.

[12] Serving with same rank in 1730. D. in 1734. He was bro. to Thomas 6th Baron Fairfax of Cameron. This nobleman inherited from his mother, Miss *Colepeper*, a large fortune and a tract of land in Virginia estimated at 5,700,000 acres !

COLONEL THOMAS SIDNEY'S REGIMENT OF DRAGOONS.
[ROYAL IRISH DRAGOONS.]

Disbanded 1798.

Lewis Griffith [1] to be Cornet to Capt. John Usher - - - - - - -	— 25 Feb. 1715/6.*i*
James Poe,[2] Esq. to be Capt.-Lieut. - -	— 10 July, 1716.*i*
Wm. Higgens [3] to be Lieut. to Lt.-Col. John Hill - - - - - - -	— ,, ,, ,, *i*
Thos. Wilson [4] to be Cornet to do. - -	— ,, ,, ,, *i*
Anthony Cope,[5] Esq. to be Capt. in room of [Major Richard] Gore - - - -	St. James's, 27 May, 1717.*b*
Wriothesley Betton,[6] Esq. to be Major in room of Richard Gore and to be Capt. of a Troop - - - - - -	,, ,, ,, ,, *b*
James Scott [7] to be Cornet to Capt. Gustavus Hamilton - - - - - -	,, ,, ,, ,, *j*
Charles Wardlaw,[8] Esq. to be Capt. in room of George Ross - - - - -	— 30 Jan. 1717/8.*j*

[1] Lieut. 8 Sept. 1725. Serving with same rank in 1740. D. in 1752. Will proved at Dublin.

[2] Third son of Emanuel Poé of co. Tipperary. Joined above Regt. as a Qr.-Mr. before 1694. Cornet, 19 June, 1702. Fought at Blenheim and in subsequent battles under Marlborough. Lieut. 24 Feb. 1708. Out of the Regt. 11 July, 1722. The will of a James Poé, Esq., of Rosneharley, co. Tipperary, was proved at Dublin in 1739.

[3] Capt.-Lieut. 11 July, 1722. Serving in 1740. His will proved at Dublin in 1759, describes him as "late Captain in the Royal Dragoons now of Dublin."

[4] Lieut. 5 Dec. 1732. Serving in 1740.

[5] Signed by George I. Comn. issued in Ireland. Appointed Cornet in above Regt. 1 Feb. 1714. Serving as senior Capt. in 1740. Appears to have belonged to the Copes of Drumully, co. Armagh.

[6] Signed by George I. Comn. issued in Ireland. Promoted Lt.-Col. 23 Sept. 1719. D. in 1731. His will, proved in London, describes him as "of the parish of St. Margaret, Westminster, Lieut.-Colonel Royal Dragoons of Ireland."

[7] Lieut. 4 March, 1735. Serving in 1740. D. in 1753. His will describes him as "Lieut. in the Royal Irish Dragoons."

[8] Serving in 1740. Belonged to the Irish branch of the ancient Scottish family of this name. D. in 1762. Will proved at Dublin.

COLONEL THOMAS HARRISON'S REGIMENT OF FOOT.

[6TH FOOT,—THE ROYAL WARWICKSHIRE REGIMENT.]

Arthur Stewart,[1] Esq. to be Capt. in room of Philip Brydall decd. - - - - - - - -	13 Jan. 1715/6.	*i*
James Duvall [2] to be Lieut. to Capt. Wm. Coward - -	22 Feb. „	*i*
Wm. Beauford (*sic*) [3] Esq. to be Capt.-Lieut. - -	3 Mar. „	*i*
Francis Morris [4] to be Lieut. to Capt. Wm. Maule - -	„ „ „	*i*
Robert Dormer,[5] Esq. to be Colonel in room of Thomas Harrison and to be Capt. of a Cy. - - - -	7 „ „	*i*
John Cotterel (*sic*) [6] to be Ens. to Capt. [John] Murray -	4 July, 1716.	*i*
John Tattershall[7] to be Lieut. to Capt. Philip Beard in room of Peter Petit - - - - - - -	15 Oct. 1717.	*j*
John Galt [8] to be Ens. to Capt. Philip Babington in room of John Tattershall - - - - - -	„ „ „	*j*
John Cottrell,[9] Esq. to be Capt. in room of Wm. Maule -	2 May, 1718.	*j*
James Cressett,[10] Esq. to be Capt. in room of Philip Babington - - - - - - - - -	24 „ „	*j*
James Dalton [11] to be Ensign to Capt. John Murray in room of John Cottrell - - - - - -	3 July, „	*j*
Robert Buggins [12] to be Lieut. to Lt.-Col. John Ramsey in room of Wm. Campbell - - - - -	1 Aug. „	*j*
Ant. Gisburn [13] to be Ens. to above Cy. in room of Robt. Buggins - - - - - - - -	„ „ „	*j*

[1] Out of the Regt. before 1727.

[2] D. in Nov. 1724.

[3] *Beaufort.* Appointed Lieut. in the Earl of Orrery's Regt. of Foot, 7 Dec. 1711. Half-pay, 1713. D. or retd. in April, 1720.

[4] Out of the Regt. before 1727.

[5] See Vol. I., p. 95, note 2.

[6] Son of Sir Chas. Cottrell, Knt., by his second marriage. Capt. 2 May, 1718. Major, 6 July, 1726. Serving in same Regt. 1737. Appointed Lt.-Col. of Col. Edward Wolfe's newly-raised Regt. of Marines, 22 Nov. 1739. Served with this Corps during the expedition to Carthagena. Succeeded to the Colonelcy, 28 April, 1741. Took part in the expedition to Cuba same year. D. in 1746.—*Gentleman's Mag.*

[7] Appointed Ens. in above Regt. 8 April, 1708. Served in Spain. Out of the Regt. before 1727.

[8] Lieut. 11 May, 1725. Serving in 1727. Out before 1736.

[9] See note 6.

[10] Out of the Regt. before 1727.

[11] Only son of John Dalton of Bedale, Yorkshire, by Jane Thornton, and great-grandson of Lt.-Col. John Dalton (only son of Sir Wm. Dalton of Hauxwell Hall, co. York) who was mortally wounded at Burton-on-Trent, 5 July, 1643, when conducting Queen Henrietta Maria from Bridlington to Oxford. James Dalton joined the 6th Regt. of Foot at the age of 18. Promoted Lieut. 21 Aug. 1721 and in 1727 was 1st Lieut. of the Grendr. Cy. After serving 21 years in Ireland he returned with his Corps to England. Sent to Scotland in 1740. Promoted Capt.-Lieut. 19 Jan. 1740. Embarked with his Regt. at Greenock, early in Sept. 1741. Took part in the expedition to Porto Bello which sailed from Jamaica early in March, 1742. His name appears in the *Gentleman's Mag.* as one of the three Captains of Guise's Regt. (6th Foot) who lost their lives in the West Indies between 8 March and 18 May, 1742. The tradition in the Dalton family is that

Capt. James Dalton.
6th Regt of Foot
D . 1742 .

(*See* p. 164, note 11.)

Capt. James Dalton was drowned when making a landing. Will proved by his widow in London, 9 May, 1743. James Dalton left an only son, John Dalton, who, after serving in Col. Jordan's Regt. of Marines, was appointed Capt. of the Grendr. Cy. in the Madras Presidency where he earned great renown. See *Memoir of Capt. John Dalton, Defender of Trichinopoly*, 1752–53, by Charles Dalton, F.R.G.S.

[12] Appointed Ens. in above Regt. 8 April, 1708. Capt. before 1726, in April of which year he d. or left the Regt.

[13] Appointed Cornet in Maj.-Gen. Evans's Regt. of Dragoons, 14 May, 1720. Out before 1727.

BRIGADIER-GENERAL HENRY MORYSON'S REGIMENT OF FOOT.

[8TH FOOT,—THE KING'S.]

Returned to Ireland from Scotland in May, 1717. For Commissions in this Regiment between 1716–17 inclusive, see Vol. I., pp. 196–218 *passim.*

Edmund Martin,[1] Esq. to be Capt. in room of Edmund Devischer - - - - - - -	14 Mar. 1717/8. *j*
Robt. Abbot[2] to be Lieut. to Capt. Jas. Beschefer in room of Thos. Redwood - - - - - -	31 ,, 1718. *j*
Robt. Eyton[3] to be [2nd] Lieut. to Capt. Arthur Usher in room of John Smith decd. - - - - -	24 Aug. ,, *j*
Wm. Gill,[4] Esq. to be Capt. in room of Burlacy (*sic*) Webb - - - - - - - -	26 ,, ,, *j*
John Letton[5] to be Ens. to Capt. John Farcy in room of John Cowley - - - - - - -	19 Sept. ,, *j*
Hayes St. Leger,[6] Esq. to be Capt. in room of Charles Stewart - - - - - - - -	2 Mar. 1718/9. *j*

[1] " A native of Sussex, a sportsman, and a *bon camarade* " (*A Duke and his Friends*). Appointed 2nd Lieut. in Wills's Marines, 2 May, 1707. Half-pay, 1713. Major of the King's Regt. 6 Dec. 1739. Lt.-Col. of Price's Regt. 7 Feb. 1741. Transferred to the King's Regt. of Foot, 1 May, 1745. Served at Falkirk and Culloden. Commanded his Corps at the battles of Roucoux and Val. Wounded at last-named engagement (*Records*). D. 26 April, 1749 (*Gentleman's Mag.*).

[2] Capt. 6 April, 1720. Serving in 1730. A certain Robert Abbot of Stepingley Park, Bedfordshire, d. in 1731.

[3] Out before 1727.

[4] Do.

[5] Comn. renewed by George II. Serving as Ens. in Gen. Whetham's Regt. (12th Foot) in 1730.

[6] Out in June, 1722.

COLONEL [THE HON.] CHARLES CATHCART'S REGIMENT OF FOOT.

[9TH FOOT,—NORFOLK REGIMENT.]

Charles Cathcart,[1] Esq. to be Colonel of Our
　　Regt. of Foot whereof Col. James Camp-
　　bell was late Colonel and to be Capt. of
　　a Company - - - - - - — 15 Feb. 1716/7.*j*
Edward Wynne[2] to be Lieut. to Lt.-Col. Wm.
　　Stuart - - - - - - — 23 Mar. ,, *j*
Nicholas Thetford[3] to be Chaplain - - — 4 May, 1717. *j*
Verney Lloyd,[4] Esq. to be Lt.-Col. in room of
　　Brigadier Wm. Steuart and Capt. of a Cy. — 8 Aug. ,, *j*
Richard Offarel (*sic*),[5] Esq. to be Major and
　　Capt. in room of Verney Lloyd - - — ,, ,, ,, *j*
Michael Doyne,[6] Esq. to be Capt. in room of
　　Richard Offarel - - - - - — ,, ,, ,, *j*
Rowley Godfrey,[7] Esq. to be Capt.-Lieut. in
　　room of Michael Doyne - - - - — ,, ,, ,, *j*
Wm. Dingley,[8] Esq. to be [1st] Lieut. of Capt.
　　John Filbrigge's Grendr. Cy. in room of
　　Rowley Godfrey - - - - - — ,, ,, ,, *j*
Robert Dowglass (*sic*)[9] to be Ens. to Capt.
　　Richard Offarel in room of Wm. Dingley — ,, ,, ,, *j*
Adam Ferguson[10] to be Ens. to Capt. Joseph
　　Shewbridge in room of Nathan Wilcocks — 20 ,, ,, *j*
James Otway,[11] Esq. to be Colonel of that
　　Regt. of Foot in Ireland whereof Col.
　　Charles Cathcart was late Colonel and to
　　be Capt. of a Cy. - - - - - Dublin Castle, 7 Jan. 1717/8.*b*
Thos. Gery,[12] Esq. to be Capt. in room of John
　　Philbridge (*sic*) - - - - - ,, ,, 17 ,, ,, *j*
John Lancaster[13] to be Ens. to Capt. Joseph
　　Shewbridge in room of Adam Ferguson - ,, ,, 1 Mar. ,, *b*
Capt. Richard Otway[14] to be Capt. in room of
　　John Ash - - - - - - - ,, ,, 16 June, ,. *j*
　　*This Regiment was sent to Minorca
　　　　in June, 1718.*
Francis Otway[15] to be Ens. to Capt. —— - St. James's, 8 Nov. ,, *b*

---

[1] See biog. notice in Vol. I., p. 224, note 81.
[2] Untraced.
[3] Serving as Chaplain to Kane's Regt. of Foot in 1727.
[4] Promoted from Major. Served as Capt.-Lieut. in the King's Regt. of Foot at Blenheim. Probably bro. to Capt. (aftds. Major) Leonard Lloyd of aforesaid Regt. Verney Lloyd served with Primrose's Regt. at Malplaquet. D. or left the Regt. in Dec. 1720.
[5] See Vol. I., p. 338, note 3.
[6] Appointed Capt.-Lieut. of above Regt. 22 Feb. 1714. Major, 4 Dec. 1739. Lt.-Col. 3 April, 1743. D. in 1749. Will proved at Dublin. He was third son of Robert Doyne, Lord Chief Justice of the Common Pleas in Ireland.

[7] Promoted from 1st Lieut. of the Grendr. Cy.   Capt. 12 Sept. 1721.   Serving in 1740. D. in 1744.   Will proved at Dublin.

[8] Promoted from Ens.   Not in any subsequent List.

[9] Appointed Major of 19th Foot, 2 July, 1747.

[10] Capt. in Anstruther's Regt. (the Cameronians), 21 March, 1719.   Serving as senior Capt. in said Corps in 1740.   A certain Major Adam Ferguson's death is recorded in the *Gentleman's Mag.* as having occurred at Ayr in 1770.

[11] See notice in Vol. I., p. 326, note 2.

[12] Appointed Major of Maj.-Gen. Evans's Regt. of Dragoons, 10 Feb. 1723.   Serving in 1730.   Out of the Army before 1740.

[13] Comn. renewed in 1727.   A certain John Lancaster had served in the former reign as 2nd Lieut. in Col. H. Holt's Regt. of Marines.

[14] Had served in the late reign as Cornet in Gen. Jas. Stanhope's Regt. of Dragoons. Half-pay, 1712.   Cornet in Col. Thos. Pitt's Horse in March, 1717.   Services untraced after 1718.   Probably son of Col. James Otway.

[15] Appointed Exempt and Capt. 3rd Tp. of Life Guards, 1 Jan. 1732. Lt.-Col. 3rd Horse, 3 May, 1744.   Serving 1749.   Out 1751.

COLONEL GEORGE GROVE'S REGIMENT OF FOOT.

[19TH FOOT,—ALEXANDRA PRINCESS OF WALES'S OWN YORKSHIRE REGIMENT.]

This Regiment took part in the Expedition to Vigo, 1719.

Philip How (*sic*),[1] Esq. to be Capt. in room of Adam Williamson - - - - - - - - -	31 Aug. 1717. *j*
Charles Mainwaring,[2] Esq. to be Capt. in room of John Fourness (*sic*) - - - - - - -	4 Nov. ,, *j*
Joseph Fourness[3] to be Lieut. to Capt. Thos. Holland in room of Charles Mainwaring - - - -	,, ,, *j*
Peter Smith[4] to be Ens. in room of Joseph Fourness -	,, ,, *j*
Nathaniel Bland[5] to be Ens. to Capt. Philip How in room of Thos. Brown - - - - - - -	11 Dec. ,, *j*
Roger Crymble[6] to be Ens. to Capt. Edward Brown in room of Robert Moore - - - - -	12 ,, ,, *j*

[1] Called "Hoar" in the List for 1736, where he appears as Capt. in above Regt., then on the Irish Establishment.   Out before 1740.

[2] Comn. renewed by George II. in 1727.   Serving in 1736.   Out before 1740.

[3] Comn. renewed in June, 1727.   Out before 1736.

[4] Out before 1727.

[5] Not in any subsequent List.   A certain Nathaniel Bland, LL.D. of Dublin, d. in 1760. Will proved at Dublin.

[6] Lieut. 11 July, 1722.   Serving with above Regt. in 1740.   Believed to have fought at Fontenoy.

THE PRINCE OF WALES'S OWN ROYAL REGIMENT OF WELSH FUZILIERS (*sic*).

[ROYAL WELSH FUSILIERS.]

This Regiment was sent to Ireland in Nov. 1718, but returned to England early in 1719.

Wm. Gent[1] to be 1st Lieut. to Capt. Griffith Jones - - - - - - -	St. James's, 15 June, 1716.*b*	
Thos. Wentworth,[2] Esq. to be Lieut.-Col. and Capt. - - - - - -	,, 10 Feb. 1717/8.*b*	
Wm. Hay[3] to be Chaplain - - -	,, 3 April, ,, *b*	
John Wilson,[4] Esq. to be Capt. of Major Henry Cookman's late Company - -	,, 16 ,, ,, *b*	
Peter Heard (*sic*)[5] to be 2nd Lieut. to Capt. John Wilson - - - - -	Kensington, 12 July, ,, *b*	
Charles Combe,[6] Esq. to be Captain - -	,, ,, ,, ,, *b*	
John Chambre[7] to be 1st Lieut. to Capt. Combe - - - - - -	,, ,, ,, ,, *b*	
Wm. Bernard[8] to be Adjt. - - -	,, ,, ,, ,, *b*	
Wm. Bissell[9] to be 2nd Lieut. to Capt. James Bissell - - - - - -	,, 26 ,, ,, *b*	
Michael Hutton[10] to be Qr.-Mr. - - -	,, ,, ,, ,, *b*	
John Hyde,[11] Esq. to be Capt. in room of Southwell Pigott [Signed in England; issued in Ireland] - - - -	Dublin, 8 Jan. 1718/9.*j*	
Wm. Bernard[12] to be 1st Lieut. to Capt. Newsham Peers in room of Malachi Hawtaque [Signed in England; issued in Ireland] - - - - -	,, 13 Mar. ,, *j*	
John Bernard[13] to be 2nd Lieut. to do. [Signed in England; issued in Ireland] - -	,, 18 ,, ,, *j*	

[1] Out before 1727. The will of a certain Wm. Gent of Dublin, gent., was proved in 1776.

[2] See biog. notice in Vol. I., p. 99, note 3.

[3] Untraced.

[4] Comn. renewed by George II. (The Gradation List for 1730 gives the date 11 April, 1718.) Major of Barrell's Regt. (4th Foot), 17 April, 1743. Believed to have served with last-named Corps at Culloden. Lt.-Col. of 49th Foot, 26 March, 1748. Out of said Corps in May, 1753.

[5] *Hewet.* Appointed Adjt. to above Regt. 1 June, 1715. Comn. as 2nd Lieut. renewed in 1727. (The Gradation List for 1730 gives the date of 16 July, 1718.) Out of above Regt. before 1740. The *Gentleman's Mag.* records the death, under date of 1740, of a certain Sir Peter Hewet, of Harrow-on-the-Hill.

[6] Promoted from 1st Lieut. Captain's Comn. renewed by George II. Out of the Regt. before 1740.

[7] Appointed 2nd Lieut. in above Regt. 5 June, 1716. Comn. as 1st Lieut. renewed by George II. Capt. in Col. Charles Douglas's newly-raised Regt. of Marines, 24 Nov. 1739. Served with said Corps at the siege of Carthagena. Major, 3 May, 1741. Serving as Major of the 27th Foot in 1749.

[8] Serving in 1727 as 1st Lieut.

[9]   Do.   Out of the Regt. 1740.

[10] Adjt. 21 March, 1719.

[11] Comn. renewed in June, 1727.

[12] See note 8.

[13] Serving in June, 1727. Out of the Regt. before 1740.

MAJOR-GENERAL PRIMROSE'S REGIMENT OF FOOT.
[24TH FOOT,—THE SOUTH WALES BORDERERS.]

This Regiment took part in the Expedition to Vigo, 1719.

Robert Maynard[1] to be Lieut. to Capt. Thos. Albritton -	—	3 Jan. 1715/6.*i*
Wm. Congreve[2] to be Lieut. to Capt. Chas. Mittford - - - - - -	—	15 Feb. ,, *i*
Thos. Addison[3] to be Ens. to do. - - -	—	,, ,, ,, *i*
Francis Tobine[4] to be Ens. to Lt.-Col. Philip Bragg - - - - - -	St. James's, 17 Mar. ,, *i*
John Bullock[5] to be Ens. to the Colonel's Cy.	—	29 ,, ,, *i*
Thos. Bosswell[6] to be Ens. to Capt. Patrick Meade - - - - - -	St. James's, 3 April, ,, *i*
Augustus Fitzgerald[7] to be Lieut. to Capt. Hector Hamon - - - -	—	28 Jan. 1716/7.*a & j*
Thomas Howard,[8] Esq. to be Colonel in room of Major-General Gilbert Primrose and Capt. of a Cy. - - - - -	—	10 Sept. 1717.*a & j*
James Nisbett[9] to be Surgeon in room of Samuel Mongin decd. - - - -	—	22 May, 1718.*j*

[1] From Ens. in Col. Handasyde's Regt. The date of this officer's Comn. as Lieut. is given in the Gradation List for 1730 as 23 Jan. 1716. Capt. 3 Nov. 1735. Serving in 1740. Appears to have been sixth son of Banastre, 3rd Baron Maynard, and according to Burke's *Extinct Peerage* d. young.

[2] Promoted from Ens. Not in any subsequent List of this Regt. A certain Wm. Congreve was appointed Lieut. in the Rl. Irish Dragoons, 5 April, 1724.

[3] Lieut. 5 Aug. 1722. Serving in same Regt. 1730. Out before 1736.

[4] The will of "Francis Tobyn, Ensign in Col. Howard's Regt." was proved at Dublin in 1721.

[5] Out before 1727.

[6] Lieut. 23 Oct. 1724. Serving as senior Lieut. in above Regt. 1740.

[7] *Augustine Fitz Gerald.* Represented an ancient family of this name in co. Clare. Was of Six Mile Bridge in said county. D. in 1776. Will proved at Dublin.

[8] See Vol. I., p. 222, note 54.

[9] Out before 1736. The will of "James Nisbet, surgeon, of Kinsale" was proved at Dublin, 1771.

COLONEL WILLIAM BARRELL'S REGIMENT OF FOOT

[28TH FOOT,—1ST BATTALION GLOUCESTERSHIRE REGIMENT.]

This Regiment took part in the Expedition to Vigo, 1719.

John Blair [1] to be Chaplain	—	1 Feb. 1715/6.*i*
John Beckwith,[2] Esq. to be Major	—	1 June, 1716.*i*
Wm. Davidson [3] to be Lieut. to Capt. Peter Morine	—	5 ,, ,, *i*
Robert Maxwell,[4] Esq. to be Capt. in room of Huntington Manning	St. James's, 28 Jan. 1716/7.*j*	
Henry Sarrau (*sic*),[5] Esq. to be Capt. in room of Peter Morine	,, ,, ,, ,, *j*	
Wm. Taylor,[6] Esq. to be Capt.-Lieut.	,, ,, ,, ,, *j*	
Dennis Sullivan [7] to be Lieut. to Capt. Lewis Liermont	,, ,, ,, ,, *j*	
Laurence Wood [8] to be Ens. to Capt. Robert Maxwell	,, ,, ,, ,, *j*	
Richard Burren (*sic*)[9] to be Ens. to Capt. [Lt.-Colonel] Wm. Davison	,, ,, ,, ,, *j*	
Wm. Græme [10] to be Ens. to Capt. Stephen Downes	—	15 Aug. 1717.*j*
Thomas Barrell [11] to be Ens. to Capt. Henry Sarrau	—	17 ,, ,, *j*
Thomas Tongue (*sic*) [12] to be Lieut. to Capt. Valentine Croome in room of Robt. Turnbull	—	23 Nov. ,, *j*
Robert Harman [13] to be Ens. to Col. Wm. Barrell in room of Thos. Tongue	—	,, ,, ,, *j*
John Nugent [14] to be Ens. to Capt. Lewis Liermont in room of Alex. Johnston	—	,, ,, ,, *j*
Elias Darassus [15] to be Ens. of Lt.-Col. Wm. Davison's Cy. in room of Richard Burren	—	31 Mar. 1718.*j*
Thomas Lumm [16] to be Ens. to Capt. George Nodes in room of John Moore	—	16 May, ,, *j*
Major John Beckwith to be Capt. of Capt. Valentine Crome's (*sic*) Cy.	—	13 Nov. ,, *j*
Robert Innes [17] to be Lieut. to Capt. [Gibson?] in room of John Ralphson decd.	—	30 ,, ,, *j*
John Lee,[18] Esq. to be Lt.-Colonel and Capt. in room of Lt.-Col. Wm. Davidson	—	18 Dec. ,, *j*
Thos. White [19] to be Ens. to Capt. Henry Sarrau in room of Thos. Barrell	—	29 ,, ,, *j*

[1] Serving with above Regt. in 1736.

[2] "Served as a volunteer at the siege of Namur, and was shot through the body at the storm of the Castle" (*Recommendations for Commissions in the New Levies,* 1706). Appointed Ens. in Col. Wm. Northcote's Regt. of Foot, 25 May, 1696. Half-pay, 1698. 2nd Lieut. in Col. Geo. Villiers's Regt. of Marines, 10 March, 1702. 1st Lieut. 10 Dec. 1702. Served at the capture and subsequent defence of Gibraltar. Capt. in Goring'

Marines, 20 March, 1712. Half-pay, 1713. Capt. in Goring's re-formed Regt. (31st Foot) in 1715. Lt.-Col. of 31st Foot, 2 July, 1737. D. at the camp near Colchester, 8 Aug. 1741. (*Gentleman's Mag.*).

[3] Out 1 March, 1720.

[4] Served previously as Capt. in Lt.-Gen. Ric. Gorges's Regt. of Foot. Out of Barrell's Regt. before 1727.

[5] Called "Serau" in previous Lists. Capt.-Lieut. of above Regt. 20 Sept. 1711. As an Ens. in same Corps he had served at Almanza, where he was taken prisoner. Out of Barrell's Regt. before 1727.

[6] Served as an Ens. in above Regt. at Almanza and was taken prisoner. Lieut. 23 Dec. 1707. Out of Barrell's Regt. in June, 1720.

[7] Ens. 28 June, 1712. Serving as senior Lieut. in 1740. Believed to have been at Fontenoy. D. in 1747 as Capt. in above Regt. Will proved at Dublin.

[8] Out before 1727.

[9] Sold his Comn. in March, 1718, to Elias Darassus, who had served two years as a volunteer in same Corps.—Letter from the Secretary-at-War to the Duke of Bolton, 20 March, 1717/8 (*S.P.D. George I.*).

[10] Out before 1727.

[11] Left 28 Dec. 1718. Probably a child.

[12] *Tonge.* Promoted from Ens. Serving in 1737. Out in 1740.

[13] Eldest son, by second marriage, of Wentworth Harman, who was Capt. of the Battle Axe Guards in 1683. Robert Harman was born in 1699, and was of Newcastle, co. Longford. Left the Army before 1727. Succeeded his uncle, Wesley Harman in the family estates in April, 1758. D.s.p. 3 Dec. 1765.

[14] Comn. renewed by George II. Lieut. 10 April, 1736. Serving in 1740.

[15] Lieut. 18 Nov. 1721. Serving with same rank in 1740. The will of a certain Elias Darassus was proved at Dublin in 1769.

[16] Left above Regt. as Capt. in May, 1727. The will of Thomas Lumm of Lumville, King's County, was proved at Dublin in 1744.

[17] Appointed 2nd Lieut. of Grendrs. in Col. Wm. Delaune's Regt. of Foot in Ireland, 30 Aug. 1708. Half-pay, 1712. Serving in Bragg's Regt. (28th Foot) in 1740.

[18] Promoted from Capt. in Maj.-Gen. Wm. Evans's Regt. of Dragoons. Comn. as Lt.-Col. renewed by George II. Lt.-Col. of the King's Regt. of Foot, 4 April, 1730. Col. of the 44th Foot, 11 March, 1743. D. in 1750. Appears to have been a cadet of the Earl of Lichfield's family and to have md. Lady Elizabeth Lee, dau. of the 1st Earl.

[19] Not in any subsequent List.

LORD MARK KERR'S REGIMENT OF FOOT.

[29TH FOOT,—1ST BATTALION WORCESTERSHIRE REGIMENT.]

John Johnston[1] to be Ens. to Major John Greenwood - - - - -	— 19 Jan. 1715/6.*i*
Wm. Ashe[2] to be Lieut. to Capt. Hugh Montgomery - - - -	Hampton Court, 28 Aug. 1716.*i*
Wm. Groves[3] to be Ens. to Capt. David Pain - - - - -	,, ,, ,, ,, *i*
Robert Kerr[4] to be Ens. to Capt. John Brooks - - - - -	,, ,, ,, ,, *i*
Benjamin Columbine,[5] Esq. to be Lt.-Colonel and Capt. of a Cy. - -	St. James's, 28 Jan. 1716/7.*j*
Wm. Kennedy,[6] Esq. to be Major and Capt. of a Cy.- - - -	,, ,, ,, ,, *j*
Mervin Pratt,[7] Esq. to be Capt. in room of John Greenwood - - -	,, ,, ,, ,, *j*
James Kerr,[8] Esq. to be Capt. in room of John Miller - - - -	— 1 Oct. 1717.*j*
Philip Parry,[9] Esq. to be Capt. in room of Hugh Montgomery - - -	-- 16 Nov. ,, *j*
Wm. Kennedy,[6] Esq. to be Lt.-Colonel in room of Ben. Columbine and Capt. of Cy. - - - -	— 9 Dec. ,, *j*
Charles Pawlet,[10] Esq. to be Major and Capt. of a Cy.- -	— ,, ,, ,, *j*
Nicholas Budiani[11] to be Lieut. to Capt. Philip Parry in room of Wm. Ashe -	— 6 May, 1718.*j*
George Collier[12] to be Ens. to Lt.-Col. Wm. Kennedy - - - -	— 30 ,, ,, *j*

[1] Appointed Lieut. in Lord Mark Kerr's Regt. 6 March, 1718/19. Adjt. before 1726. Capt. 22 Dec. 1726 in Disney's Regt. Served at the defence of Gibraltar, 1726–27. Exempt and Capt. 3rd Tp. of Life Guards, 5 July, 1735. Major, 15 Feb. 1740/41. Served at Dettingen on the Duke of Cumberland's staff. Lost a leg in aforesaid battle. Was appointed Gov. of Charlemont Fort before 1745. D. in 1770. Will proved at Dublin. A portrait of Major John Johnston is in the possession of Col. Wade-Dalton of Hauxwell Hall, Constable Burton, Yorkshire.

[2] Out 6 May, 1718.

[3] Adjt. 14 Oct. 1719.

[4] Out of above Regt. before 1727. Probably the Robert Kerr who was appointed Capt.-Lieut. of Lt.-Gen. the Hon. Wm. Ker's Dragoons, 15 Dec. 1738.

[5] See biog. notice in Vol. I., p. 356, note 3.

[6] One of the elder sons of Sir Thos. Kennedy, Knt., of Dalquharran and Dunure, Ayrshire. Capt.-Lieut. of Lord Mark Kerr's Regt. of Foot (disbanded in Nov. 1712), 28 Jan. 1709. Capt. 10 Jan. 1710. Half-pay in 1713. Lt.-Col. of Lord Mark Kerr's Regt. 9 Dec. 1717. D. as Lt.-Col. of said Corps, 1 April, 1743.

[7] Of Cabra Castle, co. Cavan. Youngest son of Joseph Pratt of Cabra. Left the Regt. in Feb. 1720. D. in 1751. Will proved at Dublin.

[8] Serving in 1740.

[9] Comn. renewed by George II. D. in 1736. Will proved at Dublin.

[10] See biog. notice in Vol. I., p. 135, note 10.

[11] Promoted Capt. 21 Jan. 1738. Serving in same Regt. 1740.

[12] Not in any subsequent List.

LORD FORRESTER'S REGIMENT OF FOOT.

[30TH FOOT,—1ST BATTALION EAST LANCASHIRE REGIMENT.]

Mem.—This Regiment embarked on board Sir George Byng's Fleet for Minorca in June, 1718, and did not return to Ireland from the Mediterranean until 1725.

George, Lord Forrester [1] to be Colonel in the room of Major-General Charles Wills and Capt. of a Cy. - - - - - - — 5 Jan. 1715/6.*i*

Wm. Davison,[2] Esq. to be Capt. in the room of Chas. Williams - - - - - St. James's, 17 April, 1716.*a*

Wm. Harvey [3] to be 2nd Lieut. to Capt. Chas. Williams's [late] Cy. - - - - — 12 May, ,, *i*

Edmund Martin [4] to be 1st Lieut. to Lt.-Col. Richard Cobham - - - - — 3 Oct. ,, *i*

John Forrester [5] to be 2nd Lieut. to Capt. Hugh Palliser - - - - - - — ,, ,, ,, *i*

Robinson Sowle,[6] Esq. to be Capt. in the room of Hugh Palliser - - - St. James's, 20 April, 1717. *b* & *j*

Philip Bureau [7] to be 2nd Lieut. to Capt. Walter Palliser - - - - — 4 May, ,, *j*

Henry Pakenham [8] to be Chaplain - - — ,, ,, ,, *j*

Nicholas Smith [9] to be 2nd Lieut. to Lord Forrester's Cy. - - - - St. James's, 3 July, ,, *b* & *j*

Edward Wolfe,[10] Esq. to be Lt.-Col. and Capt. of a Cy. - - - - - - ,, 10 ,, ,, *j*

Peter Bettsworth,[11] Esq. to be Major and Capt. of a Cy. - - - - - ,, ,, ,, ,, *j*

Brigadier-General Thos. Stanwix [12] to be Colonel in the room of Lord Forrester and Capt. of a Cy. - - - - - ,, 17 ,, ,, *b*

Andrew Forrester,[13] Esq. to be Capt. in room of Michael Medford - - - Dublin Castle, 14 Aug. 1717.*j*

Edmund Quarles [14] to be 1st Lieut. to Capt. Walter Palliser in room of James Baker - ,, ,, ,, ,, *j*

James Baker,[15] Esq. to be Capt.-Lieut. in room of Andrew Forrester - - - ,, ,, ,, ,, *j*

David Weems [16] (*sic*) to be 2nd Lieut. to Lt.-Col. Edward Wolfe in room of Edmund Quarles - - - - - - ,, ,, ,, ,, *j*

Brigadier-General Andrew Bisset [17] to be Colonel in room of Brigadier Thos. Stanwix [and Capt. of a Cy.] - Hampton Court, 25 ,, ,, *b*

Edward Stillingfleet [18] to be 2nd Lieut. to Capt. Wm. Davison in room of Wm. Harvey decd. - - - - — ,, ,, ,, *j*

Francis Peirson,[19] Esq. to be Capt. in room of Walter Palliser - - - - — ,, ,, ,, *j*

Robinson Sowle,[20] Esq. to be Major and Capt. of a Company - - - - -	—	7 May, 1718.	*j*
Peter Bettsworth,[21] Esq. to be Lt.-Col. and Capt. of a Cy. - - - - -	—	,, ,, ,,	*j*
Folliot Ponsonby [22] to be Lieut. in room of Edmund Martin - - - - -	—	8 ,, ,,	*j*
Jeffrey Gibbon,[23] Esq. to be Capt. - - -	—	15 ,, ,,	*f*
John Roper,[24] Esq. to be Capt. - - -	—	21 ,, ,,	*j*
Lieut. Peter Margarett [25] to be 1st Lieut. to Capt. John Vincent in room of John Roper	—	23 ,, ,,	*j*
John Vincent,[26] Esq. to be Capt. in room of Robinson Sowle - - -	Dublin Castle,	10 June, ,,	*b*
James Cockran,[27] Esq. to be Capt. - - -	—	13 July, ,,	*j*
Palmer Hodges [28] to be 2nd Lieut. to Capt. ——	—	24 Oct. ,,	*f*
John Horseman [29] to be 2nd Lieut. to Capt. Cochrane - - - - -	St. James's,	29 Jan. 1718/9.	*c*
Charles Jefferies [30] to be 2nd Lieut. to Capt. [Jeffrey] Gibbon - - - - -	,,	,, ,, ,,	*c*

[1] See biog. notice in Vol. I., p. 352, note 2.

[2] Appointed 2nd Lieut. in Col. Thos. Sanderson's Regt. of Marines, 17 June, 1703. 1st Lieut. 29 Sept. 1704. Capt.-Lieut. 9 Feb. 1707. Saw much service on sea and land during the war of the Spanish Succession. Half-pay, 1713. Re-appointed Capt.-Lieut. in Gen. Wills's re-formed Regt. of Foot, 25 March, 1715. D. in Feb. 1719.

[3] D. 25 Aug. 1717.

[4] See p. 165, note 1.

[5] Probably the Hon. John Forrester, youngest bro. to George Lord Forrester. Not in any subsequent List.

[6] Appointed Ens. in Lord Lucas's Regt. of Foot, 6 April, 1704. Lieut. 28 April, 1709. Capt. 13 Feb. 1712. Half-pay, 1713. Major of Brigdr. Bisset's Regt. of Foot (30th), 7 May, 1718. Lt.-Col. of Montague's Regt. (11th Foot), 23 Jan. 1732. Col. of said Corps, 21 May, 1743. Served at Fontenoy. D. or left the Army in 1746.

[7] Left the Regt. in May, 1726. He was probably son, or kinsman, to John Bureau whose will was proved at Dublin in 1720, and this document states the testator to have been a "native of Rochelle and refugee for cause of religion."

[8] Out of the Regt. in Feb. 1721.

[9] Do. before 1727.

[10] See biog. notice in Vol. I., p. 168, note 3.

[11] "A gentleman of a good estate and family in the County of Southampton and who has served his country as a J.P. and M.P. with good reputation" (*Recommendations for Commissions in the New Levies*, 1706). Capt. in Col. Wm. Evans's newly-raised Regt. of Foot, 10 April, 1703. Half-pay, 1713. Lt.-Col. of Brigdr. Bisset's Regt. 7 May, 1718. Serving in 1728.

[12] See biog. notice in Vol I., p. 166, note 1.

[13] The Hon. Andrew Forrester, younger bro. to George, 5th Lord Forrester. See his Comn. as Exempt and Capt. in 4th Tp. of Life Guards, 1 March, 1720.

[14] Appointed 2nd Lieut. in Wills's Regt. of Marines, 21 Nov. 1707. Half-pay, 1713. Re-commissioned 2nd Lieut. in Wills's Regt. of Foot, 25 March, 1715. Exchanged to the Earl of Londonderry's Regt. (3rd Foot), as Lieut. before 1727. Capt.-Lieut. 5 Nov. 1736. Serving in 1740. D. about 1742.

[15] Out of the Regt. 4 May, 1722.

[16] *Wemys.* 1st Lieut. 15 Feb. 1720. Comn. renewed by George II. Out of the Regt. before 1736.

[17] Appointed Ens. in the Earl of Dumbarton's Regt. (Rl. Scots), 1 May, 1688. Lieut. of Grendrs. in the Coldstream Guards, 31 Dec. 1688. Capt. and Lt.-Col. in do. 1 Jan. 1697. Wounded at Landen in July, 1693. Brig.-Gen. 1 Jan. 1710. Col. of the 30th Foot, 24 Aug. 1717. Maj.-Gen. 3 March, 1727. Lt.-Gen. 28 Oct. 1735. D. 22 Aug. 1742, aged 82. Bd. in Westminster Abbey.

[18] Comn. renewed by George II. 1st Lieut. 14 June, 1729. Serving in 1740.

[19] *Pierson.* Major, 27 Sept. 1732. Serving with above Regt. in Ireland 1740.

[20] See note 6.

[21] See note 11.

[22] The Gradation List for 1730 gives 2 Jan. 1717 as the date of this officer's Comn. Serving in the 27th Foot in 1727. Capt. in 28th Foot (Bragg's), 12 Feb. 1732. D. in 1746. Will proved at Dublin. He was kinsman to the Earl of Bessborough.

[23] Probably son of the Lt.-Col. Jeffrey *Gibbons* of the Coldstream Guards who lost a leg at Malplaquet. Capt. Gibbons had served in the Royal Fusiliers. He was still Capt. in 30th Foot in 1736. Out before 1740.

[24] Appointed 2nd Lieut. in Wills's Marines about 1707. 1st Lieut. 15 Nov. 1710. Half-pay, 1713. Re-appointed Lieut. in Wills's Regt. of Foot, 25 March, 1715. Comn. as Capt. renewed in 1727. D. in 1737. Will proved at Dublin. Described in said document as "late Captain in General Bisset's Regt. of Foot."

[25] Probably son of Capt. Peter Margaret of same Regt. Promoted Capt. 26 Aug. 1737. D. in 1743. Described in his will as Capt. in Gen. Bisset's Regt. of Foot.

[26] Appointed Fort Major at Fort St. Philip, Minorca, 17 Sept. 1718 (see Vol. I., p. 251). Out of Bisset's Regt. before 1727.

[27] Appointed Capt. in the Royal Fusiliers, 19 June, 1716. Lt.-Col. of Col. Chas. Douglas's newly-raised Regt. of Marines, 22 Nov. 1739. Served with said Corps at the siege of Carthagena, 1741, and succeeded to the command 26 April same year. Half-pay, 1749. Maj.-Gen. 23 March, 1754. Lt.-Gen. 14 Jan. 1758. D. same year at Hampstead.—*Gentleman's Mag.*

[28] Comn. renewed by George II. 1st Lieut. 19 Aug. 1731. Serving in 1740.

[29] Capt. in Gen. Wills's Regt. of Foot (3rd Buffs), 16 Oct. 1719. Major, 2 Sept. 1739. Lt.-Col. of Col. Daniel Houghton's newly-raised Regt. of Foot (45th), 2 Feb. 1741. Serving with said Corps in 1749. Out before 1755.

[30] One of the younger sons of Brig.-Gen. Sir Jas. Jefferys (or Jefferyes) of Blarney Castle, co. Cork. Appointed Ens. in Col. H. Rooke's Regt. 20 Nov. 1710. Half-pay, 1712. Ens. in Brig.-Gen. Alex. Grant's newly-raised Regt. of Foot, 22 July, 1715. 1st Lieut. in Bisset's Regt. 1 Sept. 1721. Capt. 1 Nov. 1734. Major, 2 April, 1742. Lt.-Col. 34th Foot, 17 Feb. 1746. Col. of 14th Foot, 3 Jan. 1756. D. in 1765.

LORD JOHN KERR'S REGIMENT OF FOOT.

[31ST FOOT,—1ST BATTALION EAST SURREY REGIMENT.]

Thos. Webb[1] to be Lieut. to Capt. John Beckwith -   - 29 Feb. 1715/6.*i*

Lancelot Lawder[2] to be Ens. to Lt.-Col. George Blakeney   „   „   „   *i*

Henry Barker[3] to be Ens. to Capt. Alex. Wilson (*sic*) 27 Mar. 1716.   *i*

Robt. Stephenson[4] to be Chaplain -   -   -   - 26 April,   „   *i*

Edward O'Bryen,[5] Esq. to be Capt. of that Cy. whereof
    John Beckwith was late Capt. -   -   -   - 14 May,   „   *i*

Ant. Ladeveze,[6] Esq. to be Capt.-Lieut. -   -   - 15   „   „   *i*

Robert Blakeney[7] to be Lieut. to the Grendr. Cy.
    whereof Fleetwood Watkins is Capt.   -   -   „   „   „   *i*

James Smith[8] to be Ens. to Capt. Edward O'Bryen   -   „   „   „   *i*

Ant. Ladeveze,[9] Esq. to be Capt. in room of Roger
    Flower   -   -   -   -   -   -   -   - 15 Aug. 1717.   *j*

Edward Thompson,[10] Esq. to be Capt.-Lieut. in room of
    Ant. Ladeveze -   -   -   -   -   -   -   „   „   „   *j*

Wm. Spicer[11] to be Lieut. to Capt. Alex. Wilson in room
    of Edward Thompson   -   -   -   -   „   „   „   *j*

Alex. Porterfield[12] to be Ens. to Capt. Ant. Ladeveze -   „   „   „   *j*

Robert Blakeney[13] to be Adjt.   -   -   -   -   „   „   „   *j*

James Baird[14] to be Lieut. to Lt.-Col. George Blakeney
    in room of Wm. Ridsdale -   -   -   -   - 1 Oct.   „   *j*

John Phillips[15] to be Chaplain in room of Robt. Steven-
    son superseded   -   -   -   -   -   - 13 Dec.   „   *j*

Thos. Sutton,[16] Esq. to be Major and Capt. of a Cy.   - 20   „   „   *j*

Edward Legard,[17] Esq. to be Capt. in room of Thos.
    Sutton   -   -   -   -   -   -   -   „   „   „   *j*

Charles Bristow[18] to be Ens. to Lt.-Col. George Blakeney
    in room of Lancelot Lawder -   -   -   - 14 Feb. 1717/8.*j*

Edward Thompson,[19] Esq. to be Capt. in room of Rupert
    Hancock -   -   -   -   -   -   -   - 8 Mar.   „   *j*

Charles Vignoles[20] to be Ens. to Capt. Alex. Wilson in
    room of Henry Barker preferred Lieut. -   -   „   „   „   *j*

Henry Barker[21] to be Lieut. to Capt. Alex. Wilson in
    room of Wm. Spicer preferred Capt.-Lieut. -   -   „   „   „   *j*

[Wm. Spicer,[22] Esq. to be Capt.-Lieut. -   -   -   „   „   „   ]

Wm. Blakeney,[23] Esq. to be Lt.-Col. in room of George
    Blakeney and Capt. of a Cy. -   -   -   - 3 April, 1718.   *j*

Robert Stephenson,[24] Chaplain, to be Chaplain in room
    of John Phillips superseded   -   -   -   - 21 Oct.   „   *j*

Archibald Kerr[25] to be Ens. to Major Thos. Sutton in
    room of Wm. Lewis -   -   -   -   - 15 Nov.   „   *j*

---

[1] Left the Regt. in June, 1719. On half-pay in 1722.

[2] Left the Regt. in Feb. 1718. Probably father of the "Lancelot Lawder, of Clove Hill, co. Leitrim, Esq." whose will was proved at Dublin in 1797.

[3] Lieut. 8 March, 1718. Out before 1727.

[4] Superseded 13 Dec. 1717. Restored 21 Oct. 1718. Out in March, 1726.

[5] Left the Regt. as Capt. in March, 1727. He appears to have been third son of Sir Edward O'Brien of Dromoland, co. Clare, Bart., a Col. of a Regt. of Militia Dragoons in co. Clare.

[6] See notice in Vol. I., p. 359, note 4.

[7] Capt. 23 April, 1720. Serving in 1740. Youngest bro. and heir to Gen. Lord Blakeney. He was of Mount Blakeney, near Kilmallock, and d. in 1763.

[8] Left the Regt. as 1st Lieut. of Grendrs. in May, 1726.

[9] See note 6.

[10] Capt. 8 March, 1718. Comn. renewed by George II. D. in 1734. Will proved at Dublin.

[11] Capt.-Lieut. 8 March, 1718. Capt. 8 Jan. 1719. Major, 25 July, 1726. Out in 1732.

[12] Out before 1727. Probably bro. to Gilbert Porterfield serving as Lieut. in above Regt. in 1727.

[13] See note 7.

[14] Capt. 20 June, 1735. Major, 27 May, 1745. Served at Fontenoy. Serving in 1749. Out before 1755.

[15] Out before 1736.

[16] From the Half-pay List. Out of above Regt. in July, 1726.

[17] Major, 3 Feb. 1741. Lt.-Col. 1 May, 1745. Served at Fontenoy. Serving in 1749. Out before 1755. Kinsman to the Lieut. Edward Legard who d. while serving in Ireland, 1678, and to whose memory a tablet was erected in Bandon Church. See *Irish Army Lists*, 1661–85, by Charles Dalton, F.R.G.S., p. 97, note 1.

[18] Lieut. 7 Sept. 1720. Comn. renewed in 1727. Out before 1736.

[19] See note 10.

[20] Lieut. 22 Oct. 1723. Served at Fontenoy and subsequent engagements in Flanders. Major of above Regt. 22 July, 1751. Lt.-Col. of 70th Foot, 13 April, 1758. D. or retd. before 1764. He belonged to a well-known Huguenot family, and was probably son of Charles Vignoles of Dublin, whose will was proved in 1727.

[21] See note 3.

[22] See note 11.

[23] Eldest son of Wm. Blakeney of Thomastown, co. Limerick. Appointed Adjt. to the Royal Irish Regt. of Foot, 9 Feb. 1699. Ens. to an additional Cy. in same Corps, 31 May, 1701. Lieut. 1 Aug. 1701. Fought at Blenheim. Capt. 25 Aug. 1704. Bt.-Major, 1 Jan. 1707. Lieut. and Capt. 1st Foot Guards, 9 March, 1708. Col. of the Inniskilling Regt. (27th), 27 June, 1737. Served as a Brig.-Gen. in the Carthagena Expedition in 1741. Defended Stirling Castle in 1745–46. Maj.-Gen. 30 March, 1745. Lt.-Gen. 11 Sept. 1747. For his gallant defence of Fort St. Philip, Minorca, Blakeney was created K.B. 27 Sept. 1756, and Baron Blakeney, in the Peerage of Ireland, a month later. D.s.p. 20 Sept. 1761, aged 91. Bd. in Westminster Abbey.

[24] Out before 1737.

[25] D. in May, 1725.

BRIGADIER-GENERAL JACOB BORR'S REGIMENT OF FOOT.

[32ND FOOT,—1ST BATTALION THE DUKE OF CORNWALL'S LIGHT INFANTRY.]

Samuel Stone,[1] Esq. to be Capt. of Brigadier Borr's late Cy. - - - - - -	—	27 Mar. 1716.*i*
John Brice[2] to be 2nd Lieut. to Capt. Humphry Cory - - - - -	—	3 May, „ *i*
Melchior Guy Dickens,[3] Esq. to be Capt. in room of Major Humphry Cory- -	Dublin Castle,	9 Aug. 1717.*j*
John Warner[4] to be 2nd Lieut. to Capt. Thos. Norton in room of John Cranwell - -	—	14 „ „ *j*
John Cranwell[5] to be 1st Lieut. to Capt. Richard Mullins in room of James Fade decd. - - - - - - - -	—	31 „ „ *j*
Westenra Crump[6] to be Chaplain - - -	—	31 „ „ *j*
Peter Marget (*sic*)[7] to be 1st Lieut. to Capt. Samuel Stone in room of John Cox decd. - - - - - - -	—	2 Sept. „ *j*
Nicholas Westby[8] to be 2nd Lieut. to Capt. Stephen Sanderson in room of Peter Marget - - - - - -	—	„ „ „ *j*
Wm. Ridsdale,[9] Esq. to be Capt. in room of Richard Mullins - - - -	—	1 Oct. „ *j*
Dawly Sutton[10] to be 2nd Lieut. to Capt. Melchior Dickens in room of John Brice decd. - - - - - - -	—	6 Jan. 1717/8.*j*
Lucius Henry Hibbin[11] to be 2nd Lieut. to Capt. Wm. Ridsdale in room of Edward Bilton decd. - - - - -	—	20 Feb. „ *j*
John Fade,[12] Esq. to be Capt. in room of Wm. Lee -	—	15 July, 1718.*j*
Charles Douglas,[13] Esq. to be Lt.-Colonel in room of [Col.] George Burston and Capt. of a Cy. - - - - - - -	—	4 Nov. „ *j*

[1] Appointed Ens. in Col. John Selwyn's Regt. of Foot (3rd Buffs), 22 Jan. 1713. Major 32nd Foot, 15 Sept. 1731. Believed to have served with the last-named Corps at Dettingen and Fontenoy. On the Staff in 1747. Out of the Regt. in July same year.
[2] D. 6 Jan. 1718.
[3] Appointed Lt.-Col. of the 47th Foot (then newly raised) 6 Feb. 1741. D. or retd. in Feb. 1751.
[4] Comn. renewed by George II. Out before 1740.   [5] Out before 1727.
[6] Md. Martha Campbell. Her will was proved at Dublin in 1755.
[7] Capt.-Lieut. 14 Aug. 1738. The will of "Peter Margaret, late Capt. in Col. Huske's Regt. of Foot" (32nd) was proved at Dublin in 1745.
[8] Comn. renewed by George II. Out before 1740. Probably son of the "Nicholas Westby, Esq., of Dublin," whose will was proved in 1716.
[9] Promoted from Sir Harry Goring's Regt. of Foot. Serving as Capt. in 32nd Foot in 1740.
[10] Lieut. 8 March, 1724. Serving in 1740.   [11] Out before 1727.
[12] Appointed Capt. in Borr's Marines, 7 Aug. 1707. Half-pay on the reduction of said Corps. D. in 1729 as Capt. in Dubourgay's Regt. of Foot (32nd). Will proved at Dublin.
[13] See notice in Vol. I., p 170, note 3.

MAJOR-GENERAL WADE'S REGIMENT OF FOOT.

[33RD FOOT,—1ST BATTALION DUKE OF WELLINGTON'S (WEST RIDING REGIMENT).]

This Regiment took part in the Expedition to Vigo, 1719.

Peter de la Faucille [1] to be Ens. to Major John Reading - - - - - - - -	— 19 Jan. 1715/6. *i*
John Bouyer (*sic*) [2] to be Lieut. to Capt. John Hauteclaire - - - - - - -	— 11 Feb. „ *i*
Henry Hawley,[3] Esq. to be Colonel in room of Major-General Wade and Capt. of a Cy. - - - - - - - -	— 19 Mar. 1716/7.*j*
John Reading,[4] Esq. to be Major and Capt. of a Cy. - - - - - - -	— 23 „ „ *j*
John Archer,[5] Esq. to be Lt.-Col. and Capt. of a Cy. - - - - - - -	— „ „ „ *j*
Wm. Norcliffe,[6] Esq. to be Capt. in room of John Reading preferred - - - -	— „ „ „ *j*
John Graydon [7] to be Lieut. to Capt. Wm. Norcliffe in room of Thos. Kerr - -	— 31 Aug. 1717.*j*
Richard Green [8] to be Lieut. to Capt. Henry Grame (*sic*) in room of John Mallet -	— „ „ „ *j*
Thos. Erle [9] to be Ens. to Lt.-Col. John Archer in room of John Martin decd. -	— „ „ „ *j*
Christopher Williams,[10] Esq. to be Capt. in the room of Wm. Norcliffe - - -	— „ „ „ *j*
Anderson Saunders [11] to be Lieut. to Capt. Richard Challenor Cobb in room of Chris. Williams - - - - - -	— 13 Sept. „ *j*
Wm. Egelston (*sic*) [12] to be Ens. to Capt. John Hauteclaire in room of Anderson Saunders - - - - - -	— „ „ „ *j*
George Robinson [13] to be Ens. to Capt. John Mallet in room of Edmund Polhill decd.	— 12 Nov. „ *j*
George Johnston [14] to be Lieut. to Capt. John Hauteclaire in room of John Bowyer -	— 21 „ „ *j*
Arthur Farewell [15] to be Ens. to Col. Hawley in room of Wm. Wade preferred - -	— 31 Mar. 1718.
Arnold James Breams [16] to be Lieut. to Lt.-Col. Archer in room of Alex. La Millière	— „ „ „ *j*
Boyle Low [17] to be Ens. to above Cy. in room of Arnold James Breams - - -	— „ „ „ *j*
Bernard Lostau,[18] Esq. to be Capt. in the room of John Hauteclaire [Signed by the Duke of Bolton] - - -	London, 6 May, 1718.*b* & *j*

[1] *De la Fausille.* Capt.-Lieut. 22 Nov. 1739. Serving in 1740.
[2] Left the Regt. in Sept. 1717.
[3] See memoir of Lt.-Gen. Henry Hawley in this vol. pp. 41–51.
[4] See biog. notice in Vol. I., p. 340, note 4.

M 2

[5] See biog. notice in Vol. I., p. 361, note 3. Retd. about 1721. He was appointed Agent to several Regts. on the Irish Establishment, and appears as such in *The Quarters of the Army in Ireland for* 1736.

[6] Appointed Cornet in the Princess Anne of Denmark's Dragoons, 1 July, 1694. Believed to have served at Almanza. Lieut. 25 Oct. 1707. Capt. in Grant's Regt. of Foot, 12 Sept. 1711. Half-pay, 1713. Left Hawley's Regt. 31 Aug. 1717.

[7] Capt. in Borr's Regt. (32nd), 7 June, 1720. Serving with same rank in 1740.

[8] Out before 1727.

[9] Lieut. in Sir Robert Rich's Regt. of Dragoons (8th), 26 July, 1722. Capt.-Lieut. 9 Aug. 1739. Major 6th Dragoons, 22 June, 1745. Lt.-Col. of the 14th Dragoons, 4 Sept. 1754. Col. 28th Foot, 15 July, 1773. D. a Maj.-Gen. in 1777. See biog. notice of his father in Vol. I., p. 112, note 2.

[10] Out 1 Dec. 1722.

[11] Comn. renewed by George II. Serving in 1730. Out before 1740. He was, according to Sir B. Burke, elder son of Robert Saunders of Dublin.

[12] Capt. 1 Dec. 1722. Major, 7 June, 1741. His proper name was *Eccleston*. D. about 1742.

[13] Lieut. 1 Dec. 1722. Serving in 1730. Out before 1740.

[14] Capt. 21 Jan. 1721. Serving in 1730. Not in any subsequent List. Believed to be the Capt. George Johnston who acted as Agent for several Regts. on the Irish Establishment in 1736 and subsequent years. In Millan's *List* for 1748, Capt. G. Johnston's address is given as " Cork Hill, Dublin."

[15] Dead in Jan. 1725.

[16] Capt.-Lieut. 16 Oct. 1722. Serving in 1727.

[17] Comn. renewed in 1727. Out before 1740.

[18] Appointed Cornet in the Rl. Dragoons, 24 July, 1711. Lieut. in the Hon. Wm. Ker's Dragoons, 15 July, 1715. D. as Capt. in Col. Hawley's Regt. of Foot in 1727. Will proved at Dublin.

LIEUT.-GENERAL RICHARD GORGES'S REGIMENT OF FOOT.
[35TH FOOT,—1ST BATTALION ROYAL SUSSEX REGIMENT.]

Wm. Wright,[1] Esq. to be Capt. in room of
—— Maxwell - - - - - — 23 Mar. 1715/6.*i*

Abel Warren[2] to be Lieut. to Capt. John
Witchalse - - - - - — ,, ,, ,, *i*

George Vickers[3] to be Lieut. to Capt. Wm.
Rice's Grenadier Cy. - - - — 20 June, 1716.*i*

George Pendred[4] to be Ens. to Capt. John
Ant. Berniere - - - - — ,, ,, ,, *i*

Henry Crofton[5] to be Ens. to Lt.-Col.
David Dunbar - - - - — 16 Oct. ,, *i*

Charles Otway,[6] Esq. to be Colonel of Our
Regt. of Foot whereof Lt.-General
Richard Gorges was late Colonel and
Capt. of a Company - - - - Hampton Court, 26 July, 1717.*b*

Wm. Collis[7] to be Chaplain in room of
Henry Matthews - - - - Dublin Castle, 17 Oct. ,, *j*

Samuel Ashton[8] to be Ens. to Capt. Wm.
Wright in room of Stephen Deane - ,, ,, 17 Dec. ,, *j*

Wm. Tenison,[9] Esq. to be Capt. of that
Cy. whereof Abel Dudley was late
Capt. - - - - - - ,, ,, 17 Apr. 1718.*j*

Michael Davey[10] to be Lieut. to Capt.
Edward Warren in room of And.
Willoughby - - - - - ,, ,, ,, ,, ,, *j*

Ensign Thos. Otway[11] to be Ens. to Capt.
Wm. Wansborough in room of
George Pendred [Signed by the Duke
of Bolton] - - - - ,, ,, 29 ,, ,, *b*

Roger Dauson,[12] Esq. to be Capt. in the
room of Edward Warren [Signed by
the Duke of Bolton] - - - ,, ,, 8 May, ,, *b*

*This Regiment was sent to Minorca
in June, 1718.*

John Winyard (sic),[13] Esq. to be Lt.-
Colonel and Capt. of a Company in
the room of David Dunbar [Signed
by the Duke of Bolton] - - - ,, ,, 10 July, ,, *b*

Thos. Vachell,[14] Esq. to be Major and
Capt. of a Company in room of John
Winyard [Signed by the Duke of
Bolton] - - - - - - ,, ,, ,, ,, ,, *b*

Cornelius O'Bryan[15] to be Lieut. to Capt.
Toby Purcell - - - - - St. James's, 1 Nov. ,, *b*

Mark Ant. Jones[16] to be Ens. to the
Colonel's own Company - - - ,, ,, ,, ,, ,, *b*

[1] Promoted Major, 23 Jan. 1724. Lt.-Col. of Brigdr. Arch. Hamilton's Dragoons (14th
Dragoons), 7 July, 1737. Serving in 1749. Out before 1754.

[2] Capt. 8 Sept. 1722. Major, June, 1745. Out before 1749. Of Lowhill, co. Kilkenny. D. in 1763. Will proved at Dublin.

[3] Promoted from Ens. Out before 1727.

[4] Out 29 April, 1718.

[5] Do.

[6] See notice in Vol. I., p. 110, note 3.

[7] The Rev. Wm. Collis, of Tralee, co. Kerry, d. in 1772. Will proved at Dublin.

[8] Serving as 1st Lieut. of the Grendr. Cy. in 1727. Out before 1736.

[9] Major, 31 Aug. 1739. Lt.-Col. of above Regt. 1 June, 1745. D. or retd. in Jan. 1750. Kinsman to the Archbishop of Canterbury of this surname who d. 1715.

[10] Out before 1727.

[11] Lieut. 3 June, 1721. Serving as Lieut. in Col. Roger Handasyde's Regt. (22nd Foot), 1727. Further services untraced. Probably a son of Col. Charles Otway.

[12] Appointed Lieut. in Col. Livesay's Regt. of Foot, 24 June, 1709. Serving as Capt. in Col. C. Otway's Regt. in 1728.

[13] Appointed Adjt. of Col. Roger Elliot's Regt. of Foot, 10 April, 1703. Served in Portugal. Half-pay, 1713. Col. of the 4th Marines, 20 Nov. 1739. Served with this Corps at the siege of Carthagena, 1741. Transferred to the Colonelcy of 17th Foot, 31 Aug. 1742 Many years C.-in-C. at Gibraltar and Port Mahon. Lt.-Gen. in Sept. 1747. D. 20 Feb. 1752. Bd. in Westminster Abbey. He was son of John *Wynyard* of Westminster (d. 1690), and was bapt. at St. Margaret's, Westminster. See Col. Chester's *Westminster Abbey Registers*, p. 2, note 1.

[14] Appointed Capt. *en second* in Col. John Hill's Regt. of Foot, 3 July, 1708. A Brigade-Major of the troops sent to Canada under Brigdr. John Hill in 1711. Out of the Army in 1724

[15] Out before 1727

[16] Probably a child. Comn. renewed by George II. Appointed Ens. in the 1st Foot Guards, 8 Jan. 1732. Lieut. and Capt. 20 April, 1743. The death of a Capt. Jones, 1st Foot Guards, is noted in *Gentleman's Mag.* for 1757.

COLONEL WM. EGERTON'S REGIMENT OF FOOT.
[36TH FOOT,—2ND BATTALION WORCESTERSHIRE REGIMENT.]

Returned to Ireland from Great Britain in Oct. 1718. Embarked for England in March, 1719. Returned to Ireland in 1720. For Commissions in this Corps during the year 1716, see Vol. I., pp. 198–202 passim.

Robert Mathison to be Chaplain	Hampton Court, 9 Feb. 1717/8.*b*	
Dudley Ackland (*sic*),[1] Esq. to be Capt. in the room of Arthur Whitmore	St. James's, 8 March, ,, *b*	
Robert Scott[2] to be Ens. to Capt. John Lloyd	,, ,, ,, ,, ,, *b*	
Samuel Cutts[3] to be Lieut. to Lt.-Col. Robert Innes	,, ,, ,, ,, ,, *b*	
John Roger Hartnoll[4] Esq. to be Capt. of that Company whereof Lt.-Col. Robt. Innes was late Capt.	,, ,, 16 April, 1718.*b*	
Wm. Hargrave,[5] Esq. to be Lt.-Colonel and Capt. of a Company	,, ,, ,, ,, ,, *b*	
Francis Flemming,[6] Esq. to be Major and Capt. of a Company	,, ,, ,, ,, ,, *b*	
Samuel Whitaker,[7] Esq. to be Capt. in the room of John Sterling	Kensington, 9 June, ,, *b*	
Wm. Braymer, Chyrurgion, to be Chyrurgion in room of Dudley Acland superseded	— 18 Dec. ,, *j*	
John Lloyd[8] to be Lieut. to Capt. Theoph. Sandford in the room of Michael Edwards decd.	— 20 Feb. 1718/9.*j*	

---

[1] Appears to have been son of Surgeon Dudley Acland, or Ackland. Promoted from Lieut. in same Regt. Major, 1 Nov. 1739. Serving on the Staff in 1742. D. in 1746. Will proved at Dublin.

[2] Capt.-Lieut. 1 Nov. 1739. Serving in 1740. Untraced after that year.

[3] Promoted from Ens. Out of the Regt. before 1727.

[4] Comn. renewed by George II. D. on active service in the West Indies, 1741 (*Gentleman's Mag.*). Held the rank of Major in Col. Cochrane's Marines at the time of his death.

[5] See biog. notice in Vol. I., p. 365, note 2.

[6] Promoted from Capt. Out of the Regt. in 1724. Serving as Major of Col. John Middleton's Regt. of Foot (25th) in 1727. He was bro. to Maj.-Gen. James *Fleming*, Col. of the 36th Foot, who d. in 1751, and in whose will were legacies to the children of his deceased bro. Francis Fleming.

[7] Comn. renewed by George II. Serving with above Regt. in 1740.

[8] Capt.-Lieut. 10 Sept. 1723. Serving in 1728.

LORD HINCHINBROKE'S REGIMENT OF FOOT.
[37TH FOOT,—1ST BATTALION HAMPSHIRE REGIMENT.]

Returned to Ireland from England in Oct. 1718. Embarked in Aug. 1719 with the Expedition to Vigo.

Thos. Lumley,[1] Esq. to be Lt.-Colonel of Lord Hinchinbroke's [late Fane's] Regt. of Foot and to be Capt. of a Company - - - - -	St. James's,	11 Dec. 1717.*b*
Russell Chapman[2] to be Ens. to Lt.-Col. Thos. Lumley - - - - -	Hampton Court,	22 Oct. 1718.*b*
Nathaniel Green[3] to be Ens. to Capt. Hall	,, ,, ,, ,,	,, *b*
Alex. Jacob,[4] Esq. to be Lt.-Colonel in the room of Lt.-Col. Thos. Lumley and to be Captain of a Company - -	Dublin Castle,	18 Dec. ,, *b*
John Wills[5] to be Ensign to Capt. Raphael Walsh in room of Samuel Watts - - - - - -	,, ,,	,, ,, ,, *j*

[1] Succeeded his bro. Richard as Earl of Scarborough in 1740. Took the additional surname of Saunderson on succeeding to the estate of the Earl of Castleton, in Ireland, in 1723. D. in 1752.

[2] Promoted Lieut. 7 Aug. 1733. Serving in 1740.

[3] Promoted Lieut. 9 July, 1728.

[4] Comn. signed by the Duke of Bolton. Appointed Capt. in Col. Theodore Vezey's Regt. of Foot, 23 Dec. 1711. Capt. in Pocock's Foot in 1715. When latter Corps was disbanded in Oct. 1718 he joined Col. Cotton's Regt. on 1 Dec. same year, but was promoted Lt.-Col. as given in the text same month. Left Lord Hinchinbroke's Regt. in May, 1722.

[5] Comn. renewed by George II. Out of the Regt. before 1736.

ENGLISH ESTABLISHMENT

CAVALRY COMMISSIONS, 1719–1727

CAVALRY COMMISSIONS, 1719–1727

1ST TROOP OF LIFE GUARDS.

James McDonald,[1] Esq. to be Exempt and eldest Captain - - - - -	St. James's, 27 Nov. 1719.c
Thos. Eaton,[2] to be Sub-Brigadier and eldest Cornet - - - - - - -	,, 17 Dec. ,, c
Wm. Cavell,[3] to be Brigadier and eldest Lieut.	,, ,, ,, ,, p
Jonathan Driver,[4] Esq. to be Exempt and eldest Capt. - - - - - -	,, 19 May, 1720.c
Daniel Leighton,[5] Esq. to be Cornet and Major - - - - - - -	,, ,, ,, , c
Edmund Wright,[6] Esq. to be Guidon and Major - - - - - - -	,, ,, ,, ,, c
James Batson,[7] Esq. to be Exempt and eldest Captain - - - - - -	,, ,, ,, ,, c
Esme Clarke,[8] to be Brigadier and eldest Lieut. - - - - - - -	,, ,, ,, ,, c
Chas. Childe,[9] to be Sub-Brigadier and eldest Lieut. - - - - - - -	,, ,, ,, ,, c
Chas. La Motte,[10] to be Chaplain - - -	Whitehall, 28 July, ,, c
Henry Herbert,[11] Esq. (commonly called Lord Henry Herbert) to be Capt. and Colonel in room of John, Duke of Montagu -	Kensington, 20 Sept. 1721.c
Wm. Herbert,[12] to be Brigadier and eldest Lieut. - - - - - - -	St. James's, 1 May, 1722.c
Richard Parsons,[13] Esq. to be Exempt and eldest Capt. - - - - - -	,, ,, ,, c
Worcester Wilson [14] to be Brigdr. and Lt. -	Kensington, 6 Oct. ,, d
Ben. Wellington [15] to be Sub-Brigdr. and Cornet - - - - - - -	St. James's, 27 Feb. 1724/5.d
Thos. Eaton [16] to be Adjt. and Lieut. - -	,, 27 May, 1725.d

[1] Appointed Brigdr. and eldest Lieut. 22 Oct. 1713. Comn. as Exempt and eldest Capt. renewed in June, 1727. Out before 1740.

[2] Exempt and Capt. 22 July, 1738. Major, 17 June, 1740. D. in 1743.

[3] Promoted from Sub-Brigdr. Exempt and Capt. 14 June, 1734. Serving in 1740.

[4] Promoted from Brigdr. First Major, 30 June, 1737. Lt.-Col. 15 May, 1742. Fought at Dettingen and Fontenoy with 4th Tp. of Life Guards. The Earl of Crawford who succeeded to the command of the cavalry at Fontenoy, on Sir James Campbell being mortally wounded, observing one of the guardsmen stoop when the cannon balls were flying about, cried out : "Don't stoop my lads, for if they are to hit you they will for all that"; upon which Col. Driver addressed himself to the men and said : "Gentlemen, you cannot have a better leader than Lord Crawford ; follow his example and you will gain immortal renown." (Rolt's *Memoirs of the Earl of Crawford*, p. 362.) Col. Driver d. in 1754.

[5] See Vol. I., p. 259, note 2.

[6] Comn. renewed in 1727.   D. in 1733.

[7] Promoted from Brigdr.   Serving in 1736.

[8] See Vol. I., p. 259, note 3.

[9] Out before 1727.

[10] Comn. signed by the Lords Justices.   The Rev. Charles La Motte, D.D., was Chaplain to the Prince of Wales.   D. 1742.

[11] Appointed Capt.-Lieut. Coldstream Guards, 23 Nov. 1716.   Capt. and Lt.-Col. 12 Aug. 1717.   Succeeded his father in 1733 as 9th Earl of Pembroke and 6th Earl of Montgomery.   Removed to the Colonelcy of King's Dragoon Guards, 22 June, 1733. Lt.-Gen. 18 Feb. 1742.   Resigned his Colonelcy in 1743.   D. 1751.

[12] The Hon. Wm. Herbert was fifth son of the 8th Earl of Pembroke and father of Henry, 1st Earl of Carnarvon.   Capt. and Lt.-Col. 1st Foot Guards in 1738.   Col. 14th Foot, 1 Dec. 1747.   D. 31 March, 1757, as a Maj.-Gen.

[13] Promoted from Brigdr.   Comn. as Exempt renewed in 1727.   Out before 1740.

[14] Comn. renewed in 1727.   D. before 1734, in which year his widow, Charlotte Wilson, was drawing a pension of £20 per annum.

[15] Comn. renewed in 1727.   Out before 1740.   Drawing half-pay in 1749.

[16] See note 2.

2ND TROOP OF LIFE GUARDS.

Samuel Lawran[ce] [1] to be Sub-Brigadier and
eldest Cornet - - - - - - Herrenhausen, 29 July, 1719.*c*

Arthur Edwards [2] to be Exempt and eldest
Capt. - - - - - - - St. James's, 16 May, 1720.*c*

John Greenhill to be Brigadier and eldest
Lieut. - - - - - - -   ,,   ,, ,,   ,, *c*

Thos. King [3] to be Adjt. and do. - - -   ,,   ,, ,,   ,, *c*

Joseph Fleming [4] to be Sub-Brigadier and
eldest Cornet - - - - -   ,   ,, ,,   ,, *c*

Dr. Robert Clavering to be Chaplain - -   8 Dec. ,, *c*

Thos. King [3] to be Brigadier and eldest Lieut.   13 Nov. 1721.*c*

Wm. Gough [5] to be Sub-Brigadier and eldest
Cornet - - - - - - -   ,   ,, ,,   ,, *c*

Samuel Lawran[ce] [1] to be Adjt. and eldest
Lieut. - - - - - - -   ,,   ,, ,,   ,, *c*

John Curwen [6] to be Sub-Brigadier and eldest
Cornet - - - - - - -   ,,   ,, ,,   ,, *c*

Wm. Merchant [7] to be do. and Cornet - -   ,,   16 Mar. 1722/3.*c*

Mark Ant. Saurin [8] to be Brigadier and Lieut.   Windsor, 29 Sept. 1724.*d*

Samuel Lawrence [1] to be do. - - - - St. James's, 8 Mar. 1724/5.*d*

Joseph Fleming [9] to be Adjt. and Lieut. -   ,,   ,, ,,   ,, *d*

Peter Prow [10] to be Sub-Brigadier and Cornet [,,]   16 Nov. 1725.*f*

---

[1] Adjt. 13 Nov. 1721. Resigned the Adjutancy 8 March, 1725. Brigdr. and Lieut. 8 March, 1725. D. in 1732 and was succeeded by Wm. Gough 3 Oct. same year as Brigdr. *and* Riding Master with rank of Lieut.—*Gentleman's Mag.*

[2] Comn. renewed in 1727. Had served at Blenheim as Ens. in Col. Emanuel Howe's Regt. (15th Foot) and was wounded. See under 2nd Life Guards in Vol. I., p. 259, and note on this officer.

[3] Out before 1727.

[4] Adjt. and Lieut. 8 March, 1725. Brigdr. and Lieut. 16 Nov. 1727. Exempt and Capt. 26 Oct. 1738. Serving in 1740.

[5] Comn. renewed in 1727. Brigdr. and Riding Master, 3 Oct. 1732. Serving in 1740.

[6]   Do.   Serving in 1730.

[7] Pomoted Brigdr. and Lieut. 21 May, 1733. Serving in 1740. D. same year. See *Gentleman's Mag.* 1740.

[8] From half-pay. Comn. renewed in 1727. Appointed Lt.-Col. of the Royal Dragoons, 24 Aug. 1746. Out of said Corps in 1754. D. in 1763.

[9] See note 4.

[10] See Vol. I., p. 154. Comn. renewed in 1727. Out before 1740.

3RD TROOP OF LIFE GUARDS

Disbanded 1746.

Harry Colt [1] to be Exempt and eldest Capt. - St. James's, 16 Dec. 1719. *c*		
Henry Bridle (*sic*), [2] to be Sub-Brigadier and eldest Cornet - - - - -	,, 4 Jan. 1719/20. *c*	
Robt. Pemberton [3] to be Surgeon - - -	,, 5 April, 1720. *c*	
John Slater [4] to be Brigadier and eldest Lieut.	,, 7 June, ,, *c*	
Henry Bridell [5] to be Adjt. and eldest Lieut. -	,, ,, ,, ,, *c*	
Ellis Cunliffe [6] to be Sub-Brigadier and eldest Cornet - - - - - - -	,, ,, ,, ,, *c*	
Edward Wills [7] to be do. and do. - - -	,, 21 ,, ,, *c*	
Mascal Cookes [8] to be Brigadier and eldest Lieut. - - - - - - -	,, ,, ,, ,, *c*	
Samuel Saville, [9] Esq. to be Exempt and eldest Capt. - - - - - - -	,, 10 July, ,, *c*	
Wm. Kreut (*sic*), [10] Esq. to be Exempt and eldest Capt. [in room of John Shaw decd.]	,, 17 Nov. 1721. *c*	
George Fowlks (*sic*) [11] to be Brigadier and eldest Lieut. - - - - -	,, ,, ,, ,, *c*	
Evan Thomas [12] to be Sub-Brigadier and eldest Cornet - - - - -	,, ,, ,, ,, *c*	
Michael Margetts [13] to be Brigadier and eldest Lieut. - - - - - - -	,, 15 Mar. 1721/2. *c*	
Geoffry Parker [14] to be Brigadier and Lieut. -	,, 18 Feb. 1722/3. *c*	
John Lloyd, [15] Esq. to be Exempt and Capt. -	,, 3 Feb. 1724/5. *d*	
James Cholmondeley, [16] Esq. to be Guidon and Major - - - - - - -	,, 12 May, 1725. *d*	
Do. to be Cornet and Major - - - -	,, 28 ,, ,, *d*	
Wm. Compton, [17] Esq. to be Guidon and Major	,, ,, ,, ,, *d*	
John Mohun, [18] Esq. to be Lieut. and Lieut.-Col.	,, ,, ,, ,, *d*	

[1] Out before 1727. Probably one of the Dutton Colt family.

[2] Adjt. 7 June, 1720. Out before 1727. His widow, Catherine *Brydal*, was drawing a pension of £20 per annum in 1734.

[3] Not in any subsequent List.

[4] Served previously as Adjt. and Lieut. Comn. as Lieut. renewed in 1727. D. before 1734, in which year his widow, Susanna Slater, was drawing a pension of £20 per annum.

[5] See note 2.

[6] Comn. renewed in 1727. Aftds. Sir Ellis Cunliffe, Knt. M.P. for Liverpool. D. in 1767.

[7] Exempt and Capt. 24 Sept. 1736. Major, 9 March, 1745. Serving in 1748.

[8] Out before 1727.

[9] Promoted 1st Major, 3 Jan. 1739. D. in 1745.

[10] *Kraut.* Promoted from Sub-Brigdr. Not in any subsequent List.

[11] Had served previously in 2nd Troop. D. in Soho Square, London, in 1732.—*Gentleman's Mag.*

[12] Comn. renewed in 1727. Out before 1740.

[13] Served previously as Lieut. in 1st Foot Guards. Serving in 3rd Troop in 1727. J.P. for Middlesex. D. in 1739.

[14] Had served as a Lieut. in Withers's Dragoons in late reign, and was made Lieut. in Gen. Evans's Dragoons, 26 Jan. 1722. Comn. in Life Guards renewed in 1727. Out before 1740.

[15] See his Comn. as Capt. in Col. Cotton's Regt. of Foot, 19 Aug. 1715, in Vol. I., p. 190. 2nd Major 3rd Tp. of Life Guards, 3 Jan. 1739. Serving in 1740.

[16] Younger bro. to George, 3rd Earl of Cholmondeley. Born 18 April, 1708. Served at Fontenoy. Was conspicuous for gallantry at the battle of Falkirk. Fought at Culloden. Col. of the 34th Foot, 18 Dec. 1742. Col. of the Inniskilling Dragoons, 16 Jan. 1750. Lt.-Gen. 2 May, 1754. D. 13 Jan. 1775.

[17] Comn. renewed in 1727. Out before 1740.

[18] Comn. renewed in 1727. D. in London, 1731. His widow, Catharine Mohun, drew a pension of £40 per annum up to March, 1735, when she remarried.

4TH TROOP OF LIFE GUARDS.

Disbanded 1746.

Francis Burton,[1] Esq. to be Lieut. and Lt.-
Colonel - - - - - - - St. James's, 25 Feb. 1718/19.*c*
George, Lord Forrester[2] to be Capt. and
Colonel in room of John, Earl of Dundonald   „   21 April, 1719. *c*
Andrew Forrester,[3] Esq. to be Exempt and
eldest Capt. - - - - -   „   1 Mar. 1719/20.*c*
Biggs Ash[4] to be Brigadier and eldest Lt. -   „   8 June, 1720. *c*
Charles Floyer[5] to be Sub-Brigadier and
eldest Cornet - - - - -   „   „ „ „ *c*
John Ball[6] to be Brigadier and eldest Lt. -   „   28 Jan. 1720/1.*c*
James Halden (*sic*),[7] Esq. to be Exempt and
eldest Capt. - - - - -   „   16 Mar.   „   *c*
Charles Floyer[5] to be do. and do. - -   „   11 May, 1721. *c*
James Haldane,[7] Esq. to be Guidon and Major   „   „ „   „   *c*
John Harbord Dod[8] to be Sub-Brigadier and
eldest Cornet - - - - -   „   9 Feb. 1721/2.*c*
Jonathan Jones to be do. and do. - -   „   20 April, 1722. *c*
Wm. Aislabie,[9] Esq. to be Exempt and Capt. -   „   26 May,   „   *f*
Ric. Gifford[10] to be Brigadier and Lieut. -   „   10 Nov.   „   *c*
John Seguin[11] to be Adjt. and Lieut. - -   „   „ „   „   *c*
John Nugent[12] to be Sub-Brigadier and Cornet   „   „ „   „   *c*
Ross Lee[13] to be Chaplain - - -   „   12 Jan. 1722/3.*c*
Richard Pyott,[14] Esq. to be Lt. and Lt.-Colonel
and rank as Lt.-Col. of Horse - -   „   22 Mar.   „   *c.*
James Miller[15] to be Sub-Brigadier and Cornet   „   3 April, 1723. *c*
Fras. Martyn[16] to be Sub-Brigadier and Cornet   „   24 May,   „   *c*
Clement Hilgrove[17] to be Brigadier and Lieut.   „   „ „   „   *c*
John Ball,[6] Esq. to be Exempt and Capt. -   „   „ „   „   *c*
John Aytoun[18] to be Sub-Brigadier and Cornet-   „   — April, 1725. *f*
Thos. Goddard[19] to be do. and do. - - Kensington, 7 July, 1726. *d*
Richard, Viscount Shannon,[20] to be Capt. and
Colonel in room of George, Lord Forres-
ter decd. - - - - - - St. James's, 9 Mar. 1726/7.*d*

---

[1] Had served at Malplaquet as Capt. in Maj.-Gen. Howe's Regt. of Foot. Major in same Corps, Jan. 1711. Comn. renewed by George I. Retd. from 4th Tp. Life Guards, 5 Jan. 1745. D. at Knightsbridge in 1753.

[2] See biog. notice in Vol. I., p. 352, note 2. His widow was drawing a pension of £50 per annum in 1735.

[3] From Capt. in Brigdr. Stanwix's (late Lord Forrester's) Regt. of Foot in Ireland. Out of 4th Life Guards before 1727. He was younger bro. to George, Lord Forrester, and was born in 1692.

[4] Appointed Sub-Brigdr. and Cornet in above Troop, 27 March, 1716. Exempt and Capt. 15 Feb. 1731. Serving in 1740.

[5] Exempt and Capt. 11 May, 1721. Comn. renewed in 1727. Out before 1740.

[6] Exempt and Capt. 24 May, 1724. Out before 1740.

[7] See biog. notice in Vol. I., p. 308, note 6.

[8] Out before 1727.

[9] See biog. notice on p. 200, note 7.
[10] Promoted from Sub-Brigdr. and Cornet.   Comn. renewed in 1727
[11] Exempt and Capt. 15 Feb. 1739.   Serving in 1740.
[12] Not in any subsequent List.
[13] Untraced.
[14] Had served in the late reign as Capt. in Col. Wm. Newton's Regt. of Foot   Serving in 4th Tp. of Life Guards in 1727.
[15] Comn. renewed in 1727.   Out before 1740.
[16] Reduced with the Tp. in 1746, and given a special annual allowance.   Living in 1758.
[17] See his Comn. as Sub-Brigdr. and Cornet in Vol. I., p. 261, and note thereto.
[18] Brigdr. and Lieut. 25 Dec. 1738.   Serving in 1740
[19] See his Comn. as Ens. in Vol. I., p. 300, note 1.
[20] See biog. notice in Vol. I., p. 308, note 1.

1st TROOP OF HORSE GRENADIER GUARDS.

Troop disbanded, 1788.

John Cope,[1] Esq. to be Lt.-Col. and rank as
Col. of Horse - - - - - St. James's, 27 April, 1720.*p*
Thos. Smyth[2] to be Adjt. and rank as Lt. of
Horse - - - - - - „ 8 June, „ *c*
John Duvernet[3] to be Sub-Lieut. and rank as
eldest Capt. of Horse - - - - „ 15 Nov. „ *c*
[Charles, Earl of March,[4] to be Guidon and
rank as eldest Captain of do. - - - „ 18 Mar. 1720/1.]
John, Lord Carmichael,[5] to be Guidon and
rank as Capt. of Horse - - - - Kensington, 5 Sept. 1722.*c*
Wm. Twisden[6] to be Sub-Lieut. and rank as
Lieut. of Horse - - - - - „ 7 „ „ *c*
John Hyde,[7] Esq. to be Lieut. and rank as
Capt. of Horse - - - - - „ 10 „ „ *c*
John Nangle[8] to be Adjt. - - - St. James's, 28 April, 1724.*d*
Lewis Dejean,[9] Esq. to be 1st Lieut. and rank
as Capt. of Horse - - - - „ 10 April, 1725.*d*
Capt. Thos. Talmash[10] to be do. and rank as do. „ 13 Jan. 1726/7.*f*

[1] Aftds. Lt.-Gen. Sir John Cope, K.B., the C.-in-C. in Scotland in 1745. His parentage has never been discovered. According to Millan's *Succession of Colonels*, Cope is said to have been commissioned a Cornet, 14 March, 1706/7. Capt. and Lt.-Col. 3rd Foot Guards, 7 Oct. 1710. Bt.-Col. 15 Nov. 1711. Lt.-Col. of Maj.-Gen. Wynne's Foot, 2 April, 1712. Half-pay, 1713. Lt.-Col. 1st Tp. H. Gr. Gds. as in the text. Col. 39th Foot, 10 Nov. 1730. Removed to the 5th Foot, 15 Dec. 1732. Brig.-Gen. 12 Nov. 1735. Col. of 9th Dragoons, 27 June, 1737. Maj.-Gen. 2 July, 1739. Col. of 7th Dragoons, 12 Aug. 1741. Lt.-Gen. 12 Feb. 1743. Commanded a division at Dettingen. Created a K.B. for distinguished gallantry after said battle. His campaign in Scotland, two years later, is a matter of history. Tried by court-martial, but acquitted of misconduct. D. 1760. See *Sir John Cope and the Rebellion of* 1745, by Gen. Sir R. Cadell, K.C.B., R.A., published in 1898.
[2] Out in April, 1724.
[3] Capt. in above Tp. 2 Oct. 1731. Lt.-Col. of do. 30 April, 1746. D. in 1756. —*Gentleman's Mag.*
[4] See p. 198, note 22, where a list of this nobleman's Comns. in the Army is given from an original MS. at Goodwood in his own writing.
[5] An A.D.C. to Gen. Earl Cadogan in 1722. Succeeded his father as 4th Lord Carmichael and 3rd Earl of Hyndford. Born in 1701. Capt. and Lt.-Col. 3rd Foot Guards in 1733. D. in 1767.
[6] *Twysden.* Appointed Guidon of above Tp. 2 Oct. 1731. Exempt and Capt. 1st Tp. of Life Guards, 9 April, 1748. Succeeded to the Lt.-Colonelcy of 1st Tp. and d. in 1784. Second son of Sir Wm. Twysden, Bart.
[7] Out before 1727.
[8] Comn. renewed in 1727. Out before 1740.
[9] Appointed Ens. in Col. Montargier's Regt. of French Foot, 2 April, 1706. Capt. in Col. Peter Carle's Regt. of Foot in 1708. Served with same in Portugal. Appointed Capt. of an Invalid Cy. in 1719. Capt. in Montagu's Regt. of Foot, 23 Nov. 1720. Lieut. and Capt. 1st Tp. H. Gr. Gds. as given in the text. Major of said Tp. 12 June, 1731. Col. 37th Foot, 9 April, 1746. Maj.-Gen. 22 Jan. 1756. Col. of the Carabiniers, 5 April, 1757. D. a Lt.-Gen. in 1764. Will proved at Dublin same year.
[10] *Tollemache.* Not in any subsequent List. Believed to have been son of the Thos. Talmash, of St. James's, Westminster, to whom a licence was given 27 May, 1703, to marry Mary Henley of same parish, he being then aged 25 and she 22. (*London Marriage Licences.*) In 1735 Catherine, widow of Capt. Talmash, of the H. Gr. Guards, was drawing a pension of £26 per annum.

2ND TROOP OF HORSE GRENADIER GUARDS.

Troop disbanded, 1788.

Henry Berkeley,[1] Esq. to be Capt. and Colonel
   in room of Lord Forrester and to rank as
   eldest Col. of Horse - - - - St. James's, 21 April, 1719.*c*
John White,[2] Esq. to be Lieut. and rank as
   eldest Capt. of Horse - - - -   ,,   7 June, 1720.*c*
James Stewart,[3] Esq. to be Guidon and rank
   as Capt. of Horse - - - -   ,,   ,, ,,   ,, *c*
James Lacon[4] to be Sub-Lieut. and rank as
   eldest Lieut. - - - - -   ,,   ,, ,,   ,, *c*
Wm. Brereton[5] to be Lieut. and rank as Capt. Kensington, 6 Sept. 1722. *c*
Alex. Hubert,[6] Esq. to be Lieut. and Lt.-Col.
   and rank as Lt.-Col. of Horse - - - St. James's, 4 Feb. 1722/3.*c*
Wm. Ducket,[7] Esq. to be Major and rank as
   Major of do. - - - - -   ,,   ,, ,,   ,, *c*
Wm. Clark,[8] Esq. to be Lieut. and rank as
   Capt. of do. - - - - -   ,,   27 May, 1723.*c*
Ant. La Melonière,[9] Esq. to be Guidon and
   Capt. - - - - - -   ,,   24 June, 1726.*d*

[1] See notice in Vol. I., p. 130, note 3.
[2] Promoted from Guidon in same Tp. Comn. renewed 1727. D. in Jan. 1739.
[3] Out in June, 1726.
[4] Not in any subsequent List.
[5] Appointed Capt.-Lieut. in Sir Roger Bradshaigh's Regt. of Foot, 13 Aug. 1707.
Capt. 31 Aug. 1710. Half-pay, 1713. Capt. in Col. James Tyrrell's Regt. of Dragoons,
22 July, 1715. Half-pay, 1718. Lieut. in 2nd Tp. of H. Gr. Gds. as in the text. Capt.
in same Tp. 14 March, 1734. Was wounded at Fontenoy, where he served as Major of said
Tp. Lt.-Col. 9 April, 1746.
[6] See his Comn. in Vol. I., p. 100, and note thereto. His widow, Elizabeth Hubert,
was drawing a pension of £40 per annum in 1735.
[7] See biog. notice in Vol. I., p. 263, note 6.
[8] From Lieut. and Capt. 3rd Foot Guards. Capt. 7 Jan. 1739. Serving in 1740.
[9] See biog. notice in Vol. I., p. 123, note 5.

ROYAL REGIMENT OF HORSE GUARDS.

Chas. Shipman [1] to be Cornet to Capt. ——	St. James's,	6 May,	1719.	c
Christopher Emilie [2] to be Cornet to Capt. ——	,,	,, ,,	,,	c
Chas. Fielding (sic) [3] to be Qr.-Mr. to Capt. Wyvil - - - - - - -	Whitehall,	22 Sept.	,,	c
George Merrick [4] to be Cornet to do. -	St. James's,	24 May,	1720.	c
Fras. Ligonier [5] to be Lieut. to Capt. Jas. Varey	,,	,, ,,	,,	c
Chas. Jenkinson, [6] Esq. to be Capt.-Lieut. -	,,	14 Jan. 1720/1.		c
Gregory Beake, [7] Esq. to be Capt. in room of Patty (sic) Byng - - - - -	,,	,, ,,	,,	c
Robt. Coke [8] to be Cornet to Capt. And. Perceval - - - - - - -	,,	,, ,,	,,	c
Thos. Taylor [9] to be Lieut. to Capt. [John] Elwes - - - - - - -	,,	,, ,,	,,	c
Robt. Bird [10] to be Cornet to Capt. Fras. Byng	,,	24 Mar.	,,	c
Fras. Burton [11] to be Qr.-Mr. to Capt. Robt. Cary - - - - - - -	,,	8 April, 1721.		c
George Eyre [12] to be Qr.-Mr. to Capt. Gregory Beake - - - - - - -	,,	1 May,	,,	c
The Rt. Hon. Lord Nassau Pawlet (sic) [13] to be Capt. in room of John Elwes - -	,,	4 June,	,,	c
Thos. Teale [14] to be Cornet to Lord Wm. Beauclerk - - - - - -	,,	8 ,,	,,	c
The Rt. Hon. Lord Wm. Beauclerck [15] to be Capt. in room of Robert Cary - - -	,,	,, ,,	,,	c
George Shaw [16] to be Lieut. to do - -	,,	,, ,,	,,	c
Thomas, Lord Fairfax, [17] to be Cornet to ——	Kensington,	15 Aug.	,,	c
Henry Migett [18] to be Adjt. - - -	,,	6 Sept.	,,	c
Wm. Elliott [19] to be Cornet to Lord Nassau Pawlet - - - - -	St. James's,	12 Feb. 1721/2.		c
Leonard Robinson [20] to be Cornet to —— -	,,	25 May, 1722.		c
[Chas.] Shipman [1] to be Lieut. to Capt. —— -	,,	30 ,,	,,	c
Chas. Herbert [21] to be Lieut. to ——	,,	,, ,,	,,	c
Chas. Lenox, [22] Esq., commonly called Earl of March, to be Capt. in room of —— Varey.	Kensington,	5 Sept.	,,	c
Abraham Lambe [23] to be Qr.-Mr. to Capt. John Wyvill - - - - - -	St. James's,	10 Nov.	,,	c
Fras. Byng, [24] Esq. to be Lt.-Col. and Capt. of a Tp. - - - - - - -	,,	5 Feb. 1722/3.		c
John Wyvill, [25] Esq. to be Major and Capt. of a Tp. - - - - - - -	,,	,, ,,	,,	c
Chas. Jenkinson, [6] Esq. to be Capt. in room of —— Fielding - - - - -	,,	,, ,,	,,	c
Sir Jas. Chamberlayne, [26] Bt. to be Capt.-Lieut.	,,	,, ,,	,,	c
Henry Baughs (sic) [27] to be Cornet to Capt. Jenkinson - - - - - - -	,,	,, ,,	,,	c
Thos. Soley [28] to be Qr.-Mr. to "Our Own Troop" - - - - - - -	,,	9 Mar.	,,	c

John Guy [29] to be Cornet to Lord Nassau
  Paulet - - - - - - - Gohre, 9 Nov. 1723.c
Sherington Talbot [30] to be Cornet to —— - St. James's, 19 Feb. 1724/5.d
Robert Ramsden [31] to be do. to the Duke of
  Richmond's Tp. - - - - ,, 17 May, 1725.d
John Mordaunt,[32] Esq. to be do. to —— - ,, 22 Feb. 1725/6.d
Henry Miget [18] to be do. to Capt. John Wyvill ,, 12 May, 1726.d
John Tempest [33] to be Qr.-Mr. to the Duke of
  Richmond's Tp. - - - - —— ,, ,, ,, d
Robert Fairfax [34] to be Cornet to —— - - St. James's, 19 Aug. ,, d
Richard Wenman [35] to be Lieut. to Capt. John
  Wyvil - - - - - - - ,, 9 Sept. .. d
John Mercer [36] to be Cornet to "Our Own
  Troop" - - - - - - ,, 22 April, 1727.d
Chas. Herbert [21] to be Lieut. to Lord Wm.
  Beauclerk - - - - - ,, ,, ,, ,, d

[1] Lieut. 30 May, 1722. Capt.-Lieut. 18 July, 1737. Serving in 1740.

[2] Out before 1727.

[3] Comm. signed by the Lords Justices in the King's absence. The Hon. Charles Feilding, bro. to the 5th Earl of Denbigh, was appointed Lieut. and Capt. Coldstream Guards, 24 Jan. 1721. Transferred to the King's Regt. of Horse in 1723. Appointed Capt. and Lt.-Col. Coldstream Guards, 7 Nov. 1739. Retd. 23 Jan. 1746. D. 6 Feb. following.

[4] Out before 1727.

[5] See biog. notice in Vol. I., p. 151, note 6. He was appointed Col. of the 13th Dragoons, 1 Oct. 1745, and died from the effects of exposure shortly after the battle of Falkirk.

[6] Appointed Lieut. in Rl. Horse Guards, 10 Oct. 1713. Capt. 5 Feb. 1723. Served at Dettingen as Major. Fought at Fontenoy. Lt.-Col. 27 May, 1745. D. in 1750. He was third son of Sir Robert Jenkinson, Bart., and father of the 1st Earl of Liverpool.

[7] Appointed Ens. in the 3rd Regt. of Foot (the Buffs), 24 Nov. 1702. Capt. 1 March, 1711. Capt.-Lieut. Rl. Horse Guards, 23 June, 1715. Capt. as in the text. Lt.-Col. of same Corps, 26 Nov. 1739. Extra A.D.C. to the C.-in-C. of the British Forces on the Continent, 11 Aug. 1742. Bt.-Col. same date. Served at Dettingen and was wounded at Fontenoy. M.P. for St. Ives, Cornwall. D. 19 June, 1749, at which time he held the post of Lt.-Gov. of Jersey.

[8] Comm. renewed in 1727. Out before 1740. Bro. to the Earl of Leicester. D. in 1750.—*Gentleman's Mag.*

[9] Adjt. 23 July, 1712. Cornet, 13 June, 1715. Comm. as Lieut. renewed in 1727. Serving in 1740.

[10] Out before 1727.

[11] Promoted Cornet, 2 Sept. 1723, in 6th Horse. Comm. renewed in 1727. Serving with same rank in 1740.

[12] Promoted Cornet, 18 July, 1737. Serving in 1740.

[13] Served previously as Cornet in Brigdr. Bowles's Regt. of Dragoons. Son of Charles, 2nd Duke of Bolton, by his third wife. Comm. as Capt. renewed in 1727. Not in any subsequent List. At the time of his death, in 1741, he was a K.B.

[14] Out before 1727.

[15] *Beauclerk.* Second son of the 1st Duke of St. Albans, and grandfather of the 4th Duke. Comm. renewed in 1727. D. in 1733. Bd. in Westminster Abbey.

[16] Out before 1727.

[17] Sixth Baron Fairfax of Cameron. Succeeded his father in 1710. " This nobleman inherited from his mother a splendid fortune, consisting of several manors in Kent, estates in the Isle of Wight, and a tract of land in Virginia, called the Northernneck comprised within the boundaries of the rivers Potowmack and Rappahanock, containing, by estimation, 5,700,000 acres. From his father he inherited Denton Hall and other property in Yorkshire, but he was obliged by his mother and grandmother to dispose of those in order to redeem the Colepepper manors. His lordship had a commission in the horse-guards, but visiting his American estates about the year 1739, he was so captivated with the soil, climate, and beauties of Virginia, that he resolved to spend the remainder of his life there ; and he soon after erected two mansions, Belvoir and Greenway Court, where he continued

ever afterwards to reside in a state of baronial hospitality. His dress was plain and simple, his manners modest and unaffected, and his style of living magnificent. Such was his generosity, that he gave up his English estates to his brother Robert, and the surplus of his American income was distributed among his poor neighbours. His principal amusement was hunting ; and after the chase he was wont to invite the whole field to partake his hospitality. He had been educated in revolutionary principles, and had imbibed high notions of republican liberty. He was lieut. and custos rotulorum of Frederick county, and presided at the provincial courts at Winchester, where, during the session, he kept an open table. His lordship d. unm., at Greenway Court, in 1782, when the title devolved upon his only surviving brother."—Burke's *Peerage*, 1839.

[18] Cornet, 12 May, 1726. Lieut. 18 July, 1737. Brigade-Major in Sept. 1743. Wounded at Fontenoy, where he served as Capt.-Lieut. of above Regt.

[19] Eldest son of Wm. *Elliot*, of Wells, co. Roxburgh. Md. in 1737 Lady Frances Nassau, eldest dau. and co-heiress of Henry d'Auverquerque, Earl of Grantham. Appointed Capt. in Col. Charles Churchill's Dragoons (10th), 12 July, 1723. Major of the 2nd Tp. H. Gr. Gds. 13 July, 1737. Lt.-Col. 28 June, 1741. Retd. in 1745. D. in 1764. (The first part of this note was kindly supplied by Miss E. Eliot, of Shenstone Lodge, Forest Hill, S.E.) Under date of 11 June, 1737, Lady Eliz. Compton, in a letter to the Countess of Northampton, thus refers to Lord Grantham's daughter's marriage : " Lady Francys (*sic*) Nassau has owned her being married to Captain Elliott to the very great grief of my Lord Grantham, which is much encreased by his discovering also now that Lady Cowper had a great share in the carrying out of the affair."—*Townshend Papers*, printed by the *Hist. MSS. Commission*, p. 248.

[20] Serving as Cornet in Lord Carpenter's Dragoons (3rd) in June, 1727. Lieut. 20 June, 1735. Dangerously wounded at Dettingen (*Records*). His death is recorded in the *Gentleman's Mag.* as having taken place in aforesaid battle.

[21] Lieut. 22 April, 1727. Illegitimate son of John Sheffield 1st Duke of Buckingham. Succeeded to the Sheffield estates in 1735, on the death of the 2nd Duke of Buckingham, and took the surname of Sheffield. Created a Bart. in 1756, and d. in 1774.

[22] See his first Comn. on p. 194. Succeeded as 2nd Duke of Richmond in 1723. A MS. at Goodwood, in this nobleman's own handwriting, gives the following list of his Commissions :—

"Guidon in 1st Troop of Horse Grenadier Guards, 18 March, 1720/21.
Troop in Royal Regt. of Horse Guards, 5 Sept. 1722.
A.D.C. to the King and Colonel, 18 April, 1724.
Brig.-Gen. 2 July, 1739.
Maj.-Gen. 1 Jan. 1741/42.
Lt.-Gen. 6 July, 1745.
Colonel Royal Regt. of Horse Guards, 13 Feb. 1749/50."

The Duke was present at Dettingen as Master of the Horse to George II. He also was at the taking of Carlisle in Dec. 1745. D. 1750. See *A Duke and his Friends*, by the Earl of March.

[23] Not in any subsequent List.

[24] See Vol. I., p. 102, note 4. His widow, Helena Byng, was drawing a pension of £40 per annum in 1735.

[25] Promoted from Capt. in same Corps. Lt.-Col. 29 Jan. 1734. D. in 1740.

[26] See biog. notice in Vol. I., p. 262, note 6.

[27] Comn. renewed in 1727. Serving in 1736. Out before 1740.

[28] Not in any subsequent List.

[29] Lieut. 29 Jan. 1734. Serving in 1740.

[30] See biog. notice in Vol. I., p. 219, note 19.

[31] Lieut. 18 July, 1737. Fought at Dettingen and Fontenoy. Fifth son of Sir Wm. Ramsden, Bart., of Byram Hall, co. York. D. in 1769.

[32] This officer must not be confounded with his namesake, Gen. Sir John Mordaunt, K.B., who was Col. of the 12th Dragoons. John Mordaunt, of the Horse Guards, was serving with the same rank in 1727. He was appointed Lt.-Col. of Kingston's Horse, 4 Oct. 1745, which Corps was disbanded in 1746. D. in 1767. (*Gentleman's Mag.*) He was younger son of John, Lord Mordaunt, and md. in 1735 the widow of Thomas, Earl of Pembroke.

[33] Untraced.

[34] The Hon. Robert Fairfax, who succeeded his bro. Thomas as 7th Baron Fairfax in 1782. Exempt and Capt. 1st Life Guards, 9 July, 1739. Serving in 1740. D.s.p. 1793.

[35] A cadet of Visct. Wenman's family. Serving in 1740 as Lieut. in above Regt.

[36] Lieut. 9 July, 1739. Serving in 1740.

THE KING'S OWN REGIMENT OF HORSE.

[1st DRAGOON GUARDS.]

Chas. Hartop[1] to be Cornet to Capt. George Burrington - - - - -	St. James's,	19 Feb.	1718/9.	c
Tindal Thompson[2] to be Cornet to Major Lisle - - - - - -	,,	21 Mar.	,,	c
Tomkyn Wardour,[3] Esq. to be Capt. in room of Galen Cope - - - - -	,,	29 Feb.	1719/20.	c
Wm. Lancaster,[4] Esq. to be Capt.-Lieut. -	,,	,, ,,	,,	c
Cuthbert Wightman[5] to be Lieut. to [Major-General] Thos. Crowther's Tp. -	,,	,, ,,	,,	c
Robt. Pemberton[6] to be Cornet to Capt. Wm. Bembowe - - - - -	,,	,, ,,	,,	c
Wm. Aislabie[7] to be Cornet to Capt. John Brown - - - - - -	,,	7 June,	,,	c
Thos. Machell[8] to be do. to Lord Irwin's Tp.	,,	8 ,,	,,	c
Richard Manning[9] to be Lieut. to Major Patrick Lisle - - - - -	,,	,, ,,	,,	c
Wm. Lancaster,[4] Esq. to be Capt. of Major-General Crowther's Tp. - -	Herrenhausen,	21 Sept.	,,	c
Wm. Duckett,[10] Esq. to be Capt.-Lieut. -	,,	,, ,,	,,	c
Samuel Strudwick[11] to be Lieut. to Capt.——	,,	,, ,,	,,	c
Samuel Garnault[12] to be Cornet to Capt. ——	,,	,, ,,	,,	c
Richard, Visct. Cobham,[13] to be Colonel in room of Viscount Irwin, and Capt. of a Tp.	St. James's,	10 April,	1721.	c
Martin Madan,[14] Esq. to be Capt. of [Capt.] Brown's late Cy. - - - -	,,	16 May,	,,	c
Wm. Walton,[15] Esq. to be Capt.-Lieut. -	,,	9 June,	,,	c
Chiverton Hartopp[16] to be Lieut. to Capt. Wm. Bembo (*sic*) - - - -	,,	,, ,,	,,	c
Richard Jones[17] to be Cornet to Capt. Geo. Burrington - - - - -	,,	,, ,,	,,	c
Wm. Thompson[18] to be Adjt. - - -	,,	,, ,,	,,	c
Henry Whitaker[19] to be Cornet to —— -	Kensington,	26 Aug.	,,	c
George Furness,[20] Esq. to be Capt. in room of —— Cole - - - - -	,,	11 Sept.	,,	c
Saml. Long[21] to be Lieut. to —— - -	,,	24 Oct.	,,	c
Thos. Strudwick[22] to be Lieut. to Capt. [Thos.] Hunt - - - - -	St. James's,	10 Feb.	1721/2.	c
Wm. Pritchard Ashurst,[23] Esq. to be Capt. in room of George Burrington - -	,,	7 Mar.	,,	c
Chas. Bembo (*sic*)[24] to be Cornet to Capt. Wm. Bembo - - - - -	,,	26 May,	1722.	c
Richard Fitz-William[25] to be Cornet to ——	Kensington,	10 July,	,,	c
Fras. Lambert,[26] Esq. to be Capt. in room of Pritchard Ashurst - - - -	St. James's,	22 Jan.	1722/3.	c
March (*sic*) Wolfe[27] to be Cornet to Capt. Fras. Lambert - - - - -	,,	,, ,	,,	c

Robert Pemberton [6] to be Lieut. to Capt.		
[Thos.] Hunt - - - -	St. James's, 22 Jan. 1722/3. *c*
[The Hon. Chas. Feilding [23] to be Capt. -	„ Feb. „]
Chas. Carter [29] to be Cornet to —— - -	„ 21 Mar. „ *c*
Conway Rand [30] to be Chaplain - - -	„ 24 May, 1723. *c*
Samuel Garnault [12] to be Lieut. to —— -	„ 10 Jan. 1723/4.*c*
Wm. Wolseley [31] to be Cornet to —— - -	„ 21 May, 1725. *d*
Thos. Merriden [32] to be Cornet to—— - -	„ 15 Feb. 1725/6.*d*
Wm. Thompson [18] to be do to —— - -	„ 26 April, 1726. *d*
John, Duke of Argyll and Greenwich [33] to		
be Colonel [and Capt. of a Tp.] - -	„ 22 Feb. 1726/7.*d*
Humphry Bland,[34] Esq. to be Capt. of Wm.		
Benbow's late Cy. - - - -	„ 25 April, 1727. *d*
Maurice Bockland,[35] Esq. to be Capt.-Lieut.	[„,] 30 May, „ *d*

[1] Apparently a clerical error in the MS. for " Chiverton Hartopp." See note 16.

[2] Appointed Capt. in Whetham's Regt. (27th), 7 July, 1721. Capt. in Lord Londonderry's Regt. of Foot (3rd), 26 Dec. 1726. Reduced with his Cy. in 1729. Drawing half-pay in 1739. A certain Tindal Thompson d. at Malton in 1775.—*Gentleman's Mag.*

[3] Son of Wm. Wardour of Whitney Court, co. Hereford. Cornet in above Regt. 24 Oct. 1707. Served at Malplaquet. Guidon and Major 2nd Tp. Life Guards, 13 Oct. 1727. Lt.-Col. 21 May, 1733. Col. of 41st Foot, 1 April, 1743. D. 13 Feb. 1752, aged 64. Bd. in Westminster Abbey.

[4] Cornet in above Regt. 24 Oct. 1707. Served at Malplaquet. Capt. 21 Sept. 1720. Serving in 1728. D. in 1733. His widow, Dinah Lancaster, received a pension of £26 per annum.

[5] Serving in 1730.

[6] Lieut. 22 Jan. 1723. Lieut. of a newly-raised Invalid Cy. 3 Nov. 1739. Serving in 1740.

[7] Son and heir of the Rt. Hon. John Aislabie of Studley Royal, Chancellor of the Exchequer, 1718–21. Young Aislabie was elected M.P. for Ripon in place of his father, 1721, and continued to represent that city until the time of his death in 1781. He was appointed Exempt and Capt. in 4th Tp. of Life Guards, 26 May, 1722. This Comn. is omitted in the War Office Entry Book, 1718–24, but is given in the Gradation List, 1730, also in the *Historical Register*, 1722.

[8] Not in any subsequent List. He was kinsman to Viscountess Irwin (*née* Machel), wife of Lord Irwin, the Col. of above Regt.

[9] Probably son of Lt.-Col. Richard Manning, of 3rd Foot Guards. Out of the Regt. before 1727.

[10] See biog. notice in Vol. I., p. 263, note 6.

[11] Out before 1727.

[12] Lieut. 10 Jan. 1724. Serving in 1728. The will of a certain " Samuel Garnou (*sic*) gent." was proved at Dublin in 1769.

[13] See special memoir, pp. 1–8.

[14] Served previously in the Coldstream Guards. Promoted Major of the King's Own Regt. of Horse, 14 June, 1734. Lt.-Col. of do. 11 May, 1742. Retd. 24 Dec. 1746. He was Gentleman of the Bedchamber to Frederick, Prince of Wales. M.P. for Wootton Bassett, 1747–54. D. 4 March, 1756, aged 55. Bd. at Bath. M.I. in Bath Abbey.—(Latter part of this note was kindly supplied by Mr. Alan Stewart, kinsman to above Col. Madan.)

[15] Exchanged to 6th Regt. of Horse (5th D.G.), with Capt.-Lieut. Maurice Boeland, 30 May, 1727. Comn. renewed same year. Out before 1737.

[16] Only son of Col. Thos. Hartopp of Quorndon. Comn. as Lieut. renewed in 1727. Capt. 41st Foot, 23 April, 1742. Bt.-Major, 4 Oct. 1745. Serving in 1758. D. in 1759. He was of Welby, co. Leicester, and left at his decease three daus. and co-heirs, the youngest of whom md. Richard, Earl Howe—the celebrtaed Admiral.

[17] Lieut. 18 Nov. 1729. Serving as Lieut. in same Regt. in 1740.

[18] Lieut. 20 Jan. 1736. Serving in 1740.

[19] Out before 1727. In 1735 his widow, Magdalen Whitaker, was drawing a pension of £16 per annum.

[20] Comn. renewed in 1727. See Vol. I., p. 291, note 8.

[21] Out before 1727. He was son and heir of Charles Long, of Longville, Jamaica, and of Hurts Hall, Suffolk. Born 1700. Said to have been a " Capt. in Queen Caroline's Dragoons " (Burke's *Landed Gentry*), but this appointment cannot be traced. D. 1757.

[22] Served in former reign as Lieut. in the Inniskilling Regt. of Foot. Serving in 1740 as Lieut. in the King's Regt. of Horse.

[23] Elder son of Robt. Ashurst, citizen of London, who bought Heveningham Estate in Essex, from Visct. Cullen. (Le Neve's *Knights*, p. 414.) Left the Regt. in Jan. 1723.

[24] Capt.-Lieut. 21 Dec. 1738. Serving in 1746 as Brigdr. and Lieut. in 3rd Tp. of Life Guards. Pensioned same year.

[25] Comn. renewed in 1727. Appointed Capt. in Col. Humphry Bland's Regt. of Foot (36th), 1 Nov. 1739. Lt.-Col. 10 March, 1742.

[26] Comn. renewed in 1727. Out before 1740.

[27] Comn. renewed in 1727. Called "Marsh" Wolfe in the Gradation List for 1727. Out before 1740.

[28] Register not given in War Office Entry Book, but his name appears in Gradation List for 1727 as Capt. in 2nd Horse. See p. 197, note 3.

[29] Comn. renewed in 1727. Exempt and Capt. in 3rd Tp. of Life Guards, 14 May, 1735. Out of said Tp. before it was disbanded in 1746.

[30] D. before 25 April, 1734, when his widow, Elizabeth Rand, was in receipt of a chaplain's widow's pension of £16 per annum.—*Pension Roll of Army Officers' Widows*, 1734–35.

[31] Had served in former reign as Cornet in Pepper's Dragoons. Serving as Cornet in the 2nd Horse (K.D.G.) in 1728. Believed to have been son of Capt. Richard Wolseley, R.N., and to have succeeded in 1730 as 5th Bart. of Wolseley, co. Stafford, and d. 1779.

[32] Lieut. 24 Dec. 1734. Killed at Dettingen, where he served as Capt. in above Regt.

[33] See special memoir in Vol. I., pp. 1–9.

[34] See biog. notice in Vol. I., p. 115, note 3.

[35] See do., p. 159, note 1.

H.R.H. THE PRINCESS OF WALES'S OWN REGIMENT OF HORSE.

[2ND DRAGOON GUARDS.]

Robt. Stringer [1] to be Cornet to Capt. Tench.	St. James's,	25 Dec.		1717.	*b*
Richard Whitworth,[2] Esq. to be Lt.-Colonel	,,		1 Jan.	1717/18.	*b*
Charles Otway,[3] Esq. to be Capt.-Lieut. -	,,	,, ,,	,,		*b*
Francis Naizon,[4] Esq. to be Major and Capt. of a Troop - - - - - -	,,	,, ,,	,,		*b*
Peter Naizon,[5] Esq. to be Capt. in room of [Lt.-Col.] Otway - - - -	,,	,, ,,	,,		*b*
Wm. Knowles (*sic*),[6] Esq., commonly called Lord Wallingford, to be Cornet to that Troop whereof —— is Capt. - -	,,	7 ,,	,,		*b*
James Low [7] to be Surgeon - - -	Kensington,	3 June,		1718.	*b*
Richard Backwell [8] to be Cornet to Capt.——	,,	26 ,,		,,	*b*
Wm. Willis [9] to be Chaplain - - -	St. James's,	17 Sept.		,,	*b*
Stephen Otway [10] to be Cornet to Capt. ——	Herrenhausen,	3 Aug.		1719.	*c*
Gerald Elrington [11] to be Adjt. - - -	St. James's,	25 May,		1720.	*c*
Wadham Wyndham [12] to be Cornet to —— -	,,	8 June,			*c*
Wm. Chaworth [13] to be Cornet to —— -	,,	8 April,		1721.	*c*
James Branston [14] to be Chaplain - -	,,	21 June,		,,	*c*
Chas. Otway,[3] Esq. to be Capt. in room of [James] Dambon - - - - -	,,	1 July,		,,	*c*
Arthur (*sic*) Renkine,[15] Esq. to be Capt.-Lieut. - - - - - - -	,,	,, ,,	,,		*c*
Thos. Denning [16] to be Lieut. to Capt. Peter Naizon - - - - - -	,,	,, ,,	,,		*c*
John Lort [17] to be Cornet to Capt. Philip Tench - - - - - - -	,,	,, ,,	,,		*c*
Gerald Elrington [11] to be Capt. - - -	[,,]	21 ,,	,,		*f*
Richard Tracey [18] to be do. - - -	[,,]	25 ,,	,,		*f*
Francis Howard,[19] Esq. to be Capt. in room of —— Walker decd. - - - -	Kensington,	14 Oct.		,,	*c*
Robt. Stringer [1] to be Lieut. to Capt. Chas. Otway - - - - - -	St. James's,	2 Jan.	1722/3.		*c*
Nicholas French [20] to be Adjt. - - -	,,	,, ,,	,,		*c*
Chas. Elstob [21] to be Cornet to Lt.-Col. Ric. Whitworth - - - -	,,	,, ,,	,,		*c*
Solomon Stevenson [22] to be do. to —— -	,,	12 Mar.	1724/5.		*d*
John, Duke of Argyll and Greenwich,[23] to be Colonel of Lord Londonderry's late Regt. of Horse - - - - -	,,	26 Aug.		1726.	*d*

[1] Lieut. 17 Jan. 1723. Serving in 1740.
[2] See Vol. I., p. 326, note 3.
[3] Called " Charles James Otway " in his Comn. as Cornet in above Regt. Doubtless son of Col. James Otway of same Regt. Capt. 1 July, 1721. Major, 9 Feb. 1741. Serving in April, 1745.
[4] Served with above Corps at Almenara in 1710 and was wounded (*Records of the 2nd D.G.*). Capt. 29 Jan. 1713. Comn. as Major renewed by George II.

[5] Appointed Cornet in above Regt. 22 Jan. 1708. Lieut. 11 March, 1712. Capt.-Lieut. 1 Aug. 1715. Major, 21 May, 1733. Lt.-Col. of 1st Dragoons, 23 Jan. 1741. Served at Dettingen. Wounded at Fontenoy. Col. of the 13th Dragoons, 17 Feb. 1746. D. in 1751.

[6] Promoted Lieut. 28 Dec. 1727. Elder son by 1st mge. of Charles *Knollys*, titular Earl of Banbury. Md. Mary Catherine, dau. of John Law, the financier. Appointed 2nd Major of the 1st Tp. of Life Guards, 15 July, 1737. M.P. for Banbury. D.s.p. 6 June, 1740. Bd. in South Audley Street Chapel.

[7] Untraced.

[8] Comn. renewed in 1727. Out before 1740.

[9] Untraced.

[10] Served previously as Lieut. in Col. Churchill's Dragoons, which Corps was disbanded in Nov. 1718. Appointed Capt. in Col. James Otway's Regt. of Foot (9th), 28 July, 1720. Comn. renewed in 1727. Major of same Corps, 19 Aug. 1743. Serving in 1748. Out before 1753.

[11] Served previously as Lieut. in Stanwix's Regt. of Foot, which was disbanded in Nov. 1718. Capt. in the 3rd Horse (2nd D.G.), 26 July, 1721. Exchanged to 3rd Foot in Dec. 1726. D. at Lichfield in 1735.—*Gentleman's Mag.*

[12] Lieut. 5 April, 1732. Serving in 1740. He was grandson of Sir Wadham Wyndham, Knt., of Norrington, co. Wilts.

[13] Lieut. 21 May, 1733. Serving in 1745.

[14] Untraced.

[15] Called "Andrew Rankine" in MS. Army List, 1717. Served as Cornet in above Regt. in former reign. Capt. 21 May, 1733. Called "Anthony Rankine" in the 1740 *Army List.* Serving in 1745.

[16] Called "Downing" in Gradation List for 1730. Further services untraced.

[17] Comn. renewed in 1727. Not in any subsequent List. He was a cadet of the old Pembrokeshire family of this name.

[18] See Vol. I., p. 223, note 67.

[19] From Capt. in Brigdr. Munden's Dragoons (13th). Appointed Capt. and Lt.-Col. in 3rd Foot Guards, 26 July, 1722. He succeeded his bro. Thomas as 7th Baron Howard of Effingham in 1725. Deputy Earl Marshal of England. Created an Earl in 1731. Col. of 2nd Tp. of H. Gr. Gds. 21 June, 1737. Col. of 4th Tp. of Life Guards, 25 Dec. 1740. D. 12 Feb. 1743. Bd. at Great Bookham.

[20] From Qr.-Mr. Not in any subsequent List.

[21] Not in any subsequent List. Appointed in 1739 joint receiver with Mr. Watson of the rents of the Earl of Derwentwater's estates.—*Gentleman's Mag.*

[22] Served previously as Lieut. in Col. James Otway's Regt. of Foot. Comn. as Cornet in the 2nd Horse renewed in 1727. Lieut. 13 May, 1735. Serving in 1745.

[23] See special memoir in Vol. I., pp. 1–9.

MAJOR–GENERAL GEORGE WADE'S REGIMENT OF HORSE.
[3RD DRAGOON GUARDS.]

Wm. Wade,[1] Esq. to be Capt. in room of Jas.
    Carpenter - - - - - St. James's, 24 Feb. 1718/9.c
Thos. Richards[2] to be Cornet to [Major] Thos.
    Hull - - - - - -   ,,   ,,   ,,   ,,   c
Robt. Morgan[3] to be Cornet to —— - - ,,   19 Mar. 1719/20.c
Wm. Bellandine (sic),[4] Esq. to be Major and
    Capt. in room of Thos. Hull - - Herrenhausen, 2 Sept. 1720.c
Thos. Hull,[5] Esq. to be Lt.-Colonel and Capt.   ,,   ,,   ,,   ,, c
Wm. Ashby,[6] Esq. to be Capt. of [Major]
    Bellandine's late Tp. - - -   ,,   ,,   ,,   ,, c
Thos. Hicks,[7] Esq. to be Capt.-Lieut. -   ,,   ,,   ,,   ,, c
Philip Fullerton[8] to be Lieut. to —— -   ,,   ,,   ,,   ,, c
—— Bowes[9] to be Cornet to Capt. Wm.
    Ashby - - - - - -   ,,   ,,   ,,   ,, c
Samuel Rolle[10] to be Lieut. to Capt. John
    Pitt - - - - - - St. James's, 15 Mar. 1720/1.c
Wm. Townshend[11] to be Cornet to do. -   ,,   ,,   ,,   ,, c
Samuel Role (sic),[10] Esq. to be Capt. in room
    of [John] Pitt - - - - -   ,,   24 Feb. 1721/2.c
Thos. Richards[2] to be Lieut. to Capt. Rolle -   ,,   ,,   ,,   ,, c
Thos. Robinson[12] to be Cornet to [Lt.-Col.]
    Hull - - - - - -   ,,   ,,   ,,   ,, c
Wm. Townshend[11] to be Lieut. to Capt. [Wm.]
    Ashby - - - - -   ,,   15 May, ,, c
Nathaniel Burroughs[13] to be Cornet to —— Kensington, 7 June, ,, c
George Jefferies[14] to be Cornet to Capt. Wm.
    Ashby - - - - - St. James's, 19 April, 1726.d
John Ball[15] to be Lieut. to —— - -   ,,   4 Feb. 1726/7.d
Col. Wm. Townshend[11] to be Capt.-Lieut. -   ,,   ,,   ,,   ,, d

[1] See his Comn. as Cornet in same Regt. in Vol. I., p. 264, and note thereto.

[2] Lieut. 24 Feb. 1722. Comn. renewed in 1727. His widow, Mary Richards, was drawing a pension of £20 per annum in 1735.

[3] Comn. renewed in 1727. Out before 1740.

[4] *Bellenden.* See biog. notice in Vol. I., p. 123, note 4.

[5] Served at Blenheim as Lieut. in above Regt. Capt. 24 Aug. 1707. Served at Malplaquet. Bt.-Major, 1 Jan. 1712. Regtal.-Major, 11 Aug. 1716. Regtal.-Lt.-Col. as in text. Comn. renewed in 1727. Out in 1733.

[6] Served in above Regt. at Blenheim and Malplaquet. Promoted from Lieut. Comn. renewed in 1727. Out before 1740.

[7] Served at Blenheim and Malplaquet. His widow, Barbara Hicks, was drawing a pension of £20 per annum in 1734.

[8] Not in any subsequent List.

[9] Do.

[10] Capt. 24 Feb. 1722. Out before 1730. Possibly son of Samuel Rolle of Heanton, Sackville, co. Devon.

[11] Third son of the 2nd Visct. Townshend and father of Charles Townshend, created Baron Bayning in 1797. The Hon. Wm. Townshend was appointed an A.D.C. to the King with rank of Col. in the Army, 24 Jan. 1727. Capt.-Lieut. of above Regt. 4 Feb. same year. Comns. renewed in 1727. D. in 1738.

[12] Serving in 1730. Out before 1740.

[13] Lieut. 10 April, 1733. Serving in 1745.

[14] Lieut. 21 Feb. 1735. Serving in 1745.

[15] Capt.-Lieut. 21 Feb. 1735. Major, 1 June, 1744. Out before 1748. His death as "Major Ball of Wade's Horse" is given in the *Gentleman's Mag.* for 1768.

THE ROYAL DRAGOONS.

Wm. Wentworth [1] to be Lieut. to Capt. ——
    Griffiths - - - - - - - St. James's, 8 May, 1719.*c*
Roger Griffith [2] to be Cornet to Capt. ——
    Thayer - - - - - - -   ,,   ,, ,,   ,, *c*
Cholmondley Rich [3] to be Lieut. to Capt. ——   ,,   30 Nov.   ,,   *c*
Arthur Jegon (*sic*) [4] to be Cornet to Capt. ——   ,, 25 Mar.1719/20.*c*
Francis Best,[5] Esq. to be Capt.-Lieut. - -   ,,   ,, ,,   ,, *c*
George Benson [6] to be Lieut. to —— - -   ,,   ,, ,,   ,, *p*
Francis Best,[5] Esq. to be Capt. in room of
    James Maule - - - - - -   ,, 11 June, 1720.*c*
Wm. Kitson,[7] Esq. to be Capt.-Lieut. - -   ,,   ,, ,,   ,, *c*
Wm. Brooke [8] to be Lieut. to Capt. Samuel
    Speed - - - - - - -   ,,   ,, ,,   ,, *c*
Allen Benson [9] to be Cornet to —— - -   ,,   ,, ,,   ,, *c*
Sir Chas. Hotham,[10] Bt. to be Colonel in
    room of Richard, Viscount Cobham, and
    Capt. of a Tp. - - - - -   ,, 10 April, 1721.*c*
John Ball [11] to be Lieut. to —— - - -   ,, 26 July, ,,   *c*
George Gibson [12] to be Cornet to Capt. —— - Kensington, 23 Aug. 1722.*c*
Thos. Frend (*sic*),[13] Esq. to be Capt.-Lieut. -   ,, 19 Sept. ,,   *c*
Richard Bendyshe [14] to be Cornet to
    Capt. —— - - - - -   ,,   ,, ,,   ,, *c*
Thos. Stevens [15] to be Lieut. to —— - -   ,,   ,, ,,   ,, *c*
Humphry Gore,[16] Esq. to be Colonel in room
    of Sir Chas. Hotham, Bt., and Capt. of a Tp. St. James's, 12 Jan. 1722/3.*c*
Samuel Gumley,[17] Esq. to be Capt. in room of
    John Griffiths - - - - - - —— 28 Mar. 1724.*c*
James Russell Madan,[18] Esq. to be Capt. in
    room of Thayer - - - - - St. James's, 14 April, ,, *d*
Wm. Gore [19] to be Lieut. to Lt.-Col. Benson - Herrenhausen,
                              10 Sept. (O.S.) 1725.*d*

John Severn [20] to be Cornet to [Major] Samuel
    Speed - - - - - - - St. James's, 16 Mar. 1725/6.*d*
Andrew Pancier,[21] Esq. to be Capt. of an
    additional Tp. - - - - -   ,, 25 Dec. 1726.*d*
John Owen [22] to be Lieut. to do. - - -   ,,   ,, ,,   ,, *d*
Francis Ransford (*sic*) [23] to be Cornet to do. -   ,,   ,, ,,   ,, *d*
Gustavus Balfour,[24] Esq. to be Capt. of an
    additional Tp. - - - - -   ,,   ,, ,,   ,, *d*
Andrew Robinson [25] to be Lieut. to do. - -   ,,   ,, ,,   ,, *d*
Lucy (*sic*) Weston [26] to be Cornet to do. -   ,,   ,, ,,   ,, *d*
Edward Poole (*sic*),[27] Esq. to be Capt. of an
    additional Tp. - - - - -   ,,   ,, ,,   ,, *d*
Thos. Parkinson [28] to be Lieut. to do. - -   ,,   ,, ,,   ,, *d*
Henry Doubleday [29] to be Cornet to do. -   ,,   ,, ,,   ,, *d*

---

[1] Promoted from Cornet. Capt. 20 Dec. 1738. Of the Earl of Strafford's family. Serving in 1745.
[2] Comn. renewed in 1727. Serving in 1730. Retd. on half-pay 1738.
[3] Out before 1738.

[4] Comn. renewed in 1727. Serving in 1745.

[5] Appointed Cornet in above Regt. in 1703. Served with the same in Spain. Capt. 11 June, 1720. Major, 25 June, 1731. Serving in 1740. Appointed Lt.-Gov. of Jersey in 1741.

[6] Son of Col. George Benson of same Regt. Out before 1727.

[7] Out 19 Sept. 1722.

[8] Called " Brooks " in *Army List*, 1740. Capt. 25 April, 1741.

[9] D. at Bewdley, Worcestershire, in 1736.—*Gentleman's Mag.*

[10] See biog. notice in Vol. I., p. 172, note 1.

[11] Exchange of Tp. He was commissioned Lieut. 22 July, 1715. Comn. renewed in 1727. Out before 1740.

[12] Comn. renewed in 1727. Out before 1740.

[13] *Friend.* Served in former reign as Adjt. of the Royal Dragoons. Comn. as Capt.-Lieut. renewed in 1727. Out before 1740.

[14] Comn. renewed in 1727. Appointed Major of the 7th Marines, 1 May, 1745. Half-pay, 1748. Lt.-Col. of the Regt. of Marines, 19 Dec. 1755. Col. 19 Feb. 1762. D. a Maj.-Gen. at Barrington Hall, Cambridge, in 1777.—*Gentleman's Mag.*

[15] Comn. renewed in 1727. Out before 1740.

[16] See biog. notice in Vol. I., p. 114, note 1.

[17] Served previously in Gore's Dragoons (10th). Comn. renewed in 1727. Major, 5 April, 1741. Lt.-Col. 22 April, 1742. Served at Dettingen and Fontenoy. 1st Major 1st Foot Guards, 29 April, 1749. Out in 1753.

[18] Born 1701. Appointed Capt. in the Royal Irish Regt. of Dragoons, 18 May, 1721. Capt. in Royal Horse Guards, 30 April, 1734. Major, 8 Feb. 1741. Retd. in 1745. Yeoman of the Robes to George II. and George III. during 50 years. D. 30 Nov. 1788.

[19] Out before 1727.

[20] *Severne.* Comn. renewed in 1727. Major 48th Foot, 21 July, 1741. Col. 8th Dragoons, 27 Nov. 1760. Son of Thos. Severne of Wallop Hall, Shropshire. Succeeded his father in 1737. D. in 1787, aged 89, as a Lt.-Gen.

[21] Appointed Cornet in the Royal Dragoons, 8 March, 1703. Served in Spain. Speculated in South Sea Stock in 1720, and had to sell his Comn. The evidence he gave against a Jacobite officer relative to a plot in 1722 was the means of his being reappointed Capt. in above Regt. as given in the text. Half-pay, 1729. Retd. in 1739.

[22] Served previously as Ens. in 3rd Foot Guards. Capt. in Lt.-Gen. the Hon. Wm. Ker's Dragoons, 15 Dec. 1738. Lt.-Col. 12th Dragoons, 12 Dec. 1747. Col. 59th Foot, 27 Dec. 1760. Maj.-Gen. 12 July, 1762. D. a Lt.-Gen. 1766. Second son of Sir Arthur Owen, Bart.

[23] Served previously as Cornet in Col. Charles Churchill's Dragoons, which Corps was disbanded in 1718. Serving in 1740 as Cornet in the Royal Dragoons. Second son of Lt.-Col. Francis Rainsford, who served many years in the Royal Fusiliers. Cornet Rainsford d. 31 July, 1770, and was bd. St. Peter ad Vincula in the Tower. He left an only son, Charles, who became a Gen. in the Army, 3 May, 1796.— *The Genealogist*, Vol. II., p. 108.

[24] This surname is sometimes spelt " Belford." From half-pay Capt. in Lord Shannon's disbanded Regt. of Marines. Comn. as Capt. in Royal Dragoons renewed in 1727. D. in Dec. 1738.—*Gentleman's Mag.*

[25] Comn. renewed in 1727. Lieut. and Capt. 3rd Foot Guards, 17 Oct. 1729. Serving in 1740.

[26] Appointed Cornet in Gen. Wade's Regt. of Horse, 10 April, 1733. Serving in 1740.

[27] Third son of Samuel *Pole*, of Rodbourne, co. Derby. Served at Malplaquet as Ens. in Brigdr. Primrose's Regt. of Foot. Half-pay as Capt. in 1713. Major, 9 March, 1732. Col. of 10th Foot, 10 Aug. 1749. D. a Lt.-Gen. 25 Dec. 1762.

[28] Retd. on half-pay in 1742.

[29] Comn. renewed in 1727. Serving in 1736.

ROYAL NORTH BRITISH DRAGOONS.

[ROYAL SCOTS GREYS.]

Paul George [1] to be Lieut. to Capt. —— -	St. James's, 31 Mar.	1720.		c
Robt. Scott,[2] Esq. to be Capt.-Lieut. - -	,, 7 June,	,,		c
Sir Thos. Hay [3] [Bt.] to be Lieut. to Capt. —— - - - - - -	,, ,, ,,	,,		c
John Dalrimple (sic) [4] to be Cornet to ——	,, ,, ,,	,,		c
Sir Thos. Hay,[3] Bt. to be Capt. in room of Thos. Agnew - - - - -	,, 11 ,,	,,		c
John Whytford (sic) [5] to be Cornet to ——	,, ,, ,,	,,		c
Wm. Lawrince (sic) [6] to be Lieut. to —— -	,, ,, ,,	,,		c
John Dalrymple [7] to be Cornet to Col. Jas. Campbell - - - - - -	,, 24 Dec.	,,		c
Alex. Spittle [8] to be Lieut. to —— - -	,, 27 Mar.	1721.		c
Wm. Wilkinson [9] to be Cornet to —— -	,, ,, ,,	,,		c
Alex. Forbes,[10] Esq. to be Capt. in room of Henry Selwyn - - - - -	Kensington, 9 Aug.	,,		c
John Gallway [11] to be Lieut. to —— - -	,, ,, ,,	,,		c
Sir Edward Gibson,[12] Bt. to be Cornet to —— - - - - - - -	,, ,, ,,	,,		c
James Erskine [13] to be Cornet to —— -	St. James's, 9 Nov.	1722.		c
Wm. Erskine,[14] Esq. to be Major and Capt. of a Tp. - - - - - -	,, 21 Mar.	1722/3.		c
James Ross,[15] Esq. to be Capt. in room of Major Pat. Robertson - - -	,, ,, ,,	,,		c
[Dougal] Campbell [16] to be Cornet to Capt. Alex. Forbes - - - - -	,, ,, ,,	,,		c
George Hay [17] to be Adjt. - - - -	,, 5 Mar.	1724/5.		d
Hugh Ross [18] to be Cornet to Capt. Robt. Hay [? Sir R. Hay] - - - -	,, 24 Dec.	1726.		d
Chas. Crosbie [19] to be Capt. of an additional Tp. - - - - - - -	,, 25 ,,	,,		d
Thos. Leslie [20] to be Lieut. to do. - -	,, ,, ,,	,,		d
Caroline Fred. Scott [21] to be Cornet to do. -	,, ,, ,,	,,		d
Thos. Leigh [22] to be Capt. of an additional Tp.	,, ,, ,,	,,		d
Jenkin Leyson [23] to be Lieut. to do - -	,, ,, ,,	,,		d
James Lyon [24] to be Cornet to do. - -	,, ,, ,,	,,		d
Charles (sic) John, Earl of Crawford,[25] to be Capt. of an additional Tp. - - -	,, ,, ,,	,,		d
James Lyndsay [26] to be Lieut. to do. - -	,, ,, ,,	,,		d
George Hay (sic) [17] to be Cornet to do. -	,, ,, ,,	,,		d

[1] Had served previously as Lieut. in Churchill's Dragoons. Appointed Lt.-Gov. of Montserrat, 25 March, 1724.

[2] Comn. renewed in 1727. Serving in 1730. Out in 1733.

[3] Major, 6 Feb. 1741. Lt.-Col. 27 May, 1742. Served at Dettingen and Fontenoy. Retd. in Feb. 1747. Sir Thos. Hay of Alderstone d. in 1769.

[4] *Dalrymple.* Second son of Hon. Wm. Dalrymple, second son of 1st Earl of Stair. Capt.-Lieut. Inniskilling Dragoons, 24 Dec. 1720. Capt. of an additional Tp. in said Corps, 25 Dec. 1726. Half-pay, 1729. Re-appointed Capt. in the Inniskillings, 17 March, 1736. M.P. for the Wigtown Burghs, 1728–34. D. at Newliston, 23 Feb. 1742.

[5] Aftds. Lt.-Gen. Sir John *Whitefoord,* Bart.   See memoir of Col. Charles Whitefoord in this vol. (pp. 65–74), and note on p. 66.

[6] *Lawrence.* Served at Malplaquet. Capt.-Lieut. 24 Sept. 1733. D. in Nov. 1740.

[7] This officer must not be confounded with his kinsman and namesake referred to in note 4. He was appointed Capt.-Lieut. in the Inniskilling Dragoons, 25 Dec. 1726. Serving in 1740. Third son of the Hon. Hew Dalrymple, one of the younger sons of 1st Visct. Stair. D. 1753. Bd. in the Old Church, Ayr.

[8] See Vol. I., p. 220, note 33.

[9] Comn. renewed in 1727. Lieut. 24 Dec. 1733. Serving in 1740.

[10] Major, 27 May, 1742. Lt.-Col. 27 May, 1745. Served at Dettingen and Fontenoy. Retd. in Feb. 1746.

[11] Not in any subsequent List.

[12] Out before 1727. Of Keirhill, co. Edinburgh. Succeeded his father, Sir Thos. Gibson, about 1713. He bought the Barony of Kinnaird, co. Fife, in Jan. 1726, which was sold after his death. D.s.p. and was bd. 2 June, 1727, at St. Mary's, Nottingham. He was succeeded by his cousin, Alex. Gibson, as 3rd Bart.—G.E.C.'s *Complete Baronetage.*

[13] Promoted Lieut. in 1740.

[14] Lt.-Col. 7th Dragoons, 21 Jan. 1741. Wounded at Fontenoy. Serving in 1748. Out in 1751.

[15] Comn. renewed in 1727. Serving in 1740.

[16]   Do.   Out before 1740.

[17] Cornet, 25 Dec. 1726. May have been the bro. of Sir T. Hay, Bart., who succeeded as 3rd Bart. of Alderstone.

[18] D. in 1739.

[19] See Vol. I., p. 302, note 5.

[20] Half-pay, 1729.

[21] This officer's first Christian name was Caroline, as given in above entry, and not "Charles," as given in subsequent Army Lists. He figures in a list of males bearing female names given in *Notes and Queries.* Serving as Cornet in 1740. Subsequently appointed Capt. in 6th Foot. Major of do. 30 Sept. 1746. Employed as an Engineer in Flanders, 1745. Chief Engineer in India, 1753. Lt.-Col. 5 Jan. 1749. D. at Calcutta, 1756.

[22] From half-pay. Had served as Capt. in Maj.-Gen. Wm. Evans's Regt. of Foot at Malplaquet. Comn. in North British Dragoons renewed in 1727. Half-pay in 1729.

[23] Serving as Lieut. in 1740. Present at Dettingen and Fontenoy.

[24] Comn. renewed in 1727. Out before 1740.

[25] John Lindsay, 20th Earl of Crawford. Comn. renewed in 1727. Appointed Col. of the Highland Regt. (Black Watch), 25 Oct. 1739. Four years previously he joined the Imperial Army on the Rhine as a volunteer, and was present at the battle of Claussen. In 1738 he served under Marshal Munich against the Turks. Subsequently joined the Imperialists near Belgrade, and fought at the battle of Kratzka, where he was severely wounded. Capt. and Col. of the Scots Troop of Horse Grenadier Guards in Dec. 1740. In 1743 was removed to the command of the 4th Tp. of Life Guards. Lord Crawford commanded the Brigade of Life Guards at Dettingen and Fontenoy. Commanded the Forces in the Lowlands of Scotland, 1745–46. Commanded a Cavalry Brigade at the battle of Roucoux, 11 Oct. 1746, and in the Netherlands, 1747–48. Col. of the Scots Greys, 28 May, 1747. D. in London, 25 Dec. 1749.

[26] "Lieut. in the Navy in 1715." Serving as Lieut. in above Regt. in 1740. Succeeded in 1746 as 5th Earl of Balcarres. D. in 1769.

EARL OF

JOHN CRAUFURD

(*See* p. 81.)

THE KING'S REGIMENT OF DRAGOONS.

[3RD HUSSARS.]

Patrick Hepburn [1] to be Qr.-Mr. to Lt.-Col. Samuel Foley's Tp. - - - -	—	24 April,	1718. *c*
Thos. Carpenter [2] to be Lieut. - - -	—	25 Dec.	,, *p*
Samuel Kempster [3] to be Cornet to Capt. Alex. Read - - - - - -	St. James's, 20 Mar.	1718/9. *c*	
Wm. Ogle, [4] Esq. to be Capt. in room of Alex. Read - - - - -	,,	16 Jan.	1721/2. *c*
John Hoare, [5] Esq. to be Capt.-Lieut. - -	,,	,, ,,	,, *c*
Henry Whitley [6] to be Lieut. to Capt. Alex. Mullen - - - - -	,,	,, ,,	,, *c*
Fairfax Norcliff [7] to be Cornet to Lt.-Col. Foley - - - - -	,,	,, ,,	,, *c*
George (*sic*) Parsons [8] to be do. to —— -	,,	,, ,,	,, *c*
Adam Maxwell [9] to be do. to Col. Joshua Guest - - - - -	9 Mar.	,, *c*	
Leonard Robinson [10] to be do. to —— - -	,,	25 April,	1722. *p*
Fairfax Norcliff [7] to be Lieut. to Col. Guest	,,	25 June,	,, *c*
Gilbert Pringle [11] to be Cornet to the Colonel's Tp. - - - - -	,,	,, ,,	,, *c*
Reginald Graham [12] to be Cornet to ——	,,	20 Dec.	,, *c*
Robert Carpenter, [13] Esq. to be Capt. of an additional Tp. - - - - -	,,	25 Dec.	1726. *d*
Edward Erle [14] to be Lieut. to do. - -	,,	,, ,,	,, *d*
Lewis Downs [15] to be Cornet to do. - -	,,	,, ,,	,, *d*
Francis Bushell, [16] Esq. to be Capt. of an additional Tp. - - - - -	,,	,, ,,	, *d*
Mathew Swinny (*sic*) [17] to be Lieut. to do.-	,,	,, ,,	,, *d*
Henry Villiers [18] to be Cornet to do. - -	,,	,, ,,	,, *d*
John Mordaunt, [19] Esq. to be Capt. of an additional Tp. - - - - -	,,	,, ,,	,, *d*
George Harman [20] to be Lieut. to do. - -	,,	,, ,,	,, *d*
Wm. Henry Durell [21] to be Cornet to do. -	,,	,, ,,	,, *d*
George Hunt [22] to be do. [in room of Durell] - - - - -	[,,]	25 Mar.	1727. *p*

[1] This Comn. was signed by Gen. Carpenter, the Col. of the Regt. Hepburn's name does not appear in any subsequent List.
[2] Comn. renewed in 1727. Serving in 1736. Out before 1740.
[3] Out before 1727.
[4] Appointed Cornet in above Regt. 23 June, 1712. Served at Dettingen.
[5] Comn. renewed in 1727. Out before 1739.
[6] Serving as Lieut. and Adjt. in 1727. Capt. 12 June, 1743. Served at Dettingen and Fontenoy. Lt.-Col. 10th Dragoons, 15 March, 1748. Col. 9th Dragoons, 6 April, 1759. Maj.-Gen. 13 Aug. 1761. D. a Lt.-Gen. in Jan. 1771.
[7] Third son of Lt.-Col. Fairfax *Norcliffe*, of Langton Hall, Yorkshire. Born at Heslington, 8 July, 1704. Lieut. 25 June, 1722. Comn. renewed in 1727. Serving in 1738. Md. in 1732 Faith, dau. of Callisthenes Brooke, of Gateforth. D.s.p. at Ripon, 24 Oct. 1739. Bd. in Ripon Minster.

o

[8] *John* Parsons. Capt.-Lieut. 12 June, 1743. Served at Dettingen. Further services untraced.

[9] Out before 1727.

[10] Lieut. 20 June, 1735. Dangerously wounded at Dettingen. Believed to have died shortly afterwards.

[11] Comn. renewed in 1727. Half-pay, 1729. Drawing half-pay in 1758.

[12] Succeeded to the Baronetcy of Norton Conyers on the death of his bro. Sir Bellingham Graham, in 1730. D. in 1755.

[13] Appointed Lieut. in Col. Toby Caulfield's Regt. of Foot, 4 Sept. 1708. Capt. in Col. Thos. Alnutt's Regt. of Foot, 10 Sept. 1712. Capt. and Lt.-Col. 3rd Foot Guards, 30 Oct. 1734. Killed at Fontenoy.

[14] Comn. renewed in June, 1727. Serving in 1736. Out before 1740.

[15]   Do.   Out before 1740.

[16] Served previously as Capt. in Col. Cholmley's Regt. of Foot. Capt. in Lord Mark Kerr's Regt. of Dragoons (11th), 31 May, 1732. Serving in 1740. See further notice of this officer on p. 305, note 6.

[17] Of Swillington, Yorkshire. Served in Spain during the War of Succession, and was taken prisoner at Brihuega in 1710. (*Treasury Papers*, CCXXXVI., No. 3.) Appointed Capt. in Lt.-Gen. the Hon. Wm. Ker's Dragoons (7th), 13 May, 1735. Major of a newly-raised Regt. of Foot, 13 Oct. 1745. Said Corps was disbanded in 1748. Major *Swiney* d. at Pontefract in 1766. (*Gentleman's Mag.*)

[18] Comn. renewed in June, 1727. Out before 1736.

[19] From Lieut. and Capt. 1st Foot Guards. Serving in 1730.

[20] Served in late reign as Ens. in Col. Kilner Brasier's Regt. of Foot. Serving in the King's Own Dragoons in 1730. Out before 1740.

[21] Out 25 March, 1727.

[22] Comn. renewed in June, 1727. Out before 1740.

MAJOR-GENERAL WM. EVANS'S REGIMENT OF DRAGOONS.

[4TH HUSSARS.]

John Lee,[1] Esq. to be Capt. of that Troop whereof [Lt.-Col. Thos.] Howard was late Capt. in above Regt. - - -	Hampton Ct., 22 Oct. 1717.*b*
James Harrison,[2] Esq. to be Capt. of that Troop whereof Peter Renovard was late Capt. in do. - - - - - -	„ „ „ „ *b*
Maurice Morgan,[3] Esq. to be Capt. of that Troop whereof [John] Lee was late Capt.	St. James's, 2 Jan. 1718/9.*b*
Wm. Maidman[4] to be Lieut. to Capt. Jas. Harrison - - - - -	„ „ „ „ *c*
Robert Bainton[5] to be Lieut. to Capt. Richard Hartshorn - - - - -	„ 13 May, 1720.*c*
Fras. Thompson to be Cornet to do. - -	„ „ „ „ *c*
Ant. Gisburne[6] to be Cornet to Capt. John Folliot - - - - - -	„ 14 „ „ *c*
George Colly,[7] Esq. to be Capt.-Lieut. - -	„ 24 Dec. „ *c*
Robert Jodrell[8] to be Lieut. to Capt. Lanoe -	„ „ „ „ *c*
John Dalrymple[9] to be Cornet to do. -	„ „ „ „ *c*
Wm. Adamson[10] to be Cornet to Col. Chas. Lanoe - - - - - - -	„ 20 Mar. 1720/1.*c*
John Brown,[11] Esq. to be Lt.-Colonel and Capt. of a Tp. - - - - - -	„ 8 May, 1721. *c*
Thos. Olivant[12] to be Cornet to Capt. Hartshorn - - - - -	„ 3 June, „ *c*
Fras. Thompson[13] to be Lieut. to —— - -	„ „ „ „ *c*
Wm. Duckett,[14] Esq. to be Major and Capt. of a Tp. - - - - - - -	„ 9 „ „ *c*
Wm. Higginson[15] to be Lieut. to —— - -	„ 28 Oct. „ *c*
Geoffry Parker[16] to be Lieut. to Capt. Morgan - - - - - - -	„ 26 Jan. 1721/2.*c*
Thos. Gery,[17] Esq. to be Capt. in room of —— Morgan - - - - -	„ 28 Feb. „ *c*
John Lockhart[18] to be Cornet to Genl. Evans's Tp. - - - - - - - -	„ 18 May, 1722. *c*
Nathaniel Halhead[19] to be Lieut. to Major Wm. Duckett - - - - -	„ „ „ „ *c*
Samuel Pashler[20] to be Cornet to —— - -	„ 26 June, „ *c*
Thos. Gery,[17] Esq. to be Major [in room of Wm. Duckett] and Capt. of a Tp. - -	„ 4 Feb. 1722/3.*c*
George Macartney,[21] Esq. to be Capt. in room of Thos. Gery - - - - -	„ „ „ „ *c*
George Fowke[22] to be Lieut. to [Major] Gery	„ 18 „ „ *c*
Wm. Adamson[10] to be Lieut. to Capt. Richard Hartshorn - - - - - -	„ 23 April, 1723.*c*
Francis Eyles[23] to be Cornet to Lt.-Col. Brown - - - - - - -	„ „ „ „ *c*

o 2

Robert Waller [24] to be Cornet to —— -	Herrenhausen, 27 Aug. 1723.*c*
Chas. Rich [25] to be do. to Capt. Knox - -	Gohre, 9 Nov. ,, *c*
Andrew Lauder [26] to be Surgeon - - -	St. James's, 18 Dec. 1724.*d*
Edward Byng [27] to be Cornet to —— - -	,, 27 May, 1725.*d*
Charles Keightley [28] to be Lieut. to Capt. Knox - - - - - - -	,, 15 Jan.1725/6.*d*
Richard Roberts,[29] Esq. to be Capt. of an additional Tp. - - - - -	,, 25 Dec. 1726.*d*
Nicholas Lee [30] to be Lieut. to do. - -	,, ,, ,, ,, *d*
Roger Townshend [31] to be Cornet to do. -	,, ,, ,, ,, *d*
Humphry Watson,[32] Esq. to be Capt. of an additional Tp. - - - - -	,, ,, ,, ,, *d*
Sir Fras. Masham,[33] Bt. to be Lieut. to do. -	,, ,, ,, ,, *d*
John Morgan [34] to be Cornet to do. - -	,, ,, ,, ,, *d*
Francis Boggest,[35] Esq. to be Capt. of an additional Tp. - - - - -	,, ,, ,, ,, *d*
Francis Eyles [28] to be Lieut. to do. - -	,, ,, ,, ,, *d*
Richard Cornwallis [36] to be Cornet to do. -	,, ,, ,, ,, *d*
Henry Bickerton [37] to be do. to —— - -	,, ,, ,, ,, *d*
Wm. Buck [38] to be Qr.-Mr. to Capt. Richard Hartshorn [signed by General Evans] -	— 8 Mar.1726/7.*d*

[1] Lt.-Col. 4th Foot, 4 April, 1730. Col. 44th Foot, 11 March, 1743. Served at Prestonpans. D. 1750.

[2] Served with the Carabiniers at Blenheim and Malplaquet. Out of Evans's Regt. before 1727.

[3] Served previously as Ens. in Lord Paston's Regt. and as Lieut. in Gen. Lumley's Regt. of Horse (1st D.G.). Capt. and Lt.-Col. 3rd Foot Guards, 16 March, 1722. Comn. renewed by George II. D. about 1740.

[4] Served previously as Capt.-Lieut. in Col. Dubourgay's Regt. of Foot. Appointed Capt. of an Invalid Cy. 28 April, 1720.

[5] Out of the Regt. 23 April, 1723.

[6] Out of the Regt. before 1728.

[7] Comn. renewed in June, 1727. Appointed Capt. of a newly-raised Indep. Cy. 13 Nov. 1739.

[8] Out of the Regt. before 1727.

[9] Do.

[10] Lieut. 23 April, 1723. Capt.-Lieut. 13 Aug. 1739. Serving in 1740.

[11] See biog. notice in Vol. I., p. 263, note 1.

[12] *Oliphant.* Under date of 3 Dec. 1724 the *Historical Register* records that : "Mr. Lewis and Mr. Oliphant Lieuts. (*sic*) in Evans's Dragoons, fought a duel at the Mitre Tavern, Charing Cross, and the former was run through the body and died immediately." Thos. Oliphant was promoted Lieut. 24 Feb. 1729. Capt. in Campbell's Regt. of Foot (Scots Fusiliers) in Nov. 1739. The death of "Thos. Oliphant, Capt. in the North British Fusiliers, aged 47," is recorded in the *Gentleman's Mag.* for 1747, and it is stated that he served at Dettingen, Fontenoy, and Culloden.

[13] Capt. of an additional Tp. in Col. Churchill's Dragoons, 25 Dec. 1726. Half-pay, 1729. Lt.-Col. of Robinson's Marines, 25 Nov. 1739. Killed at Carthagena, 1741.

[14] See biog. notice in Vol. I., pp. 263, 264, note 6.

[15] Capt. 13 Aug. 1739. Serving in 1740. Son of Capt. Wm. Higginson of Sir R. Temple's Regt. of Foot who was killed at the siege of Lille in 1708. Young Higginson was given an Ensign's Comn. in Temple's Regt. 20 June, 1709, and fought at Malplaquet.

[16] See his Comn. as Brigdr. in 3rd Tp. of Life Guards on p. 190, and note thereto.

[17] Major, 4 Feb. 1723. Retd. in Aug. 1739.

[18] Comn. renewed in June, 1727. Half-pay in 1729. Drawing half-pay, 1758.

[19] Do.   do.

[20] Lieut. 23 April, 1736. Serving in 1740.

[21] A.D.C. to Earl Cadogan, the C.-in-C., in 1722. Served previously as Lieut. and Capt. 1st Foot Guards. Serving in Sir Robt. Rich's Dragoons (late Evans's) with same rank in 1740. Believed to have been son of Lt.-Gen. Geo. *Maccartney.*

[22] Probably son of Capt. George Fowke, a Brigdr. in 2nd Life Guards. Comn. in Evans's Dragoons renewed in June, 1727. Half-pay, 1729. Living in 1739.

[23] Appears to have been son of Sir John Eyles, Knt. Lieut. in above Regt. 25 Dec. 1726. D. in 1735.

[24] Out of the Regt. before June, 1727. Major 38th Foot, 23 April, 1743.

[25] Lieut. 7 Nov. 1739. Third son of Sir Robt. Rich, Bart., of Sunning, who must not be confounded with Field-Marshal Sir Robt. Rich, Bart., of Rosehall, Suffolk.

[26] Untraced.

[27] Placed on half-pay in 1729. D. in 1756. He was younger bro. to the unfortunate Admiral John Byng executed in 1757 at Portsmouth.

[28] Served previously as Lieut. in Col. Newton's Regt. of Dragoons. Comn. as Lieut. in Evans's Dragoons renewed in June, 1727. Serving in 1738. Out in Nov. 1739.

[29] See biog. notice in Vol. I., p. 120, note 4.

[30] Comn. renewed in June, 1727. Not in any subsequent list.

[31] Capt. in Gen. Wade's Regt. of Horse (3rd D.G.), 14 Feb. 1729. Capt. and Lt.-Col. 1st Foot Guards, 8 Feb. 1741. Served at Dettingen as A.D.C. to George II. Bro. to Charles, 2nd Visct. Townshend. Gov. of North Yarmouth. D. in 1760.

[32] Appointed Capt. in the Earl of Inchiquin's Regt. of Foot, 19 Nov. 1707. Half-pay, 1712. Capt. in Sir Robt. Rich's Dragoons, 22 July, 1715. Half-pay in 1718. Capt. in Evans's as given in text. Major of Col. Edward Wolfe's Regt. of Marines, 30 Nov. 1739. Lost his life at the siege of Carthagena in 1741.

[33] Appointed Ens. in Col. Thos. Alnutt's Regt. of Foot, 10 Sept. 1712. Third son of Sir Saml. Masham, Bart., who was created Baron Masham. This Francis Masham died in the lifetime of his father and was never given a baronetcy nor did he succeed to any title.

[34] Serving in 1727. Out before 1739. A certain John Morgan was appointed Capt. in Gen. Columbine's Regt. of Foot in 1735.

[35] Promoted Regtal. Major, 11 July, 1741. He was of Hawley, Suffolk, and had served as Cornet in the Rl. Irish Dragoons at Malplaquet. Left the Army about 1745.

[36] Lieut. in Gen. Wade's Regt. of Horse, 13 Aug. 1736. Serving in 1740. Younger son to Charles, 4th Lord Cornwallis. D. at Rotterdam in 1741.—*Gentleman's Mag.*

[37] Lieut. 12 July, 1739. Serving in 1740.

[38] Placed on half-pay in 1729. Living in 1739.

THE INNISKILLING DRAGOONS.

Chas. Jas. Kirke [1] to be Cornet to the Earl of Stair	St. James's,	29 Mar.	1720.	c
Alex. Auchinleck,[2] Esq. to be Capt. in room of Lawrence Nugent	,,	24 Dec.	,,	c
John Dalrymple,[3] Esq. to be Capt.-Lieut.	,,	,, ,,	,,	c
Thos. Montgomery [4] to be Lieut. to Col. Montgomery's Tp.	,,	8 April,	1721.	c
Wm. Hamilton [5] to be Lieut. to Capt. Montagu Ferrers (*sic*)	,,	,, ,,	,,	c
Wm. Saville [6] to be Cornet to Major Augustus Duquerry	,,	,, ,,	,,	c
Robt. Wigham [7] to be do. to Lt.-Col. John Upton	,,	,, ,	,,	c
John Hamilton [8] to be Lieut. to do.	,,	;,, ,,	,,	c
Wm. Lord Crichton [9] to be Cornet to ———	,,	6 July,	,,	c
Do. to be Capt. in room of [Lt.-Col. John] Upton	,,	27 May,	1723.	c
George Abell [10] to be Lieut. to Capt. ———	,,	,, ,,	,,	c
Fras. Godolphin [11] to be Cornet to ———	Pyrmont,	4 July,	,,	c
John Dalrymple [12] to be Adjt.	St. James's,	28 April,	1724.	d
Edward Trelawney [13] to be Lieut. to Lord Crickton (*sic*)	,,	23 May,	,,	d
James Gardiner,[14] Esq. to be Major	Kensington,	20 July,	,,	d
John Dalrymple,[12] Esq. to be Capt.-Lieut.	[St. James's],	25 Dec.	1726.	f
John Dalrymple,[15] Esq. to be Capt. of an additional Tp.	,,	,, ,,	,,	d
Chas. Wm. Tonyn [16] to be Lieut. to do.	,,	,, ,,	,,	d
Chas. Gordon [17] to be Cornet to do.	,,	,, ,,	,,	d
John Whiteford,[18] Esq. to be Capt. of an additional Tp.	,,	,, ,,	,,	d
George Brodie [19] to be Lieut.	,,	,, ,,	,,	d
Wm. Dalrymple [20] to be Cornet	,,	,, ,,	,,	d
Alexander, Earl of Balcarres,[21] to be Capt. of an additional Tp.	,,	,, ,,	,,	d
John Steuart [22] to be Lieut. to do.	,,	,, ,,	,,	d
Hugh Dalrymple [23] to be Cornet to do.	,,	,, ,,	,,	d
Paul Torin [24] to be Lieut. to Lord Crichton	,,	27 April,	1727.	d
John Steuart [25] to be Adjt.	,,	6 May,	,,	d
Patrick Agnew [26] to be Lieut.	,,	31 ,,	,,	f
John Young [27] to be Cornet	,,	,, ,,	,,	f
Hugh, Lord Viscount Primrose,[28] to be Capt. of that Tp. whf. the Earl of Stair was late Capt.	,,	2 June,	,,	d

[1] Comn. renewed 20 June, 1727. Not in any subsequent List. Only son of Major George Kirke, of the Royal Horse Guards, by Adris his wife. He was baptised at St. Margaret's, Westminster, 26 Jan. 1700/1. Not named in his mother's will, which was dated 25 July, 1753, and proved 16 Dec. 1754.—Col. Chester's *Westminster Abbey Registers*, p. 387, note 6.

(*See* Vol. I., p. 110.)

[2] Promoted from Capt.-Lieut.   Served in the late reign as Lieut. in the North British Dragoons.   Comn. as Capt. renewed in 1727.   On half-pay in 1739.

[3] See p. 207, note 4.

[4] Lieut. 8 April, 1726.   Serving in 1736.

[5] On half-pay in 1739.

[6] Comn. renewed 20 June, 1727.   D. before 1733, in which year his widow, Ann Saville, was in receipt of a widow's pension of £16 per annum.

[7] D. before 1733, in which year his widow, Mary Wigham, was in receipt of a widow's pension of £16 per annum.

[8] Not in any subsequent List.

[9] There are several letters from this nobleman on regimental affairs to the Earl of Stair printed in *Annals of the Viscount and 1st and 2nd Earls of Stair*.   He was second son of the Countess of Dumfries (who had md. Lord Stair's bro. the Hon. Wm. Dalrymple). Lord Crichton succeeded his mother as Earl of Dumfries, and subsequently inherited the Earldom of Stair.   He served as A.D.C. to his uncle, Field-Marshal the Earl of Stair, at Dettingen.   Capt. and Lt.-Col. 3rd Foot Guards, 18 Jan. 1744.   K.T. 11 March, 1752. D. 1768.

[10] From half-pay.   Out of the Regt. before 1727.

[11] Comn. renewed in 1727.   Appointed Lt.-Gov. of the Scilly Isles in 1739.

[12] See p. 208, note 7.

[13] Believed to be identical with the Edward Trelawney who was third son of the Rt. Rev. Sir Jonathan Trelawney, Bishop of Bristol.   Said Edward was born 1699, and appointed Gov. of Jamaica about 1737.   He was first Col. of the 49th Regt. of Foot, which post he held till his death in 1754.

[14] The renowned Col. James Gardiner who fell at Prestonpans in 1745.   See biog. notice in Vol. VI. of *English Army Lists and Commission Registers*, 1661–1714, p. 315, note 9.

[15] See p. 207, note 4.

[16] Attained the rank of Major of above Regt. 19 March, 1745.   Serving in 1748.

[17] Comn. renewed in June, 1727.   Out before 1740.   Kinsman probably to Lady Anne Gordon, who md. Lord Crichton of above Regt.

[18] See p. 66, note 3.

[19] Serving with same rank in 1740.

[20] A younger bro. to Capt. John Dalrymple of same Corps.   Comn. renewed in 1727. Out before 1740.

[21] Fourth Earl.   Capt. and Lt.-Col. Coldstream Guards, 27 Aug. 1733.   D. 25 July, 1736.

[22] Adjt. 26 May, 1727.   Half-pay, 1729.

[23] Half-pay, 1729.   Youngest bro. to Capt. John Dalrymple, of same Corps.   D. 24 Sept. 1737.

[24] Half-pay, 1729.   Restored to full pay as Lieut. 25 Oct. 1737.   Serving in 1740.

[25] See note 22.

[26] See biog. notice in Vol. I., p. 266, note 8.

[27] Serving as Cornet in 1740.

[28] Third Visct. Primrose, stepson to the Earl of Stair, being the Countess of Stair's son by her first marriage.   "He went to the Continent with Lord Crawford, serving as a volunteer in the Imperial Army under Prince Eugene of Savoy.   He was severely wounded in an engagement at Claussen, 17 Oct. 1735.   Appointed Lieut.-Col. of the 33rd Foot in Dec. 1738, but he is styled Lieut.-Colonel of General Dalzell's Regiment in the contemporary notices of his death which occurred at Wrexham, co. Flint, 8 May, 1741, when he was in his 39th year.   He married 21 June, 1739, Anne, daughter of the Rev. Peter Drelincourt, Dean of Armagh.   She died without issue."—*The Scottish Peerage*, Vol. VII.

THE PRINCESS OF WALES'S OWN REGIMENT OF DRAGOONS.

[7TH HUSSARS.]

Thos. Crohare (*sic*) [1] to be Cornet to ———	St. James's,	7 June, 1720. *c*
David Ogilvy,[2] Esq. to be Capt. in room of Lewis Dollon	,,	28 July, ,, *c*
Wm. de la Vallie,[3] Esq. to be Capt.-Lieut.	,,	,, ,, ,, *c*
John Keate[4] to be Lieut. to Capt. Wm. Craford (*sic*)	, ,	,, *c*
——— Long[5] to be Cornet to ———	Herrenhausen, ,,	,, ,, *c*
Andrew Corner[6] to be Lieut. to Lord Torphicken	St. James's,	27 Mar. 1721. *c*
George Harrison,[7] Esq. to be Capt. in room of David Ogilvy	,,	29 July, ,, *c*
Wm. Johnston[8] to be Lieut. to Capt. [James] Livingston	,,	1 Aug. ,, *c*
David Ogilvy[9] [Junr.] to be Cornet to Lord Torphicken	,,	,, ,, ,, *c*
[John] Lumley[10] to be Cornet to ———	,,	24 Oct. ,, *c*
Thos. Fowke,[11] Esq. to be Lt.-Col. [in room of Lord Torphicken]	Kensington,	25 June, 1722. *c*
James Agnew,[12] Esq. to be Capt. in room of Sir George Dunbar	St. James's,	11 April, 1723. *c*
Robert Kerr[13] to be Lieut. to ———	,,	,, ,, ,, *c*
James Sinclair[14] to be Cornet to Capt. Livingston	,,	24 May, ,, *c*
John Lumley,[15] Esq. to be Capt. in room of [Jas.] Livingston	,,	29 ,, ,, *c*
Marcellus Laroon,[16] Esq. to be Capt. in room of ——— Crawford decd.	,,	1 Jan. 1723/4. *c*
Cornet James Ogilvy[17] to be Lieut. to Capt. George Harrison	,,	6 May, 1725. *d*
Robert Maxwell,[18] Esq. to be Capt. of an additional Tp.	,,	25 Dec. 1726. *d*
Richard Norbury[19] to be Lieut. to do.	,,	,, ,, ,, *d*
Henry Brydges, Esq., commonly called Lord Henry Brydges,[20] to be Cornet to do.	,,	,, ,, ,, *d*
Mathew Steuart,[21] Esq. to be Capt. of an additional Tp.	,,	,, ,, ,, *d*
John Rushton[22] to be Lieut. to do.	,,	,, ,, ,, *d*
Bernard Granville[23] to be Cornet to do.	,,	,, ,, ,, *d*
Philip Lloyd,[24] Esq. to be Capt. of an additional Tp.	,,	,, ,, ,, *d*
Mathew Sewell,[25] to be Lieut. to do.	,,	,, ,, ,, *d*
Harry Burrard[26] to be Cornet to do.	,,	,, ,, ,, *d*

[1] Lieut. 13 April, 1736. Serving in 1740.
[2] Promoted from Lieut. Out of the Regt. 29 July, 1721.
[3] Comn. renewed 20 June, 1727. Capt. 10 April, 1739. Serving in 1740.
[4] Promoted from Cornet. Comn. renewed in 1727. Serving in 1736.

[5] Out before 1727.

[6] Had been Lieut. in Tyrrell's Dragoons.   Comn. renewed in 1727.   Serving in 1736.

[7] Comn. renewed in 1727.   Half-pay, 1729.   Drawing half-pay in 1749.

[8] Served previously as Adjt. and Cornet.   Comn. as Lieut. renewed in 1727.   Out before 1740.

[9] Lieut. 20 Jan. 1738.

[10] The Hon. John Lumley, bro. to the Earl of Scarborough.   Capt. 29 May, 1723.   Capt. and Lt.-Col. Coldstream Guards, 31 Jan. 1732.   D. 16 Oct. 1739.

[11] Son of Capt. Thos. Fowke, of Col. Nicholas Lepell's Regt. of Foot.   On 30 June, 1707, Ens. Thos. Fowke succeeded his father as Capt. in above Regt. and, *mirabile dictu*, the father took his son's place in the Regt. as Ens. !   (See father's and son's Comns. in Vol. VI., *English Army Lists and Commission Registers*, 1661–1714, p. 243.)   This piece of family jobbery was occasioned by Capt. Fowke senr. being in declining health, and wishful to give his son a good start in his profession.   Young Capt. Fowke served in Spain during the latter part of the Spanish Succession War, and exchanged to the Inniskilling Regt. of Foot, also in Spain, 26 Dec. 1711.   Comn. in last-named Corps renewed by George I. in 1715.   Appointed Major of the Corps now known as the Somersetshire Light Infantry in 1716.   Raised the 43rd Regt. of Foot, 13 Aug. 1741.   Brig.-Gen. 1 Jan. 1745.   Served as second in command at the battle of Prestonpans.   Maj.-Gen. 18 Sept. 1747.   Was a Maj.-Gen. on the Staff in Flanders in 1748.   Appointed Gov. of Gibraltar in 1754.   For an error of judgment in refusing to send troops from Gibraltar to the relief of Port Mahon, when besieged by the French fleet in 1756, Fowke was recalled, tried by a court-martial, and cashiered.   The strong feeling in Fowke's favour induced George III. to restore this unfortunate General to his former rank in the Army, and he was appointed Maj.-Gen. in Ireland, 2 Aug. 1761.   He d. a Lt.-Gen. at Bath in 1765.

[12] See biog. notice in Vol. I., p. 111, note 4.

[13] Capt.-Lieut. 15 Dec. 1738.   Serving in 1740.

[14] Comn. renewed in 1727.   Out before 1740.

[15] See note 10.

[16] See Vol. I., p. 124, note 4.

[17] Served as Capt.-Lieut. of above Regt. at Fontenoy, and was wounded.

[18] Had served in Col. Newton's Dragoons.   In 1730 was Capt. in 5th Horse (Napier's).   Out of last-named Corps before 1736.

[19] Half-pay, 1729.   Appointed Capt. in Col. James Oglethorpe's newly-raised Regt. of Foot (Georgia Rangers), 25 Aug. 1737.   Serving in 1740.

[20] Second son of the Duke of Chandos.   Took the courtesy title of Marquess of Carnarvon at his elder bro.'s decease in 1729.   In 1744 he succeeded as 2nd Duke of Chandos.   D. in 1771.

[21] Major Mat. Stewart of same Corps.   See biog. notice in Vol. I., p. 111, note 3.

[22] Half-pay, 1729.   Drawing half-pay, 1739.

[23] Served in latter part of late reign as Ens. in Lord Slane's Regt. of Foot.   Serving as Cornet in Gen. Ker's Dragoons in 1740.

[24] Served previously as Capt. in Col. Lucas's Regt. of Foot.   Half-pay, 1729.

[25] From half-pay Pocock's Foot.   See biog. notice in Vol. I., p. 318, note 7.

[26] Comn. renewed in June, 1727.   Out before 1740.   Eldest son of Paul Burrard of Walhampton.   Created a Bart. 20 March, 1769.   D. in 1791.

BRIGADIER-GENERAL HUMPHRY GORE'S REGIMENT OF DRAGOONS.

[10TH HUSSARS.]

Henry Courtney,[1] Esq. to be Capt. in room of Philip Gery - - -	St. James's,	1 Jan.	1719/20.		c
Peter Chaban[2] to be Lieut. to [Lt.-Col.] Peter Hawker - - - - -	,,	,, ,,	,,		c
Philip Gery[3] to be Major and Capt. of a Company (sic)	,,	3 ,,	,,		p
Walter Molesworth,[4] Esq. to be Capt. in room of George Treby - - -	,,	16 ,,	,,		c
Charles Powlet,[5] Esq. to be Lt.-Col. and Capt. of Tp. - - - - -	,,	8 March,	,,		c
Barret Bowen[6] to be Cornet to —— -	,,	,, ,,	,,		c
Capt. Mat. FitzGerald to be Lieut. -	—	25 Jan.	1720/1.		c
George Buckley[7] to be Cornet to Lt.-Col. Chas. Powlet - - - -	St. James's,	24 March,	,,		c
James Manwaring[8] to be Cornet to Capt. [Henry] Courtney - - -	,,	26 Jan.	1721/2.		c
Wm. Prosser[9] to be Lieut. to do. - -	,,	,, Feb.	,,		c
Daniel Soyer[10] to be Chaplain - -	,,	2 Feb.	,,		c
Chas. Burroughs[11] to be Cornet to Capt.——[in room of Wm. Stannus]	Kensington,	10 Sept. 1722.			c
John Graham[12] to be do. to —— - -	St. James's,	8 Dec.	,,		c
Charles Churchill,[13] Esq. to be Colonel in room of Humphry Gore and to be Capt. of a Tp. - - - - -	,,	12 Jan. 1722/3.			c
John Whitworth,[14] Esq. to be Capt. in room of [Samuel] Woodward -	Herrenhausen,	12 July, 1723.			c
Wm. Elliott,[15] Esq. to be Capt. in room of Henry Courtenay - - -	,,	,, ,,	,,		c
John Jordan,[16] Esq. to be Capt.-Lieut. [in room of Israel Pressly] - -	,,	,, ,,	,,		c
George Buckley[17] to be Lieut. to [Lt.-Col.] Powlet - - - -	,,	,, ,,	,,		c
Robert Walkinshaw[18] to be Cornet to [Major] Gery - - - -	,,	29 ,,	,,		c
Edward Cater[19] to be Cornet to do. -	,,	20 Sept.	,,		c
Samuel Gumley,[20] Esq. to be Capt. in room of John Griffith - - -	,,	28 March, 1724.			c
Thomas Jekyll[21] to be Lieut. [in room of Prosser] - - - - - -	,,	26 July,	,,		d
Arthur Maynwaring[22] to be Cornet to Lt.-Col. Powlet - - - -	,,	29 April, 1725.			d
Thos. Bloodworth[23] to be do. to —— -	,,	6 May,	,,		d
Edward Goddard[24] to be Cornet to Col. Chas. Churchill - - - -	,,	17 Aug.	,,		d

Thos. Bruce [25] to be Lieut. to [Major] Philip Gery - - - -	Kensington, 19 Aug.	1726.	*d*
Fras. Thompson,[26] Esq. to be Capt. of an additional Tp. - - - - -	St. James's, 25 Dec.	,,	*d*
Ric. Lucas [27] to be Lieut. to do. - -	,, ,, ,,	,,	*d*
Peregrine Lascelles [28] to be Capt. of an additional Tp. - - - - -	,, ,, ,,	,,	*d*
Charles Hamilton [29] to be Lieut. to do. -	,, ,, ,,	,,	*d*
Edward Draper [30] to be Cornet to do. -	,, ,, ,,	,,	*d*
Wm. Gee,[31] Esq. to be Capt. of an additional Tp. - - - - -	,, ,, ,,	,,	*d*
Edward Meadows [32] to be Lieut. to do. -	,, ,, ,,	,,	*d*
Fras. Scott,[33] commonly called Lord Hermitage, to be Cornet to do. -	,, ,, ,,	,,	*d*
David Chapman (*sic*) [34] to be Cornet to Capt. Wm. Elliot - - - -	,, ,, ,,	,,	*d*
Samuel Auberry [35] to be Surgeon - -	,, 17 March, 1726/7.		*d*

[1] Left the Regt. in June, 1723.

[2] Served at Culloden with above Regt. See biog. notice in Vol. I., p. 124, note 5.

[3] Appointed Cornet in above Regt. 20 Dec. 1715. Capt. 25 Dec. 1717. Comn. as Major renewed in 1727. Out before 1739.

[4] Fifth son of 1st Visct. Molesworth. Had served as Capt.-Lieut. of Col. Thos. Allen's Regt. of Foot at close of last reign and was placed on half-pay 1713. Comn. as Capt. renewed in 1727. Half-pay, 1729. D. in 1773.

[5] *Paulet.* See biog. notice in Vol. I., p. 135, note 10.

[6] Appointed Capt. in Col. Wm. Newton's Regt. of Foot, 5 March, 1723. Out of said Regt. before 1736.

[7] Lieut. 12 July, 1723. Capt.-Lieut. 25 Aug. 1739. Serving in 1740. Half-pay Col. Churchill's Marines, 1750.

[8] Out before 1727.

[9] D. in July, 1724.

[10] Out in 1737.

[11] Serving as Cornet in the 6th Regt. of Horse (5th D.G.) in 1737. Out before 1740.

[12] Out before 1727.

[13] See biog. notice in Vol. I., p. 120, note 1.

[14] Promoted from Lieut. in Gen. Whetham's Regt. (27th Foot). Serving in Churchill's Dragoons in 1730. Out before 1740.

[15] See biog. notice on p. 198, note 19.

[16] Had served in late reign as Lieut. and Adjt. of a Huguenot Regt. of Foot in Portugal. Major of Churchill's Dragoons, 11 Dec. 1739. Appointed Col. of a Marine Regt. in 1748. Said Corps was disbanded same year and Jordan was placed on half-pay with the rest of his officers. D. in 1756. A copy of his will is in the Record Office, Dublin.

[17] See note 7.

[18] Son of Surgeon Walkinshaw. Lieut. 21 May, 1733. Serving in 1740.

[19] Accompanied Capt. Wm. Elliot of same Regt. to Denmark and North Germany in Aug. 1724, to buy horses for above Corps (see letter quoted in Introduction). Not in any List after 1724. Probably belonged to the Bedfordshire family founded by Sir Edward Cater, Knt., in 1660.

[20] See his Comn. in the Rl. Dragoons on p. 219 and note thereto.

[21] Capt. 5 Nov. 1735. Major, 24 April, 1741. Committed suicide at Canterbury in 1744. —*Gentleman's Mag.*

[22] Appointed Capt. in Maj.-Gen. Henry Harrison's Regt. (15th Foot) 25 June, 1736. D. during the Carthagena Expedition, in 1741, as Major of said Corps. He was an illegitimate son of Anne Oldfield the famous actress.

[23] Appointed Capt. in the Rl. Fusiliers, 26 Dec. 1726. Capt. and Lt.-Col. Coldstream Guards, 25 Dec. 1729. Retd. in Jan. 1739. Made Groom of the Bedchamber to the Prince of Wales in 1740. One of the representatives of Sir Thos. *Bludworth*, Knt., Lord Mayor of London, *temp.* Charles II.

[24] Lieut. 3 Nov. 1735. Capt.-Lieut. in Aug. 1743.

[25] Comn. renewed in 1727. Out before 1740.

[26] See p. 212, note 13.

[27] Half-pay, 1729.

[28] See biog. notice in Vol. I., p. 179, note 8.

[29] Promoted Capt. in Aug. 1743. Served at Culloden. See letter to him from Capt. James Wolfe on p. 48.

[30] Called "Charles" Draper in *Army List*, 1740, where he appears as Lieut. in above Regt.

[31] See biog. notice in Vol. I., p. 306, note 7. When his Tp. was reduced in 1729 he was placed on half-pay, but appointed Major of Ligonier's Horse (7th D.G.) 15 Dec. 1738. Lt.-Col. of Bligh's Foot (20th) 29 March, 1742. Killed at Fontenoy.

[32] D. at Whitehall as a Capt. in 1736.—*Gentleman's Mag.*

[33] Cornet in 3rd Horse (2nd D.G.) 28 Dec. 1727. Succeeded his father 25 Dec. 1730 as 2nd Earl of Deloraine and d.s.p. in 1739.

[34] *Chapeau.* See his Comn. on p. 301. Placed on half-pay in 1729. Restored to full-pay as Cornet in Lord Cadogan's Regt. of Dragoons (6th) 1 Feb. 1738. The *Gentleman's Mag.* for 1763 records the death of Lt.-Col. David Chapeau, Town Major of Gibraltar.

[35] Serving in 1736.

BRIGADIER-GENERAL PHILIP HONYWOOD'S REGIMENT OF DRAGOONS.

[11TH HUSSARS.]

Chas. Leman[1] to be Cornet to [Lt.-Col.]
    Archd. Hamilton - - - - St. James's, 31 Dec. 1718. *p*
—— Dawes[2] to be Cornet - - - — 24 June, 1719. *c*
Wm. Leman,[3] Esq. to be Capt. in room of
    Ben. Huffum - - - - St. James's, 3 May, 1720. *c*
[Alex.] Steuart[4] to be Lieut. to —— - — 27 „ „ *f*
Thos. Procter[5] to be Cornet to Lt.-Col.
    Hamilton - - - - - Gohre, 13 Oct. (O.S.) , *c*
Nicholas Durell[6] to be Cornet to
    Capt. —— - - - - - St. James's, 17 Dec „ *c*
Chas. Greenwood[7] to be Cornet to Brigadier
    Honywood's own Tp. - - - „ 1 May, 1721. *c*
John Bright[8] to be Cornet to —— - - „ 11 „ „ *c*
George Whitmore[9] to be Cornet to —— - „ 10 Nov. „ *c*
[James] Malcom (*sic*),[10] Esq. to be Capt. in
    room of Richard Tracy - - - Kensington, 26 July, 1722. *c*
Wm. Gardner,[11] Esq. to be Capt.-Lieut. - „ „ „ „ *c*
Ric. Honywood[12] to be Lieut. - - - „ „ „ „ *c*
Peter Wheeler[13] to be Adjt. - - - „ „ „ „ *c*
Henry Harvey[14] to be Cornet to [Lt.-Col.]
    Arch. Hamilton - - - - St. James's, 25 March, 1724.
Gustavus Hamilton[15] to be Cornet to Capt.
    Wm. Leman - - - - „ 24 Dec. 1726.
Robert Hepburn,[16] Esq. to be Capt. of an
    additional Tp. - - - - „ 25 „ „
Francis Corbet[17] to be Cornet - - - „ „ „ „
Clement Kent,[18] Esq. to be Capt. of an
    additional Tp. - - - - „ „ „ „
Daniel Tompkins[19] to be Lieut. - „ „ „ „
Charles Draper[20] to be Cornet to do. - „ „ „ „
Ralph Compton[21] to be Qr.-Mr. to do. - — „ „ „
Robert Booth,[22] Esq. to be Capt. of an
    additional Tp. - - - - St. James's, „ „ „
Guildford Killigrew[23] to be Cornet to do. - „ „ „ „
Lord George Beauclerk[24] to be Lieut. to —— „ „ „ „
James Warren[25] to be Lieut. to Capt. Booth „ 11 March, 1726/7.

---

[1] Had served as Ens. in Primrose's Regt. in late reign. Out of Honywood's Dragoons before 1727.
[2] Comn. renewed in 1727. Not in any subsequent List.
[3] See his Comn. in Vol. I., p. 271, and note thereto.
[4] Cornet in above Regt. 25 April, 1717. Capt.-Lieut. 20 Nov. 1745.
[5] Not in any subsequent List of above Regt.
[6] Served previously in Sir Robt. Rich's Dragoons. Out of Honywood's Dragoons before 1727. Appointed A.D.C. to Visct. Shannon (C.-in-C. in Ireland) before 1726.

[7] Comn. renewed in June, 1727. He had served in late reign as Ens. in Brigdr. Munden's Regt. of Foot. Capt. in Brigdr. Cornwallis's Regt. (11th Foot), 12 Oct. 1732. Major, 30 March, 1742. Out before 1746.

[5] Lieut. 5 July, 1735. Retd. same year.—*Records of 11th Hussars*, by Major G. T. Williams.

[9] "Lieut. 10 May, 1742. Capt.-Lieut. to Major Bowles's Indep. Cy. of Invalids, 13 Oct. 1755. Fort-Major Edinburgh Castle and 1st Lieut. of Cy. doing duty there, 5 May, 1756. Succeeded as Fort-Major by Alex. Bredin in 1763."—*Ibid.*

[10] Comn. renewed in 1727. Serving in 1730.

[11] "Capt. 10 May, 1742. Major, 23 April, 1746. Lt.-Col. 26 June, 1754. Retd. in March, 1761. Served during the Rebellions of 1715 and 1745 in Scotland. In April, 1760, embarked in command of the 11th Dragoons to join the Allied Army of Prince Ferdinand of Brunswick, at Fritzlar, in Lower Hesse, and served the campaign of 1760, retiring shortly afterwards. Son of Wm. Gardner of Coleraine, who commanded a Company in defence of the city of Derry. Lt.-Col. Gardner md. in 1729. His third son, Alan, entered the Royal Navy and attained the rank of Admiral of the Blue and was created a Bart. in 1794, a Peer of Ireland in 1802, and a Peer of the United Kingdom in 1806 as Baron Gardner of Uttoxeter, co. Stafford. Lt.-Col. Gardner d. 14 Aug. 1762, and was bd. at Uttoxeter."—*Ibid.*

[12] From half-pay Ens. 1st Foot Guards. Comn. renewed in June, 1727. Serving in 1730. Not in any subsequent List.

[13] See Vol. I., p. 271, note 6.

[14] *Hervey.* "Fourth son of John 1st Earl of Bristol. Md. 2 March, 1730, Catherine, eldest sister and heir to Sir Thos. Aston, Bart., of Aston Hall, co. Chester. Shortly after his marriage he went into Holy Orders and assumed by Act of Parliament the name of Aston. He became a Doctor of Divinity and Rector of Ickworth, Suffolk. D. 16 Nov. 1748."—*Records of 11th Hussars*, by Major G. T. Williams.

[15] Nephew to Col. (aftds. Lt.-Gen.) Archibald Hamilton of 11th Dragoons. Appointed Cornet in this Corps, 13 Oct. 1715. Promoted Lieut. 10 Aug. 1737. On 5 July, 1745, the aforesaid Gen. Hamilton wrote to Sir Wm. Yonge, Secretary at War, in favour of the writer's nephew, Gustavus Hamilton, being appointed Capt. in writer's Regt. (14th Dragoons) in place of Capt. Josias Patterson, "who had served upwards of 43 years and wished to retire." (*War Office Miscellanies* (P.R.O.) Bundle 16.) The will of a certain "Gustavus Hamilton, of Dublin, Esq." was proved at Dublin in 1754.

[16] See notice in Vol. I., p. 277, note 2.

[17] Comn. renewed in 1727. Half-pay, 1729.

[18] From half-pay. Had served previously as Capt. in Sir Daniel O'Carrol's Regt. of Horse in the Peninsula. Serving in 1730. Out before 1740. He was J.P. for Berkshire and d. at Thatcham in 1746.—*Gentleman's Mag.*

[19] Had served in late reign as Ens. in Col. Roger Bradshaigh's Regt. Believed to be identical with the Capt. Dan. Tompkins of Price's Foot (57th) in 1741 and subsequently Capt. in the Carabiniers.

[20] Half-pay, 1729. Lieut. Churchill's Dragoons, 15 Feb. 1739. Capt.-Lieut. 31 Aug. 1744. Capt. of an Indep. Cy. at Hull, 5 Jan. 1754.

[21] Half-pay, 1729.

[22] From half-pay. Capt. in Col. Leigh's Regt. of Foot. A certain Lieut. Robt. Booth served at Almanza as Lieut. in Gen. Maccartney's Foot and was taken prisoner. Capt. Robt. Booth of Honeywood's Dragoons was placed on half-pay in 1729.

[23] Lieut. 11 May, 1731. Serving in 1745. The following obituary notice from the *Scots Magazine* for 1751 is quoted in the *Records of 11th Hussars* by Major G. T. Williams : "Dec. 31, 1750. At Soutrahill, Lieut. Guilford Killigrew of Lord Mark Kerr's Dragoons. 'He was in his 50th year and a bachelor ; a good-natured, polite and friendly gentleman and a brave officer ; an admirer of the fair sex, and esteemed by them ; liked a moderate glass with a friend ; and ended his days with great serenity of mind and with assured hopes of that rest which is to be the portion of the righteous. He has left his whole fortune, about £800, to a natural daughter.'"

[24] See his Comn. as Ens. in the 1st Foot Guards, 29 July, 1723, and note thereto.

[25] Appointed Lieut. in Col. Montague's Regt. (11th Foot) 5 Jan. 1716. Half-pay, 1729. Re-commissioned Lieut. in 11th Dragoons, 13 Feb. 1730. Serving in 1740.

ROYAL ARTILLERY MUSTER ROLLS AND
PAY LISTS, 1719–1727;

ROYAL ARTILLERY COMMISSION REGISTERS, 1716–22;

AND

ORDNANCE WARRANTS, 1718–1722

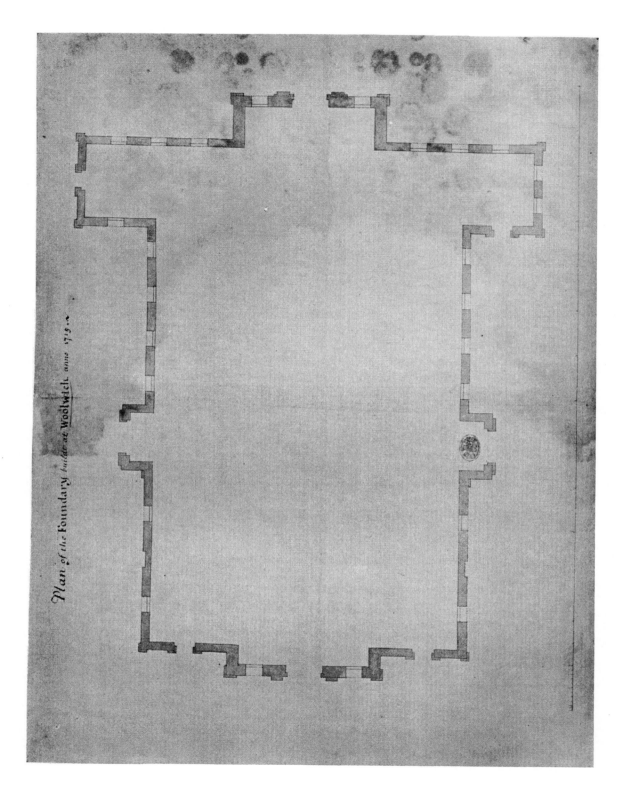

Plan of the Foundary that is at Woolwich anno 1715.

PLAN OF THE FOUNDRY AT WOOLWICH.

(*From the Original Drawing, in the British Museum, attributed to Sir John Vanbrugh.*)

EDITOR'S PREFACE

The Muster Rolls and Pay Lists of the Royal Artillery are selected from the original documents which were, until the last few years, kept at the Royal Artillery Record Office, Woolwich; they are now preserved at the Public Record Office in Chancery Lane. These Muster Rolls commence in February, 1718/19, and were formerly bound together in thick folio volumes; but the Rolls for the reign of George I., and early George II., are now devoid of covers. They are kept in bundles according to their dates. The first "volume" bears the official reference, "War Office 10, Vol. 1, 1719–1721"; the second, "Vol. 2, 1722–1725." The earliest Muster Rolls of the R.A. at Gibraltar are given in "Vol. 6"; and the Pay List for detachment of R.A. at Annapolis Royal, dated 1st August, 1727, given on p. 255, is in "Vol. 10."

These early Muster Rolls, which are now for the first time printed in their respective entirety, have a special interest of their own. They prove that the two companies of Artillery, raised by the King's Sign Manual in 1716, were almost invariably styled "Marching Companies of Gunners of the Royal Artillery," which title distinguished them from the old Ordnance Train—two companies of which were then still existent in England and another company in Scotland.

When Colonel Albert Borgard was commissioned "Colonel of his Majesty's Royal Regiment of Artillery," 1st April, 1722, all subsequent commissions to the two companies in question bore the words "in the Royal Regiment of Artillery." This fact is noteworthy, as, though the original scheme promulgated in 1716 had been for four new companies, the whole to be commanded by a Colonel with two additional field-officers, it was not till November, 1727, that the original plan for the formation of the Royal Regiment of Artillery was completed by two new companies being added; also a Major, Adjutant, Quartermaster, and Bridge-master.

In the previous March it had been found necessary to appoint a Lieut.-Colonel (Jonas Watson) to the regiment in consequence of Colonel Borgard having been appointed a Brigadier-General. When the above augmentation to the Royal Artillery took place

P

in November, 1727, Brigadier Borgard was commissioned Colonel Commandant—"the first officer holding that situation."

Some of the original R.A. Muster Rolls are in very faded ink; while here and there a name is illegible. And in one or two early Rolls the names of one or two mattrosses are missing, thus causing discrepancies in the numbers of soldiers declared to have been mustered by their officers, and the "storekeeper," who superscribed their names. Considering the course and flight of time, coupled with rough treatment, these Artillery Rolls are fairly well preserved. They form the earliest series of regimental Muster Rolls in existence. The late Colonel Cleaveland, in his valuable work *Notes on the Early History of the Royal Regiment of Artillery*, printed the names of officers from some of these early Muster Rolls; he also gave Establishment Lists as to pay and numbers, but generally omitted the names of all ranks under "fireworkers." I have made a point of giving all the sergeants, corporals, bombardiers, gunners, mattrosses, and drummers that appear in the MS. Lists I have transcribed. Not a few of the men in the lower ranks of the Royal Artillery, at the period treated of, rose to be officers in this first non-purchase corps and gained distinction in various parts of the world.

Royal Artillery Officers' Commission Registers, 1716–1722, signed by the Duke of Marlborough as Master-General of the Ordnance, are now printed for the first time. Two or three of the dates of these early commissions are missing in Kane's *List of Officers of the Royal Regiment of Artillery*; while some of the dates that are given in the last-named valuable work do not tally with those in the Commission Registers. I account for the discrepancies in question by suggesting that some of the officers' names, and dates of their respective ranks in the regiment, were taken from the early Pay Lists and not from the R.A. Commission Book (a thin folio bound in white leather with the Arms of the Board of Ordnance stamped in gold on the side) at the Public Record Office and now numbered "W.O. 55/491." I also think it well to point out that the name of Lieut. Richard Somerfield, R.A. (whose commission is given in aforesaid MS. volume) has been left out of Kane's *List*.

C. D.

ROYAL ARTILLERY MUSTER ROLLS AND PAY LISTS, 1719–1727

MUSTER ROLL OF THE DETACHMENT OF CAPT. JAMES RICHARDS MARCHING COMPA. OF GUNNERS OF THE ROYALL ARTILLERY APPOINTED TO THE TOWER DIVISION. [16TH FEBRUARY, 1718/19.]

CAPT.
James Richards.[1]

LIEUTS.
James Deall.[2]
John Brookes.[3]
George Minnens.[4]
Rich^d. Somerfield.[5]

SERJTS.
Michael Scott.[6]
Thomas James.[7]

CORPORAL.
Charles Jermain.[8]

BOMBARDIERS.
Abram Taylor.[9]
Joseph Hughes.
Henry Maynard.[10]

GUNNERS.
William Wilson.
Robert Mence.[11]
Stephen Lye.
Dan^{ll}. Morris.
Joseph Spackman.
John Hally.
Samuel Thornton.
Robert Bousfield.[12]
John Schlundt.[13]
Jonas Watson Bennett.[14]

Roger Phillips.
Rich[d]. Baxter Cookhow (?).
Thomas Crust (?).
Samuel Seaton.[15]
Stephen Copland.
John Aitkin.
Thomas Sanders.
Robert Wilson.
Isaac Hunt.
John Bondry.
Thomas Rush.
John Emmett.
William Guyes.
Francis Cope.

MATTROSSES.

Jonathan Osborn
Edw[d]. Boden.
Charles Meers.
George Deall.[16]
James Crookshank
William Downing
Anthony Ivory.
Joshua Garnett.
William Paslow.
Bartho. Perry.
Dan[ll]. Mence.[17]
John Murphy.
Francis Witherby.
William Calvert.
Christopher Newton.
Thomas Humphry.
Charles Ellis.
John Williams.[18]
Jonathan Coulson.
David Steele.
John Tomlinson.
John Baker.
John Bollands.
George Waugh.
W[m]. Smith.
John Bagford.   Deserted the same day.
Thomas Terry.
Thomas East.
Richard Tomkiss.
John Milward.
James Kenton.
George Thornworth.
William Ashwell.
Edward Danks.
Robert Farr.
George Addison

William Johnston.
John Lloyd.
Owen Harris.
James Frame.
John Lawrence.
Richard Griffiths.

[*Three names missing.*]

Musterd then the Detachm[t]. of marching gunn[rs]. appointed to the Tower division being one Captain, three Lieuts., two Serjts., one Corporall three Bomb[rs]., twenty-three Gunn[rs]., and twelve Matt[s]. for the thirty-one days of March.   One Lieut. nine days from the first to the ninth, one Gun[r]. eleven days from the twenty-first to the thirty-first.   One Mattross forty-four days.   One Mattross forty and one Mattross thirty-seven days from the sixteenth, twentieth and twenty-third of Feb[y]. to the thirty-first of March. One Mattross twenty-eight days.   Two Mattrosses twenty-five, one Mattross twenty, one Mattross nineteen, one Mattross eighteen, three Mattrosses fifteen, one Mattross thirteen, one Mattross twelve, two Mattrosses nine, six Mattrosses eight, four Mattrosses seven, two Mattrosses six, two Mattrosses five, and two Mattrosses four days from the fourth, seven, twelfth, thirteenth, fourteenth, seventeenth, nineteenth, twentieth, twenty-third, twenty-fourth, twenty-fifth, twenty-sixth, twenty-seventh and twenty-eighth to the 31st of March, One thousand Seven hundred and Nineteen.

JAMES FELTON.[19]

JAMES DEALL.
GEORGE MINNENS.
RICHD. SOMERFIELD.

[1] See Vol. I., p. 287, note 1.
[2] See   do.   p. 288, note 8.
[3] See   do.   do.   note 10
[4] The following biog. notice appeared lately in the *R.A. Journal*: "Captain-Lieutenant George Minnens (Kane No. 15), spelt in the Register of Burials, 'Minnings.' Prior to the 'Birth of the Regiment' on 26 May, 1716, he served as Adjutant of the 'Train of Artillery' in Flanders, and when placed on temporary half-pay with many others by Royal Warrant in 1715, was mentioned as having 'served well.' He also served in the Bomb Vessels, 1693–7.   On 30th December, 1718, he was commissioned in the Royal Artillery as Fireworker.   He served in the Bomb Vessels again in 1727, presumably at Gibraltar.   On 1st November of that year he was promoted Captain-Lieut.   There is no further record on hand of him until 1741, when he was reported as 'old and worn out in the Service' and superannuated.   He died in July, 1742."
[5] Had served as a Fireworker in Spain, 1710.   This officer's name is omitted in Kane's *List*.   See his Comn. as 3rd Lieut. in Capt. Richards's Cy. on p. 256.   2nd Lieut. in Capt. Pattison's Cy. 1 July, 1721.   Took part with the R.A. detachment at the Duke of Marlborough's funeral, 9 Aug. 1722.   Serving in Jan. 1723.   Untraced after that year.
[6] Served as a Master-Wheelwright with the Train of Artillery in Flanders, 1710.   See Kane's *List*, p. 171, where he is called "Mitchell Ssott."   Serving as a Sergt. at the Tower in 1726.
[7] Sergt. R.A. in 1718 (W.O. 55/491).   Served as a Fireworker in the Expedition to Vigo in Aug. 1719.   Attained the rank of Capt. R.A. 1 May, 1739.   D. 1740.   (Kane's *List*.)
[8] Comn. as Sergt. dated 28 April, 1719, "to commence 1st May" (W.O. 55/491). Serving with the R.A. Train in Hyde Park, 1723.
[9] Sergt. 28 April, 1719 (W.O. 55/491).   Attained rank of 1st Lieut. 20 Sept. 1731. D. 1739.   (Kane's *List*.)
[10] His Comn. as "Sergt. in the Royal Regt. of Artillery" was signed by the Earl of Cadogan, 1st July, 1722 (W.O. 55/491).   Serving as Sergt. in Capt.-Lieut. Holman's Cy. at Gibraltar in 1726.   Took part in the defence of Gibraltar, 1726–27.

[11] Serving as a Bombardier at Woolwich, 1723. There were two Gunners of this name in the R.A. at this date. The name is a very peculiar one. It may be that they were of the same family as Benjamin Mence, Mayor of Worcester in 1715. From his petition to the Treasury Board, dated 3 June, 1720, it appears that Benjamin Mence assisted to raise Col. Newton's Regt. of Dragoons in 1715, "for which service he was frequently insulted by the enemies of his Majesty, and was put by at the end of his Mayoralty from being an Alderman."—*Treasury Papers.*

[12] Serving as a Cadet-Gunner at Plymouth in June, 1721. Appointed a Practitioner Engineer, 31 Oct. 1721. Sub-Engineer, 10 March, 1730. Served at Gibraltar in 1727 D. in Minorca in 1732.—*List of R.E. Officers.*

[13] Serving in Minorca as a Bombardier, 1726. Belonged to the family of Maj.-Gen. John Sigismund Schlundt. See paper by Charles Dalton in *R.A. Proceedings,* Vol. XXVI.

[14] Served with the R.A. Train encamped in Hyde Park in Aug. 1723 as a Cadet-Gunner. Served in Capt.-Lieut. Holman's Cy. at Gibraltar, 1726–27, as a Corporal. Fireworker, 11 Jan. 1731. D. 1753.—Kane's *List.*

[15] Appointed a Bombardier "in the Royal Regt. of Artillery," 1 July, 1722. Comn. signed by Earl Cadogan.—W.O. 55/491.

[16] Appointed one of the Gunners in the Royal Artillery, 1 Dec. 1720. Comn. signed by the Duke of Marlborough.—*Ibid.*

[17] See note 11.

[18] Served as Mattross at the defence of Gibraltar in 1726–27.

[19] Appointed Storekeeper at Woolwich, 6 June, 1719. D. 9 April, 1734, as Storekeeper at the Royal Foundry, Woolwich.

MUSTER ROLE (*sic*) AND VOUCHER FOR SUBSISTENCE TO THE ROYALL ARTILLERY IN PORTSM°. DIVISION FOR THE MONTH OF MARCH, 1719.*

			£	s.	d.
Capt. Thomas Pattison [1]	-	-	11	12	6
Lieut. John Roope [2]	-	-	6	19	6
Corporal John Cooke	-	-	1	18	9
Bombardier Simon Thomas	-	-	1	18	9

GUNNERS.

William Stockwell [3]	-	-	1	11	0
Samuel Houlston	-	-	1	11	0
Richard Blakney	-	-	1	11	0
Pattrick Templeton	-	-	1	11	0
James Donovan	-	-	1	11	0
Dennise Dennise [4]	-	-	1	11	0
George Clenney	-	-	1	11	0
William Bland [5]	-	-	1	11	0

MATTROSSES.†

	George Coombs	-	-	-	1	3	3
	John Wathell	-	-	-	1	3	3
	Mathew Young	-	-	-	1	3	3
	Richard Weston	-	-	-	1	3	3
	John Gould	-	-	-	1	3	3
	John Warram	-	-	-	1	3	3
	John Theobalds	-	-	-	1	3	3
	Edward Alston	-	-	-	1	3	3
	George Smallwood [6]	-	-	-	1	3	3
	John Nile (*sic*)	-	-	-	1	3	3
Ent[d]. the 5th	William Crawford	-	-	-	1	0	3
„ „ 13th	Robert Spencer	-	-	-	0	14	3
„ „ 18th	Robert Leyton	-	-	-	0	10	6
„ „ 29th {	Henry Bird	-	-	-	0	2	3
	Daniel Cruse	-	-	-	0	2	3

				48	19	6

Portsm°. March the 31st 1719.

Mustred (*sic*) then the People belonging to the Detachment of the Royall Artillery commanded by Captain Thomas Pattison. The Capt.,

* Signatures of the officers and others are given after the sums received by each. Six of the recipients could not sign their names, and had to make their respective marks.

† "Soldiers in the train of artillery next below the gunners ; their duty is to assist the gunners in traversing, sponging, loading, and firing of guns, &c. They carry firelocks and march along with the store-waggons, both as a guard and to help in case a waggon should break down." (*Chalmers' Cyclopædia.*) The rank of mattross was abolished in 1783.

one Lieut., one Corporall, one Bombardier, eight Gunners, and fifteen Mattrosses, one ditto for twenty-seven days, one for nineteen days, one for fourteen days, and two for three days. The Muster being for thirty-one Days commencing the first of March and ending the thirty-first Do. One thousand seven hundred and nineteen.

JOHN ROOPE.   THOMAS PATTISON.
                 JOHN BAXTER.[7]
                 PETER STEPKIN.

[1] See Vol. I., p. 287, note 6.
[2] See do., p. 288, note 9.
[3] Serving as a Sergt. in Capt. Thos. Hughes's Cy. of R.A. at Woolwich in April, 1726.
[4] Serving as a Gunner in Capt. Hughes's Cy. at Woolwich in April, 1726.
[5] Serving at Berwick-on-Tweed in 1726.
[6] Serving in Capt.-Lieut. Holman's Cy. of R.A. at Gibraltar in Jan. 1726.
[7] Appointed Storekeeper at Portsmouth, 14 Feb. 1719.

A MUSTER ROLE OF THE MEDWAY DIVISION [OF ROYAL ARTILLERY, MARCH, 1719].

Lieut. Jonat. Lewis.[1]
Corp[l]. Michel Crosbey.[2]

GUNNERS.

Jo[n]. Pledge.
Rob[t]. Norton.
Will[m]. Davis.
Edw[d]. Jane.
Will[m]. Williams.
Joseph Bloxsom.

MATTROSSES.

Rob[t]. Baker.
Benj[n]. Drinkwater.
Sebast[n]. Hebden.
James Mattheis.
Thō. Bradley.
Jo[n]. Percivall.
Rob[t]. Borman.
Jo[n]. Lewis.
Jo[n]. Padgett.
Henry Love.
Will[m]. Moory (*sic*).
Jo[n]. Garnatt.
Jo[n]. Wright.
Joseph Pawson.
Thō. Carthwright.

Ent[d]. Mar. 9th, 1718/19.   Jo[n]. Ramsey.
Ent[d]. Mar. 11th   { Thō. Deale.
                    { Jo[n]. Oxbrow.
Ent[d]. Mar. 16th   Jo[n]. Cole.
    ,,   ,, 24th   { Rob[t]. Mote.
                    { Jo[n]. Newman.

Chatham, Mar. 31st, 1719.

Musterd then in the Medway Division One Lieut., One Corp[ll]., Six Gunners, Fiveteen Mattrosses, One Mattross twenty-three dayes, Two Mattrosses twenty-one dayes, One Mattross sixteen dayes, two Mattrosses eight dayes for thirty-one dayes commencing March 1st and ending the 31st both dayes included.

JONAT. LEWIS.

GEO. COLLETT.

[1] See Vol. I., p. 287, note 5.
[2] Promoted Sergt. 28 April, 1719.   D. as a Sergt. 21 Sept. 1719.   See p. 235.

THE MUSTER ROLL OF THE OFFICERS, GUNNERS, AND MATTROSSES [AT PLYMOUTH] FOR THE MONTH OF MARCH, 1719.

Thomas Holman,[1] Lieut.

GUNNERS.

Richard Cooper.
Thomas Pollard
Charles Pell.
John Barber.[2]
Robert Eccleston.
Henry Cockrill.
George Parry.
James Godfrey.

MATTROSSES.

	John Dutch.
	Nicholas Ginver.
Ent^d. Mar. 13th	Tristram Woolcomb.
,, ,, 21st	Richard Furnass (*sic*).
,, ,, 30th	{ Stephen Lathom.
	{ Thomas Scammell.

Plym°.
April 1st, 1719.

Then Musterd one Officer eight Gunners and six Mattrosses as above nam'd, which Muster is for thirty-one days commencing the first and ending the thirty-first day of March both days included.

THO. HOLMAN.

In the absence of
the Storekeeper
Charles Blyton.

[1] See Vol. I., p. 287, note 7.
[2] Serving as a Corporal at Plymouth in June, 1721.

MUSTER ROLL OF LIEUT. GEORGE MINNENS'S DETACH[T]. OF THE MARCHING COMP[NY]. AND GUNNERS OF THE ROYALL TRAIN OF ARTILLERY APOINTED TO THE TOWER DIVISION. [AUGUST, 1719.]

LIEUTS. { George Minnens.[1]
Richard Somerfield.[2]
Anthony Brown.[3]

SERJTS. { Michael Scott.[4]
Abram Taylor.[5]
Michael Crosby.   D. 21st Sept. 1719.

GUNNERS. { Joseph Spackman.
John Schlundt.[6]
Jonas Watson Bennett.[7]
William Guyes.
Thomas Crust.
Isaac Hunt.
Thomas Rush.
Robert Norton.

MATTROSSES.

Jon[a]. Osborn.
Edward Boden.
Thomas Humphry.[8]
George Deall.[9]
William Sumpter.[10]
Edward Dowler.
Joshua Garnett.
Christopher Newton.
John Baker.
James Kenton.
Edward Danks.
John Lloyd.   Dead Aug[t]. the 31st 1719.
John Lawrence.
Richard Griffith.
Edward Field.
Thomas Richards.
John Malpas.
William Cecill.
Daniel Enmon (sic).
John Gower.
Joseph Goodwin.
Obadiah Ragg.
Daniel Smith.
William Harrison.
Joseph Bedford.
Jacob Gregory.[11]

John Williams.
William Erle.
Lidel (*sic*) Springall.
William Kertland.
Henry Walker.
Richard Pettit.
John Holland.   Dead Augt. 9th 1719.
William Brearly.
Edward Walker.
Saml. Steele.
Sebastian Hebden.
Thomas Bradley.
John Lewis.
John Padgett.
Wroth Watson.
James Mathews.
John Oxborough.
John Newman.
Ent^d. 12th Aug. 1719.   John Mathews.   Deserted Augt. the 18th 1719.
„ 15th „   John Allwood.
Isaac de Lenauze.[12]   Returned from the Detach^t.
upon   the   Expedition
Aug. the 19th 1719.

Woolwich, Sept^m. the 1st 1719.
    Muster'd then the Detachm^t. of Marching Gunners apointed to the
Tower Division being three Live^ts. three Serjt^s. eight Gunners forty [four ?]
Mattrosses for the 31 days of Aug. one thousand seven hundred and
nineteen.

JAMES FELTON.

GEO. MINNENS.

[1] See p. 229, note 4.
[2] See do., note 5.
[3] 2nd Lieut. 1 July, 1721. Served with Capt.-Lieut. Holman's Cy. at defence of
Gibraltar in 1726–27. 1st Lieut. 1 Nov. 1727. Out before 1732.—Kane's *List*.
[4] See p. 229, note 6.
[5] See do., note 9.
[6] See p. 230, note 13.
[7] See do., note 14.
[8] Served as a Mattross in Capt.-Lieut. Holman's Cy. at Gibraltar, 1726–27. Called
" Humphries " in last-named List.
[9] See p. 230, note 16.
[10] Fireworker, 1 Oct. 1731. Attained the rank of Capt. 1 Sept. 1741. D. in Flanders,
1743.—Kane's *List*.
[11] Served at the defence of Gibraltar, 1726–27. Attained the rank of Capt., R.A., 4 Feb.
1757. Served at the defence of St. Philip's Castle, Minorca, 1756.
[12] Fireworker, 1 April, 1740. 2nd Lieut. 1 July same year. Served with the Company
of Miners in the West Indies. D. 1741.—Kane's *List*.

A MUSTER ROLE OF FIELD AND STAFF OFFICERS AND OTHER ATTENDANTS BELONGING TO HIS MAJ[TYS]. ARTILLERY GOING ON AN EXPEDITION UNDER THE COMAND OF THE HON[BLE]. COL[O]. BORGARD. [AUGUST, 1719.]*

COLONEL.

Albert Borgard.[1]

MAJOR.

William Bousfield.[2]

ENGINEERS.

John Romer.[3]
John Siliock (*sic*).[4]
Bloom Williams.[5]
[John Hargrave.][6]

FIREWORKERS.

Burnet Godfrey.[7]
Bennet Smith.[8]
George Michelson.[9]
Thomas James.[10]

SURGEON.

James Barnes.
His Mate,
William Thynne.

COM[Y]. AND PAY[MR]

Joseph Burton.[11]

CLERK OF STORES.

Sam[l]. Gibbs.

CONDUCTORS.

Francis Parker, Conductor and Cooper.
Richard Morley.
George Spens.
Samuel Thornton.
John Dunning.

Additional names given in Pay List for Oct[r]. and Nov[r].
Capt. James Richards.[12]
Lieuts. {James Deal.[13]
Jonathan Lewis.[14]
Peter Stepkins.[15]

* This siege train accompanied the Expedition to Vigo.

[1] See Vol. I., p. 284, note 1.

[2] See do., p. 281, note 1.

[3] Appointed Ens. in Col. Rooke's Regt. 1 May, 1708. Engineer-in-Ordinary, 12 Dec. 1712. Lieut. in the Queen's Own Regt. 8 April, 1713. Capt. same Regt. 19 Jan. 1740. Engineer at Annapolis, 1728. Director of Engineers, 5 July, 1742. Served in the Scottish Campaign of 1745–46, and was wounded at Culloden.

[4] *Selioke.* Appointed a Sub-Engineer, 3 May, 1705. Capt. in Col. Charles Churchill's Marines, 12 July, 1711. Serving in the 34th Foot in 1727. D. at Jamaica as senior Capt. of last-named Regt. in June, 1741.

[5] Served as a 1st Lieut. in Col. Fox's Regt. of Marines in Spain during the War of Succession. Half-pay as an Engineer in 1715. D. in 1732.

[6] Name added in Pay List. "Served at Gibraltar, 1726–27. Minorca, 1727–39. Engineer-in-Ordinary, Minorca, 31 Dec. 1739. Sub-Director and Chief Engineer, Minorca, 1 July, 1742. D. in Minorca late in 1747."—*List of Officers of the Corps of Royal Engineers*, p. 119.

[7] Served as a Fireworker with the Artillery Train in Spain, 1710. Employed on a Bomb Vessel in the Mediterranean, 1726. 2nd Lieut. 1 Sept. 1720. Out before 1732.—*Kane's List.*

[8] 2nd Lieut. 1 Sept. 1721. D. in 1728.—*Ibid.*

[9] Nephew to Gen. Borgard, and elder bro. to Borgard Michelsen. Acted as Fireworker during the Vigo Expedition, but not commissioned as such till 24 Nov. 1719 (see p. 256). 2nd Lieut. 1 July, 1721. Took part in the funeral procession of the Duke of Marlborough, 9 Aug. 1722, as Adjt. of the Royal Artillery. 1st Lieut. 1 Aug. 1729. Capt.-Lieut. 1 Jan. 1737. Served at Dettingen. D. in 1744.—*Kane's List.*

[10] See p. 229, note 7.

[11] Served as Waggon-Master at the battles of Saragossa and Villa Viciosa in 1710. See "Artillery Papers" in the Appendix to Vol. VI. of *English Army Lists*, 1661–1714.

[12]–[14] See Vol. I., pp. 287–88.

[15] 4th Lieut. (Fireworker), 30 Dec. 1718. 2nd Lieut. 1 July, 1721. 1st Lieut. 1 Aug. 1722. Served on a Bomb Vessel in the Mediterranean, 1726. According to Kane's *List* he d. in 1739 at Woolwich.

OFFICERS FOR TWO BOMB VESSELS ACCOMPANYING THE EXPEDITION UNDER LORD COBHAM.

FIREWORKERS.

Speedwell Bomb. { John Winch.[1]
Edward Backhouse.[2]

FIREWORKERS.

Furnace Bomb. { Robert Braman.[3]
Henry Harwood.[4]

[1] Fireworker in 1702 Train. Commissioned 2nd Lieut. in Capt. Thos. Pattison's Cy. 1 Sept. 1721. Served at Gibraltar, 1726–27. According to Kane's *List*, Lieut. Winch d. in 1738. He was one of the R.A. officers at the Duke of Marlborough's funeral.

[2] The name of "Edward Bacchus" appears as a Gunner in the 4th Cy. of Artillery belonging to the "Peace Train" of 1698. Placed on half-pay as a Fireworker in 1715. Untraced after 1719.

[3] Gentleman of the Ordnance, 1697. 2nd Lieut. R.A. 1 Nov. 1727. D. 1729.—Kane's *List*.

[4] Not in any subsequent List.

A MUSTER ROLE OF THE DETACHM^T. OF THE ROYAL
ARTILLERY ATT SHEERNESS, JANUARY 31st 1720/21.

Lieut. Anthony Brown.[1]
Gunner Daniel Morris.

MATTROSSES.

John Corderoy.
Robt. Mote.[2]
George Mote.[3]
John Cranfield.
Thos. Grant.
John Bollands.

Sheerness, Jan. the 31st 1720/21.

Musterd then the Detachm^t. of the Royall Artillery at this place consisting of one Lieut. one Gunner and six Mattrosses as above mentioned.

ANTHONY BROWN.

HU. DOWNMAN.[4]

[1] See p. 236, note 3.
[2] Served with Capt. Thos. Pattison's Cy. in Minorca, 1726.
[3] Do.
[4] Master of the Ordnance House at Sheerness. He was grandfather of Lt.-Col. Francis Downman, R.A., a memoir of whose services is given in *R.A. Proceedings.*

A MUSTER ROLL OF THE OFFICER, CORPORAL, GUNNERS, AND MATTROSSES FOR THE MONTH OF JUNE 1721. [AT PLYMOUTH.]

Thŏ. Holman,[1] Capt.-Lieut.

John Barbar, Corporal.

Robert Bousfield.[2]   } Cadetts.
James Wibault.[3]   } [Gunners.]

GUNNERS.

Thomas Pollard.
Charles Pell.
Robert Eccleston.
Henry Cockrill.
George Parry.
James Godfrey.

MATTROSSES.

John Dutch.
Nicholas Ginver.
Richard Furness.
Thomas Hydon.
John While.
Thomas Leton.
John Bennett.
Simon Harris.
John Ellis.
Richard Harris.

Plymᵒ. 4th July 1721.

Then muster'd one Officer, one Corporal, eight Gunners, and ten Mattrosses as above nam'd, which muster is for thirty days commencing the first and ending the thirtieth day of June both days included.

THŎ. HOLMAN.

WM. DIXON.[4]

[1] See Vol. I., p. 287, note 7.
[2] See p. 230, note 12.
[3] "Appointed Practitioner Engineer, 22 Sept. 1722. Sub-Engineer, 10 March, 1730. Engineer-Extraordinary, 28 May, 1736. Engineer-in-Ordinary, 11 Aug. 1741. Sub-Director, 8 March, 1744. Served at the defence of Gibraltar, 1727. D. at St. John's, Newfoundland, about June, 1746."—*Roll of R.E. Officers*, edited by Capt. Edwards, R.E.
[4] Appointed Storekeeper at Plymouth, 6 June, 1719.

Q

LIST OF CAPT. THOS. PATTISON'S COMPANY, JAN. 1722/3.

CAPT.

Thos. Pattison.

1st LIEUTS.

Samuell Lettle (*sic*).[1]
Jon[a]. Lewis.

2nd LIEUTS.

Richard Somerfield.
George Michelsen.

FIREWORKERS.

John Winch.
Burnett Godfrey.
Abram Kenesby.[2]
Abram Taylor.

---

[1] Serving as Lieut. of the Artillery Train at Gibraltar in 1715. Serving as Lieut. of Capt. Briscoe's Artillery Cy. at Gibraltar in 1719. Further services untraced.

[2] Served as Gunner in the Descent Train, 1692–93 ; Bombardier in the Sea Train, 1694–95 ; Fireworker in the Newfoundland Train, 1696. In 1697 proceeded with some other British Gunners to Russia and took service in the Army of Peter the Great. Fought at the battle of Narva in 1700, and was taken prisoner with his British companions. Sent to Stockholm and suffered rigorous imprisonment for many years. "The humble Petition of Abra. Kennesbe, Fireworker, Wm. Stokes and Archibald Crosier, Bombardiers, subjects of his Sacred Ma'tie of Gt. Brittaine, etc., now miserably distressed Prisoners at Stockholm in Sweden," dated "Stockholm, 24 Sept. 1701," and addressed to "The Earle of Romney, Mast'r Generall of his Ma'ties Ordnance," is printed in *Artillery Proceedings*, Vol. 25. (See article on "British Gunners at the Siege and Battle of Narva in 1701," by Charles Dalton.) Kennesbe was appointed 2nd Lieut. R.A. 1 Sept. 1720. He was commanding the detachment of R.A. at Placentia in 1728, and d. in 1731.

A MUSTER ROLL OF LIVT. LUKE SMITH'S DETACHMENT [OF ROYAL ARTILLERY ENCAMPED IN HYDE PARK, AUGUST, 1723.]

FIREWORKER-LIEU[T]. Luke Smith.[1]

SERJT. Charles Jermain.[2]

CORP[LL]. Isaac De la Nauze.[3]

BOMBARDIERS
- Robert Mence, at Woolwich.
- Pattrick Templeton.
- William Smith.

CAD[T]. GUN[RS].
- Jonas Watson Bennett.[4]
- William Sumpter.[5]
- Joseph Smith.[6]

GUNNERS.
- John Tovey, at Woolw[ch].
- Samuel Thornton.[7]
- John Enmett.
- William Calvert, at do.
- William Lightfoot.
- Benj[a]. Drinkwater.
- John Lewis.
- Joshua Garnett, at do.

DRUM[RS].
- Thomas Terry, at Woolw[ch].
- Richard Buttler.

MATTROSSES
- John Percevill (sic) at Woolw[ch].
- Mathew Toynton.
- Robert Oulton.
- Thomas Prestridge.
- William Cawser.
- Evan Powell.
- John Earl, at Woolw[ch].
- William Turner.
- Charles Williams, at do.
- John Ellis, at do.
- Henry Buttler.
- William Stevens, at do.
- Eliazar Ward.
- Henry Gould.
- John Gatehouse, at do.
- William Read.
- Edward Walker, discharged.
- John Humphrys.

Hide Park, Aug. the 31st 1723.

Muster'd then the Detachment under the comand of Lieut. Luke Smith belonging to the Company commanded by Capt.-Lieut. James Deall of the Royall Regiment of Artillery commanded by the Hon[ble]. Coll. Albert

Borgard, one Fireworker, one Serjt., one Corpl., three Bombardiers, two Drummers, three Cadet Gunners, eight Gunners and eighteen Mattrosses including one for twenty-five days and one for six days this being for thirty-one days from the first to the thirty-first of Augt. one thousand seven hundred and twenty-three.

LUKE SMITH.
JNo. BAKER.

JOHN VERHAEST.

[1] Commissioned 2nd Lieut. R.A. 1 Sept. 1720. Not in any subsequent List.
[2] See p. 229, note 8.
[3] See p. 236, note 12.
[4] See p. 230, note 14.
[5] See p. 236, note 10.
[6] Not in any subsequent List.
[7] Served as a Conductor with the siege train at Vigo in 1719.

A MUSTER ROLE OF THE DETACHMENT OF THE ROYAL ARTILLERY AT ANNAPOLIS ROYALL FOR THE MONTH OF SEPT[BER]. 1723.

LIEUT. John Melledge.[1]

BOMBARDIERS { John Dyson.[2]
Richard Deacon.

GUNNERS { Peter Feilding.
Daniell Mackcully.[3]
Mathew Hardcastle.
Samuell Douglas.[4]
George Seely.[5]

MATROSSES { Thomas Pomroy.[6]
Francis Lewis.[7]
John Perkins.[8]
John Evans.
William Jervis.[9]
William Petts.
Robert Low.[10]

Octo[br]. 1st 1723.

Then musterd before the Hon[ble]. John Doucett, Lieut.-Governour of Annapolis Royall one Lieut., two Bombardiers, five Gunners, seven Matrosses.

MASCARENE.
[Capt. in Philipps's Regt.]

JOHN DOUCETT,
Lieut.-Gov[r].
JNO. MELLEDGE.

[1] Served as a Fireworker in the Artillery Train raised for service in Scotland, Nov. 1715. 2nd Lieut. R.A. 1 Sept. 1720. Attained the rank of Capt. 1 April, 1740. Sent on an expedition to the West Indies in July, 1740. D. 1742.—Kane's *List*.
[2] Serving as a Bombardier at Annapolis in July, 1727. A certain John Dyson was appointed a Fireworker in the R.A. 16 May, 1740.
[3–5] Serving as Gunners at Annapolis in July, 1727.
[6–10] Serving as Mattrosses at Annapolis in July, 1727.

A PAY LIST FOR THE GUNNERS AT PLACENTIA FROM THE 1st OF JANUARY 1724/5 TO 31st DECEMBER 1725.

		£	s.	d.
LIEUT. Abra. Kennesbe [1]	- - -	40	1	3
Edward Hopley	- - -	19	14	8
Robert Sumpter	- - -	19	14	8
John Bright	- - -	19	14	8
John Green	- - -	19	14	8
Thomas Marsh	- - -	19	14	8
Moses Garland	- - -	19	14	8
John Lamb	- - -	19	14	8
Peter Stewart	- - -	19	14	8
		198	8	9

GUNNERS (bracketed group)

Received of John Blake Junr. One hundred ninety-eight Pounds eight shillings and nine pence due to me as Lieut. and the eight Gunners above mentioned from 1st January 1724/5 to the 31st of December 1725.

£198 : 8 : 9.   ABRA. KENNESBE.

[1] See p. 242, note 2.

A MUSTER ROLL OF THE COMPANY OF THE ROYAL REGI-
MENT OF ARTILLERY IN HIS BRITANNICK MAJ^{TYS}
GUARISON (*sic*) OF GIBRALTAR.* [JANUARY, 1725/6.]

CAPT.-LIEUT. Thomas Holman.

LEUT. Jonaⁿ. Lewis.
  ,,   Anthony Brown.
  ,,   John Winch.

SERJTS. 1. Joseph Harris.
        2. Hennry Maynard.

CORP^{LLS}. 3. Fran. Beatty.
        4. Jonas Wattson Bennett.

BUM^{BRS}. 5. John Shere.
        6. Sam^{ll}. Seaton.
        7. John Masterson.
        8. Hennry Brooks.

GUNNERS
    9. Isaac Cape (*sic*).
10. W^m. Storry (*sic*).
11. Jacob Hunt.
12. John Banstable.
13. Christopher Brown.
14. Arthur Shinkin.
15. John Belsland.
16. Robert Toe.
17. John Dearlove.
18. W^m. Knotsford.
19. Sam^{ll}. Jesser.
20. Thomas Burgess.   } reduced to a
21. George Marshal   } Mattross from
22. Charles Thompson. } the 21st Nov^{br}.

MATTROSSES
23. Allin (*sic*) Banks.
24. John Gould.
25. John Theobalds.
26. Edward Allston.
27. John Wright.
28. Edward Edwards.
29. George Smallwood.
30. W^m. Brownrigg.
31. Edm. Tipton.
32. Thomas Humphries.
33. John Baker.
34. John Ramsey.
35. Dan^{ll}. Enman.
36. John Gower.
37. Edward Danks.

	38. Dan¹. Smith.
MATTROSSES—*cont.*	39. Joseph Beadford.
	40. Jacob Gregory.
	John Williams.
	Thomas Hall.
	Edwᵈ. Hatcher.
	Wᵐ. Shadd.
	John Brown, Senʳ.
	John Brown, Junʳ.
	Thos. Milward.
	John Town.
	James Warn.
	[George Marshall].

DRUMMERS { Thomas Kensteed.
{ Dan¹. Slack.

[Signed] THO. HOLMAN.
JONAT. LEWIS.
ANTHONY BROWN.
JOHN WINCH.

Gibraltar Janu. 1st 1725.

We doe hereby certifie the Honᵇˡᵉ. Board of Ordnance that the Company of the Royal Regiment of Artillery att Gibraltar comanded by Capt.-Levt. Thomas Holman have been this day musterd by us and are effective on the Spott. One Captain-Levt., three Levts., two Serjts., two Corpˡˡˢ., four Bumbʳˢ., fourteen Gunners, twenty-eight Mattrosses, and two Drummers, and that the Subsistance of Officers and full pay of the Effectives from the 1st to the 31st of Jan. 1725/6 both days included amounts to eighty-five pounds five shillings Sterling.

JOHN PRICE.   JOHN RADCLIFFE.
                               W. HARDEMAN.

---

* This Muster Roll is almost identical with the Roll for March, 1726/7, at which time the siege of Gibraltar was at its height. Capt.-Lieut. Holman was killed in one of the batteries on 5 March. One new name of importance occurs among the Mattrosses in the March, 1727, Roll, viz. Philip Webdell. This man was, according to Kane's *List*, commissioned a Mattross 18 Aug. 1726, and attained the rank of Capt. 4 Jan. 1758. He served at the defence of St. Philip's Castle, Minorca, in 1757, as a Capt.-Lieut. R.A. Invalided Nov. 1765. Invalid Companies, 1 Jan. 1771. D. at Portsmouth, 25 May, 1780.

MUSTER ROLL OF THE COMPANY OF THE ROYAL REGIMENT OF ARTILLERY IN THE ISLAND OF MINORCA. [APRIL, 1726.]

CAPT. Thomas Pattison.

1ST LIEUT. George Aikenhead.

2ND LIEUT. George Michelsen.

FIREWORKER Robert Braman.

SERJTS. { Ivander Mackay.[1]
Will[m]. Fox.

CORPORALLS { David Lloyd.
Charles Brome.[2]

BOMBARDIERS { Arthur Trevor.
Rice Price.
John Schlundt

GUNNERS
John Beck.
Joseph Voss.
James Anderson.
Joseph Barron, Furloffe (*sic*).
John Tomlinson.
John James.
Henry More, Cittadella.
John Forbes.
John Dick.
John Grah (*sic*).
George Mote.
Robert Mote.
Will[m]. Brierly.
And[w]. Watt.
Richmond Cookhow.
John Spendelo.
Thomas Smith.
Robert Spencer.
Will[m]. Exton.
Will[m]. Guyes.

MATTROSSES

Bartho. Perry.
Charles Ellis.
John Ormond.
Willm. Smith.
Robert Main.
Willm. Pickett.
Willm. Harrison.
Robert Watkins.
Charles Hardifield.
Ambrose Hollier.
John Craufield.
Sam^ll. Jennings.
Willm. Erle.
Joseph Hawkes.
Willm. Shuter.
Thomas House.
Thō. Jado (?).
Phillip Rogers.
Thomas Bradstocks.
[illegible].
[do.].
John Lawrence.
Thō. Brooks.
Willm. Butterby.
John Stone.
John Albestone.
Willm. Withers.
James Wilson.
Charles Pell.
Peter Stepkins.
Daniell Partridge.
Thomas Layton.
Simon Harris.
Willm. Sole.
Michaell Eland.
Joseph Wright.
John Healing.
John Lindsey.
John Exton.[3]
Thomas Macally.
Phillip Hankison.
[illegible].
[do.].
Thomas Bishop.
Willm. Fisher.
James Empwater.

Furlough—James Montresoy (*sic*).[4]
att 12^d per diem—Richard Dixon.

DRUMMERS { Willm. Price.
{ Joseph Brome.[5]

THO^s. PATTISON.
GEO. AIKENHEAD.

GEORGE MICHELSEN.
ROBERT BRAMAN.

St. Phillips Castle, April the 1st 1726.

We do hereby certifie the Hon[ble]. Board of Ordnance that the Detachment of the Royal Regiment of Artillery at St. Phillips Castle in the Island of Minorca comanded by Captain Thomas Pattison has been this day muster'd by us and are Effectives on the Spot : One Captain two Lieuts. one Fireworker two Serjeants two Corporalls three Bombardiers and twenty Gunners forty-seaven Mattrosses one do at 12[d] p. diem two Drummers and that the subsistence of all the Effectives from the First to the Thirtieth of April (1726) both days included amounts to one hundred and twenty-one Pounds —— shillings or Five hundred and forty Dollars.

N.B.

The Captain and
one Mattross
receive their
pay in England.

J. SANDOZ.
GEO. MARSHALL.
NICH°. MERCADO.

---

[1] 2nd Lieut. R.A. 1 Jan. 1737. Attained the rank of Capt.-Lieut. 1 Sept. 1741. D. 1743. —Kane's *List.*

[2] 2nd Lieut. R.A. 1 July, 1740. Attained the rank of Capt. 8 March, 1751. Retd. Nov. 1760. This officer's services are given in *R.A. Proceedings*, Vol. XX., p. 293, as follows : Capture of Minorca, 1708–9 ; Scotland, 1715 ; Flanders, 1741 ; battle of Fontenoy, 1745 ; expedition to Port Lorient, 1746 ; campaign of 1755 in North America.

[3] 2nd Lieut. 1 May, 1743. 1st Lieut. 1 April, 1744. D. same year.—Kane's *List.*

[4] Believed to be identical with James *Montresor* who became Director of Engineers, 4 Jan. 1758, with the rank of Lt.-Col. This officer d. in 1776 aged 74.

[5] From the memoir of this distinguished soldier and artillerist, who attained the rank of Lt.-Gen. 12 Oct. 1793, and was many years a Col.-Commandant of the R.A., the following short summary of his war services is taken : Battle of Dettingen ; battle of Fontenoy ; battle of Culloden ; battles of Laufeldt and Roucoux ; siege of Bergen ; battles of Warbourg and Fritzler. Master-Gunner of England. D. at Woolwich, 24 April, 1796, aged 84.—See *R.A. Proceedings*, Vol. XX.

MUSTER ROLL OF CAPTAIN THOMAS HUGHES' COMPANY
OF THE ROYAL REGIMENT OF ARTILLERY. [AT WOOL-
WICH, APRIL, 1726.]

CAPT. Thomas Hughes.

1ST. LIEUT. George Minnens   } Woolwich.
    ,,   ,,   John Forbes[1]

LT.-FIREWORKER Burnett Godfrey } Berwick.
    ,,   ,,   Abra. Taylor

SERJEANTS { W^m. Downinge.
          { W^m. Stockwell,   Woolwich.

CORP^{LLS}. { George Parry,   ,,
             { Francis Cope,   ,,

BOMB^{RS}. { Richard Maurice.
             { W^m. Davice,   Woolwich.
             { Edward Jane,   ,,
             { Thos. Sanders,   ,,
             { John Boudry,   ,,
             { Francis Witherby,   ,,
             { Roger Phillip,   ,,
             { Daniel Morris.   ,,

GUNNERS { John Wathall,   Portsmouth.
        { Anthony Ivory,   ,,
        { Arch. Maxwell,   ,,
        { Hen. Cockrell,   Woolwich.
        { Denis Deneze,   ,,
        { Math^w. Hardcastle, ,,
        { John Goodyear,[2]   ,,
        { John Smith,   ,,
        { Will. Sanderson,[3]   ,,
        { Sam^{ll}. Thornton, ,,
        { Math^w. Toynton,[4] ,,
        { Robert Oulton, made Gunner the 15th day.
        { Nicholas Ginver,   Tower.
        { Willm. Bland,   Berwick.
        { John Hill,   ,,

	Richard Furness,	Berwick.
	George Cooper.	
	Thos. Bradbridge.	
	Charles Taylor.	
	Charles Williams,	Woolwich.
	Charles Blankenburgh	,,
	John Bays (sic),	,,
	Thomas Wooley,	,,
	Robert Jackson,	,,
	John Booth,	,,
MATTROSSES	Willm. Stepkins,	,,
	Willm. Wiseman,	,,
	John Owen,	,,
	John Maurice,	,,
	Frācis Ringe,	,,
	Fred^k. Delzspauch,	,,
	Willm. Buncomby, ent^d. the 5th day.	
	Thos. Bowman, ent^d. the 7th day.	
	Thos. Dickinson, do.	
	Bartho. Webster, ent^d. the 10th day.	
	Edward Hunt,	Portsmouth.

DRUM^RS.   Willm. Fitzgerald } Woolwich.
            Richard Butler   }

The following persons are not cloathed, viz. :—

SERJEANT Michael Scott,   Tower.

GUNNER Hugh Caine,   ,,

	John Reynolds,	Tower.
	Willm. Backhouse,[5]	,,
	Geo. Williamson,[6]	,,
CADET	Willm. Henry Southwick,,	
GUNNERS	Willm. Sumpter,[7]	,,
	Leonard Jackson,	Greenwich.
	Cha. Lodwick,[8]	,,
	Will. Lodwick,	,,

	John Tongue,	Whitehall.
	James Walker,	,,
MATTROSSES	Ben. Smith,	,,
	John Rowley,	,,
	Cha. Westridge,	,,

INVALID Will Johnson, Woolwich.

Woolwich, May the 2nd 1726.

Musterd then in Capt. Thomas Hughes Company one Captain two First Lieuts. two Lieut.-Fireworkers three Serjeants two Corp^ls. eight Bombardiers eight Cadet-Gunners fourteen Gunners twenty-three Mattrosses for twenty-four days two Gunners for fifteen days one Mattross for twenty-six days two Mattrosses for twenty-four days and one Mattross for twenty days. This Muster commencing the first and ending the thirtieth day of Aprill 1726 both days inclusive.

THOMAS HUGHES.   JAS. FELTON.
BURNETT GODFREY.   DAV. STEPHENSON.

[1] Serving as a Gentleman of the Ordnance in Capt. Briscoe's Artillery Cy. at Gibraltar, 1719. According to Kane's *List* he was commissioned 2nd Lieut. R.A. 1 Sept. 1720, and 1st Lieut. 1 April, 1725. Not in any subsequent List.

[2] Commissioned Gunner, 1 Dec. 1720. 2nd Lieut. 20 Sept. 1731. Capt. 1 April, 1743. Commanded the R.A. Cy. sent to India in 1747. Had the local rank of Major in India. Killed during the siege of Pondicherry in 1748. Admiral Boscawen was present when this brave officer fell. An Artillery officer, who was also present, wrote to a brother officer at Woolwich from Fort St. David's, Jan. 7, 1749 : "Had you seen him (Admiral Boscawen) on the death of Major Goodyear your heart would have bled." The writer ended his letter by remarking that he would not say who was to blame for the failure of the attack on Pondicherry, but "neither General or troops animated by his example could do more than they did against such engineers, such numbers, and such fortifications."— *London Evening Post.*

[3] Fireworker R.A. 16 May, 1740. 2nd Lieut. 1 Jan. 1745. Out before 1751.—Kane's *List.*

[4] Matthew Toynton's name appears in the R.A. Muster Roll of Capt.-Lieut. Holman's Company, at Gibraltar, for March, 1726/7. He therefore took part in the defence of Gibraltar at the date in question.

[5] Fireworker, 15 March, 1727. Served on board a Bomb Vessel in the Baltic same year. —Col. Cleaveland's *R.A. Notes.*

[6] In Feb. 1732 "George Williamson, gent." was appointed "Lieut. in Capt. Thos. Pattison's Cy. in Minorca." (Col. Cleaveland's *R.A. Notes*, p. 212.) Attained the rank of Lt.-Gen. 25 March, 1772. D. at Woolwich a Col.-Commandant R.A. 11 Nov. 1781. He commanded the R.A. at the siege and capture of Louisburg in 1758, and during the operations in North America which terminated with the capture of Montreal in 1760.

[7] See p. 236, note 10.

[8] Fireworker, 1 May, 1739. Attained rank of Capt.-Lieut. 1 April, 1743. D. 1746.— Kane's *List.*

[ROYAL ARTILLERY DETACHMENT AT ANNAPOLIS ROYAL, AUGUST, 1727.]

We whose names are under written acknowledge to have received of Jn⁰ Dyson Storekeeper the several sums specified against our names being our full subsistance for thirty-one days for the month of July 1727.

BOMBARDIER.

£ sterling

John Dyson [1] - - - - - 2 2 7½

GUNNERS.

Daniel Mackcully	-	-	-	-	1 14	2¾
Samuell Douglass	-	-	-	-	1 14	2¾
George Seely	-	-	-	-	1 14	2¾
John Evans	-	-	-	-	1 14	2¾

MATTROSSES.

Thomas Pomroy	-	-	-	-	1 4	6½
Francis Lewis	-	-	-	-	1 4	6½
John Perkins	-	-	-	-	1 4	6½
William Jervis	-	-	-	-	1 4	6½
Robert Low	-	-	-	-	1 4	6½

Muster List for 1st August 1727.

L. ARMSTRONG,
Lt.-Govʳ.

JOHN DYSON.

Samuel Collinan musterd at Canso.

[1] See p. 245, note 2.

WARRANT COMMISSIONS.*

ROYAL ARTILLERY.

1716–1722.

Capt. James Richards to be Capt. of one of the two
Companies of Gunners and Mattrosses established by
His Majesty's Sign Manual of 26 May, 1716-   -   - 26 May,   1716
The like Warrant Commission of same date to Capt. Thomas
Pattison.
Lieut. John Roope to be 1st Lieut. to Capt. James Richards's
Company   -   -   -   -   -   -   -   -   - 30 Dec.   1718
Like Commissions of same date to

Lieuts. { 2. John Brooks.
3. Jonª. Lewis.
4. Peter Stepkins.

Marginal Note.—"3rd and 4th Lieuts. were Fireworkers."
John Washington,[1] Gent. to be Lieut. of the Cy. of Gunners
at Annapolis Royal at 5 shillings p.d. -   -   -   - 1 Feb. 1718/9
Lieut. James Deal to be 1st Lieut. in room of John Roope
decd. to Capt. Richards's Company   -   -   - 24 Nov. 1719
Like Commissions of same date to

Lieuts. { 2. Jonathan Lewis in room of James Deal preferred.
3. Richard Sumerfield in room of Jon. Lewis pre-
        ferred.
4. George Michelsen in room of Richard Sumerfield,
        preferred.

Thomas James [Gent.] to be Fireworker in Capt. James
Richards's Cy.   -   -   -   -   -   -   - 31 Aug. 1720
Abraham Kennesby, Gent. to be one of the Fireworkers
and 2nd Lieut. in Capt. James Richards's Cy.   -   - 1 Sept.   „
Like Commissions of same date to

Luke Smith.
John Melledge.

Burnett Godfrey, Gent. to be Fireworker and 2nd Lieut.
in Capt. Thos. Pattison's Cy.   -   -   -   -   „   „   „
Borgard Michelsen[2] to be one of the Gunners belonging to
that Cy. of the Rl. Artillery whf ——— is Capt.   -   - 1 Dec.   „

---

* Commission Registers given in W.O. 55/591, Public Record Office, with the exception
of that to " John Washington," which appears in W.O. 55/502. None of the Commissions
below the rank of Fireworker are given by the Editor, excepting that to " Borgard Michelsen," as Gunner ; but certain Commissions below the rank of Fireworker are referred to in
the annotations to the R.A. Muster Rolls and Pay Lists. See pp. 229–254.

Thos. Holman, Esq. to be Capt.-Lieut. of Capt. Richards's Cy. of Royal Artillery - - - - - -	2 June, 1721
James Deal, Esq. to be Capt.-Lieut. of Capt. Thos. Pattison's Cy. of do. - - - - - - -	,, ,, ,,
Anthony Brown, Gent. to be one of the 2nd Lieuts. in Capt. James Richards's Cy. of the Royal Artillery -	1 July, ,,
Lieut. George Michelsen to be one of the 2nd Lieuts. in Capt. Thos. Pattison's Cy. of the Royal Artillery -	,, ,, ,,
Peter Stepkins [Gent.] to be one of the 2nd Lieuts. to Capt. James Richards's Cy. of the Royal Artillery - -	,, ,, ,,
Richard Sumerfield [Gent.] to be do. in Capt. Pattison's Cy.	,, ,, ,,
George Minnens [Gent.] to be 1st Lieut. in Capt. James Richards's Cy. of Royal Artillery - - - -	28 ,, ,,
John Winch, Gent. to be one of the Fireworkers in Capt. Thos. Pattison's Cy. and rank as 2nd Lieut. - -	1 Sept. ,,
Like Commissions of same date to	

Bennet Smith.
Robert Braman.

Albert Borgard, Esq. to be Colonel of His Majesty's Royal Regt. of Artillery at £1 1s. p. diem - - - -	1 April, 1722
1st Lieut. George Minnens to be one of the 1st Lieuts. in the Royal Regt. of Artillery, whereof Albert Borgard, Esq., is Colonel, in the room and stead of Capt.-Lieut. Thos. Holman - - - - - - - -	1 Aug. ,,
Peter Stepkins [Gent.] to be 1st Lieut. in the room of Lieut. George Minnens preferr'd - - - - -	,, ,, ,,

---

[1] Served as a Clerk of the Stores with the Artillery Train in Flanders, 1710. Gent. of the Ordnance, 1712. 2nd Lieut. R.A. 1 July, 1725. D. in 1731 at Gibraltar. Kane's *List*.

[2] Nephew to Col. Borgard and younger bro. to Lieut. George Michelsen, R.A. This juvenile Gunner was only ten years old when he received above Comn. In Vol. I. of the "R.A. Muster Rolls," at the Public Record Office, is a "Receipt from George Michelsen for his brother Borgard Michelsen's subsistence," dated "22 Aug. 1723." Borgard Michelsen was appointed Fireworker, 1 Aug. 1729, and attained the rank of Maj.-Gen. 25 June, 1759. He served at the battles of Dettingen, Fontenoy (where he lost an eye by a musket ball), Culloden, and Laufeldt. D. at Portsmouth, in 1762, as a Col.-Commandant R.A., aged 52.

ROYAL WARRANT TO THE BOARD OF ORDNANCE IN FAVOUR
OF THOS. MICKLETHWAITE, ESQ., LIEUT.-GENERAL
OF THE ORDNANCE.*

G.R.

By reason of a Grant made by our late Royal Ancestor Charles II. of
the Mansion House with the appurtenances thereunto belonging in the
Little Minories, the same is alienated from the place. . . . We do by
these presents authorise and require you to pay him the yearly sum of
£300 in lieu of the said Mansion House and premises as was allowed to
the late Thomas Erle, Esq. Given at Our Court at St. James's this 17th
day of March, 1717/8, in the fourth year of Our Reign.

* *Ordnance Warrants*, W.O. 55/502.

ROYAL WARRANT TO THE BOARD OF ORDNANCE IN
FAVOUR OF COLONEL ALBERT BORGARD AS ASSISTANT
TO THE SURVEYOR-GENERAL OF THE ORDNANCE.*

G.R.

Whereas Our Trusty and Well beloved Colonel Albert Borgard has
with great pains, diligence, and skill, and with no small expense, attended
that Service for some time past, but as yet has had no certain allowance,
We have thought it fitting and reasonable to fix a competent allowance
upon him for the same, Our Will and Pleasure therefore is and We do
hereby authorise and require you to cause the daily allowance of thirteen
shillings and fourpence to be made unto him out of Our Treasury of the
Office of Our Ordnance, in consideration of his constant attendance and
extraordinary expence in assisting to regulate Our Artillery for Sea and
Land Service, to be continued to him till otherwise provided for, &c.
Kensington, 25 April, 1718. Countersigned, STANHOPE.

* *Ibid.* W.O. 55/347, fol. 42.

ORDNANCE WARRANTS.

Wm. Skinner,[1] to be Practitioner Engineer   -   -   - 11 May, 1719
Joseph Day[2] to be Sub-Engineer   -   -   -   - 5 Aug. ,,
Peter Lamprimaudaye (*sic*)[3] to be Practitioner Engineer   -   8 Mar. 1719/20
Andrew Schalck[4] to be Master-Founder of His Majesty's
    Brass Ordnance at an allowance of £219 per annum to
    be paid quarterly   -   -   -   -   -   - 16 May, 1718

ROYAL WARRANTS.

John Armstrong,[5] Esq. to be Master-Surveyor
    of the Ordnance at £300 per annum   - St. James's, 20 Feb. 1721/2
The Earl of Cadogan[6] to be Master-General
    of the Ordnance in room of the Duke of
    Marlborough decd. -   -   -   - Kensington, 19 June, 1722

[1] Son of Thomas Skinner, a merchant of St. Kitts, West Indies. Bn. 1700. Sub-Engineer, 20 Oct. 1726. Served at the defence of Gibraltar, 1726–27. Chief Engineer at Gibraltar, 1 July, 1741. Chief Engineer in Scotland, 1746. Planned and rebuilt Fort George, which was completed in 1758. Col. in the Army and Chief Engineer, 14 May, 1757. Maj.-Gen. 18 Feb. 1761. Lt.-Gen. 30 April, 1770. D. at Greenwich, 25 Dec. 1780. There is an original portrait of this officer at the Convent, Gibraltar.—*Dict. Nat. Biog.*

[2] *S.P.D. George I.* 1719. The date of appointment in *List. of Officers of the R.E.* is given as 2 June, 1719. Engineer-in-Ordinary, 10 March, 1730. D. 1740.

[3] *W.O.* 55/502. *Laprimaudaye.* Lieut. in the Rl. Irish Regt. of Foot, 24 Dec. 1720. Engineer-in-Ordinary, 8 April, 1740. D. on service at siege of Carthagena, 24 April, 1741. Probably son of Maurice de la Primaudaye, "Seigneur de Goulan," whose will was proved at Dublin in 1705.

[4] *Ibid.* See a paper on the "Royal Arsenal," by Lieut. Grover, R.E., in the 6th Vol. of *Proceedings R.A. Institution*, where Schalck's early career is dealt with.

[5] *W.O.* 55/406. See biog. notice in Vol. I., p. 314, note 2.

[6] *S.P. Dom.* Entry Book, 178. See biog. notice in Vol. I., p. 129, note 1.

ENGLISH ESTABLISHMENT

GUARDS AND INFANTRY COMMISSIONS, 1719–1727

GUARDS AND INFANTRY COMMISSIONS, 1719–1727

FIRST FOOT GUARDS.

[THE GRENADIER GUARDS.]

Gideon Harvey,[1] Esq. to be Lieut. to Col. Philip Anstruther and rank as Capt.	St. James's,	13 Jan. 1718/9.*b*
Thos. Herbert,[2] Esq. to be Lieut. to Major-General Tatton's Cy. and rank as Capt.	,,	21 Mar. ,,	*c*
Nathaniel Goodinge[3] to be Ens. to Col. Frampton	,,	23 April, 1719.*c*
Ensign Wm. Goodrick[4] to be Qr.-Mr. to the Battalion detached out of the 1st Foot Guards in an expedition intended to be made beyond seas	Whitehall,	19 July, ,,	*c*
John Horsman,[5] Esq. to be Lieut. to Brig.-Gen. Wheeler's Cy. and rank as Capt.	Gohre,	16 Oct. ,,	*c*
Henry Cox[6] to be Chaplain	Hanover,	25 ,, ,,	*p*
Henry Wingfield,[7] Esq. to be Capt. in room of [John] Montague and rank as Lt.-Col.	St. James's,	20 Nov. ,,	*c*
George Treby,[8] Esq. to be Capt. in room of Philip Talbor and rank as Lt.-Col.	,,	12 Jan. 1719/20.*c*
John Scott[9] to be Ens. to Lt.-Col. Carpenter	,,	17 Feb. ,,	*c*
Samuel Michell[10] to be Ens. of the King's Cy.	,,	17 Mar. ,,	*c*
Chas. Russell,[11] Esq. to be Lieut. to Lt.-Col. Joshua Paul and rank as Capt.	,,	,, ,, ,,	*c*
John Rivett[12] to be Ens. to Col. John Schutz	,,	18 April, 1720.*c*
Ben. Huffum,[13] Esq. to be Capt. in room of —— Anstruther and rank as Lt.-Col.	,,	3 May, ,,	*c*
Henry Jansen,[14] Esq. to be do. in room of —— Read and rank as Lt.-Col.	,,	12 ,, ,,	*c*
Philip Monson[15] to be Ens. to ——	,,	,, ,, ,,	*c*
John Jeffreys,[16] Esq. to be Capt. and rank as Lt.-Col.	—	21 ,, ,,	*f*
Henry Strudwick,[17] Esq. to be Lieut. to Lt.-Col. John Buncombe and rank as Capt.	St. James's,	7 June, ,,	*c*
Theodore Dury[18] to be Ens. to Lt.-Col. Joshua Paul	,,	,, ,,	, *c*
John Wightman[19] to be do. to Lt.-Col. John Duncombe	,,	,, ,, ,,	*c*
Chas. Rambouillet[20] to be Qr.-Mr.	Herrenhausen,	12 July ,,	*c*

	Place	Date				
Richard Slowe [21] to be Ens. to ——	St. James's,	20 Jan.	1720/1.			c
Michael Rawlins,[22] Esq. to be Lieut. to Lt.-Col. Wingfield and rank as Capt.	,,	20 Mar.	,,			c
Daniel Webb [23] to be Ens. to Lt.-Col. Wm. Lloyd	,,	,,	,,		,,	c
Theodore Dury,[18] Esq. to be Lieut. to Lt.-Col. Ingoldsby and rank as Capt.	,,	29 Mar.	1721.			c
John Wightwick,[24] Esq. to be Lieut. to [Brig.-Gen.] Wheeler	,,	19 May,	,,			c
Richard Slowe [21] to be Adjt.	,,	24	,,		,,	c
Alex. Dury [25] to be Ens. to Lt.-Col. John Duncombe	,,	24 June,	,,			c
Wm. Pritchard Ashurst,[26] Esq. to be Lieut. to Lt.-Col. Ben. Huffum and rank as Capt.	Kensington,	7 Sept.	,,			c
Thomas Steane [27] to be Ens. to Lt.-Col. Thos. Fuller	,,	,,	,,		,,	c
Fras. Gibbon,[28] Esq. to be Lieut. to Lt.-Col. Ben. Huffum and rank as Capt.	St. James's,	11 Jan.	1721/2.			c
Erasmus Earle [29] to be Ens. to Lt.-Col. John Pitt	,,	,,	,,		,,	c
Fras. Williamson,[30] Esq. to be Capt. in room of Lt.-Col. John Howe and rank as Lt.-Col.	,,	21 Feb.	,,			c
Alex. Dury,[25] Esq. to be Lieut. to Lt.-Col. Ben. Huffum and rank as Capt.	,,	9 Mar.	,,			c
Daniel Webb,[23] Esq. to be Lieut. to Lt.-Col. Lee and rank as Capt.	,,	16 April,	1722.			c
Edward Stretton [31] to be Ens. to Lt.-Col. Wm. Lloyd	,,	,,	,,		,,	c
Wm. Earl of Cadogan [32] to be Colonel of above Regt. and Capt. of a Cy.	Kensington,	18 June,	,,			c
James Durand [33] to be Ens. to Lt.-Col. —— Hastings	,,	29	,,		,,	c
Hill Mussenden [34] to be Ens. to ——	St. James's,	1 Oct.	,,			c
Sam. Mitchell,[35] Esq. to be Lieut. to Lt.-Col. Pitts (*sic*) and rank as Capt.	,,	5	,,		,,	c
Maj.-Gen. Wm. Tatton [36] to be Lt.-Col. and Capt. of a Cy.	,,	12	,,		,,	c
Brig.-Gen. Ric. Russell [37] to be 1st Major and Capt. of a Cy.	,,	,,	,,		,,	c
Wm. Lloyd,[38] Esq. to be 2nd Major, to rank as Colonel and to be Capt. of a Cy.	,,	,,	,,		,,	c
Thos. (*sic*) Townshend,[39] Esq. to be Capt. in room of Lt.-Gen. Hy. Withers and rank as Lt.-Col.	,,	,,	,,		,,	c
Daniel Houghton,[40] Esq. to be Capt.-Lieut. and rank as Lt.-Col.	,,	,,	,,		,,	c
[John] Parker [41] to be Adjt.	,,	,,	,,		,,	c
James Guy [42] to be Qr.-Mr.	,,	21 Nov.	,,		,,	c
Robt. Urry [43] to be Ens. to Lt.-Col. Robt. Townshend	,,	24 Dec.	,,			c
Wm. Daffey,[44] Esq. to be Lieut. to Lt.-Col. John Guise and rank as Capt.	,,	,,	,,		,,	c

George Shirley [45] to be Ens. to [Lt.-Col.] Pierson - - - - - -	St. James's, 22 Jan.	1722/3.	c
Bacon Morris,[46] Esq. to be Lieut. to —— and rank as Capt. - - - - - -	,, 20 Feb.	,,	c
[John] Rivet,[12] Esq. to be Lieut. to —— and rank as Capt. - - - - - -	,, 4 Mar.	,,	c
Fras. Hildesley,[47] Esq. to be Lieut. to Lt.-Col. Geo. Treby and rank as Capt. - -	,, 18 ,,	,,	c
Thos. Apreece [48] to be Ens. to Lt.-Col. [Fras.] Williamson - - - - - -	,, 30 Mar.	1723.	c
Chas. Stanhope,[49] Esq. to be Lieut. to —— and rank as Capt. - - - -	,, 8 April,	,,	c
John Parslow [50] to be Ens. to Lt.-Col. Ingoldsby	,, 17 May,	,,	c
Do. to be Adjt. - - - - -	Herrenhausen, 12 July	,,	c
[Lord] George Beauclair (sic) [51] to be Ens. to —— - - - - - -	,, 29 ,,	,,	c
Chas. Morton,[52] Esq. to be do. to Lt.-Col. Frampton - - - - -	,, 16 Aug.	,,	c
Richard, Lord Visct. (sic) Coote [53] to be do. -	,, ,, ,,	,,	c
John Price,[54] Esq. to be Capt. in room of —— Schutz - - - - -	Gohre, 5 Oct.	,,	c
Robt. Waller [55] to be Ens. to Lt.-Col. Hy. Wingfield - - - - -	,, 9 Nov.	,,	c
John Mordaunt,[56] Esq. to be Lieut. to Lt.-Col. Inwood and rank as Capt. - -	St. James's, 1 Jan.	1723/4.	c
James Browne,[57] Esq. to be Capt. in room of Joshua Paul and rank as Lt.-Col. -	,, 19 Feb.	,,	c
John Guise,[58] Esq. to be 2nd Major, to rank as Col. and to be Capt. of a Cy. -	Kensington, 7 July,	1724.	d
Daniel Houghton,[59] Esq. to be Capt. in room of [Col. Wm.] Lloyd and to rank as Lt.-Col.	,, ,, ,,	,,	d
Richard Onslow,[60] Esq. to be Capt.-Lieut. and rank as Lt.-Col. - - - -	,, ,, ,,	,,	d
John Parker [41] to be Ens. to —— - -	Gohre, 11 Oct. (O.S.)	1725.	d
Joseph Hudson,[61] Esq. to be Lieut. to Lt.-Col. Wm. Merricke - - - - -	,, ,, ,,	,,	d
John Windus [62] to be Ens. to —— - -	St. James's, 10 Feb.	1725/6.	d
Philip Shrimpton [63] to be Ens. to [Lt.-Col. John] Price - - - - -	,, 23 Mar.	,,	d
John Mead [64] to be Ens. to —— - -	,, 29 Mar.	1726.	d
The Rt. Hon. Sir Charles Wills,[65] Knt. to be Col. and Capt. of a Cy. - - -	Kensington, 26 Aug.	,,	d
Wm. Litler (sic),[66] Esq. to be Lieut. to Lt.-Col. Frampton and rank as Capt. -	St. James's, 25 Dec.	,,	d
Ric. Brewer [67] to be Ens. to Capt. —— -	,, 26 ,,	,,	d
Barnaby Dunston [68] to be Lieut. to [Lt.-Col. Thos.] Inwood and rank as Capt. -	,, ,, ,,	,,	d
Wm. Brown [69] to be Ens. to Lt.-Col. [John] Guise - - - - - -	,, 22 Feb.	1726/7.	d
Richard Onslow,[60] Esq. to be Capt. in room of [George] Treby and rank as Lt.-Col. -	,, 9 Mar.	,,	d
Alex. Deane,[70] Esq. to be Capt.-Lieut. and rank as Lt.-Col. - - - - -	,, ,, ,,	,,	d

John Parker,[41] Esq. to be Lieut. to Lt.-Col.

[John] Price and rank as Capt.   -   - St. James's, 10 Mar. 1726/7. *d*

Thos. Robinson [71] to be Ens. to —— - -   „   „   „   „   *d*

Thos. Savill,[72] Esq. to be Capt. in room of

    Fras. Henry Lee and rank as Lt.-Col. -   „   31 Mar.   1727. *d*

James Baker [73] to be Ens. to Lt.-Col. [John]

    Buncombe - - - - - -   „   7 May,   „   *d*

MEM.—Some of the notes in the "Roll of Officers" given in Sir F. W. Hamilton's *Hist. of the Grenadier Guards* have been utilised in the annotations given below.

[1] Killed at Fontenoy.

[2] Capt. and Lt.-Col. 23 Feb. 1730. D. 1 May, 1740.

[3] Out before 1727.

[4] Bn. 1694. Fifth son of Sir John Goodricke, Bart. Ens. 1st Foot Guards, 28 Oct. 1713. Served at Vigo in 1719. Lieut. in Brigdr. Dormer's Regt. (6th Foot), 12 Dec. 1723. D. at Galway in 1728. Pension of £20 per annum to his widow Maay Goodricke.

[5] Capt. in Pearce's Regt. 20 May, 1721. Capt. of an Invalid Cy. 1 March, 1723. Transferred to Wills's Regt. 24 May, 1723. Comn. renewed in last-named Corps, 20 June, 1727. Major, 2 Sept. 1739. D. 1740.

[6] Not in the list of Chaplains given in Appendix to Vol. III. of Hamilton's *Hist. of the Grenadier Guards.*

[7] Served at Blenheim as Ens. in Howe's Regt. of Foot (15th). Exchanged to the Royal Irish Regt. and served at Malplaquet as Capt. D. at Hammersmith in 1736.

[8] Kinsman to George Treby, Secretary-at-War in 1718–24. Served previously as Capt. in Brigdr. Gore's Dragoons. Left the 1st Foot Guards in March, 1727. D. in 1763.

[9] Promoted Lieut. and Capt. 20 Jan. 1732. Exchanged as Capt. and Lt.-Col. 3rd Foot Guards, 8 April, 1743. Serving in 1746.

[10] Lieut. and Capt. 5 Oct. 1722. Capt.-Lieut. 28 Oct. 1745. Capt. and Lt.-Col. 21 Nov. 1745. Retd. 29 Nov. 1745.

[11] Son of John Russell, Gov. of Fort William, Bengal, by his first wife, and grandson of Sir John Russell, Bart., who md. Elizabeth, dau. of Oliver Cromwell. Charles Russell was appointed Capt. and Lt.-Col. in above Regt. 23 April, 1736. Served at Dettingen. Commanded 1st Batt. of his Corps at Fontenoy. A number of his letters to his wife from Flanders, 1743–45, are preserved at Chequers Court, Bucks., the residence of Mrs. Frankland-Russell-Astley. Col. Chas. Russell was appointed 2nd Major of the Coldstream Guards, 21 Nov. 1745. 1st Major, 1 Dec. 1747. Col. 34th Foot, 17 Dec. 1751. D. in Minorca, 1754. His son John succeeded as 8th Bart. of Chequers.

[12] Son of Col. Rivett. Promoted Lieut. and Capt. 4 March, 1723. Retd. 19 April, 1743.

[13] See his early services in Vol. VI., *English Army Lists*, pp. 267 and 274. Capt. in Honywood's Dragoons in 1715. Exchanged from said Corps to 1st Foot Guards as in text. Retd. in 1743.

[14] Out before 1730. Succeeded his bro. Sir Abraham Jansen as 3rd Bart. of Wimbledon. D. in Paris, 21 Feb. 1766, and was succeeded in the title by his bro. Stephen.

[15] Comn. renewed in 1727. Serving in 1730.

[16] Appointed a Gunner in the Artillery Peace Train of 1698. Was selected by Col. Michael Richards for the post of Paymaster to the Train sent to Spain, in the autumn of 1706, with Earl Rivers's Expedition. Held this command for five years. He was present at the battle of Saragossa, and was sent to Barcelona, 26 Aug. 1710, to obtain money to pay the Train. While he was detained at Barcelona the battle of Villa Viciosa (29 Nov. O.S. 1710) was fought and lost by the British and their allies ; the guns and baggage were captured, including Jeffreys' accounts and moneys for payment of the Train (see "Memorial of John Jeffreys," printed in the Appendix to Vol. VI. of *English Army Lists and Commission Registers*, 1661–1714). As a reward for his services in Spain, Jeffreys was appointed Lt.-Col. and Comptroller of the Artillery Train by Maj.-Gen. Hill, 15 Aug. 1712. Preferred to a Cy. in the Foot Guards as given in the text. Transferred to the Colonelcy of the 10th Regt. of Marines, 31 Dec. 1740. Brig.-Gen. 31 May, 1745. He was cashiered for making false musters in Aug. 1746.

[17] Served previously in the Inniskilling Dragoons. Out of the 1st Foot Guards before 1728.

[18] Believed to have been son of Theodore Dury, Chief Engineer in Scotland *temp.* Queen Anne. Lieut. and Capt. in above Regt. 29 March, 1721. Attained the rank of Lt.-Col. 62nd Foot (aftds. 51st), 30 March, 1742. Appointed Lt.-Col. of the newly-raised

Corps of Marines, 24 March, 1755. Col. of do. 6 April, 1758. Maj.-Gen. 23 Feb. 1761. Lt.-Gen. 30 April, 1770. Living in 1780.

[19] From Ens. in Maj.-Gen. Wightman's Regt. of Foot.   Out before 1727.

[20] See Vol. I., p. 220, note 35.

[21] Adjt. 24 May, 1721. Serving in 1730. D. 1733. (Gentleman's Mag.) Pension of £15 per annum to his widow.

[22] Promoted from Ens.   Serving in 1730.   Out of the Regt. before 1740.

[23] Attained the rank of Lt.-Gen. 19 Jan. 1761. Col. 8th Foot, 18 Dec. 1766. Col. 14th Dragoons, 22 Oct. 1722. He served at Dettingen as Major of the present 7th Dragoon Guards.   Commanded said Corps at Fontenoy.   D. 11 Nov. 1773.

[24] Called "Charles" Wightwick in the Gradation List for 1730. Out before 1740. A certain Charles Wightwich was appointed Capt. in the 3rd Marines, 5 Dec. 1739.

[25] Capt. and Lt.-Col. 15 Dec. 1738. Bro. to Theodore Dury. Regtal. Lt.-Col. 27 April, 1749. Maj.-Gen. 4 Feb. 1757. He commanded the Brigade of Guards in the unfortunate expedition to St. Malo, in June, 1758. Again commanded a Brigade of Guards in the descent on Cherbourg, in the autumn of same year. Gen. Dury was shot in the breast when superintending the embarkation of the troops in St. Cas Bay, and in attempting to swim to a boat was drowned.

[26] See p. 201, note 23.

[27] Out before 1730.

[28] D. 9 May, 1740.

[29] Out before 1730. He was of the ancient Norfolk family of this name, and a representative of the Col. Erasmus Earl of Cromwell's time who was a Commissioner at the Treaty of Uxbridge.

[30] See Vol. I., p. 138, note 3.

[31] Called "Strutton" in subsequent Lists. Lieut. and Capt. 25 Dec. 1733. Retd. 20 Feb. 1744.

[32] See Vol. I., p. 129, note 1.

[33] Capt. and Lt.-Col. 20 Feb. 1744. 2nd Major, 22 Dec. 1753. 1st Major, 30 Sept. 1758. Regtal. Lt.-Col. 21 July, 1760.   Maj.-Gen. 24 June, 1759.

[34] Comn. renewed in 1727. Out before 1740. The death of Hill Mussenden of Herringfleet is recorded in the Gentleman's Mag. for 1722.

[35] See note 10.

[36] See Vol. I., p. 127, note 2.

[37] See do. do. note 3.

[38] See do. do. note 6.

[39] Robert Townshend. Promoted from Capt.-Lieut. same Corps. Second son of Sir Robt. Townshend, Knt.   Comn. renewed in 1727.   Out of the Regt. before 1740.

[40] See Vol. I., p. 306, note 4.

[41] Lieut. and Capt. 10 March, 1727. Wounded at Fontenoy. Capt.-Lieut. and Lt.-Col. 21 Nov. 1745. Capt. and Lt.-Col. 11 April, 1746. Maj.-Gen. 25 Feb. 1761. Col. 41st Foot, 6 Sept. 1765.   D. at Twickenham in 1770.

[42] Out before 1727.

[43] Lieut. and Capt. 13 April, 1736.   Retd. 20 Jan. 1747.

[44] Serving in 1740.   D. at Weald, Essex, in 1771, aged 77.

[45] Lieut. and Capt. 24 Nov. 1729.   Retd. 9 July, 1739.

[46] Appointed Lieut. en second in Maj.-Gen. Wightman's Regt. of Foot (17th) in 1708. Capt. in Brigdr. Pearce's Foot, 17 Aug. 1710. Lt.-Gov. of Landguard Fort, 29 May, 1718. Gov. of said Fort, 23 Sept. 1719. Held this post until his death in 1744 (see Major J. H. Leslie's Hist. of Landguard Fort).

[47] Wounded at Fontenoy. Promoted Capt.-Lieut. and Lt.-Col. for gallantry in said battle, 29 May, 1745.   Capt. and Lt.-Col. 28 Oct. 1745.   Out of the Army before 1748.

[48] Not in any subsequent List.

[49] Out of the Regt. before 1730.

[50] Lieut. and Capt. 10 May, 1736. Capt.-Lieut. and Lt.-Col. 18 May, 1747. Capt. and Lt.-Col. 14 Feb. 1748. Col. of the 54th Regt. of Foot, 11 Sept. 1760. Maj.-Gen. 1 Nov. 1761. Transferred to the Colonelcy of 30th Foot, 30 April, 1770. Lt.-Gen. same date. D. 1786.

[51] Sixth son of the 1st Duke of St. Albans. Lieut. in Honywood's Dragoons, 25 Dec. 1726. Capt. and Lt.-Col. 1st Foot Guards, 13 Aug. 1736. A.D.C. to George II. in 1745 with rank of Col. Appointed Col. 8th Marines in 1747. Transferred to 19th Foot in 1748. Gov. of Landguard Fort, 25 Dec. 1753. C.-in-C. in Scotland in 1756. Lt.-Gen. 25 Jan. 1758.   D. 11 May, 1768.

[52] Appointed Capt.-Lieut. of 38th Foot, 23 Dec. 1738. Serving with said Corps in the West Indies, 1740.

[53] Lieut. and Capt. 17 Nov. 1731. He was Baron Coloony by courtesy, being eldest son of Richard Coote, 3rd Earl of Bellamont. He d. 23 Oct. 1740.

[54] Appointed Col. of the 57th Foot (present 46th Foot), 13 Jan. 1741. Transferred to 14th Foot in 1743. Brig.-Gen. 6 June, 1745. D. at Breda in 1747.

[55] Lieut. and Capt. 1 Feb. 1738. Left the Regt. in April, 1743.

[56] Appointed Capt. in 3rd Dragoons, 25 Dec. 1726. Serving in 1730.

[57] D. 8 April, 1743.

[58] See Vol. I., p. 127, note 9.

[59] Do. p. 306, note 4.

[60] Do. p. 221, note 44.

[61] Capt.-Lieut. and Lt.-Col. 11 April, 1746. Capt. and Lt.-Col. 21 Feb. 1747. Col. and A.D.C. to the King, 24 May, 1756. Maj.-Gen. 25 June, 1759. Lt.-Gen. — Jan. 1761. Lt.-Col. of 1st Foot Guards, 12 June, 1765. Retd. in May, 1768.

[62] Lieut. and Capt. 10 May, 1740. Left the Regt. in 1749.

[63] Transferred from Coldstream Guards. Lieut. and Capt. 6 June, 1728. D. 1734.

[64] Lieut. and Capt. 10 May, 1740. D. 12 Jan. 1747.

[65] See special memoir in Vol. I., pp. 59–70.

[66] See Vol. I., p. 221, note 51.

[67] Served previously in Gen. Wills's late Regt. of Foot. Lieut. and Capt. 25 June, 1736. Exchanged 17 June, 1740.

[68] Serving in 1740.

[69] Served previously in Gen. Wills's late Regt.

[70] From Major of Gen. Wills's late Regt. (see p. 278). Capt. and Lt.-Col. 17 Feb. 1728. Out before 1740.

[71] Out before 1740.

[72] Exchanged from Col. Cadogan's Regt. (4th Foot) with Lt.-Col. Fras. Henry Lee (see p. 282, note 9).

[73] Lieut. and Capt. 5 Nov. 1735. Serving in 1740.

THE COLDSTREAM GUARDS.

Fras. Pilliod,[1] Esq. to be Lieut. to [Lt.-Col.]
Smith and rank as Capt.   -   -   -   - St. James's, 16 April, 1719.c
George Scroop[2] to be Ens. to Lt.-Col. Chas.
Cadogan -   -   -   -   -   -   -   ,,   ,,   ,,   ,,   c
[Chas.] Howard,[3] Esq. to be Capt. in room of
Col. Cadogan and rank as Lt.-Col. -   -   ,,   21   ,,   ,,   c
Capt. Samuel Needham[4] to be Qr.-Mr. to the
Batt. to be employed in an expedition
beyond seas -   -   -   -   -   - Whitehall, 19 July   ,,   c
Stephen Cornwallis[5] to be Ens. to Sir
Tristram Dillington   -   -   -   - St. James's, 19Mar.1719/20.c
Wm. Douglas,[6] Esq. to be Capt. in room of
John Cope and rank as Lt.-Col.   -   -   ,,   3 May, 1720.c
Wm. Vachell,[7] Esq. to be Capt. in room of
—— Smith and rank as Lt.-Col.   -   -   ,,   28   ,,   ,,   c
Chas. Fielding,[8] Esq. to be Lieut. to —— and
rank as Capt. -   -   -   -   -   -   ,,   24 Jan. 1720/1.c
Samuel Needham[4] to be 1st Adjt.   -   -   ,,   28 Feb.   ,,   c
John Hodges,[9] Esq. to be Lieut. to Lt.-Col.
Poulteney and rank as Capt. -   -   -   ,,   11 Mar.   ,,   c
Thos. Macro[10] to be Ens.   -   -   -   -   ,,   14 May,   1721.f
Wm. Sotheby,[11] Esq. to be Lieut. to the Earl
of Albemarle and rank as Capt.   -   -   ,,   20   ,,   ,,   c
John Folliot,[12] Esq. to be 2nd Major and rank
as Col. -   -   -   -   -   -   -   ,,   8 July,   ,,   c
John Vernon[13] to be Lieut. and rank as
Capt. -   -   -   -   -   -   -   ,,   ,,   ,,   ,,   c
Ant. Lowther,[14] Esq. to be Capt. in room of
Sir Tristram Dillington and rank as
Lt.-Col. -   -   -   -   -   -   -   ,,   ,,   ,,   ,,   c
John Parsons,[15] Esq. to be Capt.-Lieut. [in
room of Lowther] and rank as Lt.-Col. -   ,,   ,,   ,,   ,,   c
Samuel Gumley,[16] Esq. to be Lieut. to Lt.-Col.
Wm. Douglas and rank as Capt.   - Kensington, 11 Sept.   ,,   c
Wm. Cole,[17] Esq. to be Capt. in room of
Thos. Cæsar and rank as Lt.-Col.   -   -   ,,   ,,   ,,   ,,   c
Wm. Birbero[18] to be Ens. to Lt.-Col. George
Churchill   -   -   -   -   -   -   ,,   14 Oct.   ,,   c
[Hon.] Charles Hay,[19] commonly called Lord
Charles Hay, to be Ens. to ——   -   - St. James's, 18 May, 1722.c
Richard, Earl of Scarborough to be Colonel
and Capt. of a Cy. -   -   -   -   -   ,,   18 June   ,,   c
Chas. Bodens[20] to be Ens. to ——   -   -   ,,   15 Jan. 1722/3.c
Hedworth Lambton,[21] Esq. to be Lieut. to
Lt.-Col. John Foliott and rank as Capt. -   ,,   11 Feb.   ,,   c

George Scroope,[2] Esq. to be Lieut. to Lt.-Col.
George Chudleigh and rank as Capt.   - St. James's, 13 Mar. 1722/3.*c*
Bezaleel Brownsmith [22] to be Ens. to —— -   „   18   „   „   *c*
Wm. Letheuillier,[23] Esq. to be Lieut. to
Lt.-Col. [Wm.] Douglas and rank as
Capt. - - - - - - - -   „   24 May, 1723.*c*
Thos. Hopgood [24] to be Ens. to Lt.-Col. Chas.
Howard - - - - - -   „   „   „   „   *c*
Do. to be 2nd Adjt. - - - -   „   „   „   „   *c*
Thos. Noel [25] to be Lieut. - - - -   „   „   „   „   *c*
Humphry Fish,[26] Esq. to be Lieut. to ——
and rank as Capt. - - - - -   Gohre, 5 Oct.   „   *c*
Peter Burjand,[27] Esq. to be Lieut. to Lt.-Col.
Wm. Vachell - - - - - -   St. James's, 8 Feb. 1723/4.*c*
Joseph Moxon [28] to be Ens. to [Lt.-Col.]
Hunt - - - - - - -   „   7 May, 1724.*d*
Courthope Clayton [29] to be Ens. to —— -   „   16 Feb. 1724/5.*d*
Philip Shrimpton [30] to be do. to —— - -   „   2 Mar.   „   *d*
Wm. Congreve,[31] Esq. to be Capt. in room of
[Wm.] Cole [decd.] and rank as Lt.-Col. -   „   30 Mar. 1725.*d*
Fras. Townshend [32] to be Ens. to Sir Adolphus
Oughton - - - - - - -   „   28 April, „   *d*
James Adams [33] to be Solicitor - - -   „   29 May,   „   *d*
George Putland [34] to be Surgeon - - -   „   1 Dec.   „   *d*
James Hayman [35] to be Ens. to Lt.-Col. [John]
Huske - - - - - - -   „   23 Mar. 1725/6.*d*
Robert Wilson [36] to be Ens. to —— - -   „   2 Sept. 1726.*d*
Robert Mitchenor [37] to be Solicitor - -   „   16 Feb. 1726/7.*d*
Henry Pyniot [38] to be Chaplain - - -   „   6 May 1727.*d*
Gabriel Reeve,[39] Esq. to be Lieut. to Lt.-Col.
Short and rank as Capt. - - - -   „   12   „   „   *d*
Fenwick Williamson [40] to be Ens. to Lt.-Col.
George Chudleigh - - - - -   „   „   „   „   *d*

MEM.—Some of the notes in the "Roll of Officers" given in Colonel Mackinnon's
Coldstream Guards have been utilised in the annotations given below.
    [1] Resigned in Feb. 1724.
    [2] Lieut. and Capt. 13 March, 1723. Placed on half-pay, 31 Dec. 1738.
    [3] The Hon. Charles Howard. See biog. notice in Vol. I., p. 219, note 23.
    [4] Served at Vigo. Appointed "Surveyor of Our Barracks in the Savoy and of the
Guard Rooms belonging to Our Foot Guards at the Tylt Yard and at the Royal Palaces of
St. James's and Kensington, 23 Nov. 1726." Wounded at Fontenoy. D. at Paris, 22 Dec.
1754.
    [5] "Capt. of Dragoons in Ireland, 15 Jan. 1723." Lt.-Col. of 34th Foot, 23 Jan. 1725.
Col. 11th Foot, 9 Aug. 1738. Brig.-Gen. 2 July, 1739. Maj.-Gen. 1 Jan. 1743. D. in May
same year. He was second son of 4th Baron Cornwallis.
    [6] See biog. notice in Vol. I., p. 179, note 5.
    [7] "From 5th Foot. Exchanged to half-pay of Magny's Dragoons, 1 March, 1727/8."
    [8] See biog. notice on p. 197, note 3.
    [9] Lieut. of Grendr. Cy. Comn. renewed in 1721. Capt. and Lt.-Col. 15 Dec. 1738.
"Resigned in Aug. 1745."
    [10] Lieut. and Capt. 30 Oct. 1734. "Exchanged to 10th Foot, 12 July, 1739."
    [11] Fourth son of James Sotheby of Sewardstone, Essex. Ens. in above Regt.
19 July, 1711. Capt. and Lt.-Col. 25 Aug. 1737. Retd. in 1744.
    [12] Ens. in the Coldstream Guards, 20 March, 1704. Served at the defence of Gibraltar
during the winter of 1704–5. "Received two wounds and was eight months under the
surgeon's hands . . . On his passage home he was taken prisoner and barbarously treated.

Was three months a prisoner in France." (Ens. Folliott's Petition to Prince George of Denmark, 23 April, 1706.—*Treasury Papers.*) Lt.-Gov. of Pendennis Castle in June, 1729. Gov. of Carlisle, 9 July, 1739. Lt.-Col. of 1st Foot Guards, 1 April, 1743. D. a Lt.-Gen. in 1748.

[13] " From half-pay. Replaced on half-pay, 8 May, 1730."

[14] Son of John Lowther merchant of Dantzic and nephew of 1st Visct. Lonsdale. Ens. in Earl of Barrymore's Regt. (13th), 27 Jan. 1706. Capt. in Scots Fusiliers, 1 Jan. 1708. Wounded at the battle of Malplaquet. Capt.-Lieut. and Lt.-Col. Coldstream Guards, 20 Dec. 1717. Col. of a newly-raised Regt. of Marines, 19 Nov. 1739. Maj.-Gen. in May, 1745. D. 14 Jan. 1746, aged 59. Bd. in Westminster Abbey.

[15] Lieut. and Capt. 24 April, 1708. Capt. and Lt.-Col. 6 Oct. 1729. Col. 41st Foot, 4 March, 1752. D. a Lt.-Gen. in 1764.

[16] See p. 206, note 17.

[17] Served previously as Capt. in Gen. Lumley's Horse (1st D.G.). Among the *S.P. Dom. George I.* is a document dated 1721 which states that : " Col. Wm. Cole of H.M.'s Guards claimed the personalty left by Robt. Cole deceased late Consul of Algiers who died intestate about 1714 and his relict took out letters of administration. She died in 1721 and Col. Wm. Cole claimed the moyety of personalty in right of his father Mr. Thos. Cole." Lt.-Col. Wm. Cole d. 23 March, 1725.

[18] Had been re-appointed Adjt. in 1715. D. in 1726.

[19] Second son of the 3rd Marquis of Tweeddale. Capt. in Col. Hawley's Regt. (33rd), 14 Sept. 1727. Capt. of the King's Cy. 1st Foot Guards with rank of Lt.-Col. 7 April, 1743. Commanded said Cy. at Fontenoy where he was wounded. See a true account of his famous challenge to the French Foot Guards at Fontenoy quoted in the paper on that battle given in the *Edinburgh Review* for July, 1911. Appointed Col. of the 33rd Foot, 20 Nov. 1753. Maj.-Gen. 22 Feb. 1757. D. unm. in 1760.

[20] Lieut. and Capt. 26 Jan. 1735. "Resigned in May, 1739."

[21] From Wills's Regt. of Foot (3rd). Capt.-Lieut. and Lt.-Col. 9 July, 1739. Capt. and Lt.-Col. 7 Nov. same year. Regtal. Lt.-Col. 12 May, 1753. Col. 52nd Foot, 20 Dec. 1755. Maj.-Gen. 6 Feb. 1757. Second son of Ralph Lambton of Lambton, by Dorothy, dau. and coheir of John Hedworth of Harraton. D. unm. 1774.

[22] " Dead in March, 1729."

[23] Capt. and Lt.-Col. 26 April, 1740. "Retd. on Major's half-pay in 1752."

[24] Lieut. and Capt. 10 Feb. 1736. "2nd Adjt. to Feb. 1742 when he died."

[25] Appears to have been a grandson of the 3rd Visct. Campden. "Succeeded as Lieut. by his brother Bennet Noel, 20 March, 1731."

[26] From Ens. 1st Foot Guards. "Out of the Coldstream Guards in Oct. 1728."

[27] Capt. in 30th Foot, 1 Nov. 1730. Serving in 1740.

[28] " Dead in Feb. 1725."

[29] "Cornet in the Royal Horse Guards, 17 Nov. 1727." Lieut. in the 2nd Tp. of Horse Gr. Gds. 2 Oct. 1731. Lt.-Col. of said Tp. 23 March, 1756. D. 1762.

[30] See p. 268, note 63.

[31] " From half-pay Pocock's Regt. Retd. 10 Feb. 1736 on 16s. 6d. a day being incapable from age and long services."

[32] Lieut. and Capt. 25 Aug. 1737. "Wounded at Fontenoy and died the same day."

[33] Succeeded by Robert Mitchenor, 16 Feb. 1727.

[34] " Left in March, 1734."

[35] " Dead in May, 1730."

[36] " Dead in April, 1731."

[37] D. in 1744.

[38] "Resigned, 10 May, 1742."

[39] "Died, 22 April, 1734."

[40] "Dead in Dec. 1735."

3RD FOOT GUARDS.

[THE SCOTS GUARDS.]

John Macro Blackler,[1] Esq. to be Lieut. to Lt.-Col. Ridley and rank as Capt. - -	—	9 Feb. 1718/9.c
Lewis Ducie Morton,[2] Esq. to be Capt. in room of Phineas Bowles and rank as Lt.-Col. - - - - - -	St. James's,	2 May, 1719.c
Henry Jefferies[3] to be Lieut. to [Lt.-Col.] Skelton and rank as Capt. - - -	,,	7 ,, ,, c
Capt. Wm. Murray[4] to be Qr.-Mr. to the Batt. detached to be employed in an expedition beyond seas - - - -	Whitehall,	19 July, ,, c
Henry Smith,[5] Esq. to be Capt. in room of [Lt.-Col.] Whitmore decd. and rank as Lt.-Col. - - - - - -	St. James's,	19 Nov. ,, c
Robt. Webb[6] to be Ens. to [Lt.-Col.] —— Scott - - - - - - -	,,	29 Mar. 1720. c
Samuel Lovell,[7] Esq. to be Lieut. to [Lt.-Col.] Murray and rank as Capt. - - -	,,	,, ,, ,, c
Lord John Carmichael[8] to be Ens. to Col. Geo. Howard - - - - - -	,,	23 May, ,, c
Richard Reynolds,[9] Esq. to be Lieut. to Lt.-Col. George Steuart and rank as Capt. - - - - - - -	,,	7 June, ,, c
[Hon.] Chas. Ingram[10] to be Lieut. to Lt.-Col. Wm. Murray - - - - -	,,	11 ,, ,, c
Hugh Scott[11] to be Ens. to Lt.-Col. Darby -	,,	24 Dec. ,, c
George Byng,[12] Esq. to be Capt. in room of Lord Leslie and rank as Lt.-Col. - -	,,	25 Jan. 1720/21.c
Ant. Reynolds[13] to be Ens. to the Earl of Dunmore - - - - - -	,,	17 Feb. ,, c
[Hon.] Charles Murray[14] to be Lieut. and Capt. - - - - - - -	,,	27 ,, ,, f
Henry Powlet[15] to be Ens. to —— - -	,,	24 Mar. ,, c
John Gugleman[16] to be do. to Col. Robt. Murray - - - - - -	,,	27 Mar. 1721.c
John Williams[17] to be do. to Lt.-Col. Scott -	,,	9 June, ,, c
Wm. Kingsley,[18] Esq. to be Lieut. to Lt.-Col. [Edward] Wolfe and rank as Capt. - -	,,	29 ,, ,, c
Thos. Manners,[19] Esq. commonly called Lord Thos. Manners, to be Ens. - - -	,,	29 July, ,, c
Coorte (sic) Knevit[20] to be Ens. to —— -	Kensington,	19 Aug. ,, c
Thos. Murray,[21] Esq. to be Lieut. to Lt.-Col. [Henry] Skelton and rank as Capt. - -	,,	26 ,, ,, c
Thos. Manners,[22] Esq. commonly called Lord Thos. Manners to be Lieut. to Lord Fred. Howard and rank as Capt. - - -	St. James's,	13 Mar.1721/2.c
James Russell Stapleton[23] to be Ens. to Lt.-Col. Skelton - - - - - -	,,	,, ,, ,, c

Leonard Gwyn [24] to be Ens. to ——   -   -   St. James's, 2 May, 1722.*c*

—— Gylberts [25] to be Ens. to ——   -   -   „   26   „   „   *c*

James St. Clair,[26] Esq. to be 2nd Major and
Capt. of a Cy.   -   -   -   -   - Kensington, 26 July,   „   *c*

[Hon.] Fras. Howard,[27] Esq. to be Capt. of
Jas. St. Clair's late Cy. -   -   -   -   „   3 „   „   *c*

Lionel Becher [28] to be Ens. to ——   -   -   „   3 Sept.   „   *c*

Richard Barnwell Waller,[29] Esq. to be Lieut.
to ——   to ——   -   -   -   -   „   11 „   „   *c*

Gabriel Lepipre [30] to be Ens. to Lt.-Col. Scott - St. James's, 25 Mar. 1723.*c*

Cuthbert Sheldon [31] to be Ens. to [Lt.-Col.]
Ridley   -   -   -   -   -   -   „   22 April,   „   *c*

John Edison [32] to be 2nd Adjt.   -   -   -   „   27 May,   „   *c*

Joshua Draper,[33] Esq. to be Lieut. to Lt.-Col.
George Howard and rank as Capt. -   -   „   30 „   „   *c*

Wm. Grahme,[34] Esq. to be Lieut. to —— and
rank as Capt. -   -   -   -   - Herrenhausen, 13 June,   „   *c*

Simpson Wood [35] to be Ens. to Col. Edward
Wolfe   -   -   -   -   -   -   „   20 Sept.   „   *c*

John Montgomerie,[36] Esq. to be Capt. of the
Grenadier Cy. and rank as Lt.-Col. "from
date of your former Commission " -   - Hanover, 17 Nov.   „   *c*

James Scott,[37] Esq. to be Lt.-Col. of above
Regt. and Capt. of a Cy. -   -   -   „   „ „   „   *c*

James St. Clair,[38] Esq. to be 1st Major and
to rank as Colonel and Capt. of a Cy.   -   „   „ „   „   *c*

John Darby,[39] Esq. to be 2nd Major and rank
as Colonel and Capt. of a Cy.   -   -   „   „ „   „   *c*

Robert Granville [40] to be Ens. to Lt.-Col.
Morgan   -   -   -   -   -   - St. James's, 1 Jan. 1723/4.*c*

Thos. Tuthill,[41] Esq. to be Lieut. to [Lt.-Col.]
Johnston and rank as Capt.   -   -   -   „   8 Feb.   „   *c*

Charles Legge,[42] Esq. to be Capt. in room of
George Stewart and rank as Lt.-Col.   -   „   9 Mar.   „   *c*

James Stewart,[43] Esq. to be Capt.-Lieut. [in
room of Legge] and rank as Lt.-Col.   -   „   „ „   „   *c*

John Pett [44] to be Ens. to Lt.-Col. Scott   -   „   23 April, 1724.*d*

John Owen [45] to be Ens. to ——   -   -   -   „   10 Jan. 1724/5.*d*

Chas. Leslie,[46] Esq. to be Lieut. to —— and
rank as Capt. -   -   -   -   -   „   16 Feb.   „   *d*

John Edison [47] to be Ens. to ——   -   -   -   „   12 Mar.   „   *d*

[James Stewart, Esq. to be Capt. -   -   —   — —   „   ]

Rowland Reynolds,[48] Esq. to be Capt.-Lieut.
and Lt.-Col.   -   -   -   -   - Gohre, 11 Oct. (O.S.) 1725.*d*

Arthur Owen [49] to be Ens. to [Lt.-Col.]
Moreton -   -   -   -   -   - St. James's, 6 Feb. 1726/7.*d*

Francis Cope,[50] Esq. to be Lieut. to ——   -   „   4 Mar.   „   *d*

Philip Bragg,[51] Esq. to be Capt. in room of
Lord Fred. Howard and rank as Lt.-Col. -   „   17 „   „   *d*

SUPPLEMENTARY COMMISSIONS.

George Hastings [52] to be Ens.   -   -   -   — 1 June, 1720.*f*

John Mordaunt [53] to be Ens. to ——   -   - Kensington, 26 Aug. 1721.*c*

[1] Comn. renewed in June, 1727. Out before 1740.

[2] See Vol. I., p. 278, note 3, where the date of this officer's Comn. as Capt. and Lt.-Col. in above Regt. is given as " 2 May, 1739 " instead of " 2 May, 1719."

[3] Capt. in Col. Charles Cadogan's Regt. (4th Foot), 17 May, 1721. Serving in said Corps in 1740.

[4] Served with the Vigo expedition. Untraced after 1720.

[5] Possibly Capt. Henry Smith from Wynne's Dragoons. Comn. renewed in 1727. Serving in 1730. Out before 1740.

[6] Out 9 June, 1721.

[7] Serving in 1740 with same rank.

[8] Lord Carmichael. See p. 194, note 5.

[9] D. in 1721.

[10] Capt. and Lt.-Col. 5 July, 1737. Seventh son of 3rd Visct. Irvine. Bn. 8 April, 1696. Md. Mrs. Eliz. Brace at Westminster Abbey, 9 March, 1726. He was M.P. for Horsham from 1737 till his death, 9 Nov. 1748. His only son Charles succeeded as 9th Visct. Irvine. See Chester's *Westminster Abbey Registers.*

[11] Comn. renewed 20 June, 1727. Serving in 1730. Out before 1740.

[12] See Vol. I., p. 262, note 7.

[13] Lieut. and Capt. 24 Aug. 1727. Serving in 1730. Out before 1740.

[14] Bro. to the Earl of Dunmore the Col. of above Regt. Comn. renewed in June, 1727. Serving in 1730. Out before 1740.

[15] Lieut. and Capt. 1 May, 1730. Serving in 1740. D. in 1743.

[16] Comn. renewed in 1727. Appointed Capt. of an Indep. Cy. of Foot at Sheerness, 12 Jan. 1740.

[17] Out before 1727.

[18] Appointed Lt.-Col. of above Regt. in 1752. Col. of the 20th Foot, 22 May, 1756. He served with Sir John Mordaunt's expedition to the French coast in 1757. Maj.-Gen. 20 Jan. 1758. Commanded the 2nd Infantry Brigade at Minden where he greatly distinguished himself, for which he was thanked in General Orders by Prince Ferdinand of Brunswick. Gov. of Fort William, 22 March, 1760. Lt.-Gen. 13 Dec. 1760. D. in Nov. 1769.

[19] Third son of the 2nd Duke of Rutland. D. in 1723.

[20] *Court Knyvet.* Lieut. and Capt. 30 Oct. 1734. Wounded at Fontenoy.

[21] Capt. and Lt.-Col. 22 May, 1730. Serving in 1740.

[22] See note 19.

[23] Capt. and Lt.-Col. 22 May, 1735. D. in 1743.

[24] Probably son of Capt. Leonard Gwyn, of Montague's Regt. Not in any subsequent List.

[25] Not in any subsequent List.

[26] See biog. notice in Vol. I., p. 131, note 4.

[27] See p. 203, note 19.

[28] Of Sherkin, co. Cork. Comn. renewed 20 June, 1727. Transferred as Ens. to Col. Egerton's Regt. (20th), 22 Dec. 1727. Serving in 1736. Out before 1740. D. in 1772. Will proved at Dublin.

[29] Appointed Capt. in Bisset's Regt. (30th), 5 March, 1723. Capt. in Tyrrell's Regt. in 1727. Serving in last Corps, 1730.

[30] Lieut. and Capt. 13 May, 1735. Serving in 1740.

[31] Lieut. and Capt. 18 July, 1737. Capt. and Lt.-Col. 10 Feb. 1747. Out of the Regt. before 1757. D. at Fletwick, Beds., 1765.—*Gentleman's Mag.*

[32] Ens. 12 March, 1725. Lieut. and Capt. 26 Oct. 1738. Serving in 1740.

[33] Comn. renewed, 20 June, 1727. Out before 1740.

[34] Called " Grahame " in the Gradation List for 1727. Out before 1740.

[35] Serving with same rank in 1740.

[36] Out before 1727.

[37] Served uninterruptedly in above Corps from 1 April, 1692, when he was commissioned Ens. Present at Steinkirk and other engagements in Flanders. Held the command for nearly twenty years.

[38] See note 26.

[39] Served at Malplaquet as Capt. in the Earl of Orrery's Regt. of Foot. Comn. as 2nd Major of 3rd Foot Guards renewed in 1727. D. in 1736.

[40] Serving in the Rl. Fusiliers as 2nd Lieut. in 1730. Out before 1740.

[41] Served previously as Ens. in Meredyth's Regt. (5th Foot). Killed in a duel at a London tavern, 12 Feb. 1722, by an officer of the Life Guards named Wilson.

[42] See biog. notice in Vol. I., p. 147, note 5.

[43] Of Torrence. Eldest son of Alex. Stewart of Torrence. A.D.C. to the Duke of

Argyll at Sheriffmuir. Had served in Spain and Flanders. M.P. for the Ayr Burghs, 1734–41. Gentleman Usher to George II. D. unm. 3 April, 1743.—Foster's *Members of Parliament for Scotland*.

[44] Comn. renewed in June, 1727. Lieut. in 4th Foot, 21 Jan. 1738. D. in 1750 as a Capt.

[45] See p. 206, note 22.

[46] Comn. renewed in 1727. Out before 1740.

[47] Had served as 2nd Adjt. Not in any subsequent List.

[48] Capt. and Lt.-Col. 24 Aug. 1727. Serving in 1740. D. in 1752.—*Gentleman's Mag.*

[49] Lieut. and Capt. 29 Feb. 1732. Serving in 1740. Second son of Sir Wm. Owen, Bart., who was M.P. for co. Pembroke. Arthur Owen was appointed Lt.-Col. 79th Foot, 4 Oct. 1745. Said Corps, raised by Lord Edgecumbe in 1745, was disbanded in 1746.

[50] An exchange of Company. He had been Lieut. and Capt. in same Corps since 1710. Serving in 1730. Out before 1740.

[51] Served as Ens. 1st Foot Guards at Blenheim. Capt. in Tatton's Regt. (24th), 25 Aug. 1704. Lt.-Col. of the Earl of Isla's Regt. (36th), 6 May, 1709. Col. of the 28th Foot, 10 Oct. 1734. Master of the Rl. Hospital at Kilmainham, 1733–35. Brig.-Gen. 18 Feb. 1742. Maj.-Gen. 5 July, 1743. Served at Fontenoy. Lt.-Gen. 10 Aug. 1747. D. in 1759.

[52] Comn. renewed in June, 1727. D. before 25 Dec. 1733, from which day his widow, Ann Hastings, began to draw a pension of £16 per annum which was continued till 3 July, 1735, when she remarried.—*Royal Bounty Roll to the Widows of Officers*, 25 Dec. 1733—24 Dec. 1735.

[53] Capt. and Lt.-Col. 15 July, 1731. Col. of the 58th Foot (aftds. known as the 47th Foot) 15 Jan. 1741. Brig.-Gen. 7 June, 1745. Commanded an Infantry Brigade at Falkirk in Jan. 1746. Fought at Culloden. Maj.-Gen. 22 Sept. 1747. Distinguished himself at Laufeldt in 1747. Col. 12th Dragoons 22 Dec. same year. C.-in-C. of the Expedition sent against Rochefort in 1757. The result of this descent on the French coast was a fiasco, and a Court of Enquiry was held on Mordaunt's return to England. This General had been created a K.B. some years before. He d. in 1780 aged 80.

THE PRINCESS OF WALES'S OWN REGIMENT OF FOOT.

[2ND FOOT,—THE QUEEN'S REGIMENT.]

Ralph Pennyman [1] to be Ens. - -	St. James's, 1 April, 1721.*c*
Wm. Digge,[2] Esq. to be Capt. - - -	,, 9 May, ,, *c*
Peter Heart (*sic*),[3] Esq. to Capt. - - -	,, 9 June, ,, *c*
Nathaniel Hollowes (*sic*),[4] to be Ens. to Lt.-Col. Arnot - - - - - -	,, 6 July, ,, *c*
Fras. Colome [5] to be Ens. to —— - - -	,, 9 Feb. 1721/2.*c*
Edmund Okeden [6] to be Ens. to —— - -	,, 2 Mar. ,, *c*
Wm. Graham,[7] Esq. to be Lt.-Col. and Capt. of a Cy. - - - - - - -	,, 25 Mar. 1723. *c*
John Bruce [8] to be Lieut. - - -	Herrenhausen, 13 June, ,, *c*
Walter (*sic*) Manning,[9] Esq. to be Capt. in room of [James] Giles decd. - - -	St. James's, 9 Mar. 1723/4.*c*
Robert Laton [10] to be Lieut. to Capt. Robert Laton - - - - - -	Kensington, 27 June, 1724.*d*
John Graham [11] to be Chaplain - - -	,, 8 Oct. ,, *d*
James Franks [12] to be Lieut. to Capt. Wm. Franks - - - - - - -	St. James's, 9 Mar. 1724/5.*d*
Wm. Remington [13] to be Ens. to above Cy. -	,, ,, ,, ,, *d*
Peregrine Lascelles,[14] Esq. to be Capt. in room of W. Manning - - -	Gohrde (*sic*), 11 Oct. (O.S.)1725.*d*
Mathew Sewell [15] to be Lieut. to —— -	St. James's, 4 April, 1726.*d*
Robert Barton [16] to be Ens. to —— Heart -	,, 10 Dec. ,, *d*
Paul Winkles [17] to be Lt. to —— Diggs -	,, 23 ,, ,, *d*
Ben. Theaker [18] to be Lieut. to —— - -	,, ,, ,, ,, *d*
Ben. Sladen [19] to be Lieut. to —— - -	,, 25 ,, ,, *d*
John Legg,[20] Esq. to be Capt. in room of [Peregrine] Lascelles - - - -	,, ,, ,, ,, *d*
James Nicholls,[21] Esq. to be Capt.-Lieut. -	,, ,, ,, ,, *d*
Peter Garrick [22] to be Capt. of an additional Cy. - - - - - - - -	,, 26 ,, ,, *d*
Henry Vachell [23] to be Lieut. to do. - -	,, ,, ,, ,, *d*
[Robt.] Armiger [24] to be Ens. to do. - -	,, ,, ,, ,, *d*
Philip Pennington [25] to be Capt. of an additional Cy. - - - - - -	,, ,, ,, ,, *d*
James Norman [26] to be Lieut. to do. - -	,, ,, ,, ,, *d*
Edmund Sture [27] to be Ens. to do. - -	,, ,, ,, ,, *d*

[1] Fourth son of Sir James Pennyman 3rd Bart. of Ormesby. Out of above Regt. before 1727. D. 1768 at Scampton, Yorkshire.

[2] Comn. renewed in 1727. Major 8th Dragoons, 3 Sept. 1739. D. in 1741.

[3] *Hart.* An exchange of Company. This officer was commissioned Capt. in above Regt. in 1706. Taken prisoner at Almanza. Major, 9 June, 1721. Lt.-Col. of 10th Foot 5 July, 1737. Serving in 1740.

[4] *Hallowes.* Comn. renewed in 1727. Descended from Nathaniel Hallowes of the old Derbyshire family of this surname. Out of the Regt. before 1740.

[5] Comn. renewed in 1727. Not in any subsequent List.

[6] Lieut. in Col. Philipps's Regt. 10 Dec. 1726.

[7] See biog. notice in Vol. I., p. 137, note 4.

[8] Out before June, 1727.

[9] *Walker* Manning. On 8 Nov. 1725 the King granted a "pardon to Lt.-Col. Wm. Graham of Kirke's Regt. for killing Walker Manning, a Capt. in the said Regt., in a duel, in or near Inverness in Aug. last."—*S.P. Dom. George I.*, Bundle 60.

[10] Comn. renewed in 1727. Serving in 1736.

[11] The will of the Rev. John Graham of Hockly, co. Antrim, was proved at Dublin in 1743.

[12] D. in 1733. Pension of £20 per annum to his widow Johanna *Franks*.

[13] Lieut. 14 March, 1734. Serving in 1740.

[14] See biog. notice in Vol. I., p. 179, note 8.

[15] See do. in do., p. 318, note 7.

[16] Lieut. 13 May, 1735. Serving in 1740.

[17] Comn. renewed in 1727. Serving in 1730.

[18] Capt. 22 Jan. 1738. Served as 1st Lieut. in Col. Charles Churchill's Marines in former reign. Drawing half-pay as Capt. in Gen. Cornewall's Regt. of Marines in 1758.

[19] From Wills's Foot (3rd Buffs). Had served in former reign as 2nd Lieut. in Wills's Marines. Serving in 1730.

[20] Promoted from Lieut. in same Corps. Comn. as Capt. renewed in 1727. Serving in 1730.

[21] Comn. renewed in 1727. Serving in 1730. As an Ens. in above Corps this officer had served at Almanza and was taken prisoner.

[22] Father of the celebrated dramatist David Garrick. See biog. notice in Vol. I., p. 277, note 3.

[23] Capt. 7 Nov. 1739.

[24] Comn. renewed in 1727. Capt. in the Earl of Rothes's Regt. of Foot (25th) 18 May, 1735. Capt. and Lt.-Col. 1st Foot Guards, 7 Feb. 1747. Col. 65th Foot, 21 April, 1758. Transferred to 40th Foot, 10 Dec. 1760. Served in 1759 as a Brigdr. at the reduction of Guadeloupe in the West Indies. Maj.-Gen. 25 June, 1759. Lt.-Gen. 19 Jan. 1761. Gov. of Landguard Fort, 25 May, 1768. D. 18 March, 1770, aged 68.

[25] Had served as Capt.-Lieut. in Sir Roger Bradshaigh's Regt. of Foot in 1712. Half-pay, 1713. Capt. of an additional Cy. in Stanwix's Regt. 26 Sept. 1715. Serving as Capt. in the Princess of Wales's Own Regt. of Foot in 1730.

[26] Had served in late reign as 2nd Lieut. in Holt's Marines. Untraced after 1728.

[27] From half-pay Stanwix's Regt. Untraced after 1726.

LIEUT.-GENERAL CHARLES WILLS'S REGIMENT OF FOOT.

[3RD FOOT,—THE BUFFS.]

Richard Brewer [1] to be Ens. to Capt. ——
  Wilson - - - - - - - St. James's, 5 Feb. 1719/20. *c*
Charles Wills,[2] Esq. to be Capt. in room of
  Philip Babington decd. in that Regt.
  under your command - - - -   ,,   25 Jan. 1720/1. *c*
Alex. Deane,[3] Esq. to be Major and Capt. of
  a Cy. - - - - - - -   ,,   22 Feb. ,, *c*
Wm. Pownall,[4] Esq. to be Capt. in room of
  Alex. Deane - - - - -   ,, ,, ,, ,, *c*
Henry Wilson,[5] Esq. to be Capt.-Lieut. -   ,, ,, ,, ,, *c*
John Cole [6] to be Ens. to —— - - -   ,, ,, ,, ,, *c*
Jonathan Mowbray [7] to be Lieut. to Capt.   ,, ,, ,, ,, *c*
  Thos. White - - - - -   ,, ,, ,, ,, *c*
Edward Daniel,[8] Esq. to be Capt. in room of
  [Ric.] Lowther decd. - - - Kensington, 18 Oct. 1721. *c*
Wm. Morden,[9] Esq. to be do. in room of [John]
  Greerson (*sic*) decd. - - - - St. James's, 6 Nov. ,, *c*
Fras. Corbett [10] to be Ens. to —— - -   ,, 21 April, 1722. *c*
John Farrer [11] to be Lieut. to Capt. —— -   ,, 26 July, ,, *c*
Wm. Brown [12] to be Ens. to Capt. —— -   ,, ,, ,, ,, *c*
Fras. Otway,[13] Esq. to be Capt. in room of
  Richard Otway - - - Kensington, 27 Sept. ,, *c*
John Robertson,[14] Esq. to be Capt.-Lieut. -   ,, 29 ,, ,, *c*
Ben. Day [15] to be Ens. to [Major] Deane - St. James's, 11 April, 1723. *c*
John Horsman,[16] Esq. to be Capt. in room of
  —— - - - - - - -   ,, 24 May, ,, *c*
Thos. Mason [17] to be [1st] Lieut. to Capt.
  Talbot's Grenadier Cy. - - - Herrenhausen, 12 July, ,, *c*
Chas. Fielding,[18] Esq. to be Capt. in room of
  —— Price - - - - - Gohre, 5 Oct. ,, *c*
Nathaniel Smith [19] to be [2nd] Lieut. to Capt.
  Talbot - - - - - - -   ,, 9 Nov. ,, *c*
Wm. Langhorne [20] to be Ens. to [Major]
  Deane - - - - - - -   ,, ,, ,, ,, *c*
Richard Lucas [21] to be Lieut. to Capt. Chas.
  Fielding - - - - - - St. James's, 1 Feb. 1723/4. *d*
George Storey to be Chaplain - - -   ,, 27 Nov. 1724. *d*
Wm. Crossby [22] to be Lieut. to Capt. [Thos.]
  White - - - - - - -   ,, 18 Feb. 1724/5. *d*
Fras. Thompson,[23] Esq. to be Capt. in room
  of John Wilson - - - -   ,, 19 April, 1726. *d*
Thos. Lord Londonderry [24] to be Colonel in
  room of General Sir Charles Wills and
  Capt. of a Cy. - - - - Kensington, 26 Aug. ,, *d*
Tindal Tompson (*sic*),[25] Esq. to be Capt. in
  room of [Fras.] Tompson (*sic*) - - St. James's, 26 Dec. ,, *d*

James Bolton,[26] Esq. to be Capt. of an additional Cy. - - - - - -	St. James's, 26 Dec. 1726.	*d*
Lewis Turpin [27] to be Lieut. to do. - -	,, ,, ,, ,,	*d*
Chas. Cornelius Donnovane [28] to be Ens. to do.	,, ,, ,, ,,	*d*
Gerald Elrington [29] to be Capt. of an additional Cy. - - - - - -	,, ,, ,, ,,	*d*
Timothy Vallade [30] to be Lieut. to do. - -	,, ,, ,, ,,	*d*
John Lambert [31] to be Ens. to do. - -	,, ,, ,, ,,	*d*
Ruishe Hassell [32] to be Lieut. to —— - -	,, ,, ,, ,,	*d*
Bryan Rourke [33] to be Ens. to —— - -	,, ,, ,, ,,	*d*
Wm. Deane [34] to be Lieut. to —— - -	,, ,, ,, ,,	*d*
Skrymsher Boothby [35] to be Ens. to —— -	,, ,, ,, ,,	*d*
Robert Pitt [36] to be Ens. to Capt. [Tindal] Thompson - - - - -	,, 23 Feb. 1726/7.	*d*
James Paterson,[37] Esq. to be Major and Capt. of a Cy - - - - - - -	,, 9 Mar. ,,	*d*
George Harvey [38] to be Ens. to —— - -	,, 11 ,, ,,	*d*
Gerald Elrington [39] to be Adjt. - - -	,, 15 ,, ,,	*d*
Thos. White [40] to be do. - - - -	,, 30 May, 1727.	*d*
Gerard Elrington [39] to be Qr.-Mr. - - -	,, ,, ,, ,,	*d*

[1] From Ens. in Whetham's Regt. Comn. renewed in 1727. Serving in 1730.

[2] See special memoir in Vol. I., pp. 59–70.

[3] See p. 268, note 70.

[4] See Vol. I., p. 296, note 7.

[5] Out of the Regt. 29 Sept. 1722.

[6] Lieut. 9 March, 1732. D. about 1740.

[7] D. before 1733, in which year his widow, Ann Mowbray, was drawing a pension of £20 per annum.

[8] From Capt. in Col. Fielding's Regt. of Invalids. Comn. renewed in June, 1727. Out before 1740.

[9] Comn. renewed in 1727. Serving in 1730. Out before 1740.

[10] Do. do. do.

[11] Do. do. do.

[12] Do. do. do.

[13] Exempt and Capt. 3rd Tp. of Life Guards, 1 Jan. 1732. Major 26 April, 1740. Lt.-Col. 4th Horse (3rd D.G.), 3 May, 1744. Serving in 1749. Out of the Army in 1751.

[14] Capt. 9 March, 1732. Serving in 1740.

[15] Lieut. 13 Dec. 1733. Serving in 1740. A certain Benjamin Day, J.P. for Middlesex, d. in 1773.—*Gentleman's Mag.*

[16] See p. 266, note 5.

[17] Comn. renewed in 1727. Out before 1740.

[18] See p. 197, note 3.

[19] Comn. renewed in 1727. Out before 1740.

[20] Lieut. 5 Nov. 1736. Serving in 1740.

[21] Son of Col. Richard Lucas of 38th Regt. Lieut. in his father's Regt. 11 July, 1720. Out of Wills's Regt. before 1730.

[22] Lieut. in Stanwix's Regt. 12 April, 1723. Serving in 1730. Out before 1740.

[23] See p. 212, note 13.

[24] See Vol. I., p. 326, note 1.

[25] See p. 200, note 2.

[26] From half-pay as Capt. in same Corps. See Vol. I., p. 296, note 3, where the date of his Comn. as Capt. is given as "16 June, 1719," whereas it ought to read "16 June, 1710."

[27] Had served in the late reign as Lieut. in Col. Robert Dalzell's Regt. of Foot in Spain. Serving in 1736.

[28] *Donovan.* Son-in-law to Col. Giles Spicer, Lieut.-Gov. of Guernsey. See reference to Ens. Donovan's petition in note to Col. Spicer's comn. in Vol. I., p. 243, note 3.

[29] Called "Gerard" in some Lists. Served previously as Lieut. in Stanwix's Regt. of Foot. Major, 10 Feb. 1741. Out before 1748.

[30] Serving in 1740.

[31] Reduced with the Cy. in 1729. Drawing half-pay in 1739.

[32] " D. in Hassel's Buildings, London, 1749."—*Gentleman's Mag.*

[33] Bryan *O'Rourke.* Lieut. 21 Jan. 1738. Serving in 1740.

[34] Out before 1740.

[35] Serving in 1736. Out before 1740. Called " Charles Skrymsher Boothby " in the Gradation List for 1736.

[36] Untraced after 1727 when his Comn. was renewed.

[37] Not identified with the Lt.-Col. Jas. Patterson of the 7th Marines in 1741.

[38] Out before 1740.

[39] See note 29.

[40] Out before 1740.

THE KING'S OWN REGIMENT OF FOOT.

[4TH FOOT,—THE KING'S OWN ROYAL LANCASTER REGIMENT.]

Thomas Goddard,[1] Esq. to be Capt. of Grenadiers in room of —— Dumaresq - -	St. James's, 6 Mar.	1718/9.*c*
Charles Cadogan,[2] Esq. to be Colonel in room of Henry Berkeley, and to be Capt. of a Cy. - - - - - - -	,, 21 April,	1719.*c*
James Thorn [3] to be Ens. to Capt. —— - -	,, 6 May,	1720.*c*
George Walsh,[4] Esq. to be Capt. of Grenadiers in room of Thos. Goddard - - -	,, 9 ,,	,, *c*
Henry de Vic [5] to be Ens. to —— - - -	,, 4 June,	,, *c*
Wm. Bush [6] to be Lieut. to —— - - -	,, 11 ,,	,, *c*
John Fuller [7] to be Ens. to —— - - -	,, ,, ,,	,, *c*
Wm. Newton,[8] Esq. to be Capt.-Lieut. - -	,, ,, ,,	,, *c*
Thos. Saville,[9] Esq. to be Lt.-Col. and Capt. of a Cy. - - - - - - -	,, 6 Mar.	1720/1.*c*
Thos. Shrimpton,[10] Esq. to be Capt. of Lt.-Col. Kempenfelt's Cy. - - - - -	,, ,, ,,	,, *c*
Henry Jefferies,[11] Esq. to be Capt. in room of —— Bisset - - - - -	,, 7 May,	1721.*c*
John Tucker,[12] Esq. to be Major and Capt. of a Cy. - - - - - - -	,, 17 ,,	,, *c*
Sir James Dalzell,[13] Bt. to be Ens. to Sir Chas. Mylne - - - - - - -	,, 21 April,	1722.*c*
Wm. Sumners [14] to be Qr.-Mr. - - -	,, ,, ,,	,, *c*
Robert Leigh [15] to be Ens. to above Cy. [in room of Sir J. Dalzell] - - - -	,, 29 Oct.	,, *c*
John Price,[16] Esq. to be Capt. in room of —— Pownal - - - - - -	,, 7 Nov.	,, *c*
Charles Fielding [17] to be Lieut. to Capt. ——	,, 10 ,,	,, *c*
John Knowles,[18] Esq. to be Capt. in room of James Farrell - - - - - -	,, 18 Mar.	1722/3.*c*
John Taylor [19] to be Ens. to Capt. John Trelawny - - - - - - -	,, 17 May,	1723.*c*
James Thorne [3] to be Quarter-Master - -	,, ,, ,,	,, *c*
—— Whitfield to be Chaplain - - -	,, 7 Mar.	1723/4.*c*
Chas. Vatchell (*sic*) [20] to be Lieut. to Capt. [George] Walsh - - - - -	Kensington, 9 June,	1724.*d*
John Emmenes [21] to be Lieut. to do. -	St. James's, 17 Dec.	,, *d*
John Carney,[22] Esq. to be Capt. of an additional Cy. - - - - - -	,, 26 Dec.	1726.*d*
Wm. Williams [23] to be Lieut. to do. - -	,, ,, ,,	,, *d*
Thos. Collier [24] to be Ens. to do. - -	,, ,, ,,	,, *d*
Robert Gorst,[25] Esq. to be Capt. of an additional Cy. - - - - - - -	,, ,, ,,	,, *d*
George Brereton [26] to be Lieut. to do. -	,, ,, ,,	,, *d*
Pierce Barington [27] to be Lieut. to do. - -	,, ,, ,,	,, *d*

Jasper Johnston [28] to be Ens. to do.   -   St. James's, 26 Dec. 1726. *d*
Fras. Henry Lee,[29] Esq. to be Lt.-Col. and
   Capt. of a Cy. -   -   -   -   -   -   ,,   31 Mar. 1727. *d*
Ben. Brown [30] to be Ens. to ——   -   -   -   ,,   22 April,   ,,   *d*

[1] See Vol. I., p. 297, note 1.
[2] Succeeded his bro. Earl Cadogan, in 1726, as Lord Cadogan Baron of Oakley. Transferred to the Colonelcy of the Inniskilling Dragoons in 1734, and appointed Capt. and Col. of the 2nd Tp. of Life Guards in 1742. D. a full Gen. in 1776. He was F.R.S. and a Trustee of the British Museum.
[3] Qr.-Mr. 17 May, 1723. Lieut. 1 Nov. 1733. Lt.-Col. of above Regt. 22 Jan. 1754. Believed to have been a son of Lieut. John *Thorne* of same Corps.
[4] Lt.-Col. 9th Marines, 26 Jan. 1741. Col. 49th Foot, 22 Jan. 1754. Attained the rank of Lt.-Gen. and d. in 1761. Will proved at Dublin.
[5] Lieut. in the King's Own Regt. of Horse, 5 March, 1739. Capt. 21 June, 1749. Serving in 1758.
[6] Had served in above Corps for about twelve years. Comn. renewed in 1727. Serving in 1730. Out before 1740.
[7] Serving in 1730. Out before 1740.
[8] Comn. renewed in 1727. Serving in 1730. Out before 1740.
[9] Joined above Regt. as Ens. 1 Jan. 1696. Served with same Corps on board the Fleet in the reign of Queen Anne, and was made a Bt.-Major, 1 March, 1708. Exchanged to 1st Foot Guards, 31 March, 1727. Serving in 1730. Out before 1740.
[10] Serving in 1730. Out before 1740.
[11] Serving as senior Capt. in 1740.
[12] Joined above Corps as 2nd Lieut. in 1706 and served with same on board the Fleet. Bt.-Capt. 1 March, 1708. Capt. in Regt. 13 April, 1709. Comn. as Major renewed in 1727. Serving in 1730. Out in 1736.
[13] Sir James Menteth Dalyell or Dalziell of Binns. Out of the Regt. in Oct. same year. This officer assumed the title on the death of his maternal uncle, Sir Thos. Dalyell, who d. without issue in 1719. Sir James d. 28 Feb. 1747.
[14] Not in any subsequent List.
[15] Comn. renewed in 1727. Serving in 1730. Out before 1740.
[16] Exchanged to 1st Foot Guards. See p. 268, note 54.
[17] Serving as senior Lieut. in Howard's Regt. (3rd Foot) in 1740. D. about 1741.
[18] Joined 1st Foot Guards as Ens. 13 Sept. 1708. Major of 4th Foot, 28 Jan. 1741. Lt.-Col. 4 April, 1743. Out in July, 1744.
[19] Comn. renewed in 1727. Serving in 1730.
[20] *Vachell.* From Lieut. in Pearce's Foot. Comn. renewed in 1727. Serving in 1730. Half-pay, 1729. Drawing half-pay in 1759. Belonged to the Berkshire family of this name.
[21] Served in late reign as Lieut. in Lord Paston's Regt. of Foot. Serving in 1740.
[22] From half-pay. Cy. reduced in 1729.
[23] Serving with same rank in 1740.
[24] Lieut. 2 Aug. 1734. Serving in 1740.
[25] Served in Col. Allen's Regt. in late reign. Cy. in Cadogan's Regt. reduced in 1729.
[26] Comn. renewed in June, 1727. Half-pay, 1729.
[27] This Comn. was doubtless cancelled.
[28] Out before June, 1727.
[29] From 1st Foot Guards. Serving in 1728.
[30] Half-pay, 1729. Drawing half-pay, 1739.

MAJOR-GENERAL THOMAS PEARCE'S REGIMENT OF FOOT.
[5TH FOOT,—THE NORTHUMBERLAND FUSILIERS.]

Andrew Peterson[1] to be Lieut. to Capt. Wm. Peterson	St. James's,	18 Feb.	1718/9.c	
James Paterson[2] to be do. to ——	,,	6 May,	1719.c	
John Napper,[3] Esq. to be Capt. in room of Wm. Vachell	,,	28 ,,	1720.c	
Wm. Wynn,[4] Esq. to be Capt.-Lieut.	,,	,, ,,	,,	c
Chas. Vachell[5] to be Lieut. to Capt. Bacon Morris	,,	,, ,,	,,	c
John Coultrone[6] to be Ens. to Capt. John Napper	,,	,, ,,	,,	c
James Paterson,[2] Esq. to be Capt. in room of —— Titchbourne	Whitehall,	28 July,	,,	c
Peter Bruneval[7] to be Lieut. to Capt. John Morris	,,	,, ,,	,,	c
Hercules Ogilvy[8] to be Ens. to do.	,,	,, ,,	,,	c
John Coultrone[6] to be Lieut. to Capt. John Napper	,,	29 Mar.	1721.c	
Wm. Maxwell[9] to be Ens. to do.	,,	,, ,,	,,	c
John Horsman,[10] Esq. to be Capt. in room of Bacon Morris	,,	20 May,	,,	c
Henry Houghton[11] to be Ens. to do.	,,	5 June,	,,	c
Daniel Pecqueur,[12] Esq. to be Capt. in room of Richard Hanmer	,,	9 ,,	,,	c
James Stratton[13] to be Ens. to ——	,,	9 Feb.	1721/2.c	
John Elrington,[14] Esq. to be Capt. in room of [Nicholas] Finbo	,,	24 April,	1722.c	
Gilbert Keene[15] to be Lieut. to Capt. James Paterson	,,	,, ,,	..	c
James Bennet[16] to be Ens. to Capt. Charles Pearce	,,	,, ,,	,,	c
Wm. Heele[17] to be Lieut. to Capt. Horsman	,,	,, ,,	,,	c
James Stratton[18] to be Lieut. to Lt.-Col. Peter Godby	,,	9 May,	,,	c
Robert Napier[18] to be Ens. to Capt. James Paterson	,,	,, ,,	,,	c
Robt. Cuthbertson[19] to be Ens. to do.	,,	31 ,,	,,	c
Scipio Olyphant (sic)[20] to be do. to General Pearce	Kensington,	13 July,	,,	c
John Murray[21] to be do. to Capt. [James] Paterson	,,	19 ,,	,,	c
Walter Devereux[22] to be Lieut. to Capt. ——	,,	11 Aug.	,,	c
Nicholas Skinner[23] to be Ens. to ——	,,	,, ,,	,,	c
Andrew Crewe[24] to be Lieut. to ——	,,	22 ,,	,,	c
Wm. Elrington,[25] Esq. to be Lt.-Col. and Capt. of a Cy.	,,	25 ,,	,,	c
Chas. [Wm.] Pearce,[26] Esq. to be Major and Capt. of a Cy.	,,	,, ,,	,,	c

Wm. Wynn,[4] Esq. to be Capt. in room of ——
    Godby - - - - - - - Kensington, 25 Aug. 1722. *c*
Job Elrington,[27] Esq. to be Capt.-Lieut. - -   ,,   ,,   ,,   ,,   *c*
Cary Godbey [28] to be [1st] Lieut. to [Grendr.
    Cy.] - - - - - - -   ,,   ,,   ,,   ,,   *c*
Michael Mitchell [29] to be Ens. to —— - -   ,,   ,,   ,,   ,,   *c*
Ralph Urwin (*sic*) [30] to be Lieut. to Capt. John
    Elrington - - - - - St. James's, 24 Nov.   ,,   *c*
Lambert Vanriel,[31] Junr. to be Ens. to Capt.
    Henry Owen - - - -   ,,   ,,   ,,   ,,   *c*
Christopher Alcock [32] to be Adjt. - - -   ,,   ,,   ,,   ,,   *c*
Do. to be Capt. in room of John Horsman -   ,,   9 Mar. 1722/3. *c*
John Knyvet [33] to be Lieut. to [Major] Pearce   ,,   ,,   ,,   ,,   *c*
Job Elrington,[27] Esq. to be Capt. in room of
    Henry Owen - - - - - -   ,,   24 May,   1723. *c*
James Ormsby,[34] Esq. to be Capt.-Lieut. -   ,,   ,,   ,,   ,,   *c*
Wm. Pyll [35] to be [2nd] Lieut. to Capt. Job
    Elrington - - - - - -   ,,   ,,   ,,   ,,   *c*
James Holmes,[36] Esq. to be Capt.-Lieut. - Gohre, 13 Oct.   ,,   *c*
Robert Napper [37] to be Lieut. to Capt. Dan.
    Pecqueur- - - - - - -   ,,   ,,   ,,   ,,   *c*
John Fenwick [38] to be Ens. to Capt. John
    Morice - - - - - - -   ,,   ,,   ,,   ,,   *c*
Wm. Ellis [39] to be Ens. to Capt. John Elring-
    ton - - - - - - - St. James's, 24 Jan.   1723/4. *c*
John Purcell [40] to be Lieut. to Capt. Thos.
    Giles   ,,   1 June,   1724. *c*
Ben. Gregg,[41] Esq. to be Capt. in room of
    [John] Napier decd. - - -   ,,   20 Mar. 1724/5. *d*
Robt. Napier (*sic*) [37] to be Qr.-Mr. - - -   ,,   ,,   ,,   ,,   *d*
Chas. d'Avenant [42] to be Ens. to Capt. [Ben.]
    Gregg - - - - - - -   ,,   10 May,   1726. *d*
Rowland Johnson [43] to be Chaplain - Kensington, 26 Aug.   ,,   *d*
Richard Johnston [44] to be Ens. to Capt. Wm.
    Elrington - - - - - -   ,,   18 Jan. 1726/7. *d*

---

[1] Appointed Ens. in Lord Paston's Regt. 9 Sept. 1706. Lieut. 29 Aug. 1707. Half-pay, 1712. Lieut. in Col. Ric. Lucas's Regt. before 1715. Serving as Lieut. in Pearce's Regt. in 1727. Out before June, 1728.

[2] Capt. 28 July, 1720. Major of above Regt. 1 Jan. 1736. Lt.-Col. 7th Marines, 24 Jan. 1741. Col. of the newly-raised Regt. of Marines, 19 Dec. 1755. Attained the rank of Lt.-Gen. 19 Jan. 1761. D. at Richmond in 1771.

[3] D. in March, 1725. His widow, Mary Napper, was drawing a pension of £26 per annum in 1734.

[4] Capt. 25 Aug. 1722. Comn. renewed in 1727. Out before 1736.

[5] See p. 282, note 20.

[6] Lieut. 29 March, 1721. Comn. renewed in 1727. Out before 1737.

[7] Capt. 1 Jan. 1736. Serving in 1740.

[8] Out in Oct. 1723.

[9] Out before 1727.

[10] See p. 266, note 5.

[11] Out before 1727.

[12] From half-pay. Served in late reign in Earl of Barrymore's Regt. (13th Foot). Major 5th Foot, 8 Feb. 1741. Serving in 1748.

[13] Lieut. 9 May, 1722. Capt. in the Earl of Orkney's Regt. 25 Dec. 1726. Serving with last-named Corps in Ireland, 1736. Out before 1740.

[14] Comn. renewed in 1727. Out before 1740.

[15] Capt. 20 June, 1739. Serving in 1740.

[16] Comn. renewed in 1727. Out before 1736.

[17] Called "Hale" in subsequent Lists. Capt.-Lieut. 1 Jan. 1736. Serving in Ireland, 1740.

[18] Comn. renewed in 1727. Out before 1736.

[19] Lieut. 11 March, 1732. Serving in 1740. Probably father of Lieut. Bennet Cuthbertson of same Corps, in 1758, who wrote a book entitled *A System for the Complete Interior Management and Economy of a Battalion of Infantry.*

[20] *Oliphant.* Comn. renewed in 1727. Out before 1736.

[21] Comn. renewed in 1727. Serving in 1730. D. before 1735, in which year his widow, Mary Murray, was drawing a pension of £16 per annum.

[22] Appointed Capt.-Lieut. of Handasyde's Regt. (16th Foot), 12 Jan. 1740. Not in any subsequent List.

[23] See p. 303, note 24.

[24] Serving as senior Lieut. in 1740. A certain Andrew Crew d. at Piddle Hinton, Dorsetshire, in 1759.—*Gentleman's Mag.*

[25] See biog. notice in Vol. I., p. 143, note 4.

[26] His full name was Charles William Pearce. Served previously as Capt. and Adjt. Probably son of Lt.-Gen. Thos. Pearce. Lt.-Col. 1 Jan. 1736. Serving in 1751.

[27] Had served in Portugal with above Corps in late reign. Capt. 24 May, 1723. Serving in Ireland, 1737.

[28] Serving with same rank in 1740.

[29] Lieut. 1 Jan. 1736. Serving in 1740.

[30] *Irwin.* Serving with same rank in 1740.

[31] Lieut. 1 May, 1739. His father served as Lieut. in same Corps.

[32] Comn. renewed in 1727. D. 1732.

[33] Serving as Lieut. in Ireland, 1737. Out before 1740.

[34] Out in Oct. 1736.

[35] Serving in same Corps, 1737. Capt. in Moreton's Marines, 27 Nov. 1739. Served at Carthagena in 1741, and d. in April from fever.

[36] Serving as Capt. in 1737. Out before 1740.

[37] Comn. renewed in 1727. Out before 1737.

[38] Serving as senior Ens. in 1740.

[39] Comn. renewed in 1727. Out before 1740. Son of Surgeon Wm. Ellis of same Corps. Latter d. in 1732.

[40] From Ens. in the Regt. of Invalids. Serving as Lieut. in 5th Foot, 1740.

[41] Appointed Ens. in Col. Godfrey's Regt. (16th Foot), 24 March, 1705. Served as a Lieut. at Malplaquet. Capt. in the Royal Irish Regt. 4 April, 1712. Half-pay, 1713. Major of Col. Robinson's Marines, 3 Dec. 1739. Served with same Corps in the Carthagena Expedition, 1741. Believed to have d. in the West Indies same year.

[42] Comn. renewed in 1727. He was appointed Ens. in Maj.-Gen. Newton's Regt. 12 Oct. 1711. Attained the rank of Capt. in the Army, and was given the post of Town-Adjt. at Portsmouth before 1757. D. as Town-Major to said garrison, 1773.

[43] Serving in June, 1728. Out of the Regt. before 1737.

[44] Out of the Regt. before June, 1728.

COLONEL JAMES OTWAY'S REGIMENT OF FOOT.

[9TH FOOT,—THE NORFOLK REGIMENT.]

Nicholas Romaine[1] to be Lieut. to Capt.
[Michael] Doyne - - - - - - St. James's, 9 May, 1719. *c*

Henry Cross[2] to be Ens. to —— Otway   ,,   ,,   ,,   ,,   *c*

Roger Comberbach[3] to be Capt. of Fras. Bill-
ingsley's late Cy. - - - - -   ,,   25 Nov. ,,   *c*

Henry de la Milliere[4] to be Lieut. to Major
[Ric.] Offarrell (*sic*) - - - -   ,,   22 April, 1720. *c*

Thos. Morley[5] to be Ens. to —— - - -   ,,   8 June, ,,   *c*

Stephen Otway,[6] Esq. to be Capt. in room of
Robt. Comberbach - - - - Herrenhausen, 28 July, ,,   *c*

John Campbell,[7] Esq. to be Lt.-Col. and Capt.
of a Cy. - - - - - - St. James's, 15 Nov. ,,   *c*

George Whitmore[8] to be Ens. to —— - -   ,,   25 Jan. 1720/1. *c*

Rowland Godfrey,[9] Esq. to be Capt. in room
of —— Hussey - - - - Kensington, 12 Sept. 1721. *c*

James Stewart,[10] Esq. to be Capt.-Lieut. -   ,,   ,,   ,,   ,,   *c*

Thos. Bolton[11] to be Lieut. to —— - -   ,,   ,,   ,,   ,,   *c*

Sol. Stevenson[12] to be Ens. to —— - -   ,,   ,,   ,,   ,,   *c*

Joseph Otway[13] to be do. to —— - - -   ,,   24 Oct.   ,,   *c*

Thos. Hopley[14] to be do. to —— - - - St. James's, 15 Nov. ,,   *c*

Stephen Otway,[6] Esq. to be Capt. [of Grena-
diers] in room of [Thos.] Gery - - -   ,,   10 Mar. 1721/2.*c*

James Stewart,[10] Esq. to be Capt. of Stephen
Otway's late Cy. - - - - -   ,,   ,,   ,,   ,,   *c*

Stewart Nugent[15] to be Lieut. to —— - -   ,,   ,,   ,,   ,,   *c*

John Fitz Gerald[16] to be Ens. to —— - -   ,,   ,,   ,,   ,,   *c*

Richard Dickinson,[17] Esq. to be Capt.-Lieut.   ,,   ,,   ,,   ,,   *c*

Edward Newton[18] to be Lieut to —— - -   ,,   13 June, 1722. *c*

Hopton Twynihoe[19] to be Capt. in room of
—— Le Grand - - - - Kensington, 27 July, ,,   *c*

Fras. Otway[20] to be Lieut. to Capt. Dabsac -   ,,   11 Sept. ,,   *c*

Simon Hughes[21] to be Ens. to Capt. Richard
Otway - - - - - - -   ,,   ,,   ,,   ,,   *c*

John Jordan[22] to be Surgeon - - -   ,,   20 ,,   ,,   *c*

Thos. Rainsford[23] to be Lieut. to —— - -   ,,   27 ,,   ,,   *c*

Francis Otway,[20] Esq. to be Capt. in room of
Richard Otway - - - - -   ,,   ,,   ,,   ,,   *c*

Thos. Benson[24] to be Ens. to Capt. Jas.
Stewart - - - - - - St. James's, 7 Dec. ,,   *c*

Richard Offarrell (*sic*),[25] Esq. to be Lt.-Col.
and Capt. of a Cy. - - - - -   ,,   20 ,,   ,,   *c*

Henry Dabzac,[26] Esq. to be Major and Capt.
of a Cy. - - - - - -   ,,   ,,   ,,   ,,   *c*

Ben. Darby[27] to be Lieut. to —— - -   ,,   ,,   ,,   ,,

George Lloyd[28] to be Ens. to —— - -   ,,   ,,   ,,   ,,

Joseph Dambon,[29] Esq. to be Capt. of Lt.-Col.
   John Campbell's late Cy.   -   -   -   St. James's, 20 Dec. 1722.
Sol. Stevenson[12] to be Lieut. to ——   -   -   „   25 Mar. 1723.
[Chas.] St. Maurice[30] to be Ens. to ——   -   „   „   „   „
Richard Dickinson,[17] Esq. to be Capt. in room
   of Hopton Twynihoe   -   -   -   Pyrmont,   4 July,   „   c
Peter Dumas,[31] Esq. to be Capt.-Lieut. -   „   „   „   „   c
[Thos.] Crofton[32] to be Lieut. to ——   -   -   „   „   „   „   c
Thos. Grove[33] to be Ens. to ——   -   -   St. James's, 18 Feb. 1724/5. d
Charles Elstob[34] to be Lieut. to ——   -   -   „   12 Mar.   „   d
Do. to be Qr.-Mr. -   -   -   -   -   „   „   „   „   d
James Bellenden,[35] Esq. to be Capt. in room
   of [Joseph] Shewbridge decd.   -   -   „   21 May, 1725. d
Richard Kane,[36] Esq. to be Colonel in room
   of James Otway decd. and Capt. of a
   Cy. -   -   -   -   -   Helvoet Sluys, 25 Dec.   „   d
John Hill[37] to be [2nd] Lieut. to [the Grendr.
   Cy.] -   -   -   -   -   St. James's, 29 Mar. 1726. d
Timothy Quinn[38] to be do. to ——   -   -   „   28 May,   „   d
Do. to be Qr.-Mr. -   -   -   -   -   „   „   „   „   d

[1] Comn. renewed 20 June, 1727. Capt. 14 Jan. 1737 in 30th Foot. His will was proved at Dublin in 1744.

[2] Out before 1727.

[3] D. or left the Regt. in 1720.

[4] D. in 1738 as Capt. in Lord Cavendish's Regt. of Foot. Will proved at Dublin.

[5] On half-pay in 1722.

[6] Capt. 10 March, 1722. Major, 19 April, 1743. Serving in 1748. Out in 1753.

[7] From Capt. and Lt.-Col. 3rd Foot Guards. Out of Otway's Regt. in 1722. May be identical with the Lt.-Col. Campbell who was subsequently Lt.-Gov. of Chelsea Hospital, who d. in 1773.

[8] Out before 1727.

[9] Called "Rowley Godfrey" in subsequent Lists. Comn. renewed in 1727. Serving in 1738. D. in 1744. Will proved at Dublin.

[10] Promoted from 2nd Lieut. in same Corps. Kinsman to Lt.-Gen. Wm. *Steuart*. Comn. renewed in 1727. A certain Capt. James Stewart's will was proved at Dublin in 1737.

[11] Capt.-Lieut. 12 Jan. 1740.

[12] See p. 203, note 22.

[13] Comn. renewed in 1727. Brigdr. and Lieut. in the 2nd Tp. of Life Guards, 26 Oct. 1738. In 1745 was given the command of several volunteer companies raised in the City of London, for the defence of the Metropolis, and had the rank of Lt.-Col.—*War Office Miscellany Book*, No. 21.

[14] Comn. renewed in 1727. Out before 1740.

[15] Serving as senior Lieut. in 1740.

[16] Out before 1727.

[17] Capt. 4 July, 1723. Comn. renewed in 1727. Serving in 1736.

[18] Out before 1727.

[19] Served in former reign as Capt. in Sir Robert Rich's Regt. of Foot. Half-pay, 1713. Out of Otway's Regt. 4 July, 1723.

[20] Capt. 27 Sept. 1722. Exempt and Capt. 3rd Tp. of Life Guards, 1 Jan. 1732. Major, 26 April, 1740. Lt.-Col. 9 March, 1745. Transferred to the Lt.-Coloneley of the 3rd D.G. in 1746, when the 3rd Tp. of Life Guards was disbanded. Out of 3rd D.G. in 1751.

[21] Comn. renewed in 1727. Out before 1740.

[22] Do.

[23] "Third son of Major Francis Rainsford of 7th Fusiliers (who lost an arm at the siege of Lerida, in Spain, 1707). Thos. Rainsford attained the rank of Lt.-Col. 9th Foot and d. 7 Aug. 1754. Administration of his effects granted 2 May, 1755, to Francis Rainsford, the attorney of Elizabeth his relict, then living at Kinsale in Ireland, by whom he left issue."
—*The Genealogist*, Vol. II., p. 109.

[24] Comn. renewed in 1727.   Out before 1740.

[25] See Vol. I., p. 338, note 3.

[26] *Dabsac* or *Dabzac.*   Comn. renewed in 1727.   Serving in 1736.

[27] Comn. renewed in 1727.   Serving in 1736.

[28]   Do.   do.

[29] Served previously in the Royal Fusiliers.   Serving as Capt. in 9th Foot in 1740. A copy of his will, under date of 1751, is in the Record Office, Dublin.

[30] Comn. renewed in 1727.   Serving in 1736.

[31] Capt. 19 Dec. 1735.   Serving in 1740.

[32] Serving as Lieut. in 1740.

[33] Called "Groves" in 1727 List.   Out before 1740.

[34] See p. 203, note 21.

[35] Served previously as Capt. in Col. Churchill's Dragoons and was placed on half-pay in 1718.   Comn. in Kane's (late Otway's) Regt. renewed in 1727.   Capt. in Col. Battereau's Regt. of Foot in 1742.   Placed on half-pay from said Corps in 1748.

[36] See p. 134, note 1.

[37] Comn. renewed 20 June, 1727.   Out before 1740.

[38] Comns. as Lieut. and Qr.-Mr. renewed 20 June, 1727.

BRIGADIER-GENERAL HENRY GROVE'S REGIMENT OF FOOT.

[10TH FOOT,—THE LINCOLNSHIRE REGIMENT.]

Arthur Taylor,[1] Esq. to be Capt. in room of —— Montand - - - - - -	St. James's, 5 Mar. 1719/20.	c
Alex. Durour,[2] Esq. to be Capt.-Lieut. - -	,, ,, ,, ,,	c
George Langley[3] to be Lieut. to Capt. Scipio Durour - - - - - - -	,, ,, ,, ,,	c
George Preston[4] to be Ens. to do. - - -	,, ,, ,, ,,	c
Hugh Plucknet,[5] Esq. to be Capt. in room of —— Peacock decd. - - - -	,, 27 April, 1720.	c
John Bull[6] to be Ens. to Brigadier Grove's Cy.	,, 6 June, ,,	c
John Burnet[7] to be Lieut. to Capt. Arthur Taylor - - - - - - -	,, 18 Feb. 1720/1.	c
Henry Trepsack,[8] Esq. to be Ens. to [Lt.-Col.] Columbine - - - - - -	,, 22 May, 1721.	c
Scipio Duroure,[9] Esq. to be Major and Capt. of a Cy. - - - - - - -	,, 11 Jan. 1721/2.	c
Alex. Duroure,[2] Esq. to be Capt. of Major Duroure's late Cy. - - - - -	,, ,, ,, ,,	c
Thos. Preston.[10] Esq. to be Capt.-Lieut. - -	,, ,, ,, ,,	c
John Preston[11] to be Lieut. to —— - -	,, ,, ,, ,,	c
Jas. Villettes[12] to be Ens. to —— - - -	,, ,, ,, ,,	c
Wm. Castle,[13] Esq. to be Capt. in room of Henry Poilblanc - - - - -	,, 5 Feb. 1722/3.	c
Jeremy Sambrooke[14] to be Ens. to Capt. [Arthur] Taylor - - - - -	,, 25 ,, ,,	c
Robert Pujolas,[15] Esq. to be Capt. in room of [Samuel] Buller - - - - -	,, 9 Mar. ,,	c
Wilmot Vaughan,[16] Esq. to be Capt. - -	,, 13 April, 1723.	f
Roger Dubize (sic)[17] to be Lieut. to Capt. Pujolas - - - - - - -	,, 8 May, ,,	c
Joseph Phillips[18] to be Ens. to do. - - -	,, ,, ,, ,,	c
John Littlehales[19] to be do. to Capt. Wm. Castle - - - - - - -	,, 17 ,, ,,	c
George Martyn[20] to be do. to —— - -	,, 1 Jan. 1723/4.	c
Henry Vaughan[21] to be Lieut. to [Lt.-Col.] Columbine - - - - - -	,, 16 Mar. ,,	c
Benedict Blagden[22] to be Lieut. to ——	Kensington, 24 July, 1724.	d
John Burnet,[7] Esq. to be Capt. in room of Arthur Taylor - - - - - -	St. James's, 30 Oct. ,,	d
Reginald Harrison,[23] Esq. to be Capt. in room of Robt. Pujolas - - - - -	,, 16 Jan. 1724/5.	d
Roger Lawrence,[24] Esq. to be do. in room of [Reg.] Harrison decd. - - - -	Gohre, 11 Oct. (O.S.) 1725.	d
Capt.-Lieut. Thos. Preston[10] to be Qr.-Mr.	Helvoet Sluys, 25 Dec. ,,	d
Duncan Urquhart[25] to be Ens. to Major-General Henry Grove - - - -	St. James's, 1 Feb. 1725/6.	d
George Doidge[26] to be do. to Capt. —— -	,, 25 Dec. 1726.	d

T

John Sutherland [27] to be do. to Capt. [Wilmot] Vaughan - - - - - - -	St. James's, 25 Dec. 1726.			*d*
Richard Wright,[28] Esq. to be Capt. of an additional Cy. - - - - - -	,,	26 ,,	,,	*d*
John Catesby [29] to be Lieut. to do. - -	,,	,, ,,	,,	*d*
Henry Grove [30] to be Ens. to do. - - -	,,	,, ,,	,,	*d*
Edmond Tichborne,[31] Esq. to be Capt. of an additional Cy.- - - - - - -	,,	,, ,,	,,	*d*
George Martyn [20] to be Lieut. to do. - -	,,	,, ,,	,,	*d*
Robert Rudyerd [32] to be Ens. to do. - -	,,	,, ,,	,,	*d*
Ignatius Molloy [33] to be Lieut. to —— - -	,,	,, ,,	,,	*d*
Wm. Murray [34] to be Ens. to —— - . - -	,,	11 Mar. 1726/7.		*d*

[1] Appointed Lieut. in Col. Philip Honywood's Regt. of Foot, 28 June, 1712. Half-pay, 1713. Left Grove's Regt. in Oct. 1724.

[2] See biog. notice in Vol. I., p. 219, note 26.

[3] Comn. renewed in 1727. D. before 1735, in which year his widow, Mary Langley, was drawing a pension of £20 per annum.

[4] Out before 1727.

[5] See Vol. I., p. 310, note 3.

[6] Out before 1727.

[7] Capt. 30 Oct. 1724. D. before 1735, in which year his widow, Sarah Burnett, was drawing a pension of £26 per annum.

[8] Left the Regt. before 1727.

[9] See reference to this officer and his services in biog. notice of his bro. Alexander in Vol. I., p. 219, note 26.

[10] Qr.-Mr. 25 Dec. 1725. Comn. as Capt.-Lieut. renewed in June, 1727. Out before 1740. He served at Blenheim as a Lieut. in above Regt. and at Malplaquet.

[11] Capt.-Lieut. 21 Dec. 1727. Capt. 13 May, 1735. Serving in 1740.

[12] Lieut. 25 Dec. 1728. Capt.-Lieut. 12 Jan. 1740. Drawing half-pay in 1758 as Capt. in Sir Wm. Pepperell's disbanded Regt.—*Army List*, 1758.

[13] Comn. renewed in 1727. Serving in 1730. Out before 1740.

[14] Comn. renewed in 1727. Not in any subsequent List. He was of Gobions in North Mims, Herts. Succeeded his nephew as 5th Bart. 5 July, 1740. D. unmd. 4 Oct. 1754 when the baronetcy expired. Bd. at North Mims.—G.E.C.'s *Complete Baronetage*.

[15] From half-pay. See his Comn. as Capt. in above Regt. in Vol. I., p. 215. Out of Kane's Regt. in Jan. 1725.

[16] Comn. renewed in 1727. Out before 1740. Succeeded his bro. as 3rd Visct. Lisburne in 1741. D. in 1766 leaving a son who succeeded as 4th Visct.

[17] *Debeze.* Ens. in above Regt. 1 Aug. 1711. Held an appointment under Gen. George Wade in Scotland. Capt. 12 Jan. 1740.

[18] Comn. renewed in 1727. Out before 1740.

[19]   Do.   do.

[20] From Ens. in Col. Egerton's Regt. See p. 310, note 32.

[21] Comn. renewed in 1727. Serving in 1736.

[22] Appointed Ens. in the Rl. Irish Regt. 23 March, 1711. Lieut. 25 April, 1717. Lieut. in an Indep. Cy. in Guernsey, 2 Nov. 1733. Serving with said Cy. in 1740.

[23] From half-pay as Capt. in Gen. Evans's Regt. of Foot. D. before 11 Oct. 1725.

[24] From half-pay Capt. in Elliot's Foot. Not in any subsequent List.

[25] Com. renewed in 1727. Serving in 1736. A certain Capt. Duncan Urquhart's death is recorded in the *Gentleman's Mag.* 1742.

[26] Comn. renewed in 1727. Serving in 1736.

[27]   Do.   do.

[28] From half-pay Capt. Col. Roger Townshend's Regt. of Foot. Half-pay, 1729.

[29] Serving in 1736.

[30] Half-pay, 1729. Probably son of Lt.-Gen. Henry Grove.

[31] Senior Capt. in 1740. He served with above Regt. as an Ens. at Malplaquet.

[32] Serving in 1736.

[33] Untraced after 1730.

[34] Lieut. 13 May, 1735. Serving in 1740.

COLONEL EDWARD MONTAGUE'S REGIMENT OF FOOT.

[11TH FOOT,—THE DEVONSHIRE REGIMENT.]

James Abercrombie,[1] Esq. to be Capt. in
room of [Henry] Downs [killed in
action]- - - - - - Herrenhausen, 3 July, 1719.c
Miles Thomms (sic)[2] to be Lieut. to —— - ,, ,, ,, ,, c
James Warner[3] to be do. to —— - St. James's, 8 Nov. ,, c
James Franks,[4] Esq. to be Capt. in room of
[Ric.] Hartshorn - - - - - ,, 11 Mar. 1719/20.c
Robert Brown[5] to be Lieut. to Lt.-Col.
Lawrence - - - - - - ,, ,, ,, ,, c
Maynard Jenour[6] to be Ens. to Capt. Shug-
borough - - - - - - ,, ,, ,, ,, c
Arnold Tulikens[7] to be Adjt. - - - ,, ,, ,, ,, c
Lancelot Storey[8] to be Ens. to Capt. ——
Milbourne - - - - - ,, ,, ,, ,, c
Leonard Rutter[9] to be do. to —— - - ,, 11 May, 1720.c
Jordan Wren[10] to be do. to Capt. Pat. Max-
well - - - - - - - Herrenhausen, 28 July, ,, c
John Gilby[11] to be do. to Capt. —— - - ,, 21 Sept. ,, c
Henry Domergue,[12] Esq. to be Major and
Capt. of a Cy. - - - - - St. James's, 23 Nov. ,, c
Lewis Dejean,[13] Esq. to be Capt. in room of
Henry Domergue - - - - ,, ,, ,, ,, c
Thos. Goddard[14] to be Lieut. to [Major]
Henry Domergue - - - - ,, ,, ,, ,, c
Eliot Lawrence[15] to be Ens. to [Lt.-Col.]
Herbert Lawrence - - - - ,, ,, ,, ,, c
Chas. Guerin[16] to be Lieut. to —— - - ,, 1 Feb. 1720/1.c
John Petit,[17] Esq. to be Capt. in room of
Henry Spencer - - - - - ,, 15 ,, ,, c
John Twisleton[18] to be Lieut. to —— - ,, 6 July, ,, c
Richard Scott,[19] Esq. to be Capt. in room
of —— Shugborough - - - - Kensington, 6 Sept. ,, c
Leonard Gwyn,[20] Esq. to be do. - - - — 8 Feb. 1721/2.f
Emilius Guerin[21] to be Lieut. to Major
Milburne - - - - - - Kensington, 2 June, 1722.c
James Watts,[22] Esq. to be Capt.-Lieut. - St. James's, 22 ,, ,, c
Arnoldus Tullickins,[7] Esq. to be do. - Kensington, 13 Aug. ,, c
Wm. Lee[23] to be Lieut. to Capt. —— - ,, ,, ,, ,, c
John King[24] to be Ens. to —— - - - ,, ,, ,, ,, c
Lancelot Storey[8] to be Lieut. to Capt. Ric.
Milbourne - - - - - ,, 24 May, 1723.c
Joseph Comes (sic)[25] to be Ens. to do. - ,, ,, ,, ,, c
Richardson Pack,[26] Esq. to be Major and
Capt. of a Cy. - - - - - ,, 28 Jan. 1723/4.c
Ant. Bessière[27] to be Ens. to Capt. [Richard]
Scott - - - - - - - ,, 17 July, 1724.d

T 2

Wm. Lloyd,[28] Esq. to be Capt. in room of Lewis Dejean - - - - -	St. James's, 10 April,	1725.*d*
Thos. Nugent [29] to be Lieut. to Major Pack	Kensington, 7 July,	1726.*d*
Thos. Goddard,[30] Esq. to be Capt. of an additional Cy. - - - - -	St. James's, 26 Dec.	,, *d*
John Westbrook [31] to be Lieut. to do. -	,, ,, ,,	,, *d*
Wm. Acourt (*sic*) [32] to be Ens. to do. -	,, ,, ,,	,, *d*
George Wandesford,[33] Esq. to be Capt. of an additional Cy.- - - - -	,, ,, ,,	,, *d*
John Shorthose [34] to be Lieut. to do. -	,, ,, ,,	,, *d*
[Chas.] Lawrence [35] to be Ens. to do. -	,, ,, ,,	,, *d*
Wm. Daye to be Chaplain - - - -	,, 4 Mar.	1726/7.*d*
Philip Dunbar [36] to be Lieut. to —— -	,, 11 ,,	,, *d*
Fras. Gumbleton [37] to be Ens. to —— -	,, 31 May,	1727.*d*

[1] Appointed Lieut. *en second* in the Earl of Portmore's Regt. of Foot in 1708. Capt. in Sir Charles Hobby's Regt. of Foot in America, 1 April, 1710. Served at the siege and capture of Port Royal, Nova Scotia, in the autumn of 1710. Half-pay, 1713. Served as a volunteer under Gen. Wightman at the action of Glenshiel, in July, 1719, "and was very ill wounded in the head charging with Montague's Regiment" (Letter from Gen. Wightman to Secretary Craggs, 11 June, 1719). Comn. as Capt. in Montague's Regt. renewed in June, 1727. Serving in 1730. Untraced after that year.

[2] *Thomas.* In a letter from Earl Stanhope to Secretary Methuen, from Hanover, the former writes, on "3 July, O.S. 1719," that "His Majesty has been pleased to order a commission to be prepared for Miles Thomas to be a Lieut. [in Montague's Regt.] in the room of Lieut. Granville who lost his life in action." Out of the Regt. before 1727.

[3] Out before 1727.

[4] Adjt. to above Regt. 11 July, 1708. Half-pay as Lieut. in 1713. Comn. as Capt. renewed in 1727. Out before 1740.

[5] Capt.-Lieut. 12 Jan. 1740. Killed at Fontenoy where he served as Capt. in above Corps.

[6] Second son of Sir Maynard *Jenoure*, Bart., of Much Dunmow, Essex. Not in any subsequent List.

[7] Capt.-Lieut. 13 Aug. 1722. Lt.-Col. 11 Oct. 1744. Capt. 5 June, 1733. Wounded at Fontenoy. D. same year.

[8] Lieut. 24 May, 1723. Serving in 1740.

[9] Comn. renewed in 1727. Out before 1740.

[10] Lieut. in Ponsonby's Foot (37th), 2 April, 1734. Served at Dettingen and Fontenoy; also at Culloden where Jordan Wren, then a Captain, won a medal which is still in possession of his representatives. Major of 37th, 26 Dec. 1755. Lt.-Col. 75th Foot, 20 April, 1758. Lt.-Col. 37th Foot, 24 Nov. 1759. Col. 41st Foot, 5 Aug. 1771. Maj.-Gen. 29 Aug. 1777. Lt.-Gen. 19 Feb. 1779. D. in Jan. 1784. He bequeathed his gold Cumberland medal for the battle of Culloden to his nephew, Capt. John C. Ridout, 46th Foot, of Banghurst House, Hants, as next of kin.

[11] Out before 1727.

[12] Capt. in above Regt. 6 April, 1714. Out in Jan. 1724.

[13] See p. 194, note 9.

[14] See Vol. I., p. 300, note 1.

[15] Comn. renewed in 1727. Serving in 1730. Out before 1740.

[16] Capt. 12 Jan. 1740. Major of a newly-raised Regt. 4 Oct. 1745. Half-pay, 1748.

[17] Half-pay, 1729. Drawing half-pay, 1749.

[18] Comn. renewed in 1727. Serving in 1736.

[19] Serving in 1740.

[20] Capt. in Col. Robinson's newly-raised Regt. of Marines, 18 Nov. 1739. Served during the Carthagena expedition. D. 1747.—*Gentleman's Mag.*

[21] Out of the Regt. before 1727.

[22] Do.

[23] Serving as Lieut. in 1740.

[24] Half-pay, 1729. Drawing half-pay as Ens. in 1749.

[25] Lieut. 12 Jan. 1740.

[26] Served in the late reign as Capt. in Lepell's Regt. of Foot. Comn. as Major renewed in 1727. Serving in 1730.

²⁷ From half-pay. Comn. renewed in 1727. His Christian names are given in the Gradation List for 1730 as " Mark Anthony."

²⁸ Not in any subsequent List.

²⁹ Comn. renewed in 1727. Half-pay, 1729.

³⁰ Do.   D. in 1732.

³¹ Do.   Half-pay, 1729.

³² *A'Court.* Attained the rank of Gen. 19 March, 1778, and was appointed Col. of above Regt. (11th), 21 Aug. 1765. D. in 1781. He was son of Pierce A'Court of Ivy Church, co. Wilts., by Eliz. dau. of Wm. Ashe of Heytesbury. After his father's death Wm. A'Court took the additional name of Ashe. He was M.P. for Heytesbury. His eldest son was created a Bart. and his grandson was created Baron Heytesbury in 1828.

³³ This officer's services are stated in the letter given below (see *Stowe MS.*, 247, fol. 19, Brit. Mus.) :—

Hon.rd Sir   Feb.y ye 17—1718/19

I am asham'd to trespass on yr Goodness again, but ye poor half Crown a day, which you Sir at the request of my Nephew Castle-Comer and Sir William Lowther obtain'd for me, being now under consideration, fear I shall (without the continuance of your favour) be put by of it. But least you have Sir forgot my Case, begg leave to represent it as follows. I went at my own Expence and serv'd as Voluntier both by Sea and Land to serve my King and Country during the Irish War; where I not only spent a considerable ffortune as appears by my Lord Castle-Comers Certificate (whose Estate paid it) but by the hardships I expos'd my Self to in sev'ral Seiges quite destroy'd my Health : after that warr was over I got a Captain's post in Sr Roger Bradshaig's Regiment ; and did the duty of Majr for Two Years together ; the Major of the Regiment being then in Prison for Debt ; and after that Regiment was broke Sir, I had for my good services and hardship of having a Younger Capt put Major over my head. Three half Crowns a day allow'd me upon the Establishment of Half Pay till the Year the Parliament allow'd full pay to all : and being reduc'd then from Major to Captain of Invalids, and that Company of Invalids being unfortunately broke Sixteen Months after ; Your Honour (as I shall ever most gratefully acknowledge) had the goodness to represent the hardship of my case to his Majestie at the request of my Nephew Castle-Comer and Sr Willm Lowther, and I thereupon obtain'd Half a Crown a day again, wch I constantly receiv'd tell (sic) this Examination, and all hard Cases (amongst which mine is inserted) being now under consideration and only past as half pay Captain, begg worthy Sir your protection and favour in speaking to my Lord Cadogan or Secratary att Warr, to continue wht you so justly and generously has done for a prson that has ventur'd so farr to serve his King & Country, and would do the same to shew his Gratitude if ever Occasion be for the favour you have confer'd on

Hon.rd Sir
Your most Obedient
and most humble Servt
GEORGE WANDESFORD

[Endorsed :] Maj.r Geo. Wandesford
his Case ————
[Addressed :]   To
The Right Honourable
James Craggs Esq.r
One of his Majesties Secretary's of State.

³⁴ Half-pay, 1729.

³⁵ Half-pay, 1729. Restored to full-pay before 1740, in which year he was serving as senior Ens. in same Regt.

³⁶ Half-pay, 1729.

³⁷ Do.

BRIGADIER-GENERAL THOMAS STANWIX'S REGIMENT OF FOOT.

[12TH FOOT,—THE SUFFOLK REGIMENT.]

Wm. Venner [1] to be Ens. to —— - - -	St. James's, 28 April, 1719.*c*	
John Bowes [2] to be do. to —— - - -	,, 5 Mar. 1719/20.*c*	
Wm. Whitmore,[3] Esq. to be Capt. in room of Fairfax Clement - - - - -	,, 2 June, 1720.*c*	
Jas. Wall [4] to be Ens. to Capt. Jas. Long -	,, 11 ,, ,, *c*	
Jas. Long,[5] Esq. to be Major and Capt. of a Cy.	,, 1 Dec. ,, *c*	
Jeromy (*sic*) Tullie [6] to be Lieut. to —— -	,, 24 ,, ,, *c*	
Arthur Horsman [7] to be Ens. to —— - -	,, 21 June, 1721.*c*	
Chas. Rainsford,[8] Esq. to be Capt.-Lieut. -	,, 5 Dec. ,, *c*	
Edward Phillips,[9] Esq. to be Capt. in room of Chris. Nuttall - - - - - -	,, 11 Jan. 1721/2.*c*	
Robt. Milner [10] to be Lieut. to above Cy. -	,, ,, ,, ,, *c*	
John Cossly [11] to be Adjt. - - - -	,, ,, ,, ,, *c*	
John Gilpine [12] to be Ens. to Major Long -	,, ,, ,, ,, *c*	
Lewis Ormsby,[13] Esq. to be Major and Capt. of a Cy. - - - - -	,, 28 Mar. 1722.*c*	
Fred. Hyde [14] to be Ens. to —— - - -	,, 23 April, ,, *c*	
Edmund Okeden [15] to be Ens. to —— - -	,, 25 Dec. ,, *c*	
Stanwix Nevison [16] to be Ens. to —— - -	,, 4 Feb. 1722/3.*c*	
Morris Goulston [17] to be do. to —— - -	,, 12 April, 1723.*c*	
Wm. Crosbie [18] to be Lieut. to —— - -	,, ,, ,, *c*	
John Knight [19] to be Lieut. to —— - -	Gohre, 13 Oct. ,, *c*	
John Cossley,[11] Esq. to be Capt. in room of Nat. Cossley - - - - -	Hanover, 29 Nov. ,, *c*	
Bernard Gilpin [20] to be Lieut. to —— - -	,, ,, ,, ,, *c*	
Jas. Campbell [21] to be Ens. to —— -	St. James's, 17 Jan. 1723/4.*c*	
Sampson Archer [22] to be Lieut. to —— - -	,, 19 Feb. ,, *c*	
Marsh Hollingworth [23] to be Surgeon - -	,, 2 Nov. 1724.*d*	
Major-General Thos. Whetham [24] to be Colonel in room of Brigadier Thos. Stanwix and Capt. of a Cy. - - - - - -	,, 22 Mar. 1724/5.*d*	
Wm. Watson [25] to be Lieut. to Capt. — Hayes	,, ,, *d*	
Wiltshire Castle [26] to be Lieut. to —— - -	,, 18 Feb. 1725/6.*d*	
John Letton [27] to be Ens. to —— - - -	,, 27 April, 1726.*d*	
Chas. Campbell [28] to be Ens. to —— - -	,, 2 Sept. ,, *d*	
Adam d'Huisseau [29] to be Lieut. to —— -	,, 25 Dec. ,, *d*	
Peter Carew,[30] Esq. to be Capt. of an additional Cy. - - - - - - -	,, ,, ,, ,, *d*	
Wm. Fenton [31] to be Lieut. to do. - -	,, ,, ,, ,, *d*	
—— Newton [32] to be Ens. to do. - -	,, ,, ,, ,, *d*	
Nicholas Masterson,[33] Esq. to be Capt. of an additional Cy. - - - - - -	,, ,, ,, ,, *d*	
John Burnside [34] to be Lieut. to do. - -	,, ,, ,, ,, *d*	
Edmund Wiseman [35] to be Ens. to do. - -	,, ,, ,, ,, *d*	

[1] Comn. renewed in 1727. Appointed 1st Lieut. in Col. Anthony Lowther's Regt. of Marines, 28 Nov. 1739. D. on active service in the West Indies, 1741.—*Gentleman's Mag.*
[2] Not in any subsequent List.

[3] Major, 3 Sept. 1739. Lt.-Col. 30 March, 1742. Killed at Fontenoy.—*Gentleman's Mag.*

[4] Out before 1727.

[5] Lt.-Col. 28 March, 1722. Comn. renewed in 1727. Capt. and Lt.-Col. 1st Foot Guards, 17 Nov. 1731. Col. 55th Foot, 7 Jan. 1741. Col. 4th Marines, 5 Jan. 1743. D. in 1744.

[6] Jerome Tullie. Comn. renewed in 1727. Half-pay, 1729. On half-pay, 1749.

[7] Lieut. in Col. Wm. Egerton's Regt. of Foot, 23 April, 1722. Comn. renewed in 1727. Capt.-Lieut. 31 Aug. 1739. Serving in 1740.

[8] It may be truly said of the Rainsfords that few families can boast of such a lengthy Army service. From the Civil Wars of Charles I. when Henry Rainsford (son and heir of Sir Henry Rainsford of Clifford, and of Combe, Southampton) was in arms against the Parliament, and was made prisoner at Oxford, members of this family have served the Crown continuously from the first year of the British Standing Army (1661) to the present time. Capt.-Lieut. Charles Rainsford of Stanwix's Regt. was eldest son of Major Francis Rainsford, Royal Fusiliers. He was appointed 2nd Lieut. in Col. T. Pownall's Regt. of Marines (aftds. 30th Foot), 24 May, 1705. Half-pay, 1713. Re-commissioned Ens. in Maj.-Gen. Wills's re-formed Regt. of Foot, 25 March, 1715. Capt.-Lieut. as given in the text. Capt. 2 Oct. 1731. Served at Dettingen. Major of Brigade to Marshal Wade in Flanders, 25 March, 1744 (O.S.). Was wounded at Fontenoy. Major of the Tower of London in 1749 and Deputy-Lieut. thereof, 14 Nov. 1750 "as a reward for wounds received in the Low Country Wars." Md. about 1742, Ann dau. of Lt.-Gen. Wm. Barrell, and had issue. D. 6 Feb. 1778. Bd. in St. Peter ad Vincula in the Tower, 13th of same month. His nephew, Gen. Charles Rainsford, was a very distinguished officer during the latter half of the 18th century. There is a full memoir of him in the *Dict. of Nat. Biog.* See also an admirable pedigree of the Rainsford family by Mr. F. V. Rainsford in *The Genealogist*, Vol. II., pp. 105–14.

[9] Killed at Dettingen, where he served as senior Capt.—*Gentleman's Mag.*

[10] Out before 1727.

[11] Capt. 29 Nov. 1723. Major, 30 March, 1742. Served at Fontenoy, where he was wounded. Lt.-Col. 27 May, 1745. Appointed Lt.-Gov. of Chelsea Hospital before 1748. D. as Lt.-Gov. in 1765.

[12] Comn. renewed in 1727. Serving in 1730. Out before 1740.

[13] Joined the Inniskilling Regt. of Foot, 24 April, 1705. Succeeded Col. Long as Lt.-Col. of above Regt. in 1731. D. in 1734.—*Gentleman's Mag.*

[14] Out before 1727.

[15] See p. 323, note 28.

[16] Lieut. 9 April, 1733. Serving in 1740.

[17] *Maurice* Goulston was promoted Lieut. 19 Jan. 1736. Served at Fontenoy as Capt.-Lieut. and was one of the three officers of this Regt. returned as "missing."—*An Authentic List of the Names of all the Officers Kill'd, Wounded, and Missing, at the Battle of Tournay.* London, 1745, price Sixpence.

[18] Comn. renewed in 1727. Serving in 1730. Out before 1740.

[19]   Do.   do.   do.

[20] Capt. of an Indep. Cy. of Foot at Carlisle, 26 Dec. 1738. Serving in 1740.

[21] Lieut. 7 Feb. 1739. Killed at Fontenoy as a Capt. in above Regt.

[22] Capt.-Lieut. 7 Nov. 1739. Believed to have served at Fontenoy. D. in 1754. His will describes him as of Strabane, co. Tyrone, Esq.

[23] Serving in 1727.

[24] See biog. notice in Vol. I., p. 164, note 1.

[25] Serving as senior Lieut. in 1740.

[26] Had served in late reign as 1st Lieut. in Wills's Marines (aftds. 30th Foot). Out of Whetham's (late Stanwix's) Regt. before 1727.

[27] From Pocock's Regt. Comn. as Ens. in Whetham's Regt. renewed in 1727. Not in any subsequent List.

[28] Out before 1727.

[29] Comn. renewed in 1727. Serving in 1730. Out before 1736.

[30] Appointed Ens. in Sir C. Hotham's Regt. 18 Dec. 1711. Half-pay, 1713. Capt. in Sir C. Hotham's new Regt. 19 June, 1716. Serving in 1740 as Capt. in Clayton's Regt. of Foot.

[31] Comn. renewed in 1727. Not in any subsequent List.

[32]   Do.   do.

[33] Had served as a Lieut. in Sir Ric. Temple's Regt. of Foot at the battle of Malplaquet. Half-pay, 1713. Serving in 1730.

[34] Reduced with the Cy. in 1729.

[35] Reduced with the Cy. in 1729. Only son of Sir Edmund Wiseman, Knt. He d. in 1741, leaving issue.

COLONEL STANHOPE COTTON'S REGIMENT OF FOOT.
[13TH FOOT,—THE SOMERSET LIGHT INFANTRY.]

John Severn [1] to be Ens. to Capt. —— -	Herrenhausen,	3 Aug. 1719.	c
Wm. Hargrave,[2] Esq. to be Lt.-Col. and Capt. of a Cy. - - - - - - -	St. James's,	16 April, 1720.	c
Thos. Spateman [3] to be Chaplain - - -	——	27 ,, ,,	c
Chas. Stanhope [4] to be Ens. to —— -	Herrenhausen,	2 Aug. ,,	c
Moses Moreau,[5] Esq. to be Major [and Capt. of a Cy.] - - - - - - - -	Gohre,	13 Oct. ,,	c
David Barry,[6] Esq. to be Capt. in room of —— Dilks	,,	,, ,, ,,	c
James Stewart,[7] Esq. to be do. in room of Wm. Knipe - - - - - -	,,	,, ,, ,,	c
[Jean Janvre] Quinchant,[8] Esq. to be Capt.-Lieut. - - - - - - -	,,	,, ,, ,,	c
[Thos.] Cochain (sic)[9] to be Lieut. to —— -	,,	,, ,, ,,	c
Beaumont Perkins [10] to be Ens. to —— -	,,	,, ,, ,,	c
Wm. Moone [11] to be do. to —— - - -	St. James's,	24 Dec. ,,	c
Simon Little [12] to be Lieut. to Capt. Ben. Hodder	,,	1 May, 1721.	c
Henry Bateman [13] to be do. to Capt. Edmund Webb - - - - - - -	Kensington,	4 Aug. ,,	c
Edmund Uvedall [14] to be Ens. to —— -	St. James's,	25 Dec. ,,	c
Henry Trepsack [15] to be do. to —— - -	,,	22 Dec. 1722.	c
Edward Hopson,[16] Esq. to be Ens. in room of —— - - - - - - -	,,	11 Feb. 1722/3.	c
Boteler Hutchinson [17] to be Ens. to —— -	,,	9 May, 1723.	c
Wm. Piers [18] to be Lieut. to —— - - -	,,	15 Feb. 1723/4.	c
Richard Husbands,[19] Esq. to be Capt. in room of —— Lucy - - - - - -	Windsor,	29 Sept. 1724.	d
Thos. Cardiff [20] to be Lieut. to above Cy. -	St. James's,	27 Oct. ,,	d
Arthur Maynwaring [21] to be Ens. to Lt.-Col. Hargrave - - - - - -	,,	4 Dec. ,,	d
Alex. Cummins [22] to be Lieut. to Capt. David Barry - - - - - - -	,,	10 Jan. 1724/5.	d
Thos. Cockayne [9] to be Adjt. - - - -	,,	21 ,, ,,	d
Chas. Walker,[23] Esq. to be Capt. in room of John Lloyd - - - - - -	,,	3 Feb. ,,	d
Beaumont Parkyns (sic)[10] to be Lieut. to ——	,,	22 ,, ,,	d
George Brodie [24] to be Ens. to —— - -	,,	21 May, 1725.	d
Mark Kerr,[25] Esq. (commonly called Lord Mark Kerr) to be Colonel in room of Col. Stanhope Cotton decd. - - -	Helvoet Sluys,	25 Dec. ,,	d
Jean Janvre Quinchant [8] to be Qr.-Mr. - -	,,	,, ,, ,,	d
John Farie [26] to be Ens. to —— - - -	St. James's,	10 Feb. 1725/6.	d
David Robert Delajonguiere [27] to be Ens. to Capt. Jenkins - - - - - -	,,	24 ,, ,,	d
Samuel Beecher [28] to be Lieut. to Capt. Edmund Webb - - - - -	Kensington,	18 Nov. 1726.	d
George Kerr [29] to be Ens. to Capt. Jas. Cunningham - - - - - -	,,	,, ,, ,,	d
Robt. Fielding [30] to be do. to —— - - -	,,	8 Dec. ,,	d

Wm. Burnet [31] to be Ens. to [Lt.-Col.] Wm.

   Hargrave - - - - - - Kensington, 8 Dec. 1726.*d*

Jean Janvre Quinchant [8] to be Capt. in room

   of Edmund Webb decd. - - - - St. James's, 1 Feb. 1726/7.*d*

James Charlton,[32] Esq. to be Capt.-Lieut. -   ,,   ,, ,,   ,,   *d*

John Hadzor [33] to be Lieut. to —— - -   ,,   ,, ,,   ,,   *d*

George Mackenzie [34] to be Ens. to —— - -   ,,   ,, ,,   ,,   *d*

George Hamilton [35] to be do. to —— - -   ,,   2 ,,   ,,   *d*

Edward Austin to be Qr.-Mr. - - - -   ,,   20 Mar. ,,   *d*

[1] See his Comn. as Cornet in the Royal Dragoons on p. 205, and note 20, p. 206.

[2] See biog. notice in Vol. I., p. 365, note 2.

[3] The *Gentleman's Mag.* for 1761 records the death of the Rev. Mr. Spateman, Vicar of Chiswick.

[4] Out before 1727.

[5] Lt.-Col. of above Regt. 20 Jan. 1736. Serving in 1742. Out of the Army before May, 1744.

[6] Comn. renewed in 1727. Serving in 1730. Out before 1740.

[7] Serving as senior Capt. of above Regt. in 1740.

[8] Capt. 1 Feb. 1727. Killed at Fontenoy.

[9] "Son of Francis *Cokayne* four times Mayor of Derby, by Grace his wife, and younger bro. of Francis Cokayne, Lord Mayor of London, 1750–51. He was bapt. at St. Peter's, Derby, in 1697. Lieut. in Col. Cotton's Foot, 1720. Capt. in Col. Middleton's Foot, July, 1735. Secretary to the Order of the Bath, Aug. 1735. Deputy-Judge-Advocate of the forces ordered to Flanders in April, 1742. Lt.-Col. of Pulteney's Foot (13th), 29 May, 1744, and commanded it at the battle of Culloden in 1746. He md. (settlement, 20 June, 1726) Mary, sister of Sir Wm. Mildmay, Bart. (so created in 1765), by whom he had one son, Thomas Mildmay Cokayne. He d. in London, 2 Oct. 1749, and was bd. at St. Peter's, Derby. Will dated 30 March, 1744, in which he describes himself as 'Lieut.-Colonel of Major-Gen. Pulteney's Regt. of Foot,' proved 25 Oct. 1749 in P.C.C."—(Communicated by the late G. E. Cokayne, Esq., Clarenceux King of Arms, and compiler of G.E.C.'s *Complete Peerage*, and *Complete Baronetage*.)

[10] Lieut. 10 Sept. 1723. Comn. renewed in June, 1727. Not in any subsequent List.

[11] Out before 1727.

[12] Out before 1727. The will of "Simon Little of Lisnanaugh, co. Longford, Gent." was proved at Dublin in 1741.

[13] Out before 1727.

[14] Cornet in Lord Harrington's Dragoons before 1730.

[15] Comn. renewed in 1727. Serving in 1736.

[16] Probably son of the Edward Hopson who was Deputy-Gov. of Southsea Castle in former reign. Comn. renewed in 1727. Out before 1740.

[17] Comn. renewed in 1727. Serving in 1736.

[18] Do. do.

[19] Appointed Capt. in Col. Thos. Alnut's Regt. of Foot, 6 July, 1708. Half-pay, 1713. Serving in Lord Mark Kerr's Regt. in 1727. Not in said Regt. in 1740. Appears to have belonged to the family of Sir Samuel Husbands of Shalford.

[20] Comn. renewed in 1727. Out before 1740.

[21] See p. 219, note 22.

[22] D. before 1735, in which year his widow, Ann *Cuming*, was drawing a pension of £20 per annum.

[23] Serving in 1740.

[24] See p. 215, note 19.

[25] See biog. notice in Vol. I., p. 356, note 1.

[26] Lieut. 20 Sept. 1735. Serving in 1740.

[27] Lieut. 20 Jan. 1736. Serving in 1740.

[28] Serving in 1740 as Lieut.

[29] Comn. renewed in 1727. Serving in 1736.

[30] Untraced after June, 1727.

[31] Lieut. 25 Jan. 1738. Serving in 1740.

[32] Capt. 7 May, 1729. Serving in 1740.

[33] Serving in 1740.

[34] Lieut. 19 Jan. 1740.

[35] Comn. renewed 20 June, 1727. Out before 1740.

COLONEL JASPER CLAYTON'S REGIMENT OF FOOT.

[14TH FOOT,—THE PRINCE OF WALES'S OWN (WEST YORKSHIRE) REGIMENT.]

This Regiment was on service in Scotland during the years 1716–19. It was sent to Gibraltar in the winter of 1726–27, and took part in the defence of that fortress.

John Hunt[1] to be Ens. to Capt. Henry Harrison	St. James's,	2 Feb. 1715/6.*b*	
Thos. Phillips[2] to be Lieut. to Capt. ——	,,	29 Mar. ,, *b*	
Patrick Miller[3] to be Ens. to Capt. —— Hales	,,	26 June, ,, *b*	
—— Bray[4] to be Lieut. to Capt. Barlo (*sic*) -	,,	,, ,, ,, *b*	
John Laforey,[5] Esq. to be Capt. in room of —— Hales	,,	14 July, ,, *b*	
Andrew Simpson[6] to be Lieut. to Capt. ——	,,	24 April, 1717.*b*	
Thos. Adair[7] to be Ens. to Capt. [Henry] Harrison	,,	6 June, ,, *b*	
Daniel Cole[8] to be Ens. to Lt.-Col. Kendall	Hampton Court, 4 Aug. ,, *b*		
Richard Sinnet (*sic*)[9] to be Lieut. to Capt.——	,,	26 Oct. ,, *b*	
James Sinnet (*sic*)[10] to be Ens. to do. -	,,	,, ,, ,, *b*	
James Reading,[11] Esq. to be Lt.-Colonel	St. James's, 14 Feb. 1717/8.*b*		
Robert Moore,[12] Esq. to be Capt. of the Grenadier Company in room of Wm. Jones	,,	,, ,, ,, *c*	
Wm. Jones,[13] Esq. to be Major [and Capt. of a Cy.]	,,	,, ,, ,, *c*	
John Cassell[14] to be Lieut. to Capt. Robt. Moore	,,	13 Mar. ,, *c*	
Peregrine Thos. Hobson,[15] Esq. to be Capt. of that Company whereof —— Barton was Capt.	,,	3 April, 1718.*c*	
James Hunt[16] to be Lieut. to Capt. —— Monk	Kensington, 18 July, ,, *c*		
Edmund Wright,[17] Esq. to be Capt. in room of Mat. Lafitt	,,	,, ,, ,, *c*	
George Highington (*sic*),[18] Esq. to be Capt.-Lieut.	,,	,, ,, ,, *c*	
Wm. Jones[19] to be Lieut. to Major Jones	Hampton Court, 22 Aug. ,, *c*		
Bassill (*sic*) Carty[20] to be Ens. to Capt. Ant. Welsh	,,	,, ,, ,, *c*	
John Cassell[14] to be Adjt. -	St. James's, 29 Jan. 1718/9.*c*		
James Maidman[21] to be Ens. to Capt. —— -	,,	11 Mar. ,, *c*	
Wm. Hele[22] to be do. to Capt. —— -	,,	24 May, 1719.*c*	
John Laforey,[5] Esq. to be Major and Capt. of a Cy.	,,	23 May, 1720.*c*	
Charles Strahan,[23] Esq. to be Capt. in room of John Laforey	,,	,, ,, ,, *c*	
Thos. Littleton,[24] Esq. to be Capt. in room of —— Harrison	Gohre,	13 Oct. ,, *c*	

John Scrivener [25] to be Lieut. to Capt. Chas.
   Strahan - - - - - - St. James's, 5 Mar. 1720/1.*c*
John Wiate (*sic*) [26] to be Ens. to Capt. Stanley
   Monk - - - - - - ,, 26 May, 1721] *c*
[George Heighington [18] to be Capt. - - ,, 26 May, 1721]
Thos. Baylies [27] to be Ens. to Capt. [Chas.]
   Strahan - - - - - ,, ,, ,, ,, *c*
John Bell [28] to be Ens. to —— - - - ,, 15 Jan. 1721/2.*c*
James Stewart, [29] Esq. to be Capt. in room of
   [Thos.] Littleton - - - - - ,, 9 May, 1722.*c*
Joshua Marshall [30] to be Ens. to [Capt. George]
   Heighington - - - - - ,, 12 Jan. 1722/3.*c*
Alex. Grossart [31] to be do. to —— - - ,, 18 Mar. ,, *c*
John Wiseman [32] to be Ens. to [Major] Robt.
   Reading - - - - - - ,, 11 Oct. 1723.*c*
Mat. Loo (*sic*) [33] to be Lieut. to Capt. George
   Heighington - - - - - - ,, 24 Mar. 1723/4.*c*
Ezekiel Jefferys [34] to be Lieut. to —— - Kensington, 12 June, 1724.*d*
Jasper Clayton [35] [Jun.] to be Ens. to —— - Windsor, 25 Sept. ,, *d*
Thos. Tempest, [36] Esq. to be Capt. in room of
   Jas. Stewart - - - - - - ,, 8 Oct. ,, *d*
John Gough, [37] Esq. to be Capt. in room of
   Ant. Walsh - - - - - - St. James's, 21 May, 1725.*d*
Fras. Lind [38] to be Surgeon - - - - ,, 3 May, 1726.*d*
George Archibald, Earl of Dumbarton [39] to be
   Lt.-Col. and Capt. of a Cy. - - - Kensington, 24 June, ,, *d*
Mark Jarland [40] to be Lieut. to Capt. Thos.
   Tempest - - - - - - St. James's, 8 Sept. ,, *d*
Isaac Gignoux, [41] Esq. to be Capt. of an
   additional Cy. - - - - - ,, 26 Dec. ,, *d*
Wm. Jameson [42] to be Lieut. to do. - - ,, ,, ,, ,, *d*
Peter Hawker [43] to be Ens. to do. - - ,, ,, ,, ,, *d*
George Malcolm, [44] Esq. to be Capt. of an
   additional Cy. - - - - ,, ,, ,, ,, *d*
Jasper Clayton [35] [Jun.] to be Lieut. to do. - ,, ,, ,, ,, *d*
John Campbell [45] to be Ens. to do. - - ,, ,, ,, ,, *d*
Thos. Lynn [46] to be do. to Capt. —— - - ,, ,, ,, ,, *d*

[1] Out 6 June, 1717.
[2] Out before 1727.
[3] Serving as Lieut. in same Regt. 1730.
[4] Out before 1727.
[5] The above Comn. entry, given in W.O. Entry Book, erroneously gives "to be Major in Col. Egerton's Regt. of Foot." See biog. notice of John Laforey in Vol. I., p. 149, note 5.
[6] Capt. 11 March, 1736. Serving as Capt. in 1740.
[7] Out before 1727.
[8] Comn. renewed in 1727.
[9] *Sinnot.* Promoted from Ens. Not in any subsequent List.
[10] Out before 1727.
[11] See Vol. I., p. 340, note 4.
[12] Major, 3 Aug. 1727. Lt.-Col. 3 Jan. 1739. Serving in 1742. Out of the Army before 17 Feb. 1746.
[13] D. or left the Regt. in the spring of 1720.
[14] Adjt. 29 Jan. 1719. Serving as Lieut. and Adjt. in 1730.
[15] *Hopson.* Appointed 2nd Lieut. in Lord Shannon's Marines, 25 Jan. 1703. 2nd Lieut

of Grendrs. 13 Nov. 1711. Resigned his Comn. on appointment as Ens. 3rd Foot Guards, 25 April, 1712. Major of Clayton's Regt. 3 Jan. 1739. Lt.-Col. Lord H. Beauclerk's Regt. (48th), 30 Feb. 1741. Transferred to Fuller's Regt. (29th), 1 April, 1743. Gov. of Cape Breton in March, 1748. Col. of 29th Foot, 9 June, 1748. Gov. and C.-in-C. of the Forces in Nova Scotia, 4 March, 1752. Col. 40th Foot, 4 March, 1754. Maj.-Gen. 15 Feb. 1757. Commander of an Expedition against Martinique and Guadeloupe in 1758. D. at the latter island, 27 Feb. 1759.

[16] Comn. renewed in 1727. D. before 1735, in which year his widow was drawing a pension of £20 per annum.

[17] Comn. renewed in 1727. Out before 1740.

[18] *Heighington.* Capt. 26 May, 1721. Major, 22 June, 1745. Out before 1756. Will proved at Dublin in 1757.

[19] Appointed Capt. in 13th Foot, 9 Oct. 1749. D. in 1768 as retd. Lt.-Col. of said Corps.— *Gentleman's Mag.*

[20] Comn. renewed in 1727. Not in any subsequent List.

[21] Out before 1727.

[22] See his Comn. as Lieut. in Pearce's Foot on p. 285, note 17.

[23] Comn. renewed in 1727. Serving in 1736.

[24] Out in May, 1722. Possibly Thos. Lyttleton. Lieut. in Shannon's Marines in former reign.

[25] Serving as senior Lieut. of above Corps in 1740.

[26] Out before 1727.

[27] Comn. renewed in June, 1727. Capt.-Lieut. 26 Dec. 1755. Serving in 1758.

[28] Lieut. 5 April, 1732. Major, 13 Dec. 1755. Serving in 1758.

[29] D. before 1734, in which year his widow, "Eleanor Stewart," was drawing a pension of £26 per annum.

[30] Comn. renewed in June, 1727. Serving in 1736.

[31] Do. do.

[32] Out before 1727.

[33] Called "Lowe" in List of Clayton's Regt. for June, 1727. Not in any subsequent List.

[34] See Vol. I., p. 169, note 5.

[35] Son of Lt.-Gen. Jasper Clayton of Fernhill, Berkshire. Capt. 13 June, 1734. Serving in 1740.

[36] Comn. renewed in June, 1727. D. before April, 1732, when his widow, Victoria Tempest, was in receipt of a pension of £26 per annum.

[37] Serving as Capt. in 1740.

[38] Comn. renewed in 1727. Serving as Surgeon in 1755.

[39] See biog. notice in Vol. I., p. 168, note 2.

[40] Comn. renewed in June, 1727. Serving in 1736. Out before 1740.

[41] Served at Almanza as Capt. in Col. De Nassau d'Auverquerque's Regt. of French Foot, and was taken prisoner. Half-pay, 1712. Capt. in Col. Dubourgay's Regt. 22 July, 1715. Comn. in Clayton's Regt. renewed in 1727. Capt. of a Cy. of Invalids at Carlisle, 31 Jan. 1736. D. in 1752.

[42] Comn. renewed in 1727. Out before 1740.

[43] Only son of Col. Peter Hawker, Lt.-Gov. of Portsmouth. Appointed Cornet 1st Tp. of Life Guards, 26 Dec. 1732. Brigdr. and Lieut. 14 June, 1737. Capt. in 1740. Of Long Parish House, Hants. See Burke's *Landed Gentry.*

[44] Half-pay, 1729. Capt. in 3rd Foot, 23 April, 1730. Serving in 1740.

[45] Comn. renewed in 1727. Out before 1740.

[46] Comn. as Ens. to the Colonel's Cy. renewed in June, 1727. Out before 1740.

COLONEL HENRY HARRISON'S REGIMENT OF FOOT.

[15TH FOOT,—THE EAST YORKSHIRE REGIMENT.]

This Corps was in Scotland during George I.'s reign and the early part of that of George II. Detachments were employed by General Wade in making roads through the Highlands.

Thos. Levett[1] to be Lieut. to Capt. John Pretty - - - - -	St. James's, 18 Feb.	1718/9.	c
Anthony Ligonier,[2] Esq. to be Major and Capt. of a Cy. - - - -	,, 21 Mar.	,,	c
Hugh Mackay[3] to be Ens. to Capt. How's Cy. -	Herrenhausen, 29 July,	,,	c
David Duncan[4] to be Chaplain - - -	Gohre, 19 Sept.	,,	c
Thos. Levett,[1] Esq. to be Capt. in room of Wm. Halliday - - - - -	St. James's, 30 April,	1720.	c
George Sharpless[5] to be Lieut. to above Cy.	,, ,, ,,	,,	c
Sebastian Jassen[6] to be Ens. to Capt. —— Legg - - - - - -	,, ,, ,,	,,	c
Thos. Chamberlain[7] to be Ens. to Capt. [John] Pretty - - - - -	,, 21 May,	,,	c
Wm. Strachy,[8] Esq. to be [1st] Lieut. to Capt. Jas. Whiston's Grendr. Cy. -	,, ,, ,,	,,	c
David Chapeau[9] to be Lieut. to Capt. Ant. Ligonier - - - - -	,, ,, ,,	,,	c
George Martin,[10] Esq. to be Capt. in room of Richard Legg - - - - -	,, 28 Nov.	,,	c
James Urquhart[11] to be Lieut. to Capt. Wm. How - - - - -	,, 12 May,	1721.	c
Simon Loftus,[12] Esq. to be Capt. in room of Thos. Levett - - - - -	,, 3 June,	,,	c
Richard Onslow,[13] Esq. to be Capt. in room of Wm. Tracy - - - - -	,, 10 Nov.	,,	c
Fras. Masham[14] to be Ens. to Capt. George Master - - - - - -	,, 30 May,	1722.	c
Robert Frazer (sic),[15] Esq. to be Capt. in room of John Laye - - - -	,, 7 Mar.	1722/3.	c
Charles Crosbie,[16] Esq. to be Capt.-Lieut. -	,, ,, ,,	,,	c
John Wilbraham[17] to be Lieut. to Capt. Ant. Ligonier - - - - -	,, ,, ,,	,,	c
Walter Warburton[18] to be Ens. to the Colonel's Cy. - - - - -	,, ,, ,,	,,	c
Richard Strachey[19] to be do. to Capt. Ric. Onslow - - - - - -	,, ,, ,,	,,	c
George Harman[20] to be Lieut. to ——	Herrenhausen, 13 July,	1723.	c
Lewis Marcell[21] to be Ens. to Capt. John Pretty - - - - - -	St. James's, 1 Jan.	1723/4.	c
Richard Delamarr[22] to be Lieut. to do. -	,, 19 Feb.	,,	c
Wm. Cau[l]field[23] to be Ens. to the Colonel's Cy. - - - - - - -	,, 4 Mar.	,,	c

Nicholas Skinner [24] to be Lieut. to —— - St. James's, 4 Mar.   1723/4. *c*
Robt. Carpenter,[25] Esq. to be Capt. in room
    of Jas. Whiston decd. - - - -   ,,   29 Oct.   1724. *d*
John Grant [26] to be Ens. to Capt. George
    Grant - - - - - - - -   ,,   25 Nov.   ,,   *d*
Jerome Bellingham [27] to be Ens. to Capt.
    Robt. Frazer - - - - - Helvoet Sluys, 25 Dec. 1725. *d*
Wm. Strachey [8] to be Adjt. - - - St. James's, 17 Mar. 1725/6. *d*
Edward Hawley,[28] Esq. to be Capt. in room
    of George Martin - - - - -   ,,   7 April, 1726. *d*
Robt. Thompson,[29] Esq. to be Capt. in room
    of Robt. Carpenter - - - -   ,,   25 Dec.   ,,   *d*
Thos. Levett,[1] Esq. to be Capt.-Lieut. -   ,,   ,, ,,   ,,   *d*
Thos. King [30] to be Lieut. to —— - -   ,,   ,, ,,   ,,   *d*
John Maitland [31] to be Ens. to —— - -   ,,   ,, ,,   ,,   *d*
Andrew Pringle [32] to be do to —— - -   ,,   ,, ,,   ,,   *d*
John Martindale,[33] Esq. to be Capt. of an
    additional Cy. - - - - -   ,,   26 ,,   ,,   *d*
John Charlton [34] to be Lieut. to do. - -   ,,   ,, ,,   ,,   *d*
John Morris [35] to be Ens. to do. - - -   ,,   ,, ,,   ,,   *d*
Henry Delaune,[36] Esq. to be Capt. of an
    additional Cy. - - - - -   ,,   ,, ,,   ,,   *d*
John Bell [37] to be Lieut. to do. - - -   ,,   ,, ,,   ,,   *d*
Chas. Bradshaigh [38] to be Ens. to do. - -   ,,   ,, ,,   ,,   *d*
Kingsley Robinson [39] to be Ens. to —— -   ,,   9 Mar. 1726/7. *d*

[1] Capt. 30 April, 1720. Resigned in June, 1721. Appointed Capt.-Lieut. 25 Dec. 1726. Comn. renewed in 1727. Serving in 1736. Out before 1740.

[2] Served previously as Capt. in Windress's Regt. (37th Foot). D. before 1735, in which year his widow, Mary Ligonier, was drawing a pension of £30 per annum.

[8] Served as a volunteer under Gen. Wightman at the action of Glenshiel in June, 1719, and for his gallantry was awarded £100 bounty money by His Majesty's orders, "for good services against the rebels in the late action" (*Treasury Papers* under date of 13 July, 1719). Was recommended for an Ensign's Comn. by the Lords Justices in the King's absence from England. Appointed Capt. in Col. Oglethorpe's Regt. of Foot (Georgia Rangers) at its raising in Aug. 1737. Serving in 1740.

[4] Serving in 1727.

[5] Appointed Ens. in above Regt. 23 Feb. 1711. Capt.-Lieut. 11 Jan. 1740. Served with his Regt. at Carthagena in 1741, and lost his life before Fort Lazar.

[6] Not in any subsequent List.

[7] Out of the Regt. before 1727.

[8] Adjt. 17 March, 1726. Comns. renewed in June, 1727. D. during the Carthagena expedition, where he served as Capt. in Harrison's Regt.

[9] See p. 220, note 34.

[10] Served previously as Lieut. in Gen. Sankey's Foot (39th). Capt. in the Rl. Irish Regt. 24 April, 1726. Serving in 1740 in Minorca.

[11] Comn. renewed in 1727. A certain James Urquhart was appointed Capt. in Col. Wyniard's Marines, 24 Nov. 1739, and d. on active service during the Carthagena expedition, 1741.

[12] Major, 10 Dec. 1739. Accompanied above Regt. on the expedition to Carthagena in 1741, and was wounded when serving as Lt.-Col. of same Corps. D. from the effects of said wound. (Communicated by Sir T. Fraser, K.C.B.) The will of "Hannah Loftus widow of Lt.-Col. Simon Loftus" was proved at Dublin in 1762.

[13] See biog. notice in Vol. I., p. 221, note 44.

[14] See p. 213, note 33.

[15] Col. Robert Fraser of Cuba House, Banagher. Robert Fraser was the fourth son of George ffrissell or Fraser of Parke, in the King's County, Esq. He was born *circa* 1690. Commissioned Ens. on 24 April, 1708. His Comn. as Lieut. in the 15th Foot was signed by Marlborough at St. James's on 30 Dec. 1710. He served under him from

1708 to 1711, and in 1712 under the Duke of Ormond. Became Capt.-Lieut. on 17 Sept. 1718, and Capt. 17 March, 1723, in the 15th Foot. Was aftds. Lt.-Col. to Col. Lowther's 3rd Marine Battalion in 1739. Raised large numbers of men in King's County for this Battalion. Sailed with expedition to Carthagena in 1740–1, and to Cuba in July, 1741. In June, 1741, succeeded Col. Robinson in command of the 2nd Marine Battalion. Returned with the expedition when it went home in 1742. Marine Battalions reduced in 1749, but the officers remained on half-pay. In 1750 "The Honourable" Col. R. Fraser became Military Governor of Kinsale and Fort Charles, and died in that command in 1753/4. He built Cuba House outside Banagher, and owned large estates in King's County and in Galway. He died unmarried. His nephew Col. George Fraser succeeded him.—(Communicated by Maj.-Gen. Sir Thomas Fraser, K.C.B.)

[16] See Vol. I., p. 302, note 5.

[17] Comn. renewed in June, 1727. Out before 1740.

[18] Out before 1727.

[19] Do.

[20] See p. 210, note 20.

[21] Comn. renewed in 1727. Out before 1740.

[22] Called "Delamere" in Gradation List, 1727.

[23] Comn. renewed in 1727. See biog. notice on p. 16, note 2.

[24] See his Comn. as Ens. in Pearce's Regt. on p. 283. Comn. as Lieut. renewed in 1727. Serving in 1730. D. before 1735, in which year his widow, Barbara Skinner, was drawing a pension of £20 per annum.

[25] See his Comn. as Capt. in Lord Carpenter's Regt. of Dragoons on p. 209, and note thereto.

[26] Comn. renewed in 1727. Lieut. 6 June, 1733. Serving in 1740.

[27] Do. Serving in 1730. Out before 1740.

[28] See references to Edward Hawley's parentage and early Comns. on pp. 41 and 42. After serving some years in the Cavalry he was appointed Capt. in the Rl. Irish Regt. 24 Dec. 1720. Exchanged to Harrison's Regt. in April, 1726, with Capt. George Martin, as named in the text. D. before 1735, in which year his widow, Elizabeth Hawley, was drawing a pension of £26 per annum. From a letter written by Lt.-Gen. Hawley to Marshal Wade, in 1744, quoted on p. 44, it is stated that both Gen. Hawley's brothers "were killed in the service."

[29] Serving as senior Capt. in 1740.

[30] Comn. renewed in 1727. Serving in 1730. Out before 1740.

[31] Lieut. 2 Jan. 1736. Killed before Carthagena in 1741.

[32] Lieut. 23 April, 1736. D. during the Carthagena expedition in 1741, where he served as Capt. in above Corps.

[33] Half-pay, 1729. His name is given in the *Half-Pay List*, 1739, as *Markenddle*, and it is stated that he "was provided for in Ireland, 1733."

[34] Half-pay, 1729.

[35] Lieut. 12 Jan. 1740. D. during the Carthagena expedition, 1741.

[36] Lt.-Col. 6th Marines, 15 May, 1741. Served during the Carthagena expedition. Retd. in 1746. D. same year. His will proved at Dublin in 1746, describes him as "formerly Lt.-Col. of Marines."

[37] See Vol. I., p. 302, note 8.

[38] Comn. renewed in 1727. Second son of Col. Sir Roger Bradshaigh, Bart. Appointed Exempt and Capt. 3rd Tp. of Life Guards, 12 Dec. 1738. Reduced with the Troop in 1746 and pensioned. Living in 1758.

[39] Half-pay, 1729.

COLONEL JOHN CHOLMLEY'S REGIMENT OF FOOT.

[16TH FOOT,—THE BEDFORDSHIRE REGIMENT.]

John Whiting,[1] Esq. to be Capt. in room of [John] Smelt - - - - -	St. James's, 15 Oct.	1720.	c
Wm. Mackreth,[2] Esq. to be Capt.-Lieut. -	,, ,, ,,	,,	c
George Richardson[3] to be Lieut. to Capt. Chas. Weddell - - - - -	,, ,, ,,	,,	c
Wm. Whiting[4] to be Ens. to [Major] Sam. Sleigh - - - - - -	,, ,, ,,	,,	c
George Collingwood[5] to be Adjt. - -	,, ,, ,,	,,	c
Fras. Bushell,[6] Esq. to be Capt. in room of George Heigham - - - -	,, 24 Dec.	,,	c
Chas. Maydman[7] to be Lieut. to Capt. Wm. Hook - - - - - -	,, 2 Feb.	1720/1.	c
Fenwick Dormer[8] to be do. to —— -	,, 14 June,	1721.	c
Edmund Naish[9] to be do. to Capt. Fras. Bushell - - - - -	,, 24 ,,	,,	c
Edward Fisher[10] to be do. to —— -	,, 16 Dec.	,,	c
Fras. Appleyard,[11] Esq. to be Capt. in room of —— Chiesly - - - -	Kensington, 22 Aug.	1722.	c
Walter Devereux[12] to be Lieut. to Capt. —— - - - - - -	,, ,, ,,	,,	c
Alex. Durham[13] to be do. to Capt. —— -	,, 4 Sept.	,,	c
James Erskine[14] to be Ens. to —— -	,, ,, ,,	,,	c
Chas. Draper[15] to be do. to —— -	St. James's, 9 Nov.	,,	c
[The Hon.] Charles Ingram,[16] Esq. to be Capt. in room of Fras. Appleyard -	,, 8 Feb.	1723/4.	c
Henry, Earl of Deloraine[17] to be Col. in room of John Cholmley and Capt. of a Cy. - - - - - -	,, 27 April,	1724.	d
George Cooke,[18] Esq. to be Capt. in room of Shugborough Whitney - - -	,, 28 ,,	,,	d
Richard Wenman[19] to be Lieut. to Capt. Weddell - - - - -	Kensington, 6 June,	,,	d
Henry Wroth[20] to be Lieut. to Capt. Fras. Bushell - - - - -	St. James's, 9 Sept.	1726.	d
James Draper[21] to be Ens. to —— -	,, 25 Dec.	,,	d
John Chalmers,[22] Esq. to be Capt. in room of [Fras.] Bushell - - - -	,, ,, ,,	,,	d
Sir Wm. Fleming,[23] Bt. to be Ens. to —— -	,, ,, ,,	,,	d
Peter Campbell[24] to be Ens. to —— -	,, ,, ,,	,,	d
Jacob Peachel[25] to be Capt. of an additional Cy. - - - - - - -	,, 26 ,,	,,	d
Richard Foley[26] to be Lieut. to do. - -	,, ,, ,,	,,	d
Wm. Good[27] to be Ens. to do. - - -	,, ,, ,,	,,	d
Wm. Wyvill,[28] Esq. to be Capt. of an additional Cy. - - - - -	,, ,, ,,	,,	d
John Ross[29] to be Lieut. to do. - - -	,, ,, ,,	,,	d
Mat. Reynolds[30] to be Ens. to do. - -	,, ,, ,,	,,	d

[1] Appointed Ens. in Lt.-Gen. Erle's Regt. in 1704. Lieut. 7 May, 1708. Wounded at Malplaquet. Capt.-Lieut. Durell's Regt. (16th), 31 Oct. 1712. Comn. renewed in 1727. Serving in 1737. Out before 1740.

[2] Ens. in above Regt. 1 June, 1702. Fought at Blenheim and was wounded. Lieut. 29 June, 1705. Fought at Malplaquet and was again wounded. Comn. as Capt.-Lieut. renewed in 1727. Serving in 1730. Out before 1740.

[3] Capt. 12 Jan. 1740.

[4] Lieut. 12 Sept. 1734. Serving in 1740.

[5] Capt. 12 Sept. 1734. Do.

[6] See his Comn. on p. 209. This officer commanded the detachment of above Regt. which helped to suppress the riot at Glasgow in the summer of 1725. Among the *S.P.D. George I.* at the Public Record Office is a copy of a letter from Mr. Charles Delafaye, Secretary to the Principal Secretary of State, to Mr. Hume Campbell, Deputy-Keeper of the Signet in Scotland, relative to " the indictment of Captain Bushell and other officers who suppressed the riot at Glasgow " (bundle 59). Delafaye refers to this indictment as " a very bold step." Capt. in Lord Carpenter's Dragoons, 25 Dec. 1726. Half-pay, 1729.

[7] Serving in 1730. Out before 1740.

[8] Capt. 23 April, 1736. Serving in 1740.

[9] Not in any subsequent List.

[10] Do.

[11] Served in late reign as Capt. in Sir Roger Bradshaigh's Regt. of Foot. Half-pay, 1712. Out of Cholmley's Regt. 8 Feb. 1724. The *Gentleman's Mag.* records the death of Francis Appleyard, Receiver-General of the North Riding of Yorkshire in 1747.

[12] Capt.-Lieut. 12 Jan. 1740.

[13] Comn. renewed in 1727. Serving in 1730. Out before 1740.

[14] See his Comn. in Campbell's Dragoons on p. 207.

[15] See his Comn. in Honywood's Dragoons on p. 221.

[16] See biog. notice on p. 274, note 10.

[17] See do. in Vol. I., p. 100, note 1.

[18] Comn. renewed in 1727. D. before 1735, in which year his widow, Anna Sophia *Cook*, was drawing a pension of £26 per annum.

[19] See his Comn. on p. 197, and note thereto.

[20] Served previously in the Royal Horse Guards. Lieut. in aid Corps, 23 June, 1715. Comn. in Lord Deloraine's Regt. of Foot renewed in 1727. Serving in 1730.

[21] Comn. renewed in 1727. Serving in 1730. Out before 1740.

[22] Served in late reign as Lieut. in Col. Grant's Regt. of Foot. Half-pay, 1729.

[23] Lieut. 12 Jan. 1740. " Presumably son of Sir Archibald Fleming, Bart. Bapt. 28 Dec. 1699. D.s.p. at Elgin, 25 Nov. 1746. The family estate was Farme in Rutherglen, co. Glasgow."—G.E.C.'s *Complete Baronetage.*

[24] Lieut. 7 Feb. 1739.

[25] From half-pay Capt. in Col. Wm. Stanhope's Regt. of Foot. Half-pay, 1729. D. in 1750. Will proved at Dublin.

[26] Half-pay, 1729. Appointed Capt. in Anstruther's Regt. (26th), 27 Dec. 1738. Serving in 1740. The *Gentleman's Mag.* for 1778 records the death of Capt. Richard Foley of Newent, Gloucestershire.

[27] Half-pay, 1729.

[28] Appointed Capt. in Col. James Butler's Regt. of Foot, 12 Dec. 1711. Serving as Capt. in Lord Deloraine's Regt. in 1730. Probably eldest son of D'Arcy Wyvill, second son of Sir Wm. Wyvill, Bart.

[29] Half-pay, 1729.

[30] Do.

THE ROYAL REGIMENT OF FOOT OF IRELAND.
[18TH FOOT,—THE ROYAL IRISH REGIMENT.]

This Regiment was at Minorca during the reign of George I.

James Ford [1] to be Ensign - - - -	St. James's, 24 April, 1719.*c*
[John] Montague,[2] Esq. to be Lt.-Col. [and Capt. of a Cy.] - - - - -	,, 20 Nov. ,, *c*
Wm. Sharman [3] to be Capt. in room of Henry Wingfield - - - - -	,, ,, ,, ,, *c*
Thos. Smart to be Chaplain - - - -	,, 12 April, 1720.*c*
Wm. Whitmore [4] to be Lieut. to —— - -	,, ,, ,, ,, *c*
Alex. Cosby [5] to be Ens. to —— - - -	,, 6 June, ,, *c*
Ant. Pujolas,[6] Esq. to be Major [and Capt. of a Cy.] - - - - - - -	,, 8 ,, ,, *c*
John Petit,[7] Esq. to be Capt. in room of —— d'Offranville - - - - -	,, ,, ,, ,, *c*
John Kernhen [8] to be Surgeon - - -	,, 13 Dec. ,, *p*
Edward Hawley,[9] Esq. to be Capt. in room of Robt. Tripp - - - - - -	,, 24 ,, ,, *c*
Robert Tripp [10] [Jun.] to be Ens. to Capt. ——	,, ,, ,, ,, *c*
Peter Laprimaudaye [11] to be Lieut. to Capt. John Petit - - - - - -	,, ,, ,, ,, *c*
Peter Petit [12] to be Capt. of John Petit's late Cy. - - - - - - -	,, 4 Feb. 1720/1.*c*
James Reitfield [13] to be Lieut. to —— - -	,, 28 Dec. 1721.*c*
Peter Guerin [14] to be Ens. to —— - - -	,, 17 April, 1722.*c*
Do. to be Qr.-Mr. - - - - - -	,, ,, ,, *c*
Ralph Cooke [15] to be Ens. to —— - -	Kensington, 4 June, ,, *c*
Ben. Gardiner [16] to be do. to Capt. —— -	,, 10 July, ,, *c*
Robt. Griffith [17] to be do. to —— - -	St. James's, 18 Feb. 1722/3.*c*
Abr. Pinchinat [18] to be Lieut. to —— -	Gohre, 9 Nov. 1723.*c*
John Dalbos [19] to be Lieut. to —— -	Kensington, 22 June, 1724.*d*
Chas. Nicholson [20] to be Adjt.- - - -	,, 4 July, ,, *d*
Robt. Sterling [21] to be Ens. to —— - -	,, 11 ,, ,, *d*
John Dobben [22] to be Lieut. to —— -	St. James's, 17 Dec. ,, *d*
Ant. Bissiere,[23] Esq. to be Capt. in room of Peter Petit - - - - - -	,, 27 May, 1725.*d*
Thos. Borrett,[24] Esq. to be do. in room of Peregrine Lascelles - - - -	Gohre, 11 Oct. ,, *d*
George Martin,[25] Esq. to be Capt. in room of Edward Hawley - - - - -	,, 7 April, 1726.*d*
Jas. Auchmouty [26] to be Chaplain [in room of Thos. Smart] - - - -	Kensington, 21 Nov. ,, *d*
[Emilius Guerin [27] to be Qr.-Mr. - - -	—— —— 1726/7]

[1] Out before 1727.

[2] From Capt. and Lt.-Col. 1st Foot Guards. Comn. renewed in June, 1727. One of the M.P.'s for Stockbridge, 1734. D. 2 Sept. 1734.—*Gentleman's Mag.*

[3] Appointed Ens. in Col. Kane's Regt. 25 April, 1712. Half-pay, 1713. Comn. as Capt. in the Rl. Irish Regt. renewed in 1727. Serving in 1736. Out before 1740. The will of a certain Wm. Sharman of Dublin, Esq., was proved at Dublin in 1775.

[4] See biog. notice in Vol. I., p. 219, note 32.

[5] Comn. renewed in 1727. Serving in 1730. A certain — Cosby was appointed Capt. in Irwin's Regt. of Foot in 1738. Out before 1740.

[6] See Vol. I., p. 159, note 6.

[7] See biog. notice in Vol. I., p. 223, note 69.

[8] *Kenahan.* Comn. renewed in 1727.

[9] See biog. notice on p. 303, note 28.

[10] Serving as Ens. to the Colonel's Cy. in 1727.

[11] See p. 259, note 3.

[12] See Vol. I., p. 311, note 5.

[13] Serving as Lieut. in same Regt. in 1740.

[14] Comn. renewed in 1727. Lieut. 3 May, 1734. Capt. in the King's Regt. of Foot, 20 June, 1739. D. in Feb. 1746.

[15] Comn. renewed in 1727. Serving in 1730. Out before 1740. Serving as Ens. in June, 1727.

[16] Out. before 1727.

[17] Serving as Lieut. in 1740.

[18] Serving in 1740.

[19] Appointed Ens. in Col. Fred. Sibourg's Regt. of French Foot, 2 April, 1706. Under date of Jan. 1737, Major Gillman, of above Regt., reports in a letter from Minorca to Maj.-Gen. Armstrong (Col. of same Corps), then in England : " . . . This is to acquaint you with the death of Lieut. John Dalbos of Col. Pujola's Company, who died last night of a tedious and lingering disorder attended with the gout, but in my opinion rather by old age, being 75 years."—*Campaigns and History of the Royal Irish Regt.*, by Lt.-Col. G. le M. Gretton, p. 72.

[20] Comn. renewed in June, 1727. D. in 1730. His will, proved at Dublin same year, describes him as " Lieut. and Adjt. in Royal Regt. of Ireland."

[21] Lieut. 4 Sept. 1734. Serving in 1740.

[22] From the Regt. of Invalids. His Comn. as John *Dobbin* was renewed in 1727. Out of the Regt. before 1740.

[23] Comn. renewed in 1727. Serving in 1740.

[24] Served in former reign as Capt. in Col. Humphry Gore's Regt. of Foot. Half-pay, 1712. Serving in the Rl. Irish Regt. in 1740.

[25] Exchanged from Harrison's Regt. with Capt. Edward Hawley. See p. 302, note 10.

[26] Comn. renewed in 1727.

[27] Comn. entry not forthcoming, but appears in the List of officers of above Regt. whose Comns. were renewed by George II., 20 June, 1727. This officer was appointed Lieut. of an Indep. Cy. of Foot at New York, 17 March, 1735/6. Serving in 1740.

LIEUT.-GENERAL MEREDYTH'S REGIMENT OF FOOT.

[20TH FOOT,—1ST BATTALION LANCASHIRE FUSILIERS.]

Serving at Gibraltar during all George I.'s reign.

John Monk Morgan[1] to be Ens. to ——-	St. James's, 19 Mar. 1718/9.c
Wm. Egerton,[2] Esq. to be Colonel in room of [Thos.] Meredyth decd. and Capt. of a Cy. - - - - - -	Herrenhausen, 7 July, 1719.c
John Vickers,[3] Esq. to be Capt. in room of Robt. Graham - - - - -	,, 28 May, 1720.c
Thos. Foulks,[4] Esq. to be Lt.-Col. and Capt. of a Cy. - - - - - -	Gohre, 13 Oct. O.S. ,, c
Edward Brown,[5] Esq. to be Capt. in room of Abr. Bickford - - - - -	,, ,, ,, ,, c
Ralph Bendysh,[6] to be Ens. to —— - -	,, 24 Dec. ,, c
Robt. Catherwood,[7] Esq. to be Capt. in room of Peregrine Griffith - - - -	,, ,, ,, ,, c
—— Tuthill,[8] to be Lieut. to Capt. —— -	,, 16 May, 1721.c
[Wm.] Graham[9] to be Ens. to Capt. - -	,, ,, ,, ,, c
Wm. Patten,[10] to be do. to —— - - -	,, 1 June, ,, c
Henry Pinkerton,[11] to be do. to —— -	Kensington, 12 Sept. ,, c
Rupert Oldenburgh[12] to be Lieut. to Capt. Adam Enos - - - - - -	,, 14 Oct. ,, c
Richard Capper[13] to be Ens. to —— -	St. James's, 4 Nov. ,, c
[Francis] Rousilier (*sic*)[14] to be Lieut. to ——	,, 3 Mar. 1721/2.c
Uvedal Jones[15] to be Ens. to —— - -	,, ,, ,, ,, c
Arthur Horsman[16] to be Lieut. to —— -	,, 23 April, 1722.c
Audly Lynn (*sic*)[17] to be Ens. to —— -	,, 25 ,, ,, c
John Williams[18] to be Qr.-Mr - - -	,, ,, ,, ,, c
Wm. Levingston[19] to be Ens. to —— - -	,, 25 May, ,, c
John Battereau,[20] Esq. to be Lt.-Col. and Capt. of a Cy. - - - - - -	Kensington, 25 June, ,, c
Wm. Graham,[21] Esq. to be Major and Capt. of a Cy. - - - - - -	,, ,, ,, ,, c
Robt. Johnston,[22] Esq. to be Capt. of Grenadiers in room of [Wm.] Graham -	,, ,, ,, ,, c
John Williams[18] to be Lieut. to Capt. Adam Enos - - - - - - -	,, ,, ,, ,, c
Wm. Machon (*sic*)[23] to be Adjt. - - -	,, ,, ,, ,, c
George Stanhope,[24] Esq. to be Capt. in room of Robt. Graham - - - - -	,, 16 July, ,, c
Ant. Meyrac[25] to be Ens. to Capt. ——- -	,, 8 Sept. ,, c
Wm. Cambie[26] to be Lieut. to Capt. Adam Enos - - - - - -	St. James's, 24 Nov. ,, c
Wm. Taunton[27] to be Ens. to ——- - -	,, 24 Jan. 1722/3
Walter Drax[28] to be Ens. to —— - - -	,, 19 Mar. ,,
Mordecai Abbot,[29] Esq. to be Major and Capt. of a Cy. - - - - - - -	,, 5 April, 1723

Wm. Machan,[28] Esq. to be Capt. - -	- St. James's,	5 April, 1723.
Abraham Bickford [30] to be Lieut. to ——	- ,,	,, ,, ,,
Louis la Bouchetière [31] to be Ens. to ——	- ,,	,, ,, ,,
Wm. Graham [9] to be Adjt. - - -	- ,,	,, ,, ,,
George Martyn [32] to be Ens. to —— -	- ,,	18 May, ,,
John Edgar,[33] Esq. to be Capt. in room of		
Peter Fontane - - -	- Herrenhausen, 29 July,	,,
John Furber [34] to be Ens. to —— -	- St. James's,	4 Mar. 1723/4.c
Richard Capper [18] to be Lieut. to —— -	- ,,	,, ,, ,, c
Ant. Meyrac [25] to be Adjt. - - -	- ,,	,, ,, ,, c
Philip Lloyd,[35] Esq. to be Capt. in room of		
John Edgar decd. - - -	- Windsor, 25 Sept.	1724.d
John Rogers [36] to be Lieut. to ——	- St. James's, 17 May,	1725.d
James Gendrault,[37] Esq. to be Capt. in room of		
George Stanhope - - -	- Pyrmont, 1 July, O.S. ,,	d
John Milliquet [38] to be Lieut to ——	- Herrenhausen, 10 Sept. O.S. ,,	d
Sherington Talbot,[39] Esq. to be Capt. in room		
of Wm. Graham - - -	- St. James's, 12 May,	1726.d
Henry Bellendine,[40] Esq. to be Capt. in room		
of Philip Lloyd - - -	- ,, 25 Dec. ,,	d

[1] Out before 1727. Probably son of the John Monk Morgan of Woodhouse, Bakewell, Derbyshire, whose death is recorded in the *Gentleman's Mag.* for 1774, "aged 100."

[2] See biog. notice in Vol. I., p. 365, note 5.

[3] Serving as Capt. in 1740. This officer was 1st Lieut. of the Grendr. Cy. of above Regt. on the accession of Queen Anne, and had seen much service. He d. in 1769, and his obituary notice in the *Gentleman's Mag.* records that "he was an officer in King William's reign."

[4] See biog. notice on p. 217, note 11.

[5] Comn. renewed in 1727. D. before 1735, in which year his widow, Margaret Brown, was drawing a pension of £26 per annum.

[6] Comn. renewed in 1727. Of Barrington Hall, Cambridge. See account of this family in Burke's *Landed Gentry*, 5th Ed.

[7] Major, 31 Aug. 1739. Lt.-Col. of do. 31 May, 1741. Appointed Lt.-Col. of Col. Battereau's newly-raised Regt. of Foot in 1742. Served with the same at Falkirk and Culloden. Half-pay, 1748. D. in 1749.

[8] Out before 1727.

[9] Adjt. 5 April, 1723. Out before 1727.

[10] Out before June, 1727.

[11] Do.

[12] From half-pay Lieut. in Lt.-Gen. Holt's Regt. of Marines. Not in any subsequent List.

[13] Lieut. 13 March, 1724.

[14] *Roussilière.* Capt. 31 Aug. 1739. Believed to have served at Fontenoy.

[15] Out before 1727.

[16] Capt.-Lieut. 31 Aug. 1739. Believed to have served at Fontenoy.

[17] *Lynd.* Comn. renewed in 1727. D. before 1735, in which year his widow, Hannah Lynd, was drawing a pension of £20 per annum.

[18] Lieut. 25 June, 1722. Comns. renewed in 1727. Serving as senior Lieut. in 1740.

[19] Out before 1727.

[20] See Vol. I., p. 161, note 5.

[21] Promoted from Capt. of the Grendr. Cy. D. or left the Regt. in April, 1723.

[22] Serving as senior Capt. in 1740. Believed to have served at Fontenoy.

[23] *Machan.* Capt. 5 April, 1723. Serving with above Regt. in Ireland, 1737. Out before 1740.

[24] Served previously as Cornet in Col. Wm. Stanhope's Regt. of Dragoons. Lt.-Col. 49th Foot, 10 April, 1743.

[25] Capt. 1 Aug. 1733. Wounded at Fontenoy. Major, 27 May, 1745. Serving in 1749.

[26] Serving as Lieut. in 1740. Wrongly called "Robert Cambie" in 1740 *List.* Believed to have been at Fontenoy.

[27] Out before 1727. Drawing half-pay as Ens. in 1749.

[28] Comn. renewed in 1727. Out before 1740. Drawing half-pay in 1749.

[29] See Vol. I., p. 161, note 6.

[30] Comn. renewed in 1727. D. before 1734, when holding the rank of Capt. in above Regt. His widow, Mary Bickford, was drawing a pension of £26 per annum in last-named year.

[31] Lieut. 16 Jan. 1736. Wounded at Fontenoy.

[32] Exchanged to Brig.-Gen. Henry Grove's Regt. of Foot, 1 Jan. 1724. Lieut. of an additional Cy. in same Corps, 26 Dec. 1726. Half-pay, 1729.

[33] Comn. renewed in 1727. D. in Sept. 1724. His widow, Mary Edgar, was drawing a pension of £26 per annum in 1735.

[34] Attained the rank of Capt. and Lt.-Col. 3rd Foot Guards, 6 June, 1753.

[35] Serving as Capt. in Gen. the Hon. Wm. Ker's Dragoons in 1727.

[36] Comn. renewed in 1727. Out before 1737.

[37] Serving in 1740.

[38] Comn. renewed in 1727. Out before 1737. Drawing half-pay as Lieut. in 1749.

[39] See biog. notice in Vol. I., p. 119, note 19.

[0] Comn. renewed in 1727. Out before 1737. Believed to be identical with Sir Henry *Bellenden*, Gentleman Usher of the Black Rod, who d. in 1761.

THE ROYAL NORTH BRITISH FUZILIERS.

[ROYAL SCOTS FUSILIERS.]

George Hay[1] to be [2nd] Lieut. to Capt.
——— Douglas in the Royal North British
    Fuziliers - - - - - - - St. James's, 25 April, 1718.*b*

Edward Wolfe,[2] Esq. to be Lt.-Colonel - - Kensington, 24 May, ,, *b*

Andrew Agnew,[3] Esq. to be Capt. in room of
    John Douglas - - - - - ,, ,, ,, ,, *b*

Richard Hull,[4] Esq. to be Capt. in room of
    [John] Whinyard (*sic*) - - - - ,, 26 June, ,, *b*

Thos. Michelsen[5] to be 1st Lieut. to Lt.-Col.
    Edward Wolfe - - - - - St. James's, 6 Dec. 1720.*c*

Alex. Desclousseaux[6] to be 2nd Lieut. to Capt.
    Thos. Don - - - - - - ,, ,, ,, ,, *c*

David Kerr[7] to be 2nd Lieut. to Lt.-Col. Ed-
    ward Wolfe - - - - - ,, 20 Jan. 1720/1.*c*

John Leslie[8] (commonly called Lord John
    Leslie) to be Lt.-Col. and Capt. of a Cy. - ,, 25 ,, ,, *c*

John Allerdise (*sic*)[9] to be 2nd Lieut. to Capt.
    [Alex.] Abercrombie - - - - ,, 31 May, 1721.*c*

James Dobbin[10] to be 1st Lieut. to do. - - Kensington, 11 Sept. 1722.*c*

Gabriel de la Ban[11] to be 2nd Lieut. to ——— - St. James's, 23 Jan. 1722/3.*c*

Sheffield Austen,[12] Esq. to be Capt. in room of
    Robt. Urquhart - - - - - ,, 25 May, 1723.*c*

Richard Scott to be Chaplain - - - ,, ,, ,, ,, *c*

Bernard Harrison[13] to be 1st Lieut. to Capt.
    Alex. Abercrombie [in room of James
    Dobbin] - - - - - - - ,, 30 ,, ,, *c*

Wm. Bennet Silvester[14] to be do. to Capt.
    [Sheffield] Austen - - - - Herrenhausen, 20 Sept. ,, *c*

Philip Howard[15] to be 2nd Lieut. to Major
    George Keightley - - - - Helvoet Sluys, 25 Dec. ,, *c*

George Keightley,[16] Esq. to be Major [and
    Capt. of a Cy.] - - - - - St. James's, 30 Jan. 1723/4.*c*

John Crosbie,[17] Esq. to be Capt. in room of
    Sheffield Austen - - - - - ,, 28 Mar. 1724.*d*

Peter Hacket (*sic*),[18] Esq. to be Capt. in room
    of Jeff. Prendergast - - - Herrenhausen, 10 Sept. O.S. 1725.*d*

Jeffery Prendergast,[19] Esq. to be Capt. of an
    additional Cy. - - - - - - St. James's, 26 Dec. 1726.*d*

Joseph Bentham[20] to be 1st Lieut. to do. - ,, ,, ,, ,, *d*

Thos. Leslie[21] to be 2nd Lieut. to do. - - ,, ,, ,, ,, *d*

Alex. Burnet,[22] Esq. to be Capt. of an
    additional Cy. - - - - - - ,, ,, ,, ,, *d*

John Sleddall[23] to be 1st Lieut. to do. - - ,, ,, ,, ,, *d*

Basil Cochran[24] to be 2nd Lieut. to do. - - ,, ,, ,, ,, *d*

Sir James Wood,[25] Bt. to be Colonel [in room
    of George Maccartney] and Capt. of a Cy. ,, 9 Mar. 1726/7.*d*

Mungo Mathie,[26] Esq. to be Capt. in room of
    James Ogilvie decd.   -   -   -   - St. James's, 5 May, 1727. *d*
Lewis Dick,[27] Esq. to be Capt.-Lieut. - -   ,,   ,, ,,   ,, *d*
Thos. Gordon[28] to be Lieut. to —— - -   ,,   ,, ,,   ,, *d*

[1] 1st Lieut. 7 June, 1733. Serving with same rank in 1740.

[2] See biog. notice in Vol. I., p. 163, note 3.

[3] Eldest son of Sir Jas. Agnew, Bart., of Lochnaw. Bn. in 1687. Appointed Cornet in the Rl. Scots Dragoons, 11 May, 1705. Served at Ramillies, Oudenarde, and Malplaquet. Preferred to a Company in Lord Strathnaver's Regt. of Foot, 9 Dec. 1709. Half-pay in 1713. Capt. in Col. John Pocock's newly-raised Regt. of Foot, 22 July, 1715. Major of the Royal North British Fusiliers, 16 Jan. 1737. Lt.-Col. 2 Nov. 1739. Col. of a Regt. of Marines, 15 Aug. 1746. Maj.-Gen. 3 Feb. 1756. Lt.-Gen. 3 April, 1759. Gov. of Tynemouth Castle. Succeeded as 5th Bart. in 1735. D. in 1771.

[4] Appointed Ens. in Col. Stanwix's newly-raised Regt. of Foot, 12 April, 1706. Comn. as Capt. renewed by George II. Major of Col. John Wynyard's Regt. of Marines, 7 Dec. 1739. D. on active service in the West Indies in 1741.

[5] Out before 1727.

[6] Comn. renewed in 1727. D. in 1747 as a Gentleman of the Privy Chamber.—*Gentleman's Mag.*

[7] 1st Lieut. 13 May, 1735. Serving in 1740.

[8] Afterwards Earl of Rothes. See biog. notice in Vol. I., p. 113, note 4.

[9] *Allardyce.* Not in any subsequent List. One of this family, son and heir of —— Allardyce, md. the elder dau. and co-heir of Maj.-Gen. Sir James Wood, Bart., Col. of the Royal North British Fusiliers, and called himself Sir James Allardyce Wood, of Letham, Bart., after his father-in-law's death.

[10] D. or left the Regt. in May, 1723.

[11] Appointed "Brevet Capt.-Lieut." in above Regt. 24 June, 1710. Capt.-Lieut. 7 Dec. 1739. His name is given as "Gabriel Laban" in the 1740 *List.* Served at Fontenoy as Capt. and was wounded.

[12] See his Comn. as Capt. in Sir R. Rich's Dragoons on p. 366.

[13] Comn. renewed in 1727. Serving in Ireland, 1737. Out before 1740.

[14]   Do.   Out before 1737.

[15] Appointed Capt. in Col. Edward Wolfe's Regt. of Marines, 2 Dec. 1739. D. on active service at siege of Carthagena in 1741.—*Gentleman's Mag.*

[16] See biog. notice in Vol. I., p. 119, note 3.

[17] Served at Fontenoy. Major, 25 Aug. 1746. Out in April, 1752.

[18] Major, 2 Nov. 1739. Lt.-Col. 55th Foot (aftds. numbered 44th), 2 Feb. 1741. Succeeded his father Sir Peter *Halket* as 2nd Bart. of Pitfirran in 1734. He represented Dunfermline in Parliament same year and was Lt.-Col. of Lee's Regt. (44th) at Prestonpans in 1745. "Sir Peter was taken prisoner by the Chevalier's troops, and dismissed on his parole ; and was one of the five officers (the others being the Hon. Mr. Ross, Capt. Lucy Scott, and Lieuts. Farquharson and Cumming) who refused, in Feb. 1746, to rejoin their regiments on the Duke of Cumberland's command and threat of forfeiting their commissions. Their reply, 'that his Royal Highness was master of their commissions but not of their honour,' was approved by Government ; and Sir Peter, in 1754, embarked for America, in command of the 44th Regt. He fell, with his youngest son, James, in Gen. Braddock's defeat by the Indians, 9 July, 1755. By the Lady Amelia Stewart, second dau. of Francis, 8th Earl of Moray, he had three sons : Peter, his successor ; Francis, Major in the Black Watch, d. unm. in 1760 ; and James, Lieut. 44th Regt., who fell as stated above."—*Burke's Peerage.*

[19] From half-pay. Served at Malplaquet as Capt. in Col. Sir Thos. Prendergast's Regt. of Foot. Reduced with the Cy. in 1728. Drawing half-pay, 1740. D. in 1747.

[20] Served at Malplaquet as Lieut. in Sir Ric. Temple's Regt. of Foot. Comn. as 1st Lieut. in the Royal North British Fusiliers renewed in 1727. Out before 1737.

[21] Not identified with the Capt. Leslie of same Regt. in 1740.

[22] From half-pay. Served as Ens. at Malplaquet with the Cameronians and was wounded. Serving as Capt. in the Royal North British Fusiliers in 1740.

[23] Half-pay, 1728.

[24] Serving as Lieut. in Whetham's Regt. (12th Foot) in 1740.

[25] See his Comn. as Brig.-Gen. on p. 336, and note thereto.

[26] Serving in 1740.

[27] Out before 1737.

[28] Do.

THE PRINCE ON WALES'S OWN REGIMENT OF ROYAL WELSH FUZILIERS.

[ROYAL WELSH FUSILIERS.]

Michael Hutton[1] to be Adjt. - - - - St. James's, 21 Mar. 1718/9.*c*

John Welden[2] to be 1st Lieut. to [Major]
  Ralph Whitfield - - - - „ 1 May, 1719.*c*

Robt. Layton Valentine[3] to be 2nd Lieut. to
  Capt. Chas. Combes - - - - „ „ „ „ *c*

Fras. Bolton[4] to be 2nd Lieut. to Capt. John
  Hyde - - - - - - - „ 13 Mar. 1719/20.*c*

Thos. Dudley[5] to be Qr.-Mr. - - - - „ 18 April, 1720.*c*

Newsham Peers,[6] Esq. to be Major and Capt.
  of a Cy. - - - - - - - „ 14 May, „ *c*

Wm. Sabine,[7] Esq. to be Capt. in room of
  Major Ralph Whitfield - - - - „ „ „ „ *c*

Alex. Johnston[8] to be [1st] Lieut. to Capt.
  —— Powell - - - - - - „ „ „ „ *c*

Waring Ashby[9] to be 2nd Lieut. to Capt.
  [John] Hyde - - - - - - „ „ „ „ *c*

John Jodrell,[10] Esq. to be Capt. in room of
  John Hyde - - - - - Herrenhausen, 28 July, „ *c*

Wm. Wansborough,[11] Esq. to be Capt. in
  room of Edward Thetford - - - St. James's, 24 Mar. 1720/1.*c*

Thos. Stokes[12] to be 2nd Lieut. to Capt. John
  Jodrell - - - - - - - „ 6 May, 1722.*c*

John Weaver[13] to be do. to Capt. Wm. Sabine „ 25 June, „ *c*

Newsham Peers,[6] Esq. to be Lt.-Col. and Capt.
  of a Cy - - - - - - - „ 25 Dec. „ *c*

Wm. Wansborough,[11] Esq. to be Major and
  Capt. of a Cy. - - - - - - „ „ „ „ *c*

John Waite,[14] Esq. to be Capt. of [Lt.-Col.]
  Wentworth's late Cy. - - - - „ „ „ „ *c*

Wm. Hickman,[15] Esq. to be Capt.-Lieut. - „ „ „ „ *c*

Brudenel Wansborough[16] to be 1st Lieut. to
  Capt. John Wilson - - - - - „ 24 May, 1723.*c*

Edward Pole,[17] Esq. to be Capt. in room of
  [John] Jodrell decd. - - - - „ 29 Oct. 1724.*d*

John Jemmet[18] to be [1st] Lieut. to Capt.
  John Powell - - - - - - „ 20 Mar. 1724/5.*d*

Wm. Deane[19] to be 2nd Lieut. to —— - Gohre, 11 Oct. 1725.*d*

John Barnard[20] to be Adjt. - - - St. James's, 16 Mar. 1725/6.*d*

Samuel Ashton[21] to be 1st Lieut. to —— - „ 21 May, 1726.*d*

Peter Petit,[22] Esq. to be Capt. in room of
  John Powel - - - - - - Kensington, 6 Oct. „ *d*

George Jackson,[23] Esq. to be Capt. in room of
  Edward Pole - - - - - - St. James's, 25 Dec. „ *d*

Robert Griffith[24] to be 2nd Lieut. to do. - „ „ „ „ *d*

Simon Roche,[25] Esq. to be Capt. of an additional Cy.					St. James's, 26 Dec.	1726.*d*
Fras. Bolton[4] to be 1st Lieut. to do.		,,	,,	,,	,,	*d*
Edward Baldwin[26] to be 2nd Lieut. to do.		,,	,,	,,	,,	*d*
Thos. Forth,[27] Esq. to be Capt. of an additional Cy.		,,	,,	,,	,,	*d*
Archd. Enos[28] to be 1st Lieut. to do.		,,	,,	,,	,,	*d*
Edwd. Gould[29] to be 2nd Lieut. to do.		,,	,,	,,	,,	*d*
James Drysdale[80] to be 1st Lieut. to Capt. Thos. Forth				,,	31 May,	1727.*d*

[1] Out 16 March, 1726.

[2] Comn. renewed in June, 1727. Out before 1740. Probably the third son of Walter *Weldon* of Queen's County—a collateral ancestor of the present Sir Anthony Weldon, Bart.

[8] Out before 1727.

[4] 1st Lieut. to Capt. Simon Roche's additional Cy. in above Regt. 26 Dec. 1726. Half-pay, 1728. Believed to be identical with Francis Bolton, Army agent, whose death is recorded in the *Gentleman's Mag.* for 1746.

[5] Untraced after 1727.

[6] See biog. notice in Vol. I., p. 348, note 5.

[7] Joined the Regt. as 2nd Lieut. in 1711. Comn. as Capt. renewed in 1727. Out before 1740.

[8] Serving as senior Lieut. in 1740. Fought at Dettingen and Fontenoy. Served as Capt. in last-named battle, and was one of the officers returned as "missing." Killed at Laufeldt in 1747.—*Records.*

[9] Out in May, 1722. Third son of George Ashby of Quenby by Hannah dau. and co-heir of Maj. Edward Waring. Succeeded to his father's estate of Quenby and was High Sheriff of co. Leicester in 1733. D. in 1770.—Burke's *Landed Gentry.*

[10] D. in Oct. 1724.

[11] Major, 25 Dec. 1722. See p. 144, note 5.

[12] Out before 1730.

[18] Out 25 Dec. 1726.

[14] Major, 4 Sept. 1739. Lt.-Col. 11 April, 1743. Served at Dettingen and Fontenoy. D. or left the Regt. in 1747–8.

[15] Capt. 23 March, 1731. Wounded at Fontenoy.—*Records.*

[16] Comn. renewed in 1727. Out before 1740.

[17] See biog. notice on p. 206, note 27.

[18] From Lieut. in Col. Fielding's Regt. of Invalids. Comn. renewed in 1727. Out before 1740.

[19] Comn. renewed in 1727. Lt.-Col. 37th Foot, 17 Feb. 1746. Attained the rank of Col. in the Army, 19 Nov. 1762. Gov. of Upnor Castle before 1758. Living in 1769.

[20] Called "Bernard" in subsequent Lists. 1st Lieut. 1731. Served as Capt. at Fontenoy where he was wounded. Major, 22 Feb. 1748. Out before 1756.

[21] From Lieut. in Col. Chas. Otway's Regt. Comn. renewed in 1727. Out before 1740.

[22] From Capt. in the Royal Irish Regt. See Vol. I., p. 311, note 5. Drawing half-pay in 1749.

[23] Serving as senior Capt. in 1740.

[24] Out before 1740.

[25] From half-pay Capt. in Primrose's Regt. (24th). Had served as a Lieut. with said Corps at Malplaquet. Reduced with his Cy. in 1728.

[26] Reduced with the Cy. in 1728.

[27] From Capt. in Col. Chas. Otway's Regt. of Foot. Appointed Capt. in 1st Tp. of H. Gr. Gds., Nov. 1727. Major, 10 May, 1740. Attained the rank of Col. before 1752, in which year he proved Gen. John Wynyard's will as an executor. D. in Sackville St. in 1757.

[28] Half-pay, 1728.

[29] Do.

[80] Half-pay, 1728. Restored to full pay as 1st Lieut. in above Regt. 24 Sept. 1730. Wounded at Fontenoy where he served as Capt.

BRIGADIER-GENERAL GEORGE PRESTON'S REGIMENT OF FOOT.

[26TH FOOT,—1ST BATTALION THE CAMERONIANS (SCOTTISH RIFLES).]

Adam Spittle [1] to be Ens. to Capt. —— -	St. James's, 24 Dec. 1717.	b
John Gilchrist [2] to be Lieut. to Capt. —— -	,, 27 Feb. 1717/8.	b
Charles Colvill (*sic*) [3] to be do. to Capt. —— - - - - - - -	,, 28 ,, ,,	b
George Gordon [4] to be Ens. to Capt. —— -	,, 13 Mar. ,,	b
Robert Ferguson,[5] Esq. to be Lt.-Col. and Capt. of a Company [in room of Lt.-Col. John Hope] - - - -	,, 5 April, 1718.	b
Hugh Semple,[6] Esq. to be Major and Capt. of a Company [in room of Robt. Ferguson promoted] - - - -	,, ,, ,, ,,	b
[Robert] Anstruther,[7] Esq. to be Capt. of Lt.-Col. Hope's late Company - -	,, ,, ,, ,,	b
Wm. Henderson [8] to be Lieut. to Lt.-Col. Robt. Ferguson - - - - -	Kensington, 29 May, ,,	b

Regiment embarked for Ireland in Nov. 1718. See Irish Establishment, 1719–1727.

[1] Lieut. 23 June, 1719. Serving in 1727. D. before 1735, in which year his widow, Barbara Spittle, was drawing a pension of £20 per annum.

[2] Comn. renewed by George II. Out of the Regt. before 1740.

[3] "Served as a Cadet with the 26th Regt. of Foot at Malplaquet. Wounded at the attack on the Rebels at Preston in 1715. Served at Gibraltar during the siege of 1727. Wounded at Dettingen as Major of the 21st Fusiliers, and his horse shot under him. Commanded the 21st at the battle of Fontenoy where he had three fingers of his left hand cut off and was wounded in his foot. Was at Ostend when besieged by the French in 1745. Commanded his Regt. at Culloden in 1746, and at Laffelt in 1747. Lt.-Gen. in 1770. D. at Edinburgh, 29 Aug. 1775, aged 85. Younger bro. to the 8th Baron Colville of Culross" (Douglas's *Peerage of Scotland*). Lt.-Gen. the Hon. Chas. Colville was appointed Col. of the 69th Foot in 1758.

[4] Comn. renewed by George II. Out of the Regt. in 1740.

[5] See biog. notice in Vol. I., p. 222, note 60.

[6] Succeeded as 11th Lord *Sempill*. Appointed Adjt. to above Regt. 1 Dec. 1708. Served at Malplaquet. Capt. 12 July, 1712. Half-pay in 1713. Lt.-Col. of the 19th Foot, 12 July, 1731. Col. of the 42nd Highlanders, 14 Jan. 1741. Col. 25th Foot, 9 April, 1745. Brig.-Gen. 9 June, 1745. Distinguished himself at the siege of Aeth in Flanders. Commanded the left wing of the Royal Army at Culloden. D. in Nov. 1746.

[7] Joined above Regt. as Ens. 13 Dec. 1715. Major, 15 Dec. 1738. Fought at Dettingen and Fontenoy. Lt.-Col. of above Regt. 13 July, 1745. Served at Culloden. Col. 58th Foot, 28 Dec. 1755. D. as Lt.-Gen. in Dec. 1767. Appears to have been one of the six sons of Sir Robert Anstruther, Bart. (so created 1694) by his second marriage.

[8] Capt. 11 Aug. 1737. Serving in 1740.

COLONEL CHARLES OTWAY'S REGIMENT OF FOOT.

[35TH FOOT,—1ST BATTALION THE ROYAL SUSSEX REGIMENT.]

Henry Ford [1] to be Lieut. to Capt. ——	Herrenhausen,	31 Aug.	1719.	c
Gerald Elrington [2] to be Lieut. to —— -	St. James's,	10 Nov.	,,	c
Ralph Hunt Caulfield [3] to be Ens. to —— -	,,	29 Mar.	1720.	c
James Durnford [4] to be Lieut. to —— -	,,	9 April,	,,	c
Patrick Gentleman [5] to be do. to —— -	,,	25 May,	,,	c
Edward Gibson [6] to be Ens. to —— -	,,	,, ,,	,,	c
John Twisleton [7] to be Lieut. to Capt. Wm. Campbell - - - - -	,,	15 Feb.	1720/1.	c
Mathew Sewell [8] to be Lieut to —— - -	,,	23 ,,	,,	c
Thos. Forth, [9] Esq. to be Capt. in room of Wm. Wansborough - - - -	,,	24 Mar.	,,	c
Thos. Hinkes [10] to be Lieut. to —— -	,,	,, ,,	,,	c
Thos. Otway [11] to be [1st] Lieut. to Capt. Wm. Rice's Grenadiers - - -	,,	3 June,	1721.	c
Robt. Wilson [12] to be Ens. to Capt. Thos. Forth - - - - - -	,,	,, ,,	,,	c
Richard Robinson [13] to be Lieut. to Capt. —— Gery - - - - -	,,	,, ,,	,,	c
Edward Lely [14] to be Ens. to —— - -	,,	17 July,	,,	c
Thos. Vernon [15] to be Lieut. to —— - -	,,	25 ,,	,,	c
Herbert Love [16] to be do. to Capt. [Wm.] Campbell	,,	26 ,,	,,	c
Chas. Scott [17] to be Ens. to Capt. —— Pinson	,,	24 ,,	,,	c
Richard Park [18] to be Chaplain - - -	Kensington,	24 Aug.	,,	c
Sam. Ball [19] to be Ens. to —— - -	St. James's,	9 Mar.	1721/2.	c
Sam. Ashton [20] to be Lieut. to Capt. Roger Lort - - - - - -	,,	,, ,,	,,	c
Toby Purcell, [21] Esq. to be Major and Capt. of a Cy. - - - - - -	,,	13 ,,	,,	c
John Leader [22] to be Lieut. to —— - -	,,	,, ,,	,,	c
Henry Crofton, [23] Esq. to be Capt. of Major Purcell's late Cy. - - - -	,,	,, ,,	,,	c
Robt. Carr [24] to be Ens. to —— - - -	Kensington,	18 June,	1722.	c
Wm. Wright, [25] Esq. to be Capt. of Grenadiers in room of Wm. Rice -	,,	8 Sept.	,,	c
Abel Warren, [26] Esq. to be Capt. of Wm. Wright's late Cy. - - - -	,,	,, ,,	,,	c
John Lloyd [27] to be Lieut. to —— - -	,,	,, ,,	,,	c
David Cunynghame [28] to be Ens. to —— -	,,	,, ,,	,,	c
Patrick Gentleman, [5] Esq. to be Capt.-Lieut.	St. James's,	3 Dec.	,,	c
Thos. Dunbar [29] to be Lieut. to —— - -	,,	,, ,,	,,	c
John Gwynne [30] to be Ens. to Col. Wynyard	,,	,, ,,	,,	c
Mat. Hunt [31] to be Ens. to —— - - -	,,	14 Mar.	1722/3.	c
Wm. Moor [32] to be do. to —— - - -	,,	26 April,	1723.	c
Jenkin Leyson [33] to be Lieut. to —— - -	,,	22 May,	,,	c

John Prendergast [34] to be do. to [Grendr.
 Cy.] - - - - - - Herrenhausen, 12 July, 1723.c
Wm. Wright,[25] Esq. to be Major and Capt. of
 a Cy. - - - - - - - St. James's, 24 Jan. 1723/4.c
Roger Dauson (sic)[35] to be Capt. of Grena-
 diers in room of Wm. Wright - - ,, ,, ,, ,, c
George Gumley,[36] Esq. to be Capt. of Roger
 Dauson's late Cy. - - - - ,, ,, ,, ,, c
Henry Delabene [37] to be Ens. to —— - - Kensington, 27 June, 1724.d
Thos. FitzGerald [38] to be Lieut. to —— - St. James's, 27 Mar. 1725.d
Robt. Donworth [39] to be Lieut. to —— - ,,   1 June, ,, d
Richard Bermingham [40] to be do. to —— Herrenhausen, 10 Aug. ,, d

Regiment returned to Ireland in the Autumn of 1725.
See under Irish Establishment.

[1] Out before 1727.
[2] See p. 279, note 29.
[3] Comn. renewed in 1727. Lieut. in Jan. 1735. Called "Raphael Caulfield" in 1740 List. D. 1747. Described in his will, proved at Dublin, as "Capt. in Col. Folliot's Regt. of Foot."
[4] Out before 1727.
[5] Capt. 25 April, 1736. Serving in 1740.
[6] Out before 1727.
[7] Serving as Lieut. in Montague's Regt. in 1730. Out before 1737. Son and heir of Col. Fiennes Twisleton of Broughton Castle, co. Oxford. D. in 1763.
[8] See biog. notice in Vol. I., p. 318, note 7.
[9] See p. 314, note 27.
[10] Not in any subsequent List.
[11] See p. 182, note 11.
[12] Serving in 1730. Out before 1737.
[13] Out before 1727.
[14] Lieut. 4 March, 1736. Serving in 1740. D. in 1773. Will proved at Dublin same year.
[15] Out before 1727.
[16] Do.
[17] Do.
[18] Comn. renewed in 1727. Out before 1737.
[19]   Do.   Serving in 1737. Out before 1740.
[20] See p. 314, note 21.
[21] Left the Regt. in Jan. 1724. Probably son of Col. Toby Purcell, Gov. of Duncannon Fort.
[22] Serving in 1740.
[23] D. in 1741 as Capt. in Gen. Paget's Regt. in Minorca. Will proved at Dublin.
[24] Lieut. 25 April, 1736. D. in 1742 as Lieut. in above Regt. Will proved at Dublin.
[25] Major, 24 Jan. 1724. Lt.-Col. 14th Dragoons, 7 July, 1737. Served with said Corps at Prestonpans and Culloden. Out of the Regt. in 1754.
[26] Senior Capt. in 1740. Of Lowhill, co. Kilkenny. Will proved at Dublin in 1763.
[27] Out before 1727.
[28] Capt. in Col. John Middleton's Regt. (25th) 8 April, 1723. Lt.-Col. 25 Feb. 1746. Second son of Sir David Cunynghame of Milncraig, co. Ayr, Bart. Succeeded his bro. James as 3rd Bart. in 1730. Attained the rank of Lt.-Gen. and Col. 57th Foot. D. in 1767.
[29] Attained the rank of Col. in the Army, 29 April, 1752, in which year he was Lt.-Gov. of Gibraltar. D. in 1767.—*Gentleman's Mag.*
[30] Out before 1730.
[31] Out before 1727.
[32] Do.
[33] See his Comn. on p. 207, and note thereto.
[34] Comn. renewed in 1727. Out before 1737.

[35] Called "Davson" in the Gradation List for 1730. Not in any subsequent List.

[36] Out before 1728.

[37] Appointed Capt. in Barrell's Regt. (4th Foot), 2 Nov. 1737. Out of said Regt. before 1746, on 17 April of which year Capt. (aftds. Maj.-Gen.) James Wolfe addressed a letter to Capt. Henry Delabene at York, giving a very full and interesting account of the battle of Culloden where the writer of said letter acted as A.D.C. to Gen. Hawley. The letter in question is printed in *The Genealogist*, Vol. VII., pp. 225–29.

[38] Comn. renewed in 1727. Out before 1737.

[39] Out before 1730. The will of a certain "Robert Donworth, of Cork, gent." was proved at Dublin in 1747.

[40] Comn. renewed in 1727. Out before 1737.

COLONEL WM. EGERTON'S REGIMENT OF FOOT.

[36TH FOOT,—2ND BATTALION THE WORCESTERSHIRE REGIMENT.

George Holland[1] to be Qr.-Mr. - - -	St. James's, 21 Mar. 1718/9.	c
Do. to be Lieut. to Capt. Dudley Ackland.	Herrenhausen, 23 June, 1719.	c
[Sir Chas. Hotham,[2] Bt. to be Colonel in room of Wm. Egerton and Capt. of a Cy. - - - - - - - -	,, 7 July ,,	]
Patrick Fox,[3] Esq. to be Major and Capt. of a Cy. - - - - - - -	St. James's, 29 Feb. 1719/20.	c
John Austen[4] to be Ens. to Capt. Dudley Ackland - - - - - -	,, 19 Mar. ,,	c
Chris. Hibbert,[5] Esq. to be Lt.-Col. - -	,, 6 April, 1720.	c
John Austin (sic)[4] to be Lieut. to Capt. ——— - - - - - - -	,, 23 May, ,,	c
—— Pierce[6] to be Ens. to —— - - -	,, 25 ,, ,,	c
Wm. Dobbins[7] to be Qr.-Mr. - - -	,, ,, ,, ,,	c
John Pocock,[8] Esq. to be Colonel in room of Sir C. Hotham and Capt. of a Cy. -	,, 2 Dec. ,,	c
Charles Lanoe,[9] Esq. to be do. in room of John Pocock and Capt. of a Cy. - -	,, 21 April, 1721.	c

Regiment returned to Ireland in the Winter of 1720–21.

See under Irish Establishment.

[1] D. or left the Regt. in May, 1720.

[2] See biog. notice in Vol. I., p. 172, note 1.

[3] From half-pay Major of Col. Creighton's Regt. of Foot, which Corps was reduced in 1712. Out of Sir C. Hotham's Regt. in Feb. 1724. D. in 1734.

[4] Lieut. 23 May, 1720. Comn. renewed in 1727. Out before 1740.

[5] Served previously as Lt.-Col. of Brigdr. Grant's Regt. of Foot. (See Vol. I., p. 178, note 2.) Out of the Army in Feb. 1724.

[6] Untraced among several of this name.

[7] Post reduced when the Regt. was sent to Ireland.

[8] See Vol. I., p. 180, note 1.

[9] See Vol. I., p. 223, note 77.

COLONEL RICHARD LUCAS'S REGIMENT OF FOOT IN THE WEST INDIES.

[38TH FOOT,—THE SOUTH STAFFORDSHIRE REGIMENT.]

John Osborn,[1] Esq. to be Capt. in room of
Hugh Plucknet - - - - - - St. James's, 19 Mar. 1718/9.c

Richard Holmes,[2] Esq. to be Major and Capt.
of a Cy. - - - - - - - - ,, 16 April, 1719.c

Andrew Corbet,[3] Esq. to be Capt. in room of
Philip Welsh - - - - - - ,, 20 Nov. ,, p

Ant. Hinton,[4] Esq. to be Capt. in room of
[Philip] Everard decd. - - - - ,, 29 Mar. 1720.p

Delaval Harrison[5] to be Lieut. to Capt. —— ,, 5 April, ,, p

John Morris[6] to be [2nd] Lieut. to Capt.
Watts's Grenadier Cy. - - - - ,, 17 May, ,, c

Richard Cochran Dickson[7] to be Ens. to
Capt. George Lucas - - - - ,, ,, ,, ,, c

Richard Lucas[8] [Junr.] to be Lieut. to —— - ,, 11 June, ,, c

Delaval Harrison[5] to be Adjt. - - - ,, ,, ,, ,, c

Thos. Alcroft[9] to be Lieut. to Capt. —— - ,, ,, ,, ,, c

James (sic) Allicock,[10] Esq. to be Capt.-Lieut. ,, 13 May, 1721.c

Chas. Alexander[11] to be Lieut. to Capt.
George Lucas - - - - - - ,, ,, ,, ,, c

Wm. Crafford[12] to be Ens. to do. - - - ,, ,, ,, ,, c

Chas. Pymm,[13] Esq. to be Capt. in room of
[Anthony] Hinton - - - - - ,, 13 June, ,, c

Peter Roupell[14] to be Ens. to Capt. —— - ,, 19 Oct. ,, c

James Field[15] to be Chaplain - - - ,, 10 Nov. ,, c

—— Maddan (sic)[16] to be Ens. to Capt. —— ,, 7 Feb. 1721/2.c

Thos. Wichells[17] to be do. to —— - - ,, 9 ,, ,, c

Richard Manlove (sic),[18] Esq. to be Capt. in
room of Richard White - - - - ,, 9 Mar. ,, c

Chas. Hamilton[19] to be Lieut. to Capt.
Richard Holmes - - - - - Kensington, 9 June, 1722.c

John James Deleuze[20] to be Ens. to Capt.
—— - - - - - - - - ,, 13 Aug. ,, c

John Harris,[21] Esq. to be Capt. in room of
[Thos.] Watts - - - - - - St. James's, 12 Feb. 1722/3.c

Thos. Wilson[22] to be Ens. to Capt. Morrice - ,, 1 Mar. ,, c

John Babell[23] to be Lieut. to Capt. John
Harris - - - - - - - - ,, 6 April, 1723.c

John Osborn[24] [Jun.] to be Ens. to —— - ,, ,, ,, ,, c

George Grant,[25] Esq. to be Capt. in room of
[Richard] Manlove - - - - - ,, 13 ,, ,, c

Fras. Hamilton[26] to be Ens. to Capt. —— - ,, 24 May, ,, c

John Boitoux[27] to be do. to —— - - - Pyrmont, 4 July, ,, c

Samuel Wilson[28] to be Lieut. to Capt. Pymm - St. James's, 1 Feb. 1723/4.c

Robert Griffith[29] to be Ens. to —— - - Kensington, 11 July, 1724.d

Paul George,[30] Esq. to be Capt. in room of
George Grant - - - - - - Kensington, 15 July, 1724.*d*
Andrew Vedeau [31] to be Lieut. to —— - - Gohre, 11 Oct. 1725.*d*
Andrew Doyle,[32] Esq. to be Major and Capt.
of a Cy. [in room of Richd. Holmes] - Hanover, 16 Nov.(O.S.) ,, *d*
Abraham Ponthieu [33] to be Ens. to Capt.
Paul George - - - - - - Kensington, 8 June, 1726.*d*
Alex. [De] Cubillas [34] to be Ens. to —— - ,, 10 Oct. ,, *d*
Joseph Bertin [35] to be Lieut. to —— - - St. James's, 25 Dec. ,, *d*
Thos. Sharpe [36] to be Ens. to —— - - - ,, 1 Feb. 1726/7.*d*

---

[1] Serving as senior Capt. with the above Regt. in the West Indies in 1740. Capt. of an Invalid Cy. at Hull, 12 Oct. 1751. D. in 1757. Will proved at Dublin same year.

[2] Out in Nov. 1725. A certain Richard Holmes d. at St. Christopher's, West Indies, in 1747.—*Gentleman's Mag.*

[3] Comn. renewed in 1727. Capt. of an Invalid Cy. at Hull, 25 Jan. 1731. Serving in 1740.

[4] From half-pay Capt. in Lord Mohun's Regt. of Foot. Exchanged from Lucas's Regt. in June, 1721, to Col. Robert Murray's Regt. (37th). Comn. in last-named Corps renewed in 1727. Serving in Ireland in 1737. Out before 1740.

[5] Comn. renewed in 1727. Out before 1740.

[6] Do. do.

[7] Out before 1727.

[8] See Vol. I., p. 310, note 6

[9] Out before 1727.

[10] Called "Syer Allicock" in subsequent Lists. Capt. 30 Aug. 1736. Serving in 1740.

[11] Serving in 1740. Commissioned Ens. in Queen Anne's reign when a child. Son of Col. Fras. Alexander the former Col. of above Regt.

[12] Out before 1727.

[13] Exchanged from 37th Foot with Capt. A. Hinton. Serving with same rank in 1740.

[14] Out before 1727.

[15] Comn. renewed in June, 1727.

[16] Out before 1727.

[17] D. before 1727. His widow, Emmet *Withalls*, was drawing a pension of £16 per annum in 1735.

[18] D. or left the Regt. before April, 1723. Had served in the late reign as Capt. in Col. Wm. Breton's Regt. of Foot.

[19] Out before 1727.

[20] Do.

[21] Serving as Capt. in 1740.

[22] Comn. renewed in 1727. Out before 1740.

[23] Out before 1727.

[24] Lieut. 3 Oct. 1732. Serving in 1740.

[25] Out before 1727.

[26] Comn. renewed in 1727.

[27] From Ens. in Dubourgay's Regt. See biog. notice in Vol. I., p. 169, note 6.

[28] Comn. renewed in 1727. D. before 1733, in which year his widow, Jennet Wilson, was drawing a pension of £20 per annum.

[29] Out before 1727.

[30] Lieut.-Gov. of Montserrat, 20 Aug. 1723.

[31] Comn. renewed in 1727. Out before 1740.

[32] Comn. renewed in 1727. Out before 1740. Had served in late reign as Capt. in Col. Molesworth's Regt. of Foot.

[33] Comn. renewed in 1727. D. before 1734, in which year his widow, Sarah Ponthieu, was drawing a pension of £16 per annum.

[34] Comn. renewed in 1727. D. before 1734, in which year his widow, Elizabeth De Cubillas, was drawing a *Lieutenant's* pension of £20 per annum.

[35] Comn. renewed in 1727. Out before 1740.

[36] Comn. renewed in 1727. D. before 1734, in which year his widow, Amey (*sic*) Sharpe, was drawing a pension of £16 per annum.

x

COLONEL RICHARD PHILIPPS'S REGIMENT OF FOOT.

[40TH FOOT,—1ST BATTALION THE PRINCE OF WALES'S VOLUNTEERS.]

Henry Daniel[1] to be Lieut. to Capt. Joseph
    Bennet - - - - - - Hampton Ct. 16 Aug. 1718.*b*
Robt. Wroth[2] to be Adjt. - - - - St. James's, 7 May, 1719.*c*
John Hanfield[3] to be Ens. to Lt.-Col. Purcell   ,,   26 Feb. 1719/20.*c*
Jeffery Fettiplace[4] to be do. to Capt. —— -   ,,   5 April, 1720.*c*
Wm. Hele[5] to be do. to —— - - -   ,,   ,, ,, ,, *c*
George Baker[6] to be do. to —— - - -   ,,   24 May, ,, *c*
John Barton[7] to be do. to Capt. —— -   ,,   9 June, ,, *c*
Laurence Armstrong,[8] Esq. to be Lt.-Col. and
    Capt. of a Cy. [in room of Martin Purcell]   ,,   1 Dec. ,, *c*
Alex. Cosby,[9] Esq. to be Major and Capt. of
    a Cy. - - - - - -   ,,   ,, ,, ,, *c*
Thos. Barton[10] to be Ens. to Capt. —— -   ,,   18 Feb. 1720/1.*c*
Robt. Carr[11] to be do. to Capt. —— - -   ,,   ,, ,, ,, *c*
Samuel Truebody[12] to be Chaplain - -   ,,   24 April, 1721.*c*
James Mitford,[13] Esq. to be Capt. in room of
    Wm. Moor - - - - - -   ,,   30 May, ,, *c*
Thos. Edwards[14] to be Lieut. to Capt. Chris.
    Aldridge - - - - - - Kensington, 26 Aug. ,, *c*
George Martyn[15] to be Ens. to —— - St. James's, 24 Oct. ,, *c*
Robert Handy[16] [Jun.] to be do. to —— -   ,,   24 Dec. ,, *c*
Edward Amhurst[17] to be do. to —— -   ,,   13 Mar. 1721/2.*c*
Thos. Barton[10] to be Lieut. to Capt. —— -   ,,   9 April, 1722.*c*
James Erskine[18] to be do. to Capt. —— - Kensington, 14 June, ,, *c*
Hugh Campbell[19] to be Ens. to —— -   ,,   ,, ,, ,, *c*
Henry Crofton[20] to be do. to —— -   ,,   18 ,, ,, *c*
Robt. Wroth[2] to be Ens. to —— -   ,,   25 July, ,, *c*
Fred. Jeffereyes[21] to be do. to —— -   ,,   30 ,, ,, *c*
Erasmus James Phillipps[22] to be Ens. to - St. James's, 8 April, 1723.*c*
Fras. Cavally (*sic*),[23] Esq. to be Capt. -   ,,   15 Dec. 1724.*d*
John Broadstreet (*sic*)[24] to be Ens. to above Cy.   ,,   12 Mar. 1724/5.*d*
John Hollingsworth[25] to be Lieut. to —— Hanover, 30 Nov. (O.S.) 1725.*d*
Archibald Rennie[26] to be Ens. to —— - Kensington, 7 July, 1726.*d*
John Blower,[27] Esq. to be Capt. in room of
    John Doucet decd. - - - - St. James's, 10 Dec. ,, *d*
Henry Daniel,[1] Esq. to be Capt.-Lieut. - -   ,,   ,, ,, ,, *d*
Edmund Okden (*sic*)[28] to be Lieut. to —— -   ,,   ,. ,, ,, *d*

---

[1] Capt. 22 May, 1730. Serving in 1740.
[2] His name appears in the *London Gazette* of 19 June, 1712, as one of Col. Philipps's officers in England ordered to join his Regt. at Annapolis Royal, Nova Scotia. Ens. 25 July, 1722. Comn. renewed in 1727. He appears to have exchanged to Lucas's Regt. in the West Indies, and to have d. before 1735, when the widow of Ens. Wroth of last-named Corps was drawing a pension of £16 per annum.

[3] *Handfield.* Comn. renewed in 1727. Capt.-Lieut. 3 Sept. 1739. Served as Capt. of a Cy. at Fort Minor, Nova Scotia, in July, 1749, a detachment of which was attacked and surprised by a party of Micmac Indians, the whole detachment being killed or taken prisoners, among the latter being Lieut. Hamilton and a son of Capt. Handfield (*Records*). Major, 15 Oct. 1754. Lt.-Col. 18 March, 1758. Retd. in July, 1760. His will was proved at Dublin in 1788.

[4] Not in any subsequent List.

[5] Do.

[6] D. as a Lieut. before 1733, in which year his widow, Rachel Baker, was drawing a pension of £20 per annum.

[7] Not in any subsequent List.

[8] See biog. notice in Vol. I., p. 313, note 3.

[9] See do. in do., p. 151, note 4.

[10] Lieut. 9 April, 1722. D. before 1734, in which year his widow, Mary Barton, was drawing a pension of £20 per annum.

[11] Out before 1727.

[12] D. as Rector of Stoke Clynesland, Cornwall, in 1768.—*Gentleman's Mag.*

[13] Comn. renewed in 1727. Capt. 30 Aug. 1731. Serving in 1740.

[14]   Do.   Out before 1740.

[15]   Do.   do.

[16] Son of Major Robert Handy of same Corps. Serving in 1727. Out before 1740.

[17] Lieut. 3 April, 1733. Capt.-Lieut. 25 Jan. 1749. Capt. 29 July, 1751. D. or left the Regt. before 1757.

[18] Comn. renewed in 1727. Out before 1740.

[19] D. before 1733, in which year his widow, Agatha Campbell, was drawing a pension of £16 per annum.

[20] Not in any subsequent List.

[21] Do.

[22] Comn. renewed in 1727. Succeeded his father, Sir John *Philipps*, Bart., of Picton Castle, Pembrokeshire, in 1736, and d.s.p.

[23] *Cavalier.* Served previously as Capt. in Col. Desbordes's Dragoons. Not in any subsequent List. Belonged to the Huguenot family, of which Maj.-Gen. John Cavalier was the head.

[24] *Bradstreet.* Serving in Nova Scotia as Lieut. in 1742. In the *Army List* for 1757 he appears as Lt.-Gov. of St. John's, Newfoundland. Bt.-Col. and Dep.-Qr.-Mr.-Gen. in America, 19 Feb. 1762. D. a Maj.-Gen. at New York in 1774. He was grandson of John Bradstreet who came over to Ireland with Oliver Cromwell.

[25] Comn. renewed in 1727. Out before 1740.

[26] Lieut. 12 Nov. 1733. Serving in 1740.

[27] Appointed Lieut. in Col. Wm. Walton's New England Regt. 1 April, 1710. Capt.-Lieut. 15 Aug. 1710. Served at the siege and capture of Port Royal, Nova Scotia, in autumn of same year. Half-pay, 1713. Out of Philipps's Regt. before 1740. A MS. at the War Office records that this officer was promoted from the ranks of the Rl. Horse Guards.

[28] *Okeden.* See p. 294. Comn. renewed in 1727. Serving in 1736. Out before 1740.

COLONEL EDMUND FIELDING'S REGIMENT OF INVALIDS.

[41st FOOT,—1st BATTALION THE WELSH REGIMENT.]

Edmund Fielding,[1] Esq. to be Colonel of a
Regt. of Invalids to be formed out of the
Pensioners of Our Royal Hospital near
Chelsea and likewise to be Capt. of a
Company in said Regt. -   -   - St. James's, 11 March, 1718/9. *c* & *p*

CAPTAINS.	LIEUTENANTS.	ENSIGNS.
Edmund Fielding, Col.	Michael Shute,[11] Capt.-Lieut.	Wm. Bellon [21]
George Winram,[2] Lt.-Col.	Paul Latour [12]	Leond. Robinson [22]
Wm. Maydman,[3] Major	James Martin [13]	Richard Aplin [23]
Edward Daniel [4]	John Hoyle [14]	George Welborne [24]
Philip Boisdaune [5]	Robert Catherwood [15]	Alex. Pigot [25]
Robert Baynes [6]	John Kynaston [16]	East Herbert [26]
Samuel Sedgley [7]	Wm. Pudsay [17]	Robert Gray [27]
Hopton Twynihoe [8]	John Cross [18]	Charles Clark [28]
Wm. Morden [9]	Jos. Lambert [19]	Richard Courtney [29]
Samuel Forster [10]	—— Jackson [20]	—— Merryman [30]

CHAPLAIN.

Simon Rowe [31]

SURGEON.

Alex. Littlejohn [32]

ADJUTANT.

Michael Shute [11]

SUPPLEMENTARY COMMISSIONS IN COLONEL FIELDING'S REGIMENT.

Kingsmill Eyre,[33] Esq. to be Agent and
Solicitor to above Regt. -   -   - St. James's, 16 Mar. 1718/9. *c*
Ben Willington [34] to be Ens. to Capt. Robt.
Baynes -   -   -   -   -   - Gohre,   17 Sept.   1719. *c*
George Green,[35] Esq. to be Major and Capt. of
a Cy. -   -   -   -   -   - St. James's, 21 Nov.   ,,   *c*
George Jefferies [36] to be Ens. to Capt. Phil.
Boisdaune -   -   -   -   -   ,,   25 Dec.   ,,   *c*
John Dobbyns [37] to be Qr.-Mr. -   -   -   ,,   ,, ,,   ,,   *c*

John Kerr [38] to be Lieut. to Capt. —— Herrenhausen, 28 July, 1720. *c*
Chas. Hamilton [39] to be Ens. to —— - - Hanover, 24 Sept. ,, *c*
Sampson Archer [40] to be Lieut. to —— - ,, ,, ,, ,, *c*
John Barnes, [41] Esq. to be Major and Capt. [in
   room of Wm. Maydman] - - - ,, 3 Nov. ,,
Henry Pascall [42] to be Ens. to —— - - St. James's, 5 Dec. ,, *c*
Thos. Rodd [43] to be Ens. to Capt. Hopton
   Twines (*sic*) - - - - - ,, 24 ,, ,, *c*
Chas. Clark [28] to be Lieut. to Capt. Phil.
   Boisdaune - - - - - ,, ,, ,, ,, *c*
John Green [44] to be Ens. to [Lt.-Col.] John
   Barnes - - - - - - - ,, 10 April, 1721. *c*
Ric. Applin [23] to be Lieut. to Capt. Edward
   Daniel - - - - - - ,, ,, ,, ,, *c*
Samuel Palmer [45] to be Ens. to Capt. Robt.
   Baynes - - - - - - Kensington, 7 Aug. ,, *c*
John Jammett (*sic*) [46] to be Lieut. to [Lt.-Col.]
   Barnes - - - - - - ,, 19 ,, ,, *c*
Lewis Delafaye, [47] Esq. to be Capt in room of
   Edward Daniel - - - - - St. James's, 18 Oct. ,, *c*
John Swan [48] to be Surgeon - - - ,, 19 ,, ,, *c*
Edward Strode, [49] Esq. to be Capt. of that Cy.
   whf. Lt.-Col. [John] Barnes was late
   Capt. - - - - - - - ,, 15 Nov. ,, *c*
Samuel Forster, [10] Esq. to be Major [in room of
   Lt.-Col. Barnes] and Capt. of a Cy. - ,, ,, ,, ,, *c*
John Pashler [50] to be Lieut. to —— - ,, 16 Dec. ,, *c*
Ant. Burren [51] to be Ens. to Capt. [Edward]
   Stroud - - - - - - ,, 25 ,, ,, *c*
Wm. Skeyes [52] to be Ens. to Capt. Phil.
   Boisdaune - - - - - - ,, 12 Feb. 1721/2. *c*
Alex. Gordon, [53] Esq. to be Lt.-Col. and Capt.
   of a Cy. - - - - - - ,, 28 ,, ,, *c*
Wm. Crosbie [54] to be Ens. to —— - - ,, 9 Mar. ,, *c*
John Dodd [55] to be Ens. to Capt. —— - ,, 25 April, 1722. *c*
Robt. Waller [56] to be Ens. to —— - - Kensington, 9 June, ,, *c*
James Scott, [57] Esq. to be Capt. in room of
   [Hopton] Twyniho - - - - ,, 27 July, ,, *c*
John Dobbin [58] to be Lieut. to Capt. Robert
   Bene (*sic*) - - - - ,, 15 Aug. ,, *c*
John Kynaston [16] to be Qr.-Mr. - - ,, ,, ,, ,, *c*
Thos. Phillips, [59] Esq. to be Capt. - - ,, 22 Sept. ,, *c*
Wm. Butler [60] to be Ens. to Capt. Lewis
   Delafaye - - - - - - St. James's, 11 Oct. ,, *c*
Thos. Grove [61] to be Ens. to —— - - ,, 12 April, 1723. *c*
Wm. Deane [62] to be Ens. to —— - - Herrenhausen, 31 Aug. ,, *c*
Nicholas Skinner [63] to be Lieut. to Capt.
   [Samuel] Sedgley - - - - St. James's, 24 Jan. 1723/4. *c*
James Dezières [64] to be Lieut. to —— - ,, 24 Feb. ,, *c*
John Purcel [65] to be Ens. to Capt. Sam.
   Sedgeley - - - - - - ,, 7 Mar. ,, *c*
Thos. Columbine [66] to be Ens. to Capt. Robt.
   Baynes - - - - - - ,, 14 April, 1724. *d*

John Corbet [67] to be Lieut. to Capt. [Samuel] Sedgeley - - - - - -	St. James's,	1 June, 1724.*d*
David Sinklair (*sic*),[68] Esq. to be Capt. -	„	15 July, „ *d*
James Usher [69] to be Ens. to Capt. Edward Stroud - - - - - -	Kensington,	10 Oct. „ *d*
Robt. Seton [70] to be Qr.-Mr. - - - -	„	15 „ „ *d*
Fras. Tuckey [71] to be Lieut. to —— -	St. James's,	17 Dec. „ *d*
Chas. Fell [72] to be Ens. to Capt. Sam. Sedgeley	„	18 Feb. 1724/5.*d*
Thos. Hayes [73] to be Lieut. to Capt. Stroud -	„	20 Mar. „ *d*
Park Pepper [74] to be Ens. to Capt. Robt. Baynes - - - - - -	„	22 April, 1725.*d*
Archd. McDonald [75] to be Ens. to —— -	„	21 April, 1726.*d*
John Westbrook [76] to be Ens. to [Lt.-Col.] Alex. Gordon	„	21 May, „ *d*
Thos. Moore [77] to be Lieut. to Capt. Phillips -	„	2 June, „ *d*
Chas. Clarke,[28] Esq. to be Capt.-Lieut. -	„	„ „ „ *d*
George Massey,[78] Esq. to be Capt. in room of Lewis Delafay - - - - -	„	26 July, „ *d*
Edmund Wiseman [79] to be Ens. to —— -	„	„ „ „ *d*
John Hay,[80] Esq. to be Capt. of George Massey's late Cy. - - - - -	„	26 Aug. „ *d*
Chas. Newland [81] to be Lieut. to —— - -	„	25 Dec. „ *d*
Wm. Combebrune [82] to be Ens. to —— -	„	„ „ „ *d*
Henry Spencer [83] to be do. to Lt.-Col. Alex. Gordon - - - - - -	„	„ „ „ *d*

[1] See p. 141, note 1.

[2] Appointed Ens. to his father (Major John Winram) in the Scots Foot Guards, 22 Nov. 1681. Accompanied the Guards to England in Oct. 1688. Lieut. in Col. John Buchan's Scots Regt. before 1694. Wounded at the siege of Namur. Capt. in Buchan's Regt. 1 Aug. 1697. Half-pay same year. Capt. in Lord Mark Kerr's Scots Regt. in 1706. Major early in 1707. Taken prisoner at Almanza. Placed on half-pay as Lt.-Col. in 1713. Lt.-Col. of 12 Companies of Invalids raised for Portsmouth in Aug. 1715. Retd. from the Regt. of Invalids in Feb. 1722.

[3] D. in Feb. 1723 as Capt. of an Indep. Cy. at Sheerness. Pension of £30 per annum granted to his widow, Ann Maydman. She was living in 1735.

[4] Appointed Capt. in the Queen's Regt. of Foot (2nd) in April, 1711. Half-pay in 1713. See his Comn. as Capt. in Gen. Wills's Regt. of Foot on p. 278.

[5] Comn. renewed in 1727. Out before 1740.

[6] 　　　Do.　　　　　　　do.

[7] From half-pay Capt. in Lord Mark Kerr's Regt. (29th Foot). Comn. in Fielding's Regt. renewed in 1727. Serving as senior Capt. in 1740.

[8] Out before June, 1727.

[9] From Capt. in Irwyn's Regt. of Foot. Capt. in Gen. Wills's Regt. of Foot, 6 Nov. 1721. Serving in 1730. Out before 1740.

[10] Major, 15 Nov. 1721. Comn. renewed in 1727. Out before 1740.

[11] Out 2 June, 1726.

[12] From half-pay Lieut. Kirke's Foot. Out before 1727.

[13] Out before 1727.

[14] Out before 1727. His widow, Elizabeth Hoyle, was drawing a pension of £20 per annum in 1735.

[15] See his Comn. on p. 308, and note thereto.

[16] Qr.-Mr. 15 Aug. 1722. Out before 1727.

[17] Out before 1727. His widow, Adriana Pudsay, was drawing a pension of £20 per annum in 1735.

[18] Capt. in Newton's Regt. (39th), 1 Nov. 1727. Out before 1740.

[19] D. before 1735, in which year his widow, Mary Lambert, was drawing a pension of £20 per annum.

[20] Out before 1727.

[21] Lieut. 27 Nov. 1733.   Serving in 1740.
[22] Out before 1727.
[23] Lieut. 10 April, 1721.   Serving in 1740.
[24] Out before 1727.
[25] Do.
[26] Do.
[27] D. before 1733, in which year his widow, Martha Gray, was drawing a pension of £16 per annum.
[28] Capt.-Lieut. 2 June, 1726.   Serving in 1727.   Out before 1740.
[29] Out before 1727.
[30] Do.
[31] Comn. renewed in 1727.
[32] Out before 1727.
[33] See biog. notice in Vol. I., p. 254, note 23.
[34] See p. 188, note 15.
[35] See biog. notice in Vol. I., p. 173, note 3.
[36] See his Comn. on p. 214, and note 14.
[37] Lieut. 15 Aug. 1722.   Out before 1727.
[38] Out before 1727.
[39] Do.
[40] Serving as Lieut. in Gen. Whetham's Regt. (12th) in 1727.   Capt.-Lieut. in said Corps, 7 Nov. 1739.   Described in his will, proved at Dublin in 1754, as "of Strabane, co. Tyrone, Esq."
[41] This officer's original Comn. as Major of Fielding's Corps is preserved at the Public Record Office, London.   In a "Memorial" from Lt.-Col. John Barnes to Charles Delafaye (secretary to Lord Stanhope) the writer says : "I have serv'd upwards of 30 years in succession, and was Major to Col. Frank's Regt. 11 years, and 9 years thereof Brevet Lt.-Colonel. . . . . On my return to England after the Regt. was reduced in Portugal I was taken by a Privateer, by which I lost upwards of £300." (S.P. Dom. George 1., Bundle 24, No. 263—undated.)   Appointed Town-Major of Portsmouth, 15 Nov. 1721.
[42] Out before 1727.
[43] Comn. renewed in 1727.
[44] Out before 1727.
[45] D. before 1734, in which year his widow, Martha Palmer, was drawing a pension of £16 per annum.
[46] See his Comn. on p. 314, note 18.
[47] Serving in 1727 as Capt. of an Indep. Cy. of Invalids at Sheerness.
[48] Comn. renewed in 1727.   Serving as Surgeon to above Regt. in 1758.
[49] Promoted Major, 12 Feb. 1751.   Serving in 1758.
[50] Out before 1727.
[51] Serving as Lieut. in Lord Harrington's Dragoons in 1730.
[52] Comn. renewed in 1727.   Lieut. of a newly-raised Cy. of Invalids, 13 Nov. 1739.
[53] Appointed Major of Maccartney's Scots Regt. of Foot, 1 May, 1710.   Half-pay, 1713. Held the Lt.-Colonelcy of the Regt. of Invalids until 1751.
[54] Out before 1727.
[55] John Dodd was appointed Ens. in Col. Lanoe's Regt. on the Irish Establishment.
[56] Out before 1727.
[57] Do.
[58] Name spelt "Dobbyns" in his Comn. as Qr.-Mr. on p. 324.
[59] Comn. renewed in 1727.   Out before 1740.
[60] Comn. renewed in 1727.   D. as a Lieut. before 1734, in which year his widow, Elizabeth Butler, was drawing a pension of £20 per annum.
[61] Out before 1727.
[62] Do.
[63] See his Comn. on p. 302, and note thereto.
[64] Appointed Lieut. in Desney's Regt. (29th), 1 Feb. 1727.   Capt.-Lieut. 9 July, 1739. Serving in 1740.
[65] See p. 285, note 40.
[66] Out before 1727.
[67] Comn. renewed in 1727.   Out before 1740.
[68] *Sinclair.*   Comn. renewed in 1727.   Out before 1740.
[69] Serving as Lieut. in 1727.   Out before 1740.
[70] Comn. renewed in 1727.
[71]   Do.   Serving in 1740.

[72] Comn. renewed in 1727.   Out before 1740.
[73]   Do.   do.
[74] Ens. to Capt. Graham's Cy. of Invalids in Guernsey, 25 Dec. 1722.   See biog. notice in Vol. I., p. 222, note 55.
[75] Comn. renewed in 1727.   Out before 1740.
[76] Lieut. in Col. Montague's Regt. of Foot, 25 Dec. 1726.   See p. 292.
[77] Comn. renewed in 1727.   D. before 1734, in which year his widow, Sarah *More*, was drawing a pension of £20 per annum.
[78] Out 26 Aug. 1726.
[79] See p. 295, note 35.
[80] Serving as Capt. in 1740.
[81] Comn. renewed in 1727.   D. before 1734, in which year his widow, Elizabeth Newland, was drawing a pension of £20 per annum.
[82] Comn. renewed in 1727.   Out before 1740.
[83]   Do.   do.

ENGLISH ESTABLISHMENT

NON-REGIMENTAL COMMISSIONS AND MILITARY APPOINTMENTS, 1719–1727

NON-REGIMENTAL COMMISSIONS AND MILITARY APPOINTMENTS, 1719–1727

NON-REGIMENTAL COMMISSIONS.

Sir James Wood,[1] Bart. to be Brigadier-General over all Our Forces - - - St. James's, 1 Mar. 1716/7.*p*

George Treby,[2] Esq. to be Sec. at War - - ,, 22 Dec. 1718.*p*

Lt.-General George Maccartney[3] to be Governor and Capt. of Our Town and Isle of Portsmouth and Our Castle there called South Sea Castle; and of the Forts, Blockhouses and Fortifications belonging to the same in the room of Charles Wills, Esq. - - - - ,, 15 April, 1719.*c*

Major-General Sabine[4] to be Governor of Berwick and Holy Island in room of George Maccartney, Esq. - - - ,, ,, ,, ,, *c*

Col. Samuel Gledhill[5] to be Lieut.-Governor of Placentia - - - - - - Pyrmont, 16 June (O.S.) ,, *p*

Andrew Hamilton,[6] Esq. to be Major of Brigade in H.M.'s Forces intended for an Expedition to be made beyond Seas. [Comn. signed by the Lords Justices] - Whitehall, 19 July, ,, *c*

[Richard, Lord Viscount Cobham[7] to be General and Commander-in-Chief of the Forces intended for an Expedition at Sea - - - - - - - - — 28 ,, ,,]

John Clothier[8] to be Drum-Major-General of H.M.'s Forces - - - - - - Whitehall, 8 Sept. ,, *c*

Hugh Plucknet,[9] Esq. to be Lt.-Governor of Landguard Fort - - - - - ,, 17 ,, ,, *c*

Bacon Morris,[10] Esq. to be Governor of do. in room of Fras. Hammond decd. - - ,, ,, ,, ,, *c*

Fras. Wallace[11] to be Chaplain to the Town and Garrison of Portsmouth - - - ,, 22 ,, ,, *c*

John Martyn,[12] Esq. to be Provost-Marshal-General - - - - - - - St. James's, 25 Dec. ,, *c*

John Sutton[13] to be Fort Major at West Tilbury - - - - - - - ,, 23 Jan. 1719/20.*c*

John Aldwin[14] to be Chaplain to above Fort - ,, 5 Feb. ,, *c*

Thos. Whitney,[15] Esq. to be Town Major of Portsmouth - - - - - ,, 6 April, 1720.*c*

Thos. Stewart [16] to be Adjt. to Our Royal Hospital, Chelsea - - - - -	St. James's,	23 May, 1720.	c
Charles Churchill, [17] Esq. to be Governor of Our Royal Hospital, Chelsea - - -	,,	6 June, ,,	c
Brig.-Gen. Fras. Nicholson [18] to be Capt.-General and Gov.-in-Chief of South Carolina in America - - - -	—	26 Sept. ,,	c
Alex. Stevenson to be one of the Deputy-Commissaries of the Musters of all the Forces in South Britain during Our Pleasure - - - - - -	St. James's,	5 Dec. ,,	c
Peter Davenport to be do. -	,,	17 ,, ,,	c
Col. George Treby [19] to be Capt. and Governor of Dartmouth Castle in room of Nicholas Roope - - -	,,	24 ,, ,,	c
Thos. Newman to be Fort Major at do. - -	,,	25 ,, ,,	c
Samuel Brady [20] to be Physician to Our Town and Garrison of Portsmouth - - -	,,	,, ,, ,,	c
Sydenham Fowke, [21] Esq. to be Major of the Garrison in the Tower - - - -	,,	1 Feb. 1720/1.	c
Wm. Waynes to be Town Adjt. to the Garrison of Berwick-on-Tweed - - - -	,,	25 ,, ,,	c
Brig.-Gen. Thos. Stanwix [22] to be Governor and Capt. of Our Town of Kingston-upon-Hull in room of Viscount Irwin -	,,	29 Mar. 1721.	c
Peter Rogie to be Surgeon of Sheerness Fort -	,,	,, ,, ,,	c
John, Lord Belhaven [23] to be Governor of Barbados in room of Visct. Irwin decd. - - - - - - -	—	9 April, ,,	n
Abraham Joye to be Town Major of Plymouth - - - - - - -	St. James's,	31 May, ,,	c
John Huske, Esq. to be Capt. or Keeper of Hurst Castle in Our County of Southampton - - - - - - - -	,,	8 July, ,,	c
—— Cooper to be Surgeon to the Town and Garrison of Berwick-on-Tweed - - -	,,	19 Oct. ,,	c
John Barnes, [24] Esq. to be Town Major of Portsmouth - - - - - -	,,	15 Nov. ,,	c
Henry Worsley, [25] Esq. to be Governor of Barbados in room of Lord Belhaven decd. - - - - - - - -	—	— ,, ,,	
Adam Williamson, [26] Esq. to be Adjt.-General of Our Forces in room of Metcalf Graham and rank as Colonel of Horse - - -	St. James's,	28 Feb. 1721/2.	c
Edward Hayes, [27] Esq. to be Lt.-Governor of Landguard Fort - - - - -	,,	14 May, 1722.	c
Earl of Peterboro' and Monmouth [28] to be General of all Our Marine Forces - -	,,	24 ,, ,,	p
Ben. Waide Junr. to be Surgeon to Our Garrison of Kingston-upon-Hull - -	,,	3 July, ,,	c
Sir Hans Sloane, [29] Bart. to be Physitian-General of Our Land Forces in room of Thos. Gibson decd. - - - - -	Kensington,	18 ,, ,,	c

CHARLES HOWARD

EARL OF CARLISLE.

CONSTABLE OF THE TOWER.

(*See* Vol. I., p. 232, and p. 244, note 16.)

Jonathan Hall, B.D. to be Chaplain to the Garrison of Berwick-on-Tweed - - Kensington, 22 Sept. 1722.*c*

Adam Williamson,[26] Esq. to be Deputy to the Lieut. of the Tower in room of Robert d'Oyley - - - - - ,, 29 Oct. ,, *c*

Thos. Wentworth,[30] Esq. to be Adjt.-General of all Our Forces in room of Adam Williamson and rank as Col. of Horse - ,, 29 Nov. ,, *c*

Henry Villers (*sic*),[31] Esq. to be Lt.-Governor of Tinmouth (*sic*) Castle in room of John Lewis de la Bene decd. - - - ,, 20 Dec. ,, *c*

Magnus Kempenfelt,[32] Esq. to be Lt.-Governor of Our Island of Jersey - - - - ,, 4 May, 1723.*c*

Charles, Earl of Carlisle[33] to be Governor of Windsor Castle - - - - - ,, 29 ,, ,, *c*

Henry Russell to be Surveyor of Our Barracks in the Savoy and of the Guard Rooms belonging to Our Foot Guards at the Tylt Yard and of the Royal Palaces of St. James's and Kensington - Herrenhausen, 12 July, ,, *c*

Edward Newton, Esq. to be one of the Deputy-Commissaries of the Musters and to hold the same during Our Pleasure - ,, 28 ,, ,, *c*

Chris. Whytell to be do. - - - - ,, 16 Aug. ,, *c*

Paul George,[34] Esq. to be Lt.-Governor of Montserrat in room of —— Dilks decd. - - - - - - - ,, 20 ,, ,, *p*

Samuel Horne to be Chaplain to the Garrison of Plymouth and Royal Citadel there - - - - - - ,, 20 Sept. ,, *c*

Nathaniel Terry,[35] Sen. to be Major of Dartmouth Castle - - - - - - Gohre, 9 Nov. ,, *c*

Charles Cowper, D.D. to be Chaplain to Our Town and Garrison of Portsmouth - - Hanover, 17 ,, ,, *c*

Joseph Garton[36] to be Provost-Marshal to Our Three Regts. of Foot Guards - Helvoet Sluys, 25 Dec. ,, *c*

Wm. Waynes[37] to be Barrack-Master of Our Barracks in the Savoy in room of Thos. Murphy - - - - - - - St. James's, 27 Jan. 1723/4.*c*

Wm. Townshend,[38] Esq. to be Our A.D.C. and to command and take your rank as Colonel of Foot - - - - - ,, ,, ,, ,, *c*

Wm. Crudge to be Deputy-Commissary of the Forces employed in Our Island of Scilly, to hold the said place during Our Pleasure - - - - - - ,, 23 Mar. ,, *c*

John Nathan Darley to be Chaplain at Landguard Fort - - - - - Windsor, 31 Aug. 1724.*d*

Wm. Phelps to be do. at Tilbury Fort - - ,, ,, ,, *d*

George Carlton to be do. at Sheerness - - ,, 25 Sept. ,, *d*

Wm. Day to be do. to Chelsea Hospital - Kensington, 5 Oct. ,, *d*

Laurence Armstrong,[39] Esq. to be Lt.-Governor of Our Province of Nova Scotia - - St. James's, 8 Feb. 1724/5.*d*

George Cholmondeley,[40] Esq. (commonly called Viscount Malpas) to be Governor of Our City and Castle of Chester	Kensington, 25 Feb. 1724/5.		d
George, Earl of Cholmondeley [41] to be Gov. and Capt. of Kingston-upon-Hull in room of Brig.-Gen. Thos. Stanwix	,,	20 Mar. ,,	d
Major-General Wm. Tatton [42] to be Gov. of Our Fort of West Tilbury	,,	,, ,, ,,	d
Charles Howard,[43] Esq. to be Lt.-Gov. of Carlisle Castle	,,	24 ,, ,,	d
Richard Evans,[44] Esq. to be Lt.-Governor of Sheerness Fort	Herrenhausen, 10 Sept. (O.S.) 1725.		d
Arthur Holdsworth,[45] Junr. to be Fort Major at Dartmouth	Helvoet Sluys, 25 Dec. ,,		d
Brig.-Gen. John Hobart [46] to be Gov. and Capt. of Pendennis Castle during Our Pleasure	,,	,, ,, ,,	d
Charles Le Geyt to be Dep.-Commissary of the Musters in Jersey and Guernsey	St. James's, 10 Feb. 1725/6.		d
Wm. Hicks to be Surgeon to Our Fort of Sheerness	,,	15 ,, ,,	d
Robert Nelson, Esq. to be Sec. to the Comptroller of the Accounts of the Army	—	8 April, 1726.	d
Col. Wm. Wyndham [47] to be Lt.-Gov. of Chelsea Hospital	St. James's, 15 ,,		,, d
James Howard to be Provost-Marshal to Our three Regts. of Foot Guards	Kensington, 20 July, ,,		d
Lewis Dollon,[48] Esq. to be Lt.-Gov. of Our Island of Guernsey during Our Pleasure [in room of Lt.-Col. Spicer]	,,	1 Aug. ,,	d
Samuel Needham [49] to be Surveyor of Our Barracks in the Savoy, &c.	,,	23 Nov. ,,	d
Edward Strode,[50] Esq. to be Town Major of Our Town and Garrison of Portsmouth	,,	17 Dec. ,,	d
Henry, Earl of Deloraine [51] to be Major-General over all Our Forces	St. James's, 1 Mar. 1726/7.		d
George, Earl of Cholmondeley [41] to be General over do.	,,	,, ,, ,,	d
Albert Borgard,[52] Esq. to be Brigadier-General over do.	,,	,, ,, ,,	d
Owen Wynne,[53] Esq. to be Lieut.-General over do.	,,	,, ,, ,,	d
Francis Columbine,[54] Esq. to be Brigadier-General over do.	,,	2 ,, ,,	d
Thos. Whetham,[55] Esq. to be Lieut.-General over do.	,,	,, ,, ,,	d
Richard Russell,[56] Esq. to be Major-General over do.	,,	,, ,, ,,	d
Richard Franks,[57] Esq. to be Brigadier-General over do.	,,	3 ,, ,,	d
Andrew Bisset,[58] Esq. to be Major-General over do.	,,	,, ,, ,,	d

Wm. Tatton,[42] Esq. to be Lieut.-General over do. - - - - - - -	St. James's,	3 Mar.	1726/7.		d
Joseph Sabine,[4] Esq. to be do. - - -	,,	4	,,	,,	d
Wm. Newton,[59] Esq. to be Brigadier-General over do. - - - - - - -	,,		,,	,,	d
Nicholas Price,[60] Esq. to be Major-General over do. - - - - - - -	,,		,,	,,	d
John Kerr,[61] Esq. (commonly called Lord John Kerr) to be Major-General over do. - - - - - - -	,,	5	,,	,,	d
Thos. Pearce,[62] Esq. to be Lieut.-General over do. - - - - - - -	,,		,,	,,	d
John Pocock,[63] Esq. to be Brigadier-General over do. - - - - - - -	,,		,,	,,	d
Wm. Evans,[64] Esq. to be Lieut.-General over do. - - - - - - -	,,	6	,,	,,	d
Humphry Gore,[65] Esq. to be Major-General over do. - - - - - -	,,		,,	,,	d
Charles Churchill,[66] Esq. to be Brigadier-General over do. - - - - -	,,	,,	,,	,,	d
John Hopkey,[67] Esq. to be do. - - -	,,	7	,,	,,	d
Wm. Barrell,[68] Esq. to be do. - - - -	,,	,,	,,	,,	d
George Wade,[69] Esq. to be Lieut.-General over do. - - - - - - -	,,	,,	,,	,,-	d
Philip Honywood,[70] Esq. to be Major-General over do. - - - - - - -	,,	,,	,,	,,	d
Henry Grove,[71] Esq. to be Major-General over do. - - - - - - -	,,	8	,,	,,	d
Jasper Clayton,[72] Esq. to be Brigadier-General over do. - - - - - -	,,	,,	,,	,,	d
Andrew Wheeler,[73] Esq. to be Major-General over do. - - - - - - -	,,	9	,,	,,	d
Edward Jones,[74] Esq. to be Brigadier-General over do. - - - - - - -	,,	,,	,,	,,	d
Mark Kerr,[75] Esq. (commonly called Lord Mark Kerr) to be Major-General over do.	,,	10	,,	,,	d
Robert Hunter,[76] Esq. to be do. - - -	,,	,,	,,	,,	d
Piercy Kirke,[77] Esq. to be Brigadier-General over do. - - - - - - -	,,	,,	,,	,,	d
James Crofts,[78] Esq. to be Major-General over do. - - - - - - -	,,	11	,,	,,	d
Charles Dubourgay,[79] Esq. to be Brigadier-General over do. - - - - -	,,	,,	,,	,,	d
Paul de Gually,[80] Esq. to be do. - - -	,,	12	,,	,,	d
John Moyle,[81] Esq. to be do. - - - -	,,	,,	,,	,,	d
Robert Napier,[82] Esq. to be Major-General over do. - - - - - - -	,,	13	,,	,,	d
Robert Dalzell,[83] Esq. to be do. - - -	,,	,,	,,	,,	d
Gervais Parker,[84] Esq. to be Brigadier-General over do. - - - - - - -	,,	14	,,	,,	d
James Dormer,[85] Esq. to be Major-General over do. - - - - - - -	,,	,,	,,	,,	d
David Creighton,[86] Esq. to be do. - - -	,,	15	,,	,,	d

James Tyrrell,[87] Esq. to be Brigadier-General over do. - - - - - - - St. James's,	15 Mar.	1726/7.		_d_
Edmund Fielding,[88] Esq. to be do. - - - ,,	16	,,	,,	_d_
[Richard Sutton,[89] Esq. to be Major-General over do. - - - - - - ,,	,,	,,	,,	]
John Peter Desbordes,[90] Esq. to be Brig.-Gen. over do. - - - - - - ,,	17	,,	,,	_d_
Wm. Kerr (_sic_),[91] Esq. to be do. - - - ,,	18	,,	,,	_d_
Algernon, Earl of Hertford [92] to be do. - - ,,	19	,,	,,	_d_
Sir Robert Rich,[93] Bart. to be do. - - - ,,	20	,,	,,	_d_
Wm. Anne, Earl of Albemarle [94] to be Our A.D.C. and to rank as Col. of Foot - ,,	31	,, 1727.		_d & f_
Col. David Montolieu,[95] Baron de St. Hippolite to be Brigadier-General over all Our Forces - - - - - - - ,,	22 April, 1727.			_d_
Thos. Graham, Esq. to be Apothecary-General to Our Army - - - - - - ,,	18 May,		,,	_d_
Thos. Sydenham [96] to be one of the Deputy-Commissaries during Our Pleasure - - ,,	20	,,	,,	_d_

[1] Son and heir of John Wood of "Bonyngtoun," co. Forfar (by Anne, dau. of James Ogilvy, 2nd Earl of Airlie), who was created a Bart. 11 May, 1666, and d. 1693. (G.E.C.'s _Complete Baronetage._) James Wood was appointed Capt. in Col. John Hales's Regt. of Foot, 31 Dec. 1688. Major of Lord Strathnaver's Regt. of Scots Foot in 1693. Succeeded his father as 2nd Bart. same year. Was Gov. of Dendermonde and Col. of a Regt. in the Dutch Scots Brigade. Served through Marlborough's campaigns. In 1717 Sir J. Wood was admitted as Brig.-Gen. into the British Service "in consequence of his military reputation." Col. of the Royal Scots Fusiliers, 9 March, 1726/7. Maj.-Gen. 27 Oct. 1735. D. 3 May, 1738, when the Baronetcy became extinct.

[2] Son of Sir George Treby, an eminent judge. He had been M.P. for Plympton, 1708-34. Appointed Teller of the Exchequer, 25 April, 1724. Father of George Treby, M.P. for Dartmouth, 1722-47, and Lord of the Treasury, 1741.—_Dict. Nat. Biog._

[3] See biog. notice in Vol. I., p. 253, note 3.

[4] See do. in do., p. 347, note 1.

[5] Appointed Lieut. in Lord Lucas's Regt. of Foot, 23 July, 1702. Lieut.-Col. Maccartney's Regt. of Foot, 24 Dec. 1707. Commanded Sutton's (late Maccartney's) Regt. at the siege of Douay, and was severely wounded, taken prisoner, "and dragged naked into the town." (Petition in _Treasury Papers_, dated 27 Sept. 1712.) Lieut.-Gov. of Carlisle and Capt. in Gen. Stanhope's Dragoons in 1712. D. as Lieut.-Gov. of Placentia in 1736.

[6] Not in any subsequent List.

[7] Appointed by Letters Patent. See special memoir, pp. 1-9.

[8] Comn. signed by the Lords Justices.

[9] Do. See Vol. I., p. 310, note 3.

[10] Do. From Capt. in Pearce's Regt. (5th Foot). D. 1744.

[11] Do.

[12] Do.

[13] Served previously as Major of Col. James Butler's Regt. of Foot. Half-pay, 1712. Untraced after 1720.

[14] Untraced.

[15] Believed to be identical with Lt.-Col. Thos. Whitney, of Chudleigh's Regt., see Vol. I., p. 170, note 2. He held this post at Portsmouth until Nov. 1720.

[16] Serving in 1727.

[17] See biog. notice in Vol. I., p. 120, note 1.

[18] This appointment was by Letters Patent. See special memoir, pp. 55-62.

[19] See p. 266, note 8.

[20] Held this post until Nov. 1722.

[21] See p. 156, note 17.

[22] See biog. notice in Vol. I., p. 166, note 1.

[23] Third Baron. Wrecked on the Stag Rocks, Lizard Point, on night of 10 Nov. 1721, when proceeding to Barbados on board the _Royal Anne_. Lord Belhaven was drowned

with all the passengers, officers, and crew, excepting two men and a boy who drifted on shore.

[24] See p. 327, note 41.

[25] Appointed by Letters Patent. He was second son of Sir Robt. Worsley, Bart., of Appuldercombe. Sent Envoy to Portugal, 1714. M.P. for Newport, I. of W. D. 15 March, 1747.

[26] See Vol. I., p. 223, note 78.

[27] Served previously in Pearce's Regt. (5th Foot). D. on 7 Jan. 1753, and was bd. in the graveyard of Landguard Fort. The memorial inscription on his tombstone is given in Major J. H. Leslie's *History of Landguard Fort* and is as follows :—

In Memory of

EDWARD HAYES, Esqr.,

Lieutenant-Governor

of Landguard Fort,

in this county,

who departed this life

the 7th of January, 1753,

aged 61 years.

He was Constant and Courageous

in the Execution of his Office,

Eminent for his Affability, Kindness,

and good Nature to all Mankind.

[28] Charles Mordaunt, 3rd Earl of Peterborough and 1st Earl of Monmouth. This eccentric nobleman died on his passage to Lisbon, 25 Oct. 1735.

[29] Youngest son of Alex. Sloane of Killileagh, co. Down. Bn. 16 April, 1660. Created a Bart. 3 April, 1716. Chosen President of the Royal Society, 20 March, 1727. D. 11 Jan. 1753. Bd. in Chelsea Churchyard under a handsome monument erected by his daughters.

[30] See Vol. I., p. 99, note 3.

[31] Son of Edward Villiers, a former Gov. of Tynemouth Castle. D. in 1753.

[32] See Vol. I., p. 140, note 2.

[33] Appointment by Letters Patent. See Vol. I., p. 244, note 16.

[34] D. in 1728. Pension of £26 per annum to his widow.

[35] Held this post until Dec. 1725.

[36] Held this post until 20 July, 1726.

[37] See his Comn. on p. 332.

[38] See his Comn. on p. 204, note 11.

[39] See Vol. I., p. 313, note 3.

[40] See his father's biog. notice in Vol. I., p. 97, note 1. Succeeded as 3rd Earl Cholmondeley, 7 May, 1733. Created K.B. by George II. Md. dau. of Sir Robert Walpole, 1st Earl of Orford. Raised a Regt. of Foot during the Jacobite Rebellion of 1745, and was appointed Col. thereof, 4 Oct. 1745. Said Corps was disbanded in 1746. Earl Cholmondeley attained the rank of Lt.-Gen. in 1759, and d. in 1770.

[41] See Vol. I., p. 97, note 1.

[42] See do. p. 127, note 3.

[43] See do. p. 219, note 23.

[44] Served previously as Capt. of an Indep. Cy. of Invalids.

[45] The *Gentleman's Mag.* for 1753 records the death of Arthur Holdsworth, of Dartmouth.

[46] Served previously as Capt. and Lt.-Col. Coldstream Guards. Brig.-Gen. 1 Jan. 1710. Retd. from aforesaid Regt. in 1716. D. in 1734.

[47] Appointed by Royal Warrant. Served in former reign as Lt.-Col. of the Carabineers. Sold his Comn. as Lt.-Col. in 1712.

[48] Served as a Subaltern with the Royal Dragoons in Spain, 1703–4, and was made a Bt.-Capt. in latter year. In 1715 was transferred from command of a Troop in Royal Dragoons to Col. Hon. Wm. Ker's Dragoons (7th), and retired from last-named Corps in July, 1720.

[49] Had served as Qr.-Mr. to the Batt. of Coldstream Guards sent to Vigo in 1719. See p. 269.

[50] See his Comn. as Capt. in Fielding's Regt. on p. 325, and note thereto.

[51] See biog. notice in Vol. I., page 100, note 1

[52] See do. in do., p. 284, note 1.

[53] See do. in do., p. 113, note 1.

[54] See do. in do., p. 147, note 2.

[55] See do. in do., p. 164, note 1.

[56] See do. in do., p. 127, note 3.

[57] Served as A.D.C. to the Dutch Gen. Scravemoor in 1692, at which time he was a Capt. in the Regt. afterwards known as the 6th Foot. In 1706 this officer applied to the

Duke of Marlborough for the command of a new Regt. and stated that "he had served in the Army 23 years, in Ireland, Flanders, and the West Indies as D.Q.M.G., Q.M.G., and A.G. without compensation, and that he was one of the oldest Lieut.-Colonels in the Army." (*War Office MS.*) Was given the command of a Regt. and sent to Spain in 1710. D. a Lt.-Gen. about 1743.

[58] See biog. notice on p. 174, note 17.

[59] See do. in Vol. I., p. 119, note 1.

[60] Served in former reign as Col. of a Regt. of Foot which was disbanded after the Peace of Utrecht. He was given the Colonelcy of the 28th Foot, 25 Aug. 1730. D. in 1734.

[61] See biog. notice in Vol. I., p. 98. note 2.

[62] See do. in do., p. 142, note 1.

[63] See do. in do., p. 180, note 1.

[64] See do. in do., p. 331, note 1.

[65] See do. in do., p. 114, note 1.

[66] See do. in do., p. 120, note 1.

[67] *Hopeke.* Generally called "Henry Hopkey." Henry was his second name. Served as Mate to the Firemaster in the 1689 Train. Fireworker in Gen. de Ginkell's Train of Artillery in Ireland in 1691. Major of an Ordnance Train to sail with the Fleet, 1 May, 1692. Recd. a similar appointment in 1694 and 1695. Major of the "Peace Train," 29 Nov. 1698. Lt.-Col. of the Flanders Train, 26 Feb. 1703. Fought at Blenheim. Lt.-Col. of the Artillery Train in Spain, 1 Feb. 1707. First Col. of the Artillery Train in Holland, 25 March, 1708. Recd. a similar appointment 10 Feb. 1711. Served at Malplaquet. Half-pay in 1715. D. in 1734, at which time he held the post of Comptroller of Fireworks.

[68] See biog. notice in Vol. I., p. 354, note 4.

[69] See special memoir in this volume, pp. 11–22.

[70] See biog. notice in Vol. I., p. 115, note 1.

[71] Appointed Capt.-Lieut. to the Royal Fusiliers, 1 Aug. 1692. Capt. 20 May, 1693. Wounded at the storming of the breach of Terra Nova, Namur, 20 Aug. 1695. Major to Sir Mat. Bridges's Regt. (17th) 2 June, 1700. Bt.-Lt.-Col. 6 March, 1703. Lt.-Col. of the Regt. afterwards known as 10th Foot, 25 April, 1704. Fought at Blenheim. Bt.-Col. 5 Jan. 1706. Wounded at the battle of Oudenarde. Served at Malplaquet. Brig.-Gen. 12 Feb. 1711. Col. 10th Foot, 25 June, 1715. Lt.-Gov. of Berwick in 1716. Attained the rank of Lt.-Gen. 27 Oct. 1735. D. 20 Nov. 1736. Bd. in Westminster Abbey.

[72] See biog. notice in Vol. I., p. 340, note 1. This distinguished soldier was educated at Merchant Taylors' School. He was probably eldest son of George Clayton, fourth son of Sir Jasper Clayton, Alderman of London. When his body was discovered on the battlefield of Dettingen, it was interred in Prince George of Hesse's chapel at Hanau; but is said to have been subsequently sent back to England and re-interred at Wingfield in Berkshire.

[73] See biog. notice in Vol. I., p. 127, note 4.

[74] Appointed Capt. in the Inniskilling Regt. of Foot (27th), 20 July, 1695. Served with said Corps in the West Indies and was promoted Major, 3 Sept. 1702. Lt.-Col. 1 Dec. 1703. Col. of a newly-raised Regt. of Foot in Ireland, 1708. Half-pay, 1713. Col. of the 38th Foot, 25 Dec. 1729. D. in April, 1735. Appears to have belonged to a County Wexford family.

[75] See biog. notice in Vol. I., p. 356, note 1.

[76] See do. in do., p. 245, note 19.

[77] See do. in do., p. 136, note 1.

[78] See do. in do., p. 106, note 4.

[79] See do. in do., p. 168, note 1. Sent Envoy to Berlin in 1724.

[80] Appointed Lt.-Col. of the Count de Paullin's Regt. of French Foot, 2 April, 1706. Bt.-Col. 1 Jan. 1708. Major of Col. Trapaud's Regt. of Foot in 1709. Said Corps was re-formed in Portugal same year as a Regt. of Dragoons and De Gually was appointed Col. 24 June, 1710. Half-pay in 1712. Drawing half-pay as Col. of Dragoons in 1722. Maj.-Gen. 4 Nov. 1735. D. in London, 1737.

[81] See biog. notice in Vol. I., p. 119, note 2.

[82] See do. in do., p. 328, note 2.

[83] See do. in *The Scots Army*, 1661-1688, by Charles Dalton, p. 117, note 28.

[84] See do. in Vol. I., p. 144, note 2. On the death of Field-Marshal Visct. Shannon in Dec. 1740, Lt.-Gen. Gervase Parker was appointed C.-in-C. in Ireland.

[85] See do. in Vol. I., p. 118, note 1.

[86] See do. on p. 137, note 1.

[87] See do. in Vol. I., p. 121, note 1.

[88] See do. on p. 141, note 1.

[89] See special memoir in Vol. I., pp. 55–58.

[90] Appointed Ens. in Col. Richards's Regt. (17th Foot), 29 Sept. 1688. Wounded at the storming of the breach of Terra Nova, Namur, 20 Aug. 1695. Capt. in same Corps, 31 May, 1701. Col. of a French Refugee Regt. of Dragoons in Portugal in 1709. A list of officers on half-pay of said Corps is given in the Half-pay Army List, 1714.

[91] See biog. notice in Vol. I., p. 111, note 1.

[92] See do. in do., p. 96, note 1.

[93] See do. in do., p. 122, note 1.

[94] 2nd Earl. K.G. C.-in-C. in Scotland, July, 1746. Was subsequently Ambassador at the French Court. D. at Paris, 22 Dec. 1754.

[95] Appointed Ens. in Col. de la Melonière's Regt. of French Foot, 1 April, 1689. Served under William III. in Ireland and Flanders. Attained the rank of Bt.-Col. before 1714. Maj.-Gen. 13 Nov. 1735. Lt.-Gen. 2 July, 1739. D. in 1761, aged 93.—*Gentleman's Mag.*

[96] See his Comn. as Secretary to the General of the Horse and to the General of the Foot in Vol. I., p. 230.

TEN COMPANIES OF INVALIDS FORMED OUT OF THE OUT-PENSIONERS OF CHELSEA HOSPITAL.

*Commissions dated at St. James's, 11 March, 1718/9 (c). The names marked with a * are those officers whose Commissions were renewed 20 June, 1727.*

CAPTAINS.	LIEUTENANTS.	ENSIGNS.
Robert d'Oyley.[1]	James Read.	Henry Willoughby.
Richmond Webb.*	Alex. Blackall.	Parke Pepper.*
Hugh Plucknet.[2]	Thos. Stewart.	—— Woolcombe.
Richard Jones.[3]	Alex. Frazer.	Simon Little.
Gilbert Symonds.*	John Emmenes.*	John Bowdler.
Wm. Proby.*	Samuel Ball.	Par. Donnough.
Gwyn Vaughan.[4]	John St. Aubin.	Edward Symms.
Robert Mountfort.[5]	John Ledsom.	Mich. Pouchard.
Sydenham Fowke.[6]	Thos. Moore.	John Walker.*
Richard Green.[7]	Charles Maidman.	John McDougall.*

FIFTEEN ADDITIONAL COMPANIES OF INVALIDS FORMED AS ABOVE.

Commissions dated at St. James's, 3 April, 1719. (c)

CAPTAINS.	LIEUTENANTS.	ENSIGNS.
Lewis Dejean.[8]	Edward Edmonds.*	Chas. Parkinson.*
Alex. Rinton.	Edward Mitchell.*	Stanwix Ross.
Fras. Clarke.	Wiltshire Castle.*	Sir John Hamilton.*
Robert Dove.[9]	Thos. Clutterbuck.*	John Hanning.
John Carwarden.*	Norman Macleod.*	Richard Eagan.
Fras. Wigg.*	Lewis Dufour.*	Sidney Wandesford.
Mordaunt Cratchrod [10] (sic).	Mat. Draper * [Jr.]	Henry Jackson.
Thos. Shrimpton.	James Bix.*	John Gugleman.
John Massey.[11]	Sol. Tovey.*	Wm. Pritchard.*
John Broughton.*	Wm. McCullock.	John Musgrave.*
John Crosbie.	George Ley.	Thos. Lewis.
Fras. Boggest.	Ro. Eaglesfield.*	Wm. Castle.
Ro. Byng.	John Dalway.*	Thos. Bowes.
John Shutt (sic).	Sam. Antrim.	Wm. Pyle.

SUPPLEMENTARY COMMISSIONS.

John Perceval to be Ensign to Capt. Hugh Plucknett - - - - -	-Herrenhausen,	20 Aug.	1719.c	
Thos. Lisle* to be Lieut. to Capt. Gwyn Vaughan's Cy. - - - - -	Gohre,	17 Sept. (O.S.),,	c	
Daniel Gilligan* to be Ens. to Capt. Mountfort's Cy. - - - - -	,,	13 Oct. ,,	,, c	
[John Graham [12] to be Capt. of a Cy. in Guernsey - - - - -	—	19 Dec. ,,	,,]	
Arthur Horsman to be Ens. to Capt. Hugh Plucknet - - - - -	St. James's,	15 Feb. 1719/20.c		
Hubert Marshall to be Lieut. to Capt. Wm. Proby - - - - -	,,	5 April, 1720.c		
Wm. Maidman, Esq. to be Capt. in room of Hugh Plucknet - - - - -	,,	20 ,,	,, c	
John Perkins to be Lieut. to Capt. Maidman	,,	4 June,	,, c	
Robert Colt to be Lieut. to Capt. Sydenham Fowke - - - - -	,,	6 ,,	,, c	
Henry Bernard * to be Ens. to Capt. Ric. Jones's Cy. "now doing duty in the Island of Jersey" - - -	-Herrenhausen,	28 July,	,, c	
Bryan Mahon * to be Lieut. to Capt. [John] Broughton's Cy. "now at Guernsey" -	,,	21 Sept.	,, c	
Ric. Pollard to be Lieut. to Lt.-Col. Gilbert Symonds - - - - -	Hanover,	24 ,,	,, c	

Thos. Stephens,* Esq. to be Capt. in room of Lewis Dejean - - - - -	St. James's,	23 Nov. 1720. *c*
John Heley, Esq. to be Capt. in room of Sydenham Fowke - - - -	,,	1 Feb. 1720/1. *c*
Ric. Norbury to be Lieut. to Capt. Ric. Green - - - - - - -	,,	2 ,, ,, *c*
John Broughton,* Esq. to be Capt. in room of R. Byng - - - - - -	,,	3 ,, ,, *c*
Lt.-Col. Magnus Kempenfelt* to be Capt. in room of Thos. Shrimpton - -	,,	6 Mar. ,, *c*
Paul George, Esq. to be Capt. in room of [Robert] d'Oyley - - - -	,,	24 ,, ,, *c*
Theoph. Thame* to be Ens. to Col. M. Kempenfelt - - - - - -	,,	27 Mar. 1721. *c*
Ant. Blount,* to be Ens. to Capt. Richmond Webb - - - - - -	,,	25 April, ,, *c*
Gervas Sibthorpe,[13] Esq. to be Capt. in room of John Shute - - - - -	,,	15 May, ,, *c*
Ric. Thomas to be Ens. to Capt. John Carwarden - - - - - -	,,	20 ,, ,, *c*
Wm. Orfeur to be Ens. to Capt. Wigg -	,,	21 June, ,, *c*
Noel Marchand,* Esq. to be Capt. in room of Mordaunt Cracherode - - -	,,	23 ,, ,, *c*
John Parker* to be Ens. to Capt. Fras. Wigg	,,	12 July, ,, *c*
Ventris Columbine to be Ens. to Capt. John Broughton - - - - - -	,,	13 ,, ,, *c*
Edward McBurney to be Surgeon's Mate -	,,	15 Nov. ,, *c*
Walter Manning, Esq. to be Capt. in room of —— Kelly - - - - - -	,,	,, ,, ,, *c*
Wm. Watson to be Lieut. to Capt. [Richmond] Webb - - - - - - -	,,	30 Dec. ,, *c*
Miles Parker to be Ens. to Capt. John Broughton - - - - - -	,,	26 Jan. 1721/2.*c*
Wm. Hele to be Lieut. to Capt. Paul George	,,	20 Feb. ,, *c*
Francis Meheux* to be Ens. to Capt. Fras. Wigg - - - - - - -	,,	18 April, 1722.*c*
Chas. Vachell to be Lieut. to Col.[Magnus] Kempenfelt - - - - - -	,,	21 ,, ,, *c*
Augustine Earle,* Esq. to be Capt. in room of James Stewart - - - -	,,	9 May, ,, *c*
John Hay, Esq. to be Capt. in room of Gwyn Vaughan - - - - -	,,	16 July, ,, *c*
John Wind to be Ens. to Capt. [John] Carwarden - - - - -	Kensington,	31 ,, ,, *c*
Paul Torin to be Lieut. to Capt. [John] Crosbie - - - - - -	,,	4 Aug. ,, *c*
John Rossington[14] to be Capt. in room of Robert Dove decd. - - - -	,,	22 ,, ,, *c*
John Lewis Gidoin to be Lieut. to Capt. Gilbert Symonds - - - -	——	4 Sept. ,, *c*
Peter Sadler,[15] Esq. to be Capt. of that Cy. of Invalids in Scilly whereof [John] Rossington decd. was late Capt. - -	St. James's,	6 Oct. ,, *c*

John Skeyes,* Esq. to be Capt. in room of
Ric. Jones - - - - - - - St. James's, 15 Nov. 1722. *c*

John Lee* to be Lieut. to Capt. Ric. Jones
(*sic*) - - - - - - -   ,,   20 ,,   ,, *c*

Parke Pepper to be Ens. to Capt. Graham's
Cy. of Invalids in Guernsey - -   ,,   22 Dec.   ,, *c*

John Horsman, Esq. to be Capt. of the Cy.
at Sheerness whf. Wm. Maidman was
Capt. - - - - - - -   ,,   1 Mar. 1722/3.*c*

Bacon Morris,[16] Esq. to be Capt. of the Cy.
at Landguard Fort whf. Paul George
was Capt. - - - - - -   ,,   4 ,,   ,, *c*

Daniel Tanner,[17] Esq. to be Capt. in room
of Walker Manning - - - -   ,,   9 ,,   ,, *c*

John Burnet, Esq. to be Capt. in room of
John Horsman - - - - -   ,,   24 May,   ,, *c*

Joshua Priaux * to be Ens. to Capt. John
Broughton in Guernsey - - -   ,,   ,,   ,,   ,, *c*

Joseph Maddy * to be Ens. to Capt. Bacon
Morris - - - - - - -   ,,   ,,   ,,   ,, *c*

Edward Murray * to be Lieut. to Capt.
[Daniel] Tanner - - - -   -Herrenhausen, 12 July,   ,, *c*

James Mainwaring,* Esq. to be Capt. of the
—— Cy. at Chester whf. —— Crosbie
was Capt. - - - - - -   ,,   29 ,,   ,, *c*

Rupert Oldenbourgh to be Lieut. to Capt.
John Carwarden - - - -   ,,   3 Aug.   ,, *c*

John (*sic*) Rossington to be Ens. to Capt.
[John] Hay - - - - - -   Hanover, 17 Nov.   ,, *c*

Hugh Pudsay * to be Lieut. to Capt. [James]
Mainwaring - - - - -   Kensington, 9 June, 1724.*d*

John Vincent, Esq. to be Capt. of Cy. at
Pendennis Castle whf. Gervase Sib-
thorpe was Capt. - - -   ,,   21 July,   ,, *d*

John Emmenes * to be Lieut. to Capt. John
Carwarden's Cy. at Plymouth - -   Windsor, 25 Sept.   ,, *d*

Henry Harman Vandeck [18] to be Lieut. to
Capt. [John] Burnet at Tilbury Fort -   Kensington, 9 Oct.   ,, *d*

Peter Piaget [19] to be Ens. to Capt. Noel
Marchand - - - - -   St. James's, 29 Nov.   ,, *d*

John Gage,[20] Esq. to be Capt. of the Cy. at
Tilbury Fort whf. John Burnet was
Capt. - - - - - - -   ,,   30 ,,   ,, *d*

Henry Taaff * to be Lieut. to Capt. [John]
Carwarden - - - - -   ,,   17 Dec.   ,, *d*

Jonathan Mowbray to be do. to Capt. [Fras.]
Clarke at Hull - - - -   ,,   18 Feb. 1724/5.*d*

Thos. Columbine to be Ens. to Capt. Gra-
ham's Cy. in Guernsey - - -   ,,   22 April, 1725.*d*

Chris. Hargrave to be Ens. to Capt. John
Graham - - - - - -   Gohre, 11 Oct.(O.S.),, *d*

Wm. Lloyd,* Esq. to be Capt. in room of
Leonard Gwyn - - - - -   St. James's, 7 Feb. 1725/6.*d*

John Knight * to be Lieut. to Capt. Richmond Webb's Cy. at Tilbury Fort	St. James's,	7 April, 1726.*d*
Lewis Delafay,* Esq. to be Capt. in the room of John Vincent	Kensington,	26 July, ,, *d*
Do. to be Capt. of the Cy. at Sheerness whf. John Hay was Capt.	,,	26 Aug. ,, *d*
George Massey, Esq. to be Capt. of the Cy. at Pendennis Castle whf. Lewis Delafay was Capt.	,,	,, ,, ,, *d*
Mordaunt Cracherode,[10] Esq. to be Capt. in the room of Robert Mountfort	,,	6 Oct. ,, *d*
Wm. Watkins to be Ens. to Capt. George Gage	,,	10 ,, ,, *d*
James Cole * to be Capt. in room of Francis Boggest	,,	25 Nov. ,, *d*
Abraham Gee * to be Lieut. to Capt. Wm. Lloyd	St. James's,	25 Dec. ,, *d*
John Slack * to be Lieut. to Capt. Mordaunt Cracherode's Cy. at Sheerness	,,	24 Jan. 1726/7.*d*
John Savage * to be Ens. to Capt. John Broughton in Jersey	,,	6 April, 1727.*d*
John Heath * to be Lieut. to the Cy. [in Jersey] whf. [Col.] Magnus Kempenfelt is Capt.	,,	27 ,, ,, *d*

[1] See p. 244, note 12.
[2] See Vol. I., p. 310, note 3.
[3] D. before 1735, in which year his widow was in receipt of a pension of £26 per annum.
[4] See Vol. I., p. 253, note 5.
[5] See p. 409, note 29.
[6] See p. 156, note 17.
[7] Served previously as Lieut. and Capt. in the Coldstream Guards.
[8] See p. 194, note 9.
[9] D. in Aug. 1722.
[10] *Cracherode.* See an account of this officer in Vol. I., p. 49.
[11] Serving as Capt. of an Indep. Cy. of Invalids at Hull in 1740.
[12] Comn. not forthcoming in the W.O. Registers. Serving as Capt. of a Cy. in Guernsey in 1740. Date of his appointment is given in the *Army List*, 1740.
[13] From Lieut. in the Inniskilling Dragoons. Fourth son of Gervase Sibthorp of Laneham, co. Notts. D. in 1744.
[14] D. as Capt. of Invalid Cy. at Scilly in the autumn of 1722.
[15] Serving as Capt. of an Invalid Cy. at Plymouth in 1740.
[16] See p. 336, note 10.
[17] Serving as Capt. of an Invalid Cy. at Tynemouth in 1740.
[18] Serving as Lieut. of an Invalid Cy. at Hull in 1740.
[19] Serving as Ens. of an Invalid Cy. at do. in 1740.
[20] Served in the late reign as Capt. *en second* in Visct. Mountjoy's Regt. of Foot, and was placed on half-pay in 1712. Comn. as Capt. of an Invalid Cy. renewed in 1727.

SIX NEWLY-RAISED INDEPENDENT COMPANIES OF FOOT IN THE HIGHLANDS OF SCOTLAND.

All the Commissions were dated St. James's, 24 April, 1725.   (d)

Colonel Wm. Grant,[1] Capt.
Lieut. Lewis Farquerson (*sic*), 1st Lieut.
Lieut. Lewis Grant, 2nd Lieut.

Simon, Lord Lovat,[2] Capt.
Lieut. Alex. Frazier (*sic*), 1st Lieut.
Lieut. Dugall Campbell, 2nd Lieut.

Sir Duncan Campbell,[3] Capt.
Lieut. Colin Campbell, 1st Lieut.
Lieut. Robert Stewart, 2nd Lieut.

Lieut. Colin Campbell of Skipness,[4] Commander.
Ensign John Maclain (*sic*), Ensign.

Lieut. John Campbell,[5] Commander.
Ensign Duncan Campbell, Ensign.

Lieut. George Monroe,[6] Commander.
Ensign Duncan Urquhart, Ensign.

SUPPLEMENTARY COMMISSIONS.

Peregrine Fury to be Agent and Solicitor to above six Companies - - -	St. James's,	24 April, 1725.*d*			
Alex. Stewart to be Ensign to Lieut. George Monroe - - - - -	,,	1 Feb. 1725/6.*d*			
Capt.-Lieut. John Campbell of Carrick to be Commander of an Indep. Cy. in the Highlands of North Britain - -	,,	25 Dec. 1726. *d*			
Roderick Bayne to be Lieut. to above Cy. -	,,	,,	,,	,,	*d*
John Macpherson to be Ens. to do. - -	,,	,,	,,	,,	*d*
Capt.-Lieut. Colin Campbell of Skipness to be Commander of an Ind. Cy. in the Highlands of North Britain - - -	,,	,,	,,	,,	*d*
John Maclain (*sic*)[7] to be Lieut. to above Cy.	,,	,,	,,	,,	*d*
Capt.-Lieut. George Munroe to be Commander of an Indep. Cy. in the Highlands of North Britain - - -	,,	,,	,,	,,	*d*
Alex. Stewart to be Lieut. to above Cy. -	,,	,,	,,	,,	*d*
Alex. McDonald[8] to be Ensign to do. - -	,,	,,	,,	,,	*d*

James Grant to be Ens. to Col. [Wm.]
    Grant's Cy. - - - - - - St. James's, 25 Dec. 1726. *d*
Paul McPherson [9] to be Ens. to Lord Lovat's
    Cy. - - - - - -   ,,   ,, ,, ,, *d*
John Frazier (*sic*) [10] to be [2nd] Lieut. to
    Sir Duncan Campbell - - - -   ,,   24 Jan. 1726/7. *d*

[1] Of Ballindallock. He had been appointed Capt. of an Indep. Cy. of Foot for the security of the Highlands, 24 June, 1701. Bt.-Lt.-Col. 1 Dec. 1704. D. in 1733.

[2] See biog. notice in Vol. I., p. 253, note 4.

[3] Of Lochnell. Comn. renewed in June, 1727. Out before 1739. Drawing half-pay in 1758, and described as " Sir Duncan Campbell, Bart."

[4] Capt.-Lieut. 25 Dec. 1726. Serving in May, 1739.

[5] Of Carrick. Capt.-Lieut. 25 Dec. 1726. Capt. in the Highland Regt. (Black Watch), 27 Oct. 1739. Killed at Fontenoy. Archibald Forbes, in his *Black Watch*, describes this officer as " a poet, a soldier, and gentleman . . . the object of general pride and admiration."

[6] *Munro* of Culcairn. Capt.-Lieut. 25 Dec. 1726. Capt. in the Highland Regt. (Black Watch), 29 Oct. 1739.

[7] Of Kingairlock. Lieut. in the Highland Regt. (Black Watch), 26 Oct. 1739. Removed from the Regt. in 1744, for fighting a duel with Lieut. Alex. Macdonald of same Corps.—*Records*.

[8] Lieut. in the Highland Regt. (Black Watch), 29 Oct. 1739.

[9] Do. in do. 26 Oct. 1739.

[10] Out 23 Jan. 1736.

APPOINTMENTS TO INDEPENDENT COMPANIES IN SCOTTISH GARRISONS.

Thos. Lindsay, Esq. to be Lieut. to the Earl of Rothes's Indep. Cy. in Stirling Castle - - - - - - -   St. James's, 1 Nov. 1721. *c*

David Cuningham, Esq. (*sic*) to be Ens. to above Cy. - - - - - -   ,,   ,, ,, ,, *c*

John, Earl of Rothes[1] to be Capt. of the Indep. Cy. at Stirling Castle whf. he is Constable - - - - -   ,,   22 May, 1722. *c*

David Kinloch[2] to be Ens. to the Earl of Orkney's Cy. in Edinburgh Castle [in room of James Smith] - - - -   Herrenhausen, 12 July, 1723. *c*

Wm. Kerr,[3] Esq. to be Capt. of Our Cy. in Blackness Castle and also to command any detachment of Our Troops that shall at any time be put into Our said Castle - - - - - - -   Hanover,   18 Nov. ,,   *c*

Edward Bucknal[4] to be Lieut. to the Earl of Orkney's Cy. in Edinburgh Castle, and also to be Fort Major of said Castle - - - - - - -   St. James's, 18 Feb. 1724/5. *d*

Henry Mackenzie to be Lieut. to the Earl of Orkney's Cy. in Edinburgh Castle -   ,,   25 Dec. 1726. *d*

James Hutchinson to be Lieut. to the Earl of Rothes's Indep. Cy. in Stirling Castle - - - - - -   ,,   ,, ,, ,, *d*

David Dunbar to be Ensign to the Earl of Glencairn's Indep. Cy. in Dumbarton Castle - - - - - - -   ,,   ,, ,, ,, *d*

---

[1] See biog. notice in Vol. I., p. 113, note 4.

[2] Probably a descendant of the famous Dr. John Kinloch of Aberbrothie, "physician to the Kings of Great Britain and France," who d. in 1617.

[3] Col. the Hon. Wm. *Ker.* See biog. notice in Vol. I., p. 111, note 1.

[4] Appointed Ens. in Col. Roger Elliot's Regt. of Foot, 25 Dec. 1703. Adjt. 23 Oct. 1704. Placed on half-pay as Capt. from said Corps in 1713. On 10 April, 1727, Maj.-Gen. Wade, C.-in-C. in Scotland, wrote to Lord Townshend on the subject of the defence of Edinburgh Castle :—

"I beg leave to observe to your Lordship that as the Governour and Lt.-Governour of Edinburgh Castle are generally absent, the Earl of Orkney by his attendance on his Majesty, and Brigadier Preston by his ill state of health occasioned from the wounds he received [in] the last warr, the highest officer there is the Fort Major [Bucknall], who though an experienced officer is often indisposed by sickness and [is] decayed in his constitution. I therefore am humbly of opinion that it would contribute to the security of that important place if His Majesty would be pleased to constitute a Deputy Lieut.-Governour of known zeal and experience who would constantly reside in the Castle."—*Townshend Papers,* p. 198.

MILITARY APPOINTMENTS IN SCOTLAND.

Patrick Clow to be Chaplain to the Indep. Cy. in garrison at Stirling Castle whf. John Earl of Rothes is Constable and Capt. - - - - - - -	Hampton Court, 7 Sept. 1717. *b*	
Sir Patrick Strachan,[1] Knt. to be Barrack-Master-General in Scotland - - -	St. James's, 6 May, 1719. *c*	
Dr. George Cuthbert to be Surgeon to Our Forces in Our Town and Castle of Inverness and the Barracks of Bernera Killichnituan (*sic*), and Rivan (*sic*) of Badenock - - - - -	,, 26 June, 1721. *c*	
Robert Seaton, Esq. to be Clerk of Our Courts-Martial in Scotland in room of Adam Smith - - - - -	,, 15 Jan. 1722/3.	
Richard Arnold, Esq. to be Secretary to Our Forces in Scotland - - - -	Gohre, 20 Oct. 1723. *p*	
George Wade,[2] Esq. to be Commander-in-Chief of Our Forces in Scotland and of the Barracks, Forts, and Castles there	—— 25 Dec. 1725 (*sic*). *c*	
Major-General Sibourg[3] to be Governor of Fort William during his Majesty's Pleasure only - - - - -	St. James's, 24 April, 1725.	
Col. Jasper Clayton[4] to be Govr. of Our Fort and Castle of Inverness and of all the military works and fortifications thereunto belonging - - -	,, ,, ,, ,, *d*	
Col. Alex. Spotswood[5] to be Qr.-Mr.-General of all Our Forces in Scotland -	,, ,, ,, ,, *d*	
Col. Joshua Guest[6] to be Barrack-Master-General of all Our Forces in Scotland -	,, 11 Jan. 1725/6. *d*	
John Arnot,[7] Esq. to be Adjt.-General in Scotland - - - - -	,, ,, ,, ,, *p*	
Alex. Abercrombie,[8] Esq. to be Lieut.-Governor of Fort William - - -	,, ,, ,, ,, *d*	
James Cunningham,[9] Esq. to be Dep.-Governor of Our Town, Castle, and Fort of Inverness and of all the military works and fortifications thereunto belonging	,, 25 Dec. 1726. *d*	
Henry Cunningham,[10] Esq. to be Commissary of the Musters of all Our Forces in Scotland - - - - -	,, 1 June, 1727. *d*	

[1] Of Glenkindie. Knighted in 1717. Suffered imprisonment during the '15. After he was released became very active in disarming suspected Jacobites. D. at Aberdeen, 2 Jan. 1725/6.

[2] The date "25 Dec. 1725" is manifestly an error for "25 Dec. 1724." See special memoir pp. 11–22.

[3] Royal Warrant. See biog. notice in Vol. I., p. 330, note 1.

[4] See biog. notice in Vol. I., p. 340, note 1; also in Vol. II., p. 338, note 72.

[5] Only son of Dr. Robert *Spottiswood*, Physician to the Tangier garrison. Bn. at Tangier in 1676. Ens. in the Earl of Bath's Regt. of Foot, 20 May, 1693. Lieut. 1 Jan. 1696. Capt. 9 April, 1703. D.Q.M.G. at Blenheim where he was wounded. Bt.-Lt.-Col. 1 Jan. 1707. Taken prisoner by the French in 1708. Served at Malplaquet. Dep.-Gov. of Virginia in 1710. Held this post 12 years. Col. of a Regt. of American Colonists, 26 Dec. 1739, and appointed Q.M.G. of the British Forces sent to the West Indies, in 1740, with rank of Maj.-Gen., but d. at Annapolis, Maryland, while attending to the embarkation of troops, 17 June, 1740. See Appleton's *Cyclopædia of American Biography.*

[6] See biog. notice in Vol. I., p. 109, note 2.

[7] See do. in do., p. 136, note 2.

[8] Of Glassaugh, Banffshire. Served many years in the Royal North British Fusiliers. In a petition to Lord Townshend dated from "Glassaugh, 3 Oct. 1723," this officer writes : "I have served faithfully 16 years as a Captain at all sieges, battles, and other services during the said time and at the Union. . . . Also attending the Parliament every session . . . His Majesty promised that I should be provided for in the Guards, or Dragoons, or some Deputy-Government."—*S.P. Dom. George I.*

[9] See biog. notice in Vol. I., p. 134, note 5.

[10] This Comn. appears to have been the last signed by George I.

MILITARY APPOINTMENTS AT GIBRALTAR.

Thos. Salisbury[1] to be Clerk of the Works and Barrack-Master at Gibraltar - -	—	10 Dec.	1718.
John Conduit,[2] Esq. to be Commissary of Stores of War and Provisions in room of Thos. Medlycott - - - - -	St. James's,	8 Mar.	1721/2.c
Robt. Johnston, Esq. to be Town Major -	,,	5 April,	1723. c
George Tipping to be Provost-Marshal to Our Town and Garrison of Gibraltar - -	,,	16 Jan.	1724/5.d
Col. Richard Kane[3] to be Lt.-Gov. of Our City and Garrison of Gibraltar - -	Pyrmont,	10 July,	1725.
Jasper Clayton,[4] Esq. to be do. - -	Kensington,	20 Sept.	1726. d
Dr. Wm. Neilson[5] to be Director and Purveyor of Our Hospital in Our City and Garrison of Gibraltar - - - - -	St. James's,	1 Mar.	1726/7.d
Dr. Alex. Sandilands[6] to be Physician of do.-	,,	,, ,,	,, d
Wm. Scot to be Master Surgeon of do. - -	,,	,, ,,	,, d
Ant. Robinson to be Town Adjt. - - -	,,	15 ,,	,, d
Henry Ingram,[7] Esq. to be Commissary of Stores of War and Provisions in room of John Conduit - - - - - -	,,	1 May,	1727.

[1] *Ordnance Warrant*, W.O. 55/502, fol. 155. This Comn. bears this proviso : "During so long as he shall carefully and diligently discharge this duty."

[2] Held this post in former reign. On 23 March, 1712, he was appointed Capt. in Brig.-Gen. Hunt Withers's Regt. of Dragoons in Portugal. Half-pay, 1713. D. at Paddington in 1736.—*Gentleman's Mag.*

[3] A draft copy of this Comn. is given in *Col. S.P. Gibraltar* for 1725. See biog. notice on p. 144, note 1.

[4] See biog. notice in Vol. I., p.340, note 1.

[5] Appointed Director of the Hospital erected for the service of H.M.'s Forces in Portugal, 1 March, 1709. In a letter to Brig.-Gen. Clayton, Gov. of Gibraltar, from the Duke of Newcastle, 22 Oct. 1728, the writer refers to the above-named Hospital : "During the [late] siege of Gibraltar, Sir Charles Wager consented to the Hospital, which had always been kept for the reception of the sick and hurt men belonging to H.M.'s Ships stationed in those parts, being made use of for the Soldiers. Their Lordships think that since the occasion is over the Hospital may now be restored to the Navy and the King has signified his pleasure that you accordingly give Order for the Hospital to be given up to the proper Officers of the Navy for the reception of the Sick and Wounded, His Majesty not doubting that you will be able to find other places to supply the want of an Hospital for the Garrison if there should be occasion."—*Gibraltar Papers*, C.O. 91, fol. 28.

[6] Appointed Physician to the Hospital at Dunkirk in 1712. Drawing half-pay at the rate of 10s. p.d. in 1749.

[7] Comn. given in the *Minorca and Gibraltar* [*Letter*] *Book*, No. 55.

MILITARY APPOINTMENTS IN MINORCA.

Patrick Crawford[1] to be Ordnance Store
 Keeper and Paymaster at Port Mahon   —   10 Dec.   1718. *c*
John Sutherland to be Surgeon to Fort St.
 Philip - - - - - - - St. James's, 13 ,,   ,,   *c*
Henry Crofton[2] to be Fort Major at Fort
 St. Anne - - - - - - - ,, 15 ,,   ,,   *p*
Peter Dumas[3] to be Adjt. at Fort St. Philip   ,, 30 April, 1720. *c*
Samuel Palmer, Esq. to be Capt. of the Ports
 of Fort St. Philip - - - - ,,   8 June, ,,   *c*
James Otway,[4] Esq. to be Lt.-Gov. of Fort
 St. Philip, in the absence of the Gov.
 and Lt.-Gov. of Our Island of Minorca,
 and to Command in Chief the whole
 Island and all Forts and Fortifica-
 tions - - - - - - Herrenhausen, 18 July, ,,   *c*
Walter Bacon, Esq. to be Commissary-
 General of Stores of War and Provisions
 for the Forces in Minorca in room of
 Thos. Maynard - - - - - St. James's, 22 Feb. 1721/2.*c*
Wm. Campbell,[5] Esq. to be Fort Major of
 Fort St. Philip - - - - - ,, 25 April, 1723. *c*
John Singleton to be Adjt. to Fort St. Anne ,, 24 May, ,,   *c*
Thos. Otway,[6] Esq. to be Capt. of Fort St.
 Philip - - - - - - - ,, 30 Nov. 1724. *d*
James Scot[7] to be Surgeon to do. - - ,, 24 Mar. 1724/5.*d*
John Jordan to be Surgeon's Mate to do. - ,, ,, ,, ,, *d*
Edward Montague,[8] Esq. to be Lt.-Gov. of
 Fort St. Philip in Minorca, and in
 absence of the Gov. and Lt.-Gov. to
 Command in Chief Our whole Island
 [in room of Col. Jas. Otway decd.] Helvoet Sluys, 25 Dec. 1725. *d*

[1] *Ordnance Warrant*, W.O. 55/502, fol. 155.
[2] Served previously in the Rl. Fusiliers.
[3] Served previously in Maj.-Gen. Sankey's Regt. of Foot.
[4] See biog. notice in Vol. I., p. 326, note 2.
[5] Believed to be identical with Capt. Wm. Campbell of Sankey's Foot, which Corps was
quartered in Minorca during the early part of the reign of George I.
[6] See biog. notice on p. 182, note 11.
[7] See his Comn. as Surgeon's Mate at Fort St. Philip in Vol. I., p. 238.
[8] See biog. notice in Vol. I., p. 106, note 2.

MILITARY APPOINTMENTS AT PLACENTIA, NEWFOUNDLAND.

Gerald Russell to be Commissary of the
  Musters   -   -   -   -   -   -   St. James's, 19 Dec. 1720. *c*
George Doidge, Esq. to be do.   -   -   -   Kensington, 24 Aug. 1721. *c*
Robert Hurst to be do.   -   -   -   -   St. James's, 6 May, 1725. *d*
Henry Cope to be Town Major   -   -   -   Hanover, 30 Nov. (O.S.) ,,   *d*

MILITARY APPOINTMENTS AT ANNAPOLIS, NOVA SCOTIA.

Thos. Cosby,[1] Esq. to be Fort Major -   -   St. James's, 1 May, 1722. *c*
Alex. Cosby,[2] Esq. to be Lieut.-Governor of
  Our Garrison of Annapolis Royal   -   ,,   4 Mar. 1726/7. *d*

[1] Third son of Alex. Cosby of Stradbally, Queen's County. Appointed Capt. in Gen. Wightman's Regt. (17th) 22 May, 1716. Md. Jane, sister of Nicholas, Visct. Loftus. D. 3 March, 1734.—Burke's *Landed Gentry*.
[2] Younger bro. to above Thos. Cosby. See biog. notice in Vol. I., p. 150, note 4.

TWO INDEPENDENT COMPANIES OF FOOT IN JAMAICA.

Daniel Plowman[1] to be Lieut. to Capt. Joseph
  Delaunay   -   -   -   -   -   -   St. James's, 29 Mar. 1721. *c*
Henry, Duke of Portland,[2] Capt.-General and
  Governor of Jamaica, to be Capt. of that
  Indep. Cy. whf. Sir Nicholas Laws was
  late Capt.   -   -   -   -   -   -   ,,   1 Nov.   ,,   *c*
Colonel Charles Dubourgay[3] to be Lt.-Gov.
  of above Island   -   -   -   -   -   —   —   1721. *n*
Robert Murray to be Lieut. to Capt. [Joseph]
  Delaunay   -   -   -   -   -   -   St. James's, 17 Feb. 1725/6. *d*
[Brig.-Gen.] Robert Hunter[4] to be Capt. of
  that Indep. Cy. whf. Henry, Duke of
  Portland, decd. was late Capt.   -   -   ,,   15 Feb. 1726/7. *d*

[1] D. before 1733, in which year his widow was drawing a pension of £20.
[2] Second Earl and 1st Duke. D. in Jamaica, 4 July, 1726.
[3] See biog. notice in Vol. I., p. 168, note 1.
[4] See do. in do., p. 245, note 19.

INDEPENDENT COMPANY OF FOOT IN BERMUDA.

James Maidman to be Lieut. to Capt. Benjamin
    Bennet - - - - - - St. James's, 24 May, 1720.*c*
Lt.-Colonel John Hope[1] to be Lt.-Gov. and
    C.-in-C. of Bermuda [in room of Capt.
    Bennet] - - - - - - ,, 9 Sept. 1721.*n*
[Do. to be Capt. of the Indep. Cy. - - ,, ,, ,, ,,]

[1] Held the Governorship of Bermuda until 1727. Third son of Sir Thos. Hope, Bart., of Kinross. Appointed Capt. in the 3rd Foot Guards, 3 June, 1708, with rank of Lt.-Col. Exchanged to the Cameronians as Lt.-Col. 19 July, 1716. Sold said Lt.-Colonelcy, 5 April, 1718. Col. of a Regt. of Foot (disbanded in 1748), 15 March, 1743. Succeeded to the Kinross estate and baronetcy on the death of his brother, Sir Thos. Hope. Attained the rank of Lt.-Gen. and d.s.p. in 1766.

INDEPENDENT COMPANY OF FOOT IN THE BAHAMAS.

Wm. Salter,[1] Esq. to be Commissary of the
    Musters of all Our Forces - - - St. James's, 7 Mar. 1717/8.
John Howell[2] to be Lieut. to Capt. Woodes
    Rogers - - - - - - ,, 9 June, 1720.*c*
George Phenny,[3] Esq. to be Capt. in room of
    Woodes Rogers - - - - ,, 4 July, 1721.*c*
Roger MacManus[4] to be Lieut. to Capt. George
    Phenny - - - - - - ,, 22 ,, ,, *c*
Thos. Curphy to be Chaplain - - - ,, 10 Dec. 1722.*c*
John Howell to be Surgeon - - - Herrenhausen, 16 Aug. 1723.*c*
Simon Farrell[5] to be Lieut. to Capt. George
    Phenny - - - - - - St. James's, 1 Jan. 1723/4.*c*
Kenneth Fraser[6] to be Lieut. to do. - - Windsor, 23 Sept. 1724.*d*

[1] Military Entry Book, No. 177, 1714–23.

[2] From a "Memorial of John Howell, Lt. of the Indep. Cy. at New Providence, Bahamas," to Gov. Francis Nicholson, of South Carolina, dated 15 July, 1721, the former stated that the garrison was starving and that on 25 June last there was only left in store "about one month's subsistence of flour and one month's allowance of pork." Before this "Memorial" reached Gov. Nicholson he had shipped from Charlestown, in a sloop bound for Providence, "3 months' subsistence of flour, 3 months' do. of pork and beef, 4 months' do. of rice and 2 months' allowance of rum." (Printed in the Appendix to *An Apology or Vindication of Francis Nicholson, Esq., His Majesty's Governor of South Carolina, &c.*, 1724.) Lieut. John Howell was serving in the Island of Providence, Bahamas, in 1740.

[3] Served in the former reign as Capt. in Col. Franks's Regt. of Foot. Capt.-Lieut. in Col. Phineas Bowles's Regt. (12th Dragoons), 10 March, 1720. Capt. in Borr's Regt. (32nd Foot), 7 June, 1720. Retd. 7 June same year. Appointed Gov. of Bermuda in room of Woodes Rogers in 1721. A letter from Mr. Walker of New Providence, to Col. Rhett of Charlestown, South Carolina, dated 4 Dec. 1721, records that : "His Excellency George Phenny, Esq. our Governor safe arrived to his post the 12th of last month to our joy, but to the dissatisfaction of some in this Place ; but the Governor is courteous, kind, and loving to every man and hope he'll make this Place a flourishing thriving Colony, as being a considerate wise-thinking gentleman and a soldier withall."—*S.P. Bahamas.*

[4] D. before 1734, in which year his widow, Mary MacManus, was drawing a pension of £20 per annum.

[5] From half-pay Ens. in Lord Slane's Regt. of Foot.

[6] From half-pay Ens. in Col. Franks's Regt. of Foot.

FOUR INDEPENDENT COMPANIES IN THE PROVINCE OF NEW YORK.

Andrew Nickell[1] to be Lieut. to Capt. John Riggs - - - - - - -	St. James's, 6 Mar. 1718/9.	c
Edward Richbell,[2] Esq. to be Capt. of that Cy. whf. [Colonel] Richard Ingoldsby decd. was Capt. - - - -	Pyrmont, 16 June (O.S.) 1719.	c
Wm. Helling[3] to be Lieut. to Capt. Richbell	St. James's, 8 Mar. 1719/20.	c
John Warren,[4] Esq. to be Capt. in room of Edward Richbell - - - - -	,, 8 June, 1720.	c
Wm. Burnet,[5] Esq. "Our Capt.-Gen. and Gov.-in-Chief in and over Our Province of New York and the Territorys depending thereon in America," to be Capt. of the Indep. Cy. whereof Robert Hunter, Esq. was late Capt. - -	,, 10 ,, ,,	c
James Banks[6] to be Lieut. to Capt. Jas. Weems - - - - - -	,, 26 Feb. 1721/2.	c
George Ingoldsby[7] to be Lieut. to Capt. Wm. Burnet - - - - -	,, 14 Mar. ,,	c
Do. to be Adjt. to the four Independent Companies - - - - - -	,, ,, ,, ,,	c
Lancaster Symes,[8] Esq. to be Capt. of the Indep. Cy. of Fuziliers in the Province of New York whf. James Weems was Capt. - - - - - - -	Herrenhausen, 3 Aug. 1723.	c
Edmund Blood[9] to be Lieut. to above Cy. -	,, ,, ,, ,,	c
Richard Riggs[10] to be Lieut. to Capt. Wm. Burnet, Capt.-General of the Province of New York - - - - -	,, ,, ,, ,,	p
James Orem (sic)[11] to be Chaplain to the four Indep. Companies- - - -	,, ,, ,, ,,	p
Thos. Smyth[12] to be Lieut. to Capt. Lancaster Symes - - - - -	,, 25 July, 1725.	d
John Price[13] to be Lieut. to Capt. Henry Holland - - - - - -	St. James's, 4 Feb. 1725/6.	d
Timothy Bagly[14] to be do. to Capt. John Riggs - - - - - - -	,, ,, ,, ,,	d

[1] Capt.-Lieut. 13 Nov. 1739. Called "Nicoll" in the 1740 *Army List.*
[2] Served as Capt. in Sir R. Temple's Regt. of Foot at Malplaquet. Half-pay, 1713. Major 37th Foot, 3 June, 1720. Lt.-Col. 18 May, 1722. Col. 62nd Foot, 27 March, 1742. Col. 17th Foot, 14 March, 1752. Maj.-Gen. 25 March, 1754. Served as a Brig.-Gen. in the Port L'Orient Expedition, 1746. D. in 1757.
[3] Comn. renewed in 1727. Serving in 1740.
[4] D. before 1735, in which year his widow, Elizabeth Warren, was drawing a pension of £26 per annum.
[5] Son of Dr. Gilbert Burnet, Bishop of Salisbury. Born in March, 1688, at The Hague. The Prince of Orange (William III.) was his Godfather. Appointed Lt.-Gov. of New York

z

in June, 1720 (Comn. not forthcoming).   On 15 April, 1728, transferred to the Governorship of Massachusetts, and in 1729 was given the Governorship of New Hampshire in addition. D. at Boston, 7 Sept. 1729.

[6] Out before 1740.

[7] Son of Col. Richard Ingoldsby, whose Company at New York had a "respite" on the same amounting to £1,083 0s. 8d. (*Treasury Papers.*)   Serving in 1757 as Lieut.

[8] D. before 1735, in which year his widow, Catherine Symes, was drawing a pension of £26 per annum.

[9] Serving with same rank in 1740.

[10] Capt. 14 Feb. 1729.   Serving in 1740.

[11] Serving as Chaplain in 1757.

[12] Out before 1740.

[13] Do.

[14] Serving with same rank in 1740.

INDEPENDENT COMPANY OF FOOT IN SOUTH CAROLINA.

Brigadier-General Fras. Nicholson [1] "to be Capt. of the Indep. Cy. of Foot we have thought fit to form for his Majesty's Service to be sent to South Carolina in America" - - - - - -	Whitehall, 24 Sept. 1720. c
Joseph Lambert [2] to be [1st] Lieut. to above Cy. - - - - - - -	,, ,, ,, ,, c
John Emmenes [3] to be [2nd] Lieut. to do. -	,, ,, ,, ,, c
Thos. Merryman [4] to be Ensign to do. -	,, ,, ,, ,, c
John Bowdler [5] to be do. to do. - - -	,, ,, ,, ,, c
Robert Mason [6] to be Surgeon - - -	,, ,, ,, ,, c
Thos. Hesketh [7] to be Chaplain - - -	,, ,, ,, ,, c
Joseph Ball [8] to be Surgeon [in room of Mason] - - - - - -	St. James's, 14 Feb. 1721/2. c
Roger Whitley [9] to be Ens. to Brig.-Gen. Nicholson - - - - - -	Kensington, 25 June, 1722. c
John Brafield [10] to be Chaplain [in room of Hesketh] - - - - - -	,, 1 Sept. ,, c
John Jeffreyson (sic) [11] to be Lieut. to Brig.-Gen. Nicholson - - - -	,, 11 Oct. ,, c
Charles Huddy [12] to be do. to do. - -	,, 9 Nov. ,,
Joseph Elliot [13] to be Lieut. to do. - -	,, 13 Mar. 1722/3. c
Wm. Cleland [14] to be Surgeon [in room of Joseph Ball] - - - - -	,, 28 Jan. 1723/4. c
James Watt [15] to be Lieut. to Brig.-Gen. Nicholson - - - - -	,, 29 Apr. 1725. d
Philip Delagal [16] to be Ens. to —— - -	,, 29 May, ,, d
Edward Massey, [17] Esq. to be Capt. in room of Brig.-Gen. Nicholson - - -	,, 23 Mar. 1725/6. d
Edward Dyson to be Chaplain - - -	,, 25 ,, 1726. d
Thos. Cole to be Surgeon - - - -	,, ,, ,, ,, d
Wm. Edgar to be Surgeon - - - -	Kensington, 21 June, ,, d
Thos. Farrington to be Ens. to Capt. Edward Massey - - - - - -	,, 15 Oct. ,, d

[1] Comn. signed by the Lords Justices in the King's absence abroad. See special memoir pp. 55–62.

[2] D. before 1735, in which year his widow, Mary Lambert, was drawing a pension of £20 per annum.

[3] Appointed Lieut. to an Indep. Cy. of Invalids at Plymouth, 24 Sept. 1724.

[4] See his Comn. in Vol. I., p. 247.

[5] Out before 1727.

[6] Out in Feb. 1722.

[7] Out in Sept. 1722. A certain Thos. Hesketh had been Chaplain to Col. Jacob Borr's Regt. of Foot in 1715.

[8] Out in Jan. 1724.

[9] From half-pay Ens. Col. Bowles's Regt. of Foot.

[10] Out in March, 1726.

[11] Appointed Lieut. in Brig.-Gen. John Hill's Regt. of Foot, 23 Aug. 1711 (Comn. signed by Brigdr. Hill on board H.M.S. *Windsor* in the River St. Lawrence). Half-pay, 1713. D. before 1735, in which year his widow, Hannah Jeffryson, was drawing a pension of £20 per annum.

[12] Served previously as Lieut. to an Indep. Cy. at New York. Untraced after 1722.

[13] D. before 1735, in which year his widow, Mary Elliot, was drawing a pension of £20 per annum.

[14] Out in March, 1726.

[15] D. before 1735, in which year his widow, Mary Watt, was drawing a pension of £20 per annum.

[16] A certain Capt. Delagal d. before 1735, in which year his widow was drawing a pension of £26 per annum.

[17] Appointed Capt. of an Indep. Cy. at Tilbury Fort, 20 June, 1737. Serving in 1740.

IRISH ESTABLISHMENT

REGIMENTAL COMMISSIONS, 1719–1727;
NON-REGIMENTAL COMMISSIONS AND APPOINT-
MENTS, 1719–1727

REGIMENTAL COMMISSIONS, 1719–1727

THE PRINCE OF WALES'S OWN REGIMENT OF HORSE.
[4TH DRAGOON GUARDS.]

All the Commissions were signed by the Lord Lieutenant, or in his absence from Ireland by the Lords Justices, except when stated to the contrary.

Major-General Owen Wynne [1] to be Colonel in room of Maj.-Gen. Sherington Davenport decd. - - -	6 July,	1719.*j*
Robt. Wolseley,[2] Esq. to be Capt. in room of Robt. Burton	23 Sept.	,, *j*
Luke Ogle [3] to be Lieut. to Capt. John Lister in room of Robt. Wolseley - - - - - -	,, ,,	,, *j*
Lewis Folliott [4] to be Cornet to Capt. Robt. Wolseley in room of Luke Ogle - - - - - - -	,, ,,	,, *j*
Robert Bettesworth [5] to be Cornet to Major Peter Renovard in room of Richard Corbet - - - -	14 Oct.	,, *j*
Richard Corbet [6] to be Lieut. to do. in room of Dallival (*sic*) Denton - - - - - - - -	,, ,,	,, *j*
John Lyons [7] to be Cornet to Lt.-Col. Thos. Hatton in room of Chas. Lyons - - - - - -	15 ,,	,, *j*
Wilmott Vaughan,[8] Esq. to be Capt.-Lieut. to that Tp. whf. Lt.-Col. Hatton is Capt. in room of Peter Davenport - - - - - - - - -	1 June,	1720.*j*

Mem.—*The volume of Irish Commission Registers, June 1720 to June 1724, is missing from the P.R.O. Dublin. This hiatus has partly been filled up by giving registers of Commissions from the Gradation List, 1730, now at the P.R.O. London.*

Robert Maxwell,[9] Esq. to be Capt. - - - - -	12 Jan.	1721/2.*f*
Robt. Bettsworth (*sic*) [5] to be Lieut. - - - -	27 June,	1723.*f*
Richard Corbet,[6] Esq. to be Capt.-Lieut. - - - -	,, ,,	,, *f*
Lewis Foliott (*sic*) [4] to be Lieut. - - - - -	,, ,,	,, *f*
Wm. Stopford [10] to be Cornet - - - - - -	,, ,,	,, *f*
Thos. Cox [11] to be Cornet - - - - - - -	,, ,,	,, *f*
Henry Conyngham [12] to be Lieut. to Capt. Robt. Maxwell in room of John Warburton - - - -	23 Jan. 1724/5.*r*	
John Clayton [13] to be Cornet to do. in room of Henry Conyngham - - - - - - - -	,, ,,	,, *r*
Hon. Richard Fitzwilliam,[14] Esq. to be Cornet to Capt. Richard Allen in room of Wm. Wolseley - -	22 May,	1725.*r*
Thomas Aitkin [15] to be Surgeon in room of Hannibal Hall	18 Sept.	,, *r*
Wm. Coningham [16] to be Cornet to Capt. Robt. Wolseley in room of Joseph White - - - - - -	30 Nov.	,, *r*
Wm. Hanchet [17] to be Cornet to Capt. John Lister in room of Wm. Williamson - - - - - -	26 July,	1726.*r*

[1] See biog. notice in Vol. I., p. 113, note 1.

[2] See p. 157, note 1.

[3] See p. 158, note 12.

[4] From Cornet in Gen. Wynne's Regt. of Dragoons (9th). Lieut. 27 June, 1723. Capt.-Lieut. 10 May, 1738. D. in Ireland, 1741.—*Gentleman's Mag.*

[5] Lieut. 27 June, 1723. Serving as senior Lieut. in 1740.

[6] Capt.-Lieut. 27 June, 1723. Capt. 10 May, 1738. Serving in 1740.

[7] Out before 1727.

[8] See his Comn. as Capt. in Col. Henry Grove's Regt. on p. 289, and note thereto.

[9] Comn. renewed in 1727. Exchanged to the Carabiniers, 22 Nov. 1729. Serving in 1740.

[10] Lieut. 4 April, 1734. Serving in 1740.

[11] Lieut. 27 Feb. 1737. Serving in 1740.

[12] Capt. in the Rl. Irish Dragoons, 30 Nov. 1725. Younger son of Maj.-Gen. Henry Conyngham (who was killed at St. Estevan in Spain, 1706). Styled " Captain of Horse on the Irish Establishment " in Burke's *Peerage*. He was created Baron Conyngham, 3 Oct. 1753 ; Viscount Conyngham, 20 July, 1756 ; and Earl Conyngham, 4 Jan. 1781. D.s.p. 3 April, 1781.

[13] Comn. renewed in 1727. Serving in 1730. Out before 1736.

[14] See p. 202, note 25.

[15] Serving in 1737.

[16] Comn. renewed in 1727. Serving in 1737. Out before 1740.

[17] Lieut. 10 May, 1738. Serving in 1740.

BRIGADIER-GENERAL ROBERT NAPIER'S REGIMENT OF HORSE.

[5TH DRAGOON GUARDS.]

See note at head of p. 359, and memo. on same page.

Wm. Dawes [1] to be Cornet to Capt. Daniel Crespin in room of Wm. Henry Burroughs - - - -	13 July, 1719.*j*
Thos. Bligh,[2] Esq. to be Lt.-Col. in room of Lt.-Col. Wm. Hall - - - - - - - - - - - -	2 Oct. „ *j*
John Daniel Degennes,[3] Esq. to be Major in room of Bligh - - - - - - - - - - - - -	„ „ „ *j*
Thos. Tennison [4] to be Lieut. to Capt. Daniel Paul in room of John Hall - - - - - - - -	10 Nov. „ *j*
Alexander Naper (*sic*) [5] to be Cornet to that Tp. whf. [Lt.-Col.] Wm. Hall is Capt. in room of Tennison -	„ „ „ *j*
John Bowen [6] to be Cornet to Lt.-Col. Bligh in room of Peter Ormsby - - - - - - - -	4 Mar. 1719/20.*j*
Peter Ormsby [7] to be Lieut. to Capt. Daniel Crespin in room of Wm. Portal - - - - - - -	„ „ „ *j*
Wm. Portal,[8] Esq. to be Capt. of that Tp. whf. Lt.-Col. Wm. Hall was Capt. - - - - - -	„ „ „ *j*
Chas. Levinge [9] to be Cornet to the Colonel's Tp. -	20 Nov. 1720.*p*
John Preston [10] to be Lieut. to Capt. Wm. Portal -	„ „ „ *p*
Do. to be Capt. - - - - - - - - -	4 Feb. 1721/2.*f*
Richard Reynell [11] to be Lieut. - - - - -	„ „ „ *f*
Joseph Preston [12] to be Cornet - - - - -	„ „ „ *f*
John Bowen [6] to be Lieut. - - - - -	10 Dec. 1722.*f*
Henry Stamer [13] to be Cornet - - - - -	„ „ „ *f*
John Langston [14] to be do. - - - - -	5 July, 1723.*f*
Francis Burton [15] to be do. - - - - -	2 Sept. „ *f*
Alex. Napier [5] to be Lieut. - - - - -	1 April, 1724.*f*
Henry Wallis [16] to be Cornet - - - - -	„ „ „ *f*
Chas. Burroughs [17] to be Cornet to Capt. Daniel Paul in room of Thos. Bloodworth - - - -	6 May, 1725.*r*

[1] Capt. in Bisset's Regt. of Foot (30th), 4 May, 1722. Comn. renewed in June, 1727. Out before 1737.

[2] See biog. notice on p. 160, note 11.

[3] See do. on p. 159, note 10.

[4] See do. in Vol. I., p. 328, note 4.

[5] Lieut. 1 April, 1724. Serving in 1740.

[6] Lieut. 10 Dec. 1722. Serving in 1740.

[7] See p. 159, note 9.

[8] Serving as senior Capt. in 1740.

[9] Out before 1727. Aftds. Sir Charles Levinge, Bart. D. 1762.

[10] Capt. 4 Feb. 1722. Serving in 1737. Out before 1740.

[11] Serving in 1740.

[12] Capt. 12 June, 1733. Major, 3 July, 1743. Serving in 1748. D. 1754. Will proved at Dublin.

[13] Attained the rank of Lt.-Col. of above Regt. 19 Dec. 1755. D. in 1766. His will proved at Dublin, describes him as "Colonel of Horse."

[14] Lieut. 14 Jan. 1738. Serving in 1740.

[15] Serving as Cornet in 1740.

[16] Capt. 27 April, 1756. Serving in 1759.

[17] Serving as Cornet in 1737. Out before 1740.

THE 1st REGIMENT OF CARABINIERS
[6TH DRAGOON GUARDS.]
[CARABINIERS.]

See note at head of p. 359, and memo. on same page.

John Arabin [1] to be Lieut. to Capt. Wm. Guyon in room of Wm. Finley - - - - - - -	9 June, 1720.*j*
Walter Wilson [2] to be Cornet to Col. Petry in room of Arabin - - - - - - - - -	,, ,, ,, *j*
Richard, Viscount Shannon [3] to be Colonel in room of Richard Waring and Capt. of a Tp. - - -	17 June, 1721.*p*
Wm. Hollingsworth [4] to be Cornet - - - -	29 Aug. ,, *f*
Montagu Lambert [5] to be Cornet - - -	20 Feb. 1721/2.*j*
Chas. Tassell [6] to be Lieut. - - - -	20 Mar. ,, *f*
Philip Chenevix, [7] Esq. to be Capt. - - -	19 June, 1722.*f*
Beaumont Astley, [8] Esq. to be Capt -Lieut. - - -	,, ,, ,, *f*
John Orfeur [9] to be Lieut. - - - -	26 April, 1724.*f*
Urmston Pepys [10] to be do. - - - - -	5 May, ,, *f*
Richard Stevenson [11] to be Cornet to Capt. Richard Shuckburgh in room of Richard Wolseley - -	26 Oct. ,, *r*
David Dickson [12] to be Cornet to Capt. Philip Chenevix in room of Wm. Punstoby (*sic*) - - - -	24 Mar. 1725/6.*r*
Lieut.-General George Macartney [13] to be Colonel in room of Viscount Shannon and Capt. of a Tp. -	9 Mar. 1726/7.*r*

[1] See p. 161, note 4.
[2] Lieut. 13 March, 1728. Serving in 1740.
[3] See biog. notice in Vol. I., p. 308, note 1.
[4] Comn. renewed in 1727. Serving in 1730. Brigdr. and Lieut. 3rd Tp. of Life Guards, 24 Sept. 1736. Serving in 1740.
[5] Serving as Lieut. in 1737. D. in 1740. Will proved at Dublin.
[6] Serving as senior Lieut. in 1740. The will of a certain Charles Tassell, of Kyle, co. Kilkenny, was proved at Dublin in 1758.
[7] See biog. notice on p. 161, note 1.
[8] See do. on do., note 6.
[9] "Son of Philip Orfeur and Mary, dau. of Col. Richard Kirkby, of Kirkby Ireleth, Lancashire, was gazetted 1st Lieut. to his uncle (*i.e.* Maj.-Gen. John Orfeur) 10 Jan. 1708/9, in Visct. Shannon's Regt. of Marines. In 1724 he joined Lord Shannon's Regt. of Horse, the 3rd Dragoon Guards, on the Irish Establishment, now the 6th Dragoon Guards or Carabiniers. Retd. as Capt.-Lieut. in 1745. Settled in Ireland, where he d. in 1753. He married Juliana, dau. of Col. Thomas Palliser, of Portobello, co. Wexford."—(Communicated by Col. W. O. Cavenagh.)
[10] See p. 161, note 5.
[11] Serving in 1737. Out before 1740.
[12] Serving as senior Cornet in 1740.
[13] See biog. notice in Vol. I., p. 253, note 3.

SIR JOHN LIGONIER, K.B.

MAJOR-GENERAL CHARLES SYBOURG'S REGIMENT OF HORSE.

[7TH DRAGOON GUARDS.]

See note at head of p. 359, and memo. on same page.

John Kelly[1] to be Lieut. to Capt. George Bennet in room of Samuel Pope - - -	—	25 Feb. 1718/9.*j*
Theophilus La Cour Desbrisay,[2] Esq. to be Capt. in room of Claudius Testefolle -	—	29 June, 1719.*j*
David de Charmes[3] to be Lieut. - - -	—	21 Jan. 1719/2.*f*
Wm. Waldron[4] to be Cornet - - - -	—	,, ,, ,, *f*
Charles Hotham,[5] Esq. to be Lt.-Col. in room of Lt.-Col. Wm. Bray and Capt. of a Tp. - - - - - - -	—	6 April, 1720.*f*
Ant. Morgan[6] to be Cornet to Capt. Desbrisay in room of Lord Bellew - - - -	—	9 June, ,, *f*
John Ligonier,[7] Esq. to be Colonel in room of Charles Sibourg and Capt. of a Tp. -	Herrenhausen, 18 July (O.S.) ,, *c*	
George Bennet,[8] Esq. to be Major - - -	—	25 May, 1721.*f*
Hugh Warburton,[9] Esq. to be Capt. - -	—	,, ,, ,, *f*
Charles Fitzroy[10] to be Cornet - - -	—	9 Sept. ,, *f*
Wentworth Odiarne[11] to be do. - - -	—	9 May, 1722.*f*
Walter Warburton[12] to be do. - - -	—	1 Jan. 1722/3.*f*
Edward Combe,[13] Junr. to be Chaplain in room of Edward Combe, Senr. - -	—	24 June, 1724.*r*

[1] Out before 1727.

[2] Do.

[3] Serving in 1737. Out before 1740.

[4] Lieut. 12 Jan. 1734. Serving in 1740.

[5] See his Comns. in Vol. I. He succeeded his father, Brig.-Gen. Sir Charles Hotham, Bt. in 1725, and was appointed Groom of the Bedchamber to George II. Col. of the 18th Royal Irish in Jan. 1732, and on 13 May, 1735, was transferred to the command of the 1st Tp. of H. Grendr. Gds. D. 15 Jan. 1738.

[6] Lieut. 15 Dec. 1738. Serving in 1740. Probably the "Anthony Morgan, Esq.," whose will was proved at Dublin in 1752.

[7] Comn. signed by George I. Second son of Louis Ligonier, Sieur de Monteuquet, a Huguenot. Served as a volunteer in Flanders in 1702. Capt. in the Earl of Bath's Regt. (10th Foot), 30 March, 1703. Fought at Blenheim where seven Captains of his Regt. were killed and one wounded. Bt.-Major, 1 July, 1706. At Malplaquet he had 22 shots through his clothes. Bt.-Col. 15 Nov. 1711. Lt.-Gov. of Fort St. Philip in Minorca, 12 Oct. 1713. Lt.-Col. of 4th Horse (now 3rd Dragoon Guards), 22 Nov. 1716. Served as Adjt.-Gen. in the Expedition to Vigo, 1719. Col. of the 8th Horse (now 7th Dragoon Guards), 18 July, 1720. Brig.-Gen. 14 Nov. 1735. Maj.-Gen. 2 July, 1739. Lt.-Gen. 8 Feb. 1743. Created a Knight Banneret on the field of Dettingen by George II. for conspicuous gallantry. Gained fresh laurels at Fontenoy. "At Laffeld he preserved the Allied Army from destruction, and enabled it to withdraw in good order by charging the whole line of French cavalry at the head of the British dragoons, in which charge his horse was killed, and he himself taken prisoner." Gen. of Horse, 30 Dec. 1746. Transferred to the Colonelcy of the 2nd Dragoon Guards, 24 July, 1749. Col. of the Royal Horse Guards, 27 Jan. 1753. Col. of the 1st Foot Guards, 30 Nov. 1757. Field-Marshal Commanding-in-Chief, 30 Nov. 1757. Created an Irish Visct. same year. Advanced to an English Earldom 10 Sept. 1766. D. 28 April, 1770, aged 91.

[8] See p. 162, note 9.
[9] Attained the rank of Col. of the Inniskilling Fusiliers in Sept. 1761, and d. in Sept. 1771.—*Gentleman's Mag.*
[10] Grandson of the 1st Duke of Grafton.   D. at New York in 1735.—*Ibid.*
[11] Serving in 1737.   Out before 1740.   D. in 1762 as Deputy Serjt.-at-Arms.—*Ibid.*
[12]   Do.   do.
[13]   Do.

THE ROYAL REGIMENT OF DRAGOONS OF IRELAND.

[*Disbanded in* 1798.]

See note at head of p. 359, and memo. on same page.

John Dalston[1] to be Lieut. to Major Wriothesley Betton in room of George McKean decd. - - - - - - - -	Dublin,	17 Sept.	1719.*j*
Wriothesley Betton,[2] Esq. to be Lt.-Col. in room of Lt.-Col. John Hill and Capt. of a Tp. - - - - - - - -	,,	23 ,,	,, *j*
Robert Burton,[3] Esq. to be Major in room of —— Betton - - - - - - -	,,	,, ,,	,, *j*
Richard Caulfield[4] to be Lieut. to Lt.-Col. Betton in room of John Dalston preferred	,,	3 June,	1720.*j*
James Russel Madan,[5] Esq. to be Capt. in room of John Usher - - - - -	St. James's,	18 May,	1721.*c*
James Walsh[6] to be Lieut. - - - -	—	10 July,	1722.*f*
Wm. Higgins,[7] Esq. to be Capt.-Lieut. - -	—	11 ,,	,, *f*
Nicholas Bernard[8] to be Lieut. - -	—	1 May,	1724.*f*
John Warburton,[9] Esq. to be Capt. in room of Stephen Cornwallis - - - -	—	22 Jan. 1724/5.*f*	
Gould Clarges[10] to be Cornet to Capt. Richard Madden (*sic*) in room of Lewis Griffith -	—	8 Sept.	1725.*r*
Lewis Griffith[11] to be Lieut. to Capt. Charles Wardlaw in room of Christopher Clarges	—	,, ,,	,, *r*
Wm. Cope,[12] Esq. to be Major in room of Robert Burton - - - - -	—	30 Nov.	,, *r*
Henry Conyngham,[13] Esq. to be Capt. of that Tp. whf. Robert Burton was late Capt. -	—	,, ,,	,, *r*

[1] From Cornet in Col. Bowles's Dragoons.   See biog. notice in Vol. I., p. 272, note 4.
[2] See p. 163, note 6.
[3] Served previously as Capt. in the Prince of Wales's Own Regt. of Horse.   On 1 Dec. 1725 he was appointed Capt. of the Battle Axe Foot Guards.   Said Comn. renewed by George II. in Sept. 1727.   D. in 1765.
[4] Comn. renewed in 1727.   Out before 1737.
[5] Comn. signed by George I.   See p. 206, note 18.
[6] Serving as senior Lieut. of above Regt. in 1740.
[7] See p. 163, note 3.
[8] Capt. 20 June, 1739.
[9] Lt.-Col. of above Regt. 13 May, 1747.   D. in 1750.
[10] Comn. renewed in 1727.   Out before 1737.   The death is recorded in the *Gentleman's Mag.* for 1780 of "Gould Clarges, Esq., aged 78, in Great Marlborough Street, uncle to Earl Ferrers."
[11] See p. 163, note 1.
[12] Lt.-Col. 10 May, 1740.   Out before May, 1747.
[13] See p. 360, note 12.

MAJOR-GENERAL JOHN PEPPER'S REGIMENT OF DRAGOONS.

[8TH HUSSARS.]

See note at head of p. 359, and memo. on same page.

James Johnston[1] to be Lieut. to Capt. Wm. Bland in room of Vincent Peyton	6 Mar. 1718/9.	*j*
Thos. Erle[2] to be Cornet in room of James Johnston -	,, ,, ,,	*j*
Richard Shinton[3] to be Cornet in room of Robt. Stevenson	,, ,, ,,	*j*
Phineas Bowles,[4] Esq. to be Colonel in room of Major-General John Pepper and to be Capt. of a Tp.	23 ,, ,,	*j*
Fair Jenkins[5] to be Cornet	31 Jan. 1719/20.	*f*
Charles Bowles[6] to be Lieut. to Lord Ossulston in room of John Shute decd.	13 Feb. ,,	*j*
Samuel Whitshed,[7] Esq. to be Lt.-Colonel and Capt. of a Tp. in room of Thos. Erle	2 May, 1720.	*j*
George Macartney,[8] Esq. to be Capt. in room of Edward Wills	3 June, ,,	*j*
Fras. Bailey[9] to be Cornet	31 May, 1721.	*f*
Whitney McKean[10] to be Cornet	18 Mar. 1721/2.	*f*
Thos. Erle[2] to be Lieut.	26 July, 1722.	*f*
[Major-General Richard Munden[11] to be Colonel in room of Phineas Bowles and Capt. of a Tp.	19 Nov. ,,	]
Cuthbert Ellison,[12] Esq. to be Capt.	11 April, 1723.	*f*
Sheffield Austin,[13] Esq. to be Capt. in room of James Lord Somerville[14]	15 June, 1725.	*r*
Sir Robert Rich,[15] Bart. to be Colonel in room of Major-General Richard Munden decd.	20 Sept. ,,	*r*
Wm. Barkley[16] to be Lieut. to Lt.-Col. Samuel Whitshed in room of Christopher Zobell	3 Dec. ,,	*r*
Robt. Sanderson[17] to be Cornet to do. in room of Wm. Barkley	,, ,, ,,	*r*
Richard Howard (*sic*),[18] Esq. to be Capt.-Lieut. in room of Thos. Echlin	6 May, 1726.	*r*
John Withers[19] to be Lieut. to Capt. Sheffield Austin in room of Richard Howard	,, ,, ,,	*r*
Charles Churchill[20] to be Cornet to Major Henry de Grangues	,, ,, ,,	*r*

[1] Comn. renewed in 1727. Serving with above Regt. in Ireland, 1737. Out before 1740. This officer must not be confounded with Cornet James Johnston of 13th Dragoons, which he joined in Ireland, 1 Oct. 1736. Latter officer was son of George Johnston, an Army Agent in Dublin, and after a distinguished military career at home, abroad, and on active service, d. 13 Dec. 1797, aged 76, and was bd. in Westminster Abbey.

[2] Capt.-Lieut. 9 Oct. 1739. Eventually obtained the rank of Maj.-Gen. and Col. 28th Foot. See biog. notice of his father in Vol. I., p. 112, note 2.

[3] Lieut. 4 March, 1733. Attained the rank of Capt. before 1745. The will of "Richard Shinton, Esq., Capt. in Gen. St. George's Dragoons," was proved at Dublin in 1745.

[4] See Vol. I., p. 116, note 1.

[5] Comn. renewed in 1727. Out before 1736.

[6]   Do.   do.

[7] See biog. notice in Vol. I., p. 155, note 4.

[8] See do. in do., p. 222, note 65.

[9] Lieut. 30 March, 1735. Serving in 1740.

[10] Lieut. 9 Oct. 1739. Serving in 1740.

[11] See biog. notice in Vol. I., p. 117, note 1.

[12] Eldest son of Robert Ellison, of Hebburn, Northumberland, by Eliz. eldest dau. of Sir Henry Liddell, Bart., of Ravensworth Castle. Attained the rank of full Gen. 5 May, 1772, and d. unm. 11 May, 1785.—Burke's *Landed Gentry.*

[13] See his Comn. as Cornet in above Regt. given in Vol. I., p. 268. His name there is given as "Thomas Sheffield Austin." Serving with same rank in 1740.

[14] The register of Lord Somerville's Comn. as Capt. in above Regt. is not forthcoming owing to the gap in the Irish Comn. Registers referred to on p. 359. James 13th Lord Somerville succeeded in 1700, but his claim to the title being disputed, it was not till 27 May, 1723, that the House of Lords confirmed his claim. Chosen a Scottish representative peer in 1741.

[15] See biog. notice in Vol. I., p. 122, note 1.

[16] *Berkeley.* Serving as senior Lieut. in 1740.

[17] Serving as senior Cornet in 1740.

[18] "Comn. signed in England, issued in Ireland." Called "Harwood" in subsequent Lists. Capt. 9 Oct. 1739. The death of a certain "Major Harwood in Ireland" is recorded in the *Gentleman's Mag.* for 1750.

[19] "Comn. signed in England, issued in Ireland." Out before 1736.

[20]   Do.   do.

MAJOR-GENERAL OWEN WYNNE'S REGIMENT OF DRAGOONS.

[9TH LANCERS.]

See note on p. 359 and memo. on same page.

Thos. Burroughs,[1] Esq. to be Capt. in room of Hon. Chas. Howard - - - -	—	23 May, 1719.*j*
Fras. Rannells (*sic*) to be Cornet to Lt.-Col. Wm. Duncombe in room of Chris. Adams	—	1 July, ,, *j*
Brig.-Gen. James Crofts[2] to be Colonel in room of Maj.-Gen. Wynne - - -	—	6 ,, ,, *j*
Paul Malide,[3] Esq. to be Capt. - - -	—	7 Oct. ,, *f*
John Foliott[4] to be Lieut. to Capt. Andrew Knox in room of Edward Whitway -	—	11 Nov. ,, *j*
Peter Renaut[5] to be Cornet to Capt. Thos. Burroughs in room of John Foliott	—	,, ,, ,, *j*
Loftus Bolton[6] to be Cornet to do. in room of Lewis Foliott - - - - -	—	4 Mar. 1719/20.*j*
Edward Webster[7] to be do. to the Colonel's Tp. in room of Ant. Morgan - - -	—	1 May, 1720.*j*
John Foliott,[4] Esq. to be Capt. of that Tp. whf. Col. Wm. Douglas was Capt. - -	—	1 June, ,, *j*
Wm. Green[8] to be Cornet to Capt. Thos. Burroughs in room of Peter Renaut -	—	,, ,, ,, *j*
Roger Pemberton[9] to be Lieut. to Lt.-Col. Wm. Duncombe in room of Jacob Warns (*sic*)	—	5 ,, ,, *j*
Theodore Amyand[10] to be Cornet to Major John Dunbar in room of Roger Pemberton	—	,, ,, ,, *j*
James Hill[11] to be Lieut. - - - -	—	19 Aug. 1721.*f*
Fras. Ligonier,[12] Esq. to be Capt. - - -	—	5 May, 1722.*f*
Wm. Green[8] to be Lieut. - - - -	—	15 Aug. ,, *f*
Sir Wm. Gostwick[13] to be Cornet - - -	—	,, ,, ,, *f*
Thos. Aston[14] to be do. - - -	—	15 April, 1723 *f*
James Gardiner,[15] Esq. to be Major and Capt. of a Tp. - - - - -	- Kensington, 1 June, 1724.*r*
Henry Goddard,[16] Esq. to be Major and Capt. of a Tp. [in room of James Gardiner] -	—	25 July, ,, *r*
Nathaniel Preston[17] to be Cornet to Capt. Fras. Ligonier in room of Chris. Gilbert -	—	14 Mar. 1725/6.*r*
Edward Clayton[18] to be Cornet to [Lt.-Col.] Wm. Duncombe in room of Fras. Rannalls	—	21 ,, ,, *r*
Fras. Rannalls[19] to be Lieut. to do. in room of Chris. Russell - - - - -	—	21 May, 1726.*r*

[1] From half-pay Capt. in Maj.-Gen. Sibourg's Regt. of Foot. Out of the Army before June, 1727.

[2] See biog. notice in Vol. I., p. 106, note 4.

[3] From Lieut. in Lord Cobham's Dragoons. Major of 9th Dragoons, 12 July, 1737. D. in 1747 on full pay. Will proved at Dublin.

[4] Out before 1727. Believed to be identical with the John *Folliot* who d. as Lt.-Gov. of Kinsale in 1765.—*Gentleman's Mag.*

[5] Probably son of Capt. Peter Regnaud, who was a Capt. in Sir Ric. Temple's Regt. of Foot at Malplaquet. The Cornet named in the text left the Regt. in June, 1720.

[6] Out before 1736.

[7] Serving in 1737.

[8] Lieut. 15 Aug. 1722. Out before 1736.

[9] Out before 1736.

[10] Do.

[11] Serving in 1737. Out before 1740.

[12] See biog. notice in Vol. I., p. 151, note 6. At the time of his death, a few days after the battle of Falkirk, where he had distinguished himself, he was Col. of the 13th Dragoons, to which he had been appointed 1 Oct. 1745.

[13] Lieut. 12 July, 1737. Serving in 1740. The last Bart. of Willington, co. Bedford. He succeeded his grandfather in 1722. D.s.p. in 1766.

[14] Serving as Cornet in 1737. Out before 1740.

[15] Comn. signed by George I. See Vol. I., p. 108, note 6.

[16] Appointed Capt. of the Grendr. Cy. in the Earl of Inchiquin's Regt. of Foot in Ireland, March, 1704. Major, 28 May, 1710. Bt. Lt.-Col. 1 Jan. 1711. Half-pay, 1712. Comn. as Major of Crofts's Dragoons renewed in 1727. D. in 1748. Will proved at Dublin.

[17] Comn. renewed in June, 1727. Out before 1737. The will of a certain "Nathaniel Preston, Esq., of Swainstown, co. Meath," was proved at Dublin in 1760.

[18] Comn. "signed and sealed in England." Serving as senior Cornet in 1740. Attained the rank of Major of the 9th Dragoons, 9 April, 1756.

[19] Comn. "signed and sealed in England." Serving in 1740. Called "Reynolds" in the *Army List*, 1740.

MAJOR-GENERAL JOHN ORFEUR.

(*See* Vol. I., p. 116, note 3.)

(*From an Original Portrait in the possession of the Rer. F. J. Cannon,
Plealey House, Pontesford, Shrewsbury.*)

BRIGADIER-GENERAL PHINEAS BOWLES'S REGIMENT OF DRAGOONS.

[12TH LANCERS.]

See note at head of p. 359 and memo. on same page.

Phineas Bowles,[1] Esq. to be Colonel in room of Brigdr.-Gen. Phineas Bowles and Capt. of a Tp. - - - - -	—	23 Mar. 1718/9 *j*
John Carmichael[2] to be Lieut. to Major Thos. Brown in room of Hugh Hilton decd. -	—	29 Aug. 1719.*j*
John Knox[3] to be Lieut. to Capt. John Prideaux in room of John Dalston -	—	17 Sept. ,, *j*
George Macartney,[4] Esq. to be Capt. in room of Major Giles Stevens - - -	—	17 Feb. 1719/20.*j*
George Phenney,[5] Esq. to be Capt.-Lieut. in room of Wm. Bourden - - -	—	10 Mar. ,, *j*
Thos. Cooke[6] to be Cornet to the Colonel's Tp. in room of Wm. Pomfret - -	—	5 April, 1720.*j*
Edward Wills,[7] Esq. to be Major in room of Thos. Brown decd. and Capt. of a Tp. -	—	3 June, ,, *j*
John Dalston,[8] Esq. to be Capt. in room of George Macartney - - - - -	—	7 ,, ,, *j*
John Johnston,[9] Esq. to be Capt.-Lieut. in room of George Phenney preferred -	—	,, ,, ,, *j*
Brett Norton[10] to be Lieut. to Capt. John Dalston in room of John Johnston - -	—	,, ,, ,, *j*
John Alder[11] to be Cornet to do. in room of Brett Norton - - - - - -	—	,, ,, ,, *j*
John Carmichael,[2] Esq. to be Capt. in room of John Prideaux - - - - -	—	9 ,, ,, *j*
Richard Honeywood[12] to be Lieut. to Capt. Carmichael - - - - -	—	,, ,, ,, *j*
Wm. Long[13] to be Cornet to Capt. John Pierson in room of Richard Honeywood	—	,, ,, ,, *j*
Jasper Tryce,[14] Esq. to be Lt.-Colonel - -	—	15 Aug. 1722.*f*
Charles Bernard[15] to be Lieut. - - -	—	27 Nov. 1723.*f*
John Leslie[16] to be do. - - - - -	—	2 May, 1724.*f*
[John Smith, Esq. to be Major and Capt. -	—	,, ,, ,,]
Wm. Wray[17] to be Cornet - - - -	—	,, ,, ,, *f*
Wm. Piers[18] to be Lieut. to Major John Smith.	Kensington,	11 July, ,, *r*
Christopher Clarges,[19] Esq. to be Capt. of [Lt.-Col.] John Orfeur's Tp. - - -	—	8 Sept. 1725.*r*
Gavin Hamilton,[20] Esq. to be Major and Capt. of a Tp. in room of John Smith decd. -	—	12 Feb. 1725/6.*r*

[1] Son of the late Brig.-Gen. Phineas Bowles, the former Col. of above Regt. Transferred to the Carabiniers, 20 Dec. 1740. Attained the rank of Lt.-Gen. 12 May, 1745. D. in 1746 as Gov. of Derry. A copy of his will is in the Dublin Record Office.

[2] See his Comn. as Major of Munden's Dragoons on p. 371.

A A

[3] Out before 1727.

[4] See biog. notice on p. 212, note 21.

[5] See do. on p. 352, note 3.

[6] Out before 1727.

[7] From Capt. in Pepper's Dragoons. In previous reign he had served in Col. Fras. Langston's Regt. of Horse as Qr.-Mr. to the Colonel's Tp. and subsequently as Lieut. in Lord Cutts's Dragoons in Ireland. Out of Bowles's Dragoons in 1724.

[8] See biog. notice in Vol. I., p. 272, note 4.

[9] Serving as senior Capt. in 1740.

[10] Capt. 20 June, 1739. D. in 1765. Will proved at Dublin.

[11] Lieut. 25 Aug. 1733. Serving in 1740.

[12] See Vol. I., p. 272, note 1.

[13] Out before 1727.

[14] From Major of Handasyde's Regt. (22nd Foot). Serving in 1739. D. or left the Regt. in Aug. same year.

[15] Lieut. 20 Feb. 1736. Serving in 1740.

[16] Serving as Lieut. in 1737. Out before 1740.

[17] Comn. renewed in 1727. Serving in 1737. Out before 1740. Believed to be one of the Wrays, of Castle Wray, co. Donegal. Mention is made of this family in the Introduction to *The Wrays of Glentworth* by Charles Dalton, F.R.G.S.

[18] Capt.-Lieut. 20 June, 1739.

[19] Major, 5 Sept. 1739. D. at Chingford, Essex, in 1780. Will proved at Dublin.

[20] See his Comn. on p. 132, and note thereto.

BRIGADIER-GENERAL RICHARD MUNDEN'S REGIMENT OF DRAGOONS.

[13TH HUSSARS.]

See note at head of p. 359, and memo. on same page.

Abraham Swift,[1] Esq. to be Capt. in room of Sutton Lister - - - - - - - - -	1 Aug.	1719.*j*
Stratford Eyre[2] to be Cornet - - - - - -	5 ,,	,, *f*
Nathan Forth[8] to be Cornet to Col. Clement Nevill in room of Richard Henson - - - - -	15 Sept.	,, *j*
Richard Pyott,[4] Esq. to be Lt.-Col. in room of Samuel Freeman and Capt. of a Tp. - - - -	1 June,	1720.*j*
Charles Dilke,[5] Esq. to be Major and Capt. of a Tp. -	8 ,,	,, *j*
John Carmichael,[6] Esq. to be Major [in room of Dilke] -	22 Nov.	,, *f*
Richard Evans,[7] Esq. to be Capt. - - - -	14 Oct.	1721.*f*
Peter Kerr,[8] Esq. to be Lt.-Colonel and Capt. of a Tp. -	24 Mar. 1721/2.*f*	
Edward Southwell[9] to be Cornet - - - -	5 June,	1722.*f*
[Sir Robert Rich,[10] Bart. to be Colonel in room of Richard Munden and Capt. of a Tp. - - - -	19 Nov.	,,]
Wm. Crofton[11] to be Cornet - - - - -	5 July,	1723.*f*
John West[12] to be do. - - - - - -	2 April, 1724.*f*	
Richard Downe[18] to be Lieut. - - - - -	21 ,,	,, *f*
Lodowick Peterson,[14] Esq. to be Capt.-Lieut. - -	24 June,	,, *f*
Ant. Burren[15] to be Lieut. to Capt. Shugbrough Whitney in room of Henry Dawson - - - -	23 Oct.	,, *r*
Fras. Russell[16] to be Surgeon in room of Nicholas Hansard - - - - - - -	28 June,	1725.*r*
Wm. Stanhope,[17] Esq. to be Colonel in room of Sir Robt. Rich, Bart. and Capt. of a Tp. - - - -	20 Sept.	,, *r*
Robert Walker[18] to be Lieut. to Capt. Abr. Swift in room of Maurice Keating - - - - -	23 Oct.	,, *r*

[1] See p. 135, note 10.

[2] Grand-nephew of Edward Eyre, M.P. Comn. renewed in 1727. Appointed Capt. in Col. Battereau's Regt. of Foot, 29 March, 1742. In 1747 he was appointed Gov. of the town and port of Galway. An account of his residence there is given in *Old Irish Life*, by J. W. Callwell, published in 1912.

[8] Lieut. in Col. Clement Nevill's Dragoons (14th), 1 Jan. 1726. Placed on half-pay as Lieut. but re-appointed Lieut. in Nevill's Dragoons, 20 June, 1739. Serving in 1740.

[4] Appointed Lieut. and Lt.-Col. 4th Tp. of Life Guards, 22 March, 1723. Comn. renewed in 1727. Out before 1740. Appears to have belonged to the Staffordshire Pyotts.

[5] Brigdr. and Lieut. 1st Tp. of Life Guards, 30 Jan. 1701. Lieut. in Lord Cobham's Dragoons, 3 Oct. 1715. Out of Munden's Dragoons in Nov. 1720.

[6] From Capt. in Bowles's Dragoons. Serving in 1730. Out before 1736.

[7] Serving in 1736. Out before 1740.

[8] Served in Sir John Wittewrong's Regt. of Foot in late reign and was made Major thereof, 1 Aug. 1711. Half-pay, 1712. Serving as Lt.-Col. of the 13th Dragoons in 1737. Out before 1740. D. in 1744. Will proved at Dublin.

[9] Comn. renewed in 1727. Probably the Edward Southwell who eventually succeeded as Baron de Clifford, and d. in 1777.

[10] See biog. notice in Vol. I., p. 122, note 1.

[11] Lieut. 2 April, 1733.   Capt.-Lieut. 30 Nov. 1745.   Wounded at Prestonpans.   Served at Falkirk.   Capt. 26 Feb. 1746.   Out in Sept. 1754.

[12] Capt. 1 Sept. 1739.

[13] Capt. 20 June, 1739.   Called "Downes" in 1740 *Army List.*   Out in 1747.

[14] Attained rank of Lt.-Col. of above Regt. 26 Feb. 1746.   Out before 1748.

[15] Comn. renewed in 1727.   Out before 1736.

[16] Out before 1736.

[17] Created Earl of Harrington.   See biog. notice in Vol. I., p. 124, note 1.

[18] Out before June, 1727.

BRIGADIER-GENERAL JAMES DORMER'S REGIMENT OF DRAGOONS.

[14TH HUSSARS.]

See note at head of p. 359, and memo. on same page.

Peter Lasalle[1] to be Qr.-Mr. to Capt. James Stevens -	1 June, 1719.*j*
Cuthbert Smith,[2] Esq. to be Capt.-Lieut. in room of Henry Lasalle - - - - - - -	17 July, „ *j*
Thos. Delahay[3] to be Lieut. to Lt.-Col. Wm. Boyle in room of Cuthbert Smith - - - - - -	„ „ „ *j*
Henry Boyle[4] to be Cornet to Capt. Peter Morin in room of Thos. Delahay - - - - - - -	„ „ „ *j*
James Newcomen[5] to be Cornet to Capt. Beverley Newcomen in room of Robert Bettesworth - - -	14 Oct. „ *j*
George Hoey[6] to be Lieut. to do. in room of James Fleming decd. - - - - - - -	1 Mar. 1719/20.*j*
Beverley Newcomen,[7] Esq. to be Major in room of Thos. Digges and Capt. of a Tp. - - - -	5 April, 1720.*j*
Cuthbert Smith,[2] Esq. to be Capt. of Beverley Newcomen's late Tp. - - - - - -	„ „ „ *j*
Thos. Ellis[8] to be Lieut. to Capt. Peter Morin in room of Jonathan Pyrke - - - - - -	„ „ „ *j*
James [Russell] Madan[9] to be Cornet to do. in room of Thos. Ellis - - - - - - -	„ „ „ *j*
Jonathan Pyrke,[10] Esq. to be Capt.-Lieut. in room of Cuthbert Smith - - - - - -	„ „ „ *j*
Clement Nevill,[11] Esq. to be Colonel in room of James Dormer and Capt. of a Tp. - - - -	9 „ „ *j*
Wm. Hamilton[12] to be Lieut. - - - - -	20 Aug. 1720.*f*
Beverley Newcomen,[7] Esq. to be Lt.-Colonel - - -	1 Dec. „ *f*
Josias Patterson,[13] Esq. to be Capt.-Lieut. - -	13 Sept. 1721.*f*
Reginald Molineux[14] to be Lieut. - - - -	„ „ „ *f*
James Baillie[15] to be Cornet - - - -	„ „ „ *f*
Wroth Watson[16] to be do. - - - -	2 Jan. 1721/2.*f*
Michael O'Brien Dilke[17] to be Capt. - - -	15 June, 1723.*f*
Peter Smith[18] to be Cornet - - - -	14 April, 1724.*f*
Richard Bowles[19] to be Capt. - - - -	1 May, „ *f*
David Lesley[20] to be Cornet - - - -	5 „ „ *f*
Nathan Forth[21] to be Lieut. to Capt. O'Brien Dilke in room of Thos. Delahay - - - - -	1 Jan. 1725/6.*r*
Henry Echlin[22] to be Cornet to the Colonel's Tp. in room of Forth - - - - - - -	„ „ „ *r*
Gavin Hamilton,[23] Esq. to be Major in room of Michael Moore decd. - - - - - - -	21 „ „ *r*
Cuthbert Smith,[2] Esq. to be Major in room of Gavin Hamilton preferred - - - - - -	12 Feb. „ *r*

[1] Out before 1736.

[2] Capt. 5 April, 1720. Major, 12 Feb. 1726. Left the Regt. in 1737. D. in 1742. Will proved at Dublin.

[3] Out 1 Jan. 1726.

[4] Not in any subsequent List.

[5] Serving as Cornet in the 7th Horse (6th D.G.) in 1730. Lieut. in do. 1 May, 1738. Serving in 1740.

[6] Out before 1727.

[7] Served at Malplaquet as Lieut. in the Rl. Irish Dragoons. Lt.-Col. of Col. Nevill's Dragoons, 1 Dec. 1720. D. in 1731. (*Gentleman's Mag.*) He was fifth son of Sir Thomas Newcomen, Bart., of Kenagh, who was killed at the siege of Enniskillen in 1689.

[8] Serving as senior Lieut. in 1740.

[9] See p. 206, note 18.

[10] Out in Sept. 1721.

[11] See biog. notice in Vol. I., p. 117, note 2.

[12] Serving in 1736. On half-pay in 1739.

[13] On 5 July, 1745, Maj.-Gen. Arch. Hamilton, Col. 14th Dragoons, wrote to the Secretary-at-War asking him to transmit his letter to the King, at Hanover, which was to the effect that Capt. Josias Paterson had served upwards of 43 years, and, being worn out with age, was ready to retire ; Hamilton requested that the vacancy thus caused might be given to his (Gen. Hamilton's) nephew (*W.O. Miscellanies*, Vol. 16). Capt. Josias Paterson d. in 1753. Will proved at Dublin.

[14] Comn. renewed in 1737. Out before 1740.

[15] Lieut. 28 June, 1739.

[16] Serving in 1737. Out before 1740.

[17] *Dilkes.* Lt.-Col. 14 Nov. 1745. Attained the rank of Lt.-Gen. 11 Nov. 1759. Gov. Rl. Hospital, Dublin, 1755. Col. 50th Foot, 3 Feb. 1774. D. in 1775.

[18] Serving as senior Cornet in 1740.

[19] Major, 13 March, 1742. Served at Prestonpans and Falkirk. Appointed Major of the 81st Foot (a Corps of Invalids), 13 Oct. 1755. Lt.-Col. of the 71st Foot (Invalids), 5 April, 1759. Lt.-Gov. of Pendennis Castle. D. at Bristol, 1769.—*Gentleman's Mag.*

[20] Serving in 1730. Out before 1736.

[21] See p. 371, note 3.

[22] Serving in 1737. He was younger son of Sir Henry Echlin, Bart., and d. in 1740, leaving a son, Henry, who succeeded as 3rd Bart.—Burke's *Baronetage.*

[23] See p. 132, note 3.

THE ROYAL REGIMENT OF FOOT.

[THE ROYAL SCOTS.]

See note at head of p. 359, and memo. on same page.

Paul Rycaut,[1] Esq. to be Capt. in room of Robt. Kerr - - - - - - -	—	2 Mar. 1718/9.*j*
Chas. Gordon[2] to be Lieut. to Capt. Wm. Brisban in room of Paul Rycaut - -	—	,, ,, ,, *j*
Wheeler Barington[3] to be Ens. to Capt. John Ramsay in room of Chas. Gordon -	—	,, ,, ,, *j*
Wm. Cunningham[4] to be Ens. to Capt. Paul Rycaut in room of Alex. Napier - -	—	16 April, 1719.*j*
Rochfort McNeal[5] to be Lieut. to Capt. Jas. Hamilton in room of George Inglish	—	4 July, ,, *j*
Wm. Hodder[6] to be Ens. to Capt. Alex. Ruthven in room of Rochfort McNeal -	—	,, ,, ,, *j*
Wm. Becket[7] to be do. to Capt. Wm. Brisban in room of Alex. Brodie - - -	—	,, ,, ,, *j*
Alex. Gordon,[8] Esq. to be Capt. in room of Wm. Brisbane - - - - - -	—	17 Feb. 1719/20.*j*
Henry Vignoles[9] to be Ens. to Lt.-Col. Irwin	—	29 Nov. 1720.*p*
Michael Smith[10] to be Ens. to Capt. Robt. Hamilton - - - - - -	St. James's, 22 May,	1721.*c*
Archibald Hepburn[11] to be Ens. - - -	—	11 July, 1722.*f*
Wm. Forster[12] to be do. - - - - -	—	,, ,, ,, *f*
Sir George Hope[13] to be Capt. - - -	—	,, ,, ,, *f*
Claud Frazer (*sic*)[14] to be Lieut. - - -	—	,, ,, ,, *f*
Wheeler Barrington[3] to be do. - - -	—	26 Nov. ,, *f*
Lord Riccarton[15] to be Capt. - - - -	—	6 May, 1723.*f*
James Forrester,[16] Esq. to be do. - - -	—	22 Nov. ,, *f*
George Davidson[17] to be Lieut. - - -	—	23 Oct. 1724.*f*
Kenneth Mackenzay (*sic*)[18] to be Adjt. in room of Thos. Parker - - - - -	—	— Mar. 1724/5.*r*
John Coningham (*sic*)[19] to be Ens. to Capt. Paul Rycaut in room of Wm. Coningham	—	30 Nov. 1725.*r*
Walter Innis,[20] Esq. to be Capt. in room of Robt. Straton - - - - -	—	29 Jan. 1725/6.*r*
James Streton (*sic*),[21] Esq. to be Capt.-Lieut.	—	,, ,, ,, *r*
Gilbert Brown[22] to be Lieut. to the Earl of Balcarras (*sic*) in room of James Streton	—	,, ,, ,, *r*
John Hamilton[23] to be Adjt. in room of Gilbert Brown - - - - - -	—	,, ,, ,, *r*
John Douglass[24] to be Ens. to Lt.-Col. Alex. Irwin in room of David Dickson - -	—	24 Mar. ,, *r*
Patrick Hamilton[25] to be do. to [Major] James Horne in room of Alex. McGowan - -	—	1 Nov. 1726.*r*
Donald Clark[26] to be do. to the Earl of Balcarras in room of James McCulloch -	—	,, ,, ,, *r*

James Favier [27] to be do. to Capt. Wm. Weir in room of Robert Trippe - - -	—	29 Nov. 1726.*r*
James Streton,[21] Esq. to be Capt. in room of the Earl of Balcarras - - - -	—	25 Dec. „ *r*
Patrick Stewart,[28] Esq. to be Capt.-Lieut. in room of James Streton - - - -	—	„ „ „ *r*
Alex. Farquhar [29] to be Lieut. to Capt. Wm. Weir in room of Patrick Stewart - -	—	„ „ „ *r*

[1] Embarked with his Company from Cork, in Oct. 1741, on an Expedition to the West Indies (see *London Daily Post and General Advertiser*, 6 and 8 Oct. 1741). D. in the West Indies, 1742.—*Gentleman's Mag.*

[2] Comn. renewed in 1727. Described in his will, proved at Dublin in 1735, as " of Moraick, Aberdeenshire, and Lieut. in the Earl of Orkney's Regt. of Foot."

[3] Lieut. 26 Nov. 1722. Serving in Ireland, 1740. D. in 1754. Will proved at Dublin.

[4] Left the Regt. in Nov. 1725.

[5] Comn. renewed in 1727. Out before 1737.

[6] Lieut. 11 July, 1734. Serving in 1740.

[7] Out before 1727.

[8] Do.

[9] Comn. renewed in 1727. Out before 1737.

[10] Placed on half-pay in Ireland in 1726, " on account of his labouring under a disorder which has affected his senses."—*Treasury Papers*, Vol. CCLXII., No. 2.

[11] Lieut. 15 Feb. 1735. The will of " Archibald Hepburn, Lieut. in Royal Scotch Regt. of Foot " was proved at Dublin in 1741.

[12] Lieut. 29 Aug. 1735. Attained the rank of Lt.-Col. 2nd Batt. 1st Foot, 24 Dec. 1755. Serving in 1758. Out before 1768. D. in 1771. His will was proved at Dublin.

[13] From 3rd Foot Guards. Comn. renewed in 1727. Out before 1737.

[14] Third son of George ffrisell or Fraser, of Parke, Esq., and his wife Elizabeth d'Angennes. Ens. in the Rl. Regt. of Foot, 21 Nov. 1717. Lieut. 11 July, 1722. Capt.-Lieut. early in 1741. Capt. before Oct. same year, when he embarked with his Company from Cork on an Expedition to the West Indies. Retired in 1747. D. at his place, Grace Dieu, Waterford, in 1749. Will proved same year.—(Communicated by Maj.-Gen. Sir Thos. Fraser, K.C.B.)

[15] William Hamilton, eldest son of John, Earl of Ruglen and Visct. Riccarton (so created in April, 1697). Bn. 1695. D. unm. at Edinburgh in Feb. 1742. During his latter years he was known as Lord Daer, his father having succeeded as Earl of Selkirk in 1739.—*Extinct Peerage.*

[16] Major, 20 April, 1741. Embarked with his Company from Cork in Oct. same year on an Expedition to the West Indies. Serving as Major, 1749. Capt. and Lt.-Col. 3rd Foot Guards, 23 Dec. 1752. Believed to be the Col. Forrester appointed Gov. of Belle Isle, France, after that island had been captured by the British, who d. in 1765.

[17] Serving as Lieut. in 1740. Attained the rank of Capt. in above Regt. and d. in 1746. Will proved at Dublin.

[18] Capt. 4 April, 1734. Serving in 1740.

[19] Lieut. 3 Aug. 1736. Capt. 1 April, 1744. Serving in 1758 as senior Capt.

[20] Wounded at Blenheim as Ens. in above Regt. Fought at Malplaquet. Serving in 1740.

[21] *Stratton* or *Stretton.* Capt. 25 Dec. 1726. Serving in 1737. Out before 1740.

[22] Serving in 1737. Out before 1740.

[23] Lieut. 1 Aug. 1727. Served as Lieut. to Capt. Peter Rycaut's Company in the Expedition to the West Indies, 1741–42. Identical with the " Capt. John Hamilton " who d. in the West Indies, 1742.—*Gentleman's Mag.*

[24] Comn. renewed in June, 1727. Out before 1737.

[25] " Comn. signed and issued in England." Lieut. 10 July, 1737. Served with the Expedition to the West Indies in 1741–42.

[26] Lieut. 8 Sept. 1736. Serving in 1740.

[27] " Comn. signed in England and issued in Ireland." Lieut. 14 Aug. 1738. Accompanied the Expedition to the West Indies in Oct. 1741. Attained the rank of Major, 2nd Batt. above Regt. 4 Sept. 1754. Serving in 1758.

[28] " Comn. signed and issued in England." Capt. 25 Oct. 1727. Serving in 1740. This officer's name is given as " Peter Stewart " in a former Comn. He was wounded at the battle of Schellenberg when serving as Ens. in above Regt. He also fought at Malplaquet.

[29] " Comn. signed and issued in England." Serving in 1728. Out before 1737.

COLONEL THE HON. ROBERT DORMER'S REGIMENT OF FOOT.

[6TH FOOT,—THE ROYAL WARWICKSHIRE REGIMENT.]

See note at head of p. 359, and memo. on same page.

Richard Miller,[1] Esq. to be Capt. in room of Robert Bradley - - - - - - - -	6 Feb. 1718/9.	*j*
Albert de Breze (*sic*)[2] to be Ens. to Capt. John Cottrell in room of Nathaniel Mitchell - - - -	,, ,, ,,	*j*
George Bell[3] to be Surgeon in room of Richard Miller	,, ,, ,,	*j*
Nathaniel Mitchell[4] to be Lieut. to Capt. Philip Beard	,, ,, ,,	*j*
John Sweetenham (*sic*)[5] to be Ens. to Capt. Richard Miller in room of John Clarke - - - -	23 Feb. ,,	*j*
Henry Jolly[6] to be Ens. to the Colonel's Cy. in room of Henry Price - - - - - - -	30 April, 1719.	*j*
Elias Landy,[7] Esq. to be Capt.-Lieut. in room of Wm. Beauford - - - - - - - -	1 May, ,,	*j*
George Bell[8] to be Lieut. to Capt. Edward Columbine in room of Samuel Reynolds [decd.] - - -	,, ,, ,,	*j*
Wm. Hamilton[9] to be do. to Major Chas. Harrison in room of Landy - - - - - - - -	,, ,, ,,	*j*
Brigadier-General James Dormer[10] to be Colonel in room of Robert Dormer and to be Capt. of a Cy. -	9 April, 1720.	*j*
Albert Debreze[2] to be Lieut. to Capt. John Cottrell in room of Nathaniel Mitchell - - - - -	1 June, ,,	*j*
Nathaniel Mitchell,[4] Esq. to be Capt. - - - -	,, ,, ,,	*j.*
Thos. Freeman[11] to be Ens. to do. in room of Debreze -	,, ,, ,,	*j*
Davis Baylie[12] to be Ens. - - - - - -	31 May, 1721.	*f*
Arthur Brereton,[13] Esq. to be Capt. - - - -	29 Aug. ,,	*f*
Lancelot Baugh[14] to be Ens. - - - - -	,, ,, ,,	*f*
James Dalton[15] to be [1st] Lieut. [of Grenadiers] -	,, ,, ,,	*f*
John Swettenham[5] to be Lieut. - - - - -	,, ,, ,,	*f*
Ancketel Moutray[16] to be Ens. - - - -	18 Jan. 1721/2.	*f*
Francis Lestrange[17] to be do. - - - -	20 Oct. 1722.	*f*
Wm. Goodricke[18] to be do. - - - - -	12 Dec. 1723.	*f*
Fras. Mercier[19] to be Adjt. in room of James Duvall decd. - - - - - - - - -	15 Nov. 1724.	*r*
Chas. Nelson[20] to be Lieut. in room of do. - - -	,, ,, ,,	*r*
Wm. Robinson[21] to be Ens. to Capt. Robt. Saunders -	,, ,, ,,	*r*
John Galt[22] to be Lieut. to Richard, Earl of Cavan, in room of Benjamin Harrington decd. - - -	11 May, 1725.	*r*
Wm. Burrard[23] to be Ens. to Capt. Nathaniel Mitchell in room of John Galt - - - - - -	,, ,, ,,	*r*
Frederick Gore,[24] Esq. to be Capt. in room of Robert Buggins - - - - - - - -	5 April, 1726.	*r*
John Cottrell,[25] Esq. to be Major in room of John Murray - - - - - - - - -	6 July, ,,	*r*

John Murray,[26] Esq. to be Lt.-Colonel in room of the
Earl of Cavan [and Capt. of a Cy.] - - -   6 July, 1726. *r*
Edward Southwell,[27] Esq. to be Capt. of the Earl of
Cavan's late Cy. - - - - - - -   ,, ,, ,, *r*
Henry Jolly [6] to be [2nd] Lieut. to Capt. Philip Beard
in room of Southwell - - - - - -   ,, ,, ,, *r*
Wm. Jenkins [28] to be Ens. to the Colonel's Cy. in room
of Jolly - - - - - - - - -   ,, ,, ,, *r*
John Johnstone [29] to be Chaplain in room of Robt.
Cocking - - - - - - - - -   23 ,, ,, *r*
Oliver Walsh [30] to be Ens. to Capt. Robt. Saunders in
room of Wm. Robinson - - - - -   1 Jan. 1726/7. *r*

---

[1] Serving as senior Capt. in 1740. Took part in the early operations against the Jacobites in Scotland in 1745. See Cannon's *Records 6th Foot*, p. 62.

[2] *De Brisay.* Lieut. 1 June, 1720. Comn. renewed in 1727. Out before 1736.

[3] Serving in 1737.

[4] Capt. 1 June, 1720. Major, 19 Jan. 1740. Served with his Regt. in the Expedition to the West Indies in 1741–42. Lt.-Col. of the 1st Marines, 22 Sept. 1742. Half-pay, 1748.

[5] *Swettenham.* Lieut. 29 Aug. 1721. Capt. in 1742. Served with above Regt. in the West Indies, 1742. He was in Scotland with his Regt. when Prince Charles Edward landed, and was taken prisoner by a party of Jacobites, but soon released on parole (Cannon's *Records 6th Foot*, p. 62). He came to London and gave evidence before the Privy Council relative to the outbreak of the rebellion.—*Ibid.*

[6] 2nd Lieut. of Grendrs. 2 July, 1726. Killed in a military fracas at Galway a year or two later. See account of this affair in *Old Irish Life*, by J. W. Callwell, 1912. There is a tablet in St. Martin's Church, Galway, to Lieut. Jolly's memory, but the date of his death is not recorded.

[7] D. on active service in the West Indies in the spring of 1742. A pension of £20 per annum was given to his widow, Ann Landy.

[8] Capt. 19 Jan. 1740. D. on active service in the West Indies in the spring of 1742.— *Gentleman's Mag.*

[9] Out before 1727.

[10] See biog. notice in Vol. I., p. 118, note 1.

[11] Comn. renewed in 1727. Out before 1736.

[12] Lieut. 25 Jan. 1730. D. on active service in the West Indies in the spring of 1742. Pension of £20 per annum was given to his widow, Ann *Bailie.*

[13] Serving in 1740.

[14] Exchanged to 1st Foot Guards, 20 Feb. 1730. Lieut. and Capt. 8 April, 1743. Attained the rank of Lt.-Gen. in 1787 and appointed Col. of the 6th Foot, 18 April same year. D. in April, 1792. Will proved at Dublin.

[15] See biog. notice on p. 164, note 11.

[16] Lieut. 3 July, 1733. D. on active service in the West Indies in 1742. Will proved at Dublin.

[17] Comn. renewed in 1727.

[18] See biog. notice on p. 266, note 4.

[19] Lieut. 16 April, 1733. D. on active service in the West Indies, 1742. Pension of £20 per annum to his widow, Mary Mercier.

[20] Comn. renewed in 1727. Out before 1736.

[21] Out in Dec. 1726.

[22] See p. 164, note 8.

[23] Comn. renewed in 1727. Out before 1736.

[24] "Comn. signed in England and issued in Ireland." Serving in 1740.

[25] Comn. signed as above. See biog. notice on p. 164, note 6.

[26] Do. Retd. in Oct. 1741.

[27] Comn. signed as above. Serving in 1730. Possibly the "Edward Southwell of Portarlington, Esq.," whose will was proved at Dublin in 1736.

[28] Comn. signed and issued in England. Serving in 1737. Out before 1740.

[29] Do. do. do.

[30] Lieut. 26 Aug. 1737. D. on active service in the West Indies, 1742.—*Gentleman's Mag.*

THE ROYAL FUSILIERS.

See note at head of p. 359, and memo. on same page.

[Rupert] Pratt[1] to be Lieut. - - - -	—	13 July, 1718.	*f*
Wm. Cropp,[2] Esq. to be Capt. in room of Richard Baynes - - - -	—	30 April, 1719.	*j*
John Harris[3] to be Lieut. to Lt.-Col. Jarvis Parker in room of Wm. Cropp - -	—	,, ,, ,,	*j*
John Peachy,[4] Esq. to be Capt. in room of Wm. Cropp -	Pyrmont, 16 June (O.S.) ,,		*c*
Edward Higgins,[5] to be Lieut. to Capt. Jas. Fleming in room of George Speke Petty -	—	12 Aug. ,,	*j*
Ben Jones,[6] Esq. to be Capt. in room of Pierce Griffith - - - -	—	17 Nov. ,,	*j*
John Godfrey[7] to be Lieut. to Capt. James Brown in room of Wm. Cook - - -	—	5 April, 1720.	*j*
[John] Darassus[8] to be Lieut. - - -	—	17 Nov. 1721.	*f*
Roger Hale,[9] Esq. to be Capt. - - -	—	9 May, 1722.	*f*
John Adlercron,[10] Esq. to be Capt. - - -	—	4 Aug. ,,	*f*
[Meredith] Everard[11] to be [2nd] Lieut. - -	—	7 Sept. ,,	*f*
Thos. Maule,[12] Esq. to be Capt. - - -	—	24 Mar. 1722/3.	*f*
Ben Jones,[6] Esq. to be Major - - - -	—	,, ,, ,,	*f*
Henry Ormsby[13] to be Lieut. - - - -	—	20 May, ,,	*f*
Marcus Smith,[14] Esq. to be Capt. in room of Thos. Proby - - - - -	—	4 Nov. 1724.	*f*
Edward Ford[15] to be [2nd] Lieut. to the Colonel's Cy. in room of Marcus Smith -	—	,, ,, ,,	*r*
Ant. Bligh[16] to be do. to do. in room of Ford -	—	,, ,, ,,	*r*
James Clarke[17] to be [2nd] Lieut. to Capt. Marcus Smith in room of Guy Johnson -	—	26 Sept. 1726.	*r*
Wm. Elwes[18] to be [1st] Lieut. to Capt. Thos. Maule - - - - - - -	—	20 Oct. ,,	*r*
Lovelace Gilby,[19] Esq. to be Capt. in room of Wm. Gee - - - - - -	St. James's, 25 Dec. ,,		*d*
August Pinniot,[20] Esq. to be Capt. of an additional Cy. - - - - -	,, 26 ,, ,,		*d*
Robt. Conduit[21] to be [1st] Lieut. to do. -	,, ,, ,, ,,		*d*
Philip Craddock[22] to be [2nd] Lieut. to do. -	,, ,, ,, ,,		*d*
Thos. Bloodworth,[23] Esq. to be Capt. of an additional Cy. -	,, ,, ,, ,,		*d*
George Watkins[24] to be [1st] Lieut. to do. -	,, ,, ,, ,,		*d*
[Wm.] Kellet[25] to be [2nd] Lieut. to do. -	,, ,, ,, ,,		*d*
John Fleming[26] to be Lieut. to Capt. August Pinniot - - - - - -	,, ,, ,, ,,		*d*

Mem.—*Regiment embarked for England in Jan. 1727.*

[John] Congreve Chillcot[27] to be Qr.-Mr. - St. James's, 15 Mar. 1726/7. *d*

[1] " Capt.-Lieut. 9 Feb. 1751. Capt. 3 June, 1752. D. in Ireland, — June, 1753."— Wheater's *Historical Records of the Royal Fusiliers.*

[2] " Major, 3 Sept. 1733. D. in England, 20 July, 1740." (*Ibid.*) Will proved at Dublin in 1754.

[3] Capt. in Wolfe's Marines, 25 Nov. 1739. Killed before Carthagena in 1741.

[4] Not in any subsequent List. Succeeded his father, the 2nd Bart. of West Dean, Sussex, in 1737, and d. in 1744.

[5] Comn. renewed in June, 1727. Out before 1740.

[6] Major, 24 March, 1723. D. in July, 1733. Pension of £30 per annum to his widow, Ann Jones.

[7] Comn. renewed in 1727. Out before 1740.

[8] Capt. 13 Dec. 1739. " Retd. in Dec. 1752."—Wheater's *Records.*

[9] " D. at Gibraltar, 1 Dec. 1732."—*Ibid.*

[10] See p. 161, note 7.

[11] " D. 1750."—Wheater's *Records.*

[12] " D. 1734."—*Ibid.*

[13] Serving as Lieut. in 1740.

[14] See p. 143, note 13.

[15] The word " Vacated " is written in the margin of this Comn. entry.

[16] Comn. renewed in June, 1727. Out before 1740.

[17] " Comn. signed in England, issued in Ireland." Serving in 1730. Out before 1740.

[18] " D. or retd. 1754."—Wheater's *Records.*

[19] Appointed Capt. in Sir Chas. Hotham's Regt. of Foot, 27 Sept. 1710. Half-pay, 1713. Out of the Rl. Fusiliers before 1730.

[20] " Retd. 8 May, 1749."—Wheater's *Records.*

[21] From half-pay Gore's Regt. of Foot. Reduced with his Cy. in 1729.

[22] Half-pay, 1729. He had served previously in Borr's Regt. of Foot.

[23] See p. 219, note 23.

[24] Half-pay, 1729.

[25] " Exchanged to the Coldstream Guards, 8 May, 1730. Capt. and Lt.-Col. in do. 9 Feb. 1741. D. of wounds received at Fontenoy."—Wheater's *Records.*

[26] Capt. 22 Sept. 1742. Son of Robt. Fleming, bro. of Maj.-Gen. Jas. Fleming. He was residuary legatee of his uncle, Gen. Fleming, and was also residuary legatee and executor of Lt.-Gen. Wm. Hargrave, the Col. of the Rl. Fusiliers. John Fleming was created a Bart., as of Brompton Park, Mdx., 22 April, 1763, but d.s.p. a few months later, when the title expired. His widow remarried Baron Harewood. Sir John Fleming was bd. in Westminster Abbey. See Col. Chester's *Westminster Abbey Registers,* pp. 403–4, note 9.

[27] Appointed Lieut. in above Regt. 18 Jan. 1740. " Capt.-Lieut. 3 June, 1752. Capt. 16 Dec. 1752. Exchanged to half-pay as Quartermaster, 25 March, 1755." (Wheater's *Records.*) Drawing half-pay in 1769.

BRIGADIER-GENERAL HENRY MORYSON'S REGIMENT OF FOOT.

[8TH FOOT,—THE KING'S REGIMENT.]

See note at head of p. 359, and memo. on same page.

James Wilson[1] to be Surgeon in room of James Chambers - - - - -	—	30 April, 1719.*j*	
John Spranger,[2] Esq. to be Capt. in room of Arthur Usher - - - -	—	29 June, ,,	*j*
John Young[3] to be Lieut. to Lt.-Col. Wm. Congreve in room of Peter Ribton -	—	6 July, ,,	*j*
Edward Fynn[4] to be Ens. to Capt. Hayes St. Leger in room of Wm. Rowland -	—	,, ,, ,,	*j*
John La Fauçille[5] to be Ens. to Capt. Wm. Gill in room of Young - - -	—	,, ,, ,,	*j*
Wm. Rowland[6] to be [2nd] Lieut. to Capt. Henry Moryson in room of Samuel Palmer	—	,, ,, ,,	*j*
Malcolm Hamilton[7] to be Ens. to [Lt.-Col.] Wm. Congreve in room of Peter Renaut	—	1 Sept. ,,	*j*
John Letton[8] to be Ens. to Capt. John Farcy in room of John Cowley - -	—	19 ,, ,,	*j*
Abraham Devischer,[9] Esq. to be Capt. of that Cy. whf. Wm. Congreve was late Capt.	—	17 Nov. ,,	*j*
Edward Hayes[10] to be Lieut. to Capt. Wm. Gill in room of Theophilus Nicholls -	—	5 April, 1720.*j*	
Abraham Devischer,[9] Esq. to be Lt.-Col. and Capt. of a Cy. in room of Lt.-Col. Chas. Hotham - - - - - - -	—	6 ,, ,,	*j*
John Farcy,[11] Esq. to be Major in room of Abr. Devischer and Capt. of a Cy. -	—	,, ,, ,,	*j*
Robt. Abbott,[12] Esq. to be Capt. of Major Farcy's late Cy. - - - - -	—	,, ,, ,,	*j*
John Dallons[13] to be Ens. to Capt. James Beschefer in room of Paul Pigou -	—	,, ,, ,,	*j*
Paul Pigou[14] to be Lieut. to do. in room of Robt. Abbott - - - - -	—	,, ,, ,,	*j*
[Sir Charles Hotham,[15] Bart. to be Colonel in room of Henry Moryson - - -	—	3 Dec. 1720]	
[John Pocock,[16] Esq. to be Colonel in room of Sir C. Hotham - - - -	—	21 April, 1721]	
Peter Ribton[17] to be Lieut. -	—	2 May, ,,	*f*
Gilbert, Lord Lambert,[18] to be Ens. to the Colonel's Cy. - - - - -	—	29 Sept. ,,	*j*
Thos. Adams,[19] Esq. to be Capt. in room of Hayes St. Leger - - - -	- Kensington,	9 June, 1722.*c*	
John Dallons[18] to be Lieut. - -	—	24 ,, 1723.*f*	
John Pierse Cook[20] to be Ens. - -	—	1 Jan. 1723/4.*f*	

George Banastre,[21] Esq. to be Capt. in room of Thos. Adams decd. - - - -	—	23 Oct. 1724.*r*
Conductor (*sic*) Ball,[22] Esq. to be Capt.-Lieut. in room of George Banastre - - -	—	,, ,, ,, *r*
John White[23] to be [1st] Lieut.. of the Grenadier Cy. whf. John Spranger is Capt. in room of Ball - - - -	—	,, ,, ,, *r*
Arthur Loftus[24] to be Ens. to the Colonel's Cy. in room of John White - - -	—	,, ,, ,, *r*
Wm. Robinson[25] to be Ens. - - - -	—	15 Nov. ,, *f*
Thos. Gee[26] to be Chaplain in room of Thos. White - - - - - -	—	1 May, 1725.*f*
Christopher Mitchell[27] to be Ens. to Capt. Robt. Abbott in room of Wm. Moody -	—	1 Feb. 1725/6.*r*
Wm. Catherwood[28] to be Surgeon in room of Wilson - - - - -	—	16 Mar. ,, *r*
John Ekins[29] to be Ens. to [Major] John Farcy in room of John Letton- - -	Dublin,	27 April, 1726.*d*
Thos. Nugent[30] to be [2nd] Lieut. to the Grenadier Cy. in room of Wm. Rowland	—	12 Nov. ,, *d*
Thos. Gilson[31] to be Ens. to [Lt.-Col.] Abr. Devischer in room of Thos. Nugent -	—	,, ,, ,, *d*
John Lafossile (*sic*)[5] to be Lieut. to Capt. Abbott in room of Chas. Chambers -	—	,, ,, ,, *d*
Chas. Duterne[32] to be Lieut. - - -	—	23 Dec. ,, *d*
Nehemiah Donnellan[33] to be Ens. - -	—	,, ,, ,, *d*

Regiment returned to England in December 1726 and embarked for Gibraltar early in 1727.

John Trevanion,[34] Esq. to be Capt. of an additional Cy. - - - - -	St. James's,	26 Dec. 1726.*d*
Wm. Boyd[35] to be Lieut. to do. - - -	,,	,, ,, ,, *d*
John Jennings[36] to be Ens. to do. - -	,,	,, ,, ,, *d*
Joseph Duberry[37] to be Capt. of an additional Cy. - - - - - - -	,,	,, ,, ,, *d*
Wm. Bernard[38] to be Lieut. - - -	,,	,, ,, ,, *f*
Wm. Brodie[39] to be Ens. - - - -	,,	,, ,, ,, *d*
John Cowley[40] to be Ens. to Capt. Joachim Goudet - - - - - - -	,,	,, ,, ,, *d*
John Grey[41] to be Capt.-Lieut. - - -	—	1 Jan. 1726/7.*f*

[1] Out in March, 1726.

[2] Appointed Major of Col. Wm. Gooch's 2nd Batt. American Regt. in 1739. D. at the siege of Carthagena in 1741.

[3] Comn. renewed in 1727. Out before 1737.

[4] Out before 1727. The will of Edward Fynn was proved at Dublin in 1752.

[5] *La Fausille.* Attained the rank of Maj.-Gen. and was Col. 66th Regt. "Served at Dettingen, Fontenoy, Falkirk, Culloden, Roucoux, and Val. In the last of these battles he was wounded. D. [at sea] 19 Jan. 1763."—*Records of the King's Regt.*

[6] Out in Nov. 1726.

[7] Lieut. 2 July, 1721. "Capt. 15 June, 1743. D. 17 Feb. 1746."—*Ibid.*

[8] See p. 165, note 5.

[9] See biog. notice in Vol. I., p. 309, note 2.

[10] Served as Ens. in Pearce's Foot. Out of the King's Regt. before 1727.

[11] Served at Blenheim as Capt. in the King's Regt. Fought also at Malplaquet. D. as Lt.-Col. of the King's Regt. in 1731. Will proved at Dublin.

[12] Comn. renewed in 1727.   Out before 1737.

[13] Capt. 31 Aug. 1733.   Wounded at Fontenoy.   "D. 16 Feb. 1746."—*Records.*

[14] Serving as Adjt. in 1737.   The will of "Paul Pigou, of Wexford, Esq." was proved at Dublin in 1760.

[15] See biog. notice in Vol. I., p. 172, note 1.

[16] See do. in do., p. 180, note 1.

[17] Serving in 1737.   Out before 1740.

[18] Gilbert, Lord *Lambart*, was eldest son of Richard, 3rd Earl of Cavan, Lt.-Col. of Dormer's Regt. of Foot.   This young nobleman d. young and predeceased his father.

[19] D. in Oct. 1724.

[20] Comn. renewed in 1727.   Out before 1737.

[21] Left the Regt. in June, 1743.—*Records.*

[22] Believed to be son of Capt. Charles Ball, Wagon-Master-Gen. to the Train of Artillery in Flanders in 1704, and subsequently Conductor Ball of the King's Regt. got his Comn. as Ens. in said Corps, 24 March, 1705.   Served at Malplaquet.   Out in Dec. 1726.

[23] Serving in 1740.

[24] "Lieut. 23 Aug. 1735.   Capt.-Lieut. 14 July, 1743.   Capt. 4 Oct. 1743.   Major, 27 April, 1749.   Wounded at Fontenoy.   D. 25 Aug. 1753."—*Records.*

[25] "Lieut. 20 June, 1739.   Wounded at Dettingen."—*Ibid.*

[26] Out before 1737.

[27] Serving in 1730.   Out before 1737.

[28] Serving in 1737.

[29] "Lieut. 11 Sept. 1736.   Capt.-Lieut. before 1745.   Wounded at Fontenoy.   D. 15 Aug. 1750."—*Records.*

[30] " Comn. signed and issued in England."   Retd. 13 May, 1742.—*Ibid.*

[31]   Do.   Not in any subsequent List.

[32]   Do.   "Promoted 12 Jan. 1740."—*Records.*

[33] " Comn. signed and issued in England."   Lieut. 12 Jan. 1740.   Promoted Capt. 29 Nov. 1745.   (*Ibid.*)   Major, 27 Aug. 1753.   Out in 1757.

[34] Half-pay, July, 1727.

[35] " Serving in 1739."—*Records.*

[36] Half-pay, July, 1727.

[37]   Do.   Drawing half-pay in 1739.

[38]   Do.   do.

[39] Out of the Regt. before 1740.

[40] " Served at Dettingen, and commanded this Regt. after the Lt.-Col. and Major had both been wounded.   Promoted Major after the death of Major Barry, 14 July, 1743."—*Records.*

MAJOR-GENERAL JOSEPH WIGHTMAN'S REGIMENT OF FOOT.

[17TH FOOT,—THE LEICESTERSHIRE REGIMENT.]

This Regiment was sent to Ireland in Sept. 1721.

Joseph Hill[1] to be Lieut. to Capt. ——   - St. James's, 24 Mar. 1717/8.*b*

Amand Dupperron,[2] Esq. to be Capt. in room
of Wm. Lloyd   -   -   -   -   -   -   „   16 April, 1718.*b*

James Marquis[3] to be Lieut. to Capt. Edward
Tyrrell   -   -   -   -   -   -   -   „   1 Nov.   „   *b*

John Knapp[4] to be Ens. to Capt. Richard
Andrew Pope   -   -   -   -   -   -   „   „   „   „   *b*

Charles Burrough[5] to be do to Capt. ——   -   „   22 „   „   „   *b*

Solomon Stevenson[6] to be Qr.-Mr.   -   - Kensington, 13 July,   „   *b*

Chas. Strahan[7] to be Lieut. to Capt. ——   - St. James's, 19 Mar. 1718/9.*c*

John Walter,[8] Esq. to be Lt.-Col. and Capt. of
a Cy.   -   -   -   -   -   -   -   „   „ „   „   *c*

Thos. Lutton[9] to be Ens. to Capt. ——   -   „   5 Mar. 1719/20.*c*

Thos. Morris[10] to be Lieut. to Capt. Andrew
Richard Pope   -   -   -   -   -   „   23 May,   1720.*c*

Arthur Morris[11] to be Ens. to do.   -   -   „   „ „   „   *c*

Thos. Chase[12] to be Ens. to ——   -   - Dublin,   11 April, 1722.*c*

Chris. Russell,[13] Esq. to be Lt.-Col. and Capt.
of a Cy.   -   -   -   -   -   -   „   5 June,   „   *c*

Thos. Dalyell[14] to be Ens. to Capt. Jas.
Fonzubrand (*sic*)   -   -   -   -   „   18 Aug.   „   *c*

Thos. Ferrers,[15] Esq. to be Colonel in room of
Major-General Wightman [decd.] and
Capt. of a Cy.   -   -   -   -   - Kensington, 28 Sept. 1722.*c*

James Tyrrell,[16] Esq. to be Colonel in room of
Brig.-Gen. Thos. Ferrers decd. and Capt.
of a Cy. -   -   -   -   -   -   - St. James's, 25 Oct.   „   *c*

Andrew Booth[17] to be [2nd] Lieut. of
Grenadiers   -   -   -   -   -   „   26 Nov.   „   *c*

Arthur Mathers[18] to be Ens. to Capt. [Edward]
St. George   -   -   -   -   -   -   „   „ „   „   *c*

Regiment sent to Minorca in June, 1725.

Thos. Talmash,[19] Esq. to be Capt. in room of
And. Ric. Pope decd.   -   -   - St. James's, 10 Feb. 1724/5.*d*

John Leighton[20] to be Capt. in room of
[Edward] St. George   -   -   - Helvoet Sluys, 25 Dec.   1725.*d*

Philip Lywood[21] to be Ens. to Capt. Dan
Herring -   -   -   -   -   - St. James's, 8 Mar. 1725/6.*d*

Andrew Booth[17] to be Adjt.   -   -   -   „   12 „   „   *d*

John Brown,[22] Esq. to be Capt. of Grenadiers
in room of Loftus Cosby   -   -   „   8 Apr. 1726/7.*d*

Edward Crofts[23] to be Lieut. to ——   -   „   „ „   „   *d*

John Dumaresque [24] to be Qr.-Mr.   -   -   St. James's, 8 April 1727. *d*
Chris. Forster [25] to be Lieut. to Capt. John
   Wallis - - - - - - -   ,,   ,, ,,   ,,   *d*
Chas. Hayes [26] to be Ens. to Capt. Thos.
   Weldon - - - - - -   ,,   ,, ,,   ,,   *d*

[1] Out before 1727.

[2] *Armand* Duperron was appointed 2nd Lieut. in the North British Fusiliers, 1 Aug. 1715. Major 17th Foot, 4 Feb. 1741. D. in 1749 as Lt.-Col. Will proved at Dublin.

[3] Serving as senior Lieut. of above Regt. in 1740.

[4] Out before 1727.

[5] Appointed Cornet in the 6th Regt. of Horse (5th D.G.) in 1727. Serving with said Corps in Ireland, 1736. Out before 1740.

[6] Appointed Cornet in the 3rd Regt. of Horse, 18 May, 1735. Serving in 1740.

[7] Out before June, 1727.

[8] Left the Regt. in June, 1722.

[9] Comn. renewed 20 June, 1727. D. before 1735, in which year his widow, Mary Lutton, was drawing a pension of £16 per annum.

[10] See biog. notice in Vol. I., p. 342, note 7.

[11] Lieut. 27 May, 1732. Attained the rank of Lt.-Col. of above Regt. 21 Sept. 1756. D. in 1767.

[12] Comn. renewed 20 June, 1727. Out before 1740.

[13] Comn. signed by the Duke of Grafton. See biog. notice in Vol. I., p. 342, note 3.

[14] Comn. renewed 20 June, 1727. Out before 1740.

[15] See biog. notice on p. 132, note 1.

[16] See do. in Vol. I., p. 121, note 1.

[17] Adjt. 8 March, 1726. Comns. renewed in 1727. Serving in 1740.

[18] Called "Mather" in 1727 List. Out before 1740.

[19] Major of above Regt. before 20 June, 1727. Comn. not forthcoming.

[20] Lt.-Col. 2nd Marines, 24 April, 1741. Serving in 1757 as Lt.-Gov. of Fort William.

[21] Called "Leywood" in the 1727 List. Out of the Regt. before 1740.

[22] Serving as Capt. in 1740.

[23] Comn. renewed 20 June, 1727. Out before 1740.

[24] Capt. 5 July, 1735. Serving in 1740.

[25] Comn. renewed 20 June, 1727. Out before 1740.

[26]   Do.   do.

COLONEL GEORGE GROVE'S REGIMENT OF FOOT.

[19TH FOOT,—ALEXANDRA PRINCESS OF WALES'S OWN YORKSHIRE REGIMENT.]

See note at head of page 359, and memo. on same page.

Joshua Green[1] to be Lieut. to Capt. [Edward] Brown in room of Mathew Waller - -	—	25 Feb. 1718/9.*j*
Henry Southwell[2] to be Ens. to Capt. —— in room of Joshua Green preferred - -	—	,, ,, ,, *j*
Leming Richardson[3] to be Lieut. to —— in room of Simmons preferred Capt.-Lieut. -	—	2 Mar. ,, *j*
—— Simmons,[4] Esq. to be Capt.-Lieut. in room of Samuel Norman - - -	—	,, ,, ,, *j*
Wm. Gardiner[5] to be Ens. to —— in room of Leming Richardson - - -	—	,, ,, ,, *j*
Randolph Baron[6] to be Lieut. to Capt. James Philips in room of John Massey - -	—	1 July, 1719.*j*
Bartholomew Stacpole,[7] Esq. to be Ens. to Major Ric. Hawley in room of Randolph Baron - - - - - - -	—	,, ,, ,, *j*
George Speke Petty,[8] Esq. to be Capt. of that Cy. whf. the Colonel himself was Capt. -	—	15 Aug. ,, *j*
Mat. Bunbury[9] to be Ens. to Capt. Thos. Holland in room of Wm. Rousby - -	—	30 May, 1720.*j*
Richard Dixie[10] to be Ens. - - - -	—	10 Oct. 1721.*f*
Wm. Rousby[11] to be Lieut. to Capt. Edward Brown in room of Joshua Green - -	—	,, ,, ,, *f*
Newdigate Dalgarno[12] to be Ensign - -	—	11 July, 1722 *f*
Roger Crymble[13] to be Lieut. - - -	—	,, ,, ,, *f*
Wm. Taylor,[14] Esq. to be Capt. in room of —— Bellamy decd. - - - - -	St. James's, 2 Nov. ,, *c*
Edward Lyster[15] to be Ens. to Capt. Joseph Stysted - - - - - - -	,, 22 ,, ,, *c*
Henry Southwell[2] to be Lieut. - - -	—	25 Mar. 1723.*f*
John Lyons,[16] Esq. to be Capt. - - -	—	22 April, 1724.*f*
Thos. Southwell[17] to be Ens. to Capt. Thos. Woodhouse in room of Thos. Burton -	—	15 Feb. 1724/5.*r*
Nicholas Rylands[18] to be Lieut. to Capt. Wm. Hoar in room of Thos. Clift decd. -	—	18 ,, ,, *r*
Daniel Webb,[19] Esq. to be Capt. in room of Edward Browne - - - -	—	22 May, 1725.*r*
Richard Hawley[20] [Junr.] to be Ens. to Major Ric. Hawley in room of Edward Goddard - - - - - - - -	—	1 Sept. ,, *r*
Edward Gibbon[21] to be Ens. to Capt. Joseph Stisted in room of Philip Sucklin decd. -	—	,, ,, ,, *r*
Thos. Leake[22] to be Ens. to above Cy. in room of Philip Sucklin decd. - - -	—	,, ,, ,, *r*

John Freke [23] to be Ens. to Capt. John Lyons in room of Wm. Gardiner - - -	—	15 Mar. 1725/6.	*r*
George Dobson [24] to be Chaplain in room of Thos. Visey (*sic*) - - - - -	—	22 ,,	,, *r*
Richard Lowndes [25] to be Lieut. - - -	—	3 Sept. 1726.	*f*
Thos. Burton, [26] Esq. to be Capt.-Lieut. in room of Mounser (*sic*) Simons - - -	—	23 Dec. ,,	*r*
Mounser Simons, [4] Esq. to be Capt. in room of Thos. Woodhouse - - - - -	—	,, ,,	,, *r*
Nicholas Ford [27] to be Ens. to Capt. Thos. Handasyde in room of Thos. Burton -	—	24 ,,	,, *r*
John Adams, [28] Esq. to be Capt. of an additional Cy. - - - - -	St. James's, 25 ,,	,, *d*
Wm. Arnaud [29] to be Lieut. to do. - - -	,, ,, ,,	,, *d*
John Lambert [30] to be Ens. to do. - - -	,, ,, ,,	,, *d*
Thos. Webb, [31] Esq. to be Capt. of an additional Cy. - - - - - - -	,, ,, ,,	,, *d*
James Grove [32] to be Lieut. to do. - - -	,, ,, ,,	,, *d*
Thos. Master [33] to be Ens. to do. - - -	,, ,, ,,	,, *d*
Elisha Grove [34] to be Qr.-Mr. - - - -	,, ,, ,,	,, *d*

Mem.—*Regiment returned to England in Jan.* 1727.

Newdigate Delgardno [12] to be Adjt. - -	—	15 Mar. 1726/7.	*d*
Edward Gibbs [35] to be Ens. to ―――― - -	—	22 April, 1727.	*d*

[1] Out in Oct. 1721.

[2] Lieut. 25 March, 1723. Capt. in Guise's Regt. (6th Foot), 28 Jan. 1736. Serving in 1740.

[8] Lieut. in Ligonier's Regt. of Horse (7th D.G.), 15 Nov. 1734. Serving in 1740. Appointed Fort-Major of Duncannon Fort, 18 Feb. 1745. (*London Gazette.*) The copy will of " Lemynge Richardson, Lieut. in Colonel Ligoniere's Regt. of Horse," dated 1752, is at the Irish Record Office, Dublin.

[4] *Simonds.* This officer's Christian name has been variously spelt as "Monier" and "Mounser." He served with above Regt. in Flanders as a Lieut. and is believed to have been present at Malplaquet. Capt. 23 Dec. 1726. Serving in 1730. Out before 1737.

[5] Out in March, 1726.

[6] Out before 1730.

[7] Do.

[8] Served previously in the Rl. Fusiliers. D. in 1722. Will proved at Dublin. He doubtless belonged to the Dorsetshire family of Petty, represented on the female side by the Marquis of Lansdowne.

[9] Lieut. 16 May, 1733. Serving in 1740.

[10] Serving in 1730. Out before 1736.

[11] Serving in 1740.

[12] Adjt. 15 May, 1727. Serving as Lieut. and Adjt. in 1737. Out before 1740.

[13] See p. 167, note 6.

[14] Serving in 1737. Out before 1740.

[15] Comn. renewed in June, 1727. Out before 1740.

[16] Serving in 1737. Out before 1740.

[17] Out before 1727.

[18] " Of Callan, co. Kilkenny, fourth son of Charles *Ryland* of Dungarvan, co. Waterford. Serving in 1737. Out in 1740."—(Communicated by Major M. L. Ferrar.)

[19] See p. 267, note 23.

[20] Lieut. 18 Nov. 1736. Serving in 1740.

[21] " Vacated " written in margin of the Comn. entry.

[22] " Capt. 21 Jan. 1743. Taken prisoner at the battle of Roucoux, 1746."—(Communicated by Major M. L. Ferrar.)

[28] Comn. renewed in 1727. Out before 1737.

[24] Serving in 1737.

[25] Serving in 1730.   Out before 1737.   A certain Richard Lowndes was M.P. for Bucks. in 1756.

[26] " Comn. signed and issued in England."   Capt. 1 March, 1737.   Serving in 1740.

[27] " Comn. signed and issued in England."   Lieut. 7 Nov. 1739.   " Adjt. 21 Jan. 1742/3. Capt.-Lieut. 20 Oct. 1746.   Capt. 2 July, 1747."—(Communicated by Major M. L. Ferrar.)

[28] From half-pay Capt. in Lord Mark Kerr's Regt. of Foot.   Reduced with the Cy. in 1729.

[29] From half-pay Cornet in Baron de Borle's Regt. of Dragoons.   Reduced with Capt. Adams's Cy. in 1728.

[30] Reduced with the Cy. in 1728.

[31] From half-pay Capt. in Sir Chas. Hotham's Regt. of Foot.   Reduced with his Cy. in Grove's Regt. 1728.   Drawing half-pay in 1749.—*Half-Pay List.*

[32] Reduced with the Cy. in 1728.   Appointed Lieut. in Grove's Regt. 3 May, 1728. Serving in 1740.

[33] Reduced with the Cy. in 1728.

[34] Placed on half-pay in 1728.   Drawing half-pay in 1739.

[35] Out before 1737.

COLONEL ROGER HANDASYDE'S REGIMENT OF FOOT.

[22ND FOOT,—THE CHESHIRE REGIMENT.]

See note at head of p. 359, and memo. on same page.

Henry de Ponthieu[1] to be [2nd] Lieut. to
Capt. Wm. Horler in room of Philip
Chapman - - - - - - — 15 Jan. 1718/9.*j*

Richard Ellis[2] to be Lieut. to Capt. ——
Walsh in room of Hyde Howard - - — 28 Feb.   ,, *j*

George Humes[3] to be do. to —— in room of
Thos. Wood - - - - - - — 22 June, 1719.*j*

Chas. Archer[4] to be Ens. to —— in room of
Geo. Humes - - - - - — ,, ,,   ,, *j*

John Lyon[5] to be Lieut. to Capt. George
Lisle in room of Wm. Geekie - - - — 14 Oct.   ,, *j*

Chas. Pinfold[6] to be Ens. to Capt. Robt.
Hunt in room of John Lyon - - - — ,, ,,   ,, *j*

Chas. Gordon[7] to be do. to Capt. Fras. Leighton in room of Archibald Campbell - — 15 Feb. 1719/20.*j*

Archibald Campbell[8] to be Lieut. to Major
Jasper Tryce in room of Edward Thornycroft - - - - - - - — ,, ,,   ,,   *j*

Edward Thornycroft,[9] Esq. to be Capt.-Lieut.
in room of John Gordon - - - - — ,, ,,   ,,   *j*

Robt. Staniard[10] to be Lieut. to —— in room
of Richard Francks - - - - — 5 Mar. ,,   *j*

Michael Delabene,[11] Esq. to be Capt. in room
of Daniel Houghton - - - - - — 14 May, 1720.*f*

Thos. Otway[12] to be Lieut. - - - - — 3 June, 1721.*f*

Thos. Maynard[13] to be Lieut. - - - — 31 July, ,, *f*

Henry Crofton,[14] Esq. to be Capt. - - - — 13 Mar. 1721/2.*f*

Francis Leighton,[15] Esq. to be Major and
Capt. of a Cy. - - - - - - — 15 Aug. 1722.*c*

Peter de la Fausille[16] to be Lieut. - - - — ,, ,,   ,, *f*

Gerrard Leighton,[17] Esq. to be Capt. in room
of Fras. Leighton - - - - - — ,, ,,   ,, *c*

George Hume,[8] Esq. to be do. - - - — 25 Mar. 1723.*f*

Peter Schaak[18] to be Lieut. - - - - — ,, ,,   ,, *f*

Thos. Handasyde[19] to be Ens. to Capt. Henry
Walsh in room of Thos. Taylor - - — 23 Oct. 1724.*r*

James Burleigh[20] to be Ens. to the Colonel's
Cy. in room of John Pluckenett - - — 8 Mar. 1724/5.*r*

Archibald Douglas[21] to be Ens. to Major
Fras. Leighton in room of Marmaduke
Constable - - - - - - — 30 June, 1725.*r*

John Porter[22] to be do. to Major Fras. Leighton in room of Marmaduke Constable - — 3 Aug. ,, *r*

Mem.—*Regiment returned to England during the winter of 1725, and
from thence embarked for Minorca.*

Edward Molesworth,[23] Esq. to be Capt. in
   room of George Gumley - -   -   Helvoet Sluys, 25 Dec. 1725.*d*
Wheeler Fletcher,[24] Esq. to be Capt. in room
   of Henry Walsh decd. -   -   -   - St. James's, 10 Feb. 1725/6.*d*
Richard Nugent [25] to be Ens. to Capt. Edward
   Molesworth - -   -   -   - Kensington, 25 June, 1726.*d*
George Forbes [26] to be do. to Capt. George
   Hume - -   -   -   -   -   ,,   6 Oct.   ,,   *d*
Lovelace Gilby,[27] Esq. to be Capt. in room of
   Wheeler Fletcher - -   -   -   ,,   29 Nov.   ,,   *d*
Chas. Handasyde,[28] Esq. to be Capt.-Lieut. -   ,,   ,, ,,   ,, *d*
Thos. Collier,[29] Esq. to be Capt. in room of
   [George] Lisle decd. - -   -   ,,   ,, ,,   ,, *d*
Henry Dawson [30] to be Lieut. to ——— - -   ,,   ,, ,,   ,, *d*
Fras. Hayes,[31] Esq. to be Capt. in room of
   Lovelace Gilby - -   -   - St. James's, 25 Dec.   ,, *d*

[1] Out before 1727.

[2] Capt. 13 Aug. 1736. D. in 1756. Will proved at Dublin.

[3] *Hume.* Capt. 25 March, 1723. Comn. renewed in 1727. Out before 1740.

[4] Lieut. 13 May, 1735. Serving in 1740.

[5] Comn. renewed in 1727. Serving in 1730. Out before 1740.

[6] Out before 1727. Probably son of Lt.-Col. Wm. Pinfold of above Regt.

[7] Out before 1727.

[8] Comn. renewed in 1727. Capt.-Lieut. 13 Aug. 1736. Serving in 1740.

[9] Not in any subsequent List. Appears to have been a grandson of Edward Thornicroft, of Thornicroft in Cheshire, and kinsman to the Elizabeth Thornicroft (dau. of the baronet of that name) who md. Brig.-Gen. Roger Handasyde, Col. of above Regt.

[10] Not in any subsequent List. Appears to have belonged to the family of *Stannard,* of Stannard Grove, co. Cork.

[11] From Col. Henry Harrison's Regt. of Foot. Comn. as Capt. in Handasyde's Regt. renewed in 1727. Served subsequently in Lord Molesworth's Regt. of Dragoons, and was drawing half-pay from said Corps as a Lt.-Col. in 1749.—*Half-Pay List.*

[12] Comn. renewed in 1727. Serving in 1730. Out before 1740. See p. 182, note 11.

[13]   Do.   do.   do.

[14] Serving as senior Capt. in 1740. D. in 1741 in Minorca. Will proved at Dublin.

[15] "Comn. signed in London by the Duke of Grafton." See biog. notice in Vol. I., p. 306, note 9.

[16] Comn. renewed in 1727. Serving in 1730. Out before 1740.

[17] See his Comn. as Sub.-Brigdr. 2nd Tp. of Life Guards in Vol. I., p. 259, and note thereto.

[18] Comn. renewed in 1727. Out before 1740.

[19] Lieut. 7 Feb. 1736. Called "Thos. Handasyde, Sen." in 1740 *Army List.*

[20] Lieut. 5 Nov. 1735. Served as Capt. of Marines in 1741. Appointed Major of Lord Falmouth's Regt. of Foot raised in Oct. 1745, and was placed on half-pay in 1746 as Capt. of Marines. Drawing half-pay in 1749.

[21] "Vacated" written in margin of Comn. entry.

[22] "Comn. signed and issued in England."

[23] Major, 9 July, 1737. D. at Dublin in 1768.—*Gentleman's Mag.*

[24] Left the Regt. in Nov. 1726.

[25] Lieut. 1 Jan. 1736. Serving in 1740.

[26] Out before 1730.

[27] See p. 380, note 19.

[28] Capt. 19 Sept. 1729. Major, 26 March, 1747. Under the date of 1766 the *Gentleman's Mag.* records the death of "Lt.-Colonel Handasyde, aged 97"!

[29] D. before 1735, in which year his widow, Mary Collyer, was in receipt of a pension of £26 per annum.

[30] Comn. renewed in 1727. Serving in 1730. Out before 1740.

[31] D. in 1732.

COLONEL THOMAS HOWARD'S REGIMENT OF FOOT.

[24TH FOOT,—THE SOUTH WALES BORDERERS.]

See note at head of p. 359, and memo. on same page.

Amateur Borough,[1] Esq. to be Capt. in room
   of [Charles] Mitford decd. - - -   —   14 Mar. 1718/9.*j*

Wm. Usher[2] to be Ens. to Capt. Ben. Drake
   in room of Ralph Lisle - - -   —   31 July, 1719.*j*

Ralph Lisle[3] to be Lieut. to Capt. Thos. Al-
   britton in room of Samuel Furniss -   —   ,, ,,   ,, *j*

John Clements[4] to be Ens. to Capt. Ric. Har-
   ward in room of Gabriel Maturin -   —   1 Aug.   ,, *j*

Wm. Whitshed[5] to be Ens. to Capt. Ben. Lar-
   wood in room of Fras. Tobine decd. -   —   1 Jan. 1719/20.*j*

Benjamin Drake,[6] Esq. to be Major in room of
   Thos. Pollexfen - - - - -   —   7 June, 1720.*j*

John Gore[7] to be Lieut. - - - -   —   19 Mar. 1721/2.*f*

Antonio Pinsum[8] to be Ens. - - -   —   17 April, 1722.*f*

Thos. Addison[9] to be Lieut. - - -   —   5 Aug. ,, *f*

John Parr,[10] Esq. to be Capt. - - -   —   15 ,,   ,, *f*

Christopher Garey,[11] Esq. to be Capt.-Lieut. - St. James's, 1 Dec.   ,, *c*

Wm. Usher[2] to be Lieut. to Capt. Gilbert
   Primrose - - - - - - ,,   ,, ,,   ,, *c*

Samuel Medland[12] to be Ens. to Major Ben.
   Drake - - - - - - - ,,   ,, ,,   ,, *c*

Ant. Harman[13] to be Lieut. to Capt. Hector
   Hamon - - - - - -   ,,   ,, ,,   ,, *c*

Wm. Godfrey[14] to be Ens. - - -   —   15 May, 1723.*f*

Chris. Garey[11] to be Capt. - - -   —   18 June, ,, *f*

Ralph Lumley[15] to be Ens. - - -   —   16 April, 1724.*f*

John Ballard,[16] Esq. to be Capt.-Lieut. - -   —   ,,   ,,   ,, *f*

Wm. Rufane[17] to be Lieut. - - -   —   17 ,,   ,, *f*

Thos. Boswell[18] to be do. to Capt. Thos. Al-
   britton in room of Ralph Lisle decd. -   —   23 Oct.   ,, *r*

Charles Scott[19] to be Ens. to Capt. Chris.
   Gavey in room of Thos. Boswell - -   —   ,,   ,,   ,, *r*

George Dowding[20] to be do. to Capt. Hector
   Hamon in room of Henry Stanton -   —   5 Jan. 1724/5.*r*

Edward Winder[21] to be Chaplain in room of
   Jas. Greenshields - - - - -   —   25 May, 1725.*r*

George Howard[22] to be Ens. to Capt. John
   Parr in room of Wm. Whitshed - -   —   28 Feb. 1725/6.*r*

John Kenny[23] to be Surgeon in room of James
   Nesbitt - - - - - - -   —   21 July, 1726.*r*

Richard Kyffin[24] to be Ens. to Capt. Amateur
   Borough - - - - - -   —   27 Oct.   ,, *r*

Patrick Bairde[25] to be Surgeon - - - St. James's, 25 Dec.   ,, *r*

[1] Called "Bouchereau" in a former Comn. Served at Malplaquet as Capt. in Lord Orrery's Regt. of Foot. Comn. as Capt. in Howard's Regt. renewed in 1727. Serving in 1737. Out before 1740.

[2] Lieut. 15 Aug. 1722. Comn. renewed in 1727. Capt.-Lieut. before 1737. Out before 1740.

[3] D. in Oct. 1724.

[4] Comn. renewed in 1727. Out before 1740.

[5] Out in Feb. 1726.

[6] His will as "Lt.-Col. of Howard's Regt." was proved at Dublin in 1733.

[7] Capt.-Lieut. 16 Aug. 1737. D. before Carthagena in 1741.

[8] Comn. renewed in 1727. Lieut. 10 May, 1729. Called "Pinson" in *Army List*, 1740.

[9] Comn. renewed in 1727. Capt. in the Army, 9 June, 1740. Serving as senior Capt. in 28th Foot in 1758.

[10] Served as Ens. with above Regt. at Blenheim, and as Lieut. at Malplaquet. Out of above Regt. before 1737.

[11] Served as a Lieut. at Malplaquet. Capt. 18 June, 1723. D. while serving at the siege of Carthagena in 1741. His proper name was *Geary*.

[12] Comn. signed by the King. Comn renewed in 1727. Out before 1737.

[13] Comn. signed by the King. Capt. 10 Jan. 1736. Fifth son of Wentworth Harman, Capt. of the Battleaxe Guards. Serving in 1740.

[14] Lieut. 7 April, 1732. Major of 24th Foot, 4 March, 1751. D. in 1763 as Major 28th Foot and Bt. Lt.-Col. Will proved at Dublin.

[15] Lieut. 20 May, 1732. D. as Capt. before Carthagena in 1741.

[16] Out before 1727.

[17] Attained the Lt.-Colonelcy of above Regt. 27 Feb. 1751. Col. 76th Foot, 16 Jan. 1761. Served at the capture of Belle Isle. Also served with distinction in the West Indies. Maj.-Gen. 10 July, 1762. Col. 6th Foot, 14 June, 1765. Lt.-Gen. in May, 1772. D. in Feb. 1773.

[18] Serving as senior Lieut. in 1740.

[19] Comn. renewed in 1727. Out before 1740.

[20] Serving as Lieut. in 1737. Out before 1740.

[21] Serving in 1737.

[22] Aftds. Field-Marshal Sir George Howard, K.B. This officer was son of Lt.-Gen. Thos. Howard, and was bn. in 1718, so that he received his first Comn. as a child of barely eight years. Capt. in 3rd Buffs (then commanded by his father), 1 Sept. 1739. Commanded said Corps at Fontenoy, Falkirk, and Culloden. Received the gold Culloden medal which is still preserved by his lineal representative. Commanded the Buffs at Val, and in 1749 succeeded his father as Col. of said Corps. Served with distinction as Maj.-Gen. in Germany during the Seven Years' War. He was given a sword, set with jewels, by Prince Ferdinand of Brunswick ; also that Prince's portrait. Transferred to the 7th Dragoons in 1763, and created K.B., Field-Marshal, Gov. of Chelsea Hospital, and a member of the Privy Council. D. 16 July, 1796. Bd. at Great Bookham, Surrey.

[23] Out in Dec. 1726.

[24] "Comn. signed and issued in England." Serving in 1737. Out before 1740.

[25]   Do.   Out before 1737.

LIST OF COLONEL JOHN MIDDLETON'S REGIMENT OF FOOT IN 1727.*

[25TH FOOT,—THE KING'S OWN SCOTTISH BORDERERS.]

CAPTS.	LIEUTS.	ENSIGNS.
John Middleton,[1] [17 June, 1721 *p*], Col.	Alex. Moncreif.	Robert Bennet.
Edmond Devischer,[2] [17June,1721 *p*],Lt.-Col.	Chas. Mackie, [10 July, 1725 *r*]	John Mitchell.
Francis Fleming,[3] [1 Feb. 1720 *j*], Major.	James Hamilton.	Wm. Lucas.[14]
Peter Ronalds,[4] [Grs.]	John Maitland,[11] Wm. Baird.[12]	
James Biggar.[5]	Lewis Meares [23 Oct. 1724 *r*].	George Middleton.
Wm. Spence.[6]	Wm. Brodie.	David Watson [15] [10 July, 1725 *r*].
Wm. Stevens.[7]	Frederick Bruce.[13]	Chas. Stevens.
Jas. Dalrymple.[8]	Samuel Creech [28 Oct. 1719 *j*].	Jas. Hamilton.
David Cunningham.[9]	Alex. Biggar.	David Douglas [29 Oct. 1726 *r*].
Wm. Campbell.[10]	Chas. Maitland.	George Scott.[16]

STAFF OFFICERS.

Thos. Pattison, Chaplain.
Wm. Baird,[12] Adjt.
John Murray, Surgeon.

---

* This Regt. was sent to Gibraltar in Dec. 1726, and took part in the defence of that fortress. Owing to the loss of the Commission Entry Book for 1720–23 at the Dublin Record Office some of the Comn. Registers for the period named are not forthcoming. The above List gives all the officers to whom George II. granted fresh Comns. under date of Sept. 1727. The List in question is at the Dublin Record Office (Military Commissions, 1724–30). The dates between brackets are added by the Editor and references are given.

[1] Of Seaton, co. Aberdeen. Fifth son of George Middleton, D.D., Minister of Glamis. Capt. in the Duke of Argyll's Regt. of Foot, 24 May, 1709. Lt.-Col. Maitland's Regt. 18 March, 1711. Bt.-Col. 15 Nov. 1711. Lieut.-Gov. of Tynemouth Castle, 28 Jan. 1715. Transferred to the Colonelcy of the 13th Foot, 29 May, 1732. Brig.-Gen. 13 Nov. 1735. D. 4 May, 1739. Was M.P. for Aberdeen Burghs and Gov. of Holy Island.

[2] Capt. in the King's Regt. of Foot, 23 March, 1709. Served at Malplaquet. Called " De Fisher " in previous Lists. Out of above Regt. before July, 1737.

[3] Younger bro. to Maj.-Gen. Jas. Fleming. Served previously as Capt. in 36th Foot. Out of 25th Foot before July, 1737. See his Comn. on p. 183 and note thereto.

[4] Appointed Capt. in above Regt. 15 May, 1711. Out before 1740. Called "Ronald" in previous Lists.

[5] Major, 19 July, 1732. Lt.-Col. 37th Foot, 27 March, 1742. Killed at the battle of Falkirk, 1746.

[6] Out before 1740.

[7] Do.

[8] Major, 7 May, 1742. Wounded at Fontenoy. The death of a certain Major Jas. Dalrymple is recorded in the *Gentleman's Mag.* for 1766 as having taken place at Munran, Scotland.

[9] Lt.-Col. of above Regt. 25 Feb. 1746. Called "Sir David Cunningham" in the *Army List* for 1758. See p. 317, note 28.

[10] Out before 1740.

[11] Capt. 1 March, 1739.

[12] Serving as senior Lieut. in 1740.

[13] Capt.-Lieut. 1 March, 1739.

[14] Lieut. 13 June, 1732. Wounded at Fontenoy, where he served as Capt.

[15] Served on the Staff in Flanders, 1748, as Commissary-Gen. of Musters. Col. 63rd Foot, 21 April, 1758. Col. 38th Foot, 12 Oct. 1660—11 Nov. 1761.

[16] Attained the rank of Lt.-Col. of 25th Foot, 22 March, 1757.

BRIGADIER-GENERAL GEORGE PRESTON'S REGIMENT OF FOOT.

[26TH FOOT,—1ST BATTALION THE CAMERONIANS.]

See note at head of p. 359, and memo. on same page.

Adam Ferguson,[1] Esq. to be Capt. in room of Wm. Drummond - - - - -	—	21 Mar. 1718/9. *j*
Robt. Ross[2] to be Lieut. to Capt. Wadham Sprage in room of George Gordon decd. -	—	4 April, 1719. *j*
Adam Spittall[3] to be Lieut. to Capt. Adam Ferguson in room of Robt. Pringle - -	—	22 June, ,, *j*
Alex. Leslie[4] to be Ens. to Capt. Robt. Anstruther in room of Adam Spittall -	—	,, ,, ,, *j*
John Johnston,[5] Esq. to be Capt. in room of Alex. Ogilvie - - - - -	—	10 Sept. ,, *j*
George Somerville,[6] to be Ens. to Major Hugh Sempill in room of John Johnston -	—	,, ,, ,, *j*
Philip Anstruther,[7] Esq. to be Colonel in room of Brigdr. George Preston and Capt. of a Cy. - - - - - - -	—	31 Mar. 1720. *j*
Wm. Henderson[8] to be Lieut. - - -	—	28 Sept. 1721. *f*
Sir Henry Wardlaw,[9] Bt. to be Ens. - -	—	20 July, 1722. *f*
Philip Anstruther,[10] Esq. to be Capt. - -	—	18 June 1723. *f*
[George] Moncrief[11] to be Lieut. - - -	—	,, ,, ,, *f*
—— Holbourn[12] to be Ens. - - - -	—	25 Nov. ,, *f*
George Anstruther[11] to be Lieut. - - -	—	12 Dec. 1726. *f*
David Main[13] to be Qr.-Mr. - - - -	Kensington, 25 ,, ,, *d*
Richard Harris[14] to be Lieut. to Capt. Wadham Spragg - - - - - - -	Dublin, 28 Mar. 1727. *r*
James Thompson[15] to be Ens. in room of Richard Harris - - - - -	,, ,, ,, ,, *r*

Regiment returned to England in Dec. 1726, and embarked for Gibraltar from Portsmouth the end of Jan. 1727.

[1] See p. 167, note 10.
[2] Out in March, 1727.
[3] Comn. renewed in 1727.   Out before 1740.
[4] Out before 1727.
[5] Do.
[6] Comn. renewed in 1727.   Serving in 1730.   Out before 1740.
[7] See biog. notice in Vol. I., page 127, note 10.   He was M.P. for Anstruther Easter, Fifeshire, 1715–41 and 1747–54.—Foster's *Members of Parliament for Scotland.*
[8] Capt. 11 Aug. 1737.   Serving in 1740.
[9] Only son and heir of Sir George Wardlaw, Bart.   Comn. renewed in 1727.   Subsequently he was a "private soldier in the 2nd Foot Guards and as such made his will, 20 June, 1739."   Said will "was proved at St. Andrews, 15 July following."—G.E.C.'s *Complete Baronetage.*
[10] Comn. renewed in 1727.   Serving in 1730.   Out before 1740.
[11] Attained the Lt.-Colonelcy of above Regt. 18 Dec. 1755.
[12] Comn. renewed in 1727.   Serving in 1730.   Out before 1740.
[13] Appointed on the Regt. being placed on the English Establishment.
[14] Capt.-Lieut. 12 July, 1739.   Serving in 1740.
[15] Lieut. 28 June, 1735.   Serving in 1740.

MAJOR-GENERAL THOMAS WHETHAM'S REGIMENT OF FOOT.

[27TH FOOT,—1ST BATTALION THE ROYAL INNISKILLING FUSILIERS.]

See note at head of p. 359, and memo. on same page.

Wm. Grinfield [1] to be Ens. to the Colonel's Cy. in room of George Middleton - - -	—	13 Mar. 1718/9.*j*
John Edgar [2] to be Surgeon - - - -	—	21 ,, ,, *j*
John Wiseman [3] to be Ens. to Capt. Tokefield in room of Richard Brewer - - - -	—	5 April, 1720.*j*
Fell Tokefield, [4] Esq. to be Capt. in room of Jeffery Stevens - - - - - -	—	18 ,, ,, *j*
Henry Massey [5] to be Ens. to —— in room of Leonard Forrester - - - -	—	30 ,, ,, *j*
Leonard Forrester [6] to be Lieut. to Capt. Edmond Strudwick in room of Thos. Strudwick -	—	,, ,, ,, *j*
Thos. Strudwick, [7] Esq. to be Capt.-Lieut. in room of John Petit - - - - -	—	,, ,, ,, *j*
James Steuart, [8] Esq. to be Major in room of Henry Cope and Capt. of Cy. - - -	—	8 June, ,, *j*
Philip Lethbridge [9] to be Ens. - - - -	—	19 Mar. 1722.*f*
Robert Forster, [10] Esq. to be Capt.-Lieut. -	—	27 April, ,, *c*
Thos. Scroggs [11] to be Lieut. - - - -	—	,, ,, ,, *f*
Thos. Griffith [12] to be Ens. - - - -	—	,, ,, ,, *f*
Fras. Thompson, [13] Esq. to be Capt. in room of John Hay - - - - - -	Dublin,	12 May, ,, *c*
Wm. Rutherford [14] to be Lieut. to Capt. Tokefield in room of Chichester Fortescue - -	—	20 Jan. 1724/5.*r*
Alex. Dallway [15] to be Ens. to Capt. Lewis Givin in room of Wm. Rutherford - - -	—	,, ,, ,, *r*
Hon. Robert (*sic*) Molesworth, [16] Esq. to be Colonel in room of Major-General Thos. Whetham -	Dublin,	22 Mar. ,, *r*
Solomon Blossett, [17] Esq. to be Capt. in room of John Wilson - - - - -	—	27 Oct. 1726. *r*
Angus Macleod, [18] Esq. to be do. in room of John Whiteford preferred - - -	—	25 Dec. ,, *r*
Peter Carnac, [19] Esq. to be do. in room of Tindall Thompson - - - - - -	Dublin,	,, ,, ,, *r*

[1] Lieut. 5 July, 1735. Serving in 1740.
[2] Serving in 1737.
[3] Out before 1727.
[4] Called "Gilbert" Tokefield in Gradation List for 1730. "Fell" may have been a second name.
[5] Out before 1727.
[6] Do.
[7] See his Comn. on p. 199 as Lieut. in the King's Regt. of Horse, and note thereto.
[8] Comn. renewed in 1727. Serving in 1730. Out before 1737.

A. Penni   Jn. Brooks fecit

The R.ᵗ Hon.ᵇˡᵉ Richard Viscount Molesworth
Lievt. General of his MAJESTY'S Forces and
Master General of the Ordnance of IRELAND.

(*See* Vol. I., pp. 85, 86.)

[9] Comn. renewed in 1727.   Out before 1737.   Probably a son of Christopher Lethbridge, of Westaway, Devon, by Margaret, dau. of Philip Bouchier.

[10] Capt. 3 April, 1733.   Serving in 1740.

[11] Comn. renewed in 1727.   Serving in 1730.   Out before 1740.

[12] Lieut. 27 Aug. 1737.   D. on active service in the West Indies, 1742.—*Gentleman's Mag.*

[13] Exchanged to 3rd Foot, 19 April, 1726.   See p. 278 ; also p. 212, note 13.

[14] Capt. 8 March, 1740.   D. on active service in the West Indies, 1742.—*Gentleman's Mag.*

[15] Comn. renewed in 1727.   Out before 1737.

[16] See memoir in Vol. I., of Field-Marshal *Richard*, Viscount Molesworth.

[17] Serving in 1740.   D. 1749.   Will proved at Dublin.

[18] " Comn. signed and issued in England."   Out before 1740.

[19] " Comn. signed and issued in England."   Appears to have been son of Surgeon Peter Carnac, who served at Blenheim as Surgeon to the 24th Foot.   Peter Carnac, junior, served at Malplaquet as Lieut. in 24th Regt.   His Comn. as Capt. in 27th Foot was renewed in 1727.   Out of the Regt. before 1737.

COLONEL WILLIAM BARRELL'S REGIMENT OF FOOT.

[28TH FOOT,—1ST BATTALION THE GLOUCESTERSHIRE REGIMENT.]

Regiment embarked with the Expedition to Vigo in Aug. 1719, and returned to Ireland three months later.

Eusebius Holmes [1] to be Qr.-Mr. - - -	Whitehall, 19 July,	1719.*c*
Charlton Whitlock (*sic*) [2] to be Ens. to Col. Barrell's Cy.—Comn. signed by Viscount Cobham on board H.M.S. *Ipswich* - -	23 Sept.	„ *j*
Robert Harman, [3] Esq. to be Capt. in room of George Noades.—Signed as above - -	29 „	„ *j*
Thomas Holmes [4] to be Ens. to Capt. Robt. Maxwell.—Signed as above - -	„ „	„ *j*
Paul Malide, [5] Esq. to be Capt. in room of John Champfleury.—Signed as above -	7 Oct.	„ *j*
John Roos [6] to be Adjt. in room of Wm. Davidson - - - - -	Dublin, 1 Mar. 1719/20.*j*	
Do. to be Lieut. to Capt. Robt. Harman in room of Wm. Davidson - - -	„ „ „	„ *j*
Charles Gignous (*sic*), [7] Esq. to be Capt. in room of Lewis Leirmont - - -	„ 5 April,	1720.*j*
Marmaduke Sowle [8] to be Lieut. to Lt.-Col. Lee in room of Chas. Gignons preferred -	„ „ „	„ *j*
Daniel Pinsun [9] to be Ens. to Capt. —— in room of Marmaduke Sowle preferred -	„ „ „	„ *j*
Scot Floyer, [10] Esq. to be Capt.-Lieut. in room of Wm. Tayleur - - - - -	„ 9 June,	„ *j*
Wm. Greemes (*sic*) [11] to be Lieut. to Capt. Robt. Maxwell in room of Scot Floyer preferred	„ „ „	„ *j*
Chas. Gookin [12] to be Ens. to Capt. Stephen Downes in room of Wm. Greems - -	„ „ „	„ *j*
Elias Darassus [13] to be Lieut. - - -	— 18 Nov.	1721.*f*
Charleton Whitelock, [2] Esq. to be Capt. -	— 15 Mar.	1721/2.*f*
Henry Cossard [14] to be Lieut. - - -	— „ „	„ *f*
Thos. Buck [15] to be Ens. - - - -	— 9 Aug.	1722.*f*
Richard Babington [16] to be do. - - -	— 31 Aug.	1723.*f*
Francis Nesbitt [17] to be do. - - -	— 15 Jan.	1723/4.*f*
John Stevenson [18] to be do. - - -	— 1 May,	1724.*f*
Daniel Pinsun [9] to be Lieut. - - - -	— „ „	„ *f*
Cyrus de la Millière, [19] Esq. to be Capt. - -	— „ „	„ *f*
Isaac Sailly [20] to be Lieut. - - - -	— „ „	„ *f*
James Johnston [21] to be Lieut. to [Lt.-Col.] John Lee in room of Henry Holmes preferred - - - - - -	Dublin, 11 May,	1727.*r*
Henry Holmes, [22] Esq. to be Capt. in room of Chas. Gignous - - - - - -	„ „ „	„ *r*

Marmaduke Sowle [8] Esq. to be Capt. in room
 of Thos. Lumm - - - - - Dublin, 11 May, 1727. *r*
Thos. Burton [23] to be Lieut. to Capt. Cyrus
 de la Millière in room of M. Sowle preferred - - - - - - - ,, ,, ,, ,, *r*
Roger Holt [24] to be Ens. to Capt. Charleton
 Whitelock in room of Thos. Johnson - ,, ,, ,, ,, *r*

[1] Placed on half-pay when above Regt. returned to Ireland in Oct. 1719.

[2] *Carleton Whitelocke.* Major, 10 Feb. 1741. He md. 15 April, 1726, Anne, elder dau. of George Roche, of Limerick, by his second wife, and had two sons, the elder of whom was given the family name of "Bulstrode." Major Whitelocke d. in 1776, and his will, in which he is described as "of Priorswood, co. Dublin," was proved at Dublin same year.

[3] See biog. notice on p. 171, note 13.

[4] Out before 1727.

[5] See p. 367, note 3.

[6] Serving as Adjt. and Capt. in 1737. Out before 1740.

[7] Out in May, 1727. D. in 1735. Will proved at Dublin.

[8] Appointed Ens. in above Regt. 10 Dec. 1711. Transferred to the 3rd Buffs, 17 March, 1732. Major of 11th Foot, then commanded by Col. Robinson Sowle, 15 Aug. 1745. Believed to have served with the Buffs at Fontenoy. Serving as Major 11th Foot in 1748.

[9] Lieut. 1 May, 1724. Serving in 1740.

[10] Capt. 8 July, 1737. Serving in 1740.

[11] *Graeme.* Out before 1727. The Surgeon to same Regt. was Wm. Graham.

[12] Not in any subsequent List.

[13] See p. 171, note 15.

[14] Serving in 1740.

[15] Serving as senior Ens. in 1740. Attained the Lt.-Colonelcy of 51st Foot, 20 Dec. 1755.

[16] Comn. renewed in 1727. Out before 1737.

[17] Serving as Ens. in 1740. The will of a certain "Francis Nesbitt, gent." was proved at Dublin in 1766.

[18] Comn. renewed in 1727. Out before 1737.

[19] Comn. renewed in 1727. Out before 1737. He had served in the late reign in Col. La Fabreque's French Dragoons.

[20] Wounded at Fontenoy.

[21] Out before 1737. Called "Thos. Johnson" in the Gradation List, 1730.

[22] Serving in 1740.

[23] Out before 1737.

[24] Wounded at Fontenoy where he served as Capt. in above Regt.

LORD MARK KERR'S REGIMENT OF FOOT.

[29TH FOOT,—1ST BATTALION THE WORCESTERSHIRE REGIMENT.]

See note at head of p. 359, and memo. on same page.

John Johnston [1] to be Lieut. to Capt. —— in
    room of Wm. Lake -   -   -   -   —   6 Mar. 1718/9.*j*

Allen Johnston [2] to be Ens. to Capt. —— in
    room of John Johnston -   -   -   —   ,, ,,   ,, *j*

Fras. Salisbury [3] to be Lieut. to Capt. James
    Kennedy's Grendr. Cy. in room of Thomas
    Peirson -   -   -   -   -   —   10 Sept. 1719.*j*

Edmund Bradshaw [4] to be Ens. to Capt. Philip
    Parry in room of Fras. Salisbury -   —   ,, ,,   ,, *j*

Wm. Grove [5] to be Adjt. in room of Andrew
    Charleton -   -   -   -   -   —   14 Oct. ,, *j*

Wm. Fullarton, [6] Esq. to be Capt. in room of
    David Pain -   -   -   -   -   —   6 Nov. ,, *j*

Simon Sandys [7] to be Lieut. to Capt. Ruben
    Callindine (*sic*) in room of Jas. Stewart
    decd. -   -   -   -   -   —   20 Feb. 1719/20.*j*

David Kennedy, [8] Esq. to be Capt. in room of
    Mervin Pratt -   -   -   -   —   ,, ,,   ,, *j*

Josiah Cook, [9] Esq. to be Capt. of Major
    Chas. Pawlet's late Cy. -   -   —   ,, ,,   ,, *j*

James Kennedy, [10] Esq. to be Major in room
    of [Major] Chas. Pawlet -   -   —   15 April, 1720.*j*

Daniel Callaud [11] to be Lieut. -   -   —   18 Sept. 1721.*f*

John Charleton, [12] Esq. to be Capt. -   —   4 Mar. 1722/3.*f*

Chas. Collins [13] to be Lieut. -   -   —   10 Aug. 1723.*f*

Wm. Johnston [14] to be do. -   -   —   29 Nov. ,, *f*

Arthur Nesbit [15] to be Ens. -   -   —   9 April, 1724.*f*

George Mure [16] to be Lieut. -   -   —   28 ,,   ,, *f*

Robt. Fielding [17] to be Lieut. to Capt. —— Kensington, 8 Dec. 1725.*d*

Henry Desney, [18] Esq. to be Colonel in room
    of Lord Mark Kerr and Capt. of a Cy. Dublin, 25 ,,   ,, *r*

Chas. Collins [13] to be Adjt. in room of John
    Johnston -   -   -   -   -   ,,   22 Dec. 1726.*d*

John Johnston, [1] Esq. to be Capt. in room of
    John Brooks -   -   -   -   ,,   ,, ,,   ,, *d*

Edmund Bradshaw [4] to be 2nd Lieut. to
    [Major] Jas. Kennedy in room of John
    Johnston -   -   -   -   -   ,,   ,, ,,   ,, *d*

Edward Lovibond [19] to be Ens. to Capt.
    Philip Parry -   -   -   -   ,,   ,, ,,   ,, *d*

Wm. Hunt [20] to be Qr.-Mr. to above Regt. - St. James's, 25 ,,   ,, *d*

James Desières [21] to be Lieut. to [Lt.-Col.] Wm. Kennedy - - - - -	—	1 Feb. 1726/7.*d*
Richard Marriot [22] to be Ens. to Capt. John Charlton in room of Smyth Magennis -	—	26 Mar. 1727.*d*

[1] See biog. notice on p. 172, note 1.

[2] Out before 1727. A certain " Allen Johnston, of Drumin, co. Cavan," d. in 1763, and his will was proved at Dublin.

[3] Out before 1727.

[4] Capt. 9 July, 1739.

[5] D. or left the Regt. before 1724.

[6] Comn. renewed in 1727. Out before 1740. The *Gentleman's Mag.* records the death of a " Capt. Wm. Fullerton of the Guards," under date of 1732.

[7] Out before 1727.

[8] Comn. renewed in 1727. Serving in 1730. Drawing half-pay 1739. Believed to have been bro. to Major James Kennedy.

[9] Out before 1727.

[10] See biog. notice in Vol. I., p. 108, note 7.

[11] Capt. 8 May, 1730. Serving in 1740. Probably son of Capt. Reuben *Caillaud* of same Corps, who d. in 1732. A member of this family, Capt. John Caillaud, distinguished himself in Southern India in 1753, and d. a Maj.-Gen.

[12] Comn. renewed in 1727. Out before 1740.

[13] Adjt. 22 Dec. 1726. Comns. renewed in 1727. Out before 1740.

[14] Comn. renewed in 1727. Out before 1740.

[15] Lieut. 21 Jan. 1738. Called " Andrew Nesbitt " in *Army List*, 1740.

[16] Comn. renewed in 1727. Out before 1740.

[17] Do.   do.

[18] See biog. notice in Vol. I., p. 365, note 3. It is a curious fact that though his name is given as " Desney " on his tablet in Westminster Abbey Cloisters, this officer signed his name " Disney " in his will.

[19] Son of Henry Lovibond, Master in Chancery. D. a Capt. in 1733.—*Gentleman's Mag.*

[20] Appointed on return of the Regt. to England.

[21] Capt.-Lieut. 9 July, 1739.

[22] Out before 1740.

BRIGADIER-GENERAL ANDREW BISSET'S REGIMENT OF FOOT.

[30TH FOOT,—1ST BATTALION THE EAST LANCASHIRE REGIMENT.]

This Regiment was placed on the Irish Establishment 14 Aug. 1725.

Richard Onslow,[1] Esq. to be Capt. in room of [Wm.] Davison decd. - - - -	St. James's,	16 Feb. 1718/9.		c
Wm. Sherman[2] to be Lieut. to Capt. Roper -	,,	25 ,,	,,	c
James Mossman[3] to be 2nd Lieut. to Capt. Wm. Scott	,,	,, ,,	,,	c
Henry Sowle[4] to be 1st Lieut. to Robinson Sowle, Esq. - - - - - -	,,	24 April, ,,		c
Ventris Scott[5] to be 2nd Lieut. to Brigadier Bisset - - - - - -	,,	6 May,	,,	c
Joseph Dussaux[6] to be 1st Lieut. to Capt. —————— - - - - - -	,,	20 Nov.	,,	c
Bryan J'Anson[7] (sic) to be 2nd Lieut. to Lt.-Col. Betsworth - - - -	,,	15 Feb. 1719/20.		c
David Weems[8] to be 1st Lieut. to Capt. Fras. Pierson - - - - - -	,,	,, ,,	,,	c
Richard Henley,[9] Esq. to be Capt. in room of Andrew Forrester - - - -	,,	1 Mar. 1720.		c
Wm. Cook[10] to be Lieut. to Capt. ——— - -	,,	5 April,	,,	c
Henry Ravenhill[11] to be 2nd Lieut. to ——— Cochran - - - - - -	,,	21 May,	,,	c
James Auchmuty[12] to be Chaplain - -	,,	13 Feb. 1720/1.		c
James Mosman (sic)[3] to be 1st Lieut. to ———	,,	29 Mar.	,,	c.
Robt. Throgmorton[13] to be 1st Lieut. to Lt.-Col. Peter Betsworth - - - -	,,	17 May,	,,	c
Moses La Porte[14] to be 2nd Lieut. to [Capt. Richard] Henley - - - - -	,,	5 July,	,,	c
Wm. Orfeur[15] to be do. to ——— - - -	,,	12 ,,	,,	c
Charles Janvre de la Bouchetière[16] to be 2nd Lieut. to ——— - - - - -	,,	1 Sept.	,,	c
Charles Jefferies[17] to be 1st Lieut. to Capt. Vincent - - - - - -	,,	,, ,,	,,	c
George Lovell[18] to be 2nd Lieut. to Major Scott - - - - - -	,,	28 Oct.	,,	c
Wm. Tracy,[19] Esq. to be Capt. in room of Richard Onslow - - - -	,,	10 Nov.	,,	c
Charles Bouchetière[16] to be 1st Lieut. to [Lt.-Col.] Sowle - - - -	,,	5 Dec.	,,	c
Charles Cotterell[20] to be 2nd Lieut. to ——— Gibbons - - - - -	,,	,, ,,	,,	c
Chichester Hamilton[21] to be Qr.-Mr. - -	,,	28 April, 1722.		c
Wm. Daws,[22] Esq. to be Capt. in room of [Jas.] Baker - - - - -	,,	4 May,	,,	c

Henry Vaughan,[23] Esq. to be 1st Lieut. to [Lt.-Col.] Betsworth - - - -	St. James's, 4 May,	1722.*c*
Chas. Blunt[24] to be do. to Capt. Wm. Tracy -	Kensington, 1 Sept.	,, *c*
Charles Jefferies[17] to be Adjt. - - -	,, 7 ,,	,, *c*
Wm. Cook,[10] Esq. to be Capt. - - - -	,, ,, ,,	,, *c*
Richard Barnwell Waller,[25] Esq. to be Capt. in room of Ric. Henley - - - -	St. James's, 5 Mar. 1722/3.*c*
David Brevet[26] to be 2nd Lieut. to Peter Betsworth, Esq. - - - - -	,, 8 Feb. 1723/4.*c*
Daniel Herring,[27] Esq. to be Capt. in room of Wm. Tracy - - - - -	,, ,, ,, ,, *c*
Henry Ravenhill,[11] Esq. to be Capt.-Lieut. -	,, ,, ,, ,, *c*
James Abercrombie[28] to be 2nd Lieut. to —— - - - - - - -	,, 7 Mar. ,, *c*
Wm. Palmer[29] to be [1st] Lieut. to [Lt.-Col.] Betsworth - - - - - -	,, 16 ,, ,, *c*
Thos. Baldwin[30] to be 2nd Lieut. to [Capt.] Roper - - - - - -	Kensington, 22 June, 1724.*d*

Regiment sent to Gibraltar in the winter of 1726–27.

George McLaughlan[31] to be Qr.-Mr. -	St. James's, 23 Mar. 1725/6.*d*
Alex. Hutchinson[32] to be 2nd Lieut. to —— -	,, 7 May, 1726.*r*
Thos. Smart[33] to be Chaplain - - -	,, 21 Nov. ,, *d*

[1] See biog. notice in Vol. I., p. 221, note 44.

[2] Out before 1727.

[3] Capt. 1 March, 1738. Major 4th Marines, 7 Oct. 1742. Retd. about 1748.

[4] Capt. in Lord John Kerr's Regt. (31st), 26 July, 1721. Serving in 1730. Out before 1740.

[5] First Lieut. 26 Sept. 1732. Out before 1740.

[6] Serving as Lieut. in Tyrrell's Regt. in 1727. Capt. 13 Aug. 1739. Appointed Lt.-Col. of the Earl of Halifax's Regt. in 1745. Placed on half-pay as Captain in 1746. Drawing half-pay in 1758.

[7] Out in Feb. 1724.

[8] Comn. renewed in 1727. Out before 1737.

[9] Out in March, 1723.

[10] Capt. 7 Sept. 1722. Comn. renewed in 1727. Out before 1757.

[11] Capt. 14 June, 1729. Major, 14 June, 1729. Lt.-Col. 22 June, 1745. Served with above Corps on board the Fleet in 1746. D. or retd. in 1750.

[12] Out in Nov. 1726.

[13] Out in April, 1722.

[14] First Lieut. 27 Sept. 1732. Serving in 1740.

[15] Comn. renewed in 1727. Serving in 1730. See his Comn. as Ensign to Capt. Wigg's Invalid Cy. on p. 341. "Will dated 1 Dec. 1729 ; proved in London, — April, 1733. Had a house in Chelsea. Believed to have been elder bro. to Capt. John Orfeur, of the Carabiniers." (Communicated by Col. Cavenagh.)

[16] Appears to have been son of Col. Charles de la Bouchetière who is noticed on p. 134, note 1. Capt.-Lieut. 1 March, 1738. Serving in 1740.

[17] See biog. notice on p. 175, note 30.

[18] Comn renewed in 1727. Serving in 1730. Lieut. in Col. John Irwin's Regt. of Foot (5th), 20 June, 1739. The will of "George Lovell, Esq., reformed Capt. in Gen. Irwin's Regt." was proved at Dublin in 1749.

[19] Out in Feb. 1724.

[20] Comn. renewed in 1727. Serving in 1730. Out before 1740.

[21] Placed on half-pay when the Regt. was sent to Ireland in Aug. 1725.

[22] Appointed 2nd Lieut. in above Regt. (when it was a Marine Corps), 9 Nov. 1703. Comn. as Capt. renewed in 1727. Serving in 1730. Out before 1737.

[23] Exchanged to Brigdr. Grove's Regt. (10th), in March, 1724. See his Comn. on p. 289 and note thereto.

[24] Comn. renewed in 1727. Out before 1737.

[25] Out before 1727.

[26] Comn. renewed in 1727. First Lieut. 28 Jan. 1735. Serving in 1740.

[27] Left the Regt. before 1727. On 5 Oct. 1745 he was appointed Lt.-Col. of a newly-raised Regt. of Foot which Corps was disbanded in 1746 and Lt.-Col. Herring reverted to the half-pay list as a Capt. D. at Bath in 1777.

[28] Appointed 2nd Lieut. of the Grendr. Cy. in Visct. Shannon's Regt. (25th), 27 Aug. 1717. Became Capt. in the Royal Regt. of Foot (1st), 18 June, 1736. Lt.-Col. of the 1st Batt. at the attempted relief of Hulst in 1747 where he was wounded. Bt.-Col. 19 April, 1746. Maj.-Gen. 31 Jan. 1756. Col. of a Regt. of Foot (50th), 18 Dec. 1755. C.-in-C. of the Land Forces in America, 2 April, 1756. The troops under Abercrombie's command were signally defeated at the attack on Fort Ticonderoga in July, 1758. Abercrombie was recalled to England and removed from the Colonelcy of the 60th Regt. (Rl. Americans) to which he had been appointed in Dec. 1757. He d. as Gen. and Col. 44th Foot in 1781.

[29] Comn. renewed in 1727. Out before 1737.

[30] Out before 1727.

[31] Qr.-Mr. appointed on the Regt. being ordered to England.

[32] Comn. renewed in 1727. Out before 1737.

[33]   Do.   do.

LORD JOHN KERR'S REGIMENT OF FOOT.

[31st FOOT,—1st BATTALION THE EAST SURREY REGIMENT.]

See note at head of p. 359, and memo. on same page.

Robert Pollock,[1] Esq. to be Capt.-Lieut. - - -	8 Jan. 1718/9.	*j*
Wm. Spicer,[2] Esq. to be Capt. in room of Cutts Hassan	,, ,, ,,	*j*
John Peirson[3] to be Lieut. to Capt. Edward O'Brien in room of Thos. Webb - - - - -	22 June, 1719.	*j*
Frederick Porter[4] to be Ens. to the Colonel's Cy. in room of John Peirson - - - - -	,, ,, ,,	*j*
David Kennedy[5] to be Lieut. to Capt. Fleetwood Watkins in room of John Blackney (*sic*) decd. - - -	1 Feb. 1719/20.	*j*
Robert Blakeney,[6] Esq. to be Capt. in room of Fleetwood Watkins - - - - - - -	23 April, 1720.	*j*
Thos. Pennefeather[7] to be Lieut. to Capt. Alex. Wilson in room of Robert Blakeney - - - -	,, ,, ,,	*j*
Henry Caldecot,[8] Esq. to be Capt.-Lieut. in room of Robert Pollock - - - - - - -	1 June ,,	*j*
John Pollock[9] to be Lieut. to Major Thos. Sutton in room of Henry Caldecott - - - -	5 ,, ,,	*j*
Henry Soule (*sic*)[10] Esq. to be Capt. - - - -	26 July, 1721.	*f*
Robert Ryves[11] to be Ens. - - - - -	25 Sept. ,,	*f*
Frederick Porter[4] to be Lieut. - - - -	17 Nov. ,,	*f*
Francis Mears[12] to be Ens. - - - - -	,, ,, ,,	*f*
James Vignoles[13] to be do. - - - - -	15 Dec. ,,	*f*
Anesley Gore[14] to be do. - - - - -	29 Nov. 1723.	*f*
Wm. Pollock[15] to be do. - - - - -	11 Feb. 1723/4.	*f*
Henry Hyat[16] to be do. - - - - -	21 Mar. ,,	*f*
Wm. Allen[17] to be Ens. to Major Thos. Sutton in room of Archibald Kerr - - - - -	23 Oct. 1724.	*r*
Archibald Kerr[18] to be Lieut. to Capt. Robert Blakeney	,, ,, ,,	*r*
Charles O'Hara[19] to be Ens. to Major Thos. Sutton in room of Wm. Allen decd. - - - -	15 April, 1725.	*r*
Wm. Northcote[20] to be Lieut. to Capt. Robert Blakeney in room of Archibald Kerr decd. - - -	23 May, ,,	*r*
Ant. Gavin[21] to be Chaplain in room of Robert Stephenson - - - - - - - - -	23 Mar. 1725/6.	*r*
Benson Cushin[22] to be Lieut. to Capt. Ant. Ladeveze in room of Lionel Seaman decd. - - -	27 Mar. 1726.	*r*
Gilbert Porterfield[23] to be 1st Lieut. to Capt. Robt. Blakeney in room of James Smith - - -	27 May, ,,	*r*
Chas. Cockburne[24] to be Ens. to Capt. Henry Sowle in room of James Hamilton - - - -	6 July, ,,	*r*
Wm. Spicer,[2] Esq. to be Major in room of Thos. Sutton and Capt. of a Cy. - - - - -	25 ,, ,,	*r*
Wm. Williamson,[25] Esq. to be Capt. in room of Wm. Spicer - - - - - - - - -	,, ,, ,,	*r*

George Wallace [26] to be Surgeon in room of James Scott   12 Jan. 1726/7. *r*
Wm. Drummond,[27] Esq. to be Capt. in room of Edward
    O'Bryan - - - - - - - - - - - 20 Mar. „
John Poujad (*sic*) [28] to be Surgeon in room of Wallace - 26 May, 1727. *r*

[1] Out 1 June, 1720.
[2] Major, 25 July, 1726. Comn. renewed in 1727. Serving in 1730. Out in 1732.
[3] Out before 1727.
[4] Lieut. 17 Nov. 1721. Wounded at Fontenoy, where he served as senior Lieut.
[5] See p. 401, note 8.
[6] See p. 177, note 7.
[7] See p. 145, note 14.
[8] D. or left the Regt. in the summer of 1727.
[9] Capt.-Lieut. 21 Feb. 1736. Killed at Fontenoy, where he served as Capt.
[10] Son of Col. Robinson Soule (or Sowle). See p. 403, note 4.
[11] Lieut. 30 Nov. 1730. Serving in 1740.
[12] Lieut. 11 Aug. 1730. Serving in 1740.
[13] Lieut. 6 Nov. 1732. Major, 18 Aug. 1756. D. in 1779. Will proved at Dublin.
[14] Comn. renewed in 1727. Out before 1737. The will of a certain " Annesley Gore of Belleck, co. Mayo, Esq." was proved at Dublin in 1782.
[15] Comn. renewed in 1727. Serving in 1730. Out before 1737.
[16] Lieut. 23 Feb. 1733. Serving in 1740.
[17] D. in April, 1725.
[18] D. in May, 1725.
[19] Lieut. 20 June, 1735. Serving in 1740.
[20] Comn. renewed in 1727. Out before 1737.
[21] Out before 1737.
[22] Comn. renewed in 1727. Out before 1737. Probably son of Capt. John Cushing, of the Rl. Hospital, Dublin, who d. in 1718.
[23] " Comn. signed and issued in England."   Comn. renewed in 1727. Out before 1737.
[24]   Do.   Lieut. 21 Feb. 1736. Serving in 1740.
[25]   Do.   Serving in 1740.
[26]   Do.   Out in May, 1727.
[27]   Do.   Serving in 1740.
[28] Serving in 1737.

BRIGADIER-GENERAL JACOB BORR'S REGIMENT OF FOOT.

[32ND FOOT,—1ST BATTALION THE DUKE OF CORNWALL'S LIGHT INFANTRY.]

See note at head of p. 359, and memo. on same page.

Francis Cashell[1] to be 2nd Lieut. to Capt. Robt. Kemp in room of Thos. Hoysted -	—	10 Feb. 1718/9.*j*
Wm. Dixon[2] to be do. to Capt. Bernard Dennett in room of Philip Craddock (*sic*)	—	,, ,, ,, *j*
Wm. Bryan[3] to be 2nd Lieut. to Capt. Peter Coulbron (*sic*) in room of Wm. Vause -	—	22 June, 1719. *j*
Christopher Adams,[4] Esq. to be Capt. in room of Peter Coulborne -	—	1 July, ,, *j*
Philip Cradock[5] to be 1st Lieut. to Capt. Melchior Guy Dickens in room of John Hollinsworth - - - - -	—	24 Aug. ,, *j*
John St. John[6] to be 1st Lieut. to Capt. John Fade in room of Thos. Fitzgerald - -	—	25 Dec. ,, *j*
Charles Demarais[7] to be 1st Lieut. to Capt. Wm. Ridsdale in room of John Cranwell decd. - - - - - -	—	1 Feb.1719/20.*j*
Wm. Scott[8] to be 2nd Lieut. to Lt.-Col. Charles Douglas in room of Robt. Brudenall - - - - -	—	24 May, 1720. *j*
John Warner[9] to be 1st Lieut. to Capt. Melchior Guy Dickens in room of Philip Cradock - - - - - -	—	2 June, ,, *j*
Knowles Kinsey[10] to be 2nd Lieut. to Capt. Thos. Norton in room of John Warner -	—	,, ,, ,, *j*
Stephen Sanderson,[11] Esq. to be Major in room of Robt. Kempe - - - -	—	7 ,, ,, *j*
George Phenney,[12] Esq. to be Capt. in room of [Thos.] Norton decd. - - - -	—	,, ,, ,, *j*
John Graydon,[13] Esq. to be Capt. of Major Kempe's late Cy. - - - -	—	,, ,, ,, *j*
Robert Graydon[14] to be 2nd Lieut. - -	—	29 Aug. 1721. *f*
[Charles Dubourgay,[15] Esq. to be Colonel in room of Jacob Borr and Capt. of a Cy. -	—	28 June, 1723.]
Wm. Price[16] to be 2nd Lieut. - - -	—	7 May, 1724. *f*
Charles Child[17] to be 1st Lieut. to Capt. Samuel Stone - - - - -	Kensington, 10 Oct. ,, *r*
Anthony Kendall[18] to be Adjt. in room of James Nowland - - - -	—	25 Jan. 1724/5.*r*
Esther (*sic*) Shepherd[19] to be 1st Lieut. to Capt. John Graydon in room of Fras. Sullivan - - - - - -	—	8 Feb. ,, *r*

Dawley Sutton [20] to be do. to Capt. Samuel Stone in room of Charles Child decd. -	—	8 Mar. 1724/5. *r*
John Plukenett [21] to be 2nd Lieut. to Capt. Melchior Guy Dickens in room of Dawley Sutton - - - - - - -	—	,, ,, ,, *r*
Bernard Dennett, [22] Esq. to be Major in room of Stephen Sanderson decd. and Capt. of a Cy. - - - - - - -	—	24 May, 1725. *r*
Mordaunt Cracherode, [23] Esq. to be Capt. in room of Bernard Dennett - - -	—	,, ,, ,, *r*
John Greenville [24] to be 2nd Lieut. to Lt.-Col. Charles Douglas in room of Boyle Ashbury decd. - - - - - -	—	10 June, ,, *r*
Philip Cecill [25] to be do. to do. in room of do. -	—	,, ,, ,, *r*
Henry Clement [26] to be 2nd Lieut. to Capt. Melchior Guy Dickens in room of John Plucknett - - - - - -	—	22 Mar. 1725/6. *r*
Wm. Killett [27] to be 2nd Lieut. to Capt. Mordaunt Cracherode in room of Richard Sanders - - - - - -	—	24 ,, ,, *r*
Wm. Dickson [2] to be 1st Lieut. to Capt. Gerald Elrington in room of John Goodwin	—	20 Aug. 1726. *r*
James Douglass [28] to be 2nd Lieut. to [Major] Bernard Dennett in room of Wm. Dickson	—	,, ,, ,, *r*
Robert Mountfort, [29] Esq. to be Capt. in room of Mordaunt Cracherode - - -	—	6 Oct. ,, *r*
Wm. Bryan [3] to be 1st Lieut. to Capt. Gerald Elrington in room of Wm. Dickson -	—	1 Nov. ,, *r*
Peter Parr [30] to be 2nd Lieut. to Capt. Samuel Stone in room of Wm. Bryan - - -	—	,, ,, ,, *r*
John Douglass [31] to be do. to [Major] Bernard Dennet in room of James Douglas - -	—	18 Dec. ,, *r*
James Macdonald [32] to be do. to [Major] Dennet in room of Wm. Kellett preferred - -	—	26 ,, ,, *r*
Hugh Jones, [33] Esq. to be Capt. in room of Gerald Elrington - - - - - -	—	,, ,, ,, *r*

[1] Out before 1727.
[2] Called "Dickson" in a subsequent Comn. 1st Lieut. 20 Aug. 1726. Out before 1737.
[3] 1st Lieut. 1 Nov. 1726. Serving with same rank in 1740.
[4] Serving in 1740.
[5] Out in June, 1720.
[6] Out before 1727.
[7] Do.
[8] Comn. renewed in 1727. Out before 1737. Possibly the Lieut. Wm. Scott who d. "in Dublin Barrack, 1733," and his will proved same year.
[9] Out before 1727.
[10] 1st Lieut. 8 Dec. 1731. Serving in 1740.
[11] Served in the former reign as Capt. in Borr's Marines. D. in May, 1725.
[12] See p. 352, note 3.
[13] Serving in 1740.
[14] 1st Lieut. 31 March, 1733. Serving in 1740.
[15] See biog. notice in Vol. I., p. 168, note 1.
[16] Comn. renewed in 1727. Out before 1737.
[17] "Comn. signed by his Majesty." D. in March, 1725.
[18] Serving as Adjt. and 1st Lieut. in 1737.

[19] Not in any subsequent List.

[20] Serving as senior Lieut. in 1740.

[21] Out in March, 1726.

[22] Lt.-Col. 15 Sept. 1731. Left the Regt. in April, 1744. D. 1760.—*Gentleman's Mag.*

[23] See biog. notice on p. 343, note 10.

[24] "Vacated" written in margin of Comn. entry.

[25] Comn. renewed in 1727. Out before 1737.

[26] Capt. in 33rd Foot, 2 April. 1733. Lt.-Col. of said Corps, 24 Sept. 1744. Killed at Fontenoy. Will proved at Dublin.

[27] Appointed 2nd Lieut. to an additional Cy. in the Rl. Fusiliers, 26 Dec. 1726. See p. 380, note 25.

[28] Out in Dec. 1726.

[29] From Capt. of an Indep. Cy. of Invalids. See p. 339. This officer had served as a Lieut. in Brigdr. Blood's Regt. (17th Foot) at Almanza, and had been taken prisoner.

[30] "Comn. signed and issued in England." 1st Lieut. 8 Aug. 1734. Serving in 1740.

[31]   Do.   Serving in 1737. Out before 1740.

[32] "Comn. signed and issued in England." Comn. renewed in June, 1727. Called "Macdaniel" in the Gradation List for 1730.

[33] "Comn. signed and issued in England." From half-pay Capt.-Lieut. in Brigadier Humphry Gore's Regt. of Foot. Serving as Capt. in 32nd Foot in 1740.

COLONEL HENRY HAWLEY'S REGIMENT OF FOOT.

[33RD FOOT,—1ST BATTALION THE DUKE OF WELLINGTON'S (WEST RIDING) REGIMENT.]

See note at head of p. 359, and memo. on same page.

Edward Erle[1] to be Ens. to Capt. Chris. Williams in room of Thos. Erle - -	—	6 Mar. 1718/9.*j*
John Longfield[2] to be Ens. to Capt. Henry Grant in room of Peter Reynolds - -	—	31 July, 1719.*j*
Anthony Harman[3] to be Ens. to Col. Henry Hawley's Cy.—Comn. signed by Viscount Cobham on board H.M.S. *Ipswich* -	29 Sept.	„ *j*
John Gore,[4] Esq. to be Capt.-Lieut.—Signed as above - - - - - - -	„ „	„ *j*
James Obrien,[5] Esq. to be Capt. in room of Oliver Wheeler.—Signed as above -	„ „	„ *j*
Thomas Lacey[6] to be Lieut. to Capt. James Obrien.—Signed as above - - -	„ „	„ *j*
Richard Chaloner Cobbe,[7] Esq. to be Major in room of John Reading - - -	—	31 Mar. 1720.*j*
Arthur Farewell[8] to be Lieut. to Capt. John Mallett in room of John Graydon - -	—	7 June, „ *j*
Wrothe Wattson[9] to be Ens. to Lt.-Col. John Archer in room of Arthur Farewell -	—	„ „ „ *j*
Richard Chaloner Cobbe,[7] Esq. to be Lt.-Col.	—	5 Oct. 1721.*f*
Richard Harward,[10] Esq. to be Major - -	—	„ „ „ *f*
Robt. Eccles[11] to be Ens. - - - -	—	15 Aug. 1722.*f*
George Johnson,[12] Esq. to be Capt. in room of [James] O'Bryen (*sic*) - - - -	St. James's, 16 Oct.	„ *c*
Arnold James Breams,[13] Esq. to be Capt.-Lieut.	„ „ „	„ *c*
Wm. Eckleston[14] to be Lieut. to Lt.-Col. Cobb	„ „ „	„ *c*
Fras. Cooper[15] to be Ens. to do. - - -	„ „ „	„ *c*
Wm. Cobbe,[16] Esq. to be Capt. in room of John Mallet - - - - - -	„	26 Nov. „ *c*
Wm. Eckleston,[14] Esq. to be do. in room of Chris. Williams - - - - - -	„	1 Dec. „ *c*
George Robinson[17] to be Lieut. to Capt. ——	„	„ „ „ *c*
David Roberts[18] to be Ens. to Capt. —— -	„	„ „ „ *c*
Fras. Mills[19] to be do. to Capt. John Reading	„	15 „ „ *c*
John Longfield[2] to be Lieut. - - - -	—	30 Aug. 1723.*f*
—— Townshend[20] to be Ens. - - - -	—	„ „ „ *f*
Peter Daulhat[21] to be do. - - - -	—	21 April, 1724.*f*
Thos. Wood[22] to be Lieut. to Capt. Wm. Cobbe in room of Arthur Farewell decd.	—	26 Jan. 1724/5.*r*
Humphry Brown,[23] Esq. to be Capt. in room of John Reading - - - - - -	—	21 April, 1725.*r*

Digby Berkeley [24] to be Ens. to Capt. Henry Grame in room of Anthony Turner	—	29 Mar.	1726.*r*
John Toovey [25] to be Lieut. to Capt. Bernard Lostau in room of Edward Erle preferred	—	26 Dec.	„ *r*
James Normand (*sic*) [26] to be Ens. to Capt. George Johnston in room of John Toovey preferred	—	„ „	„ *r*
Arundel Strangeways [27] to be Ens. to Capt. Richard Haward (*sic*)	—	„ „	„ *r*
Lucas Savage [28] to be Ens. to Capt. George Johnston in room of James Norman preferred	—	26 May,	1727.*r*

[1] See his Comn. as Lieut. in Lord Carpenter's Dragoons on p. 209, and note thereto.

[2] Lieut. 30 Aug. 1723. Serving in 1740.

[3] See p. 392, note 13.

[4] Out in Oct. 1722.

[5] Do.

[6] Capt. 22 Nov. 1739. Wounded at Fontenoy. Major, 27 May, 1745. Serving in 1748.

[7] Lt.-Col. 5 Oct. 1721. D. or retd. in 1738. Eldest son of Thos. Cobbe, Gov. of the Isle of Man. Col. Cobbe md. Mary, dau. of Francis Godolphin, the Gov. of Scilly.

[8] D. in Jan. 1725.

[9] See his Comn. as Cornet in Nevill's Dragoons on p. 373, and note thereto.

[10] Comn. renewed in 1727. Out before 1737. D. in Ireland, 1751.—*Gentleman's Mag.*

[11] Lieut. 3 Feb. 1728. Serving as Lieut. and Adjt. in 1740. Wounded at Fontenoy, where he served as Captain.

[12] *Johnston.* See p. 180, note 14.

[13] See p. 180, note 16.

[14] See do., note 12.

[15] Out before 1727.

[16] Younger bro. to Lt.-Col. Chaloner Cobbe. Comn. renewed in 1727. Serving in 1737. Out before 1740. D.s.p. in 1749.—Burke's *Landed Gentry.*

[17] Comn. renewed in 1727. Out before 1737.

[18] Lieut. 13 May, 1735. D. in 1740. Will proved at Dublin.

[19] Out before 1727.

[20] Comn. renewed in 1727. Out before 1737.

[21] Lieut. 13 Aug. 1739. Believed to have served at Fontenoy. Attained the rank of Major, 1 Sept. 1756. D. in 1758. Will proved at Dublin. Appears to have been son of Surgeon Daulhat of same Corps.

[22] Comn. renewed in 1727. Serving in 1740.

[23] From half-pay Capt. in Brigdr. Humphry Gore's Regt. of Foot. Serving in 33rd Foot in 1740.

[24] Lieut. 22 Nov. 1739. Major in the Army, 11 June, 1753. Appointed Capt. of an Invalid Cy. at Sheerness, 8 Dec. 1756.

[25] "Comn. signed in England, issued in Ireland." This officer, subsequently Lt.-Col. Royal Dragoons, is believed by genealogists to have been an illegitimate son of Lt.-Gen. Hawley, who, in his will dated 29 March, 1749, left his whole fortune between his only sister, Anne Hawley, Capt. Wm. Toovey, and Lt.-Col. John Toovey, both of his own Regt., sons of Mrs. Elizabeth Toovey, widow, who was to life-rent most of what Capt. Wm. Toovey succeeded to. The testator went on to say that the said Mrs. Toovey had "been for many years his friend and companion, often his careful nurse, and in his absence a faithful steward."—*The Genealogist*, Vol. I., p. 162.

[26] "Comn. signed in England, issued in Ireland." Appointed Lieut. to an additional Cy. in Kirke's Regt. (2nd), 26 Dec. 1726. See p. 276.

[27] "Comn. signed in England, issued in Ireland." Serving as senior Ens. in 1740.

[28] Do. Serving as Ens. in 1740.

COLONEL THOMAS CHUDLEIGH'S REGIMENT OF FOOT.

[34TH FOOT,—1ST BATTALION THE BORDER REGIMENT.]

Regiment returned to England from Ireland in March, 1719. Served in the Expedition to Vigo same year; then returned to Ireland, and embarked for Gibraltar in 1726.

Maurice Powell [1] to be Ens. to Capt. Fras. Mutis in room of Wm. Wickham	—	6 Mar. 1718/9.	*j*
Wm. Wickham,[2] Esq. to be Capt. of the Cy. whf. Robt. Hays was late Capt.	—	7 ,,	,, *c*
Chris. Phillips [3] to be Qr.-Mr.	St. James's, 21 ,,		,, *c*
Gilbert Geddes,[4] Esq. to be Capt. in room of Henry Whitney	,,	,, ,,	,, *c*
Thos. Adams,[5] Esq. to be Capt. in room of Doidge decd.	,,	19 May,	,, *c*
Thos. Speedy [6] to be Lieut. to [Lt.-Col.] Robt. Hays in room of Thos. Chudleigh	—	18 July,	,, *j*
Thos. Chudleigh [7] to be Ens. to do in room of Thos. Speedy preferred	—	,, ,,	,, *j*
Samuel Daniell,[8] Esq. to be Adjt. in room of Adjt. Thos. Chudleigh	—	,, ,,	,, *j*
Solomon White,[9] Esq. to be Capt. in room of Richard Pigott	—	15 April, 1720.	*j*
Toby Molloy,[10] Esq. to be Capt. in room of Fras. Mutys	—	22 ,,	,, *j*
Michael Studholm [11] to be Lieut.	—	9 June, 1722.	*f*
John Berkeley [12] to be Ens.	—	9 July, ,,	*f*
Robert Hayes,[13] Esq. to be Colonel in room of Thos. Chudleigh and Capt. of a Cy.	Dublin,	18 Feb. 1722/3.	*c*
Henry de la Millière [14] to be Capt.	—	28 Mar. 1723.	*f*
Henry Freeman [15] to be do.	—	4 July, ,,	*f*
Hugh Montgomery [16] to be do.	—	8 Dec. ,,	*f*
Robt. Freeman [17] to be Ens. to Capt. Humphry Brown	Kensington,	1 Aug. 1724.	*r*
Rowland Leffever [18] to be Adjt. in room of John Hely	—	15 Dec. ,,	*r*
Stephen Cornwallis,[19] Esq. to be Lt.-Col. in room of —— Hayes	—	23 Jan. 1724/5.	*r*
Timothy White,[20] Esq. to be Capt.-Lieut. in room of Wm. Hayes	—	1 Mar. ,,	*r*
John Brushfield [21] to be Lieut. to Capt. Wm. Freeman in room of Timothy White	—	,, ,,	,, *r*
Henry Hart [22] to be Ens. to Capt. Henry de la Millière in room of Thos. (*sic*) Brushfield	—	,, ,,	,, *r*
Thos. Parker [23] to be Lieut. to Capt. John Hely in room of Thos. Price decd.	—	13 Mar. 1725.	*r*

Robt. Chamier [24] to be Ens. to above Cy. in room of Thos. Parker - - - -	—	30 Mar. 1725. *r*
Hon. Stephen Cornwallis [19] to be Capt. of that Cy. whf. Humphry Brown was late Capt.	—	21 April, „ *r*
Michael Phillips [25] to be Lieut. to Capt. Michael Brandreth in room of Chris. Phillips - - - - - - -	—	9 July, 1726. *r*
Michael Studholm [11] to be Adjt. in room of Rowland Leffever - - - - -	—	21 Nov. „ *r*
Philip Parsons [26] to be Qr.-Mr. - - -	St. James's, 25 Dec.	„ *d*

Regiment returned to England in Dec. 1726, and embarked for Gibraltar early in 1727.

[1] See biog. notice in Vol. I., p. 309, note 6.

[2] Out before 1727.

[3] Served as Lieut. in above Regt at the defence of Gibraltar, 1726–27. He had a duel with Lieut. Roger Sterne of same Corps at Gibraltar, and the latter was seriously wounded. (See Introduction to Vol. I., p. xlvi.) Phillips is said to have been promoted Captain in above Corps. Out before 1737.

[4] Out in 1730.

[5] Do.

[6] Capt. 20 May, 1731. Lt.-Col. 9 Oct. 1741. Drawing half-pay, 1746.

[7] Lieut. 28 Aug. 1737. Called "Sir Thomas Chudleigh" in *Army List*, 1740. Succeeded his uncle, Sir George Chudleigh, as Bart. in Oct. 1738. D. at Aix-la-Chapelle in 1741.

[8] Major 37th Foot, 18 May, 1722. Lt.-Col. 15th Foot, 2 July, 1737. Served at siege of Carthagena in 1741, and d. from fever on 24 April, when in command of the 5th Marines.

[9] Out before 1730.

[10] From half-pay, Sir Daniel Carrol's Regt. of Dragoons. Serving in 34th Regt. in 1730. Out before 1740.

[11] Capt. 15 Dec. 1731. Major, 21 April, 1743. Out before 1746.

[12] Lieut. 22 July, 1731. Serving in 1740.

[13] D. at Jamaica in 1731.—*Gentleman's Mag.*

[14] See p. 286, note 4.

[15] Comn. renewed in 1727. Serving in 1730. Out before 1740.

[16]   Do.   do.   do.

[17]   Do.   do.   do.

[18] The "Lieut. Le Fever" of Laurence Sterne's *Tristram Shandy*. Serving in 1730. Out before 1737.

[19] Col. of 11th Foot, 9 Aug. 1738. See biog. notice on p. 270, note 5.

[20] Serving as Capt. in 1737. Out before 1740.

[21] Serving as Lieut. and Adjt. in 1737. Out before 1740.

[22] Comn. renewed in 1727. Serving in 1737. Out before 1740.

[23]   Do.   Out before 1737.

[24] Lieut. 20 Nov. 1731. Serving in 1740.

[25] "Comn. signed in England, issued in Ireland." Serving as senior Lieut. in 1740.

[26] Not in any subsequent List.

COLONEL CHARLES OTWAY'S REGIMENT OF FOOT.

[35TH FOOT,—1ST BATTALION THE SUSSEX REGIMENT.]

This Regiment returned to Ireland in the autumn of 1725.

John Stanhope,[1] Esq. to be Capt. in the room
   of Pinsent decd. - - - - - Gohre, 11 Oct. O.S. 1725.*d*
James Murphy[2] to be Ens. to ——— - - ,, ,, ,, ,, ,, *d*
James Hay[3] to be Lieut. to ——— in room of
   Matthewes Sewell - - - - - — 4 April, 1726.*r*
Edmund Leslie,[4] Esq. to be Capt. in room of
   Thos. Forth - - - - - - — 6 May, ,, *r*
Wm. Bernard[5] to be Lieut. to Capt. Roger
   Lort in room of James Aston - - - — 31 ,, ,, *r*
Thos. Burges[6] to be Ens. to Capt. Edmund
   Leslie in room of Robt. Wilson - - - — 2 Sept. ,, *r*
John Johnston[7] to be Ens. to Capt. Abel
   Warren in room of Samuel Bates - - — 24 Dec. ,, *r*
Thos. Moore[8] to be do. to Capt. Wm. Campbell
   in room of Wm. Moore - - - - — 27 Jan. 1726/7.*r*

---

[1] Serving in 1740. The will of "John Stanhope, late Capt. in Brigdr. Otway's Regt. of Foot," was proved at Dublin in 1747.
[2] Out before 1727.
[3] "Comn. signed and issued in England." Serving as Lieut. in 1740.
[4]   Do.   Serving as Capt. in 1740.
[5]   Do.   Serving as Lieut. in 1737. Out before 1740.
[6] "Comn. signed and issued in England." Comn. renewed in June, 1727. Out before 1737.
[7] "Comn. signed and issued in England." Lieut. 31 Aug. 1739.
[8]   Do.   Serving as senior Ens. in 1740.

COLONEL CHARLES LANOE'S REGIMENT OF FOOT.

[36TH FOOT,—2ND BATTALION THE WORCESTERSHIRE REGIMENT.]

Regiment sent to Ireland in the autumn of 1721.

Wm. Sheyne,[1] Esq. to be Capt. - - - - -	1 Dec. 1722.*f*
Edward Whitmore [2] to be Lieut. - - - - -	1 June, 1723.*f*
Robert Scott [3] to be Lieut. - - - - - -	15 Aug. ,, *f*
John Lloyd,[4] Esq. to be Capt.-Lieut. - - -	10 Sept. ,, *f*
John Bodville [5] to be Ens. - - - - - -	,, ,, ,, *f*
Charles Barton [6] to be Lieut. - - - - -	,, ,, ,, *f*
Lambert Pepper,[7] Esq. to be do. - - - -	19 Feb. 1723/4.*f*
Michael Cheape [8] to be Ens. - - - - -	,, ,, ,, *f*
John Grant,[9] Esq. to be Lt.-Col. - - - -	,, ,, ,, *f*
Theophilus Sandford [10] to be Major - - -	,, ,, ,, *f*
Stephen Thompson [11] to be Lieut. - - - -	4 May, 1724.*f*
John Cuppage [12] to be Ens. - - - - -	,, ,, ,, *f*
John Westbrook [13] to be do. to Capt. Samuel Whitaker in room of Hugh Murray - - - -	8 Feb. 1725/6.*r*
John Dodd [14] to be Ens. to do. in room of John Westbrook - - - - - - - -	21 May, 1726.*r*

[1] Serving in 1737. D. in 1739. Will proved at Dublin.

[2] See biog. notice in Vol. I., p. 365, note 4.

[3] Capt.-Lieut. 1 Nov. 1739. Believed to be identical with Robert Scott appointed Lt.-Col. 6th Foot, 8 Jan. 1756, and Bt.-Col. 19 Feb. 1762. D. 1770.—*Gentleman's Mag.*

[4] Comn. renewed in 1727. Out before 1737.

[5] Lieut. 27 June, 1734. Killed before Carthagena in 1741.

[6] Comn. renewed in 1727. Out before 1737.

[7] Serving as a Capt. in 1737. Out before 1740. Described in his will, proved in 1776, as of "Mata, co. Tipperary, Esq."

[8] Lieut. 12 June, 1736. Killed before Carthagena in 1741.

[9] Col. 5th Marines, 1741. Killed before Fort Lazar, Carthagena, when leading the stormers. See p. 68.

[10] Killed at the siege of Carthagena as Lt.-Col. of 24th Foot.

[11] Comn. renewed in 1727. Out before 1737.

[12] Lieut. 26 June, 1726. Serving in 1740.

[13] See p. 293, note 31.

[14] "Comn. signed and issued in England." Serving in 1730. Out before 1740.

VISCOUNT HINCHINBROKE'S REGIMENT OF FOOT.

[37TH FOOT,—1ST BATTALION THE HAMPSHIRE REGIMENT.]

See note at head of p. 359, and memo. on same page.

John Bickerstaff,[1] Esq. to be Capt. in room
of Ant. Ligonier - - - - - St. James's, 21 Mar. 1719.*c*

*Regiment returned to Ireland after taking part in the Vigo Expedition
Aug.–Oct. 1719.*

Charles Pym,[2] Esq. to be Capt. in the room of Raphael Walsh - - - - -	—	11 May, 1720.*j*
James Butler,[3] Esq. to be Lt.-Col. in room of Alex. Jacobs and Capt. of a Cy. - -	—	2 June, „ *j*
Edward Richbell,[4] Esq. to be Major in room of James Butler preferred and Capt. of a Cy. - - - - - - -	—	3 „ „ *j*
John Cozens [5] to be Lieut. - - - -	—	29 April, 1721.*f*
Thos. Butler [6] to be do. - - - - -	—	23 May, „ *f*
John Povey,[7] Esq. to be Capt. - - -	—	4 Oct. „ *f*
Thos. Doucett [8] to be Lieut. - - - -	—	16 Mar. 1721/2.*f*
Richard Bassett,[9] Esq. to be Capt. - - -	—	11 April, 1722.*f*
Chas. Rook [10] to be do. - - - - -	—	18 May, „ *f*
Samuel Daniel,[11] Esq. to be Major - - -	—	„ „ „ *f*
[Hon. Robert Murray [12] to be Colonel and Capt. of a Cy. - - - - - -	—	4 Aug. 1722.]
Wm. Strode [13] to be Lieut. - - - -	—	6 „ „ *f*
George Bell [14] to be do. - - - - -	—	8 Feb. 1723/4.*f*
Henry Montfort [15] to be Ens. - - - -	—	„ „ „ *f*
Thos. Timpson,[16] Esq. to be Capt.-Lieut. in room of John Chilcot decd. - - -	—	1 Sept. 1725.*r*
Henry Wetheral [17] to be 2nd Lieut. to Capt. John Pickering's Grendr. Cy. in room of Thos. Timpson preferred - - - -	—	„ „ „ *r*
Henry Merriden [18] to be Adjt. in room of John Chilcot decd. - - - - -	—	„ „ „ *r*
Samuel Bouchier [19] to be Ens. to Capt. John Southey (*sic*) in room of Henry Wetheral preferred - - - - -	—	3 „ „ *r*
Thos. Bradley (*sic*) [20] to be Lieut. to Capt. John Povey in room of Henry Merriden decd. - - - - - - -	—	2 Jan. 1725/6.*r*
Thos. Butler [6] to be Adjt. in room of do. -	—	„ „ „ *r*
Edward Loftus [21] to be Ens. to above Cy. in room of Thos. Bradley preferred - -	—	„ „ „ *r*
Robt. Bailey [22] to be Ens. to Col. Murray in room of Wm. Agnew - - - -	—	17 Aug. „ *r*

Charles Berthe,[23] Esq. to be Capt. in room of John Sotheby - - - - - -	—	20 Dec.	1725/6.*d*
James Scott,[24] Esq. to be Capt. of an additional Cy. - - - - - - -	St. James's, 26	,,	,,	*d*
Edward Northall[25] to be Lieut. to above Cy. -	,,	,,	,,	,,	*d*
Patrick Maxwell[26] to be Ens. to do. - -	,,	,,	,,	,,	*d*
Patrick Murray,[27] Esq. to be Capt. of an additional Cy. - - - - -	,,	,,	,,	,,	*d*
Sir John Murray[28] to be Lieut. to do. - -	,,	,,	,,	,,	*d*
Wm. Musgrave[29] to be Ens. to do. - -	,,	,,	,,	,,	*d*
Fras. Franckfort,[30] Esq. to be Capt. in room of —— Greene - - - - -	,,	25 Mar.	1727.*d*
Burkin Everson[31] to be Qr.-Mr. - - -	,,	22 April,	,,	*d*

Regiment returned to England in Dec. 1726.

---

[1] Out before 1727. The will of "John Bickerstaff, of Dublin, Esq." was proved at Dublin in 1751.

[2] Capt. in 38th Foot, 13 June, 1721. Serving as Capt. in said Corps, then in West Indies, in 1740.

[3] Appointed Adjt.-Gen. in Ireland, 29 Sept. 1722. Called the "Hon. James Butler" in said Comn.

[4] See biog. notice on p. 353, note 2.

[5] Comn. renewed in 1727. Out before 1737.

[6] Serving as Capt. in 1737. Out before 1740.

[7] Comn. renewed in 1727. Out before 1737.

[8] Do. do.

[9] Major, 15 Jan. 1740. Bt.-Lt.-Col. 1745. D. in 1746. Will proved at Dublin.

[10] Serving in 1737. Out before 1740.

[11] See biog. notice on p. 413, note 8.

[12] Bro. to John, Earl of Dunmore, the Col. of the 3rd Foot Guards. Appointed Ens. in the 3rd Foot Guards, 18 June, 1705. Capt. and Lt.-Col. 4 Sept. 1710. Transferred from Colonelcy of 37th Foot to that of 38th Foot, 13 May, 1735. Brig.-Gen. 29 Nov. same year. D. unm. 9 March, 1738. Bd. at Stanwell, Middlesex.

[13] Comn. renewed in 1727. Out before 1737.

[14] Capt.-Lieut. 1 May, 1739. Serving in 1740.

[15] Serving as Ens. in 1737. Out before 1740.

[16] Capt. 7 Dec. 1734. Serving in 1740.

[17] Serving as senior Lieut. in 1740.

[18] D. before Jan. 1726.

[19] Lieut. 11 May, 1735. Serving in 1740.

[20] Called "Brady" in subsequent Lists. Serving in 1740.

[21] Lieut. 7 March, 1737. Serving in 1740.

[22] "Comn. signed and issued in England." Serving in 1730. Out before 1737.

[23] Comn. signed by the King. Serving in 1730. Out before 1737.

[24-29] Comns. signed by the King. Placed on half-pay when the Corps returned to Ireland about 1730.

[30] From half-pay Capt. in Col. Chas. Churchill's Regt. of Foot. Services untraced after 1727.

[31] Placed on half-pay when the Regt. returned to Ireland.

D D

LIEUTENANT-GENERAL N. SANKEY'S REGIMENT OF FOOT.

[39TH FOOT,—1ST BATTALION THE DORSETSHIRE REGIMENT.]

See note at head of p. 359, and memo. on same page.

Isaac Courtiers[1] to be Ens. to Capt. Daniel Negus in room of Henry de Ponthieu preferred - - - - - - -	? Dublin,	15 Jan. 1718/19.*j*
Brigadier Thos. Ferrers[2] to be Colonel of the Regt. of Foot whf. Lt.-Gen. Nicholas Sankey was Colonel, and to be Capt. of a Cy. -	—	11 Mar. 1719/20.*j*
Richard Pyott,[3] Esq. to be Major in room of Edmond Keating decd. and to be Capt. of a Cy. - - - - - - -	—	15 April, 1720.*j*
George Lucy[4] to be Ens. to Capt. Walter Breams in room of Nicholas Sankey decd. - -	—	21 „ „ *j*
Nicholas Bunbury,[5] Esq. to be Major in room of Richard Pyott and to be Capt. of a Cy. -	—	1 June, „ *j*
Worcester Wilson[6] to be Ens. to Capt. Lewis Ormsby in room of Wm. Stuart decd. -	—	2 „ „ *j*
Barret Bowen,[7] Esq. to be Capt. - - -	—	5 Mar. 1721/2.*f*
Philip Savage,[8] Esq. to be do. - - -	—	9 „ „ *f*
John Harrison,[9] Esq. to be Major - - -	—	„ „ „ *f*
[Wm. Newton,[10] Esq. to be Colonel and Capt. of a Cy. - - - - - - - -	—	28 Sept. 1722]
Edward Gosnell[11] to be Ens. - - - -	—	15 Mar. 1722/3.*f*
Arthur Balfour,[12] Esq. to be Capt. - - -	—	1 Sept. 1723.*f*
Arthur Forster[13] to be Ens. - - - -	—	25 Jan. 1723/4.*f*
Isaac Coutier (*sic*)[1] to be Lieut. - - -	—	„ „ „ *f*
Thos. Newton[14] to be Ens. to the Colonel's Cy. in room of Henry Keene - - - -	—	14 Feb. 1725/6.*r*
Henry Keene[15] to be Lieut. to Capt. Wm. Morrice in room of John Hoare decd. - -	—	„ „ „ *r*
Thos. Townsend (*sic*)[16] to be Lieut. to [Col.] Walter Breams in room of Michael Riggs -	—	29 March, 1726.*r*
Edward Williams[17] to be Ens. to Lt.-Col. Thos. Townsend in room of Thos. Townsend preferred - - - - - - - -	—	„ „ „ *r*

Regiment sent to England in Dec. 1726, and embarked for Gibraltar early in 1727.

Hugh Edgar[18] to be Qr.-Mr. - - -	St. James's,	25 Dec.	1726.*d*
George Lucy[4] to be Lieut. - - - -	—	3 May,	1727.*f*
Adam Speed[19] to be Ens. - - - - -	—	23 „	„ *f*

[1] Lieut. 25 Jan. 1724. Capt. 19 Nov. 1731. Serving in 1740. Probably son of Lieut. Augustine de Courtier, of Sankey's Regt. *temp.* Queen Anne.
[2] See biog. notice on p. 132, note 1.
[3] See p. 193, note 14 ; also p. 371, note 4.
[4] Lieut. 3 May, 1727. Capt. 2 Aug. 1731. Serving in 1740.

⁵ Out in 1723. He had served in late reign with Sankey's Regt. in Portugal, and had received a Brevet of Major in 1712.

⁶ See p. 188, note 14.

⁷ Serving in 1730. Out before 1737.

⁸ Lt.-Col. 18 Aug. 1739. Out before 1748. He had served as a Subaltern with Sankey's Regt. in Portugal.

⁹ Comn. renewed in 1727. Out in 1731.

¹⁰ See biog. notice in Vol. I., p. 119, note 1.

¹¹ Serving in 1730. Out before 1737.

¹²   Do.   do.

¹³   Do.   do.

¹⁴   Do.   do.

¹⁵ Capt. 22 July, 1731. **Serving in 1740.**

¹⁶ Son of Lt.-Col. Thos. *Townshend* of same Regt. Attained the rank of Lt.-Col. of 57th Foot, 3 Aug. 1757. Bt. Col. 19 Feb. 1762. Serving in Ireland, 1769.

¹⁷ Capt. 31 Aug. 1739.

¹⁸ Comn. signed by the King. Lieut. in same Regt. Not in any subsequent List.

¹⁹ Lieut. 17 March, 1731. Serving in 1740.

NON-REGIMENTAL COMMISSIONS AND APPOINT-MENTS, 1719–1727

NON-REGIMENTAL COMMISSIONS, 1719–1727

See note at head of p. 359, and memo. on same page.

Samuel Forbes to be Barrack Master at Athlone, Banagher, and Portumny in room of Hugh Galbraith - - - -	—	23 April, 1719.*j*
James Jefferyes,[1] Esq. to be Govr. of the City of Cork and the Forts adjacent in room of Sir James Jefferyes decd. - - -	—	29 ,, ,, *j*
Edward Spragg, Esq. to be Barrack Master at Mullingar, Trym, Tullamore, and Philipstown in room of Edward Page decd. -	—	25 May, ,, *j*
John Titchborne (*sic*),[2] Esq. to be Govr. of Charlemont in room of Lord Santry -	—	19 June, ,, *j*
Henry Barry, Baron of Santry [3] to be do. of the City of Londonderry and Fort of Culmore in room of Thos. Meredyth decd.	—	,, ,, ,, *j*
Richard Bermingham to be Barrack Master at Longford, Roscommon, Lanesborow, and Finae in room of Nathan Forth -	—	15 Sept. ,, *j*
Lord Harry Powlett [4] to be Govr. of Kinsale and Charles Fort in room of Wm. Earl of Inchiquin decd. - - - - -	—	25 Dec. ,, *j*
Do. to be Capt. of the Company of Foot Guards armed with Battle Axes in room of Wm. Southwell decd. "and also to take rank, place, and precedence as Colonel of Foot in the Army in the said Kingdom." - - - - -	—	24 Jan. 1719/20.*j*
Archibald Cathcart to be Barrack Master at Enniskillen, Ballyshannon, and Clonawly in room of John Moore - - - -	—	5 April, 1720.*j*
Brigadier - General Phineas Bowles [5] to be Qr.-Mr.-General and Barrack-Master-General in room of Col. Richard Morris decd. - - - - - - - -	—	30 May, ,, *j*
Thos. Rose to be Barrack Master at Charlevil (*sic*), New Market, Cullen, and Colecorrunch (?) in room of Thos. St. Leger -	—	1 June, ,, *j*
Richard, Viscount Shannon [6] to be Commander-in-Chief of all Our Forces in Ireland - - - - - - -	Gohre,	13 Oct. ,, *p*

Gervas Parker,[7] Esq. to be Qr.-Mr.-General in Ireland in room of Phineas Bowles and also to be Barrack-Master-General - -	—	4 Aug. 1722.
The Hon. James Butler,[8] Esq. to be Adjt.-General in Ireland - - - - -	—	29 Sept. ,,
James Clement to be Barrack Master at Carrickfergus, &c. - - - - -	—	5 June, 1724.r
Lt.-Col. George Bate[9] to be Lt.-Govr. of Kinsale and Charles Fort - - -	—	1 Aug. ,, r
Wm. Thattford to be Barrack Master at Carrickfergus, Belfast, Downpatrick, and Newry Town in room of James Clement -	—	12 Dec. ,, r
James Ribett Vigie, Junr. to be do. at Gallway, Headford, and Loughrea in room of Henry Nisbett - - - -	—	28 Feb. 1724/5.r
Stephen Haydocke to be do. at Kilkenny, Callen, Thurles, Longford, Pass of Killinaule, in room of Chris. Hewetson - -	—	24 April, 1725.r
Walter Pendergast to be do. at Bantry, Macroom, Kilmeeky, Roscarbery, and Inchegeela in room of James Dennis decd. - - - - - -	—	27 ,, ,, r
James Nesbett to be do. at Nenagh, Roscrea, and Silvermines in room of Francis Cornwall - - - - -	—	1 July, ,, r
Garves (sic) Parker,[7] Esq. to be Lt.-Govr. of Kinsale and Charles Fort in room of George Bate decd. - - - -	—	31 Aug. ,, r
Robert Burton, Esq. to be Capt. of the Company of Foot Guards armed with Battle Axes in room of Lord Henry Powlett and to take rank as Colonel of Foot - -	—	1 Dec. ,, r
Thos. Parker to be Barrack Master at Cork and Mallow in room of Robert Parker -	—	8 Feb. 1725/6.r
St. John Noble to be one of the six Commissaries of the Musters in Ireland in room of Wm. Moore - - - - -	—	1 Mar. ,, r
John Shaw, Junr. to be Barrack Master of the several barracks at Clonmel, Carrickneshure, Nine Mile House, Four Mile Water, Dungarvan and Cashell, in room of John Shaw, Senr. - - - -	—	5 ,, ,, r
John Craggs to be do. at Ross Castle, Tralee, Dingle, &c., in room of Thos. Church -	—	23 ,, ,, r
Samuel Walter Whitshed,[10] Esq. to be Govr. of Wicklow Castle in room of Henry Piercy - - - - - - -	—	25 Mar. 1726.r
Christopher Gilbert to be Barrack Master at Bray, Wicklow, Arklow, Enniscorthy, and Wexford in room of John Mosely -	—	31 ,, ,, r
John Coghlan to be one of the six Commissaries of the Musters in Ireland in room of James Maule - - - - -	—	28 Sept. ,, r

Robert Butler, Esq. to be Lieut. of the Com-
    pany of Foot Guards armed with Battle
    Axes and rank as Capt. of Foot in room
    of Humphry Butler - - - -   —   29 Nov. 1726.*r*
Owen Wynne,[11] Esq. to be Lieut.-General of
    all our Forces - - - - - - St. James's, 1 Mar. 1726/7.*r*
Wm. Heath[12] to be Provost-Marshall-General Dublin,   17 April, 1727.*r*
[Charles, Lord Moore[13] of Tullamore to be
    Muster-Master-General, n.d.]

[1] See memoir pp. 85–89.

[2] Served in former reign as Major of Col. Thos. Pierce's Regt. of Foot. Fourth son of Sir Wm. Tichborne, of Beaulieu, co. Louth, Bart. D. in 1745.

[3] See biog. notice on p. 156, note 37.

[4] *Paulet.* See biog. notice on p. 123, note 6.

[5] See do. on p. 116, note 1.

[6] Comn. signed by the King. See biog. notice in Vol. I., p. 308, note 1.

[7] A copy of this Comn. is given in *Add. MS.* 23636. See biog. notice in Vol. I., p. 144, note 2.

[8] Do. See p. 416.

[9] See biog. notice in Vol. I., p. 120, note 2. Called "Bates" in previous Lists.

[10] See do. in do., p. 155, note 4.

[11] See do. in do., p. 113, note 1. Above Comn. was signed by the King.

[12] "Comn. signed in England, issued in Ireland. Fees remitted." Comn. renewed by George II. at Kensington, 13 Sept. 1727.

[13] His name appears in the *Military List* (Ireland) 1726. He succeeded his father as 2nd Baron in Sept. 1725. Created Earl of Charleville, 15 Sept. 1758. D.s.p. 17 Feb. 1764.

RICHARD, VISCOUNT SHANNON, COMMANDER-IN-CHIEF IN IRELAND, 1720-1740.

(*See* Vol. I., p. 308, note 1.)

(*From an Unfinished Portrait by Sir Godfrey Kneller, painted for the Kit-Kat Club.*)

GENERAL OFFICERS ON THE IRISH ESTABLISHMENT, 1726.*

All the names given below, excepting Lieut. Durell, have been annotated.

GENERAL AND COMMANDER-IN-CHIEF.

Richard, Viscount Shannon.

LIEUT.-GENERAL.

George Maccartney.

MAJOR-GENERALS.

Owen Wynne.
Wm. Evans.
Thos. Pearce.

RRIGADIER-GENERALS.

Earl of Deloraine.
Lord Mark Kerr.
Lord John Kerr.
James Crofts.
Robert Napier.
Philip Honywood.
Andrew Bisset
Richard Russell.

A.D.C.'S TO THE LORD-LIEUTENANT.

Hon. Stephen Cornwallis.
John Montagu.

A.D.C. TO VISCOUNT SHANNON.

Lieut. Nicholas Durell.[1]

* Printed in the *Civil and Military List*, Dublin, 1726. *Add. MS.* 23636, *Brit. Mus.*
[1] Served in former reign as Cornet in Brigdr. Hunt Withers's Regt. of Dragoons.

ENGLISH ESTABLISHMENT

EXTRACTS FROM THE OFFICIAL ACCOUNTS OF
THE RIGHT HON. SIR SPENCER COMPTON, K.B.,
PAYMASTER-GENERAL
MARCH 1722—DECEMBER 1723

EDITORIAL NOTE

THE parchment roll from which the following extracts are taken is one of a series, for the latter part of George I.'s reign, recently sold with other "Townshend Papers" at Messrs. Sotheby & Wilkinson's auction rooms. It is endorsed "Accompts of the Rt. Hon. Sir Spencer Compton, Knight of the Bath, as Receiver and Paymaster General of his Majesty's Guards, Garrisons and land Forces." This rare and interesting parchment has been thus described by an expert:

"The roll is throughout carefully written in a bold hand of the Chancery type. It measures in length 34 ft. 6 in. and is 12 in. in width. It is composed of fourteen pieces of parchment joined together with stitches. The total amount accounted for is £1,565,950 18s. 4¾d., and the period covered is from 15 March 1721/2 to 24 Dec. 1723."

ENGLISH ESTABLISHMENT

EXTRACTS FROM THE OFFICIAL ACCOUNTS OF THE RIGHT HON. SIR SPENCER COMPTON, K.B., PAYMASTER-GENERAL. MARCH 1722—DECEMBER 1723.

	£	s.	d.
Ger. Andrews, Esq. Pay as Deputy-Commissary, 25 Apr. 1722 to 15 Aug. 1723	239	0	0
Col. Armstrong. Pay as Quart.-Mast.-Gen., 25 Apr. 1722 to 24 Dec. 1723	609	0	0
Marmaduke Bealing, Esq., in full for executing the Office as Secretary to the Board of Gen¹. Officers for inspecting the clothing and an Allowance on the Establishments of Guards and Garrisons from 25 Dec. 1721	365	0	0
Lt.-Col. Bland. Pension or Reward from H.M. Bounty, 25 Apr. 1722 to 24 Dec. 1723	182	14	0
Ensign Ric. Brown of Maj.-Gen. Elliot's Regᵗ. of Foot. Payment to from H.M. Bounty, "being left out of the Establishment for the year 1723 for not appearing at the Gen¹. Examination of the Reduced Officers occasioned by the neglect of his Agent, from 25 Dec. 1722 to 24 Dec. 1723"	33	9	2
James Bruce, Esq. } Pay as Comptrollers of Accounts of Sir Phil. Medows, Knt. } Army, 25 Apr. 1722 to 24 Dec. 1723	2,502	11	10
Sir Phil. Meadows } Comptrollers of the Accounts of the Army, and John Bruce } for incidents at their Office, without Accoᵗ, and setled at £900 per Ann., between lady day 1722 and 24 Dec. 1723	1,575	0	0
Col. Burges, from H.M. Bounty, without deduction for his long and faithful Services	365	0	0
Thos. Byde, Esq., for extraordinary pains as Judge-Advocate-Gen¹. of the Forces, 1 Aug. 1714 to 19 Sept. 1715	415	0	0
Dan¹. Cabrol, without deduction, for his merit and length of faithfull Service (H.M. Bounty)	45	12	6
Col. Cadogan, in full for Trophys for the Regimᵗ. of Foot under his command	200	0	0
Chelsea Hospital, Allowance for	27,000	0	0
viz. for 1722, £15,000.			
„ 1723, £12,000.			
Col. Cholmley, in full of Pay as Aid-de-Camp to his Maᵗⁱᵉ, 25 Apr. to 24 Dec. 1722	100	0	0
Hen. Cholmley, his executor, from thence to 24 Dec. 1723	150	0	0
Col. Churchill, Pay as A.-de-C. to Gen¹., 25 Apr. 1722 to 11 Jan. 1722/3	131	0	0
Joⁿ. Cloathier, Pay as Drum-Major-Gen., 25 Apr. 1722 to 24 Dec. 1723	50	1	0

	£	s.	d.

Ric. Tempest Culliford. *See* with John Righton.

Sir Jo. Cuningham. Payment from H.M. Bounty, 25 Apr. 1722 to 24 Dec. 1723 - - - - - - - - - 76 13 4

Dr. Cuthbert. Pay as Surgeon to the Town and Castle of Inverness and Barracks of Bernera &c., 25 Apr. 1722 to 24 Dec. 1723 - - - - - - - - - 182 14 0

Pet. Davenport. *See* with John Righton.

Major Alex. Dean. Paym. from H.M. Bounty, 25 Apr. 1722 to 24 Dec. 1723 - - - - - - - - 152 5 0

Col. Geo. Douglas. Paym. from H.M. Bounty, 25 Apr. 1722 to 24 Dec. 1723 - - - - - - - - 304 10 0

Jo. Durell, Esq. Pay. as Dep.-Commissary at Jersey and Guernsey, 25 Apr. 1722 to 24 Dec. 1723 - - - - 76 2 6

Lt. Jo. Emmenes, Paym. from H.M. Bounty, 9 Nov. 1722 to 17 Oct. 1723 - - - - - - - - 40 0 4

Kingsmill Eyre, Esqr., for Robt. Mason, Surgeon of Brig^r. Nicholson's Independent Co^y., for his pay, 21 May to 17 Oct. 1723 - - - - - - - - 30 0 0

Capt. Jo. Farrer. Paym. from H.M. Bounty, 25 Apr. 1722 to 24 Dec. 1723 - - - - - - - - 471 19 6

Abra. Fowler. Paym. from H.M. Bounty, " without deduction as his Mat^{y's} Royal Bounty " - - - - - 50 0 0

Dr. Gibson. Pay as Phys.-General, 25 Apr. 1722 to 17 July of same year - - - - - - - - - 42 0 0

Maj. Gifford, Town Major of Berwick. Pay as Turnkey - - - - - - - - - - 40 0 0

Alex. Gordon. *See* with John Righton.

Col. Geo. Grove's Irish Reg^t. Pay from day of embarkation from Ireland for H.M. Service in Gr. Britain to the day of disembarking again in Ireland, in consideration of losses and Expences in Recruting notwithstanding their want of Muster Rolls : 22 Aug. 1722 to 31 Dec. following, deducting £389 5s. 2d. for Offreckonings - - - 3,174 14 2

(*See* also with Col. Pococke.)

John Gumley, Esq. Pay as Dep^y.-Commissary-Gen., 25 Apr. 1722 to 24 Dec. 1723 - - - - - - - - 700 7 0

Col. Roger Handasyde's Irish Reg^t. Pay (same as Col. Geo. Grove's), 23 Aug. to 28 Dec. 1722, deducting £375 18s. 10d. for Offreck^{gs}. - - - - - - - - - 3,065 1 4

(*See* also with Col. Pococke.)

Col. Hawley. Pay as A.-de-C. to Gen. in succession to Col. Churchill, 11 Jan. to 24 Dec. 1723 - - - - 173 10 0

Col. Hen. Hawley's Irish Reg^t. Pay (same as Col. Grove's), 23 Aug. 1722 to 1 Jan. 1722/3, deducting £385 14s. 3d. for Offreck^{gs}. - - - - - - - - 3,147 5 1

(*See* also with Col. Pococke.)

Lady Dowager Hinchingbrook, for late Lord H. (in full pay as A.-de-C. to his Maj^{tie}), 25 Apr. 1722 to 4 Oct. of same year - - - - - - - - - - 88 17 9

Maj.-Gen. Holmes. Paym. from H.M. Bounty, 25 Apr. 1722 to 7 May 1723 - - - - - - - - - 283 10 0

Sir Wm. Hope, Do., 25 Apr. 1722 to 24 Dec. 1723 - - - 433 18 3

	£	s.	d.
Col. Thos. Howard's Irish Reg^t. Pay (same as Col. Grove's), 22 Aug. to 30 Dec. 1722, deducting £387 9s. 9d. for offreck^{gs}. - - - - - - - - - - - - *(See* also with Col. Pococke.)	3,159	6	9
Col. Huffum. Paym. from H.M. Bounty, 25 Apr. 1722 to 24 Dec. 1723 - - - - - - - - - -	152	5	0
Edw. Hughes, for Incidents at the Judge-Advocate's Office, from Midsummer 1722 to 24 Dec. 1723 - - - -	195	14	6
Do. for extraordinary trouble in attending the Genl. Officers, from 25 Apr. 1722 to 24 Dec. 1723 - - - -	609	0	0
Edw. Hughes, Esq. Paym. as Judge-Advocate-Gen. and 3 men attending his Office, 25 Apr. 1722 to 24 Dec. 1723 - -	746	0	6
Dr. Inglis. Pay as Surgeon-Gen., 25 Dec. 1722 to 24 Dec. 1723 - - - - - - - - - - -	182	10	0
Ja. Johnson. Paym. from H.M. Bounty for serving as Surgeon in Sterling Castle, from 12 June 1723 to 24 Dec. following	19	12	0
Capt. John Kelly. Paym. from H.M. Bounty till he shall be provided for, from 25 Apr. 1722 to 24 Dec. 1723 - -	152	5	0
Martin Killigrew, Esq., for Rent of Castlehill in Cornwall, for a year and three quarters to 24 Dec. 1723 - - -	350	0	0
Lord Kilmaine, in full of Pay as Aid-de-Camp to his Matie, from 25 Apr. 1722 to 24 Dec. 1723 - - - - -	300	0	0
Chas. King, Esq., for Incidents at the Judge-Advocate's Office, for half year to Midsummer 1722 - - - - -	68	17	0
Col. Lascels. Pay as Deputy-Q.M.-Gen., 25 Apr. 1722 to 24 Dec. 1723 - - - - - - - - - -	304	10	0
Col. Lloyd, in full of Pay as Aid-de-Camp to his Matie to 24 June 1722 - - - - - - - - - -	400	0	0
more, from thence to 24 Dec. 1723 - - - - -	300	0	0
Capt. Lockhart. Paym. from H.M. Bounty, 25 Apr. 1722 to 24 Dec. 1723 - - - - - - - - - -	304	10	0
Capt. Lockhart. Do., in full Satisfacçon of his demands on acco^t of his Pay from 24 Dec. 1717 to 24 June 1720 -	456	5	0
Hen. Lowman, Esqr., to pay for the damages of 3 Gardens contiguous to his Ma^{is}. Palace at Kensington by Soldiers doing Duty in the Summer, 1723 - - - - -	15	0	0
Cornet Justin McCartney of Col. Newton's Regt. of Dragoons. Paym. from H.M. Bounty, in consideraçon of his being struck off the Establishm^t. for not appearing at the Genl. Examination of the Reduced Officers occasioned by the Neglect of his Agent, from 25 Dec. 1722 to 24 Dec. 1723	45	12	6
Jo. Martin. Pay as Provost-Marshal-Gen., 25 Apr. 1722 to 24 Dec. 1723 - - - - - - - - -	152	5	0
Robert Mason. *See* under Kingsmill Eyre.			
Medows or Meadows (Sir Phil.). *See* entries under James Bruce and John Bruce (page 429).			
Maj. Mohun, Major of Brigade to the Horse Guards, for his Pay for a year ended 24 Dec. 1723 - - - - -	182	10	0
The Marquis of Montandre. Paym. from H.M. Bounty, in consideraçon of his being struck off the Establishment for not appearing at the Genl. Examination of the Reduced Officers occasioned by the Neglect of his Agent, from 25 Dec. 1722 to 24 Dec. 1723 - - - - - -	237	5	0

	£	s.	d.
Col. David Montolieu de Santipolite. Paym. (as previous entry) from 28 June 1723 to 24 Dec. foll^g. - - -	108	0	0
Tho. Morphy. Pay as Barrack Mastr. to the Savoy, 25 Apr. 1722 to 24 Dec. 1723 - - - - - - - -	100	1	9
Edward Newton, Esq. Pay as Dep^y.-Comissary, as successor to Geo. Righton, from 28 July to 24 Dec. 1723 - -	74	10	0
Sir Adolphus Oughton, Bart. For the pay of 3 hautbois to the Cold Stream Reg^t. of Foot Guards for 2 years ended Xmas. 1723 - - - - - - - - - -	164	5	0
Major Ovray. Paym. from H.M. Bounty for 2 years to 24 Dec. 1723 - - - - - - - - - -	182	10	0
Elizth. Lady Dowager Paston. Paym. from H.M. Bounty for 2 years to 24 Dec. 1723 - - - - - - -	600	0	0

Col. Philips. Deduction from pay of non-coms. of his reg^t. at Anapolis Royal and Placentia, 25 Apr. 1722 to 24 Oct. 1723 - - - - - - - - (separate sum not stated)

| Col. Pitt, in full as A.-de-C. to his Matie, from 25 Dec. 1722 to 24 Dec. 1723 - - - - - - - - - - | 150 | 0 | 0 |
| Col. Pocock's Irish Reg^t. Pay from day of embarkation from Ireland for H.M. Service in Gr. Britain, &c. (*see* entry under Col. Geo. Grove), 24 May 1722 to 2 Jan. 1722/3, deducting £657 16*s*. 8*d*. for Offreckonings - - | 5,365 | 18 | 8 |

Six Irish Regiments of

    Col. Pococke
    Col. Howard
    Col. Grove   } reimbursed for difference
    Col. Handasyde   } of pay upon the foot of
    Col. Hawley   } the English Establish-
    Col. Tyrrell   } ment.

Note.—This is mentioned generally at the beginning of the roll. There are also separate entries for each regiment for their losses and expences, for which see under the names.

Geo. Preston. Paym. from H.M. Bounty as Surg.-Major and Mate, 25 Apr. 1722 to 24 Dec. 1723 - - - - -	166	13	4
Capt. Read. Pay as another A.-de-C. to the Gen., 25 Apr. 1722 to 24 Dec. 1723 - - - - - - -	304	10	0
Geo. Righton, Esq. Pay as Dep^y.-Comissary, 25 Apr. 1722 to 28 July 1723 - - - - - - - - -	230	0	0

John Righton - - - -   } Pay as
Ric. Tempest Culliford - - - } Deputy
Alex. Stevenson - - - - } Comissaries,   1,522 10 0
Alex. Gordon - - - - - } 25 Apr. 1722 to
Pet. Davenport - - - - } 24 Dec. 1723

| Lt.-Col. Rose, of Lt.-Gen. Wills' Regt. Paym. to from H.M. Bounty, 25 Apr. 1722 to 24 Dec. 1723 - - - | 60 | 18 | 0 |

Maj.-Gen. Sabine. *See* with Brig. Stanwix.

Sir Hans Sloan. Pay as succ^r. to Dr. Gibson as Phys.-Gen., 18 July 1722 to 24 Dec. 1723 - - - - - -	262	10	0
Dr. Smith. Pay as Chaplain-Gen., 25 Apr. 1722 to 24 Dec. 1723	263	16	8
Tom. Smith. Pay as Dep.-Comissary at Scilly, 25 Apr. 1722 to 24 Dec. 1723 - - - - - - - - - -	40	12	0

	£	s.	d.
Col. Geo. Somerville. Paym. from H.M. Bounty, 25 Apr. 1722 to 24 Dec. 1723 - - - - - - - - -	243	12	0
Maj.-Gen. Sabine (for their Expence and trouble in examᵍ and { the Reduced Officers and Out Pensioners Brig. Stanwix (of Chelsea hospital in the year 1722	300	0	0
Alex. Stevenson. *See* with John Righton.			
Maj. Steward. Paym. from H.M. Bounty, 25 Apr. 1722 to 24 Dec. 1723 - - - - - - - - -	471	19	6
Dr. Stewart, Do. (same dates) - - - - - -	166	13	4
Sir Pat. Strachan. Pay as Barrack-Mastr.-Gen. in North Britain, 25 Apr. 1722 to 24 Dec. 1723 - - - -	609	0	0
Sir Wm. Strickland, Bart. Pay as Commissary-Gen. of Musters and Clerks, 25 Apr. 1722 to 24 Dec. 1723 - -	685	2	6
Do., Comissary-Genᵃˡ. of the Musters. For the Incidents of his Office, without deduction, for 2 years ended 24 Dec. 1723 - - - - - - - - - - -	91	5	0
Capt. Strudwicke, for colours &c. for Brigᵈ. Morrison's Regt. of Foot - - - - - - - - - - -	240	0	0
Thos. Sydenham, Esq., Secretary to the Genᵃˡ. for Incidents of his Office, 25 June 1722 to 24 Dec. 1723 - - -	67	19	8
Elizᵗʰ Tichborne. Paym. from H.M. Bounty, 25 Apr. 1722 to 24 Dec. 1723 - - - - - - - -	166	13	4
Geo. Treby, Esq. Pay as Sec. to the Forces, 25 Apr. 1722 to 24 Dec. 1723 - - - - - - - -	609	0	0
Geo. Treby, Esq., Sec. at War. House rent for a year and three quarters to Christmas, 1723 - - - - -	350	0	0
Robt. Trelawney. Paym. from H.M. Bounty, 25 Apr. 1722 to 24 Dec. 1723 - - - - - - - -	152	5	0
Maj.-Gen. Trelawney, late Govʳ. of Plymouth and St. Nichᵒ. Island; as an Additional Allowance from 1 Aug. to 25 Dec. 1714 (deducting £20 17s. 5d. for Poundage and one day's Pay) - - - - - - - - -	374	17	0
Geo. Turbill, Esq., without deduction, for Incidents at the Office of Sec. at War, between lady day 1722 and 24 Dec. 1723 - - - - - - - - - - -	2,420	16	3
Robt. Turnbull. Paym. from H.M. Bounty, for a year to Christmas, 1723 - - - - - - - -	73	0	0
Col. Tyrrell. *See* with Col. Pococke.			
Col. Jas. Tyrrell's Irish Regt. of Foot. Pay (same as Col. Grove's), 23 Aug. 1722 to 30 Dec. of same year, deducting £354 15s. 6d. for Offreckonings - - -	2,901	16	2
Col. Tyrrell. Paym. from H.M. Bounty, without deduction, not being provided for - - - - - - -	1,000	0	0
Ant. Vezian, for his trouble in examᵍ. half-pay Officers in the year 1722 - - - - - - - - - -	50	0	0
Maj. Jo. Vincent. Paym. from H.M. Bounty, without deduction, for his faithfull services - - - - -	160	0	0
Hugh Warren. Pay as Surveyor of the Guards, 25 Aprʳ. 1722 to 24 Dec. 1723 - - - - - -	76	2	6

	£	s.	d.
Col. [Jonas] Watson. Pay as Firemaster to the Grenadiers, 25 Apr. 1722 to 24 Dec. 1723- - - - - - -	91	7	0
Col. Wentworth. Pay as Adj.-Gen. in succession to Col. Adam Williamson, 29 Nov. 1722 to 24 Dec. 1723 - -	391	0	0
Col. Wentworth, for his Expences in going to Gloucester -	80	0	0
Christ^r. Whytell, Esq. Pay as Dep.-Comissary in succession to Ger. Andrews, 16 Aug. to 24 Dec. 1723 - - -	65	10	0
Col. Adam Williamson. Pay as Adj.-Gen., 25 Apr. 1722 to 28 Nov. 1722 - - - - - - - - -	218	0	0
Jane Willson, Widow of Capt. Willson, late lieut.-Govern^r. of the Island of Jersey, for his Subsisting 3 Papist secured there coming from France to enlist themselves in the Foot Guards - - - - - - - - -	16	9	6

INDEX

A

B